MARGARET MORGAN
and
MARY MORGAN PEDLOW

Memorial

RIVERSIDE   PUBLIC   LIBRARY

Mexican Political Biographies, 1884–1935

MEXICAN POLITICAL BIOGRAPHIES, 1884–1935

by Roderic A. Camp

 UNIVERSITY OF TEXAS PRESS, AUSTIN

Requests for permission to reproduce
material from this work should be sent to
Permissions, University of Texas Press, Box
7819, Austin, Texas 78713-7819.

♾The paper used in this publication meets
the minimum requirements of American
National Standard for Information
Sciences—Permanence of Paper for Printed
Library Materials, ANSI Z39.48–1984.

For reasons of economy and speed this
volume has been printed from computer-
generated disks furnished by the author, who
assumes full responsibility for its contents.

**Library of Congress Cataloging-in-
Publication Data**

Camp, Roderic A.
    Mexican political biographies, 1884–1935 /
by Roderic A. Camp. — 1st ed.
        p.   cm.
    Includes bibliographical references.
    ISBN 0-292-75119-2 (cloth)
    1. Mexico—Biography.   2. Statesman—
Mexico—Biography.
    I. Title.
F1233.5.C28   1991
920.72–dc20   90-39352
                                          CIP

To John and Mary Minassian, grandparents who brought history alive, and to the memory of Carl Solberg, a wonderful teacher

CONTENTS

A NOTE TO THE READER

IN 1968, while conducting research on Mexican cabinet figures for my dissertation topic, I encountered a serious gap in biographical reference materials on leading national political figures. In the ensuing years, I published *Mexican Political Biographies, 1935–75* (Tucson: University of Arizona Press, 1976), *Mexican Political Biographies, 1935–81* (Tucson: University of Arizona Press, 1982), *Biografías políticos mexicanos, 1935–1988* (Mexico City: Fondo de Cultura Económica, 1991); and *Who's Who in Mexico Today* (Boulder: Westview Press, 1988), all of which deal with contemporary political figures since 1935. The need for biographical information on public figures is reflected in the demand for these four successive books. Yet, since the initial publication, many individuals interested in Mexico have asked for a complementary volume which would cover the earlier part of the twentieth century.

The purpose of the present volume is to provide short, accurate biographies of leading public figures, comparable to those included in my earlier books, extending back to the second administration of Porfirio Díaz, beginning in 1884 through 1934. This period in Mexican political history has been more neglected in English literature than the post-1935 period. Inaccuracies abound, and much information about leading figures is just not available without engaging in primary research.

The biographies include presidents, cabinet secretaries, assistant secretaries, *oficiales mayores*, senators, repeating federal deputies, Supreme Court justices, party leaders, prominent ambassadors, military commanders, governors, and other figures. In the appendixes, I have included complete lists of all cabinet secretaries and, for selected agencies, assistant secretaries, all Supreme Court justices, senators and federal deputies and their alternates, state governors, selected ambassadors, and their dates in office. Thus, the reader can readily find the name of an individual by the position held or, if the individual's name is known, consult the biographical section.

Furthermore, I have designed this work stylistically to approximate the initial volumes, so they can easily be used together. Both the biographical entries and the appendixes, where possible, are comparable. I have especially

attempted to follow political families back into the nineteenth century, and references in the biographical entries are made to individuals who are descendants of prominent figures in the present volume and who have distinguished themselves in the post-1935 era.

It has taken nearly two decades to accumulate this information. I believe, therefore, that anyone interested in contemporary political life will also find this volume extremely insightful, since an essential ingredient in Mexican politics in the last century is the persistence of family clans, over many generations, in leadership positions, readily illustrated by the notable descendants of the Sierra, Paz, Madero, Calles, Cárdenas, and other families.

I believe these biographical data, and the appendixes, will be useful to anyone interested in Mexican public life. Collectively, these data provide a portrait of Mexico's political and military elite, their social origins, their ties to leading intellectual and economic figures, and their influence over multiple generations. Although I will be presenting an analytical study of Mexican political figures from 1884 to 1988 in another work, this volume alone makes it possible to understand better the connections of the present leadership with their ancestors, and the changing characteristics of political leadership over time.

ACKNOWLEDGMENTS

THIS WORK has taken two decades to complete. It is the type of project which is never complete. Biographical information on such a range of figures can always be improved and made more accurate. Although working on many other projects over the years, I have kept an eye open for bits and pieces of biographical information on numerous political figures. Many libraries have aided this lengthy process, including the Nettie Lee Benson Latin American Collection at the University of Texas at Austin, the Library of Congress, and the Colegio de México library. I would especially like to thank Dolores Martin for facilitating my research at the Library of Congress, 1983–84, and Jorge Carpizo, who obtained access for me at the National Autonomous University of Mexico archives, 1985. I also want to express my thanks to Peter H. Smith for giving me his old files, and to Stuart Voss and Michael Conniff for critiquing parts of this manuscript.

HOW TO USE THIS BOOK

BIOGRAPHICAL ENTRIES are entered by the father's surname, followed by the mother's maiden name. Many Mexicans, however, do not use their mother's maiden name, or do so inconsistently, thus making it confusing to identify an individual's career. When the mother's maiden name appears in parentheses, it indicates that the individual typically uses only his father's name. The date of death, if known, appears below the individual's name in the biography. If the date is not known, the word *deceased* appears. Several individuals, at the time of publication, may still be alive. In such cases, of course, no information appears to the right of the name.

The biographical information in the entries is divided into twelve categories, to correspond with the early volumes. When information for any category is unavailable, the word *unknown* is entered. The word *none* indicates that the category did not apply to the individual biographee, such as no union activities or military service. When a position is *italicized* in a biography, it means that the position is also listed in the appendixes. When a person's name is *italicized* in the biography, that individual has his or her own biographical entry. A name *italicized* in the appendix means that a biography of that individual appears in this book.

The appendixes can be used to reconstruct the leadership of a given agency over time. These appendixes make it possible to examine governmental positions without knowing the names of the officeholders. Also, for hundreds of important and lesser figures, whose biographies do not appear in this volume, a skeletal career of one's positions, that is to say, a political outline of an individual, can be sketched by examining positions held. This can be particularly useful for numerous minor figures about whom biographical information would be difficult, if not impossible, to locate.

The categories are:

A] Date of birth.

B] Birthplace, city and state, sometimes including the municipality if the city is a small village, mining community, or farm.

C] Education: primary, secondary, preparatory, professional, and college education with the dates of attendance and graduation, if possible. Most

individuals who attended college went to regional institutions, or professional schools in Mexico City which became the National University of Mexico (later the National Autonomous University of Mexico—UNAM) in 1910. The schools which form the antecedent of the National University are the School of Mines (later the National School of Engineering), the National School of Medicine, and the National School of Law, all located in Mexico City. I have added the word *National* to the names of these schools to indicate they are the antecedents of those schools. The military college, which many of the military-political figures attended, is referred to in the biographies as the National Military College, the antecedent of the Heroic Military College. In the nineteenth century, many individuals were certified as lawyers by the courts, and not by the schools themselves. When those institutions and the date of certification are known, they are included in the biography. The entry "no degree" indicates that the individual never completed professional or university studies. Teaching and administrative positions at any level of education are also included in this category.

D] Elective positions: any positions which at least nominally are attained through the electoral process, from council member to president. Provisional, interim, and substitute governors are not included in this category, but under the appointive governmental positions category. During the Porfiriato, 1884–1911, some individuals were elected simultaneously to more than one position as federal deputies; thus duplicate dates and different states and districts are not errors. The individual could serve in only one post, and his alternate was required to take the alternate post.

E] Party positions: any known affiliations to a political party or campaign are included. Candidates for office are also included.

F] Appointive governmental positions: any appointive office at the local, state, national, and international levels. I have attempted, if possible, to list these in chronological order, to give a clearer notion of the individual's career. Many individuals hold multiple appointive posts, or appointive posts simultaneously with elective offices, and duplicate dates are not in error.

G] Group activities, including intellectual, student, labor, and other organizations. Only selected, numbered members in cultural or professional academies are noted.

H] Nongovernmental positions: excluding education and the military, these include professional jobs, self-employment, ownership of land and firms, and, generally, any post in the private sector. Also, if the individual is a significant author, poet, or artist, that information will appear in this entry.

I] Grandparents, parents, spouses, siblings, friends: relevant family data, including father's occupation, as well as information about relatives and friends who have held important governmental positions. Particular care has been taken to try to identify other relatives who have held prominent political offices, or who are married to such individuals. The occupation of the parent is the most difficult variable about which to obtain information. I

have used extensive genealogical sources to provide more information about family background. Political mentors are also identified.

J] Military experience: detailed career information, if available, including date and rank of entry into service, date of rank, highest rank reached, important battles, if known, and faction supported during periods of rebellion. Many of the entries are based on Secretariat of War data. Guerrilla and revolutionary activities also are included.

K] Miscellaneous information: unusual information about an individual's career, including imprisonment, exile, cause of death, if not natural, duels, or some notable feat.

L] Addition sources: books, reference works, government directories, newspapers, magazines, educational files. Biographical monographs about an individual are not cited, since they can be easily found in the card catalog. The word *letter* indicates that some of the information was confirmed by a relative or by correspondence from another source or agency.

HOW PERSONS WERE SELECTED FOR INCLUSION

INDIVIDUALS CHOSEN for inclusion in this work were selected on the basis of positional and reputational criteria, and on the completeness and accuracy of the biographical information available. From an original sample of approximately 2,000 biographies, I had satisfactory data on 1,000 persons. Of those, more than 700 were selected for inclusion. Their biographies were the most complete, and I could cross-check the information for accuracy, preferably in official government records as well as in published sources.

To be included in this work, an individual had to hold one of the following positions: president of Mexico; vice-president of Mexico; cabinet secretary; subsecretary or *oficial mayor*; governor of a state; territory, or the Federal District; senator; repeating federal deputy; justice of the Supreme Court; ambassador to the United States, the United Kingdom, the Soviet Union, France, or Cuba; private secretary to the president; chief of the presidential staff; chief of staff of the Secretariat of War; zone commander; presidential candidate; and party leader, opposition, or official.

Naturally, the disadvantage of a positional approach as the basic criterion for selection is that some leaders, intellectual, religious, guerrilla, or otherwise, who may have had an impact on the period do not qualify under this criterion. The argument can be made that during historical periods when political institutions are weak, or in flux, the number of these leaders increases. This is undoubtedly so, but remarkably, during the fifty-year period this book covers, with the exception of 1910–11, 1913–16, and 1919–20, that is, 6 years, the political institutions remain strong, and more important, most political figures, especially of national importance, hold one or more of the above-mentioned positions. Indeed, the long-term trend throughout this period is one of increasing institutionalization. It is the leaders of these institutions that I wish to portray collectively, since they are the ones responsible for political development after 1934.

I make no claim that all such figures are included, first because of inadequate information, and second, because once you move from the realm of objective criteria, given its particular limitations, to subjective judgments

about whom to include and exclude, even broader criticisms can be raised. I have stuck with these criteria because they are clear, they are consistent, and they are compatible with the first volume. I believe this consistency sacrifices very little in terms of the broad sweep of political biography during the last century and clearly documents the "victors" of Mexico's institutional structures.

I have made a special effort to include constitutional deputies, 1916–17, and federal deputies elected under Madero, 1912–13, even if they only held a position once, since, as most observers have concluded, these elections were among the freest in Mexican history, and the occupants actually earned their seat in the Chamber from the electorate, rather than being repeatedly appointed as the candidate of Díaz or some succeeding post-revolutionary regime. Constitutional deputies are given special consideration, too, because they are considered Mexico's twentieth-century founding fathers.

No matter how important the individual, no biography was included if information was missing for three or more categories. Although I have cross-referenced information in these biographies in multiple sources, it does not mean that the information contained in the appendixes or biographies is infallible, since government and nongovernmental sources prove to be inaccurate. In fact, I have had to make numerous decisions about dates of birth, dates of death, and years positions were held, since contradictory information was common to most individuals included in the biographical section. Government records have helped to clarify career data, but, unfortunately, even government records use inconsistent spellings or wordings for individual officeholders, making it difficult to separate individuals with similar names.

ABBREVIATIONS OR TERMS USED IN THE TEXT

THESE HAVE been kept to a minimum, for purposes of clarity. Several terms are not readily translated and therefore deserve mention.

CEN
National Executive Committee (Comité Ejecutivo Nacional), used by the government parties to designate its executive administrative structure

Great Committee
(Gran Comisión), the most important committee in the Chamber of Deputies, made up of the head of each state delegation. The president of this body would have the status of a majority leader

Oficial Mayor
No logical translation exists for this position in the national and state executive branches. At the national level, this post is often third in rank, in prestige and power, after that of a secretary and subsecretary

Political Boss
(Jefe Político), although we use the term in political language to refer to a machine-style politician, such as Richard Daley of Chicago, in the biographies, during the Porfiriato, this was a formal political post, below that of governor, which had executive powers at the local level or over large regions, including territories, such as Nayarit, which later became states.

UNAM
National Autonomous University of Mexico or National University (Universidad Nacional Autónoma de México)

SOURCE ABBREVIATIONS

Abreu Gómez
Ermilo Abreu Gómez, *Sala de retratos* (Mexico City: Secretaría de Educación Pública, 1947)

Aguilar Camín
Héctor Aguilar Camín, *La frontera nómada: Sonora y la revolución mexicana* (Mexico City: Siglo XXI, 1977)

Agraz, 1958
Gabriel Agraz García de Alba, Ofrenda a México (Guadalajara, 1958)

Album de la Paz
Ireneo Paz, *Album de la paz y el trabajo* (Mexico City: Ireneo Paz, 1911)

Almada
Francisco R. Almada, *Gobernadores del estado de Chihuahua* (Mexico City: Cámara de Diputados, 1950)

Almada, 1968
Francisco R. Almada, *Diccionario de historia, geografía y biografía chihuahuenses* (Chihuahua: 1968)

Almada, Colima
Francisco R. Almada, *Diccionario de historia, geografía y biografía de Colima* (Colima, 1939)

Almanaque de Aguas
Almanaque de Aguascalientes (Mexico City: Almanaque de México, 1982)

Almanaque de Chiapas
Almanaque de Chiapas (Mexico City: Almanaque de México, 1982)

Almanaque de Oaxaca
Almanaque de Oaxaca (Mexico City: Almanaque de México, 1982)

Almanaque de Puebla
Almanaque de Puebla (Mexico City: Almanaque de México, 1982)

Almanaque de Sonora
Almanaque de Sonora (Mexico City: Almanaque de México, 1982)

Almanaque de Tabasco
Almanaque de Tabasco (Mexico City: Almanaque de México, 1982)

Alvarez Coral — Juan Alvarez Coral, *Galería de gobernadores de Quintana Roo* (Mexico City: Gobierno de Quintana Roo, 1972)

Amigos — Sociedad de Amigos del Libro Mexicano, *Directorio de escritorios mexicanos* (Mexico City, 1956)

Andrade — Cayetano Andrade, *Antología de escritores nicolaitas, 1540–1940* (Mexico City: Vanguardia Nicolaita, 1941)

Aranda Pamplona — Hugo Aranda Pamplona, *Biobibliografía de los escritores del estado de México* (Mexico City: UNAM, 1978)

Armijo — Raymundo Armijo Rodríguez, *Este día en la historia* (Mexico City: Editorial Letras, 1968)

Azpurua — Ramón Azpurua, *Biografías de hombres notables de Hispano América* (Mexico City, 1877)

Balmori — Diana Balmori et al., *Notable Family Networks in Latin America* (Chicago: University of Chicago Press, 1984)

Blue Book — *Blue Book of Mexico* (Mexico City, 1901)

Bojórquez — Juan de Dios Bojórquez, *Forjadores de la revolución mexicana* (Mexico City, 1960)

Bonavit — Julián Bonavit, *Fragmentos de la historia del Colegio Primitivo* (Morelia, 1910)

Bulnes — Pepe Bulnes, *Gobernantes de Tabasco* (Mexico City, 1978)

Bustillos — Antonio Bustillos Carrillo, *Apuntes históricos y biográficos* (Mexico City, 1953)

Carrasco Puente — Rafael Carrasco Puente, *Datos históricos iconografía de la educación en México* (Mexico City: Secretaría de Educación Pública, 1960)

Carreño — Alberto María Carreño, *La Academia Mexicana Correspondiente de la Española, 1875–1945* (Mexico City: Secretaría de Educación Pública, 1946)

C de D — Cámara de Diputados, *Memoria*, each legislature, date, 1880–1988

C de S — Cámara de Senadores, *Memoria*, each legislature, date 1880–1988

Chiapas — *Chiapas, 1925* (no publisher or date)

Cockcroft — James D. Cockcroft, *Intellectual Precursors of the Mexican Revolution, 1900–13* (Austin: University of Texas Press, 1968)

Colliman	Daniel A. Moreno, *Colliman*, 2 Vols. (Mexico City, 1952–1953)
Cordero	Enrique Cordero y Torres, *Diccionario General de Puebla* (Puebla, 1958)
Covarrubias	Ricardo Covarrubias, *Los 67 gobernadores de México independiente* (Monterrey, 1952)
Covarrubias, I-IV	Ricardo Covarrubias, *Las calles de Monterrey*, 4 Vols. (Monterrey, 1970)
Cruzado	Manuel Cruzado, *Bibliografía jurídica mexicana* (Mexico City: Oficina de Estampillas, 1905)
Cuéllar Valdés	Pablo Cuéllar Valdés, *Historia del estado de Coahuila* (Saltillo: Universidad Autónoma de Coahuila, 1979)
Cuevas	Gabriel Cuevas, *El glorioso Colegio Militar mexicano en un siglo 1824–1924* (Mexico City, 1937)
CyT	Enrique Cordero y Torres, *Diccionario biográfico de Puebla*, 2 Vols. (Mexico City, 1972)
Dávila	José María Dávila, *El ejército de la revolución* (Mexico City: Slyse, 1938)
DBGM, 1984	*Diccionario biográfico del gobierno mexicano* (Mexico City: Presidencia de la República, 1984)
DBM68	*Diccionario biográfico de México, 1966–68* (Monterrey: Editorial Revesa, 1968)
DGF50	Mexico, Dirección Técnica de Organización, *Directorio del gobierno federal*, 1950
DGF51	Mexico, Dirección Técnica de Organización, *Directorio del gobierno federal*, 1951
DGF56	México, Dirección Técnica de Organización, *Directorio del gobierno federal*, 1956
de Parrodi	Enriqueta de Parrodi, *Sonora, hombres y paisajes* (Mexico City: Editorial Pafim, 1941)
Dicc mich	Jesús Romero Flores, *Diccionario michoacano de historia y geografía* (Morelia, 1960)
Dir social	*Directorio Social* (Mexico City, 1935)
DP70	*Diccionario Porrúa* (Mexico City: Editorial Porrúa, 1970)
DPE61	*Directorio del poder ejecutivo, 1961* (Mexico City, 1961)
Dulles	John W. F. Dulles, *Yesterday in Mexico* (Austin: University of Texas Press, 1961)
EBW	*Biographical Encyclopedia of the World* (New York: Institute for Research in Biography, 1946)

Enc Mex	*Enciclopedia de México* (Mexico, various years)
Enc de Yucatán	Carlos A. Echanove Trujillo, *Enciclopedia yucatense* (Mexico City: Gobierno de Yucatán, 1944–1947)
Enc Reg Coah	*Diccionario enciclopédico regional del estado de Coahuila* (Mexico: Fernández, 1966)
Estrada	Genaro Estrada, *Poetas nuevos de México* (Mexico City: Ediciones Porrúa, 1916)
Excélsior	*Excélsior* (Mexico City)
FSRE	*Funcionarios de la Secretaría de Relaciones Exteriores, desde el año de 1821 a 1940* (Mexico City: SRE, 1940)
Func	Sergio Serra Domínguez and Roberto Martínez Barreda, *México y sus funcionarios* (Mexico: Litográfico Cárdenas, 1959)
Fusco	Federico M. Fusco and Félix M. Iglesias, *Los hombres que rodean al señor general Porfirio Díaz* (Mexico City: La Paz Pública, 1896)
García Cubas	Antonio García Cubas, *Diccionario geográfico, histórico y biográfico de los Estado Unidos Mexicanos* (Mexico City: Antigua Imprenta de Murguía, 1888–1891)
García de Alba	Gabriel Agraz García de Alba, *Jalisco y sus hombres* (Guadalajara, 1958)
García Purón	Manuel García Puron, *México y sus gobernantes, biografías* (Mexico: Porrúa, 1964)
García Rivas	Heriberto García Rivas, *150 biografías de mexicanos ilustres* (Mexico City: Diana, 1964)
Garrido	Luis J. Garrido, *El partido de la revolución institucionalizada* (Mexico City: Siglo XXI, 1982)
Ghigliazza	Manuel Mestre Ghigliazza, *Apuntes para una relación de los gobernantes de Tabasco* (Mérida, 1984)
Godoy	José F. Godoy, *Enciclopedia biográfica de contemporáneos* (Washington, D.C.: Globe Printing Office, 1898)
Gómez	Marte R. Gómez, *Biografías de agrónomos* (Mexico City: Escuela Nacional de Agricultura, 1976)
González Dávila	Amado González Dávila, *Diccionario geográfico, histórico, biográfico y estadístico del estado de Sinaloa* (Culiacán, 1959)
González de Cossío	Francisco González de Cossío, *Xalapa* (Mexico City, 1957)

González de la Garza	Rodolfo González de la Garza, *Mil familias de Tamaulipas, Nuevo León, Coahuila y Texas*, 2 Vols. (Mexico City, 1980)
Gordillo y Ortiz	*Diccionario biográfico de Chiapas* (Mexico City: Costa Amic, 1977)
Grimaldo	Isaac Grimaldo, *Apéndice de mexicanos distinguidos* (Mexico City, 1946)
Gruening	Ernest Gruening, *Mexico and Its Heritage* (New York: D. Appleton–Century, 1928)
Guerra	F. X. Guerra, *Le Mexique: De l'Ancien Régime a la Revolution*, 2 Vols. (Paris: L'Harmattan, 1985)
HA	*Hispano Americano* or *Tiempo*
Holms	P. G. Holms, *The Directory of Agencies, Mines and Haciendas, 1905–06* (Mexico City: American Book and Printing Company, 1905)
Hombres prominentes	Ireneo Paz, *Hombres prominentes de México* (Mexico City: La Patria, 1888)
Ind biog	Arturo Blancas and Tomás L. Vidrio, *Indice biográfico de la XLIII Legislatura Federal* (Mexico City, 1956)
Illescas	Francisco R. Illescas and Juan Bartolo Hernández, *Escritores veracruzanos, reseñas biográfica-antológica* (Veracruz, 1945)
Inguíñiz	Juan B. Inguíñiz, *Bibliografía biográfica mexicana* (Mexico City: UNAM, 1969)
Ipiña de Corsi	Matilde Ipiña de Corsi, *La familia Hernández Soto de San Luis Potosí* (San Luis Potosí, 1966)
Ipiña de Corsi, 1956	Matilde Ipiña de Corsi, *Cuatro grandes dinastías en los descendientes de los hermanos Fernández de Lima y Barragán* (San Luis Potosí, 1956)
Iturribarría	Jorge Fernando Iturribarría, *La generación oaxaqueña del 57* (Mexico City, 1956)
JSH	*Biografías de amigos y conocidos* (Mexico: Cuadernos Americanos, 1980)
Justicia	*Justicia* (Mexico City legal review)
Langston	William S. Langston, "Coahuila in the Porfiriato, 1893–1911," Unpublished Ph.D. dissertation, Tulane University, 1980.
Lanuza	Agustín Lanuza, *Historia del Colegio de Guanajuato* (Guanajuato, 1924)
Leight	Hugo Leight, *Las calles de Puebla* (Puebla, 1967)
Libro azul	Rosario Sansores Pren, *Libro azul de la sociedad mexicana* (Mexico City, 1946)

Libro de oro   H. Ruiz Sandoval, Jr., *El libro de oro de México* (Mexico City, 1967–1968)

Linajes   Torsten Dahl, *Linajes en México* (Mexico City: Casa Editora de Genealogía Ibero Americana, 1967)

López   José López Escalera, *Diccionario biográfico y de historia de México* (Mexico City: Editorial del Magistrado, 1964)

López, Héctor   Héctor F. López, *Diccionario geográfico, histórico, biográfico y lingüístico del estado de Guerrero* (Mexico City: Pluma y Lápiz, 1942)

López González   Valentín López González, *Los compañeros de Zapata* (Morelos, 1980)

Lutrell   Estelle Lutrell, *Mexican Writers* (Tucson, 1920)

MAH   Academia Mexicana de Historia, *Memorias* (Mexico City, various years)

Márquez   Joaquín Márquez Montiel, *Hombres célebres de Chihuahua* (Mexico City: Editorial Jus, 1953)

Martínez Alomía   Gustavo Martínez Alomía, *Historiadores de Yucatán* (Campeche: El Fénix, 1906)

Mata Torres   Ramón Mata Torres, *Personajes ilustres de Jalisco* (Mexico City, 1978)

Medina, No. 20   Luis Medina, *Historia de la revolución mexicana, periodo 1940–1952*, Vol. 20 (Mexico: El Colegio de Mexico, 1979)

Mellado   Guillermo Mellado, *Tres etapas políticas de Don Venustiano* (Mexico City, 1916)

Mestre   Manuel Mestre Ghigliazza, *Efemérides biográficas* (Mexico City: Antigua Librería Robredo, 1945)

México y sus hombres *México y sus hombres* (Mexico City, 1905)

Meyer, No. 12   Lorenzo Meyer, et al., *Historia de la revolución mexicana periodo 1928–1934*, Vol. 12 (Mexico City: Colegio de Mexico, 1978)

Montejano   Rafael Montejano y Aguinaga, *Biobibliografía de los escritores de San Luis Potosí* (Mexico City: UNAM, 1979)

Morales Jiménez   Alberto Morales Jiménez, *Hombres de la revolución mexicana* (Mexico City: Talleres Gráficos de la Nación, 1960)

Moreno   Daniel Moreno, *Colima y sus gobernadores* (Mexico City, Ediciones Studium, 1953)

Mundo Lo   Sarah de Mundo Lo, *Index to Spanish Ameri-*

	can Collective Biography, Vol. 2 *Mexico* (New York: G. K. Hall, 1982)
Naranjo	Francisco Naranjo, *Diccionario biográfico revolucionario* (Mexico City: Editorial Cosmos, 1935)
Nakayama	Antonio Nakayama, *Sinaloa, el drama y sus actores* (Mexico City: INAH, 1975)
NYT	The *New York Times*
O'Campo	Aurora O'Campo and Ernesto Prado Velázquez, *Diccionario de escritores mexicanos* (Mexico City: UNAM, 1967)
Ortega	Ricardo Ortega, Pérez Gallardo, *Historia genealógica de las familias más antiguas de México* (Mexico City: A. Carranza, 1908)
Palavicini	Félix F. Palavicini, *Grandes de México* (Mexico City: Sociedad Bolivariana, 1948)
Parrodi	Enriqueta de Parrodi, *Sonora, hombres y paisajes* (Mexico City: Editorial Pafím, 1941)
Pasquel	Leonardo Pasquel, *Educadores veracruzanos* (Mexico City: Editorial Citlaltepetl, 1983)
Pasquel, 1972	Leonardo Pasquel, *La generación liberal veracruzana* (Veracruz: Editorial Citlaltepetl, 1972)
Pasquel, Jalapa	Leonardo Pasquel, *Xalapeños distinguidos* (Jalapa: Editorial Citlaltepetl, 1983)
Pavía	Lázaro Pavía, *Los estados y sus gobernantes* (Mexico City: Escalerillas, 1890)
Pavía, breves	Lázaro Pavía, *Breves apuntes biográficos de los miembros más notables del ramo de hacienda de la república mexicana* (Mexico City: Dublán, 1895)
Pavía, judges	Lázaro Pavía, *Apuntes biográficos de los miembros más distinguidos del poder judicial* (Mexico City: Barroso, 1893)
Peña	Antonio de la Peña y Peña, *Vidas y tiempos* (Havana: El Renacimiento, 1915)
Peral	Miguel Angel Peral, *Diccionario biográfico mexicano* (Mexico City: Editorial PAC, 1945?)
Peral 47	Miguel Angel Peral, *Diccionario biográfico mexicano suplemento* (Mexico: Editorial PAC, 1947)
Pérez Galaz	Juan de Dios Pérez Galaz, *Diccionario geográfico e histórico de Campeche* (Campeche, 1944)
Pérez López	Abraham Pérez López, *Diccionario biográfico hidalguense* (Mexico: Imprenta Unión, 1979)

Política	*Política*
Puente	Ramón Puente, *La dictadura, la revolución y sus hombres* (Mexico City, 1938)
QesQ	Carlos Morales Díaz, *Quién es quien en la nomenclatura de la ciudad de México* (Mexico City: Costa Amic, 1971)
QesQM	*Quién es cada quien en Monterrey* (Monterrey, 1952)
Quirós	Roberto Quirós Martínez, *El momento actual* (Mexico City, 1924)
Ramírez	Alfonso Francisco Ramírez, *Hombres notables y monumentos coloniales de Oaxaca* (Mexico City, 1948)
Rev de Ejer	*Revista de Ejército y Fuerza Aérea*
Rice	Jacqueline Ann Rice, "The Porfirian Political Elite: Life Patterns of the Delegates to the 1892 Unión Liberal Convention," Unpublished Ph.D. dissertation, UCLA, 1979.
Romero Aceves	Ricardo Romero Aceves, *Maestros colimenses* (Mexico City: Costa Amic, 1975)
Romero Flores	Jesús Romero Flores, *Maestros y amigos* (Mexico City: Costa Amic, 1971)
Romo	Joaquín Romo de Vivar y Torres, *Guadalajara* (Guadalajara: Banco Industrial de Jalisco, 1964)
Rouaix	Pastor Rouaix, *Diccionario geográfico, histórico y biográfico del estado de Durango* (Mexico City: Instituto Pan Americano de Geografía e Historia, 1946)
Sánchez García	Alfonso Sánchez García, *Historia elemental del estado de México* (Toluca: Gobierno del Estado, 1983)
Santamaría	Francisco J. Santamaría, *Semblanzas tabasqueñas* (Mexico, 1946)
Sec of War	México, Secretaría de Guerra y Marina, *Escalafón general de ejército* (Mexico City, 1902, 1911, 1914)
Serrano	T. F. Serrano, *Episodios de la revolución en México* (El Paso: Modern Printing, 1911)
Siempre	*Siempre* (Mexico City)
Sierra	Carlos J. Sierra, *Historia de la administración hacendaria en México* (Mexico City: Secretaría de Hacienda Pública, 1970)
Siliceo	Rosario Siliceo Ambia, *Perfiles de gloria* (Puebla: Centro de Estudios Históricos, 1969)
Sociedad	México, Sociedad Mexicana de Geografía y Estadística, *Boletín de la Sociedad Mexicana de*

	Geografía y Estadística
Sosa	Francisco Sosa, *Biografías de mexicanos distinguidos* (Mexico City: Secretaría de Fomento, 1884)
Teixidor	Felipe Teixidor, *Exlibris y bibliotecas en México* (Mexico City: Secretaría de Relaciones Exteriores, 1931)
Torre Villar	Ernesto de la Torre Villar, *Mexicanos ilustres*, Vol. 2 (Mexico City: Jus, 1979)
Torres Martínez	Gonzalo Torres Martínez, *Los Torres de Jaen en México* (Mexico City: Editorial Jus, 1975)
UNAM, ENP	*Inscripciones* (UNAM, National Preparatory School, official registration records, all years)
UNAM, law	*Inscripciones* (UNAM, National School of Law, official registration records, all years)
UNAM, med	*Inscripciones* (UNAM, National School of Medicine, official registration records, all years)
UTEHA	*Diccionario Enciclopedia UTEHA* (Mexico: UTEHA, 1950)
Valdés Acosta	José María Valdés Acosta, *A través de las centurias* (Mérida, 1931)
Velasco	Alfonso Luis Velasco, *Porfirio Díaz y su gabinete, estudios biográficos* (Mexico City: Editores, 1889)
Velásquez Bringas	Esperanza Velásquez Bringas and Rafael Heliodoro Valle, *Indice de escritores* (Mexico City: Herrero, 1928)
Villa, 1937	Eduardo W. Villa, *Educadores Sonorenses* (Mexico City, 1937)
Villaseñor	Ramiro Villaseñor y Villaseñor, *Bibliografía general de Jalisco* (Guadalajara: Gobierno del Estado, 1957)
WB48	*World Biography* (New York: Institute for Research in Biography, 1948)
WB54	*World Biography* (New York: Institute for Research in Biography, 1954)
Wright	Laureana Wright de Kleinhans, *Mujeres notables mexicanas* (Mexico City: Económica, 1910)
WWLA35	Percy A. Martin, *Who's Who in Latin America* (Stanford: Stanford University Press, 1935)
WWLA40	Percy A. Martin, *Who's Who in Latin America* (Stanford: Stanford University Press, 1940)
WWM45	Percy A. Martin, *Who's Who in Latin America* (Stanford: Stanford University Press, 1945)

Mexican Political Biographies, 1884–1935

A

Abarca Pérez, Juan
(Deceased) A] June 24, 1893. B] Penjamillo, Michoacán. C] Primary studies, Penjamillo; preparatory studies, Morelia, 1907; no degree. D] *Federal deputy* from the State of Michoacán, Dist. 19, 1926–28, 1928–30. E] None. F] None. G] None. H] Journalist, began working for *La Sátira*; reporter, *El País*; founded various newspapers during the Revolution. I] Unknown. J] Joined the Constitutional Forces, 1913; paymaster, Constitutional Army; rank of captain; fought under General *José María Maytorena*. K] None. L] Mundo Lo, 28; Romero Flores, 10; Peral, 10.

Acosta (Guajardo), Miguel N.
(Deceased April 1, 1947) A] September 16, 1891. B] Chihuahua, Chihuahua. C] Early education unknown; no degree; director, National Military College, 1925–27. D] None. E] None. F] Oficial mayor of the Secretariat of War, 1924; *secretary* of communications and public works, 1932–34. G] None. H] None. I] Son of Domingo Acosta and Epifania Guajardo; married Enriqueta Schneider. J] Fought against *Pascual Orozco*, reserve forces, 1912–13; joined the Constitutionalists, San Luis Potosí, 1913, rank of 2nd captain; captured and imprisoned, 1913; served under the command of *Lucio Blanco*, Sonora, 1914; rank of lt. colonel, January 9, 1914; rank of brigade general, 1915; commander, 1st Brigade, 6th Division, 1916–17; commander of military operations, Eastern Sector, Michoacán; garrison commander, Ciudad Camargo, Chihuahua; supported the Plan of Agua Prieta, 1920; secretary of the Council of War which sentenced *Felipe Angeles* to death, 1920; commander, 1st Special Regiment, Federal District, 1923; fought against the de la Huerta rebellion, 1923; rank of division general, October 21, 1924; fought against Jesús M. Aguirre in Veracruz, 1929; commander, 22nd Military Zone, Veracruz, 1934; special assignment, Rochester, New York; unassigned, Secretariat of War, 1936. K] None. L] Almada, 1968, 9; Rev de Ejer, Sept., 1976, 124; Peral, 13; Dávila, 88; Dir social, 1935, 51;

Enc Mex, I, 58; DP70, 17; WWM45, 1; López, 15–16.

Acuña, Jesús
(Deceased January 3, 1931) A] March 22, 1886. B] Saltillo, Coahuila. C] Primary studies in Coahuila; secondary studies unknown; law degree, National School of Law, UNAM; enrolled, 1906. D] *Constitutional deputy* from the Federal District, Dist. 8, 1916–17. E] None. F] *Governor* of Coahuila, 1914–15; *secretary* of government, 1915–16; *secretary* of foreign relations, 1915–16. G] Member of the radical group of the First National Student Congress. H] Unknown. I] Son of Jesús Acuña and Mariana Narro. J] Joined the Constitutionalists, 1913; representative to the Convention of Aguascalientes, 1914–15. K] None. L] Peral, 14; Enc Mex, I, 64; Enc Reg Coah, 6.

Adame (Alatorre), Julián
(Deceased) A] January 14, 1882. B] San Francisco de los Adame, Zacatecas. C] Primary and secondary studies, San Francisco de los Adame; preparatory studies, Scientific and Literary Institute of Zacatecas; engineering degree, National School of Mines. D] Mayor of Zacatecas, Zacatecas, 1916; *constitutional deputy* from Zacatecas, Dist. 2, 1916–17. E] None. F] Interim governor of Zacatecas; member of the National Agrarian Commission, 1924–28; engineer, National Irrigation Commission, Sinaloa; delegate of the Department of Agrarian Affairs, Guerrero; engineer, Secretariat of Hydraulic Resources, 1950. G] Founder and president of the Local Agrarian Committee, Zacatecas, 1915. H] None. I] Son of José Adame Elías and Rafaela Alatorre Ocampo. J] None. K] None. L] C de D, 1916–17.

Aguilar (Vargas), Cándido
(Deceased March 19, 1960) A] Feb. 12, 1888. B] Congregación de Palma y Monteros, Veracruz. D] *Governor* of Veracruz, June 20, 1914–June 24, 1917; *constitutional deputy* from the State of Veracruz, Dist. 15, 1916–17, first vice-president of the convention; senator from Veracruz, 1934–40; federal deputy from the State of Veracruz, Dist. 8, 1943–46. E] Presi-

dent of the Party of the Mexican Revolution (PRM), 1951. F] Secretary of foreign relations, 1918; confidential ambassador to the United States and Europe, 1919. G] Founder of the League of Agrarian Communities in Veracruz. H] Milkman before the Revolution. I] Son-in-law of President *Venustiano Carranza*; married Virginia Carranza; brother of *Silvestre Aguilar*; uncle of Hesiquio Aguilar Marañón, federal deputy from Veracruz, 1967–70; great uncle of Hesiquio Aguilar de la Parra, federal deputy from Veracruz, 1979–82. J] Joined the Anti-Reelectionist movement under *Francisco Madero* in 1910, served under General *Gabriel Gavira*, and became a Constitutionalist in 1913; served as a chief of operations, but left the army after President Carranza was killed; rank of division general, 1944; commander of the Legion of Honor, 1950. K] Remained loyal to Carranza, 1920; joined the de la Huerta rebellion in 1923 and was exiled; lived in San Antonio, Texas, 1920–25; publicized the corruption in the PRM and was thrown out of the official party on June 10, 1944; went into self-exile in Cuba and El Salvador, 1952–54; imprisoned for political reasons in Veracruz, 1952. L] Peral 47, 5–6, DP70, 35, letter, Gruening, 584, UTEHA, 284; López, 21.

Aguilar, Jr. (Vargas), Silvestre
(Deceased 1955) A] 1914. B] Córdoba, Veracruz. C] Primary studies in Córdoba, Veracruz, and San Antonio, Texas; secondary studies in St. Louis and Chicago; law degree, School of Law, University of Veracruz, Jalapa. D] *Constitutional deputy* from the State of Veracruz, Dist. 11, 1916–17; federal deputy from the State of Veracruz, Dist. 9, 1937–40; federal deputy from the State of Veracruz, Dist. 6, 1943–46; federal deputy from the State of Veracruz, Dist. 9, 1949–51, member of the Committee on Forest Affairs, the Library Committee, the First Balloting Committee, and Executive Secretary of the First Instructive Committee for the Grand Jury. E] None. F] Employee of the Secretariat of Government; oficial mayor of the State of Veracruz under Governor Jorge Cerdán, 1940–43; treasurer of Veracruz, 1946. I] Brother of *Cándido Aguilar*, son-in-law

of *Venustiano Carranza* and his secretary of foreign relations; son, Hesiquio Aguilar Marañón, was a federal deputy from Veracruz, 1967–70; grandson, Hesiquio Aguilar de la Parra, was a federal deputy from Veracruz, 1979–82. K] In exile in the United States and Cuba, 1920. L] Peral, 20; C de D, 1937–40, 5; C de D, 1943–46, 5; C de D, 1949–51, 61; DGF51, 26, 30, 34.

Aguilar y Maya, José
(Deceased November 30, 1966) A] July 28, 1897. B] Jerécuaro, Guanajuato. C] Primary, secondary, and preparatory; Seminario de Morelia, Michoacán, and Colegio de Guanajuato; law degree, National School of Law, UNAM; professor of Spanish and literature, Preparatory School, Guanajuato; professor of general theory and of public law, UNAM, for ten years, during which he gained national recognition; head, Department of Justice and Public Instruction, Guanajuato. D] *Federal deputy* from the State of Guanajuato, Dist. 13, 1924–26; *federal deputy* from the State of Guanajuato, Dist. 12, 1926–; *federal deputy* from the State of Guanajuato, Dist. 21, 1928–30; *federal deputy* from the State of Guanajuato, Dist. 7, 1937–40; governor of Guanajuato, 1949–55. E] None. F] *Attorney general* of the Federal District and Federal Territories, 1928; attorney general of the Federal District and Federal Territories, 1930–32; attorney general of Mexico, 1940–46; attorney general of Mexico, 1955–58. G] None. H] Director general of Seguros de México, SA, 1948; author of many works and emergency war legislation for President Avila Camacho. I] Brother of Guillermo Aguilar y Maya, federal deputy and attorney general of the Federal District; friend of Senator *Enrique Colunga*, governor of Guanajuato, 1923–27, and minister of government under President Alvaro Obregón; married María Tinajero; father was a small landowner. J] None. K] Attributes his nomination as governor of Guanajuato to teaching students who later became pivotal men in the Mexican political system; leader of political faction in Guanajuato known as the "Reds"; supported candidacy of Ernesto Hidalgo as governor, 1943. L] WWM45, 1; HA, 18 Feb. 1957, 6;

HA, 28 Sept. 1953; DP70, 38; Gruening, 429; Peral, 18–19; Enc Mex I, 214–15; WWLA35, 16; López, 25.

Aguilera (Serrano), José Guadalupe
(Deceased March 13, 1941) A] February 5, 1857. B] Mapimí, Durango. C] Primary studies in Mapimí; secondary studies at the Juárez Institute of Durango, on a scholarship from Mapimí; prefect, Juárez Institute of Durango; preparatory studies, National Preparatory School, 1876–77; engineering degree, School of Mines, 1877–82; preparer of applied and analytical chemistry, School of Mines, 1879–82; professor of mineralogy, geology, paleontology, petrology, National School of Engineering; professor of mineralogy, general geology, Mexican geology, paleontology, and soils, National School of Agriculture; professor, National Military College; subdirector, Geological Institute, 1891–95; director, Geological Institute, 1895–1914; director of Geology and Geography, School of Graduate Studies, National Autonomous University of Mexico (UNAM). D] None. E] None. F] Subsecretary of development, 1914. G] None. H] Resident at the Smithsonian Institution, 1884–86. I] Son of José Guadalupe Aguilera and María Serrano; married Lillie Goudille; disciple of Antonio del Castillo. J] None. K] Cofounder of the Geological Institute, 1891; considered the father of Mexican geology. L] Dir social, 52; Carreño, V, 5–22; Rouaix, 19–20; Gómez, 17; DP70, 39.

Aguirre Benavides, Adrián
(Deceased 1968) A] 1879. B] Parras de la Fuente, Coahuila. C] Early education unknown; law degree, National School of Law, UNAM. D] *Federal deputy* from the State of Coahuila, Dist. 5, 1912–13; *federal deputy* from the State of Coahuila, Dist. 2, 1922–24. E] None. F] Legal adviser to *Francisco I. Madero*; official, Secretariat of Water Resources, 1946. G] None. H] None. I] Son of Rafael Aguirre, tax administrator, and Jovita Benavides; brother of *Eugenio Aguirre Benavides*, revolutionary and subsecretary of war, 1914–15; related to Francisco I. Madero; brother of Luis Aguirre Benavides, private secretary to *Gustavo A. Ma-*

dero. J] Joined Villa, 1913. K] Awarded the Belisario Domínguez Medal, October 7, 1964. L] Enc Mex, I, 165; Gómez, 22–23.

Aguirre Benavides, Eugenio
(Deceased June 2, 1915) A] September 6, 1884. B] Parras de la Fuente, Coahuila. C] Primary studies in Parras de la Fuente, 1892; abandoned studies in 1900 because of eyesight. D] Mayor of Torreón, Coahuila, 1912–13. E] None. F] *Subsecretary* of war, 1914–15. G] None. H] Began working on a ranch, 1900. I] Son of Rafael Aguirre, tax administrator, and Jovita Benavides; brother Alfonso managed *Francisco Madero*'s grape ranches after the Revolution; brother *Adrián Aguirre Benavides* was a federal deputy; brother Luis was *Gustavo Madero*'s secretary; related to Madero on mother's side. J] Fought under *Francisco Villa* early in the Revolution, 1910; opposed *Pascual Orozco*, 1912–13; joined the Constitutionalists, 1913; secretary of Francisco Villa at the Convention of Aguascalientes, 1914; captured and executed by General Nafarrate, Matamoros, Coahuila. K] None. L] Gómez, 22–23; Moreno, 201–04; Peral, 21; Enc Mex, I, 165.

Aguirre Berlanga, Joaquín
(Deceased March 28, 1939) A] May 22, 1885. B] San Antonio de las Alazanas, Municipio de Arteaga, Coahuila. C] Secondary studies at the Ateneo Fuente, Saltillo; no degree. D] *Constitutional deputy* from the State of Jalisco, Dist. 16, 1916–17; *federal deputy* from the State of Jalisco, Dist. 16, 1917–18, 1918–20. E] None. F] Employee, Department of Labor, State of Jalisco, 1939. G] None. H] Author. I] Brother of *Manuel Aguirre Berlanga*, secretary of government, 1917–20; son of Esiquio Aguirre Berlanga and María de los Angeles Berlanga. J] Unknown. K] Supported *Francisco I. Madero*, 1911. L] HA, 21 Feb. 1987, 37.

Aguirre Berlanga, Manuel
(Deceased October 4, 1953) A] January 28, 1887. B] San Antonio de las Alazanas, Municipio de Arteaga, Coahuila. C] Secondary studies at the Ateneo Fuente, Sal-

tillo, Coahuila; preparatory studies at the Scientific and Literary Institute of San Luis Potosí; law degree, National School of Law, UNAM, 1910; professor of constitutional law, University of Guadalajara; professor of administrative law, University of Guadalajara. D] Mayor of Piedras Negras, Coahuila; local deputy to the state legislature of Coahuila, 1913; *constitutional deputy* from the State of Coahuila, Dist. 1, 1916–17. E] Candidate of the Independent Liberal party for federal deputy. F] Posts in the state government of Coahuila, 1911–12; secretary general of government of the State of Jalisco, 1914; *governor* of Jalisco, 1915–16; *subsecretary* of government, 1916–17; *secretary* of government, 1917–20; justice of the Superior Tribunal of Justice of the Federal District. G] None. H] Practicing lawyer; author. I] Brother of *Joaquín Aguirre Berlanga*, constitutional deputy, 1916–17; son of Esiquio Aguirre Berlanga and María de los Angeles Berlanga; married Matilda Rangel. J] Military commander of Jalisco under General *Manuel Diéguez*,1914–15. K] Remained loyal to *Venustiano Carranza* in 1920; retired from public life after Carranza's murder; represented Carranza in the United States. L] Peral, 21; DP70, 41; Dir Social, 1935, 52.

Aguirre Colorado, Ernesto
(Deceased 1939) A] November 6, 1889. B] Huimanguillo, Tabasco. C] Primary studies in Huimanguillo; secondary studies at the Hidalgo Institute, Villahermosa, Tabasco; first year of preparatory studies, Juárez Institute, Villahermosa, Tabasco; continued preparatory studies at the National Preparatory School; left studies to join the Revolution, 1911; no degree. D] *Federal deputy* from the Federal District, Dist. 5, 1917–18; *federal deputy* from the Federal District, Dist. 7, 1920–22. E] Founded the Anti-Reelectionist Club, Huimanguillo, Tabasco, July 31, 1909. F] Tax administrator, Lagos de Moreno, Jalisco, 1920; director, Department of Cavalry, Secretariat of National Defense; chief of staff, Secretariat of National Defense. G] None. H] None. I] Brother of Fernando Aguirre Colorado, federal deputy from Tabasco, 1920–22; brother of General Rafael Aguirre Colorado; nephew

of Aureliano Colorado, justice of the Superior Tribunal of Justice of Tabasco. J] Joined the Revolution under General Ignacio Gutiérrez in Tabasco, April 1911; captured by General Blanquet, 1913; rank of 1st captain, April 5, 1913; fought against Victoriano Huerta's forces, 1913; rank of colonel, September 1914; rank of brigadier general , October 20, 1914; attended the Convention of Aguascalientes, 1914–15; served under General *Salvador Alvarado* in Yucatán, 1915; military commander of the State of Tabasco, 1915; garrison commader in Oaxaca and Guadalajara; commander of the 1st Mixed Brigade against the forces of *Adolfo de la Huerta*, in Veracruz, 1923; rank of brigade general, June 1, 1924; inspector general of the army, 1926; commander of the 16th Military Zone, Irapuato, Guanajuato, 1926; commander of the 31st Military Zone, Tapachula, Chiapas. K] Detained by General *Samuel García Cuéllar*, inspector of police, Mexico City, for political activities, 1910; left school to support Madero's forces in Tabasco, 1911. L] DP70, 41; Dávila , 139–40; Peral, 21–22; Enc Mex, I, 166.

Aguirre (del Hierro), Gabriel
(Deceased September 15, 1908) A] 1826. B] Mineral de Batopilas, Andrés del Río, Chihuahua. C] Primary studies in Mineral de Batopilas; law studies, San Luis Potosí, 1857–61; law degree before the National College of Lawyers, October 19, 1861. D] Federal deputy from the State of Chihuahua, 1857–58; federal deputy from the State of San Luis Potosí, 1861; federal deputy from the State of Chihuahua, 1873–75; senator from the State of Chihuahua, 1875–76; senator from the State of Chihuahua, 1880–84; local deputy to the state legislature of Chihuahua, 1884–88; *alternate federal deputy* from the State of Michoacán , Dist. 9, 1892–94; *alternate federal deputy* from the State of Chihuahua, Dist. 6, 1904–06. E] Joined the Liberal party, 1857. F] Secretary to the political boss of the Matamoros Canton (District), 1847; first councilmember, Matamoros Canton; political boss of Matamoros, 1855–56; director of the Treasury Department, San Luis Potosí, San Luis Potosí, 1858–59; paymaster general,

General Juan Zuazua's troops, 1859; district court judge, Chihuahua, Chihuahua, 1864–65, 1866–68, 1869–73; district court judge, San Luis Potosí, 1868–69; interim governor of Chihuahua, 1880; district court judge, Chihuahua, 1908. G| None. H| Concession from federal government to develop his hacienda Alamos de Peña, 1897; operated coach line between Chihuahua, Chihuahua, and Guerrero, Chihuahua. I| Son of Pablo José de Aguirre and María de Jesús del Hierro. J| Captain, national guard. K| Supported the political group headed by *Luis Terrazas* against *Carlos Pacheco,* 1887. L| Almada, 1968, 199; Almada, 374–77.

Aguirre Escobar, Juan
(Deceased August 14, 1954) A| May 16, 1874. B| Hacienda La Florida, Municipio de Patos (General Cepeda), Coahuila. C| Primary studies at the Villa de Patos Public School until 1887; preparatory studies at the Ateneo Fuente, Saltillo, 1888–89; abandoned studies to help support his family; no degree. D| *Constitutional deputy* from the State of Zacatecas, Dist. 8, 1916–17; *federal deputy* from the State of Zacatecas, Dist. 8, 1917–18, president of the Great Committee (majority leader of the Chamber). E| Supported the prerevolutionary political movement of *Ricardo Flores Magón,* 1906. F| Official, Secretariat of War, 1915. G| None. H| Laborer, United States, 1892–93; miner, Concepción del Oro, Zacatecas, 1893–10; co-owner, San Marcos Mine. I| Son of Jesús Aguirre Charles and Ignacia Escobar. J| Fought under *Eulalio Gutiérrez* in the revolution, 1910; served in the Constitutionalist forces under Luis Gutiérrez, 1913–16; represented General Luis Gutiérrez at the Convention of Aguascalientes, 1914–15; rank of brigadier general, 1924; retired from active duty, 1944. K| Participant in a revolt against government authorities, Concepción del Oro, 1900. L| Peral, 22.

Aguirre (Santiago), Amado
(Deceased August 22, 1949) A| February 8, 1863. B| San Sebastián, ex-canton (district) of Mascota, Guadalajara, Jalisco. C| Primary and secondary studies in San Sebastián; preparatory studies at the Liceo de Varones, Guadalajara; mining engineering degree, University of Guadalajara; director, National Military College, 1925. D| *Constitutional deputy* from the State of Jalisco, Dist. 11, 1916–17; *senator* from the State of Jalisco, 1917–18. E| None. F| Ambassador to the United States; ambassador to various South American countries; director, Department of History, Secretariat of War; director, Department of Cavalry, Secretariat of War; subsecretary of development, 1917–20; subsecretary of agriculture, 1920; *secretary* of communications and public works, 1921–24; *governor* of Quintana Roo, 1925; subsecretary of war; *governor* of Baja California del Sur, 1927–29. G| None. H| Manager of mines, San Andrés de la Sierra, Durango; mining official, Pachuca and Real del Monte mines. I| Son of Amado Ignacio Aguirre, prominent journalist, mining engineer, and Liberal, and Mariana Santiago. J| Supported Madero with money and arms, 1910; joined the Constitutionalists as a major of engineers under General *Lucio Blanco,* 1913; rank of colonel, January 2, 1915; commander of the 2nd Brigade; chief of staff, General *Manuel Diéguez,* commander of the Fort of Guadalajara, 1916; commander of the 15th Military Zone, Guadalajara, Jalisco, 1916; commander of the 15th Military Zone, Guadalajara, Jalisco, 1924; rank of brigade general, November 13, 1924; rank of division general. K| Supported General Escobar, 1929. L| DP70, 40; López, 26–27; Rev de Ejer, Sept. 1976, 123; Peral, 23; Alvarez Corral, 93; Agraz, 1958, 161; Villaseñor, 11.

Ahumada (Saucedo), Miguel
(Deceased August 6, 1917) A| September 29, 1844. B| Colima, Colima. C| Primary studies in various colegios in Guadalajara; abandoned studies to fight in the Reform. D| Local deputy to the state legislature of Colima, 1876; syndic of City of Colima, 1880; *governor* of Chihuahua, 1892–03; *governor* of Jalisco, 1903–11; *governor* of Chihuahua, 1911; *federal deputy* from the State of Jalisco, Dist. 11, 1913–14. E| None. F| Alternate prefect of the Central District of Colima, 1873–75; prefect of the Central District of Colima, 1875–76; president of the Welfare Board,

1892. G] President of the Society of Federal Employees. H] Carpenter; customs guard, Manzanillo; interventor, Bank of Commerce, Chihuahua; stockholder in Minera de la Reina y de Sagunto Company. I] Son of Ramón Ahumada and Dolores Saucedo. J] Private, Liberal forces, French Intervention; fought under Donato Guerra and *Ramón Corona*, Jalisco; commander of the garrison, Colima, 1876; rank of colonel, national guard, 1876; supported President Lerdo de Tejada, 1876–77; captured and amnestied by general *Francisco Tolentino*, 1877; commander of the Naval Customs Station, Guaymas, Sonora, 1880; chief of the 3rd Tax Police Zone, 1881–86; chief of the 2nd Tax Police Zone, Chihuahua, 1886. K] Went into exile in El Paso, Texas, 1914–17, after Huerta's forces were defeated. L] Márquez, 278–81; Mata Torres, 61; Album de la Paz; Almada, 11–12; DP70, 45; Mestre, 258; Enc Mex, I, 180–81; Godoy, 172; Almada, 426–34; Almada, 1968, 21; Peral, appendix, 8.

Alamillo, José Trinidad
(Deceased October 16, 1937) A] June 9, 1847. B] Villa de Chávez, Colima. C] Primary studies in the Colima School for Boys, Colima; no degree. D] Local deputy to the state legislature of Colima, 1891–97; *alternate federal deputy* from the State of Zacatecas, Dist. 2, 1906–08; *alternate federal deputy* from the State of Coahuila, Dist. 4, 1908–10; *alternate federal deputy* from the State of Coahuila, Dist. 4, 1910–12; *governor* of Chihuahua, 1911–13. E] None. F] Official, secretary general of government, State of Colima, 1874; official, Criminal Judicial District, Colima; customs official, Colima; director, Government Printing Office and the *Diario Oficial* of Colima, 1885–87; political prefect of the 1st District, Colima, under Governor *Gildardo Gómez*, 1887–91. G] None. H] Printer; journalist. I] Son of Mateo Alamillo, fought the French in the 1860s, and Jesús Carrillo; married Paula Guizar. J] Supported *Victoriano Huerta* in the Revolution, 1913. K] Brought the first linotype to Colima. L] DP70, 49; Moreno, 61–64; Peral, appendix, 10; Mestre, 293; Pavía, 321–30.

Alarcón, Manuel
(Deceased December 15, 1908) A] 1851. B] Hacienda Buenavista, Santa María, Municipio de Cuernavaca, Morelos. C] Early education unknown; no degree. D] Local deputy to the state legislature of Morelos, 1884; *governor* of Morelos, 1896–08. E] None. F] Political boss of Cuautla, Morelos, 1883–84; political boss of Cuernavaca, 1887; *interim governor* of Morelos, 1895–96. G] None. H] Rancher, 1876–77. I] Parents were peasants. J] Volunteer under a Colonel Castelló against the French, 1866; rejoined forces in Tepoztlán, Morelos, under Prisciliano Rodríguez and General Francisco Leyva, 1866; attached to the forces under *Porfirio Díaz*, 1867; chief of public security, Yautepec and Tetecala, 1868–76; supported the Revolution of Tuxtepec, 1876; retired to civilian life, 1876–77; joined the 5th and later 10th Rural Forces, 1877; rank of colonel, cavalry reserves, March 11, 1890; appointed commander of the military forces in Morelos by Governor *Carlos Quaglia*. K] None. L] DP70, 52; Mestre, 233; Album de la Paz; México y sus hombres.

Albístegui, Francisco
(Deceased 1912) A] 1841. B] Hidalgo del Parral, Chihuahua. C] Early education unknown; no degree. D] Local deputy to the state legislature of Chihuahua, various years, 1880s; *federal deputy* from the State of Chihuahua, Dist. 2, 1894–96, 1896–98, 1898–1900; *senator* from the State of Guanajuato, 1900–04, 1904–08, 1908–12. E] None. F] Unknown. G] None. K] Hid *Porfirio Díaz* from government authorities, 1872. L] DP70, 55.

Alcaraz Romero, Salvador
(Deceased 1949) A] 1880. B] Huetamo, Michoacán . C] Primary studies in Huetamo; began preparatory studies at the Auxiliary Colegio of the Seminary of Morelia; completed preparatory studies at the Colegio de San Nicolás, Morelia, Michoacán; civil engineer degree from the Free School of Engineering, Guadalajara, Jalisco, 1909. D] *Constitutional deputy* from the State of Michoacán, Dist. 7, 1916–17; *federal deputy* from the State

of Michoacán , Dist. 7, 1922–24. E] Supported Madero, 1910. F] None. G] None. H] Civil engineer. I] Student at the Colegio de San Nicolás with *Jesús Romero Flores*, constitutional deputy, 1916–17; student of Ambrosio Ulloa at the Free School of Engineering. J] Fought *Victoriano Huerta's* forces under General J. Rentería Luviano, Michoacán , 1913–14; represented General Alfredo Elizondo at the Convention of Aguascalientes, 1914–15. K] None. L] Flores Romero, 225–28; DP70, 58; Dicc mich, 16–17.

Alcérreca, Félix María
(Deceased 1937) A] May 18, 1845. B] Puebla, Puebla. C] Primary studies, Palafox Seminary, Puebla; graduated as a notary public and lawyer, Mexico City, 1867; enrolled in the Conservatory of Music, Mexico City, to study the violoncello under Agustín Caballero, 1868. D] *Federal deputy* from the State of Querétaro, Dist. 3, 1892–94, 1894–96; *federal deputy* from the State of Querétaro, Dist. 2, 1896–98, pro-secretary of the Chamber of Deputies; *federal deputy* from the State of Querétaro, 1898–1900, 1900–02; *federal deputy* from the State of México, Dist. 4, 1902–04; *federal deputy* from the State of Querétaro, Dist. 3, 1904–06, 1906–08, 1908–10, 1910–12. E] None. F] None. G] President of the National College of Notaries; director of the Philharmonic Society. H] Notary public; journalist for many Mexico City dailies; Director of *Musical Chronology*; founder of the Conservatory Orchestra and first violoncello; composer. I] Related to General Agustín Alcérreca and General Agustín Alcérreca, Jr. J] None. K] Orphaned at the age of fourteen. L] Mestre, 229; Godoy, 8–9; CyT, 25.

Alcocer, Ignacio
(Deceased May 2, 1936) A] December 21, 1870. B] Saltillo, Coahuila. C] Early education unknown; medical degree. D] *Senator* from the State of Coahuila, 1914–16. E] None. F] *Governor* of Coahuila, 1913; *subsecretary* in charge of government,1913–14; *secretary* of government, 1914. G] None. H] Physician; author of many books. I] Unknown.

J] None. K] None. L] Enc Mex, I, 211; Mestre, 291.

Alcolea (Sastre), Leandro M.
(Deceased September 18, 1909) A] December 8, 1842. B] Veracruz, Veracruz. C] Primary studies, public schools, Veracruz; studies in law in Havana, Cuba; completed legal studies in Mérida, Yucatán, 1864; law degree before the College of Lawyers, Puebla, and the Superior Tribunal of Justice of Puebla, 1867. D] Local deputy to the state legislature of Veracruz, 1875; federal deputy from the State of Veracruz, 1875–77; mayor of Veracruz, 1885–88, 1892, 1894–96; *federal deputy* from the State of Veracruz, Dist. 1, 1896–98, president of the chamber, 1896; *federal deputy* from the State of Veracruz, Dist. 1, 1898–1900, 1900–02, 1902–04, 1904–06, 1906–08, 1908–09. E] None. F] Syndic of the 2nd Council of Veracruz, 1869; judge of the 4th District, Veracruz, 1870–71; political chief of Veracruz Canton (District), 1871–74; interim district court judge, Veracruz, 1881–83; secretary general of government of the State of Veracruz, 1883; first magistrate of the Superior Tribunal of Justice, 1884; syndic of 1st Council of Veracruz, 1884–85; *interim governor* of Veracruz, 1892. G] Member of the Political Military Association of Veracruz, 1870. H] Employee of Muriel, Ulibarri & Co., 1856. I] Son of Diego R. Alcolea and Felipa Sastre; son Rafael Alcolea served as an alternate federal deputy from Veracruz, 1902–06, and federal deputy, 1910–12; daughter Isabella Alcolea married *Félix Díaz*, nephew of *Porfirio Díaz* and presidential chief of staff; close political associate of *Teodoro A. Dehesa*, governor of Veracruz. J] None. K] Joined father, exiled for political activities, in Cuba in 1856. L] Peral; DP70, 61; Pasquel, 9–10; Mestre, 236; Album de la Paz.

Alessio Robles, Miguel
(Deceased November 10, 1951) A] December 5, 1884. B] Saltillo, Coahuila. C] Early education unknown; preparatory studies at the Ateneo Fuente, Saltillo; legal studies at the National School of Law, UNAM, 1903–08, law degree, 1909. D] *Federal deputy* from the State of Coa-

huila, Dist. 1, 1920–22. E] None. F] Confidential mission to Spain for *Venustiano Carranza*, 1916; director of the National Library; private secretary to President *Adolfo de la Huerta*, 1920; ambassador to Spain, 1921–22; *secretary* of industry and commerce, 1922–23. G] None. H] Director of the magazine *Todo*; regular contributor to *El Universal*; author of many books. I] Son of Domingo Alessio, Italian, and Cristina Robles; married Josefina Fernández; son Miguel is a lawyer and director general of Sidermex, 1982–88; daughter-in-law is Beatriz Landa Berriozábal, descendant of a prominent 19th-century family; brother *Vito Alessio Robles*, a prominent revolutionary; brother José, a career officer. J] Torre Villar, 11; Libro de Oro, 8; WWM45, 3; López, 38; Peral, 37.

Alessio Robles, Vito
(Deceased June 11, 1957) A] August 14, 1879. B] Saltillo, Coahuila. C] Primary studies at the Colegio de San Juan Nepomuceno and the Instituto Pestalozzi; preparatory studies at the Ateneo Fuente, Saltillo, Coahuila; enrolled in the Colegio Militar, 1897, graduating as a lieutenant of construction engineering, 1903; professor of military tactics, Colegio Militar, 1902; professor, Colegio Civil of Monterrey, 1904; professor of history and mathematics, UNAM, 1935–44; professor, School of Military Aspirants, 1909–13. D] *Federal deputy* from the Federal District, Dist. 4, 1920–22, member of the Great Committee; *senator* from the State of Coahuila, 1922–26. E] President of the Anti-Reelectionist party, 1927–29; supported *José Vasconcelos* for president, 1927–29; opposed *Nazario S. Ortiz Garza* for governor of Coahuila, 1929. F] Subsecretary of justice under the Convention Government, 1914; *governor* of the Federal District under the Convention Government, 1915; ambassador to Sweden, 1925–26. G] Member of the Mexican Academy of History, 1937–57; member of the Seminar of Mexican Culture, 1943–57. H] Contributor to *El Universal, La Prensa, Excélsior*; director of *El Heraldo de México*, 1920; director of *El Demócrata*, 1920–23; author of many historical works. I] Son of Domingo Alessio, Italian, and Cristina

Robles; married Trinidad Cuevas; brother *Miguel Alessio Robles* was private secretary to *Adolfo de la Huerta*, 1920; brother José a career officer. J] Served in the Engineering Corps, army, 1903–11; reached rank of lt. colonel of engineers in the army, 1909; fought Yaquis; fought original Maderistas in the battle of Casas Grandes, 1911; inspector general of police in the Federal District, 1911–12; chief, general staff, President Madero, 1912; military attaché, Rome, Italy, 1912–13; joined the Constitutionalists, 1913; secretary of the Convention of Aguascalientes, 1914, representing General Eduardo Carrera. K] Arrested by the government of General Huerta, 1913; exiled, 1929. L] Carrasco Puente, 235; Enc Mex, I, 220; WWM45, 3; López, 38; Peral, 37; Cuevas, 356; Libro de Oro, 8; MAH, 1957, 217–19.

Alfaro, Francisco
(Deceased) A] Unknown. B] Saltillo, Coahuila. C] Preparatory studies in Saltillo, Monterrey, and San Luis Potosí; completed preparatory in Mexico City; law degree, Seminary of Mexico City; awarded law degree in Tlaxcala; law degree, University of Havana (recognized by Spain), 1878. D] Alternate federal deputy from Tacubaya (Federal District), 1877; *alternate federal deputy* from the State of Oaxaca, Dist. 8, 1894–96; *federal deputy* from the State of Guerrero, Dist. 1, 1904–06, 1906–08, 1908–10; *senator* from the Federal District, 1910–12. E] None. F] Public defender, 1880–86. G] Vice-president of the Associated Press in Mexico, 1886. H] Owner and editor of *Foro*; practicing lawyer, 1872–. I] Son of General Joseph Marian Alfaro, division commander; father exiled for political reasons. J] None. K] None. L] Hombres prominentes, 281–83.

Algara (Cervantes), José
(Deceased March 10, 1908) A] April 23, 1849. B] Mexico City. C] Preparatory studies at the Colegio de San Ildefonso, Mexico City; law degree, School of Law, Mexico City, 1870; professor of international law, penal law, and administrative law, School of Law, Mexico City. D] *Federal deputy* from the Federal District, Dist. 9, 1906–08. E] None. F] Syndic,

City Council of Mexico City; member, City Council of Mexico City; adviser, Secretariat of Foreign Relations, *subsecretary* of foreign relations, 1901–08; *subsecretary* in charge of the Secretariat of Foreign Relations, 1903. G] Original shareholder in the Jockey Club; secretary, Chamber of Commerce, Mexico City. H] Practicing lawyer. I] Son of Ignacio Algara y Gómez and Ana María Cervantes y Ozta; grandson of General José María Cervantes y Velasco, Marquis of Salinas, 12th Count of Santiago, and Ana María Ozta y Cotera, daughter of 3rd Marquesa of Rivascacho. J] None. K] None. L] Inguíñiz, 1203; Peral, 37–38; FSRE, 139; Mestre, 230–31; DP70, 67; Blue Book, 1901, 87; Ortega, 12; UNAM, law, 1868–69, 22.

Almada, Francisco R.
A] October 4, 1896. B] Chínipas, Chihuahua. C] Early education unknown; completed secondary education; no degree; teaching assistant, public schools, 1914–16; director of a rural school, 1916–19, 1926–28; director, Department of Historical Research, University of Chihuahua. D] Mayor of Chínipas, Chihuahua, 1918, 1919–20, 1921–22; local deputy to the state legislature of Chihuahua, 1922–24, 1928–30, 1947–59; *federal deputy* from the State of Chihuahua, Dist. 5, 1924–26; *federal deputy* from the State of Chihuahua, Dist. 4, 1932–34. E] None. F] Tax collector, Ciudad Juárez; assistant inspector of schools, State of Chihuahua, 1926–28; *interim governor* of Chihuahua, 1928, 1929–30; oficial mayor of the government of the State of Chihuahua, 1936, 1942, 1955; secretary general of government of the State of Chihuahua, 1937; secretary of the Education Commission, State of Durango, 1942–44; vice-president, Literacy Council, State of Chihuahua, 1953–55; director, Federal Treasury Office, Colima; director, National Census, Second Division, 1960. G] Member, Mexican Academy of History, 1963. H] Employee, private firm, 1911–13; employee, mining company, 1914–22; prominent regional historian. I] Unknown. J] None. K] None. L] Enc Mex, I, 241–42; Almada, 574; Mundo Lo, 64.

Almeida, Jesús Antonio
(Deceased March, 1957) A] 1888. B] Bachíniva, Guerrero, Chihuahua. C] Primary studies at Public School No. 73, Ciudad Guerrero; no degree. D] *Governor* of Chihuahua, 1924–27. E] None. F] None. G] None. H] Businessman; rancher; practicing physician (no degree), learned medicine in army. I] Student of Professor Mariano Irigoyen in Ciudad Guerrero; political enemy of Fernando Orozco E.; from a family of small ranchers; married Susanna Nesbitt Becerra, daughter of important Urique mining family. J] Supported Orozco, 1912; organized the municipal guards of Chihuahua, 1916; officer, Army Health Section, 1911–17, under Colonel *Samuel García Cuéllar*; opposed *Venustiano Carranza*, May 1920; director of social defense, State of Chihuahua, 1921–23; reached rank of colonel. K] Deposed by the state legislature as governor, April 15, 1927; in exile in the United States, 1927. L] Almada, 559; Gruening, 410–11; Almada, 1968, 30.

Alonzo Romero, Miguel
(Deceased December 25, 1964) A] September 29, 1887. B] Tekax, Yucatán. C] Primary studies, Tekax; secondary and preparatory studies, Literary Institute, Mérida, Yucatán; medical degree, School of Medicine, University of Yucatán; advanced studies in Paris, Berlin, London, and Vienna. D] *Constitutional deputy* from the State of Yucatán, Dist. 5, 1916–17, president of the chamber, 1917; *federal deputy* from the State of Yucatán, Dist. 6, 1917–18; *federal deputy* from the State of Yucatán, Dist. 6, 1920–22, president of the chamber, 1920; mayor of Mexico City, 1922. E] President of the Party in Defense of the Revolution, 1939–40. F] Director, Department of Health, Yucatán, 1915, 1922; director of medical services in the Southeast, 1915; ambassador to Japan and China, 1929–32; ambassador to Japan, 1933–34; ambassador to Venezuela, 1935; ambassador to Nicaragua, 1954–58. G] President, Student Congress of Yucatán, 1913–14; president, Ateneo Popular, 1916. H] Physician; founder, and director of *El Federalista*, a political weekly, 1921; author. I] Son of Crescencio Alonzo and Regina Romero. J] None.

K] Self-imposed exile studying health systems in Europe, Africa, and Asia, 1923–29; remembered for his congressional debates with *Antonio Díaz Soto y Gama.* L] DP70, 75; Peral, 41; Dir social, 1935, 270.

Altamirano, Manlio Fabio
(Deceased June 25, 1936) A] October 12, 1892. B] Jalapa, Veracruz. C] Primary studies in Jalapa and Mexico City; preparatory studies, Mexico City; law degree, National School of Law, UNAM. D] *Federal deputy* from the State of Veracruz, Dist. 1, 1918–20; *federal deputy* from the State of Veracruz, Dist. 8, 1920–22, member of the Great Committee; *federal deputy* from the State of Veracruz, Dist. 6, 1922–24, member of the Great Committee; *federal deputy* from the State of Veracruz, Dist. 6, 1924–26; *federal deputy* from the State of Veracruz, Dist. 7, 1926–28; *senator* from the State of Veracruz, 1928–32; *federal deputy* from the State of Veracruz, Dist. 5, 1934–37; governor-elect of Veracruz, 1936. E] *Secretary* of press of the National Executive Committee (CEN) of the National Revolutionary party (PNR), 1928; *secretary* of the exterior and labor of the CEN of PRI, 1931; leader of radical socialist groups in Veracruz. F] Director general of the Talleres Gráficos de la Nación. G] None. H] Director general of *El Nacional.* I] Came from a working-class family. J] None. K] Assassinated in the Café Tacuba, June 25, 1936, before taking office as governor. L] Peral, 43; Enc Mex, I, 249; DP70, 78; López Esc, 45; QesQ, 17–18.

Alvarado, Salvador
(Deceased June 9, 1924) A] July 20, 1880. B] Culiacán, Sinaloa. C] Began primary studies in Pótam, Sonora, and completed in Hermosillo; no degree. D] None. E] Supported Madero, 1909–11; active member of the Anti-Reelectionist party, 1910; cofounder of the Socialist Party of the Southeast, 1918, at the Socialist Workers Congress. F] President of the Electoral Board, Hermosillo, Sonora, 1906; *governor* of Yucatán, 1915–18; *secretary* of the treasury, 1920. G] None. H] Employee, pharmacy, Guaymas, Sonora; small businessman, Pótam, Sonora, 1906; grocery store owner, Cananea, Sonora. I] Son of

Timoteo Alvarado; from a middle-class family; married Laura Manzano; knew *Adolfo de la Huerta* since residence in Pótam; became friend of federal deputy Manuel I. Villaseñor in 1919. J] Joined the forces of Colonel Juan G. Cabral, 1911, to support Madero; rank of major, 1911; fought against the rebellion of General *Pascual Orozco,* 1912–13; rank of lt. colonel, 1912; joined the Constitutionalists, 1913; chief of the Central Zone of Sonora under Governor *Ignacio L. Pesqueira,* 1913; rank of colonel, 1913; rank of brigadier general, 1913; commander of the parade ground of Mexico City, 1914; commander of the Army of the Southeast; military commander of Yucatán, 1915–18; rank of division general, 1915; supported *Adolfo de la Huerta's* rebellion against General Obregón, 1923; chief of de la Huerta's military forces, 1924; killed at La Hormiga hacienda, Chiapas, by the forces of Federico Aparicio. K] None. L] Enc Mex, I, 260–61; DP70, 85; QesQ, 19; Peral, 44–45; González Dávila, 24–26; Bojórquez, 148–51; Morales Jiménez, 223; Moreno, 307–09; Natayama, 243–49.

Alvarez, Alfredo
(Deceased July 15, 1939) A] January 1, 1876. B] Teziutlán, Puebla. C] Primary and secondary studies in Teziutlán; preparatory studies in Puebla; no degree. D] *Federal deputy* from the State of Puebla, Dist. 13, 1912–13; *federal deputy* from the State of Michoacán, Dist. 12, 1922–24. E] Joined the Anti-Reelectionist party, 1909; president of the Anti-Reelectionist party in Veracruz. F] Director, presidential residences, 1911; organized the tax service under President *Venustiano Carranza;* inspector general of taxes; Treasurer of the Official Committee to Commemorate Mexico's Independence, 1924. G] None. H] Railroad employee, Tabasco; businessman, Veracruz. I] None. J] Joined Carranza, 1913. K] None. L] Mundo Lo.

Alvarez (Benítez), Diego
(Deceased January 28, 1899) A] November 12, 1812. B] Coyuca de Benítez, Guerrero. C] Early education unknown; enrolled in preparatory studies, 1826; began legal studies, but abandoned for a

military career; no degree. D] Local deputy to the state legislature of Puebla, 1845; federal deputy (twice); governor of Guerrero, 1862; governor of Guerrero, 1873–76; *governor* of Guerrero, 1882–85; *senator* from the State of Guerrero, 1894–99. E] None. F] None. G] None. H] Owner of La Providencia Hacienda, Acapulco, Guerrero. I] Son of General Juan Alvarez, governor of Guerrero and independence leader, and María Faustina Benítez. J] Joined the forces of Vicente Guerrero, 1830; aide to father in the battle for Acapulco, 1832; colonel, auxiliary forces, 1842; aide to General Nicolás Bravo, 1842; second-in-command, Southern Division, 1843; fought North Americans, 1846; fought in many battles against the Conservatives, 1850–58; rank of brigade general, November 30, 1865; fought the French in Acapulco, 1865; rank of division general, November 30, 1865; commander of the 2nd and 3rd brigades, Southern Division, 1867; commander under *Porfirio Díaz* in taking Mexico City, 1867. K] Grew up in the mountains, living off the land, when father was hiding from Spanish troops, 1812–24. L] Enc Mex, I, 244–46; Mestre, 204; Hombres prominentes, 251–52.

Alvarez del Castillo, Juan Manuel
(Deceased) A] November 14, 1891. B] Guadalajara, Jalisco. C] Early education unknown; degree unknown. D] *Constitutional deputy* from the State of Jalisco, Dist. 4, 1916–17; *federal deputy* from the State of Jalisco, Dist. 4, 1918–20, 1920–22, 1922–24. E] None. F] Represented *Adolfo de la Huerta* in Washington, D.C., 1923; represented General Escobar in Washington, D.C., 1929; ambassador to Peru, 1933–36; ambassador to the Dominican Republic, 1936; ambassador to Norway, 1940; ambassador to Portugal, 1940–43; ambassador to Colombia, 1944–45; ambassador to Argentina, 1945–51; ambassador to Canada, 1952–53; ambassador to Brazil, 1954–56; resigned from the Foreign Service, 1959. G] None. H] Unknown. I] Unknown. J] Supported *Alvaro Obregón* against *Venustiano Carranza*, 1920. J] None. K] None. L] López, 49; Peral, 46; Villaseñor, 28; Agraz, 1958, 178.

Alvarez García, Higinio
(Deceased 1967) A] 1889. B] Colima, Colima. C] Early education unknown; no degree. D] Local deputy to the state legislature of Colima, 16th session; *senator* from Colima, 1924–28. E] Founder and president of the Independent party of Colima; candidate for senator from Colima on the Colima Independent party ticket, 1952. F] *Interim governor* of Colima, 1920. G] None. H] Unknown. I] Son of Miguel Alvarez, local deputy to the state legislature of Colima and prefect of the Central District of Colima; brother of *Miguel Alvarez García*, governor of Colima, 1921–23; uncle of Griselda Alvarez, governor of Colima, 1980–86; grandson of General Manuel Alvarez, first governor of Colima; related to General *Juan José Ríos*. J] Participated in the Revolution; reached rank of brigadier general, 1923; supported General *Alvaro Obregón* against *Adolfo de la Huerta*, 1923. K] Proclaimed governor of Colima by the local legislature, August 6, 1931, but the Senate declared his powers nonexistent, November 16, 1931; opposed President *Plutarco Elias Calles* as a senator, 1924; considered to be the power behind the throne in his brother's administration. L] DP70, 89–90; Almada, Colima, 18–19; Colliman, 114.

Alvarez García, Miguel
(Deceased December 14, 1931) A] 1880. B] Colima. C] Early education unknown; no degree. D] Alternate deputy to the state legislature of Colima; *governor* of Colima, 1919–20; *governor* of Colima, 1921–23. E] None. F] None. G] None. H] Unknown. I] Son of Miguel Alvarez, local deputy to the state legislature of Colima and prefect of the Central District of Colima; grandson of General Manuel Alvarez, first governor of Colima; brother of *Higinio Alvarez García*, governor of Colima, 1921; father of Griselda Alvarez, governor of Colima, 1980–86; related to General *Juan José Ríos*; close friend of *Gilberto Valenzuela* and *Francisco Solórzano Béjar*, governor of Colima, 1925–27. J] Major, Constitutional Army; supported *Venustiano Carranza*, but converted to *Alvaro Obregón* overnight, 1920. K] local legislature removed him from office, but he was reinstated by the federal govern-

ment, 1920; brother considered to be the real power in his administration. L] DP70, 90; Moreno, 9–12, 73; Peral, Appendix, 18; Almada, Colima, 18, 20.

Alvarez y Alvarez de la Cadena, José
(Deceased 1970) A] April 10, 1885. B] Zamora, Michoacán. C] Primary, secondary, and preparatory studies, Zamora; private accounting degree. D] Mayor of Morelia, Michoacán, 1915; *constitutional deputy* to the State of Michoacán, Dist. 11, 1916–17. E] Entered politics, 1906; founder and secretary of the Francisco I. Madero Democratic Club, 1911; member of the radical Jacobin socialist group as constitutional deputy. F] Political chief of Zamora, Michoacán, 1912–13; private secretary to the governor of Michoacán, 1916; chief of staff, 1924–28; representative of the National Lottery in Cuernavaca, Morelos, 1960s. G] Mason. H] Accountant for the Bank of Jalisco, Bank of Michoacán, Bank of Guerrero, and the Singer Sewing Machine Company. I] Son of Dr. José María Alvarez y Verduzco and Manuela Alvarez de la Cadena y Ugarte; brother of Rafael Alvarez y Alvarez, senator from Michoacán, 1926–30. J] Joined the revolutionary forces under *Joaquín Amaro* as a 2nd lieutenant, 1914; chief of staff to General Amaro for many years; rank of brigade general. K] None. L] Enc Mex, I, 266

Amaro, Joaquín
(Deceased 1952) A] August 16, 1889. B] Corrales de Abrego, Sombrerete, Zacatecas. C] Early education unknown; no degree; director, Military College, 1931–35. D] None. E] None. F] *Subsecretary* of the secretariat of war and navy, 1924–29; *secretary* of the secretariat of war and navy, 1924–25, 1929–30, 1930–31; director of military education, 1935–36. G] None. H] None. I] Married Elisa Izaguirre. J] Joined the Revolution in 1910, serving under *Gertrudis Sánchez*; fought against the forces of *Bernardo Reyes*, 1911; fought against the forces of *Emiliano Zapata*, 1913; participated in the battle of Celaya, 1915; joined *Plutarco Elías Calles* and *Alvaro Obregón* in support of the Plan of Agua Prieta against *Venustiano Carranza*, 1920; rank of division general, 1920; commander of the

5th Division of the North, 1920; fought against the forces of *Adolfo de la Huerta* in the Bajío region, 1923; director of the military prison camps, 1924; commander of the military zones of Chihuahua, Durango, Nuevo León, Coahuila, and San Luis Potosí; commander of the 28th Military Zone, Oaxaca, Oaxaca, 1947. K] Precandidate for presidency of Mexico, 1939; considered a leading contributor to the army's professionalization. L] Libro de oro, 1935–36, 21; Enc Mex, I, 1977, 277–78; DP70, 94–95; López, 52; NYT, 18 Feb. 1940, 23; WWM45, 4.

Amaya, Juan Gualberto
(Deceased) A] April 17, 1889. B] Santa María del Oro, Durango. C] Early education unknown, no degree. D] *Governor* of Durango, 1928–29. E] None. F] None. G] None. H] Travel agent, 1912–13; farmer and rancher. I] Unknown. J] Joined General Orozco's forces as a 2nd captain, January 1911, in support of Madero; joined the Constitutionalists under General *Francisco Murguía*'s forces in Piedras Negras, 1913; rank of lt. colonel, 1914; rank of colonel, 1915; rank of brigadier general, 1920; rank of brigade general, February 12, 1924; chief of operations in the Isthmus of Tehuantepec; chief of operations in Saltillo, Coahuila; chief of operations in Puebla, 1925–26; supported the rebellion of General *José Gonzalo Escobar*, 1929. K] In exile in the United States, 1929–36; reincorporated into the army by President Manuel Avila Camacho. L] Peral, Appendix, 23; Rouaix, 29–20.

Amézcua (Amézcua), Genaro
(Deceased) A] April 3, 1887. B] Mexico City. C] Primary and secondary studies in Huastusco, Orizaba, Jalapa, Veracruz, and Mexico City, in public schools and under private teachers; no degree. D] None. E] Member of the Liberal party, the Democratic party, and the Anti-reelectionist party; met *Francisco I. Madero* and began working for his movement, 1908; supporter of Flores Magón. F] Oficial mayor in charge of the Secretariat of War, Convention Government, 1915. G] None. H] Wrote for *El Mundo* and *La Nación* from exile in the United States and Havana, 1917–20. I] Unknown. J] Joined

Madero, 1910–11; joined the Zapatistas, 1911–15; rank of lt. colonel, December 25, 1911; rank of colonel, November 20, 1912; represented General Eufemio Zapata at the Convention of Aguascalientes, 1914–15; rank of brigadier general, December 10, 1914; rank of brigade general, 1916; retired from active duty, 1920. K] Imprisoned in Huajuapan de León for demonstrating publicly in favor of Madero in Tehuacán, 1910–11. L] DP70, 99; Peral, 52–53; López González, 23–24.

Anaya (y Aranda), Buena ventura
(Deceased 1898) A] September 20, 1857. B] Lagos, Jalisco. C] Early education unknown; law degree, School of Law, Guadalajara, 1876; professor, National School of Law. D] *Federal deputy* from the State of Guerrero, Dist. 6, 1890–92, 1892–94. E] None. F] Agent of the Superior Tribunal of Justice of the State of Jalisco; president of the Superior Tribunal of Justice of Jalisco; *interim governor* of Jalisco, 1889–90. G] None. H] Practicing lawyer. I] Son of Jesús Anaya Torres and Higinia Aranda; married María Alvarez del Castillo y Villaseñor; daughter María Guadalupe married engineer Juan Martín del Campo, chief of the Mexico–United States International Boundary Committee. J] None. K] None. L] Holms, 289; Rice, 230; Torres Martínez, 507.

Ancona Albertos, Antonio
(Deceased February 22, 1954) A] June 1, 1883. B] Mérida, Yucatán. C] Preparatory studies at the Literary Institute of Yucatán; no degree. D] *Federal deputy* from the State of Yucatán, Dist. 2, 1912–14; *constitutional deputy* from the State of Yucatán, Dist. 1, 1916–17; *federal deputy* from the State of Yucatán, Dist. 1, 1917–18; *senator* from Yucatán, 1918–20, 1920–24, 1924–26. E] Cofounder of the Anti-Reelectionist party in Yucatán, 1909. F] Private secretary to *José María Pino Suárez*, governor of Yucatán, 1911; *provisional governor* of Yucatán, 1920; *governor* of Quintana Roo, 1926–27; director of the Civil Registry, Department of the Federal District, 1952–54. G] None. H] Journalist, *El Peninsular*, 1904–07; journalist, *La Campaña*, 1907; journalist, *Diario Yucateco*, 1907; director, *La Voz*

de la Revolución, 1915; director, *El Heraldo de México*, 1920; editorial writer, *El Nacional*. I] Son of *Eligio Ancona Castillo*, politician, lawyer, and justice of the Supreme Court, 1890–93, and Manuela Albertos Zavalegui; longtime collaborator with *José María Pino Suárez*, beginning with his career as a journalist; later collaborator with *Salvador Alvarado*. J] Joined the Constitutionalists, Hermosillo, Sonora, 1914. K] Imprisoned by Huerta in the Juárez Penitentiary with other federal deputies, 1913; exiled to Cuba and the United States, 1913–14; wrote under the pseudonym Mónico Neck. L] López, 53; Valdés Acosta, 2, 56–57; Enc Mex, I, 301; DP70, 104; Alvarez Coral, 103–04.

Ancona (y Castillo), José Eligio
(Deceased April 3, 1893) A] December 1, 1836. B] Mérida, Yucatán. C] Preparatory studies at the Conciliar Seminary of San Ildefonso, Yucatán; law degree, Literary University of Yucatán, 1862; founded the Literary Institute of Yucatán. D] Member of the City Council of Mérida, Yucatán; federal deputy from Yucatán, 1867, 1868–70, 1870–72; interim governor of Yucatán, 1868, 1874–76. E] None. F] Secretary general of government of the State of Yucatán, 1867; judge of the Circuit Court of Yucatán; *justice* of the Supreme Court, 1890–93. G] None. H] Practicing lawyer; founded *La Píldora*; founded *Yucatán*, 1866; author of numerous historical works and novels. I] Son of Antonio María de Ancona y Cárdenas and Fernanda del Castillo y Echavarría; grandson of regidor Juan Ramón de Ancona y Cepeda; descendant of lawyer Francisco Ancona de Ancona y Cepeda; married Manuela Albertos Zavalegui; son *Antonio Ancona Albertos* served as deputy and senator from Yucatán. J] Joined the forces of General Cepeda Peraza, 1867. K] Imprisoned in Cozumel, 1866–67. L] Enc de Yucatán, 5, 829; García Rivas, 220–22; Romero Flores, 52–58; Mestre, 182; Valdés Acosta, 2, 37, 52–53; Martínez Alomía, 232–36; Pavía, judicial, 48–59.

Andrade López, Cayetano
(Deceased June 10, 1962) A] August 7, 1890. B] Moroleón, Guanajuato. C] Primary studies at Public School No. 1, 1898–

1902; preparatory studies from the Colegio de San Nicolás, 1903–08; medical studies on a scholarship, School of Medicine, Colegio de San Nicolás, 1909–14, graduating January 23, 1914. D] *Constitutional deputy* from the State of Michoacán, Dist. 3, 1916–17, president of the chamber; *federal deputy* from the State of Michoacán, Dist. 2, 1918–20; *federal deputy* from the State of Guanajuato, Dist. 12, 1924–26; local deputy to the state legislature of Guanajuato, 1928–32; federal deputy from the State of Guanajuato, Dist. 3, 1952–55. E] Participated in a student strike, 1910; supported Madero. F] Director, official paper, under General *Gertrudis G. Sánchez*, Morelia; school inspector, Morelia, Michoacán; physician, Medical Department, Secretariat of Health, 1935–51; director general of information, Secretariat of Government, 1955–58; director, *Diario Oficial*, Secretariat of Government, 1958–62. H] Journalist, 1909–16; editor of *El Girondino*; published student magazine *Flor de Loto*; physician, Morelia; physician, Mexico City, 1918–24. I] Son of Dr. Ramón Andrade and Francisca López. J] None. K] None. L] Dicc mich, 22; DP70; Romero Flores, 395–98; Peral, appendix, 24.

Andreu (Andrew) Almazán, Juan
(Deceased October 9, 1965) A] May 12, 1891. B] Olinalá, Guerrero. C] Primary studies in Olinalá; preparatory studies at the Colegio de Puebla, 1903–08; medical studies, Colegio de Puebla, 1908–10, no degree. D] None. E] None. F] *Secretary* of communications and public works, 1930–32. G] None. H] Director of the Anáhuac Construction Company. I] Son of Juan Andreu and María Almazán Nava, wealthy landowners; friend of revolutionary precursor Aquiles Serdán; brother of *Leonides Andreu Almazán*. J] Joined the Revolution in 1910 under *Francisco I. Madero*; fought under *Emiliano Zapata*, 1911; rank of brigadier general, May 3, 1911; opposed *Francisco I. Madero*, 1911–12; joined General *Victoriano Huerta*, 1913; fought against Rómulo Figueroa; opposed *Venustiano Carranza*, 1915; one of the youngest revolutionary generals; joined Obregón, 1920; rank of division general, January 1, 1921; opposed the

Adolfo de la Huerta rebellion, 1923; commander of the 5th Military Zone, Monterrey, Nuevo León, 1924–34; commander of a military column against General *José Gonzalo Escobar*, 1929; commander of the 6th Military Zone, Torreón, Coahuila. K] Went into exile after General Huerta was defeated, 1914; resigned from the army in 1939 to become a presidential candidate of the Revolutionary Party of National Unification; after defeat went into exile in Panama, Cuba, and the United States, 1940–47, but later returned to Mexico. L] DP70, 107; Enc Mex I, 407; NYT, 1 Aug. 1938; Peral, 55; NYT, 11 Oct. 1965, 39.

Andreu (Andrew) Almazán, Leonides
(Deceased January 18, 1963) A] August 8, 1896. B] Olinalá, Guerrero. C] Preparatory studies in Puebla; medical degree from the National School of Medicine, UNAM, 1923; hygienist at the University of Paris; professor of medicine at the Military Medical School. D] *Governor* of Puebla, 1929–33, resigned shortly before completion of term. E] None. F] *Ambassador* to Great Britain, 1935; minister to Germany, October 27, 1935–38; head of the Department of Health, 1938–39. G] None. H] Chief of the Clinic of the Necker Institute in Mexico City; chief of urological services of the Military Hospital in Mexico City; chief of the Pharmacy Department of the Mexican Institute of Social Security; adviser to the Mexican Institute of Social Security. I] Brother of *Juan Andreu Almazán*; resigned as head of the Health Department to direct brother's campaign for president, 1939; son of Juan Andreu and María Almazán Nava, wealthy landowners; related to Miguel Andreu Almazán, federal deputy from Guerrero, Dist. 4, 1937–39. J] Fought with *Emiliano Zapata* during the Revolution. L] Peral, 55; DP70, 106–07.

Angeles (Ramírez), Jr., Felipe
(Deceased November 26, 1919) A] Zacualtipan, Hidalgo. B] June 13, 1869. C] Primary studies, Molango, Huejutla, and Pachuca, Hidalgo; scholarship to the National Military College, 1883; cadet instructor, National Military College; studies in powder manufacturing in the United

States; studies in France, 1910–11; director, National Military College, 1912. D] None. E] None. F] *Subsecretary* of war, 1913; military commission to Europe, 1913. G] None. H] None. I] Son of Colonel Felipe Angeles, veteran of the war against the French and commander of various districts, and Juana Ramírez; brother Alberto J. Angeles was a military engineer and poet. J] Career artillery officer; rank of brigadier general, 1911; fought Zapatistas for Madero; commanding general of artillery, 1912–13; defended President *Francisco I. Madero* against *Félix Díaz*; joined the Constitutionalists, 1913; joined *Francisco Villa*, 1914, becoming a key adviser; represented at the Convention of Aguascalientes, 1914–15; fought against *Venustiano Carranza*, 1919. K] Exiled in El Paso and later New York City, 1915–18; considered one of the leading artillery technicians in the army; captured in Chihuahua and executed. L] DP70, 108; López, 54–55; QesQ, 29–30; Pérez López, 40–42.

Aragón (León), Agustín
(Deceased March 30, 1954) A] August 28, 1870. B] Jonacatepec, Morelos. C] Primary studies in Joncatepec; preparatory studies at the National Preparatory School, 1884–88; geological engineering studies, National School of Engineering, 1889–91, degree in topographical and geographical engineering, 1891; degree in hydrological engineering, 1893; degree in civil engineering; studies in medicine, National School of Medicine, 1893–94 (completed second year); dean, National School of Agriculture, 1914–15. D] *Federal deputy* from the State of Veracruz, 1900–02, Dist. 3, 1900–02; *federal deputy* from the State of Michoacán, Dist. 15, 1902–04, 1904–06, 1906–08, 1908–10. E] Supported *Bernardo Reyes* against *Porfirio Díaz*; member of the Anti-Reelectionist party; candidate for governor of Morelos, 1912. F] Aide, Boundary Commission, Mexico–United States, 1891–92; first official, National Property Office, 1894; oficial mayor of development, Convention Government, 1914; subsecretary of development, Convention Government, 1914–15; adviser to the president of Mexico, 1954. G] Dean, Mexican Society of Geogra-

phy and Statistics; president, National Academy of Sciences. H] Founder and editor of *Revista Positivista*, 1901–14. I] Son of José Hermenegildo Aragón and Victoria León; son, Agustín Aragón Leiva, writer and journalist; student of *Porfirio Parra*; related to Rosario Aragón, prominent military leader during the French intervention. J] None. K] Defended *Jose López Portillo y Rojas* against the government in the Chamber of Deputies. L] Enc Mex, I, 344; López, 57; Carreño, 347–48; DP70, 125; García Rivas, 4, 176–77; Gómez, 31–32; Peral, 59; WWM45, 5.

Aranda Valdivia, Manuel
(Deceased February 8, 1952) A] 1869. B] Purísima del Rincón, Guanajuato. C] Primary and secondary studies in Purísima del Rincón; preparatory studies in León, Guanajuato; mining engineering degree from the University of Guanajuato, 1900; senior professor, University of Guanajuato; rector of the University of Guanajuato. D] *Alternate federal deputy* from the State of Guanajuato, Dist. 9, 1912–13; mayor of Guanajuato (appointed by Jesús Carranza); *constitutional deputy* from the State of Guanajuato, Dist. 9, 1916–17; local deputy to the state legislature of Guanajuato, 1922–23, 1932–34. E] Candidate for governor of Guanajuato, 1923. F] Technical engineer, Secretariat of the Treasury; representative of the Secretariat of the Treasury, State of Puebla; political chief of Guanajuato, 1912; chief, Treasury Department, State of Guanajuato, 1920–22. G] None. H] None. I] Son of Matías Aranda Ruiz and Lucia G. Valdivia. bJ] None. K] None. L] C de D, 1916–17; C de D, 1912–13.

Araujo (y Araujo), Emilio
(Deceased October 23, 1953) A] August 9, 1892. B] Tuxtla Gutiérrez, Chiapas. C] Early education unknown; law degree, National School of Law, UNAM, 1913–17. D] Mayor of Tuxtla Gutiérrez; *federal deputy* from the State of Chiapas, Dist. 1, 1917–18, 1918–20, president of the Chamber; federal deputy from State of Chiapas, Dist. 3, 1937–40; interim governor of Chiapas, 1938; senator from Chiapas, 1940–46; president of the Senate, 1942; president of the First Justice Committee,

secretary of the Constitutional Affairs, Foreign Relations, and Consular and Diplomatic Service committees, and member of the First Balloting Group. F] Judge of the lower court in Chiapas; legal adviser to the Department of the Federal District; legal adviser to the Mexican delegation at the United Nations Conference in San Francisco, 1945; secretary general of government of the State of Chiapas (twice). G] None. H] Member of various commercial and scientific commissions in Europe, 1920–37; lawyer for the Mexico City Chamber of Commerce in Europe, 1927. I] Close to President *Venustiano Carranza* during constitutionalist movement, fled with Carranza in 1920; law partner with Ezequiel Padilla; secretary of foreign relations; married Eloísa Ana Mónica Mendizábal Gutiérrez; son Roberto Araujo Mendizábal is a lawyer with the firm of Padilla and Araujo. J] None. K] President of the Mexican Democratic party, which ran Ezequiel Padilla for president in 1945–46. L] WWM45, 5; DP70, 129; Peral, 61; letter; Medina, No. 20, 61; C de D, 1917–18; C de D, 1918–20.

Arce, Francisco O.
(Deceased August 10, 1903) A] March 15, 1831. B] Guadalajara, Jalisco. C] Primary studies in Guadalajara; mining engineering studies, School of Mines, Mexico City, but abandoned to join the army, 1847; no degree. D] Governor of Guerrero, 1869–73; federal deputy from the State of Guerrero, Dist. 6, 1880–82; alternate federal deputy from the State of Guerrero, Dist. 6, 1882–84; *governor* of Guerrero, 1885–93; *senator* from the State of Aguascalientes, 1892–96; *alternate senator* from Campeche, 1896–1900. E] None. F] Judge of the Supreme Court of Military Justice, 1901–03. G] Founder of the Masonic Lodge, Durango, Durango. H] None. I] Son of Sixto Arce and Soledad Otarola. J] Joined the national guard as a volunteer, 1847; fought the U.S. invasion in the Victoria Battalion; lieutenant, customs guard, Chihuahua, 1849–56; joined the Liberal forces; captain and adjutant to President Ignacio Comonfort, 1857; rank of lt. colonel, 1859; commander of the garrison, Durango, under general Santos Degollado; rank of colonel,

1859; commander of the 8th Cavalry, 1860; fought in the battle of Puebla, 1862; rank of brigadier general, 1863; captured by and escaped from French, 1866; commander of the 2nd Division, 1867; rank of brigade general, November 14, 1867; fought in the siege of Querétaro, 1867; sent to pacify Guerrero by President Juárez, 1867–68; defeated La Noria revolt in Sinaloa and Tepic; military commander of Sinaloa, 1873. K] Abandoned the governorship after a rebellion by General Canuto A. Neri, 1893. L] Enc Mex, I, 355; QesQ, 34–35; Godoy, 197–98; DP70, 130–31; López, Héctor, 64–66; Pavía, 188–91; Peral, 61; Mestre, 217; Almada, 1968, 12; Sec of War, 20.

Aréchiga, Jesús
(Deceased July 16, 1923) A] 1843. B] Jalpa, Zacatecas. C] Early education unknown; no degree. D] *Federal deputy* from the State of Aguascalientes, Dist. 4, 1884–86; *senator* from the State of Zacatecas, 1886–88; *governor* of Zacatecas, 1888–90; *senator* from the State of Zacatecas, 1890–92; *alternate senator* from the State of Guerrero, 1896–98; *senator* from the State of Guerrero, 1898–02, 1904–06; *senator* from the State of San Luis Potosí, 1914–16. E] None. F] None. G] None. H] None. I] None. J] Joined the national guard as a young boy, Zacatecas; fought during the Reform War and the French invasion; supported *Porfirio Díaz* in the Tuxtepec Rebellion, 1876; stationed in Zacatecas, 1877; rank of brigadier general in the cavalry reserves, March 8, 1877; rank of brigade general, April 23, 1914. K] None. L] Hombres prominentes, 361–62; DP70, 133; Godoy, 275; Pavía, 430; Peral, 62; Sec of War, 1901, 25; Sec of War, 1914, 29; C de S, 1900, 6; Mestre, 271; C de S, 1904; C de S, 1914, 23.

Arellano, Felipe
(Deceased October 28, 1907) A] 1833. B] Mazatlán, Sinaloa. C] Early education unknown; no degree. D] Alternate federal deputy from the State of Chihuahua, 1871–72; federal deputy from the State of Chihuahua, 1877–78; *senator* from the State of Chihuahua, 1884–88; *federal deputy* from the State of Veracruz, Dist. 1,

1892–94; *federal deputy* from the State of Veracruz, Dist. 2, 1894–96; *alternate federal deputy* from the State of Guanajuato, Dist 16, 1896–98; *alternate federal deputy* from the State of Guanajuato, Dist. 1, 1898–1900, 1900–02, 1902–04, 1904–06. E] None. F] Political boss of Arteaga Canton (District), 1869; political boss and military commander of Hidalgo del Parral Canton, Chihuahua; director of taxes in the Federal District, 1880–84; director of Customs, Ciudad Juárez, Chihuahua; director of customs, Mazatlán; director general of customs. G] None. H] Publisher of *La Nueva Era*; owned a mining operation in Urique, Chihuahua; owned a mining operation in Las Yedras, Chihuahua. I] Father was a businessman who had difficulties with General *Ramón Corona*; married Felicitas Milán; son Lorenzo J. Arellano Milán was a political boss and alternate federal deputy; son Felipe Arellano Milán graduated from the National School of Law. J] Supported the Plan of Urique, part of the Plan of La Noria, 1872; commander of military forces in Chihuahua, 1872; rank of colonel in infantry; supported the Plan of Tuxtepec, 1876. K] Had to move to Urique Mine, Chihuahua, because of father's conflict with General Corona. L] Almada, 1968, 43–44; UNAM, 1891–96, 159.

Arredondo (Garza), Eliseo
(Deceased October 18, 1923) A] 1871. B] Villa Nava, Cuatro Ciénegas, Coahuila. C] Primary studies in Cuatro Ciénegas; preparatory studies at the Ateneo Fuente, Saltillo, Coahuila; legal studies, Ateneo Fuente, (first two years); completed law degree from the National School of Law, 1896. D] Local deputy to the state legislature of Coahuila; *federal deputy* from the State of Coahuila, Dist. 4, 1912–14. E] Member of the Anti-Reelectionist party. F] Judge; secretary general of government of the State of Coahuila, 1911–12, under *Venustiano Carranza*, confidential agent of Carranza, Washington, D.C., 1914; subsecretary of government, in charge of the secretariat, 1914; *ambassador* to the United States, 1915; ambassador to Spain and Portugal, 1920. G] None. H] Practicing lawyer; in practice with *Jacinto Pallares*, one of the most distinguished

lawyers of his generation. I] Son of Juan Arredondo and Inés Garza. J] Joined the Constitutionalists, 1913. K] Considered by some observers to be an important behind-the-scenes figure in the early Carranza era. L] DP70, 147; Peral, 70; UNAM, 1891–96, 111.

Arrieta, Domingo
(Deceased November 18, 1962) A] August 4, 1874. B] Municipio de Candelas, Durango. C] Early education unknown; no degree. D] *Governor* of Durango, 1917–20; senator from Durango, 1936–40. E] None. F] *Governor* of Durango, 1914–16. G] None. H] Before joining the Revolution was a miner and a muleteer in Durango. I] Brother of Mariano Arrieta, an early revolutionary leader in the State of Durango who became governor of Durango for several months in 1915, and continued career as a military officer; brothers Andrés and Eduardo were revolutionary generals; son of Teófilo Arrieta; father of Atanasio Arrieta García, senator from Durango, 1946–52. J] Joined the Revolution under Madero, 1910; commander of the garrison of Durango, 1911–13; fought against *Victoriano Huerta* in 1913; general of the revolutionary forces which took Durango, 1913; became military commander of Durango, 1914–16; fought against *Francisco Villa*, 1914–16; constitutionalist, 1916–20; opposed General *Alavaro Obregón*, 1920; became a division general on November 16, 1940; retired from the army August 1, 1944. K] Remained faithful to *Venustiano Carranza* when he fled the presidency; pardoned by Obregón, May 7, 1924; rejoined the army September 11, 1927. L] DP70, 149–50; Peral, 72; QesQ, 43–45; Enc Mex, Annual, 1977, 478–79; Rouaix, 38–39.

Arrioja Isunza, Eduardo
(Deceased) A] August 31, 1884. B] Puebla, Puebla. C] Early education unknown; law degree, University of Puebla. D] *Federal deputy* from the State of Puebla, Dist. 6, 1918–20, member of the Great Committee; *federal deputy* from the State of Puebla, Dist 6, 1920–22, 1922–24; *federal deputy* from the State of Puebla, Dist. 5, 1932–34. E] None. F] Actuary, First Division, State Supreme Court,

Puebla, 1914; consulting lawyer, commanding officer, 4th Army of the East, 1914; civil judge, 4th District, Mexico City, 1917–18; director, Legal Department, comptroller general of Mexico, 1918; director, Legal Department, Secretariat of Industry and Commerce, 1927–28; justice, Superior Tribunal of Justice of the State of Puebla, 1928; judge of the first instance, 1935; justice of the Superior Tribunal of Justice of the Federal District and Territories, 1949. G] None. H] Notary public, Tehuacán, Puebla, 1935. I] Possibly son of Manuel M. Arrioja, judge and interim governor of Puebla, 1885. J] Supported General *Pablo González*, January 4, 1920. K] None. L] Almanaque de Puebla, 128; Hombres prominentes, 459–60.

Arróniz, Abraham
(Deceased) A] March 16, 1833. B] San Luis de Potosí. C] Early education unknown; moved to Mexico City for studies, 1841; no degree. D] Member of the City Council of Puebla. E] Member of the Liberal party, 1850s–60s. F] Prefect of Atotonilco el Grande, Hidalgo; prefect of Tulancingo, Hidalgo, 1881; prefect of Pachuca, Hidalgo, 1888; political boss of Baja California del Sur, 1900–02; *political boss* (see governor) of Baja California del Norte, 1902–03. G] None. H] Businessman; landowner. I] Son of Spanish merchant Vicente Arróniz and Carmen del Conde. J] Fought against the French; rank of lt. colonel, but not a career military officer. K] None. L] López, 66; Hombres prominentes, 465–66.

Arroyo Ch., Agustín
(Deceased April 24, 1969) A] August 28, 1891. B] Irapuato, Guanajuato. C] Primary studies at Pueblo Nuevo; secondary at private schools in Guanajuato; no degree. D] Local deputy to the state legislature of Guanajuato; *federal deputy* from the State of Guanajuato, Dist. 7, 1920–22; *federal deputy* from the State of Guanajuato, Dist. 10, 1922–24; *governor* of Guanajuato, 1927–31. F] Subsecretary of government, 1935–36; first director of the Department of Press and Publicity (which became PIPSA), 1936–40; secretary of labor and social welfare, 1940; president of

the Administrative Council of PIPSA, 1958–62; publisher of the official government newspaper *El Nacional*, 1962–68; member of the board of PIPSA, 1967–69. G] None. H] Post office employee, Celaya, Guanajuato, 1915; worked in the Department of General Provisions, under *Francisco Múgica*. I] Close personal friend of Governor *Enrique Colunga* of Guanajuato, 1923–27, who imposed Arroyo Ch. as governor; also a friend of Governor *Antonio Madrazo*, 1920–23; early supporter of *Francisco Múgica* for president, 1939–40; political adviser of *Lázaro Cárdenas*; married Carolina Damián; son Agustín was a federal deputy from Guanajuato, 1955–58, 1964–67. J] Participated in the Revolution. K] He and Colunga controlled state politics in Guanajuato for many years. L] Dulles; HA, 29 Dec. 1958, 8; Peral, 73; Gruening, 427, 487–88; Enc Mex I, 303; NYT, 21 Jan. 1940, 21.

Arroyo de Anda, Agustín
(Deceased 1917) A] August 28, 1853. B] Sayula, Jalisco. C] Primary studies in Sayula; secondary and preparatory studies, Guadalajara, Jalisco; law degree, National School of Law, Mexico City. D] *Federal deputy* from the State of México, Dist. 6, 1886–88; *federal deputy* from the Federal District, Dist. 10, 1888–90, 1890–92; *federal deputy* from the Federal District, Dist. 8, 1892–94; 1894–96, 1896–98; *alternate federal deputy* from the State of Durango, Dist. 3, 1900–02. E] None. F] Public defender; director, Public Defender's Office, Mexico City; personal adviser to President *Porfirio Díaz*; government orator. G] Cofounder and vice-president of Associated Press of Mexico. H] Practicing criminal lawyer; owner of *La Prensa*, Mexico City; director of various political and scientific magazines. I] Brother of Rafael Arroyo de Anda, journalist and federal deputy; brother of Francisco Arroyo de Anda, journalist; from a prominent family; related to (probably grandson of) José Francisco Arroyo de Anda, deputy to the Spanish cortes; related to (probably great-grandson of) Mariano Arroyo de Anda, lawyer, and Margarita Villagómez. J] None. K] None. L] Villaseñor, 51; Godoy, 251–52; DP70, 152.

Aspe (Arriola), Francisco de P.
(Deceased June 19, 1914) A] July 18, 1835. B] Veracruz, Veracruz. C] Primary studies in Veracruz; no degree. D] Federal deputy several times; *senator* from the State of Veracruz, 1890–92, 1894–98, 1898–1902, 1902–06, 1906–10, 1910–14. E] Delegate to the Unión Liberal Congress. F] Customs administrator, Tampico and Veracruz, 1872–76. G] None. H] Broker in Veracruz; broker in Mexico City; left business career to join army. I] Son of Alonso José Aspe and Ana Arriola; married Dolores de Emparán, a native Cuban, daughter of José de Emparán; daughter Enriqueta Aspe married *Emilio Pardo, Jr.,* senator from Tlaxcala. J] Joined the Liberal army as a 2nd lieutenant of artillery; rank of 1st lieutenant, 1854; wounded in the Battle of Chiquihuite, 1854; secretary to general Ignacio de la Llave; rank of captain of Artillery; reached rank of colonel in the Liberal forces. K] None. L] Godoy, 114–15; Rice, 231; C de S, 1904, 18.

Avila (Chacón), Fidel
(Deceased September 22, 1954) A] April 14, 1875. B] Satevó, Chihuahua. C] Early education unknown; no degree. D] None. E] None. F] *Governor* of Chihuahua, 1914–15. G] None. H] Worked as an agricultural laborer until 1911; lived in El Paso, Texas, 1915–29; returned to Ciudad Juárez, Chihuahua, 1929–54. I] Son of Nieves Avila and Cesárea Chacón, peasants. J] Joined *Francisco I. Madero's* forces under *Francisco Villa,* January 5, 1911, with the rank of captain; served with Villa until 1912, and returned home to work; rejoined Villa 1912 to fight against *Pascual Orozco,* 1912–13; joined the Constitutionalists, 1913; colonel in Villa Brigade, 1913; rank of brigadier general, March 1914; commander of the garrison, Ciudad Juárez, 1914; president of the Council of War which judged William Benton, 1914; served in the Division of the North under Villa; represented *Francisco Lagos Cházaro* at the Convention of Aguascalientes, 1914–15; military commander of the State of Chihuahua, 1914–15. K] In exile, El Paso, Texas, 1915–29. L] Enc Mex, I, 502; Almada, 522–23; Almada, 1968, 53.

Avilés (Inzunza), Cándido I.
(Deceased December 17, 1964) A] April 15, 1881. B] Culiacán, Sinaloa. C] Primary studies in Culiacán; three years of preparatory studies at the Colegio Civil Rosales, Culiacán; no degree. D] Local deputy to the state legislature of Sinaloa, 1912–13; mayor of Mazatlán, Sinaloa, 1914; *constitutional deputy* from the State of Sinaloa, Dist. 4, 1916–17; *federal deputy* from the State of Sinaloa, Dist. 2, 1922–24. E] Cofounder of an Anti-Reelectionist Club, 1909; supported *Francisco I. Madero,* 1910–11. F] Prefect of the Mocarito District, Sinaloa, 1912; prefect of Mazatlán, Sinaloa, 1912; treasurer of Maritime Customs, Port of Mazatlán, 1913; director of taxes, Mazatlán, 1915–16, 1917; treasurer of Mazatlán, 1925; tax collector, Cosalá, Sinaloa, 1925; assistant treasurer of the State of Sinaloa, 1929–32; prison administrator, Islas Marías, 1933; treasury inspector and tax collector, Mazatlán, 1936–37. G] None. H] Managed a store owned by his uncle, Mocorito, Sinaloa; business agent, Nogales, Sonora, 1913; rancher, 1937–64. I] Son of Víctor P. Avilés, farmer and administrator of textile factory, and Jesús Inzunza; married Jesús de la Rocha. J] Chief of the mounted guard, Angostura, Sinaloa; 1st captain and adjutant, 1st Sinaloa Battalion, 1913. K] Imprisoned by *Victoriano Huerta,* 1913. L] Almanaque de México, 507; letter.

Avilés Maya, Uriel
(Deceased 1956) A] January 25, 1885. B] Zitácuaro, Michoacán. C] Primary studies in a public school, Zitácuaro; no degree. D] *Constitutional deputy* from the State of Michoacán, Dist. 4, 1916–17, elected as an alternate but in functions; *federal deputy* from the State of Michoacán, Dist. 2, 1918–20; *federal deputy* from the State of Michoacán, Dist. 1, 1920–22. E] Joined the Liberal party, 1909; propagandist for government opposition, 1907–11. F] None. G] None. H] Carpenter; printer; journalist; founded *La Idea,* opposed to the Díaz administration, 1909; cofounder of *Libre Prensa, El Día,* and *La Gaceta.* I] Son of Ramón Avilés and María Teresa Maya. J] Fought in the Revolution, 1913–16; reached rank

of colonel. K| Imprisoned by the government for opposition to *Porfirio Díaz*; mother defrauded out of family's inheritance, thus leaving them poor. L| DP70, 181; Peral, 78.

Ayala González, Abraham
(Deceased 1958) A| 1898. B| San Pedro de las Colonias, Coahuila. C| Preparatory studies at the Ateneo Fuente, Saltillo, Coahuila; medical degree, with a specialty in gastroenterology, National School of Medicine, UNAM, 1919. D| None. E| None. F| *Chief*, Department of Health, 1934–35. G| Founded Mexican Association of Gastroenterology; president, Mexican Academy of Medicine, 1944–45. H| Director, General Hospital, Mexico City; founded special section devoted to gastroenterology, General Hospital. I| Wife served as a personal secretary to General *Plutarco Elías Calles*. J| None. K| None. L| Libro de oro, 18; DP70, 183; Enc Mex I, 514; Peral, 79.

Azcárate, Juan F.
(Deceased ?) A| September 8, 1896. B| Dr. Arroyo, Nuevo León. C| Primary studies at a private school in St. Louis, Missouri; secondary studies at the Jackson Academy of St. Louis; studies at Washington University; aeronautical engineering degree, New York University, 1927. D| None. E| None. F| Chief of the Mexican air force, 1929–31; chief of staff, President *Abelardo Rodríguez*, 1932–33; ambassador to Germany, 1937–39, 1940–41; special ambassador, Central and South America, 1944. G| None. H| Director and founder of Aviones Azcárate, 1930. I| Son of José Ignacio Azcárate and Urbina Pino; married Eva del Pulgar; grandson of Miguel Azcárate, governor of the Federal District; great-grandson of Juan F. Azcárate y Ledesma, ambassador, lawyer, and judge. J| Captain, constitutional army, 1913; rank of major, 1915; rank of lt. colonel, 1916; commander, 4th Cavalry Regiment, 1916–29; rank of colonel, 1917; rank of brigadier general, 1927; director, military aeronautics factory, 1928–29; chief, Aeronautics Department, Secretariat of National Defense, 1931–32; military attaché to the United States, 1933–37; rank of brigade general, 1937; director of

veterinary services, Secretariat of National Defense, 1939–40; commander of the Gulf of Mexico Military Region, 1942. K| None. L| DP70, 188; WWM45, 7; Peral, 80; EBW, 1143.

Aznar Cano, Tomás
(Deceased August 29, 1923) A| Unknown. B| Mérida, Yucatán. C| Early education unknown; medical degree. D| *Senator* from the State of Campeche, 1902–06; *governor* of Campeche, 1905–10. E| None. F| None. G| None. H| Physician. I| Son of Tomás Aznar y Barbachano, lawyer, federal deputy, and governor of Campeche, and Paula Manuela Concepción Cano y Cano; grandson of Tomás de Aznar y Peón, military officer, and María Concepción Barbachano; nephew of poet Luis Aznar y Barbachano; uncle of Antonio J. Aznar Zetina, subsecretary of the navy, 1965–70. J| None. K| None. L| Martínez Alomía, 207–08; DP70, 189; C de S, 1904, 18; Pérez Galaz, 37–40; Enc de Yucatán, V, 828; Valdés Acosta, 2, 111–12; Mestre, 271.

Azpiroz (Ureta), Manuel
(Deceased March 24, 1905) A| June 9, 1836. B| Puebla, Puebla, C| Preparatory studies at the Palafoxian Conciliar Seminary, 1852; completed preparatory studies at the University of Mexico, 1856; legal studies, Autonomous University of Puebla, Puebla, 1857; completed law degree at the Palafoxian Seminary, 1859; professor of civil law, Autonomous University of Puebla, 1861–62; secretary of the Autonomous University of Puebla, 1861–62; professor of law, Autonomous University of Puebla, 1883–90. D| Constitutional deputy, 1857; senator from the State of Puebla, 1867; senator from the Federal District, 1876–80. E| None. F| Clerk, government of the State of Puebla, 1857; secretary of government of the State of Chihuahua, 1866; official mayor of the secretary of foreign relations, 1867–71; represented Mexico in the case of the Californias Pious Funds, 1868; political boss of Puebla, 1871–72; agent and lawyer, Mixed Claims Committee, Mexico–United States, 1872–73; consul, San Francisco, California, 1873–75; official, Secretariat of Foreign Relations; secretary of the trea-

sury, State of Puebla, 1883–85; director, General Hospital of Puebla, 1883–1890; judge, Superior Tribunal of Justice of Puebla, 1887; member, City Council of Puebla; *subsecretary* of foreign relations, 1890–99; *secretary* of foreign relations, 1890; *secretary* of foreign relations, 1898; *ambassador* to the United States, 1899–1905. G] None. H] Practicing lawyer, 1860–61. I] Son of Manuel Javier de Azpiroz and María de la Luz Ureta. J] Joined the Liberals under General Zaragoza as a 2nd lieutenant of artillery, May 4, 1862; rank of captain, July 15, 1862; fought at the battle of Puebla, 1862; captured by the French, 1862; escaped from the French, 1863, and joined General Negrete's staff; battalion commander, June 15, 1863, General Negrete's forces; staff, Reserve Division, Army of the East, 1863; rank of major, 1864; special mission for Benito Juárez, 1864; captured and freed by the Conservatives, 1865; commander in the taking of Chihuahua, 1866; adjutant to General *Mariano Escobedo*, 1867; military attorney on the war council which condemned Maximilian, 1867; retired from the service, June 14, 1867; rank of colonel, reserves, January 30, 1899. K] None. L] Enc Mex, I, 523; CyT, 67; Peral, 81; Mestre, 222; Almada, 1968, 54; Cruzado, 69–75; Godoy, 173–74; FSRE, 113–14; Sec of War, 1902; Márquez, 239–41.

B

Badillo, Basilio

(Deceased July 25, 1935) A] July 14, 1885. B] Zapotitlán, Jalisco. C] Primary studies in Colima; teaching certificate, National Teachers School, on a scholarship from governor *Enrique O. de la Madrid*; studies at the Conciliar Seminary; rural schoolteacher, near Zapotitlán, Colima; director of the public school of Zapotitlán, 1903; teacher, Preceptora, Colima, 1906–07; director, Ramón de la Vega School, Colima, 1908. D] F*ederal deputy* from the State of Jalisco, Dist. 18; 1917–18; 1918–20, 1920–22. E] *President* of the National Executive Committee of the National Revolutionary Party (PNR), 1930. F] Director general of education, State of Colima, 1915–17; *governor* of Jalisco, 1921–22; *ambassador* to the Soviet Union,

1922–27; ambassador to Norway and Denmark; represented Mexico at the 7th Pan American Conference, 1931; ambassador to Uruguay, 1931–35. G] Leader of the Revolutionary Student Group; president of the Local Agrarian Commission, Colima. H] Published *El Discípulo*, Zapotitlán, 1902–03; collaborator on *El Observador*, Ciudad Guzmán, Jalisco, 1904; director of *El Baluarte*, Colima. I] Poor orphan. J] None. K] General *Alvaro Obregón* allegedly wanted him to serve as secretary of public education his second term. L] QesQ, 54; DP70, 199; Romero Aceves, 187–90; Política, 62.

Bandala (Patiño), Abraham

(Deceased November 8, 1916) A] Papantla, Veracruz. B] May 12, 1838. C] Early education unknown; no degree. D] *Federal deputy* from the State of Tabasco, Dist. 2, 1888–90, 1890–92, 1892–94; *federal deputy* from the State of Tlaxcala, Dist. 1, 1894–96; *governor* of Tabasco, 1895–99, 1900–10; *federal deputy* from the State of Guerrero, Dist. 8, 1910–12. E] None. F] *Governor* of Tabasco, 1887; *interim governor* of Tabasco, 1894 G] None. H] None. I] Son of wealthy Cuban physician, José Bandala, and María Rosalia Patiño, from a landowning family in Papantla; married Margarita Cortona; son Abraham a military engineer. J] Enlisted in the national guard as an ordinary soldier, 1858; battalion commander, 1860; fought under *Porfirio Díaz* against the French; garrison commander, 1863; commander of the garrison of Tabasco, 1866; participant in the siege of Puebla, April 1867; rank of lt. colonel, national guard, Puebla, July 22, 1868; commander in the campaign against the Yaquis, 1882–83; rank of brigadier general, September 28, 1883; commander of the 11th Military Zone, Tabasco, 1885–87; rank of brigade general, February 23, 1892; governor of the national palace, 1911–13; retired from the army, February 3, 1913. K] None. L] Sec of War, 1911, 16; Peral, appendix, 43; Pasquel, 17–22; Mestre, 256; Cuevas, 378; Bulnes, 136; 20–21; Almanaque de Tabasco, 149.

Bandera y Mata, Gabino
(Deceased 1926) A] 1887. B] Huitzingo, Guerrero. C] Early education unknown; no degree. D] *Constitutional deputy* from the State of Puebla, Dist. 14, 1916–17; *federal deputy* from the State of Puebla, Dist. 13, 1917–18; *federal deputy* from the State of Guerrero, Dist. 6, 1918–20, member of the Great Committee. E] Member of the Anti-Reelectionist party. F] None. G] None. H] Pharmacist; railroad postal agent; traveling agent for an insurance company. I] Unknown. J] Fought under *Ricardo Flores Magón* in the pre-Revolutionary battles of Viesca, Coahuila, 1908; rank of 1st captain, 1910; fought *Félix Díaz* and *Manuel Mondragón*, 1913; joined the Constitutionalists, 1913; rank of lt. colonel, 1913; fought under General Antonio Medina, Matamoros Brigade, 3rd Division of the East, 1913; military commander of San Luis Potosí and Durango; rank of colonel, 1914; representative of General *Gabriel Gavira*, Convention of Aguascalientes, 1914–15. K] Exiled to Cuba, 1913; murdered in 1926. L] CyT, 73–74; C de D, 1917–18; C de O, 1918–20.

Baranda (y Quijano), Joaquín
(Deceased May 21, 1909) A] May 7, 1840. B] Mérida, Yucatán. C] Primary studies at the Liceo González Arfián, Campeche; preparatory studies at the Colegio San Miguel de Estrada, Campeche; law degree, Campeche Institute, 1862; professor of Spanish, rhetoric, and poetry, Campeche Institute. D] Federal deputy from the State of Campeche, 1867–69, 1869–71; federal deputy from the Federal District, 1869–71; governor of Campeche, 1871–75, 1875–77; senator from the Federal District, 1881–82, president of the Senate; *senator* from the Federal District, 1884–88; *senator* from the State of México, 1908–09. E] Member of the Liberal party. F] Judge of the first instance, Matamoros, 1863; civil and criminal judge, Campeche, 1863; adviser to the director of the treasury, State of Tamaulipas, 1863; fiscal attorney, State of Tamaulipas, 1863; secretary general of government, State of Tamaulipas, 1866; ambassador to Guatemala; circuit court judge, Yucatán, Campeche, Tabasco, and Chiapas, 1881; secretary of justice, 1882–84; interim governor of Campeche, 1883; *secretary* of foreign relations, 1884–85; *secretary* of justice, 1884–1901. G] None. H] Journalist. I] Son of Pedro Sáinz de Baranda y Borreiro, prominent Spanish naval officer in the battle of Trafalgar and later vice-governor and governor of Yucatán, 1834–35, and Joaquina Quijano; grandson of Pedro Sáinz y Baranda y Cano, lawyer and royal minister of treasury in Mexico; married Elvira MacGregor y Estrada, daughter of his father's business partner, cofounder of the first steam-operated thread factory in Mexico; brother of Pedro Sáinz de Baranda, governor and military commander of Tabasco, deputy to the 1857 Constitutional Convention, commander of the 11th Military Zone, 1891, and governor of Campeche. J] None. K] Exiled to Tamaulipas for helping opposition, 1862; imprisoned for opposing the empire; supported Lerdo de Tejada, 1877. L] Valdés Acosta, 475–78; Mestre, 235; DP70, 218; Enc Mex, II, 48; Godoy, 145; Carreño, 164; Peral, appendix, 45; Hombres prominentes, 37–40; Peña, 94–95; FSRE, 136; Pavía, 9–17; Velasco, 133.

Bárcena, Mariano
(Deceased April 10, 1898) A] June 25, 1848. B] Ameca, Jalisco. C] Primary studies in Ameca; studies in drawing, painting, sculpture, and piano in Guadalajara on a loan from a family friend; studies in painting, San Carlos Academy, Mexico City, 1865–66, on a scholarship from a local hacendado; preparatory studies in geology and botany, San Carlos Academy, 1867; engineering degree with a specialization in topographical geology, National School of Engineering, 1871; professor of assaying, National School of Engineering. D] Local deputy to the state legislature of Jalisco; *senator* from the State of Chiapas, 1890–98. E] None. F] Assayer, National Mint, 1874–76; founder and director of the Meteorological Observatory, Mexico City, 1876–77; *governor* of Jalisco, 1889–90. G] None. H] Learned harness- and saddle making from his father; prominent scientist; author of numerous works; represented Mexico in international exposi-

tions in Philadelphia, 1876, New Orleans, 1885, Paris, 1889, and Chicago, 1893. I] Father a harness maker; studied music under Cruz Balcázar in Guadalajara. J] None. K] Discovered many new species of vegatables and a new form of mercury. L] Enc Mex, II, 53–54; García Rivas, 226–27; Pavía, 210–14; Godoy, 252; DP70, 222; Mata Torres, 51; Peña, 97–98.

Barocio Barrios, Enrique
A] April 25, 1891. B] Federal District. C] Primary and secondary studies in Mexico City; abandoned medical studies to join the Revolution, 1911; medical degree, National School of Medicine, UNAM, October 27, 1922. D] None. E] None. F] Member of the presidential staff under Colonel Julián Avitia, 1924; *interim governor* of Quintana Roo, 1924–25; industrial hygiene physician, secretariat of Labor, 1937–38; director, Coordinating Services, Secretariat of Health, 1938–41; specialist, Federal Workers Social Services Institute; director of the General Hospital, Baja California, 1963. G] None. H] Practicing physician, Baja California, 1947–63. I] Son of Teófilo Barocio Ongarza and Lucia Barrios Heath. J] Joined the Revolution in support of *Francisco I. Madero* under the forces of Martín Triana in Torreón, 1911; abandoned medical internship, February 9, 1913, in Santa María de la Ribera, to join the Constitutionalists; fought in the Belisario Domínguez Battalion, 2nd Division, under the command of General García, Puebla, 1914; rank of lt. colonel, July 8, 1918; military physician, 1923; rank of lt. colonel, regular army, November 21, 1925. K] None. L] Alvarez Corral, 87–88.

Barragán (Rodríguez), Juan
(Deceased September 28, 1974) A] August 30, 1890. B] Ríoverde, San Luis Potosí. C] Primary and secondary studies in San Luis Potosí; preparatory studies at the Scientific and Literary Institute of San Luis Potosí; completed fourth year of law school. D] *Federal deputy* from the State of San Luis Potosí, Dist. 6, 1917–18; *senator* from the State of San Luis Potosí, 1918–20; federal deputy from the State of San

Luis Potosí, 1964–67, Dist. 1, member of the Military Industry Committee, the Military Justice Committee; federal deputy from the State of San Luis Potosí, Dist. 10, party deputy for the Authentic Party of the Mexican Revolution (PARM), 1970–73, member of the Department of the Federal District Committee, the Legislative Studies Committee, General Means of Communication and Transportation, and the Public Security Committee. E] President of PARM, 1965–74. F] None. G] None. I] Great-grandfather Miguel Francisco Barragán was interim president of Mexico in 1836; grandfather was a senator under Benito Juárez; son of Juan Francisco Barragán Anaya, a rancher, who served as mayor of Ciudad del Maíz; sister, María, married to Mariano Moctezuma, subsecretary of industry and commerce, 1936–38; intimate collaborator of *Jacinto B. Treviño*, cofounder of PARM; married to Teresa Alvarez; son Juan was a candidate for federal deputy from PARM, 1967. J] Joined the Revolution in 1913, served under *Jesús Agustín Castro*; lt. colonel in 1920; chief of staff for President *Venustiano Carranza*, 1920; career army officer, rank of general; incorporated back into the army by President *Lázaro Cárdenas*. K] Organized a strike at the Scientific and Literary Institute of San Luis Potosí in support of *Francisco I. Madero*; imprisoned after the murder of Venustiano Carranza, 1920; escaped into exile in the United States and Cuba; supported the Serrano-Gómez rebellion in 1927. L] HA, 28 May 1973, 9; C de D, 1970–72, 102; C de D, 1964–66, 87; letter; DP70, 566; HA, 7 Oct. 1974, 11; López, 85.

Bassols, Narciso
(Deceased July 24, 1959) A] October, 1897. B] Tenango del Valle, México. C] Preparatory studies, National Preparatory School, Mexico City, 1911–15; law degree, National School of Law, UNAM, May 29, 1920; professor of ethics, logic, and constitutional law at the National School of Law, UNAM, 1920–31; director of the National School of Law, UNAM, 1928–29. D] None. E] Founder of the League of Political Action with Vicente Lombardo Toledano; founder and vice-president of the

Popular party, 1947–49. F] Secretary general of Government of the State of México under Governor *Carlos Riva Palacio*, 1925–26; *secretary* of public education, 1931–34; *secretary* of government, 1934; *secretary* of the treasury, 1934–35; ambassador to Great Britain, 1935–37; delegate to the League of Nations, 1937; ambassador to France, 1938–39; ambassador to Russia, 1944–46; adviser to Adolfo Ruiz Cortines, 1952–54. G] None. H] Founder of the National School of Economics, UNAM; author of the Agrarian Law of 1927; author of many articles. I] Longtime friend of Vicente Lombardo Toledano; student with Gilberto Loyo and Rafael de la Colina at the National Preparatory School and at UNAM; studied sociology under Antonio Caso at UNAM; father, Narciso Bassols, was a judge; greatnephew of Sebastián Lerdo de Tejada; mentor to Ricardo J. Zevada and Víctor Manuel Villaseñor; married Clementina Batalla, daughter of *Diódoro Batalla*. J] None. K] Participated in the gubernatorial campaign in Aguascalientes, 1919, writing campaign speeches; *Plutarco Elías Calles* considered him a possible successor to *Pascual Ortiz Rubio* as president of Mexico, 1932; ran for federal deputy from the State of México and lost; resigned as director of the law school after a student rebellion against the introduction of a trisemester system; considered one of the most brilliant law professors at UNAM. L] WWM45, 9; DP70, 235; letters, EBW, 212; Peral, 96; Enc Mex, II, 533; *Excélsior* 14 Nov. 1949; NYT, 17 Oct. 1954, 16.

Batalla (Leones), Diódoro
(Deceased June 3, 1911) A] May 3, 1867. B] Veracruz, Veracruz. C] Early education unknown; enrolled National Law School, 1880; law degree, National School of Law. D] *Alternate federal deputy* from the State of Veracruz, Dist. 6, 1904–06, 1906–08; *alternate federal deputy* from Veracruz, Dist. 7, 1908–10, under *Félix Díaz*; *federal deputy* from the State of Veracruz, Dist. 1, 1910–11. E] None. F] Unknown. G] Prominent student leader during law school days. H] Journalist. I] Son of Lucas Batalla and Sotera Leones; married Clementina Torres; daughter Clementina Batalla married *Narciso Bassols*, secretary of public education, 1931–34, and prominent intellectual. J] None. K] Remembered for his distinguished oratory as a deputy and his opposition to the científicos. L] Illescas, 258; Mestre, 240; UNAM, law, 1880–91, 13.

Bátiz, Juan de Dios
(Deceased May 20, 1979) A] April 2, 1890. B] Zataya, Sinaloa. C] Early education unknown; began engineering studies in Culiacán, completed at the National Military College, 1908–12; cadet, 1st Company. D] *Federal deputy* from the State of Sinaloa, Dist. 1, 1922–24, member of the Great Committee; *federal deputy* from the State of Sinaloa, Dist. 3, 1924–26; *federal deputy* from the State of Sinaloa, Dist. 2, 1930–32; *senator* from the State of Sinaloa, 1932–34. E] *Treasurer* of the National Executive Committee (CEN) of the National Revolutionary party (PNR), 1931. F] *Interim governor* of Sinaloa, 1926–27; director of technical education, Secretariat of Public Education, 1934–36; founder of the National Polytechnic Institute (IPN), 1936; director of social welfare, secretariat of labor, 1936–40; director general of the National Mortgage Bank, 1940–46. G] None. H] Manager of various private firms, 1946–70. I] Married Laura Pérez; son Juan de Dios was a director general in the Secretariat of Industry and Commerce, 1961; related by marriage to *Lázaro Cárdenas*'s sister. J] Participated in the Revolution; served in the 1st Artillery Regiment under Colonel *Felipe Angeles*; participated in the battle for Nazas, Durango, 1912; fought against Orozco, 1912; rank of 2nd captain, February 10, 1913; officer, 3rd Artillery Regiment; fought in Torreón in the Nazas Division under General J. Refugio Velasco; commander in the 3rd Artillery Regiment; rank of 1st captain, 1914; rank of major, 1914; joined the Constitutionalists, 1915; military governor of Nayarit. K] President Cárdenas allegedly offered him the position of secretary of public education in 1934, but he turned it down in order to found the IPN. L] HA, 28 May 1979, 14; *Excélsior*, 21 May 1979, 4; Peral, 97; *Excélsior*, 22 May 1979, 30; DPE61, 66; Rev de Ejer, June 1971, 5–6.

Baz (Arrazola), Gustavo A.
(Deceased March 14, 1904) A] September 3, 1852. B] Federal District. C] Preparatory studies at the National Preparatory School, Mexico City; engineering degree, National School of Engineering, UNAM. D] Federal deputy, 1876–77; *federal deputy* from the State of México, Dist. 15, 1886–88; *federal deputy* from the State of Jalisco, Dist. 7, 1888–90; *federal deputy* from the State of Michoacán, Dist. 16, 1902–04. E] None. F] Attaché, Mexican legation in Paris, 1881; second secretary, Mexican legation in Madrid; secretary of the Mexican legation in Lisbon; official, Secretariat of Foreign Relations, 1885–86; first secretary, Mexican legation in Paris, 1888–98; chargé d'affaires, Mexican embassy, Paris, 1904. G] None. H] Journalist in youth. I] Son of Liberal politician Juan José Baz, secretary of government, 1876, and Luciana Arrazola; brother Maximiliano Baz was a public defender in the Federal District. J] None. K] Supported Lerdo de Tejada in 1877; accompanied Lerdo de Tejada into exile, 1877. L] Godoy, 199; DP70, 239; Mestre, 219; Peña, 109–10; QesQ, 62–63; Villaseñor, 132–33; Pavía, judges, 495.

Beltrán, Joaquín
(Deceased 1946) A] 1856. B] Unknown. C] Early education unknown; enrolled, National Military College, 1878, graduated as an engineer; director, National Military College, 1906–12. D] None. E] None. F] *Governor* of México, 1913–14. G] None. H] Journalist; author of numerous books. I] Classmate of *Victoriano Huerta, Angel García Peña,* and *Enrique Torroella* at the National Military College. J] Career army officer; rank of colonel, August 2, 1890; rank of brigadier general, September 15, 1904; rank of brigade general, September 12, 1911; fought against General Higinio Aguilar, las Cumbres de Acalzingo, 1912; commander, 2nd Cavalry Regiment; director of recruitment, Jalisco, Guanajuato, Querétaro, Zacatecas, and San Luis Potosí; rank of division general, January 7, 1914; officer, Legion of Honor, France. K] Loyal to *Francisco I. Madero,* 1912–13; apprehended *Félix Díaz* in Veracruz, 1912; later supported *Victoriano Huerta,* 1913.

L] Cuevas, 342, 350, 375; Sec of War, 1914, 17; Peral, appendix, 51–52; DP70, 247; López, 104–05.

Benítez, Daniel
A] 1890s. B] Amacueca, Jalisco. C] Primary studies at Autlán de la Granja; preparatory studies at the Liceo de Varones, Guadalajara, Jalisco; law degree, Liceo de Varones, 1914; professor of law, sociology, and political economy, Preparatory School of Guadalajara, 1914; subdirector of the Preparatory School of Guadalajara, 1914. D] *Federal deputy* from the State of Jalisco, Dist. 13, 1922–24; *governor* of Jalisco, 1926–27. E] None. F] Judge, Superior Tribunal of Justice of Sonora; secretary general of the State of Sonora; oficial mayor of the State of Sonora; attorney general of the State of Sonora; secretary general of Baja California del Sur, 1920; governor of Baja California del Sur; legal adviser to *Gilberto Valenzuela,* secretary of government, 1920; oficial mayor of the Secretariat of Government, 1924; subsecretary of government, 1924. G] None. H] Practiced law; law partner with Gilberto Valenzuela, I] Member of Gilberto Valenzuela's political clique; met him at the Liceo de Varones in Guadalajara; parents were from a humble backgound. J] Gruening, 446–51; Quirós, 375–78.

Benítez (Martínez), José
A] January 1, 1891. B] Linares, Nuevo León. C] Secondary studies at the Colegio Civil of Monterrey; preparatory studies at the National Preparatory School; enrolled, National School of Law, UNAM, May 8, 1909, graduating with a law degree; advanced studies from the University of Heidelberg, and in Berlin, Munich, and Vienna. D] None. E] None. F] Private secretary to *Aarón Sáenz;* director, Department of Chancelleries, Secretariat of Foreign Relations; chargé d'affaires, Washington, D.C., and Guatemala, 1921–24; interim governor of Nuevo León, 1925, 1928–29, 1930–31; secretary of government of the State of Nuevo León, 1927; secretary general of the Department of the Federal District, 1932–35. G] None. H] Adviser to various banking firms; lawyer, Cía. Fundidora de Fierro y Acero de Monterrey; member of the board of Cré-

dito Industrial de Monterrey, Banco General de Monterrey, and Cía. Manufacturera de Tubos de Aceros. I] Son of engineer Francisco Benítez Leal and Adelaida Martínez; married Eva Gómez; probably nephew of Pedro Benítez Leal, governor of Nuevo León, 1900–02; Eduardo Bustamante Vasconcelos, secretary of government properties, served as his adviser, 1927. J] None. K] None. L] WWM45, 11; UNAM, law, 1906–12, 80; QesQM, 27–28.

Bernal, Arturo
(Deceased 1945) A] 1882. B] Zitácuaro, Michoacán. C] Primary studies at the School of Arts, Morelia, Michoacán; no degree. D] *Federal deputy* from the State of Michoacán, Dist. 6, 1926–28. E] None. F] Oficial mayor of the Secretariat of War; *governor* of Baja California del Norte, 1930; attached to staff, Secretariat of National Defense, 1937. G] None. H] Telegrapher, La Piedad and Jiquilpan, Michoacán. I] Grandson of guerrilla leader Félix Bernal of Zitácuaro. J] Joined the Constitutionalists, 1913; officer in the forces of *Joaquín Amaro*; chief of staff, under General Amaro, secretary of war; rank of brigade general, May 16, 1929; commander of the 23rd Military Zone, Tlaxcala, Tlaxcala. K] None. L] Dávila, 112; Romero Flores, 53; Peral.

Berriozábal, Felipe B.
(Deceased 1900) A] August 23, 1829. B] Zacatecas, Zacatecas. C] Early education unknown; enrolled at the National School of Engineering; interrupted studies to fight the North American invasion, 1846–47; engineering degree, April 1849. D] Federal deputy, 1868–69; federal deputy, 1873–74. E] Supporter of the Liberals. F] Boundary surveyor for the States of México, Tlaxcala, and Michoacán; provisional governor and military commander of México, 1859–62; secretary of war, 1863; governor and military commander of Michoacán, 1863–64; secretary of war, 1876; secretary of government, 1880; *secretary* of war, 1896–1900. G] Stockholder in and member of the Jockey Club. H] Engineer in the States of México and Tlaxcala, 1849–53. I] Orphaned at a young age; from a very poor family. J] Saw first military action as a lieutenant of engineers, July 22, 1847, under General José Joaquín de Herrera; commander of Toluca District, 1855–58, for the Liberal forces; rank of captain of engineers, National Guard, State of México, January 15, 1856; rank of lt. colonel of engineers, August 22, 1856; participated in the attack on Mexico City, 1858; colonel of cavalry reserves under General Santos Degollado, 1859; fought in the battles of Calamanda, Ahorcado, and Tacubaya, 1859; commander of the 1st Division, Army of the East, at the siege of Puebla, 1863; governor and military commander of Veracruz, 1863; rank of division general, May 25, 1863; military commander of Coahuila, Nuevo León, and Tamaulipas, 1866–67; left the army, 1876–77. K] Captured by the French at Orizaba, but escaped, 1863. L] Godoy, 200; DP70, 258; QesQ, 72; Enc Mex, II, 105–06; Hombres prominentes, 75–77; Rev de Ejer, July, 1968, 21–27; Dicc mich, 54; Peña, 118–19; Sánchez García, 235.

Blanco, Lucio
(Deceased 1922) A] 1879. B] Nadadores, Coahuila. C] Early education unknown; no degree. D] None. E] Joined the Anti-Reelectionists, 1909. F] *Secretary* of government, Convention Government, 1915. G] None. H] Unknown. I] Son of peasants. J] Joined the Maderistas, 1910; supported *Francisco I. Madero*'s forces against the Orozco rebellion, 1912, reaching the rank of major; fought under *Jesús Carranza* and Luis Alberto Guajardo; rejoined the Constitutionalists as a major, March 4, 1913, with sixty men from the Libres del Norte Regiment in Arteaga, Coahuila; signed the Plan of Guadalupe, March 26, 1913, as a lt. colonel; rank of colonel, 1913; rank of brigadier general, June 1, 1913; took the city of Matamoros, Tamaulipas; commander of the cavalry in the Army of the Northeast under *Alvaro Obregón*; supported *Francisco Villa* against Obregón, 1915; separated from Villa. K] In cooperation with *Francisco J. Múgica* responsible for the first land redistribution in Tamaulipas, for which he was removed from his command by *Venustiano Carranza* and sent to serve under Obregón in Hermosillo, Sonora; exiled to Laredo, Texas, 1915; exiled after the death

of Carranza, 1920; murdered in Nuevo Laredo, after initiating a movement against Obregón, 1922. L] QesQ, 74; DP70, 267; Enc Mex, II, 122.

Blanquet, Aureliano
(Deceased April 15, 1919) A] December 31, 1848. B] Morelia, Michoacán. C] Primary and secondary studies, Colegio de San Nicolás, Morelia; no degree. D] None. E] None. F] *Secretary* of war, 1913–14. G] None. H] Unknown. I] Son, Aureliano, Jr., served as an alternate federal deputy from Hidalgo, 1914–15. J] Joined the army as a 2nd lieutenant, February 4, 1877; rank of brigadier general, December 13, 1911; chief of military operations in the State of México, 1912–13; conspired against President *Francisco I. Madero* with *Félix Díaz* and *Victoriano Huerta*; rank of brigade general, February 18, 1913; rank of division general, March 20, 1913; joined the forces of Félix Díaz against *Venustiano Carranza*, 1918. K] Exiled to Cuba, 1914–18; killed by the troops of Guadalupe Sánchez at Chauaxtla, Veracruz; was a member of Maximilian's execution squad, 1868. Blanquet's head was exhibited in Veracruz on order of *Francisco Urquizo*. L] Mestre, 262; Dicc mich, 55; Rouaix, 57–58; DP70, 269; Enc Mex, II, 123; Sec of War, 1914, 17.

Bojórquez (León), Juan de Dios
(Deceased July 27, 1967) A] March 8, 1892. B] San Miguel Horcasitas, Sonora. C] Primary studies at the Colegio de Sonora, Hermosillo; agricultural engineering degree, National School of Agriculture, San Jacinto, 1908–12, on a scholarship; professor of Mexican history, Normal School, Hermosillo, Sonora, 1918. D] *Alternate constitutional deputy* from the State of Sonora, Dist. 4, 1916–17; *federal deputy* from the State of Sonora, Dist. 2, 1920–22; senator from Sonora, 1964–67. E] None. F] Governor of Baja California del Sur; private secretary to the oficial mayor of development, *Ignacio Bonillas*, 1913; director general of agriculture, State of Veracruz, 1914; subsecretary of agriculture, 1914; private secretary to General Lino Morales, commander of the 20th Sonora Battalion, 1915; minister to Honduras; minister to Guatemala, 1922; director

general of agriculture, 1925; *minister* to Cuba, 1926; director, Department of Statistics, 1926–31, 1932; *secretary* of labor, 1933–34; *secretary* of government, 1934–35; chief of the National Tourism Commission, 1950; director of the Small Business Bank of the Federal District, 1950–52. G] Organized the local Agrarian Commission of Sonora, 1916; secretary of the local Agrarian Commission of Sonora; founder and president of the Intellectual Workers Bloc. H] Agricultural engineer, Sonora, 1913; author of many books; worked in Los Angeles, California, 1913; publisher; director of three newspapers, 1915–17; director of *El Nacional*, 1931; president and director general of Telegraph News Agency of Mexico, 1935–41; director general of Maíz Industrializado, S.A., 1964. I] Son of Antonio Bojórquez and Jesús León. J] Joined the Constitutionalists, 1913. K] None. L] DP70, 273; Parrodi, 119–21; WWM45, 13–14; Gómez, 148–58; Peral, 115.

Bolaños Cacho, Miguel
(Deceased May 19, 1928) A] February 9, 1869. B] Oaxaca, Oaxaca. C] Primary studies at the Colegio del Sagrado Corazón de Jesús under Father Luis G. Santaella; secondary studies at the Liceo Mexicano in Mexico City; legal studies, Institute of Arts and Sciences, Oaxaca; law degree, University of Puebla, September 1889; professor, Scientific and Literary Institute of Chihuahua; professor, Institute of Arts and Sciences of Oaxaca. D] Local deputy to the 20th state legislature of Chihuahua; *alternate federal deputy* from the State of Oaxaca, Dist. 6, 1896–98; *federal deputy* from the State of Oaxaca, Dist. 3, 1898–1900, 1900–02; *federal deputy* from the State of Chihuahua, Dist. 3, 1902–04; *senator* from Tamaulipas, 1906–10; *alternate senator* from the State of Tamaulipas, 1910–12; *federal deputy* from the State of Oaxaca, Dist. 8, 1912–13; *governor* of Oaxaca, 1912–14. E] None. F] Secretary, Judicial District, Chihuahua, 1889–90; secretary general of the government of Chihuahua; district court judge, Oaxaca, 1895; secretary, Judicial District, Mexico City, 1901–02; *interim governor* of Oaxaca, 1902; district court judge, San Luis Potosí, 1903; *justice* of the Supreme

Court, 1904–06. G] Member of the Antonio Alzate Academy (National Academy of Sciences) and the Ateneo Mexicano. H] Editor, *El Chihuahuense*, 1890–93; prolific author; poet. I] Son of Dr. Ramón Bolaños Echeverría and Sabina Cacho y Apezechea; grandson of Aurelio Bolaños, lawyer, judge, and governor of Oaxaca; grandson of Julián Cacho, wealthy landowner from Tehuacán, Puebla; married María Maceyra; uncle of Demetrio Bolaños Espinosa, federal deputy from Oaxaca, 1934–37, 1940–43; uncle of Raúl Bolaños Cacho, senator from Oaxaca, 1964–70. J] Adviser to the army with a rank of colonel, 2nd Military Zone, Chihuahua, 1890. K] Exile in El Paso, Texas, 1914; exile in San Diego, California, 1914–28. L] Márquez, 69–74; Album de la Paz; DP70, 274; Ramírez, 113–18; Mestre, 280; Almanaque de Oaxaca, 130; Almada, 1968, 71.

Bonilla, Adolfo
(Deceased) A] June 24, 1880. B] Tlaxco, Tlaxcala. C] Primary education in Huamantla, Tlaxcala; no college degree. D] *Governor* of Tlaxcala, 1933–37. E] None. F] President of the Military Tribunal in Puebla, 1927. G] None. H] None. I] Father of Ignacio Bonilla Vázquez, who served as his inspector of police and himself became governor; political enemy of Luciano Huerta Sánchez, governor of Tlaxcala, 1970–76. J] Became active in the Anti-Reelectionist movement in 1910 and joined the Revolution in 1911; reached the rank of general in the army, November 17, 1915; supported *Francisco Villa* until 1920; commander of the 98th Regiment against the de la Huerta rebellion, 1923. K] Dissolved the Puebla state legislature, November 15, 1935. L] Peral, 116.

Bonilla, Manuel
(Deceased 1957) A] 1867. B] Sinaloa. C] Early education unknown; some secondary in the United States; engineering degree, with a specialty in mathematics, in the United States. D] Member of the City Council of Culiacán, Sinaloa, 1893–94, 1900, 1902; *senator* from Sinaloa, 1912. E] Supporter of José Ferrel, gubernatorial candidate in Sinaloa, 1909; foun-

der of the Anti-Reelectionist Club, Sinaloa, 1910; supported *Francisco I. Madero*'s campaign, 1909–10; opposed *Adolfo de la Huerta*, 1923; supported *José Vasconcelos* for president, 1929. F] Employee of the treasury of the State of Sinaloa; tax inspector for the federal treasury, 1909; *secretary* of communications and public works, 1911–12; *secretary* of development, 1912–13; supernumerary judge of the Superior Court of Justice of the State of Sinaloa. G] None. H] Mine administrator, Culiacán District, 1890s; editor, *El Correo de la Tarde*, 1910; employee of the Naviera del Pacífico Company; administrator of Industria El Colos, owned by *Joaquín Redo*. I] Son, Manuel Bonilla Gaxiola, revolutionary and newspaper editor. J] Commissioned by Madero to establish order in Sonora and Sinaloa, 1911, organized rurales in Mazatlán, Sinaloa; commissioned by *Francisco Villa* to solve agrarian problem in Chihuahua, 1914. K] Jailed for political articles, 1910; first supported, then exiled by *Venustiano Carranza*, 1913–14. L] Enc Mex, II, 142; DP70, 279.

Bonillas, Ignacio
(Deceased 1942) A] 1858. B] Magdalena, Sonora. C] Primary studies, public school, Tucson, Arizona; engineering degree, Technical Institute of Boston, on a scholarship from the governor of Arizona. D] Mayor of Magdalena, 1884, 1887–89; local deputy to the state legislature of Sonora, 1911–13; mayor of Nogales, Sonora, 1897, 1900, 1901. E] Supported *Francisco I. Madero*, 1910; candidate of the Carrancistas for president of Mexico, 1920. F] Prefect, Magdalena District, 1891–93; prefect, Arizpe District, Sonora, 1913; judge of the first instance, Magdalena, Sonora; oficial mayor of communications, 1914–15; *subsecretary* of communications, in charge of the secretariat, 1915–17; *ambassador* to the United States, 1917–20. G] None. H] Mining agent in Magdalena, Sonora; employee of many mining companies. I] Parents were very poor; father a blacksmith; helped support his family by shining shoes; became friends with the governor of Arizona by shining his shoes. J] Fought the Apaches, 1890. K] Accompanied *Venustiano Ca-*

rranza to Tlaxcalantongo, Veracruz, 1920; exiled in the United States, 1920–42. L] Enc Mex, II, 142; Bojórquez, 122–14; López, 120; DP70, 280.

Bórquez, Flavio A.
(Deceased October 17, 1928) A] 1869. B] Quiriego, Sonora. C] Primary studies in Alamos, Sonora; no degree. D] Local deputy to the state legislature of Sonora, 1911–13, with *Carlos Plank* and *Ignacio Bonillas*; *constitutional deputy* from the State of Sonora, Dist. 2, 1916–17; *senator* from Sonora, 1917–18; *senator* from Sonora, 1922–26. E] Joined the Anti-Reelectionist party, 1910; supported *Francisco I. Madero*, 1910; supported *Venustiano Carranza*, 1915; signed the Plan of Agua Prieta, 1920. F] Secretary to the political boss of the Canton (District) of Matamoros, Sonora; director of the Treasury Department, State of Sonora, 1914–15; Treasurer of the State of Sonora, 1915, under General *Plutarco Elías Calles*; secretary general of government of the State of Sonora, 1920, under *Adolfo de la Huerta*; *substitute governor* of Sonora, 1920–21; comptroller general of the nation, 1921–23, 1923–24; *provisional governor* of Sonora, 1923; *ambassador* to Peru, 1926–27. G] President (first) of the Local Agrarian Committee, Sonora, 1915. H] Merchant since youth. I] Son of Flavio Bórquez, secretary to the political boss of Matamoros district, and Dolores Velderráin, daughter of a large landowner; married Rosario Gil Samaniego; grew up in the mountains of Chihuahua. J] Fought against *Pascual Orozco*, 1912. K] Jailed in Hermosillo, Sonora, 1911; voted to not recognize *Victoriano Huerta*, 1913, as a local deputy. L] HA, 21 Feb. 1987, 36; López, 121; DP70, 283; Almanaque de Sonora, 127.

Borrego, Ignacio
(Deceased November 1931) A] Unknown. B] Durango. C] Early education unknown; no degree. D] *Federal deputy* from the State of Durango, Dist. 1, 1912–13, member of the Great Committee; *federal deputy* from the State of Durango, Dist. 1, 1920–22. E] President, Durango Democratic party, 1909; organized reception for an opposition gubernatorial candidate, July 12, 1909; helped publicize

Francisco I. Madero's campaign for president, 1910. F] *Secretary* of foreign relations, Convention Government, 1915; employee, Secretariat of Development, 1916. G] None. H] Unknown. I] Son of General Tomás Borrego, governor of Durango, 1871–72. J] Joined the Constitutionalists, 1913; represented *Roque González Garza* at the Convention in Mexico City, 1915. K] Jailed by *Victoriano Huerta's* government, 1913. L] C de D, 1912–13; 1920–22.

Bósques Saldívar, Gilberto
A] July 20, 1892. B] Villa de Chiahutla, Puebla. C] Primary studies in Chiahutla, completed his studies at the Normal Institute of the State of Puebla; continued his studies in 1911; teaching certificate; professor at the Normal Institute of Puebla; teacher at the primary and secondary levels in Puebla; professor of Spanish, Higher School of Construction, Secretariat of Industry and Commerce. D] *Federal deputy* from the State of Puebla, Dist. 7, 1922–24; *federal deputy* from the State of Puebla, Dist. 6, 1934–37, president of the Chamber of Deputies. E] Secretary of press and publicity for the National Executive Committee (CEN) of the Mexican Revolutionary party (PRM), 1937–39. F] Employee of the Department of Technical Education for Women, Secretariat of Public Education; employee of the Press Department, Secretariat of the Treasury, 1929; director general of *El Nacional*, 1938; first consul general, Paris, France, 1938–42; chargé d'affaires, Vichy, France, 1939–42; minister to Portugal, 1946–50; minister to Finland, 1950–53; ambassador to Cuba, 1953–64; retired from the Foreign Service, 1967. G] President of the Executive Committee of the Association of Normal Students, 1910; director of the Maderista student movement of the State of Puebla, 1910. H] Journalist, Mexico City, 1920. I] Son of Cornelio C. Bósques, merchant, and María de la Paz Saldívar; grandson of Antonio Bósques, who fought against Maximilian; participated in the Aquiles Serdán conspiracy; organized students and teachers against *Victoriano Huerta*, 1913; good friend of *Narciso Bassols*; prisoner in Germany, 1942–44; precandidate for governor of Puebla, 1949. L] DBP, 721–22;

letter; CyT, 115; *Excélsior*, 7 Oct. 1984, 11, 26.

Bravo, Ignacio A.
(Deceased April 11, 1918) A] 1835. B] Guadalajara, Jalisco. C] Early education unknown; no degree. D] None. E] None. F] Political boss and first *governor* of Quintana Roo, 1902–12. G] None. H] None. I] Unknown. J] Career military officer; rank of brigade general in the artillery, November 27, 1884; chief of the 11th Military Zone, Zacatecas, Zacatecas; distinguished for cruelty against the Mayas in the Yucatán campaign, 1901; rank of division general, May 12, 1903; commander of the 10th Military Zone, Durango, Durango; fought the Maderistas, 1911; commander of the Nazas Division, which opposed *Francisco Villa's* forces in Torreón, 1913; commander of the parade ground of Mexico City, 1914. K] Exiled to the United States, 1914–18. L] Sec of War, 1911, 15; Peral, appendix, 58; Mestre, 259; Enc Mex, II, 158; Alvarez Corral, 37; Sec of War, 1914, 17.

Breceda (Mercado), Alfonso
A] 1890s. B] Ciudad Lerdo, Durango. C] Early education unknown; one year of studies at the Juárez Institute, Durango; enrolled at the National School of Agriculture, San Jacinto, 1910–12; left San Jacinto after the school was militarized; enrolled at the National Preparatory School, Mexico City, 1912–13. D] *Federal deputy* from the State of Durango, Dist. 4, 1917–18, 1918–20; *alternate senator* from the State of Durango, 1932–34. E] Remained loyal to *Venustiano Carranza*, 1920. F] Secretary in the Secretariat of Government; aide to Venustiano Carranza, 1914–16. G] Participated in the Xochimilco and Xochimangas student plot against *Victoriano Huerta's* government with *Rafael Cal y Mayor, Jesús M. Garza, Aarón Sáenz, Jorge Prieto Laurens.* H] In real estate, 1921– . I] Parents were from Matamoros, Coahuila; parents were good friends of *Alvaro Obregón;* brother *Alfredo Breceda Mercado* was a prominent revolutionary general and governor of the Federal District, 1918. J] Left school to join the Revolution with other students, including *Manuel Pérez Treviño;*

aided by *Federico González Garza* and *Rafael Zubarán* to join the Constitutionalist forces in the North, 1913; Aarón Sáenz, Jesús M. Garza, and Breceda were apprehended; crossed into the United States at Brownsville, Texas, and traveled to Piedras Negras via the United States; made a captain in the Constitutionalist forces at Piedras Negras, 1913; paymaster, Ochoa Column, 1913. K] Exiled to Europe, 1920–21. L] Gómez, 77–80; DP70, 293; Enc Mex, II, 164.

Breceda (Mercado), Alfredo
(Deceased 1966) A] 1886. B] Matamoros, Coahuila. C] Early education unknown; no degree. D] *Federal deputy* from the State of Coahuila, Dist. 3, 1918–19. E] Member of the Democratic Anti-Reelectionist party, 1908; signed the Plan of Guadalupe, 1913. F] Private secretary to *Venustiano Carranza;* sent to the United States to buy equipment to manufacture small arms, 1915; director general of military industries, 1915–16; oficial mayor in charge of the Secretariat of Government, 1916; *governor* and military commander of the State of San Luis Potosí, 1917; *governor* and military commander of the State of Coahuila, 1917; *governor* of the Federal District, 1918, 1919; ambassador to Sweden, 1937–40; ambassador to Panama, 1941. G] None. H] Author; businessman. I] Parents were good friends of *Alvaro Obregón;* brother *Alfonso Breceda Mercado* served as a federal deputy from Durango, 1917–20. J] Joined the forces of Madero as a 2nd captain of the cavalry, and fought against federal troops at Río Yaqui, Sonora, 1910; rank of 1st captain, July, 1911; joined the Constitutionalists under Carranza, February 21, 1913; participated in the battle of the Hacienda of Anhelo, March 7, 1913; fought against Huerta's forces in Saltillo, Coahuila, March 22–23, 1913; rank of major, October, 1913, participated in the battle of Culiacán under General Obregón; rank of lt. colonel, September 27, 1914; commander of forces in Yucatán, 1915; rank of colonel, February 16, 1915; rank of brigadier general, 1917. K] Responsible for introducing the use of radium in the General Hospital of Mexico City, August, 1917; discovered large quantities of sul-

pher in Mexico, 1944. L] DP70, 293; Enc Mex, II, 164.

Buelna Pérez, Eustaquio
(Deceased April 30, 1907) A] September 20, 1830. B] Villa de Mocorito, Sinaloa. C] Preparatory studies at the Conciliar Seminary of Sinaloa, Culiacán, 1841; graduated from the School of Law, Guadalajara, December 24, 1854, law degree recognized by the Superior Tribunal of Justice of Jalisco, January 13, 1855. D] Local deputy to the State Legislature of Sinaloa, 1865, 1869–71; senator from Sinaloa, 1875; *alternate federal deputy* from the State of Sinaloa, Dist. 1, 1886–88, under *Justo Sierra*, 1886–88. E] Candidate for governor of Sinaloa, 1867. F] Prefect of Culiacán, 1855; provisional governor of Sinaloa, 1856; secretary of government of the State of Sinaloa, 1863; judge of the 1st Instance, Sinaloa, 1867; district court judge, Mexico City, 1867–68; justice of the Superior Tribunal of Justice of Sinaloa, 1868–69; secretary of government of the State of Sinaloa, 1871; governor of Sinaloa, 1871; *justice* of the Supreme Court, 1886–1907; *president* of the Supreme Court, 1897. G] None. H] None. I] Related to Rafael Buelna, revolutionary general; son of José Miguel Buelna and Estefana Pérez; uncle Basilio Pérez, a priest, helped him attend school. J] Joined the guerrilla forces of Plácido Vega; supported the Plan of Ayutla, 1854; fought in the Liberal forces against the French. K] None. L] Pena, 141–42; González Dávila, 64–65; Pavía, judges, 28–36; Godoy, 61; DP70, 297; Nakayama, 179–83; Mestre, 227; Blue Book, 1901, 29.

Bulnes, Francisco
(Deceased September 22, 1924) A] October 4, 1847. B] Mexico City. C] Early education unknown; studies at a private school, 1864–65; engineering degree in mining, School of Mines, Mexico City; civil engineering degree, National School of Agriculture; professor, National Preparatory School; professor, School of Mines. D] *Federal deputy* from the State of Morelos, Dist. 4, 1984–86; *federal deputy* from the State of Morelos, Dist. 1, 1886–88, 1888–90, 1890–92; *federal deputy* from the State of Michoacán, Dist. 15, 1892–94,

1894–96; *federal deputy* from the State of Michoacán, Dist. 10, 1896–98; *federal deputy* from the State of Michoacán, Dist. 6, 1898–1900; *federal deputy* from the State of Michoacán, Dist. 12, 1900–02; *federal deputy* from the Federal District, Dist. 8, 1902–04, 1904–06; *federal deputy* from Quintana Roo, Dist. 1, 1908–10, member of the Great Committee; *federal deputy* from Baja California del Sur, Dist. 1, 1910–12, member of the Great Committee; *senator* from Morelos, 1913–14. E] None. F] Represented Mexico on a cultural mission to Japan, 1874. G] None. H] Leading intellectual of his era; philosopher, anthropologist, astronomer, biologist, chemist, and mathematician. I] Son of Spanish immigrant Manuel Bulnes and María Muñoz Cano; uncle an important merchant and landowner in Tabasco. J] Secretary to General Carbo during the Reform; supported Lerdo de Tejada, 1877. K] Considered an independent positivist; exiled to Havana, Cuba, 1913. L] DP70, 301; Enc Mex, II, 172; Godoy, 118; García Rivas, 225–26; Puente, 33–36; Rice, 232.

C

Caballero, Luis G.
(Deceased June 26, 1915) A] 1851. B] Morelia, Michoacán. C] Early education unknown; law degree, Colegio de San Nicolás, Morelia, 1875; professor of philosophy, Colegio de San Nicolás; professor of constitutional law, Colegio de San Nicolás. D] Alternate federal deputy from the State of Michoacán, Dist. 2, 1882–84; *alternate federal deputy* from the State of Michoacán, Dist. 10, 1892–94; *federal deputy* from the State of Michoacán, Dist. 1, 1894–96, 1896–98, 1898–1900; *federal deputy* from the State of Michoacán, Dist. 8, 1900–02, 1902–04, 1904–06, 1906–08; *federal deputy* from the State of Michoacán, Dist. 7, 1908–10, member of the Great Committee; *federal deputy* from the State of Michoacán, Dist. 6, president of the Great Committee, 1910–12. E] Supported *Francisco I. Madero*, 1910–11; secretary of the Unión Liberal Convention. F] Judge of the first instance, Tacambaro, Zitácuaro, and Maravatio, Michoacán, 1875–83; judge of the Superior Tribunal of Justice of Michoacán, 1885–89; justice of

the Superior Tribunal of Justice of Michoacán, 1913–14. G| None. H| Practicing laywer, Morelia. I| Father of Luis Caballero, Jr., justice of the Supreme Court, 1938; married Isabel Escobar. J| None. K| None. L| DP70, 309–10; Rice, 232; Dicc mich, 61–62; Bonavit, 323.

Caballero, Luis
(Deceased 1930) A| 1880. B| Jiménez, Tamaulipas. C| Primary studies in public school, Jiménez; no degree. D| None. E| Ran for governor of Tamaulipas against General César López; declared himself the winner but his victory was not recognized by the federal government, 1918, when the Senate nullified the elections. F| Governor and military commander of Tamaulipas, 1913–15; ambassador to Guatemala, 1922. G| None. H| Businessman, rancher, and owner of La Concepción hacienda, Jiménez. I| Unknown. J| Supported *Francisco I. Madero*, 1910; participated in the rural forces of Tamaulipas against the supporters of *Bernardo Reyes*, 1911; rank of lt. colonel, 1913; fought under General *Lucio Blanco* against the Huertistas, 1913; rank of colonel, 1913; fought under General *Pablo González* in the battle for Matamoros, 1913; rank of brigadier general, 1913; in the battle for Ciudad Victoria, November 16–18, 1913; represented Colonel Bibiano Zaldívar Cervantes at the Convention of Aguascalientes, 1914; inspector of the army and chief of operations, Huasteca region, 1915; remained loyal to *Victoriano Carranza*, 1920. K| Wounded *Emilio Portes Gil* in a duel in Chapultepec Park, Mexico City. L| QesQM, 87; López, 133.

Cabral (González), Juan C.
(Deceased October 16, 1946) A| April 3, 1883. B| Minas Prietas, Sonora. C| Primary studies in a public school in Minas Prietas; secondary studies at the Colegio de Sonora; university studies at the University of Arizona. D| None. E| Active in Anti-Reelectionist campaign, 1910. F| Inspector of consulates, Secretariat of Foreign Relations, 1914; customs inspector, 1921; ambassador to Panama, 1923–27; ambassador to Ecuador, 1927; ambassador to Peru, 1928–32; *director general* of the Federal District Department, 1932; subsec-

retary of government, 1932–34, in charge of the Secretariat, 1934. G| Participated in the strike against the Cananea Mining Company. H| Box maker and cashier for a lumber yard; cashier, Cananea, 1906–07. I| Son of Portuguese Juan Cabral and Trinidad González. J| Joined *Francisco I. Madero's* forces; rank of colonel of cavalry, May 6, 1911; commander of revolutionary forces in Sonora, 1911; supported Madero against *Pascual Orozco*, 1912; commander of the Fiscal Police, 3rd Military Zone, La Paz, Baja California del Sur, 1912–13; rank of brigadier general, June 6, 1913; chief, Department of War, State of Sonora, 1913; pressured Governor Maytorena not to recognize *Victoriano Huerta's* government, February 22, 1913; joined the Constitutionalists under *Venustiano Carranza*, March 4, 1913; took Nogales, May 13, 1913; commander of military operations, Northern Sonora, 1913; commander of a military column, Army of the Northeast, 1913–14; brigade commander, Army of the Northeast, 1914; commander of the parade ground, Mexico City, 1914; commander of military operations in Sonora, 1914; represented Agustín Preciado at the Convention of Mexico City, 1915; tried to reconcile Generals *Alvaro Obregón* and *Francisco Villa*, 1915; supported the Convention forces against Obregón, 1915; reintegrated into the army, November 11, 1921, as a brigade general; attached to the chief of staff, Secretariat of National Defense, 1934; rank of division general, January 1, 1939. K| Jailed as a student for making an antigovernment speech, 1900; exiled to Arizona and California, 1910–11; 1915–21. L| Villa, 17–18; López, 134; de Parodi, 61–70; QesQM, 87–88; DP70, 313; Dávila, 111; Morales Jiménez, 197–99; Aguilar Camín, 122.

Cabrera (Lobato), Alfonso
(Deceased June 30, 1959) A| July 2, 1881. B| Zacatlán, Puebla. C| Primary studies in Zacatlán; secondary studies at the Colegio de Puebla; preparatory studies in Puebla and at the National Preparatory School, Mexico City; medical degree, National School of Medicine. D| *Federal deputy* from the State of Puebla, Dist. 17, 1912–13; *constitutional deputy* from the State of Puebla, Dist. 17, 1916–17; *gover-*

nor of Puebla, 1917–20. E] None. F] Director of the Central Military Hospital, 1940; chief of medical services, Department of the Federal District Hospital; director of Disinfection Department, Secretariat of Health; member of the Superior Council of Health, 1952–59. G] Organizer of the National Student Congress, opposed to *Porfirio Díaz*, 1910. H] Wrote for *El Hijo del Ahuizote*. I] Son of Cesáreo Cabrera, baker, and Gertrudis Lobato; nephew of Daniel Cabrera, cartoonist and publisher of *El Hijo del Ahuizote*, opposed to Díaz government; uncle of Enrique Cabrera Cosío, physician and cofounder of the National Liberation Movement; brother of *Luis Cabrera*, secretary of the treasury, 1914–17; father of Lucio Cabrera Acevedo, professor at the National School of Law; married Esperanza Acevedo. J] Director of medical and health services, Constitutionalist Army; remained loyal to *Venustiano Carranza*, 1920. K] Publicly opposed *Victoriano Huerta* as a federal deputy, 1913; exiled to New Orleans and Panama, 1920. L] López, 134; CyT, 122; Almanaque of Puebla, 130; Dir social, 1935, 65; DP70, 315; Libro azul, 104; letters.

Cabrera (Lobato), Luis
(Deceased 1954) A] July 17, 1876. B] Zacatlán, Puebla. C] Primary studies in Zacatlán; preparatory studies at the National Preparatory School, 1889–93; enrolled at the National School of Law, 1901, graduated with a law degree, 1901; schoolteacher in Tecomaluca, Tlaxcala, 1893–94; professor at the National School of Law, 1907–08; dean, National School of Law, 1912. D] *Federal deputy* from the Federal District, Dist. 11, 1912–13; *federal deputy* from the State of Puebla, Dist. 14, 1917–18. E] Supported *Bernardo Reyes* for president, but when Reyes would not oppose Díaz, Cabrera supported *Francisco I. Madero*; a founder of the Anti-Reelectionist party; offered the candidacy of the Anti-Reelectionist party for the presidency, but declined, 1933; offered the candidacy of the National Action party for the presidency, but declined, 1946. F] *Secretary* of the treasury, 1914–17; president of the Mixed United States–Mexico Claims Commission, 1916–17; envoy of Mexico

to South America, 1918; *secretary* of the treasury, 1919–20. G] None. H] Prolific author under the pseudonym of Blas Urrea; journalist, 1892; reporter, *El Noticiero*, 1906; practiced law with *Rodolfo Reyes*, son of *Bernardo Reyes* and his costudent at the National School of Law; lawyer with the firm of William A. McLaren and Rafael Hernández. I] Son of Cesáreo Cabrera, a baker, and Gertrudis Lobato; legal dependent at law school of his uncle, Daniel Cabrera, publisher of an anti-Díaz newspaper; married Elena Cosío; son Enrique was a cofounder of the National Liberation Movement in the 1960s. J] Joined *Venustiano Carranza*, 1913; special agent of Carranza in the United States, 1913; remained loyal to Carranza, 1920; accompanied Carranza to Tlaxcalantongo, Veracruz, 1920. K] Offered subsecretary of government by President *Francisco León de la Barra*, but ran for federal deputy, 1911; Madero's advisers vetoed him as too liberal as his choice for secretary of development, 1912; deported to Guatemala by the Mexican government for criticisms of *Pascual Ortiz Rubio*, 1931. L] López, 135; CyT, 123–24; Enc Mex, II, 194; DP70, 314; Dir soc, 1935, 65; Bojórquez, 17–19; Justicia, March, 1971; UNAM, law, 1891–96, 70.

Cahuantzi, Próspero
(Deceased January 9, 1915) A] July 29, 1834. B] Santa María Yxtulco, Municipio del Entro, Tlaxcala. C] Primary studies in Tlaxcala; some military studies after 1856; no degree. D] Senator from Tlaxcala. E] None. F] Oficial mayor of the Secretariat of War; political boss of Huamantla, Tlaxcala; secretary of government of the State of Tlaxcala; *governor* of Tlaxcala, 1885–1911. G] None. H] Author of a book on military history. I] Son of an Indian peasant; one of the few Indians prominent in national Mexican politics under *Porfirio Díaz*. J] Fought with General Comonfort against General Santa-Anna; fought in Wars of the Reform; joined the national guard, 1856; commander of a troop of rurales; fought against the French Intervention as a lieutenant and captain; supported Díaz in 1876; rank of colonel in the cavalry, August 10, 1877. K] Died in the Chihuahua

penitentiary. L] Pavía, 378–79; Hombres prominentes, 333–34; Mestre, 252; DP70, 320; López, 137; Godoy, 254.

Calderón, Esteban Baca
(Deceased March 29, 1957) A] May 6, 1876. B] Santa María del Oro, Nayarit. C] Primary in Ixtlán del Río, secondary and preparatory studies; assistant in the Higher School of Tepic, Nayarit; director of a boys' school, Buenavista, Sonora, 1911; rank of 2nd lieutenant from a military school, 1902. D] *Constitutional deputy* from the State of Jalisco, Dist. 17, 1916–17; coauthor of Article 123; *provisional governor* of Nayarit, 1928–29; *senator* from Jalisco, 1918–20; *senator* from Nayarit, 1930–34; senator from Nayarit, 1952–58, member of the Rules Committee, first secretary of the Second National Defense Committee, the First Navy Committee, and the Social Welfare Committee. E] Cofounder with General *Manuel Diéguez* of the Liberal Union of Humanity in Cananea, Sonora, which was affiliated with the Flores Magón brothers, 1906. F] *Governor* and military commander of Colima, 1914–15; director general of taxes, State of Jalisco; director of customs in Nuevo León, 1929; president of the National Claims Commission, 1918; president of the Federal Board of Material Improvement, 1925–27; director of the Purchasing Department, National Railroads of Mexico, 1937. G] Leader of the Cananea mining strike, 1906; sentenced to 15 years in prison, 1909; imprisoned with Manuel Diéguez in San Juan de Ulloa. H] Worked in the mining fields of Sonora, 1904–06. I] Son of Jesús B. Calderón and Vita Ojeda, from the middle class. J] Organizer of volunteers with *Pablo Quiroga* and Manuel Diéguez to oppose *Victoriano Huerta*, 1913; fought under General *Alvaro Obregón*; fought against *Francisco Villa*, 1915; rank of brigade general, April 27, 1917; rank of division general, 1939. K] Opposed *Venustiano Carranza's* imposition of a successor in 1920. L] DGF56, 7, 9–12; Ind biog., 30–32; Morales Jiménez, 55–59; Dávila, 111.

Calero (y Sierra), Manuel
(Deceased August 19, 1929) A] December 28, 1868. B] Hacienda de Paso de Toro, Veracruz. C] Early education unknown; enrolled National School of Law, January 4, 1890, graduating with a law degree. D] *Federal deputy* from the State of Yucatán, Dist. 1, 1902–04, 1904–06, 1906–08; *federal deputy* from the State of Veracruz, Dist. 14, 1908–10, 1910–12; *senator* from México, 1912–13. E] None. F] *Subsecretary* of Development, 1909; *secretary* of justice, 1911; *secretary* of development, 1911; *secretary* of foreign relations, 1911–12; *ambassador* to the United States, 1912–13. G] None. H] Practicing lawyer; author; banker. I] Son of Bernardo Calero and María Sierra; related to Vicente Calero Quintana, senator and historian, and to *Justo Sierra*. J] None. K] None. L] Martínez Alomía, 184; UNAM, law, 1880–91, 21; FSRE, 113; Mestre, 283; Armijo, 579–80; DP70, 327; QesQ, 90–91; López, 140.

Caloca, Lauro G.
(Deceased October 17, 1956) A] August 18, 1884. B] San Juan Bautista del Teul, Zacatecas. C] Primary studies in Zacatecas, Zacatecas; law degree from the Institute of Sciences of Zacatecas on a fellowship; professor at the Institute of Sciences of Zacatecas; director of the library, Institute of Sciences of Zacatecas. D] *Federal deputy* from the State of Zacatecas, Dist. 6, 1924–26; *senator* from Zacatecas, 1928–30, 1932–34, 1952–56. E] None. F] Secretary general of government of the State of Puebla; interim governor of Zacatecas; provisional governor of Puebla; adviser to the secretary of agriculture, 1920–24. G] None. H] Cofounder of the rural school program in Mexico, 1921; director of *La Voz* of Zacatecas, 1913; director of *El Independiente* of Zacatecas, 1920; writer for *El Universal*, Mexico City; poet and short story writer. I] Brother of General José R. Caloca; worked as a peasant and carpenter to support mother. J] Fought in the Revolution under *Francisco Villa* and *Emiliano Zapata*. K] None. L] DGF56, 8; López, 142; Enc Mex, II, 236; QesQ, 91.

Camacho, Sebastián
(Deceased) A] 1823. B] Jalapa, Veracruz.
C] Primary studies in Jalapa; preparatory
studies at the Colegio de Jalapa; civil engineering degree, National School of Mines,
Mexico City. D] Member of the City
Council, Mexico City, 1880; *alternate
senator* from the State of Jalisco, 1888–90,
1890–92, 1892–94, 1896–98; mayor,
Mexico City, 1894; *federal deputy* from
the State of Guanajuato, Dist. 15, 1894–96,
1896–98, president of the Chamber, 1894–
96; *senator* from the Federal District,
1900–02, 1902–04, 1904–06, 1906–08,
1908–10, 1910–12, 1913–14. E] None.
F] Assayer of the mint, Mexico City; represented Mexico on an industrial commission, New Orleans, 1894–95. G] Jockey
Club member since 1883; stockholder,
1901. H] Mining and industrial businesses; president of the National Bank,
1907; publisher of *La Libertad*, Mexico
City. I] Father a distinguished diplomat,
governor, and statesman who accumulated
a large fortune in business with Angel
Lerdo de Tejada; married Loreta Pizarro.
J] None. K] None. L] López, 144; Rice,
233; Blue Book, 1901, 89; Godoy, 280–81;
Pasquel, Jalapa, 67–68; C de S, 1900–02,
6; C de S, 1904–06, 18.

Cámara Valles, Nicolás
(Deceased) A] Unknown. B] Yucatán.
C] Primary and secondary studies at the
Colegio of Primary and Secondary Instruction, directed by Benito Ruz y Ruz; medical degree, Germany. D] *Governor* of Yucatán, 1912–13. E] None. F] *Interim
governor* of Yucatán, 1911. G] None.
H] Practicing physician, Mérida, Yucatán.
I] Son of Raymundo Cámara y Luján;
grandson of Nicolás de la Cámara y Castillo and Carmen Valles y Castillo; descendant of Juan de la Cámara , conquistador;
brother-in-law of *José María Pino Suárez*,
vice-president of Mexico, 1911–13.
J] None. K] None. L] Valdés Acosta, I,
419–20.

Campillo Seyde, Arturo
(Deceased May 25, 1958) A] August 14,
1884. B] Paso del Macho, Orizaba, Veracruz. C] Primary studies in Córdoba, Veracruz; no degree. D] *Federal deputy*
from the State of Veracruz, Dist. 11,
1920–22; *federal deputy* from the State of
Veracruz, Dist. 14, 1922–24, 1924–26;
federal deputy from the Federal District,
Dist. 4, 1926–28; *senator* from Veracruz,
1928–32, leader of the National Revolutionary Bloc, secretary of the Permanent
Committee of Congress; federal deputy
from the State of Veracruz, Dist. 10,
1934–37. F] *Governor* of Quintana Roo,
1930–31; federal customs official, Reynosa, 1952. J] Supporter of General *Félix
Díaz* during the Revolution; supported
Alvaro Obregón against *Venustiano Carranza*, 1920; rank of brigadier general,
January 1, 1924; zone commander of Tlaxcala and Querétaro. K] Expelled from the
National Revolutionary party in 1930 as a
leader of the "Whites" on the permanent
committee of Congress. L] Peral, 138;
DP70, 342; López, 147; Meyer, No. 12,
114, 125; Alvarez Coral, 115; Dávila, 194.

Cándano, Mauro
(Deceased July 31, 1938) A] 1855.
B] Villa de Tianguistengo, Hidalgo.
C] Primary studies in Tianguistengo; pre-
paratory studies at the National Prepara-
tory School; professor of mathematics,
Scientific and Literary Institute of
Hidalgo. D] Local deputy to the state leg-
islature of Chihuahua, 1888–90, 1891–93.
E] Propagandist in Chihuahua for *Félix
Díaz's* candidacy for president, 1913.
F] Political boss, Bravos District (Ciudad
Juárez), Chihuahua, 1887–88; *interim
governor* of Chihuahua, 1889. G] None.
H] President, Streetcar Company of Ciudad Juárez; accountant, Banco Mexicano,
1896–97. I] Married Aurelia González,
cousin of *Abraham González*, governor of
Chihuahua; second wife, Carmen Sagredo.
J] Joined the 3rd Regiment, March 20,
1876, as a 2nd lieutenant; initially opposed the Tuxtepec rebellion led by General *Porfirio Díaz*, 1876; joined the Porfi-
ristas under General *Francisco Tolentino*,
1876; rank of 1st lieutenant, 1876; rank of
2nd captain, Durango, 1880; rank of captain of cavalry, July 20, 1881; rank of major under Colonel Santiago Nieto's forces,
1884–85; private secretary to General Ramón Reguera, commander of the 2nd Military Zone, Baja Califonia de Norte, 1885;

rank of lt. colonel, June 30, 1888; military legal instructor, headquarters, 1st Military Zone, Federal District, 1899–02; rank of colonel, 1913; supported Félix Díaz in revolt against *Francisco I. Madero*; abandoned support when Abraham González was murdered, 1913. K] None. L] Almada, 416–18; Almada, 1968, 84–85; Sec of War, 1900, 163.

Cañedo (Belmonte), Francisco
(Deceased June 5, 1909) A] 1840.
B] Ranchería, Bayona, Nayarit. C] Early education unknown; no degree. D] Senator from Sonora, 1880–82; *senator* from Sonora, 1892–1904; *governor* of Sinaloa, 1884–88, 1892–1909. E] None. F] Prefect of Culiacán, Sinaloa; *governor* of Sinaloa, 1877, 1878; substitute governor of Sinaloa, 1879. G] None H] Employed as a porter, Culiacán, Sinaloa; employee in Manuel Izurieta's store, Culiacán; employee of Vasabilbazo brothers, Mazatlán, Sinaloa; wealthy businessman in later life; owner of several businesses in Sinaloa. I] Married into the Bátiz family; close friend of *Joaquín Redo*, senator from Chihuahua. J] Joined the Guerrero Battalion, national guard, to fight the French, fought with Colonel Antonio Rosales and General *Ramón Corona*; supported *Porfirio Díaz's* Plan de La Noria, 1871; rank of brigadier general of the cavalry, October 3, 1883. K] Imprisoned and sentenced to death for supporting Díaz, but sentence commuted to exile, 1871; accused of being the intellectul author of the murder of José Cayetano Valdés, a Mazatlán journalist, 1878. L] Godoy, 282–83; Mestre, 235; Album de la Paz; Villaseñor, 192; Balmori, 120; Sec of War, 1901, 23; González Dávila, 82–84; Almada, 1968, 86; C de S, 1900–02, 6.

Cañete, Rafael P.
(Deceased 1925) A] April 23, 1856.
B] Puebla, Puebla. C] Primary studies at a private school in Puebla, completed in 1870; secondary studies, Seminary of Puebla, 1870–75; legal studies, Colegio de Puebla, 1876–81, graduating with a law degree, February 24, 1881. D] *Senator* from Puebla, 1912–13; *constitutional deputy* from the State of Puebla, Dist. 2, 1916–17. E] President of the Anti-

Reelectionist party of Puebla. F] Judge of the first instance, Cholula, Chiautla, and Chicomula, Puebla; *provisional governor* of Puebla, 1911; *justice* of the Supreme Court, 1912. G] None. H] Practicing lawyer. I] Unknown. J] None. K] None. L] CyT, 145–46.

Canseco, Alberto
(Deceased 1929) A] 1854. B] Juchitán, Oaxaca. C] Primary studies in Juchitán, Oaxaca; graduated as a 2nd lieutenant of construction engineers, National Military College, 1886. D] None. E] None. F] *Interim governor* of Zacatecas, 1913–14. G] None. H] Engineer, various petroleum companies, 1914–29. I] Student at the National Military College with *Samuel García Cuéllar, David de la Fuente, Alberto Robles Gil*; brother Mauro graduated in 1887 from the National Military College as a construction engineer. J] Career army officer; attached to a sapper battalion, 1887–88; served in Oaxaca reconstructing the ruins of Mitla, 1889–1904; rank of 1st captain of the engineers, January 19, 1892; rank of colonel, August 14, 1908; subdirector, Department of Engineers, Secretariat of War; commander, sapper battalion, opposed to the Zapatistas, State of México, 1912; director, Department of Engineers, Secretariat of War, 1913; fought under General *Felipe Angeles*, 1913; rank of brigadier general, February 10, 1913; commander of the 11th Military Zone, Zacatecas, Zacatecas, 1913–14; rank of brigade general of engineers, Jan. 1, 1914. K] None. L] DP70, 352–53; Sec of War, 1914, 20; Peral, appendix, 69; Cuevas, 350.

Canseco, Agustín
(Deceased) A] August 28, 1832. B] Oaxaca, Oaxaca. C] Secondary studies, Conciliar Seminary, Oaxaca, Oaxaca; law degree, Institute of Sciences, Oaxaca, May 2, 1859. D] Local deputy to the state legislature of Oaxaca, 1867; *senator* from Oaxaca, 1888–90; *senator* from Zacatecas, 1890–1900. E] None. F] Judge, 1859–66; District Court judge, Oaxaca, Oaxaca, 1867; attorney for the Supreme Court, 1872–77; *justice* of the Supreme Court, 1877–86, 1886–87; *interim governor* of Oaxaca, 1886; *governor* of Oaxaca, 1887–

88. G] None. H] Practicing lawyer.
I] Unknown. J] None. K] None.
L] Godoy, 175–76; C de S, 1880–90; C de
S, 1890–92.

Cantón Rosado (y Rosado), Francisco
(Deceased January 30, 1917) A] Valladolid, Yucatán. B] April 2, 1833. C] Early
education unknown; no degree. D] Federal deputy, 1877–79; *federal deputy* from
the State of Yucatán, Dist. 5, 1884–86;
governor of Yucatán, 1898–1902. E] None.
F] Governor of Yucatán, 1867–68.
G] None. H] Rancher in youth; owner of
the Kanto hacienda; owner of the Mérida
to Valladolid Railroad; obtained a government concession in 1880; sold his line in
1902 for $5 million. I] Son of Juan Can-
tón y Rosado and Rita Rosado y Pérez;
grandson of Pedro Cantón y Meléndez and
Rafael Rosado; descendant of a prominent
Spanish family of regidores and officers;
lawyer son *Francisco Cantón Rosado* directed his railroad and served as a federal
deputy from Yucatán; married Domitila
Sabido, no children; second wife, Rudesinda Rosado y Casanova. J] Captain under Colonel Lázaro Ruz, fought Indian
rebels, 1854; as a colonel defended Chi-
chimila from the Mayas, 1861; fought Mayas under General Navarrete, 1865–66;
recognized Maximilian and fought against
the Republicans, 1863–67; revolted
against the government, Yucatán, March
13, 1872; chief of the Eastern Military
Line, 1873; supported *Porfirio Díaz*, Tuxtepec rebellion, 1876; rank of brigadier
general, 1877. K] Exiled to Havana, Cuba,
1867; imprisoned in Mexico City, 1869;
defended by *Joaquín Baranda* and ab-
solved, 1869. L] México y sus hombres,
78; DP70, 354; Godoy, 229; Valdés Acosta,
II, 497–500; Mestre, 257.

Cantón Rosado y Rosado, Francisco
(Deceased) A] Unknown. B] Valladolid,
Yucatán. C] Secondary and preparatory
studies at the Colegio Católico de San Ildefonso, Mérida, 1877–86; legal studies,
private law school under José Rivero Figueroa, 1886–90, graduating January 1, 1890.
D] *Federal deputy* from the State of Yucatán, Dist. 5, 1898–1900, 1900–02, 1902–
04, 1904–06. E] None. F] None.
G] None. H] Founder and editor of *El*

Amigo del País, a Catholic weekly,
1883–87; cashier, Mérida-Valladolid Railroad, 1892–96; superintendent, Mérida-
Yucatán Railroad; author of many books.
I] Son of *Francisco Cantón Rosado*, governor of Yucatán, and Rudesinda Rosado y
Casanova; married Delfina Cano y Mane,
daughter of lawyer Bernardo Cano Caste-
llanos and Delfina Mane y Navarrete.
J] None. K] None. L] Acosta Valdés, III,
483, 500–01.

Cantú Jiménez, Esteban
(Deceased 1966) A] November 27, 1880.
B] Linares, Nuevo León. C] Primary stud-
ies in Linares, Nuevo León; special classes
in Morelia, Michoacán; enrolled in the
National Military College, 1897. D] Sen-
ator from the State of Baja California del
Norte, 1952–58, president of the Second
Naval Committee, second secretary of the
Military Health Committee, member of
the Second Balloting Group. E] None.
F] *Governor* and military commander of
Baja California del Norte, 1917–20.
G] None. I] Brother of José T. Cantú, federal deputy from Baja California, 1917–18.
J] Career army officer; served in the 7th
Cavalry Regiment, Mexico City; instructor in the Second Army Reserve, Chihuahua, Jalisco, and Zacatecas, 1902–03;
fought against the Yaquis in Sonora,
1903–06; rank of major, 1911; fought in
the Cuesta del Gato, Chihuahua; supported *Francisco Villa*, 1914; Constitutionalist nominally, but really independent, 1915; commander of the federal
garrison, Mexicali, 1914–17; reached the
rank of colonel. K] Had to flee to the
United States in 1913 for opposing the assassination of *Francisco I. Madero*; lived
in Los Angeles, California, during the
1920s and 1930s. L] Ind biog, 32–33;
DP70, 354.

Caraveo, Marcelo
(Deceased March 15, 1955) A] 1885.
B] San Isidro, Orozco, Chihuahua.
C] Primary studies at a public school, Ciudad Guerrero, Chihuahua, where he studied
under *Mariano Irigoyen*, later federal
deputy from Chihuahua; no degree. D] Alternate senator from Chihuahua; *governor*
of Chihuahua, 1928–29. E] None.
F] *Provisional governor* of Durango, 1914;

director of customs, Ciudad Juárez, 1951–
55. G] None. H] Rancher. I] Unknown. J] Supported General *Pascual
Orozco*, 1910–11; rank of major in Orozco's forces; supported Orozco against
Francisco I. Madero, 1912; rank of brigadier general, 1912; commander of the 24th
Rural Group, 1912; rank of brigade general
in the cavalry, November 11, 1913, after
defending Chihuahua against *Francisco
Villa*; supported General *Victoriano
Huerta*, 1913–14; fought in the Nazas Division, 1913; rank of division general, May
1914; returned to fight against Pershing's
troops, 1916, but imprisoned by General
Jacinto B. Treviño in the Santiago Tlatelolco Military Prison, Mexico City; escaped from prison, 1917; fought against
Venustiano Carranza under General Manuel Peláez, 1920; reintegrated into the
army by General *Alvaro Obregón*, 1920;
chief of military operations in the Isthmus
of Tehuantepec, Durango, and México,
1921–25; supported Obregón against the
de la Huerta rebellion, 1923; chief of military operations in Chihuahua, 1925–28;
supported the Escobar rebellion, March
5–April 3, 1929, defeated in Reforma, Chihuahua, April 3, 1929; reintegrated into
the Mexican army as a divison general,
December 11, 1947; retired, 1951. K] In
exile, 1914–16; 1929–40. L] DP70, 359;
López, 156; Almada, 569–70; Almada,
1968, 86; Sec of War, 1914, 20.

Cárdenas, Miguel
(Deceased) A] 1850s. B] San Buenaven-
tura, Monclova, Coahuila. C] Primary
studies under private tutors; law degree,
National School of Law, Mexico City.
D] *Governor* of Coahuila, 1897–1909.
E] None. F] Secretary of government of
the State of Coahuila, 1880–84, under
Julio Cervantes; secretary of government
of the State of Coahuila, 1884–86; *interim
governor* of Coahuila, 1894–96. G] None.
H] Lawyer, land developing company; one
of the 16 largest landholders in Coahuila.
I] Parents were wealthy landowners.
I] Political disciple of *Bernardo Reyes*;
son-in-law of Cayetano Ramos Falcón, political enemy of *José María Garza Galán*,
governor of Coahuila, 1890–93; boyhood
friend of *Venustiano Carranza* and his
brother. J] None. K] Helped oust Garza

Galán from the governorship, 1893; resigned from the governorship after *Porfirio
Díaz* sent his mentor, Bernardo Reyes,
abroad. L] Album de la Paz; Cuellar
Valdés, 192; Langston, 135, 45.

Cárdenas (del Río), Lázaro
(Deceased October 19, 1970) A] May 21,
1895. B] Jiquilpan de Juárez, Michoacán.
C] Primary studies in Jiquilpan de Juárez;
no formal education after 1909. D] *Governor* of Michoacán, 1928–32, with numerous leaves of absence; president of
Mexico, 1934–40. E] *President* of the
National Executive Committee of the National Revolutionary party, 1930–31.
F] *Interim governor* of Michoacán, 1920;
secretary of government, August 28–
October 15, 1931; *secretary* of war and
navy, 1933; secretary of national defense,
1942–45; executive director of the Cuenca
del Tepalcatepec, 1947–60; executive
director of the Cuenca del Río Balsas,
1960–70. G] None. H] Worked as a
printer, 1911–13. I] Brother of Dámaso
Cárdenas, governor of Michoacán; married
Amalia Solórzano; father a small grocer;
father of Cuauhtémoc Cárdenas, governor
of Michoacán and presidential candidate
of the National Democratic Front, 1988.
J] Joined the Revolution, 1913, under the
forces of General Guillermo García Aragón as a 2nd captain and member of his
staff; fought under General *Alvaro Obregón* against *Emiliano Zapata*, 1914; major
in charge of a detail of the 22nd Cavalry
Regiment; fought under the forces of *Lucio Blanco*, 1914; fought against the forces
of *Francisco Villa* under General *Plutarco
Elías Calles*, 1915; fought against the de la
Huerta rebellion during which he was captured by *Enrique Estrada*, 1923; rank of
brigadier general, 1924; commander of the
military zone of Tampico, 1925; rank of
division general, 1928; fought against the
Cristeros, 1928; commander of the 19th
Military Zone, Puebla, November 1,
1933–January 1, 1934; commander of special Pacific Defense Zone, 1941–42.
K] Saved General *Enrique Estrada* from
military execution (1924), who later
served as a federal deputy during Cárdenas's presidency; active in the National
Liberation Movement in the 1960s; leader
of one of the largest political groups in

Mexico until his death. L] WWM45, 18–19; DGM68, 114; EBW, 29; DGF56, 414; DP70, 362–63, 2374–75; DGF50, II, 451; WB54, 162; QesQ, 100–01; Enc Mex, II, 361–67; NYT, 20 Oct. 1970.

Carpio, Manuel
(Deceased November 4, 1929) A] 1877. B] Aguascalientes, Aguascalientes. C] Primary and secondary studies at the Liceo for Boys, Guadalajara; no degree. D] *Federal deputy* from the State of Aguascalientes, Dist. 2, 1924–26; *senator* from Aguascalientes, 1926–28; *governor* of Aguascalientes, 1928–29. E] Supported *Ignacio Bonillas* for president of Mexico, 1920. F] Employee, state government of Guadalajara; official, Secretariat of Foreign Relations. G] None. H] Poet, journalist; contributor to *El Pueblo*, Mexico City; founder of *Crónica*, January 1, 1907; director, *La Voz de la Revolución*, Yucatán. I] Possibly related to Manuel Carpio Hernández, poet. J] None. K] Exiled to the United States, 1914, 1920; returned to Mexico, 1920, under the protection of General *Salvador Alvarado*, 1920; killed in a plane crash in Villa del Carbón, Mexico, while serving as governor. L] Almanaque de Aguascalientes, 104; DP70, 371.

Carranza (de la Garza), Venustiano
(Deceased May 21, 1920) A] January 14, 1860. B] Cuatro Ciénegas, Coahuila. C] Primary studies at the Ateneo de la Fuente, Saltillo, Coahuila; secondary and preparatory at the Ateneo de la Fuente; preparatory studies at the National Preparatory School, 1875; medical studies, National School of Medicine, but dropped out of school because of illness. D] Local deputy to the state legislature of Coahuila; mayor of Cuatro Ciénegas, Coahuila, 1887–89, 1889–91, 1894–95, 1896–97, 1898; *alternate federal deputy* from the State of Coahuila, Dist. 1, 1898–1900; *senator* from the State of Coahuila, 1904–06, 1906–08, 1908–10, 1910–12; *governor* of Coahuila, 1912–13; *president* of Mexico, 1914–20. E] A founder of the Democratic party, 1900; organized opposition to Governor *José María Garza Galán*, 1890. F] *Interim governor* of Coahuila, 1908; secretary of war and navy in *Fran-*

cisco I. Madero's rebel government in Ciudad Juárez, 1911. G] None. H] Owner of El Venado hacienda, Cuatro Ciénegas, Coahuila. I] Grandson of Rafael Carranza Ramos and Ignacia Neyra Jiménez, and Juan Nepomuceno de la Garza and María de Jesús; son of Colonel Jesús Carranza Neyra, Liberal and Juarista, who was a large landholder, and María de Jesús de la Garza; married Virginia Salinas, daughter of José María Salinas Arreola and Catarina Balmaceda; daughter Julia married *Cándido Aguilar*, revolutionary and governor of Veracruz; son Rafael Carranza Hernández was a leader of the Authentic Party of the Mexican Revolution and a senator from Coahuila; brother Jesús was a revolutionary general. J] Second lieutenant in the Reyista 2nd Reserves; chief of the Constitutionalist Army, 1913–15; author of the Plan of Guadalupe, March 26, 1913. K] Murdered in Tlaxcalantongo, Puebla, by the forces of Rodolfo Herrero. L] Morales Jiménez, 241–49; González de la Garza, 169–70; Mellado, 17ff; Holms, 255; Covarrubias, I, 211–18; C de S, 1904–06, 18; C de S, 1906–08, 19; QesQ, 105; López, 165; Moreno, 117–38.

Carrascosa, Manuel
(Deceased 1920s) A] May 2, 1840. B] Comitán, Chiapas. C] Early education unknown; law degree. D] Member of the City Council of Comitán; mayor of Comitán; federal deputy, 1864; federal deputy, 1877; *federal deputy* from the State of Chiapas, Dist. 3, 1882–84; *federal deputy* from the State of Chiapas, Dist. 5, 1884–86, 1886–88; *governor* of Chiapas, 1887–91; *senator* from the State of Chiapas, 1894–96; *federal deputy* from the State of Puebla, Dist. 5, 1904–06, 1906–08; *federal deputy* from the State of Puebla, Dist. 6, 1908–10, 1910–12. E] None. F] Judge, Comitán; political boss of Comitán. G] None. H] Practicing lawyer; rancher in Guatemala; large landowner in Chiapas. I] From a landowning family. J] Supported *Porfirio Díaz* in his revolt in 1872; exiled to Guatemala, 1872–76. K] Introduced innovative ideas in the cultivation of corn, coffee, and other crops. L] Godoy, 203; Pavía, 121; Almanaque de Chiapas, 117; Hombres prominentes, 289–90.

Carreón, Donaciano
(Deceased 1944) A] 1873. B] Zinapécuaro, Michoacán. C] Primary studies
only. D] *Federal deputy* from the State of
Michoacán, Dist. 9, 1930–32; federal
deputy from the Federal District, Dist. 3,
1934–37. E] None. F] Tax official; chief
of the treasury office, Ario de Rosales, Jiquilpan, and Zamora, Michoacán; treasurer general of the State of Michoacán;
treasurer of the National Lottery. G] None.
H] Operated own printing firm in Jiquilpan; publisher of *El Ensayo.* I] Employed
Lázaro Cárdenas, president of Mexico,
1934–40, in his print shop; brother Angel
Carreón served as interim governor of Michoacán, 1912. J] None. K] None.
L] C de D, 1930–32; C de D, 1934–37.

Carrillo (Aguayo), Lauro
(Deceased March 6, 1910) A] April 2,
1841. B] Sahuaripa, Sonora. C] Primary
studies in Moris, Chihuahua; no degree.
D] Mayor of Moris, Chihuahua, 1874; local deputy to the state legislature of Chihuahua, 1878–80, 1880–82, 1884–86;
alternate senator from Chihuahua, 1884–
88; *governor* of Chihuahua, 1888–92;
senator from Morelos (never served),
1890; *senator* from Chihuahua, 1892–96;
federal deputy from the State of Puebla,
Dist. 16, 1896–98; *federal deputy* from
the State of Puebla, Dist. 20, 1900–02.
E] Head of the *Carlos Pacheco* political
group in Chihuahua, 1887–92. F] Director of development, colonization, and in-
dustrialization, State of Chihuahua; *substitute governor* of Chihuahua, 1887–88.
G] None. H] Small businessman, 1858–
65; surveyor and miner, 1858–65; mining
employee, Mineral de Barranca del Cobre,
1874; partner in the firm of Salinas de Palomas y de la Unión. I] Son of Juan José
Carrillo and Teresa Aguayo; daughter María married prominent revolutionary general and politician *Jacinto B. Treviño*;
granddaughter Adela Palacios married intellectual *Samuel Ramos,* oficial mayor of
the Secretariat of Public Education, 1931–
32; married Adelaida Gutiérrez; business
associate of *Jesús E. Valenzuela,* federal
deputy from the State of Chihuahua; political disciple of General *Carlos Pacheco,*
secretary of development. J] Rank of col-

onel, but never served in guard or army.
K] Removed from the Senate for dueling, 1894; found guilty of dueling by the
courts, but pardoned by the Senate, 1895.
L] Pavía, 127–28; Almada, 408–15; Hombres prominentes, 197–98; Mestre, 237;
Romero Aceves, 642–43.

Carrillo Puerto, Felipe
(Deceased January 3, 1924) A] November
8, 1874. B] Motul, Yucatán. C] Primary
studies in public school of Motul, Yucatán; primary studies in Mérida, Yucatán;
no degree. D] Local deputy to the state
legislature of Yucatán; *federal deputy*
from the State of Yucatán, Dist. 1, 1920–
22; *governor* of Yucatán, 1922–23. E] Organized workers in the Socialist Workers
party (later Socialist Party of the Southeast), 1916, and president of the party,
1917. F] None. G] None. H] Laborer,
woodcutter, and railroad worker, 1880s
and 1890s. I] Son of Justiniano Carrillo
Pasos, small businessman, and Adela
Puerto; family lower middle class; daughter Dora Carrillo Palma married Javier
Erosa, mayor of Mérida, 1920s; grandson
Raúl Erosa Carrillo, local deputy to the
state legislature of Yucatán; brother Gualberto, senator from Yucatán, 1934–40;
sister Elvia, a federal deputy. J] None.
K] Executed by the *Adolfo de la Huerta*
forces under Hermenegildo Rodríguez and
Ricárdez Broca after watching his brothers
Wilfrido, Edesio, and Benjamín killed first;
sent aid to Lenin; name appears in gold
letters in Red Square, Moscow. L] Letter;
Morales Jiménez, 229–33; DP70, 381;
QesQ, 107–08; Bustillos, 13ff.

Carvajal (Gual), Francisco S.
(Deceased September 30, 1932) A] December 9, 1870. B] Campeche, Campeche. C] Early education unknown;
legal studies, National School of Law,
1890–95; law degree, National School of
Law. D] *Alternate senator* from the State
of Campeche, 1904–06; *senator* from the
state of Campeche, 1906–08, 1908–10.
E] Member of *José Yves Limantour's* political group. F] *Justice* of the Supreme
Court, 1908–14; *chief justice* of the Supreme Court, 1908, 1913–14; *secretary* of
foreign relations, 1914; *interim president*

ot Mexico, 1914. G] None. H] Practicing lawyer. I] Son of Francisco Carbajal and Mercedes Gual. J] Chief delegate of President *Porfirio Díaz* at the peace conference with *Francisco I. Madero*, 1911. K] None. L] Law, UNAM, 1880–91, 134; FSRE, 162; Mestre, 287; Covarrubias, 1952, 94; C de S, 1906–08, 19; C de S, 1908–10, 20.

Casanova Casao, Pedro
(Deceased 1975) A] 1880s. B] Cárdenas, Tabasco. C] Early education unknown; law degree. D] Local deputy to the state legislature of Tabasco, 1918–20. E] Active anti-reelectionist in *Manuel Mestre Ghigliazza*'s group, 1906; member of the Tabasco Liberal party, 1911. F] *Interim governor* of Tabasco, 1921; judge, Veracruz; assistant attorney general of the State of Veracruz; judge of the Superior Tribunal of Justice of Veracruz. G] None. H] Pharmacist, Bótica Nueva, San Juan Bautista (Villahermosa); notary public and lawyer, Veracruz, Veracruz, 1923. I] Close political friend of Carlos Greene, governor of Tabasco, 1920. J] Constitutionalist, fought with General Carlos Greene, 1913; private secretary to General Carlos Greene, 1914–19. K] Signed the Constitution of Tabasco, 1919. L] Bulnes, 259–60.

Casas Alatriste, Roberto
(Deceased 1967) A] August 5, 1893. B] Tezuitlán, Puebla. C] Early education unknown; public accounting degree, School of Business and Administration, UNAM, 1910; dean, School of Business, UNAM; professor emeritus, School of Business, UNAM; member, Governing Board of UNAM, 1953–62. D] *Federal deputy* from the State of Sinaloa, Dist. 1, 1918–20; federal deputy from the Federal District, Dist. 9, 1920–22; *federal deputy* from the State of Puebla, Dist. 4, 1922–24. E] None. F] Represented Mexico at the de la Huerta–Lamont negotiations, 1920; general accountant, Secretariat of the Treasury, 1922; financial agent, Mexican government, New York City, 1922–23; auditor, Bank of Mexico, 1929. G] President of the Association of Accountants of Mexico. H] Certified public accounting

firm (one of the first in Mexico); founder of *Finance and Accounting* magazine, 1934. I] Married Adolfina Hernández; first cousin of Sealtiel Alatriste, director general of the Social Security Institute, 1964–66. J] Supported *Alvaro Obregón*, 1920. K] None. L] Dir soc, 1935, 67; WWM45, 21; Libro azul, 111.

Casasús (González), Joaquín D.
(Deceased February 25, 1916) A] December 22, 1858. B] Frontera, Tabasco. C] Primary studies in Campeche, Campeche; preparatory studies at the Scientific and Literary Institute of Mérida, Yucatán, graduating with a program in science, 1876; law degree, National School of Law, March 15, 1880; professor, National School of Engineering; professor, National School of Law; founder and dean of the National School of Business; professor of history, Juárez Institute; professor of political economy, National School of Engineering, 1886–98. D] *Federal deputy* from the State of Tabasco, Dist. 1, 1886–88, 1888–90, 1890–92, 1892–94, 1894–96, 1896–98, 1898–1900, 1900–02, member of the Great Committee, and president of the Chamber, 1903; *federal deputy* from the State of Tabasco, Dist. 1, 1902–04, member of the Great Committee, 1904–06; *senator* from Veracruz, 1908–10, 1910–12. E] Treasurer, Unión Liberal Convention; member of the Liberal party. F] Judge, Teapa, Tabasco, 1880; secretary of government of the State of Tabasco, 1881; editor, *Diaro Oficial*, Tabasco; secretary of the Pan American Union, 1901–09; *ambassador* to the United States, 1905–06. G] None. H] Businessman; banker; international law practice, Mexico City and New York City; leading intellectual figure; author and translator. I] Grandson of José Casasús y Fotosaus, sailor and merchant from Spain; son of Francisco Asis Casasús Echazaralta, boat builder and carpenter in Campeche, and Ramona González; brother Carlos was a federal deputy from Mexico, 1894–1912; his mentor was Sánchez Roca, father of *Juan Sánchez Azcona*, senator from Campeche, who wanted to send him to Italy when Juan was ambassador; closest friend was *Miguel S. Macedo*, subsecretary of

government, 1906–11; political protector of intellectuals Amado Nervo, Victoriano Salado, and Enrique González Martínez; brother Carlos related by marriage to *Olegario Molina*, landower and governor of Yucatán; brother-in-law of Catalina Altamirano, daughter of Ignacio Altamirano, prominent intellectual and political figure; niece Evangelina Casasús married Manuel Sierra, son of *Justo Sierra*. J] None. K] None. L] Carreño, 154–55; DP70, 390; López, 174; Rice 233–34; Godoy, 147; Puente, 347–50; Palavicini, 79–81.

Castañeda, Francisco de P.
(Deceased) A] 1839. B] Guanajuato. C] Preparatory studies at San Ildefonso, graduating 1856; no degree. D] *Federal deputy* from the State of Guanajuato, Dist. 2, 1886–88; *federal deputy* from the State of Guanajuato, Dist. 8, 1888–90; *senator* from Guanajuato, 1894–1900, 1900–02. E] Delegate, Unión Liberal Convention, 1892. F] None. G] None. H] Owner, La Purísima, Marfil, Guanajuato; owner, Mesquite Gordo hacienda, Pénjamo, Guanajuato; banker; owner, agricultural implement store; partner, La Compañía del Ferrocarril de Celaya a León, Guanajuato. I] Unknown. J] None. K] None. L] Holms, 186, 275; Rice, 234.

Castañeda y Nájera, Vidal de
(Deceased May 9, 1903) A] April 28, 1836. B] Mexico City. C] Early education unknown; law degree, National School of Law, 1856; director, National Preparatory School, 1885–98. D] Federal deputy from the State of Puebla, 1862; *senator* from Puebla, 1890–92, 1892–94, 1894–96, 1896–98, 1898–1900, 1900–02. E] None. F] Attorney of the Supreme Court of Military Justice, 1883; attorney general of the Federal District, 1886. G] Secretary of the College of Lawyers of Mexico, 1867–75. H] Practicing lawyer, 1858; administered estates of father and uncle. I] Son of Manuel Castañeda Nájera, wealthy lawyer and Supreme Court justice, 1873, and Dolores González Escalante; grandson of José Castañeda and Josefa de Nájera; married Clotilde Espinosa de Monteros. J] None. K] None. L] Hombres prominentes, 463–64; Godoy, 93; Rice, 234–35; Teixidor, 54.

Castañón, José
A] 1893. B] Tuxtla Gutiérrez, Chiapas. C] Preparatory studies begun in Toluca, México; completed preparatory at the National Preparatory School, Mexico City; law degree, National School of Law, UNAM, April 24, 1912. D] *Federal deputy* from the State of Chiapas, Dist. 5, 1920–22; *federal deputy* from the State of Chiapas, Dist. 6, 1926–28; federal deputy from the State of Chiapas, Dist. 4, 1946–49, member of the Great Committee. E] None. F] Judge of the first instance; attorney general of the State of Chiapas; judge of the Superior Tribunal of Justice of the State of Mexico; secretary general of government of the State of Chiapas, under general Carlos A. Vidal, 1925–26; secretary general of government of the State of Chiapas, under Rafael P. Gamboa, 1940–44; president of the Superior Tribunal of Justice of Chiapas, 1944–46. G] None. H] Unknown. I] Son of Ezequiel Castañón and Lasuigilda Esponda. K] None. L] UNAM, law, 1912–16, 7.

Castaños, Fernando
(Deceased December 9, 1956) A] 1888. B] San Juan del Río, Durango. C] Early education unknown; no degree. D] *Constitutional deputy* from the State of Durango, Dist. 4, 1916–17. E] None. F] Judge, 5th Collegiate Circuit Court, Veracruz; oficial mayor of the State of Durango, 1913; secretary general of government of the State of Durango, under General Mariano Arrieta, 1915–16; *provisional governor* of Durango, 1916; judge of the Superior Tribunal of Justice of Durango, 1917–22; correctional judge, Mexico City, 1923; judge, Criminal Court, Mexico City, 1930–34; district court judge, Tlaxcala, 1935–41. G] None. H] None. I] From an established family in San Juan del Río; brother Salvador was a colonel in the Revolution. J] Supported *Francisco I. Madero*, 1910. K] None. L] López, 176; Rouaix, 83; HA, 21 Feb. 87, 37.

Castelló, Juan B.
(Deceased) A] Unknown. B] Tampico, Tamaulipas. C] Primary studies in Tamaulipas; law degree, National School of Law. D] *Federal deputy* from the State of

Hidalgo, Dist. 5, and the State of Tamaulipas, Dist. 3, 1886–88 (served in the latter post), 1888–90, 1890–92, 1892–94, 1894–96, 1896–98, 1898–1900, 1900–02, 1902–04, 1904–06, 1906–08; *governor* of Tamaulipas, 1908–11. E] None. F] None. G] None. H] Practicing lawyer. I] Unknown. J] None. K] None. L] Album de la Paz; C de D, 1888–90; C de D, 1906–08.

Castellot (Batalla), José
(Deceased April 7, 1938) A] 1856. B] Campeche, Campeche. C] Primary and secondary studies, Campeche; no degree. D] *Federal deputy* from the State of Hidalgo, Dist. 6, 1898–1900, 1900–02; *senator* from Chiapas, 1902–04, president of the Senate; *governor* of Chiapas, 1903; *senator* from Chiapas, 1908–12; *senator* from Yucatán, 1912–14, 1914–16. E] None. F] *Interim governor* of Campeche, 1902. G] Sovereign commander of the Supreme Council of Masonic Lodges, 1909. H] Banker; financier; journalist, wrote for *Alborada*, Campeche; cofounder of the Banco Central Mexicano, Banco de Michoacán, Banco de Hidalgo, Banco de Campeche, and the Banco Agrícola e Hipotecario de México; partner of Castellot Brothers; cofounder of the General Warehouse of Mexico and Veracruz; and cofounder of Cía. Bancaria de Fomento y Bienes Raíces. I] Son, José Castellot, Jr., served as a federal deputy from many states, including Tabasco, 1902–16; daughter-in-law, Ernestina Madrazo Torres, is the sister of *Manuel F. Madrazo Torres*, director of the Department of Health, 1933. J] None. K] None. L] UNAM, law, 1891–96, 3; Carreño, 285–88; Album de la Paz; Mestre, 294; C de S, 1904–06, 18; 1902–04; DP70, 397.

Castilla Brito, Manuel
(Deceased) A] 1872. B] Campeche. C] Preparatory studies at the Colegio Católico of Monsignor Norberto Domínguez, Mérida, Yucatán; no degree. D] *Governor* of Campeche, 1911–13. E] None. F] Political boss of Hecelchakán, 1903–05; political boss of Campeche. G] None. H] Unknown. I] Son of Marcelino Castilla and Rosario Brito; grandson of Manuel Antonio de Castilla y Suárez; sister

Ana married *Carlos MacGregor*, governor of Campeche, 1899–1903; married Vicenta MacKinney y Huerta. J] Supported Madero, 1910–11, with a rank of colonel in the rebel forces; Constitutionalist, rank of brigadier general, 1913; represented at the Convention of Mexico City, January 10, 1915; supported the *Adolfo de la Huerta* rebellion, 1923. K] Executed with two sons in Mamantel, Campeche. L] López, 178; Valdés Acosta, II, 123–24.

Castillo (Corzo), Víctor Manuel
(Deceased December 15, 1946) A] December 25, 1863. B] Tuxtla Gutiérrez, Chiapas. C] Primary studies in San Cristóbal; secondary and preparatory studies at the Scientific and Literary Institute of Chiapas; law degree, National School of Law, November, 15, 1884; professor, Scientific and Literary Institute of Chiapas, 1885; prefect, National School of Law, 1886–93; professor of international public law, National School of Law, 1889–1912; professor of international public law, Free Law School, 1912; professor of Roman law, Institute of San Cristóbal de las Casas; director, Institute of San Cristóbal de las Casas. D] Local deputy, state legislature of Chiapas, and president of the legislature; *alternate federal deputy* from the State of Chiapas, Dist. 2, 1892–94; *federal deputy* from the State of Chiapas, Dist. 2, 1894–96, 1896–98, 1898–1900, 1900–02, 1902–04, 1904–06, 1906–08, secretary of the Great Committee, 1908–10; *senator* from Campeche, 1910–12, 1912–14; *senator* from Chiapas, 1914–16. E] None. F] Syndic, City Council of Mexico City, Tacuba, and Azcapotzalco; director, official paper, State of Chiapas, 1884–86; private secretary to *Justino Fernández*, secretary of justice, 1901–10; represented Mexico at the International Maritime Congress, Brussels, Belgium, 1909–10. G] President of the Mexican Bar; member of the Bankers Club. H] Practicing lawyer; cofounder of the *Revista de Legislación y Jurisprudencia*, with *Emilio Rabasa*. I] Son of Cesáreo Agustín Castillo and Teófila Corzo; grandson of General Angel Albino Corzo, governor of Chiapas many times. J] None. K] None. L] UNAM, law, 1886–91, 20–21; DP70,

402; Gordillo y Ortiz, 40; Blue Book, 113; Chiapas, 151–52.

Castillo Lanz, Angel
A] November 1, 1898. B] Isla de Champotón, Campeche. C] Primary studies in Champotón; law degree, School of Law, University of Campeche. D] *Governor* of Campeche, 1923–27; *federal deputy* from the State of Campeche, Dist. 2, 1928–30, member of the Great Committee, secretary of the Chamber; *federal deputy* from the State of Campeche, Dist. 1, 1930–32, member of the Great Committee; *federal deputy* from the State of Campeche, Dist. 1, 1932–34, member of the Great Committee; senator from the State of Campeche, 1934–40. E] None. F] Oficial mayor of the Chamber of Deputies, 1934; director, Accounting Office, Chamber of Deputies, 1951–56. G] None. J] None. K] Some sources considered him to have been the political boss of Campeche. L] Enc Mex, II 301; DGF56, 38; C de S, 1934–40.

Castillo Ledón, Luis
(Deceased 1945) A] January 17, 1880. B] Santiago Ixcuintla, Nayarit. C] Preparatory studies from the Liceo de Varones, Guadalajara; professor of Spanish and Mexican history, National Preparatory School; oficial mayor of UNAM. D] *Federal deputy* from the State of Nayarit, Dist. 3, 1914–16; *alternate federal deputy* from the State of Nayarit, Dist. 3, 1918–20; governor of Nayarit, 1930–31. E] None. F] Secretary of the National Library, 1906; organized the Publishing Department, Secretariat of Public Education; secretary and director, National Museum of Anthropology and History, 1914; oficial mayor of the National Archive. G] Member of the Seminar of Mexican Culture, 1942; member of the Mexican Academy of History. H] Author of many historical works; editor, *Revista Moderna*, 1904; cofounder, *Savia Moderna*; wrote for *El Mundo, El Universal*, and *El Imparcial*, Mexico City; editor, *El Monitor Occidental*, Guadalajara; director, *Anales* of the National Museum of Anthropology and History. I] Married Amalia González Caballero, intellectual and political figure. J] None. K] WWM40, 113–14; López, 180; JSH,

86–97; O'Campo, 72; Velázquez, 52–55; DP70, 402–03.

Castillo Nájera, Francisco
(Deceased 1954) A] November 25, 1886. B] Durango, Durango. C] Primary and secondary studies in Durango; preparatory at the Juárez Institute of Durango; medical degree from the National School of Medicine, UNAM, 1903; advanced studies at the University of Paris and the University of Berlin; professor of urology at the Military Medical College, 1917–27; professor of forensic medicine at the National School of Medicine, UNAM, 1920–22, 1924; professor of general pathology at the National School of Medicine, UNAM, 1927; professor of urology for postgraduate students, UNAM, 1927. D] None. E] None. F] Director of the Juárez Hospital, Mexico City, 1918–19; director of the Military Medical College, 1920; head of the Council of Legal Medicine for the Federal District, 1919–21; minister to China, 1922–24; ambassador to Belgium, 1927–30; ambassador to Holland, 1930–32; head of the Department of Health and Welfare, 1932; ambassador to Sweden, 1932; *ambassador* to France, 1933–35; ambassador to the League of Nations, 1934; ambassador to the United States, 1935–45; secretary of foreign relations, 1945–46; president of the National Securities Commission, 1946–54. G] None. H] Founding member of the Mexican Medical Association, president of the National Academy of Medicine. I] Close personal friend of *Lázaro Cárdenas*; brother of Marino Castillo Nájera, federal deputy from Durango, 1943–45; and senator, 1946–52; son Francisco was a captain in the navy and subdirector of the Naval Medical Center; other son, Guillermo, was head of the Department of Security of the General Administration of the Consular Service of the Secretariat of Foreign Relations; brother José died in the Revolution, 1914; son of Rosa Nájera and Romualdo Castillo, political boss of Inde, Durango; married Eugenia Dávila Zayas. J] Career army medical officer; lt. colonel and surgeon, Oct. 11, 1915; director of medical services, Laveaga Brigade; director of the military hospitals in León and Torreón, 1915; director of sanitary ser-

vices, Sonora, 1915; director of sanitary services, Baja California, 1915–17; rank of colonel, July 21, 1916; rank of brigadier general, January 21, 1922; rank of brigade general, January 11, 1939. K] Precandidate for president, 1939. L] DP70 403; Peral, 162–63; Enc Mex, II, 420; HA, 29 Mar. 1946; Medina, 20, 11.

Castillo (Ramírez), Apolinar
(Deceased March 30, 1902) A] July 23, 1849. B] Oaxaca, Oaxaca. C] Early education unknown; pharmacy degree, Institute of Arts and Sciences of Oaxaca; professor of chemistry, Institute of Arts and Sciences, Oaxaca, 1870; teacher, Orizaba, Veracruz, 1875. D] Member of the City Council, Oaxaca, Oaxaca, 1869–70; local deputy, state legislature of Oaxaca, 1871; mayor of Orizaba, 1877–78; *federal deputy* from the State of Veracruz, 1878–80; *senator* from the State of Veracruz, 1878–80; *governor* of Veracruz, 1880–83; *federal deputy* from the State of Morelos, Dist. 3, 1884–86; *federal deputy* from the State of Jalisco, Dist. 10, 1886–88; *senator* from Yucatán, 1896–98; *alternate senator* from Yucatán, 1900–02. E] None. F] Political boss and military commander of Oaxaca, 1871; political boss of Córdoba, Veracruz, 1878. G] None. H] Owner of the Hacienda Ekal, Yucatán; land developer in Michoacán; director, Mexico City Streetcar Company, publisher; journalist. I] Son of Evaristo Castillo and Juana Ramírez; son-in-law of José Santos del Prado and Luz Arcos; married Concepción Santo Prado. J] None. K] None. L] Rice, 235; Mestre, 213.

Castillo Torre, José
A] 1891. B] Mérida, Yucatán. C] Early education unknown; law degree, University of Yucatán, 1914; member of the University of the Southeast Council, 1922. D] Councilman for Mérida, Yucatán, 1918; *federal deputy* from the State of Yucatán, Dist. 3, 1918–20; president of the Chamber of Deputies, 1919; *federal deputy* from the State of Yucatán, Dist. 1, 1922–24; *federal deputy* from the State of Yucatán, Dist. 3, 1924–26; *senator* from the State of Yucatán, 1926–30, president of the Senate, 1926; senator from the State of Yucatán, 1940–46, secretary of the Sen-

ate; president of the First Public Education Committee, president of the Second Foreign Relations Committee; federal deputy from the State of Yucatán, 1949–52, member of the Legislative Studies Committee (1st and 2nd years), the First Committee on Government, and the Foreign Relations Committee; member of the Great Committee. E] None. F] Member of the State Commission to Revise the Legal Codes of Yucatán, 1916; assistant lawyer for the secretary general of government of the State of Yucatán, 1917; representative of the State of Yucatán in Mexico City, 1922; president of the Editorial Commission of the Secretariat of Foreign Relations; legal adviser to the Mexican delegation to the United Nations Conference on International Organizations, San Francisco, 1945. G] None. H] Consulting lawyer to the state government of Yucatán, 1918, 1924; lawyer for railroads of Yucatán in Mexico, 1922; lawyer for the Secretariat of Foreign Relations, 1934, 1937; lawyer for the Consulting Office of the attorney general of Mexico, 1938–39; author of many legal articles. J] None. K] None. L] WWM45, 23; C de D, 1949–51, 67; DGF51, 27, 29, 32, 33, 36; Enc Mex, II, 210; Peral, 164; WB48, 1026.

Castillo (Zamudio), Eusebio
(Deceased October 7, 1897) A] December 15, 1834. B] San Juan Bautista, Tabasco. C] Early education unknown; no degree. D] *Governor* of Tabasco, 1885–87. E] None. F] Substitute governor of Tabasco, 1882–83. G] None. H] Owner, Angustias hacienda, Pichucalco, Chiapas. I] Son of Marcial Castillo and María Josefa Zamudio; married Leonarda Hernández. J] Rank of colonel in the infantry, auxiliary militia, October 1, 1867. K] None. L] Ghigliazza, 122–24; Mestre, 198.

Castrejón (Castrejón), Adrián
(Deceased March 15, 1954) A] May 10, 1894. B] Apaxtla, Aldama, Guerrero. C] Primary studies in Apaxtla; enrolled in the Heroic Military College as a brigadier general, April 11, 1921. D] *Governor* of Guerrero, 1929–33. E] None. F] None. G] None. H] None. I] Son of Leopoldo Castrejón Guerrero and Agustina Castre-

jón Maneses; married Esperanza Jaimes. J] Joined the Revolution 1910, under Salvador González, a Maderista; chief of "Los Colorados," Guerrero, 1911; fought under *Emiliano Zapata*, Morelos, 1913; rank of lt. colonel, 1913; commander of own forces, April 22, 1913; rank of colonel, 1914; incorporated into the regular army as a brigadier general, 1920; commander of the 24th Military Zone, Guerrero, January 1, 1924; organized the 109th and 153rd regiments, 1924; fought against *Adolfo de la Huerta*, 1923; rank of brigade general, July 24, 1924; served in Chiapas, Tabasco, and Veracruz, 1924–29; commander of the 18th Military Zone, Pachuca, Hidalgo, 1934–41; rank of division general, January 1, 1939; commander of 27th Military Zone, Iguala, Guerrero, 1947. K] None. L] Blue Book, 113; López, 183; López González, 63–64; Dávila, 134; Cuevas, 393.

Castrejón , Martín
(Deceased 1920) A] 1879. B] Hacienda de San Pedro Jorulla, Michoacán. C] Secondary and preparatory studies, Colegio de San Nicolás, Morelia, Michoacán; began university studies, Colegio de San Nicolás, Morelia, but abandoned studies to farm. D] *Constitutional deputy* from the State of Michoacán, Dists. Nos. 9 and 10, 1916–17. E] Member of the Liberal party. F] Prefect of Tacámbaro, Michoacán, 1913. G] None. H] Rancher. I] Unknown. J] Joined the Constitutionalists under General *Gertrudis G. Sánchez*, governor of Michoacán, and General *Joaquín Amaro*, 1913; fought in the battle for Uruapan, Michoacán, June 24, 1913; commander of military zone in Uruapan, Michoacán, 1914; commander of forces in Veracruz, Veracruz; represented Colonel Salvador Herrejón at the Convention of Aguascalientes, 1914; chief of Group A, Legion of Honor; remained loyal to *Venustiano Carranza*, 1920. K] Killed in a battle supporting Carranza. L] DP70, 405; Dicc mich, 78–79.

Castro, Cesáreo
(Deceased March 1, 1950) A] 1856. B] Cuatro Ciénegas, Coahuila. C] Early education unknown; law degree. D] None. E] Member of the Anti-Reelectionist party, 1909; delegate to the Anti-Reelectionist

Convention, Mexico City, 1909. F] *Governor* and military commander of Puebla, 1916–17; chief of the Civil Registry, 1932–34. G] None. H] Rancher. I] Brother, General Celso Castro, mayor of Torreón, 1918–19, executed by General Contreras in 1923 because Cesáreo supported *Adolfo de la Huerta*. J] Joined the Revolution as a Maderista, November 20, 1910; fought against *Pascual Orozco*, 1912; signed the Plan of Guadalupe, 1913; rank of lt. colonel, 1913; fought under General *Pablo González* and General *Lucio Blanco* against *Victoriano Huerta*; wounded in the battle for Nuevo Laredo, January 2, 1914; chief of cavalry under *Alvaro Obregón* at the battles of Celaya and León against *Francisco Villa*, 1915; remained loyal to *Venustiano Carranza* as military commander of Torreón, 1920; supported de la Huerta, 1923; supported Escobar, 1929; rejoined army, 1940; retired as a division general, 1942. K] Exiled, 1920; arrested for sedition, May 1, 1927, but released; exiled, 1929–32; returned to Mexico, 1932. L] DP70, 406; CyT, 164; QesQ, 115; Enc Mex, III, 422; López, 184; Moreno, 69–70; Almanaque de México, 130.

Castro (Rivera), Jesús Agustín
(Deceased March 22, 1954) A] August 15, 1887. B] Rancho de Eureka, Ciudad Lerdo, Durango. C] Primary in the public schools of Durango, had to leave school for economic reasons; no degree. D] *Governor* of Durango, 1921–24; *senator* from the State of Durango, 1924–28. E] None. F] *Governor* of Chiapas, 1914–15; *governor* of Oaxaca, 1915–16; *subsecretary* of war, 1917–18, in charge of the secretariat; secretary of national defense, 1939–40. G] None. H] Conductor for a streetcar company, 1910. I] Son of José F. Castro, a middle-class rancher; close friend of *Enrique Nájera*, who followed Castro as governor of Durango, 1924–27, when Castro was military commander of the state; Castro's personal political organization supported Nájera; had one of the largest groups of political disciples in the post–1935 period. J] Led 127 men against the *Porfirio Díaz* government, November 20, 1910; joined the Revolution, 1911, serving under General *Pablo Gonzá-*

lez; rank of colonel, 1911; fought under
Francisco I. Madero; joined *Venustiano
Carranza*, 1913; rank of brigade general,
October 17, 1914; division general, 1920;
military commander of Tlaxcala, Puebla,
Veracruz, 1918; commander of the 10th
Military Zone, Durango, 1935–36; com-
mander of the 5th Military Zone, Chihua-
hua, Chihuahua, 1936–39. K] Ran for
president of Mexico, 1946. L] DP70, 406;
Gruening, 423–25; Peral, 166–67; EBW,
1133; QesQ, 115–16; Enc Mex, II, 423;
López, 184; NYT, 28 Jan. 1946, 9; Dávila,
81–82.

Cauz, Eduardo M.
(Deceased September 19, 1937) A] 1852.
B] Jalapa, Veracruz. C] Early education
unknown; graduated as a 2nd lieutenant in
cavalry, National Military College. D]
None. E] None. F] *Governor* and military commander of Veracruz, 1913–14.
G] None. H] None. I] Son of Antonio
Cauz, a Spaniard who built the Cauz Theater, and Joaquína Cervantes, daughter of
the Count of Santiago, owner of the Ma-
huixtlan hacienda. J] Career army officer;
adjutant, staff of General Juan Enríquez,
governor of Veracruz; supported *Porfirio
Díaz* in the Tuxtepec rebellion, 1876; rank
of lt. colonel, May 10, 1890; rank of brigadier general, March 8, 1909; inspector of
rural forces; director, Department of Cavalry, Secretariat of War, 1912; commander
of the 1st Cavalry Regiment; rank of brigade general, February 10, 1913; rank
of division general, January 1, 1914.
K] Went into exile for many years, 1914;
died poor and blind in Mexico City.
L] Mestre, 293; Sec of War, 1900, 163; Sec
of War, 1914, 17; Pasquel, Jalapa, 119–20;
Peral, appendices, 81.

Ceballos, Ciro B.
(Deceased August 13, 1938) A] January
31, 1873. B] Tacubaya, Federal District.
C] Preparatory studies at the National Preparatory School; began legal studies, National School of Law; no degree; professor
of history, School of Military Prosecutors.
D] *Constitutional deputy* from the Federal District, Dist. 11, 1916–17. E] None.
F] Director, National Library, 1917–18;
chief, War Archives, 1919–21; member,
History Commission, Staff Archives, Sec-

retariat of War, 1922–24; adviser, National Department of Statistics, 1929.
G] Member of the Modernist group of
writers, including Nervo, Urbina, and
Campos. H] Journalist; literary critic;
author of numerous books; director, *El
Intransigente*, 1912–13; writer for *El Imparcial* and *El Universal*; director, *El Imparcial*, 1914; director, *El Liberal*; director, *Revista Moderna*. I] Son of José
María Ceballos and Manuela Bernal.
J] None. K] None. L] Dir social, 1935,
211; Enc Mex, III, 436; DP70, 416; Peral,
appendices, 81; WWLA35, 89.

Ceballos, José
(Deceased April 19, 1893) A] 1831.
B] Durango, Durango. C] Primary studies, Durango, Durango; studies at the National Military College, 1851–52; graduated from the National Military College as
a 2nd lieutenant of artillery, October 22,
1852; director of the Polytechnic School,
Guatemala. D] Federal deputy from the
State of Sinaloa; senator from Sonora,
1882–84; *senator* from Durango, 1884–
96, 1886–88, 1888–90, 1890–92, 1892–
94. E] None. F] Governor and military
commander of Jalisco, 1870s; *governor* of
the Federal District, 1884–93. G] None.
H] None. I] None. J] Corporal of cadets,
National Military College, 1851; sergeant
of cadets, National Military College, 1852;
rank of 1st lieutenant of artillery, December 27, 1852; rank of captain, May 18,
1855; rank of 1st captain of artillery, July
5, 1856; rank of lt. colonel of infantry, December 21, 1860; rank of colonel, January
15, 1864; participated in the assault on
Puebla against the French, April 2, 1867;
served under General *Porfirio Díaz* in taking Mexico City, June 21, 1867; rank of
brigade general, March 30, 1870; rank of
division general, September 2, 1873; military governor of Yucatán. K] Exiled to
San Francisco, 1877. L] González Dávila,
107–08; Cuevas, 382; Pavía, 141–42;
Hombres prominentes, 65–66; Mestre,
182.; Armijo, 163–64; Romo, 139ff.

Cedaño, Marcelino
(Deceased August 12, 1962) A] June 18,
1888. B] Teocuitatlán de Corona, Jalisco.
C] Primary, secondary, and preparatory
studies completed; teaching certificate;

studies at a private business school; attended a university, studies in literature, philosophy, and two years of medicine; schoolteacher. D] *Constitutional deputy* from the Territory of Tepic (Nayarit), Dist. 2, 1916–17. E] None. F] School inspector in the State of Sonora; official, Federal Treasury Office, Guadalajara, 1913; agent of the federal government and military commander, Acaponeta, Tepic, 1916; technical official, Special Technical Committee on Social Welfare, Chamber of Deputies, 1924; inspector of the Boards of Conciliation and Arbitration, State of México, 1926–27; director, Department of Labor, State of Guadalajara, 1927–28; director, Department of Labor, and president of the State Board of Conciliation and Arbitration, State of Nayarit, 1928–29. G] None. H] Unknown. I] Son of J. Merced Cedaño and Severa Mora; parents poor. J] Supported the Revolution as an intellectual, 1910; joined the Constitutionalists, 1913; fought *Francisco Villa*, 1915; opposed *Adolfo de la Huerta*, 1923; reached rank of major, 1915. K] None. L] C de D, 1916–17.

Cedillo, Saturnino
(Deceased January 11, 1939) A] 1890. B] Rancho de Palomas, San Luis Potosí. C] Only completed primary school. D] *Governor* of San Luis Potosí, 1927–31. E] Active member of the National Agrarian party; head of the Agrarian Sector of the National Revolutionary party, 1934. F] *Secretary* of agriculture, 1931; secretary of agriculture and livestock, 1935–37. G] None. H] Auxiliary judge in Palomas, San Luis Potosí, 1912. I] Brothers Magdaleno and Cleofas fought with Saturnino under *Emiliano Zapata* and were killed during the Revolution; longtime friend of *Gildardo Magaña*, since they were companions fighting under Zapata; tried to persuade Magaña to support him in his fight against President *Lázaro Cárdenas*; parents were peasants. J] Joined the Revolution in 1911; commander of military operations in San Luis Potosí, 1920–27; fought against the *Adolfo de la Huerta* rebellion in 1923; commander-in-chief of the Central Division, 1926; rank of division general, 1928; supported the govern-

ment against Escobar, 1929; commander of military operations in San Luis Potosí, 1935. K] Imprisoned by *Victoriano Huerta*, 1913–14; supporter and later political enemy of Governor *Aurelio Manrique*, 1924–25; gave Lázaro Cárdenas the decisive help of the agrarian sectors, 1934–35; resigned his cabinet post to protest government policies and become head of a rebellious military movement, 1938; killed in the fighting, 1939; member of the Inner Circle, 1934–37. L] Gruening, 311; DP70, 417; Dulles; QesQ, 117–18.

Ceniceros y Villarreal, Rafael
(Deceased 1933) A] July 11, 1855. B] Durango, Durango. C] Secondary studies at the Conciliar Seminary, Durango; law degree, 1878. D] *Governor* of Zacatecas, 1913. E] None. F] *Interim governor* of Zacatecas, 1912–13. G] None. H] Practicing lawyer, Zacatecas, 1878– ; novelist, dramatist; founder of *La Revista Forense*. I] Unknown. J] None. K] None. L] Peral, appendices, 82; Lutrell.

Cepeda de la Fuente, Rafael
(Deceased August 25, 1947) A] October 5, 1872. B] Villa de Arteaga, Coahuila. C] Early education unknown; medical degree. D] *Governor* of San Luis Potosí, 1911–13; *constitutional deputy* from the State of San Luis Potosí, Dist. 3, 1916–17; *senator* from San Luis Potosí, 1918–20; mayor of Mexico City. E] Member of the Anti-Reelectionist party. F] *Governor* and military commander of the State of San Luis Potosí, 1910–11; *governor* and military commander of the State of México, 1916–17. G] None. H] Physician. I] Son of Francisco Cepeda, a military officer, and Manuela de la Fuente; uncle of Román Cepeda Flores, governor of Coahuila, 1951–57; friend of Miguel Alemán, president of Mexico, 1946–52; uncle of Ignacio Cepeda Dávila, governor of Coahuila, 1945–47; relative of Delfín and Reginaldo Cepeda, federal deputy and senator, respectively, from Coahuila; brothers Abraham and Román were Anti-Reelectionists. J] Supported *Francisco I. Madero*, 1910; Constitutionalist, 1913; supported *Venustiano Carranza*, 1920; president, Legion of Revolutionaries; op-

posed *Adolfo de la Huerta*, 1923. K] Exiled, 1920. L] Cuevas, 59–60; Montejano, 92.

Cepeda Medrano, Manuel
(Deceased) A] September 24, 1886.
B] Piedras Negras, Coahuila. C] Early education unknown; teaching certificate; teacher. D] *Constitutional deputy* from the State of Coahuila, Dist. 5, 1916–17; *federal deputy* from the State of Coahuila, Dist. 1, 1917–18; *senator* from Coahuila, 1918–20, 1920–22, 1922–24. E] Supporter of *Ricardo Flores Magón*. F] Collaborated with *Venustiano Carranza*, 1913; treasurer, State of Coahuila, under Venustiano Carranza; treasurer general of Mexico, 1920; director, National Army Savings Bank; department head, Department of the Federal District, 1947–49; president of the Board of Material Improvement and customs official, Torreón, Coahuila, 1953–66. G] None. H] Normal teacher. I] Unknown. J] Remained loyal to Carranza, 1920. K] None. L] C de S, 1918–20, 1920–22.

Cerísola (Salcido), Alejandro
(Deceased) A] March 7, 1886. B] Mazatlán, Sinaloa. C] Early education unknown; medical degree. D] *Federal deputy* from the State of Veracruz, Dist. 16, 1924–26; *federal deputy* from the State of Veracruz, Dist. 6, 1926–28, 1928–30; *federal deputy* from the State of Veracruz, Dist. 3, 1930–31; federal deputy from the State of Veracruz, Dist. 4, 1934–37. E] None. F] *Subsecretary* of public education, in charge of the secretariat, 1931. G] None. H] Physician. I] Son of Alejandro Cerísola, naval captain and commander of Acapulco; married Juana Mange, from Valparaíso, Chile. J] None. K] None. L] Dir soc, 1935, 69; Sec of War, 1902, 29; Sec of War, 1900, 297; Carrasco Puente, 85; Blue Book, 115.

Cervantes, Daniel
(Deceased November 1, 1925) A] December 6, 1857. B] San Juan de los Lagos, Jalisco. C] Primary and secondary studies in Guadalajara; chemical pharmacy degree, Guadalajara; professor of chemistry, Institute of Sciences, Aguascalientes.

D] Local deputy to the state legislature of Aguascalientes; *constitutional deputy* from the State of Aguascalientes, Dist. 2, 1916–17. E] None. F] Political boss of Aguascalientes; *interim governor* of Aguascalientes, 1911; director, Department of Storage, Military Industries, Secretariat of War. G] President of the Chamber of Commerce of Aguascalientes. H] Pharmacist, operated own business. I] Son of José Refugio Cervantes, small businessman, and Refugio Gutiérrez. J] None. K] None. L] C de D, 1916–17.

Cervantes, Julio María
(Deceased October 26, 1909) A] 1839.
B] Puebla, Puebla. C] Early education unknown; attended the National Military College, graduating as a 2nd lieutenant of infantry, October 25, 1853. D] *Governor* of Coahuila, 1884–90; *senator* from Coahuila, 1886–90, 1890–94, 1894–98. E] None. F] Provisional governor of Coahuila; governor of Querétaro; inspector of national lines, 1909. J] Career military officer; rank of 1st lieutenant, August 27, 1856; rank of captain, 1860; battalion commander, January, 1861; rank of colonel, September 20, 1863; breveted brigadier general, November 29, 1866; rank of brigadier general, July 4, 1882; commander of the 3rd Military Zone; commander of the 1st Military Zone, 1888. K] *Porfirio Díaz* imposed Cervantes to control powerful competing political interests in the state. L] Cuéllar Valdés, 177; Mestre, 238; Cuevas, 382; Hombres prominentes, 233–34.

Cervantes, Laureano
(Deceased) A] 1894. B] Colima, Colima. C] Primary studies in Colima; private accounting degree, Colima. D] Local deputy to the state legislature of Colima, 1926–28; *governor* of Colima, 1927–31. E] None. F] None. G] None. H] Businessman in lumber. I] Unknown. J] Volunteer for service under *Victoriano Huerta*'s forces, 1913; fought against the Cristeros. K] Local legislature tried to dissolve his powers, 1929; Senate dissolved his powers August 6, 1931, for supporting General Higinio Alvarez's gubernatorial candidacy against the National

Revolutionary party's choice; according to Moreno, his administration was in the hands of Carlos Véjar, his secretary general of government. L] Moreno, 81–82; Peral, appendices, 84; Colliman, 126.

Chao, Manuel
(Deceased June 26, 1924) A] September 26, 1883. B] Tuxpán, Veracruz. C] Early education unknown; no degree; director, Nombre de Dios School, Durango, 1900–03; aide, Public School No. 138, Chihuahua, 1903; aide, public school, Balleza region, Chihuahua, 1903; teacher, public schools, Chihuahua, 1903–10. D] None. E] Joined the Anti-Reelectionist party, 1910. F] *Governor* of Chihuahua, 1914; *governor* of the Federal District, 1914. G] None. H] Worked as agricultural laborer in youth; operated own forestry business, Chihuahua, 1910. I] Son of Angel Chao and Ramona Rovira; married Ignacia Loya. J] Joined the Revolution, Baqueteros, 1910; rank of lt. colonel, Rural Forces, 1911; organized the Hidalgo Regiment to oppose *Pascual Orozco* under General *Victoriano Huerta*, 1912; rank of colonel, 1912; joined the Constitutionalists, 1913; chief of military operations in Southern Chihuahua, 1913; commander of the Chao Brigade, Division of the North, 1913; broke with *Francisco Villa*, 1914; withdrew recognition of *Venustiano Carranza* as first chief of the Constitutionalist forces, 1914; represented self at the Convention of Aguascalientes, 1914; rank of division general, January 2, 1915; supported the *Adolfo de la Huerta* rebellion, 1923–24. K] Captured by the forces of General Escobar, 1924, and executed by the Council of War as a rebel; lived in exile in New Orleans, 1915, and later in Costa Rica until 1923; involved in Costa Rican politics, offered secretary of war, but refused. L] Almada, 513–18; Almada, 1968, 133; Rouaix, 118.

Chapa, Pedro A.
(Deceased) A] May 8, 1890. B] Dr. Arroyo, Nuevo León. C] Primary studies at the Liceo Francés, Nuevo León, and at the Colegio Civil de Monterrey; secondary studies at the Western Military Academy, Alton, Illinois; attended the University of Pennsylvania. D] *Constitutional deputy* from the State of Tamaulipas, Dist. 1, 1916–17; *federal deputy* from the State of Tamaulipas, Dist. 1, 1917–18; *federal deputy* from the State of Nuevo León, Dist. 5, 1920–22. E] None. F] Chief of the Mexican delegation, Civil Aviation Conference, Montreal, 1944, and Chicago, 1945. G] President of the National Chamber of Transportation; president of the National Chamber of Industries (Concamin), 1946–48. H] Businessman; vice-president of the Mexican Aviation Company, 1957. I] Possibly related to Leobardo Chapa, governor of Nuevo León, 1910–11. J] Rank of colonel in the army. K] None. L] López, 253; C de D, 1916–17, 1920–22.

Chavero (y Cardona), Alfredo
(Deceased October 24, 1906) A] February 1, 1841. B] Mexico City. C] Secondary and preparatory studies at El Colegio de San Juan de Letrán; law degree, San Juan de Letrán, 1861; professor of administrative law, San Juan de Letrán; director, Colegio de las Vizcaínas, Mexico City. D] Federal deputy from the State of Guerrero, 1862; *federal deputy* from the State of Veracruz, Dist. 11, 1886–88; *federal deputy* from the State of Zacatecas, Dist. 9, 1888–90; *federal deputy* from the State of Zacatecas, Dist. 10, 1890–92, and president of the Chamber; *federal deputy* from the State of Zacatecas, Dist. 9, 1892–94, 1894–96, 1896–98, 1898–1900, president of the Chamber, 1900–02, president of the Chamber; *federal deputy* from the State of San Luis Potosí, Dist. 9, 1902–04, member of the Great Committee; *federal deputy* from the State of Puebla, Dist. 10, 1904–06, 1906–08, member of the Great Committee. E] None. F] Oficial mayor of the Secretariat of Foreign Relations, 1877; judge, Superior Tribunal of Justice of the Federal District; subdirector of the Musuem of the Government of the Federal District; syndic, Mexico City. G] None. H] Dramatist; historian; author; director of *El Siglo XIX*, 1867; poet; practicing lawyer, 1861–62. I] Grandfather of Alfredo Chavero Hijar, dean, School of Business, UNAM, 1934–38; married Guadalupe Rosas y Soriano; son Ernesto Chavero y Rosas served as a federal deputy from the State of México, 1900–12. J] Supported

Juárez against the French intervention, 1862; captured by the French; accompanied Juárez when he abandoned Mexico City. K] Traveled to Europe, 1872–76. L] Enc Mex, III, 280; López, 254; DP70, 590; Godoy, 257; Carreño, 173; Linajes, 80–81.

Chávez, Gregorio
(Deceased July 15, 1901) A] 1830. B] Oaxaca, Oaxaca. C] Primary studies at the Colegio de Oaxaca; graduated from the National Military College as a 2nd lieutenant in artillery, September 20, 1852. D] *Federal deputy* from the State of Oaxaca, Dist. 1, 1886–88; *federal deputy* from the State of Oaxaca, Dist. 1, 1888–90; *governor* of Oaxaca, 1890–94. E] None. F] None. G] None. H] None. I] Unknown. J] Career army officer; opposed the Plan of Jalisco, 1853; supported the Plan of Ayutla, 1854; rank of 1st lieutenant, September 5, 1856; rank of captain, May 31, 1859; division commander, November 20, 1860; fought in the battle for Oaxaca, 1865; captured by the French, 1865; freed from the French by *Porfirio Díaz*, 1866; fought with General Díaz in the assault on Puebla, April 2, 1867; fought Juchitán rebels, 1870; rank of lt. colonel, February 26, 1870; supported Díaz's rebellion, 1871, but captured by government forces; rank of colonel, February 2, 1876; supported Díaz's rebellion, 1876; commander of the 1st Artillery Battalion; rank of brigade general, September 26, 1884; commander of the 10th Military Zone, 1901. K] None. L] Mestre, 208; Pavía, 273–77; Almanaque de Oaxaca, 1982, 130; Sec of War, 1900, 89.

Chávez, Ezequiel A.
(Deceased 1946) A] September 19, 1868. B] Aguascalientes, Aguascalientes. C] Primary studies under mother in Mexico City and at Celso Bernal's private school, Aguascalientes; first year of preparatory studies at the Anglo-French-Mexican Institute, Mexico City, 1881–82; preparatory studies from the National Preparatory School, 1882–85; legal studies, National School of Law, UNAM, 1886–91, graduating 1891, with a thesis on the philosophy of political institutions; honorary Ph.D., UNAM, 1910; professor, National Prepara-

tory School, 1891, 1893–1905, 1911–16, 1918; professor, UNAM, 1891–41; professor emeritus, UNAM, 1941; visiting professor, University of California–Berkeley, 1906, 1909, visiting professor, Cambridge University, 1916–17, University of Madrid, 1927, University of California–Los Angeles, 1932; professor, Free Law School; professor, Normal School for Women; director of the preparatory program of the School of Higher Studies; rector of UNAM, 1913–14, 1923–24; founder of the Graduate School, UNAM, 1910; director, School of Higher Studies (Graduate School), UNAM, 1921–23. D] *Alternate federal deputy* from the State of Zacatecas, Dist. 7, 1898–1900; *alternate federal deputy* from the State of Chiapas, Dist. 1, 1900–02; *alternate federal deputy* from the State of Chihuahua, Dist. 2, 1904–06; *federal deputy* from the State of Chihuahua, Dist. 2, 1906–12. E] Founding member of the National Action party, 1939. F] Official, Secretariat of Justice and Public Education, 1895–1905; *subsecretary* of public education, 1905–11. G] None. H] Practiced law with *Rafael Dondé*, senator from Sonora. I] Son of Dr. *Ignacio T. Chávez*, a physician and prominent educator who served as senator and governor from Aguascalientes, and Guadalupe Lavista; grandson of Ignacio Chávez Alonso, carpenter; student of Ignacio M. Altamirano and *Justo Sierra*. J] None. K] In exile, New York City, 1916. L] DP70, 591; WWM45, 29; Carreño, 174–75; UNAM, law, 1880–91, 66; Dir soc, 1935, 70.

Chávez, Ignacio T.
(Deceased July 4, 1908) A] April 16, 1837. B] Aguascalientes, Aguascalientes. C] Primary studies in Aguascalientes; preparatory studies, Institute of la Purísima, Aguascalientes; initiated medical studies at the School of Medicine, University of Guadalajara; medical degree, School of Medicine, Mexico City, 1865; director, Industrial School for Orphans, Mexico City; founder of the Institute of Sciences of Aguascalientes. D] Federal deputy from the State of Aguascalientes; governor of Aguascalientes; *senator* from Aguascalientes, 1882–86, 1898–1902; 1902–06, 1906–08. E] None. F] Founder and director, Public Poor House, Mexico City.

G] None. H] Founder of the Civil Hospital of Aguascalientes; physician, Morelos Hospital, Mexico City. I] Son of Ignacio Chávez Alonso, carpenter; father of *Ezequiel Chávez*, subsecretary of public education. J] None. K] None. L] C de S, 1902–04, 1904–06, 1906–08; López, 255; DP70, 592; C de S, 1900–02, 5; Mestre, 232.

Cienfuegos y Camus, Adolfo
(Deceased 1943) A] September 27, 1889. B] Tixtla, Guerrero. C] Incomplete primary studies; studies toward a normal certificate, Atliaca, 1906; scholarship student to the Normal School, Mexico City, 1910–14; abandoned studies to join the Revolution; completed teaching certificate, 1916; teacher, history of teaching, Normal School for Women; professor of applied sociology of education and political economy, Normal Night School; professor of the sociology of education, Graduate School, UNAM, 1926–28; professor of sociology, School of Philosophy and Letters, UNAM. D] *Federal deputy* from the Federal District, Dist. 11, 1917–18, president of the Chamber; *federal deputy* from the State of Guerrero, Dist. 5, 1920–22. E] Candidate for governor of Guerrero. F] First secretary, Costa Rica, 1918–19; chargé d'affaires, Costa Rica, 1919–20; director of administration, Secretariat of Foreign Relations, 1923–24; oficial mayor of foreign relations, 1924–28; *ambassador* to Cuba, 1930–33; ambassador to Chile, 1934–36; ambassador to Guatemala, 1936–38. G] None. H] Worked as an agricultural laborer. I] Married Guadalupe Jiménez. J] Joined the Constitutionalists, 1914; chief of staff to General *Alvaro Obregón*, 1914–16; chief of staff, Secretariat of War and Navy, 1916–17. K] None. L] López, 195; DP70, 432–33; Gruening, 432; Dir soc, 1935, 269.

Colorado (Calles), Aureliano
(Deceased October 15, 1945) A] January 16, 1876. B] Huimanguillo, Tabasco. C] Primary studies in Huimanguillo; law degree, Juárez Institute, Villahermosa, on a fellowship from Manuel Jamet. D] *Senator* from Tabasco, 1917–18, 1920–22.

E] Member Anti-Reelectionist party, 1910. F] Judge of the Superior Tribunal of Justice of Tabasco, 1911–14; secretary general of the State of Tabasco, 1915, 1916. G] None. H] Practicing lawyer. I] Son of Cornelio Colorado, who died exploring the Usumacinta River, and María Eligia Calles; married Anita Iris; son Mario Colorado Iris, was a federal deputy, 1949–52; brother Pedro Colorado Calles was governor and military commander of Tabasco, 1915; son Cornelio was killed by troops of Vicente González Fernández; cousin of Fernando and *Ernesto Aguirre Colorado*, revolutionaries and federal deputies. J] Joined *Francisco I. Madero*'s movement, 1910; supported *Venustiano Carranza*, 1913. K] Conspirator against *Porfirio Díaz*, 1902; supporter of *Flores Magón* brothers, 1906; arrested by *Victoriano Huerta*, nearly executed. L] López, 206–07; Bulnes, 71, 116–17.

Colunga, Enrique
(Deceased December 6, 1946) A] August, 1876. B] Celaya, Guanajuato. C] Primary and secondary studies in León, Guanajuato; law degree, University of Guanajuato, 1893. D] *Constitutional deputy* from the State of Guanajuato, Dist. 10, 1916–17; local deputy to the state legislature of Guanajuato, 1917; *alternate federal deputy* from the State of Guanajuato, Dist. 16, 1917–18; member of the City Council of Celaya, 1920; *senator* from Guanajuato, 1922–24; *governor* of Guanajuato, 1924–27. E] Candidate for governor of Guanajuato, 1911. F] Judge, State of Guanajuato, 1911; *justice* of the Supreme Court, 1917–18; *provisional governor* of Guanajuato, 1920; *secretary* of government, 1923–24; circuit court judge, 1927–46. G] None. H] Practicing lawyer, Celaya, 1894–1911. I] Political friendships with *Enrique Hernández Alvarez*, *Federico Medrano*, *Cayetano Andrade*, and *Agustín Arroyo Ch.* J] None. K] None. L] López, 207; DP70, 472; Morales Jiménez, 267–70; letter; Quirós, 344–46; Gruening, 426.

Coral (Heredía), Pascual
(Deceased April 16, 1955) A] May 17, 1882. B] Cozumel, Quintana Roo.

C] Early education unknown; no degree. D] Member of the City Council of Payo Obispo, 1902. E] None. F] Employee, Maritime Customs, Bahía de Ascensión, 1903; *governor* of Quintana Roo, 1921; customs administrator, Payo Obispo, 1943. G] None. H] Traveled with father on business trips in youth; dredged Chetumal, 1904; self-employed, Bacalar, 1907–12; businessman, Payo Obispo, 1912; rancher in Bacalar; timber and chicle business, Bacalar; experimented with agriculture, Bacalar. I] Son of José Luis Coral, businessman, and Lucia Heredia Viana. J] None. K] None. L] Alvarez Corral, 77.

Córdoba (y Herrera), César
(Deceased 1958) A] August 24, 1882. B] Pichucalco, Chiapas. C] Secondary studies in Tabasco; law degree, 1918. D] None. E] None. F] Career Foreign Service officer; served in Europe; reached rank of ambassador; director, Department of Industry and Commerce, 1923; *provisional governor* of Chiapas, 1924–25; subdirector of the Department of Agrarian Affairs. G] President of the Lions Club. H] Unknown. I] Married Esperanza Ramírez from Pichucalco. J] None. K] None. L] Almanaque de Chiapas, 119; Blue Book, 118.

Corona (Mac Entee), Ramón
(Deceased April 25, 1936) A] November 12, 1869. B] Mazatlán, Sinaloa. C] Early education unknown; law degree. D] *Federal deputy* from the State of Guerrero, Dist. 5, 1900–02; *federal deputy* from the State of Jalisco, Dist. 5, 1900–02, 1902–04, 1904–06, 1906–08, 1908–10. E] None. F] *Governor* of the Federal District, 1914. G] None. H] Stockholder in Corona, Mac Entee, and Rodríguez; adviser to La Nación Insurance Company. I] Son of General *Ramón Corona*, governor of Jalisco, 1886–89; married Isabel Sánchez Juárez. J] Career army officer; rank of brigadier general in the army reserves, November 26, 1913; rank of brigade general, April 26, 1914; supported *Victoriano Huerta*, 1913–14. K] None. L] QesQ, 133–34; López, 228; Hombres prominentes, 30–31; Sec of War, 1914, 29; Mestre, 291; Dir soc, 1935, 71.

Corona (Madrigal), Ramón
(Deceased November 11, 1889) A] October 18, 1837. B] Hacienda de Puragua, Tuscueca, and Tizapán el Alto, Chapala, Jalisco. C] Primary studies in Teocuitatlán; left school to work. D] *Governor* of Jalisco, 1886–89. E] None. F] Minister to Portugal and Spain, 1867–84. G] None. H] Employee, Teocuitatlán, Jalisco; worked for Castaños brothers in warehouse in Tepic until 1856; employee, Hacienda de Motague; self-employed, 1885–86. I] Son of Esteban Corona and Delores María Madrigal, peasants; mother died and father moved to California, leaving Ramón to live in Tepic and later with relatives in Guadalajara and Tuscueca, Jalisco; son *Ramón Mac Entee Corona* was governor of the Federal District. J] Joined the Liberals under Generals Santos Degollado and Pedro Ogazón, 1858; rank of major, 1859; commander of the Tepic Section, 1861; commander of the Jalisco and Sinaloa brigades against the French, 1865; rank of brigade general, June 21, 1865; commander of the Army of the East during the French Intervention; rank of divison general, November 2, 1866; received Maximilian's sword after the Conservative surrender, 1867; remained loyal to Lerdo de Tejada government, 1871. K] Assassinated by a deranged woman while governor of Jalisco, 1889. L] DP70, 522–23; Hombres prominentes, 61–64; Ríos, 297–308; Rev de Ejer, May 1968, 36–44; Covarrubias, I, 1947, 292–98; Romo, 155; Mestre, 167; García de Alba, 1958, 160; Armijo, 502–04.

Coronado (Flores), Fernando G.
A] December 14, 1898. B] Unknown. C] Teaching certificate, National Normal School, Mexico City; preparatory studies, National Preparatory School; law degree, National School of Law, UNAM, 1927. D] Member of the City Council of Tacuba, Federal District; mayor of Tacuba, Federal District. E] None. F] Director, Legal Department, Secretariat of Communications and Public Works; oficial mayor of communications and public works; subsecretary of communications and public works, 1934. G] None. H] Practicing lawyer; author of many books on law and communications. I] Son of Manuel Coro-

nado and Agustina Díaz; married Laura
Flores. J] Participated in the Revolution;
reached rank of lt. colonel; secretary of
the First Military Court. K] None.
L] WWM45, 31.

Corral (Verdugo), Ramón
(Deceased November 10, 1912) A] January 10, 1854. B] Hacienda Las Mercedes,
Alamos, Sonora. C] Primary studies under father in Alamos; no degree. D] Alternate local deputy (in functions) to the
state legislature of Sonora, 1877–78; local
deputy from Alamos to the state legislature of Sonora, 1879; federal deputy from
the State of Sonora, 1881–82; *governor* of
Sonora, 1895–99. E] Joined the political
group of Colonel *Luis E. Torres*, 1876.
F] Private secretary to Colonel *Luis E. Torres*, 1876; secretary general of government
of the State of Sonora, 1879–80, 1883–87;
vice-governor of Sonora, 1887–91; *governor* of the Federal District, 1900–03; *secretary* of government, 1903–04, 1904–11,
1910–11; vice-president of Mexico,
1904–10, 1910–11. G] Founded the Sociedad Mutualista de Artesanos, 1873.
H] Clerk, First Judicial District of Alamos,
1868; printer; employee, Hacienda de Beneficio de Justina, 1868–73; accountant,
light company, Hermosillo and Guaymas;
director, *El Fantasma*, Alamos; director,
La Voz de Alamos, 1872; stockholder,
Bank of Sonora; built a flour mill; invested
in mining companies. I] Son of Fulgencio
Corral, administrator of José María Almada's hacienda, Alamos; small storekeeper, Palmarejo, 1859–63, and mayor of
Chínipas, and Francisca Verdugo; daughter
Amparo Corral y Escalante married Guillermo Obregón y Gómez Vélez, founder
of the Mexican Bankers Association and
the Obregón law firm; political enemy of
the uncles of Antonio and Raúl Ortiz
Mena, leading political figures in the 1960s.
J] Opposed the reelection of Governor *Ignacio Pesqueira*, 1872, and took up arms
against him; worked for the overthrow of
Governor Mariscal, 1878; worked for the
overthrow of Governor Carlos Ortiz, 1883.
K] Signed a protest against the monarchy
with his father, August 2, 1863; self-exile
to Paris, 1911–12. L] Mestre, 244; Pavía,
331–34; Hombres prominentes, 225–26;
Godoy, 94; Enc Mex, IV, 158–59; López,

230–31; DP70, 525; Villa, 1937, 431–32;
Linajes, 190.

Correa Nieto, Juan
(Deceased) A] June 28, 1890. B] Villahermosa, Tabasco. C] Primary studies at
the Annex to the Normal School of Mexico; preparatory studies from the National
Preparatory School; law degree, National
School of Law, UNAM, March 23, 1915;
professor of mercantile law, civil law,
and tax law, UNAM, 1917. D] None.
E] None. F] Public defender, 1919–22;
criminal judge, Mexico City, 1923–26; *attorney general* of the Federal District and
Federal Territories, 1926–28; consulting
lawyer to the secretary of government,
1929; representative of the Department of
the Federal District for revising the tax
laws; adviser to the secretary of public
education, 1931; private secretary to the
secretary of foreign relations, 1933–34.
G] None. H] Practicing lawyer. I] Son of
Alberto Correa and Sofía Nieto; married
Luz López Arias. J] None. K] None.
L] Dir social, 1935, 212–13.

Cortázar (Sada), Joaquín
(Deceased December 11, 1905) A] 1846.
B] Monterrey, Nuevo León. C] Early education unknown; law degree, School of
Law, University of Nuevo León. D] Federal deputy from the State of Monterrey,
Dist. 2, 1882–84; local deputy to the state
legislature of Chihuahua, 1895–1901.
E] None. F] Judge, District of Hidalgo,
Chihuahua, 1889–91; judge, Bravo District, Chihuahua, 1891–93; secretary
general of government of Chihuahua,
1893–1903, 1903–05; *interim governor*
of Chihuahua, 1903, 1904. G] None.
H] Practicing lawyer. I] Son of Antonio
Cortázar, military officer (captain) killed
by the French, and Soledad Sada; grandson
of General Cortázar, governor of Guanajuato; son Joaquín Cortázar, Jr., local
deputy, married Adela Creel, daughter of
Enrique Creel. J] None. K] None.
L] DP70, 532; Almada, 1868, 122; Dir social, 1935, 71.

Cortés y Frías, José
(Deceased July 20, 1893) A] August 9,
1842. B] Jalapa, Veracruz. C] Early education unknown; enrolled, National Mili-

tary College, 1857, graduating as a 2nd lieutenant in artillery, January 1, 1861. D] None. E] None. F] *Provisional governor* of Veracruz, 1883–84. G] None. H] None. I] Son of General José María Cortes Gallardo, first director of the National Military College; army pal of General Juan de la Luz Enríquez, governor of Veracruz. J] Career army officer; rank of 1st lieutenant, 1862; fought the French, 1862–67; participated in the battle of Puebla, May 5, 1862; captured by the French and escaped, 1863; rank of captain, 1863; battalion commander, national guard, 1864; rank of lt. colonel, national guard, 1865; commander of the forces in Veracruz, Veracruz, 1867; rank of colonel, national guard, February 20, 1868; commander of the 18th Battalion, 1876; rank of brigadier general, 1884; rank of brigade general, May 20, 1893. K] None. L] Cuevas, 382; Hombres prominentes, 285; Pasquel, 1972, 49; Mestre, 184.

Coss, Francisco
(Deceased October 7, 1961) A] August 15, 1880. B] Ramos Arizpe, Coahuila. C] Early education unknown; no degree. D] None. E] Precursor of the Revolution; supported the Flores Magón brothers, Villa Acuña, Coahuila, 1906; member of the Liberal party. F] *Governor* of Coahuila, 1914; *provisional governor* and commander of military operations, Puebla, 1915. G] None. H] None. I] Unknown. J] Joined Madero's forces as a 2nd sergeant, Parras, Coahuila, 1910; commander of irregular forces in Coahuila; joined the Constitutionalists, 1913; commander of the 2nd Division of the Army of the East under *Pablo González*, 1913; rank of brigade general, 1913; represented at the Convention of Aguascalientes, 1914; fought against the Zapatistas in Puebla, 1914; rank of division general, July 31, 1915; commander of military operations in Tlaxcala, 1916; supported the *Adolfo de la Huerta* rebellion, 1923; reintegrated into the army, 1942. K] Exiled to the United States, 1923–42. L] QesQ, 139–40; DP70, 539; CyT, 192; Almanaque de Puebla, 129.

Covarrubias, José F.
(Deceased 1935) A] 1861. B] Jalapa, Veracruz. C] Preparatory studies from the Colegio Preparatorio de Jalapa; civil engineering degree, College of Mines. D] None. E] None. F] *Subsecretary* of communications, 1912–13; oficial mayor of communications, 1917–18; subdirector of the mails; director of the national lottery, 1920–32. G] President of the public welfare, Federal District. H] Practicing engineer. I] Son of José Miguel Covarrubias and Juliana Acosta; grandson of poet and general José de Jesús Covarrubias; nephew of Francisco Díaz Covarrubias, his mentor, who served as subsecretary of development under President Lerdo de Tejada; disciple of *Manuel Fernández Leal*, secretary of development, 1891–1903; married Elena Duclaud y Fuerero; son Miguel, an anthropologist; son Luis, a painter; nephew of José Díaz Covarrubias, lawyer, federal deputy, and secretary of education under President Lerdo de Tejada; brother of *Miguel Covarrubias*, secretary of foreign relations, 1920; best friends included Octavio Dubois; *Agustín Aragón*, federal deputy and intellectual; and Pastor Roque. J] None. K] None. L] Pasquel, Jalapa, 149–50, 169–71; Dir social, 1935, 72.

Covarrubias, Miguel
(Deceased July 7, 1924) A] January 29, 1856. B] Jalapa, Veracruz. C] Preparatory studies, National Preparatory School, 1872; law degree, National School of Law; librarian, National Preparatory School, 1876; professor of English, National Preparatory School, 1876. D] None. E] None. F] Career foreign service officer; 3rd secretary to the Mexican embassy, United States, 1880, under *Matías Romero*; 2nd secretary to the Mexican embassy, Italy, 1890–92; 1st secretary, Mexican embassy, United States, 1893; 1st secretary to the Mexican embassy in Belgium, Germany, and Russia; chargé d'affaires, Russia, 1900; minister to South America, 1901; chargé d'affaires, Germany, 1902; ambassador to Peru, 1903; ambassador to Chile, 1903–05; *ambassador* to Great Britain, 1907–13; *ambassador* to Russia, 1913; designated ambassador to the United States by *Francisco I. Ma-*

dero, but the president was killed before Covarrubias's appointment was carried out; *secretary* of foreign relations, 1920; ambassador to Germany, 1921. G] None. H] None. I] Son of José Miguel Covarrubias and Juliana Acosta; grandson of poet and general José de Jesús Covarrubias; nephew of Francisco Díaz Covarrubias, subsecretary of development under President Lerdo de Tejada; nephew of José Díaz Covarrubias, secretary of education under President Lerdo de Tejada; studied at the National Preparatory School under uncle Francisco, who helped him obtain a position there when his father died; brother *José F. Covarrubias* was subsecretary of communications, 1912. J] None. K] He was the only ambassador in the diplomatic corps to resign when Madero was assassinated, 1913. L] Pasquel, Jalapa, 149, 151–53, 169–71; Mestre, 273; FSRE, 174.

Cravioto (Mejorada), Alfonso
(Deceased September 11, 1955) A] January 24, 1884. B] Pachuca, Hidalgo. C] Secondary studies at the Scientific and Literary Institute of Pachuca, Hidalgo; preparatory studies from the National Preparatory School; law degree, National School of Law. D] Secretary, City Council, Mexico City, 1911; *federal deputy* from the State of Hidalgo, Dist. 6, 1912–14; *constitutional deputy* from the State of Hidalgo, Dist. 7, 1916–17; *federal deputy* from the State of Hidalgo, Dist. 7, 1917–18; *senator* from Hidalgo, 1918–22; president of the Senate, 1921, and 1922–26; senator from Hidalgo, 1952–55. E] Vice-president, Club Redención Antireeleccionista, 1903; organized the National Independent party, May 1911. F] Director general of fine arts, 1914; official mayor of the Secretariat of Public Education; *subsecretary* of public education, 1914–17; ambassador to Guatemala, 1927–28; ambassador to Chile, 1928–32; ambassador to Holland and Belgium, 1932–33; *ambassador* to Cuba, 1934–35; ambassador to Bolivia, 1943. G] President of the Ignacio Ramírez Student Society at the National School of Law. H] Art critic; cofounder of *Savia Moderna* with *Luis Castillo Ledón*; man of letters. I] Son of prominent political figure and

governor of Hidalgo General *Rafael Cravioto Moreno* and Laura Mejorada; married Elena Vázquez Sánchez; nephew of Simón Cravioto Moreno, governor of Hidalgo; nephew of *Francisco Cravioto Moreno*, governor of Hidalgo. J] None. K] None. L] Dir soc, 1935, 72; WWM45, 32; Carreño, 348–49.

Cravioto (Moreno), Francisco
(Deceased) A] Unknown. B] Huauchinango, Puebla. C] Early education unknown; no degree. D] *Governor* of Hidalgo, 1885–97. E] Member of the Liberal party. F] Interim governor of Hidalgo, 1877. G] None. H] Ran father's business in Huauchinango. I] Son of Simón Cravioto, businessman, and Luz Moreno; brother Simón, governor of Hidalgo; brother of *Rafael Cravioto Moreno*, governor of Hidalgo; son Roberto was a local deputy to the state legislature of Hidalgo, 1896, and an industrialist and hacendado; nephew *Alfonso Cravioto Mejorado* was subsecretary of education, 1914–17. J] Career army officer; joined the Liberal forces, 1853; taken prisoner by the Conservatives in the battle of Huauchinango; fought under General *Porfirio Díaz* in the Army of the East; participated in the battle of Puebla, May 5, 1862; prefect of Huauchinango, Puebla, 1867; supported Díaz in the Tuxtepec Rebellion in Hidalgo, 1876; tried to take the Fort of Tulancingo, March 11, 1876; military commander of Hidalgo under brother Rafael's governorship, 1877. K] None. L] Album; Pérez López, 107; Hombres prominentes, 275–76.

Cravioto (Moreno), Rafael
(Deceased November 28, 1903) A] October 24, 1829. B] Huauchinango, Hidalgo. C] Early education unknown; no degree. D] Senator from Puebla, 1880–84; *senator* from Hidalgo, 1886–90; *alternate federal deputy* from the State of Hidalgo, Dist. 11, 1894–96; *alternate federal deputy* from the State of Hidalgo, Dist. 4, 1896–98. E] None. F] Interim governor of Hidalgo, 1877. G] None. H] Owner, Zoquital hacienda; hacendado, 1895–1903. I] Son of Simón Cravioto, businessman, and Luz Moreno; brother of *Francisco Cravioto*

Moreno, governor of Hidalgo; brother of *Simón Cravioto Moreno,* governor of Hidalgo; uncle of Adrián Cravioto Leyzaola, general and engineer; father of *Alfonso Cravioto Mejorada,* subsecretary of education, 1914–17; married Laura Mejorada. J] Career army officer; joined the national guard as a captain, Huauchinango Battalion, 1847; supported the Liberals in the Plan of Ayutla; fought during the War of the Reform under General Manuel González; fought the French, 1862–67; rank of brigade general, June 4, 1863; supported *Porfirio Díaz* in the Tuxtepec Rebellion, 1876. K] None. L] Pavía, 202–05; Sec of War, 20; Holms, 286; Mestre, 217–18; Pérez López, 107; Loera y Chávez, 11.

Cravioto (Moreno), Simón
(Deceased June 3, 1905) A] 1840. B] Pachuca, Hidalgo. C] Early education unknown; no degree. D] Local deputy to the state legislature of Puebla, 1867–70; senator from Puebla, 1875; *governor* of Hidalgo, 1881–85; *federal deputy* from the State of Hidalgo, Dist. 7, 1886–88, 1888–90, 1890–92, 1892–94, 1894–96, 1896–98. E] None. F] None. G] None. H] Unknown. I] Son of Simón Cravioto, businessman, and Luz Moreno; brother of *Francisco Cravioto,* governor of Hidalgo; brother of *Rafael Cravioto Moreno,* senator from Hidalgo; uncle of Adrián Cravioto Leyzaola, general and engineer; uncle of *Alfonso Cravioto Mejorada,* subsecretary of public education, 1914–17. J] Enlisted in the 9th Reserve Battalion against the French; captured by the Austrians and sentenced to death, but sentence commuted by Maximilian, 1865; rank of colonel, 1867; supported the Plan of Tuxtepec, 1876. K] None. L] UNAM, law, 1900–06, 75; Mestre; Hombres prominentes, 405–06.

Creel (Cuilty), Enrique C.
(Deceased August 17, 1931) A] August 31, 1854. B] Chihuahua, Chihuahua. C] Primary studies in Chihuahua; self-educated; honorary law degree, University of Pennsylvania. D] Member of the City Council, Chihuahua, 1875–76; syndic, City Council, Chihuahua, 1878–79; member of the City Council, Chihuahua,

1880–81; local deputy to the state legislature of Chihuahua, 1882–83, 1884–85; *alternate federal deputy* from the State of Chihuahua, Dist. 4, 1892–94; local deputy to the state legislature of Chihuahua, 1897–98, 1899–1900; *federal deputy* from the State of Durango, Dist. 1, 1900–02; *federal deputy* from the State of Chihuahua, Dist. 5, 1902–04, 1904–06; *governor* of Chihuahua, 1907–10. E] None. F] *Interim governor* of Chihuahua, 1904–07; *ambassador* to the United States, 1907–08; *secretary* of foreign relations, 1910–11. G] President of the Chamber of Commerce of Chihuahua, 1889; president of the Casino of Chihuahua, 1898; president of the Bankers Association of Mexico, 1899; president of the Mexican Society of Geography and Statistics, 1929; vice-president of the National Academy of Science Antonio Alzate, 1931. H] Founding stockholder and manager, Mining Bank of Chihuahua, 1883; president of the Telephone Company of Chihuahua and Durango, 1885; founding stockholder and president, La Mexicana Insurance Company, 1887; adviser, Chihuahua Mining Company, 1888; president of the Industrial Mexicana Company, 1883; president of the Streetcar Company of Chihuahua, 1894; founding stockholder and president, Central Mexican Bank, 1900; president of the Mining Railroad of Chihuahua, 1900; founding stockholder and president, Agricultural and Mortgage Bank of Mexico, 1901; vice-president of the Chihuahua-Pacific Railroad, 1902; vice-president of the Kansas City Railroad, 1902; director, Central Mexican Railroad, 1903; president of the Board of the Yucatán Railroad. I] Son of Rubén W. Creel, businessman and American consul in Chihuahua, and Paz Cuilty, sister of Carolina Cuilty, wife of *Luis Terrazas,* governor of Chihuahua; mother is the daughter of Colonel Gabio Cuilty and María de la Luz Bustamante; grandson of Eligel Creel; daughter Adela married *Joaquín Cortázar,* governor of Chihuahua, 1903; in business with *Juan Terrazas Cuilty,* brother of Luis, *Ernesto Madero Farías,* uncle of Francisco, and brother Juan Creel. J] None. K] Started in father's business at age 14; original name was Henry Clay Creel. L] Album;

Hombres prominentes, 481–82; Enc Mex, IV, 189; López, 242; DP70, 548, Godoy, 257; Mestre, 285; Almada, 437–47; Márquez, 178–80; Almada, 1968, 124; FSRE, 143; Carreño, 23–68.

Crespo y Martínez, Gilberto
(Deceased 1916) A] August 17, 1853. B] Veracruz, Veracruz. C] Primary, secondary, and preparatory studies, Seminary of Jalapa, Veracruz; preparatory studies at the Colegio de Puebla; studies, Liceo Jalapa; studies in engineering, School of Mines, Mexico City, 1865–70, graduating with an engineering degree, 1876; secretary, School of Mines, 1876; professor of geology and paleontology, School of Mines, 1878–79. D] *Federal deputy* from the State of Morelos, Dist. 2, 1886–88, 1888–90, *federal deputy* from the State of Morelos, Dist. 1, 1892–94, 1894–96, 1896–98, 1898–1900, 1900–02; *federal deputy* from the State of Michoacán, Dist. 15, 1894–96. E] None. F] Official, first level, Secretariat of Agriculture, 1882; consul to Cuba, 1885–86; represented Mexico at the International Exposition, New Orleans, 1886; department head, secretariat of development, 1886–88; oficial mayor of the Secretariat of Development, 1889–91; *subsecretary* of development, 1892–1900; consul to Cuba, 1900; *ambassador* to Cuba, 1902–05; ambassador to Austria, 1906–10; *ambassador* to the United States, 1911–12; ambassador to Austria, 1912–14. G] None. H] Engineering intern, Real del Monte mine. I] Married Adela de la Serna y Campbell; son Jorge Juan Crespo Serna, artist; student in Jalapa with *Teodoro A. Dehesa*, governor of Veracruz, and supported a political group with Dehesa and *Manuel Fernández Leal* in favor of moderate political change. J] None. K] Remained in post as ambassador to Austria although he had been officially removed, 1914–16. L] DP70, 549; Pasquel, 69–70; Godoy, 147–48.

Cruz, Ausencio Conrado
(Deceased 1963) A] May 27, 1898. B] Tetela de Ocampo, Puebla. C] Early education unknown; no degree. D] Local deputy to the state legislature of Tabasco; *governor* of Tabasco, 1927–28, 1929–30;

senator from Tabasco, 1932–34. E] *Secretary* of publicity of the National Revolutionary party, 1934–35. F] *Interim governor* of Tabasco, 1924–25; aide to *Tomás Garrido Canabal*, governor of Tabasco, 1923–26; inspector general of police, Tabasco. G] None. H] Unknown. I] Married Jacoba Padrón (died 1935); second wife, María de la Luz Lafarja, poet and member of the Mexican Communist party; good friend of Carlos Madrazo, president of PRI. J] Sergeant in the 230th Regiment, Tabasco, 1919; opposed the *Adolfo de la Huerta* rebellion, 1923; rank of 1st captain; participated in conflict between supporters of Garrido and Rodulfo Brito Foucher in Villahermosa, 1935. K] Persecuted Catholics as governor and responsible for destroying the Cathedral of Tabasco. L] López, 243; Bulnes, 460; Almanaque de Tabasco, 153; Romero Aceves, 632.

Cruz, Manuel Encarnación
(Deceased 1925) A] 1859. B] Tuxtla Gutiérrez, Chiapas. C] Primary studies in Tuxtla Gutiérrez; preparatory studies in San Cristóbal las Casas; normal certificate; law degree, 1882; teacher, Agrimensura, 1878. D] None. E] None. F] Director, Legal Department, Secretariat of Industry, Commerce, and Labor; president of the Superior Tribunal of Justice of the Federal District; *justice* of the Supreme Court, 1917–18; legal adviser to President *Alvaro Obregón*, 1922–23; *interim governor* of Chiapas, 1923–24. G] None. H] Practicing lawyer, Pichucalco, Chiapas, Jalapa, Veracruz, and Mexico City; author of many books. I] Unknown. J] None. K] None. L] DP70, 555; Gordillo y Ortiz, 52–53; Almanque de Chiapas, 119; letter.

Cruz (Medina), José Ciriaco
(Deceased September 7, 1957) A] June 18, 1888. B] Villa de Pozos, San Luis Potosí. C] Early education unknown; normal studies at the Literary Institute of San Luis Potosí with studies in philosophy, rhetoric, and poetry, 1901–06; normal certificate, 1906; director, private school, 1901–02; joined public school system, 1902; returned to teaching, 1932–57; schoolteacher, Urique and Batopilas, Chihuahua. D] Mayor of Cedral, San

Luis Potosí, 1911; local deputy to the state legislature of San Luis Potosí; *federal deputy* from San Luis Potosí, Dist. 2, 1917–18; *senator* from San Luis Potosí, 1924–28. E] Represented *Francisco A. Madero* in San Luis Potosí, 1909–10; member of the Executive Board, Anti-Reelectionist party. F] Director general of education, San Luis Potosí, 1919; federal inspector of education, Puebla, 1929; federal inspector of education, Querétaro and San Luis Potosí. G] None. H] Wrote for clandestine newspapers, 1909. I] Unknown. J] None. K] Lost teaching positions for supporting Madero. L] QesQ, 143; DP70, 557; Montejano, 103.

Cuéllar, José T.
(Deceased 1894) A] 1830. B] Mexico City. C] Early education unknown, enrolled National Military College, 1846; no degree; teacher, secondary school for girls. D] None. E] None. F] First secretary to the Mexican legation, Washington, D.C.; *subsecretary* of foreign relations, 1886, 1887–90. G] Corresponding member of the Royal Academy of Spain; member of the Liceo Hidalgo literary group. H] Began writing, 1848; journalist; novelist; dramatist; contributor to *El Semanario de las Señoritas* and *La Ilustración Mexicana*. I] Unknown. J] Defended Chapultepec Castle against the North American invasion as a cadet. K] None. L] Hombres prominentes, 373–74; Peña, 310–12; Cuevas, 382.

Cuéllar, José María
(Deceased) A] Unknown. B] Jalisco. C] Early education unknown; no degree. D] Mayor of Guadalajara, Jalisco; *federal deputy* from Jalisco, Dist. 14, 1918–20, 1920–22; *federal deputy* from the State of Jalisco, Dist. 9, 1922–24; *federal deputy* from State of Jalisco, Dist. 4, 1924–26, 1928–30. E] Candidate for governor of Jalisco, 1926. F] Clerk, Tax Department, State of Jalisco, 1910–14; *provisional governor* of Jalisco, 1929–30. G] None. H] Unknown. I] Married widow of General Melitón Albáñez; intimate friend of Jorge Prieto Laurens, governor of San Luis Potosí, 1923. J] Served in the forces of Colonel Melitón Albánez as 2nd lieutenant, 1914; rank of lt. colonel K] Impli-

cated in the murder of Gudelio Jiménez during the Badillo-Zuno campaign for governor of Jalisco. L] Gruening, 444–46; C de D, 1918–20, 1922–24, 1928–30.

Cuéllar, Rómulo
(Deceased) A] 1840. B] San Fernando de Presas, Tamaulipas. C] Early education unknown; no degree. D] Senator from Tamaulipas, 1880–84; *governor* of Tamaulipas, 1884–88; *senator* from Tamaulipas, 1888–92, 1892–96, 1896–1900, 1900–04, 1904–06, 1910–12. E] None. F] *Governor* of Guanajuato, 1913–14. G] None. H] Owner of the Barra hacienda, San Fernando, Tamaulipas. I] Unknown. J] Career army officer; joined the army, 1860; fought against the French; rank of brigade general, June 6, 1877; commander of federal troops in Tamaulipas, 1880–81; commander of the 3rd Military Zone, 1881–84; no military post, 1901; commander of military operations in Tamaulipas, 1911; rank of division general, June 27, 1913; commander of the Division of the Center, 1913–14; joined the Constitutionalists, 1914. K] None. L] C de S, 1904–06, 18; C de S, 1910–12, 21; Holms, 342; Peral, appendix, 94; C de S, 1900–02, 6–7; López, 246; Sec of War, 194, 1902.

Curiel (C.), Luis del Carmen
(Deceased March 18, 1930) A] March 15, 1846. B] Guadalajara, Jalisco. C] Primary studies in Guadalajara, Jalisco, and Durango, Durango; law degree, 1874; interrupted law studies to support *Porfirio Díaz* against the government, 1871. D] Senator from Guerrero, 1878–82, president of the Senate; *federal deputy* from the State of Jalisco, Dist. 10, 1888–90, 1890–92, 1892–94; *governor* of Jalisco, 1889–91, 1895–1903; *senator* from Yucatán, 1902–06, 1906–10, 1910–12, 1912–13. E] None. F] Subsecretary of government, 1877; subsecretary of justice, 1877; governor of the Federal District, 1877–80; consul in Paris, France; *substitute governor* of Jalisco, 1893–95; *subsecretary* of war, 1903–07; *governor* of Yucatán, 1911. G] None. H] Practicing lawyer and journalist, 1874. I] Son Luis Curiel, Jr., served as a federal deputy from Oaxaca, 1906–08, 1910–12. J] Joined the Tuxtepec Rebellion in support of Díaz as a cav-

alry colonel, 1876; rank of brigade general, January 1, 1892; returned to active duty November 11, 1912; retired from the army July 2, 1913. K] None. L] Godoy, 284–85; Sec of War, 1901, 19; Mestre, 284; C de S, 1904–06, 18; 1906–08, 19; 1908–10, 20; Peral, appendix, 97.

Curiel (Gallegos), Rafael G.
(Deceased March 29, 1955) A] December 30, 1883. B] Ciudad Valles, San Luis Potosí. C] Primary studies in Ciudad Valles and Puebla, Puebla; preparatory and professional studies, Scientific and Literary Institute of San Luis Potosí, San Luis Potosí, completed studies in engineering, mining engineering degree, National School of Engineering, January 4, 1936. D] *Federal deputy* from the State of San Luis Potosí, Dist. 10, 1912–14; *constitutional deputy* from the State of San Luis Potosí, Dist. 10, 1916–17; *federal deputy* from the State of San Luis Potosí, Dist. 10, 1917–18; local deputy to the state legislature of San Luis Potosí, 1919. E] None. F] *Interim governor* of San Luis Potosí, 1919–20; tax auditor, comptroller general of Mexico, 1921–23; general fiscal inspector of petroleum, Tampico, 1923–26; employee, Secretariat of Agriculture and Livestock, 1927–28; petroleum and mining engineer, Department of Mines and Petroleum, Secretariat of National Economy, 1936–38. G] None. H] Engaged in farming and mining, Zacactecas, 1928–34; retired, 1936. I] Son of Emeterio Curiel, cattle rancher and farmer, and Everarda Gallegos. J] Joined the Revolution in support of *Francisco I. Madero*, 1910; fought under General *Jesús Agustín Castro*, 1910–11; joined the Constitutionalists, 1913; fought under General Nicolás Flores, 1913–16; reached rank of lt. colonel. K] None. L] Peral, appendix, 97; C de D, 1912–14, 1916–17, 1917–18.

D

Dávalos (Vázquez), Marcelino
(Deceased September 19, 1923) A] April 26, 1871. B] Guadalajara, Jalisco. C] Secondary and preparatory studies, Liceo de Varones, Guadalajara; law degree, School of Law, Guadalajara, 1900; manual arts

teacher, Liceo de Varones, Guadalajara; professor, National Conservatory, Mexico City. D] *Alternate federal deputy* from the Federal District, Dist. 4, 1912–13, under *Eduardo Hay; constitutional deputy* from the State of Jalisco, Dist. 2, 1916–17. E] None. F] Private secretary to General Ignacio Bravo in Quintana Roo, 1903–04; political boss of Quintana Roo, 1903–07; adviser to the commander of the 10th Military Zone, 1907–08; secretary general of government of the State of Coahuila; oficial mayor of the Secretariat of Foreign Relations, 1914–15; consulting lawyer to the Secretariat of Communications and Public Works, 1917–19. G] None. H] Practicing lawyer; painter; writer; joined a theater company, 1895; editor of *Excélsior*. I] Son of Angel Dávalos and Ignacia Vázquez, a very poor family; considered his mentor to be Aurelio Ortega, his teacher in Guadalajara. J] None. K] Imprisoned by *Victoriano Huerta* for 7 months and exiled briefly to Texas, 1913–14. L] FSRE, 163; Villaseñor, 263–68; Enc Mex, III, 415–16; DP70, 622; López, 262.

Dávila Peña, Encarnación
(Deceased February 1, 1943) A] March 25, 1847. B] La Aurora, Saltillo, Coahuila. C] Primary studies in Saltillo; no degree. D] Local deputy to the state legislature of Coahuila, 1884; local deputy to the state legislature of Coahuila, president, 1907; *alternate senator* from Coahuila, but replaced *Venustiano Carranza* when he became governor of Coahuila, 1910–12; president of the Senate, 1912. E] Supported the political group of *Miguel Cárdenas*, governor of Coahuila, 1896–1909, against *José María Garza Galán*, governor of Coahuila, 1890–93; supported *Francisco I. Madero* during presidential campaign, 1910. F] Governor of Coahuila, 1883. G] None. H] Unknown. I] Son of Lorenzo Dávila and Guadalupe Peña; friends included *Porfirio Díaz, Justo Sierra, Joaquín Casasús*, and *José Yves Limantour*; close friend of Evaristo Madero, grandfather of *Francisco I. Madero*. J] None. K] In exile in San Antonio, Texas, 1913–16; Carranza offered him a post in his government, but he refused,

1916. L] Moreno, 103–05; C de S, 1910–12.

de Alba, Pedro
(Deceased November 10, 1960) A] December 17, 1887. B] San Juan de los Lagos, Jalisco. C] Primary in San Juan de los Lagos, Jalisco; secondary and preparatory studies at the Institute of Sciences, Aguascalientes; medical degree from the National School of Medicine, UNAM, graduated as a surgeon; studies in medicine at the Medical-Military Practical School of the Army, 1913; diploma in ophthamology in Paris; professor of general history and of Spanish literature at the National Preparatory School and the School of Philosophy and Letters, UNAM; director of the Preparatory School in Aguascalientes, 1919; director of the Institute of Sciences of Aguascalientes; director of the National Preparatory School, 1929–33; commissioned by the secretary of public education of the State of Nuevo León to organize the University of Monterrey, 1933; member of the Technical Advisory Council to the Secretariat of Public Education, 1935. D] *Federal deputy* from the State of Aguascalientes, Dist. 1, 1920–22; *senator* from Aguascalientes, 1922–26, president of the Senate, member of the Foreign Relations Committee; senator from the State of Aguascalientes, 1952–58, member of the Great Committee, the Public Welfare Committee, the first Public Education Committee, and the Health Committee. F] Counselor of public education in Aguascalientes, 1917; director of the Health Service in Aguascalientes, 1918; assistant director of the Pan American Union, 1936–47; ambassador to Chile, 1947; ambassador to the International Organization of Labor, 1948–51; delegate to UNESCO, 1951. G] None. H] Author of several books. I] Nephew Alfonso de Alba Martín served as a federal deputy from Jalisco, 1967–70; father, Lamberto de Alba, was a partner in the cattle ranching business; grandfather, Blas de Alba, was a small rancher; maternal grandfather, a general under *Porfirio Díaz*. J] Major in the Mexican army. K] None. L] WWM45, 3; DP70, 54; DGF56, 5, 8, 9, 10, 12; DGF51, 110, 117; WB48, 1383; Ind. biog., 49–50.

de Anda, J. Guadalupe
(Deceased) A] December 12, 1882. B] San José de los Lagos, Jalisco. C] Early education unknown; no degree. D] *Federal deputy* from the State of Jalisco, Dist. 6, 1918–20; *federal deputy* from the State of Jalisco, Dist. 10, 1926–28; *federal deputy* from the State of Jalisco, Dist. 8, 1928–30, member of the Great Committee. E] None. F] Telegrapher, National Railroads of Mexico; station chief, National Railroads of Mexico, Guanajuato; superintendent of the National Railroads of Mexico, Guadalajara; assistant to the director general of the National Railroads. G] None. H] Unknown. I] Son of Silverio de Anda, poet, journalist, and schoolteacher. J] Supported General *Alvaro Obregón* against *Venustiano Carranza*, 1920; opposed the Cristeros, 1926–29. K] None. L] C de D, 1918–20, 1926–28, 1928–30.

de Dios Bátiz, Juan
(Deceased May 20, 1979) A] April 2, 1890. B] Zataya, Sinaloa. C] Early education unknown; began engineering studies in Culiacán, completed at the National Military College, 1908–12; cadet, 1st Company. D] *Federal deputy* from the State of Sinaloa, Dist. 1, 1922–24, member of the Great Committee; *federal deputy* from the State of Sinaloa, Dist. 3, 1924–26; *federal deputy* from the State of Sinaloa, Dist. 2, 1930–32; *senator* from the State of Sinaloa, 1932–34. E] Treasurer of the National Executive Committee (CEN) of the National Revolutionary party (PNR), 1931. F] *Interim governor* of Sinaloa, 1926–27; director of technical education, Secretariat of Public Education, 1934–36; founder of the National Polytechnic Institute (IPN), 1936; director of social welfare, secretary of labor, 1936–40; director general of the National Mortgage Bank, 1940–46. G] None. H] Manager of various private firms, 1946–70. I] Married Laura Pérez de Bátiz; son Juan de Dios was a director general in the Secretariat of Industry and Commerce, 1961; wife related to *Lázaro Cárdenas*'s sister. J] Participated in the Revolution; served in the 1st Artillery Regiment under Colonel *Felipe Angeles*; participated in the battle

for Nazas, Durango, 1912; fought against
Orozco, 1912; rank of 2nd captain, February 10, 1913; officer, 3rd Artillery Regiment; fought in Torreón in the Nazas Division under General J. Refugio Velasco;
commander in the 3rd Artillery Regiment;
rank of 1st captain, 1914; rank of major,
1914; joined the Constitutionalists, 1915;
military governor of Nayarit. K] President Cárdenas allegedly offered him the
position of secretary of public education
in 1934, but he turned it down in order to
found the IPN. L] HA, 28 May 1979, 14;
Excélsior, 21 May 1979, 4; Peral, 97; *Excélsior*, 22 May 1979, 30; DPE61, 66; Rev
de Ejer, June 1971, 5–6.

de Herrera, Manuel
(Deceased November 1, 1898) A] January
19, 1830. B] Villa de Concepción (Ciudad
Guerrero), Chihuahua. C] Primary studies in Villa de Concepción; no degree.
D] Local deputy to the state legislature of
Chihuahua, 1863–64, 1871–72, 1873–74,
1877–79, 1881–82, 1883–84, 1887–88,
1889–90; *alternate senator* from Morelos,
1890–94, 1894–96; *senator* from Morelos,
1894–96. E] None. F] Employee, Tax
Office, Guerrero Canton (District), 1849;
employee, office of the political boss of
Guerrero Canton, Chihuahua; political
boss of Guerrero Canton, 1862; political
cal boss of Iturbide Canton, Chihuahua, 1873–74, 1877; governor and military commander of Chihuahua, 1876.
G] None. H] Went into business with
Celso González and Juan María Salazar;
acquired properties in the 1880s; stockholder, Streetcar Company of Chihuahua;
stockholder, real estate company, with
Jesús E. Valenzuela. I] Son of Gil de Herrera and Joséfa Mendoza; married Gertrudis González. J] Colonel, national guard;
commander, Guerrero Battalion, against
the La Noria rebellion of *Porfirio Díaz*,
1872; quartermaster, Chihuahua forces
under Governor *Luis Terrazas*, 1872;
opposed the rebellion of Porfirio Díaz,
1876; commander of military operations
in Chihuahua, 1876; rank of colonel,
1877. K] Supported a movement to restore
Lerdo de Tejada to the presidency, 1877.
L] DP70, 987; Enc Mex, VI, 418; Almada,
333–37; Almada, 1968, 251.

Dehesa (y Méndez), Teodoro A.
(Deceased September 25, 1936) A] October 1, 1848. B] Jalapa, Veracruz. C] Primary studies at Señorita Torres's Amigas
School and at the Santo Domingo Public
School, Jalapa, Veracruz; secondary studies
at the Colegio Juan Rodríguez, Veracruz;
preparatory studies at the Liceo de Jalapa;
abandoned studies to enter business when
father died. D] Local deputy to the state
legislature of Veracruz, 1873–75; *governor* of Veracruz, 1892–1911. E] None.
F] Customs inspector, Veracruz, 1876–80;
director of customs, 1880–92. G] None.
H] Employee and bookkeeper, Manuel
Loustau Clothing Store; secretary to Manuel Loustau; owner of El Rincón de la
Miel hacienda, Misantla, Veracruz. I] Son
of Teodoro Dehesa y Bayona, Spanish immigrant who owned a candy store in Veracruz, Veracruz, and Antonia Méndez y
Ruiz; married Teresa Núñez; son, Raúl
Dehesa y Núñez, journalist and federal
deputy, married Emma García Peña,
daughter of General *Angel García Peña*;
cousin or brother of Francisco Dehesa, federal deputy from Veracruz, 1890s. J] Supported *Porfirio Díaz* during the Plan of La
Noria, helping him to escape from Veracruz, September 1, 1871; supported Díaz
during the Plan of Tuxtepec, 1876. K] Exiled, 1871, for supporting Díaz; apprehended and jailed for supporting Díaz,
1876; exiled to Havana, Cuba, 1913; properties confiscated by the revolutionaries,
1914, and returned by *Venustiano Carranza*, 1915; exiled to Florida and Havana, 1915–20; returned to Mexico during
the *Alvaro Obregón* administration.
L] Enc Mex, III 421; DP70, 628–29; Pasquel, 75–76; López, 267–69; Hombres
prominentes, 363–64; Mestre, 291–92;
album; Peral, appendix, 101–02; Godoy,
19–20; Holms, 352.

de la Garza, Pablo A.
(Deceased August 11, 1932) A] January
12, 1876. B] Monterrey, Nuevo León.
C] Primary studies in Monterrey, 1882–
88; preparatory studies at the Colegio
Civil, Monterrey, 1888–94; law degree, University of Nuevo León, 1899.
D] None. E] None. F] Judge, Sabinas Hidalgo, Nuevo León, 1899; attorney, 1st

Military Zone, 1899–04; military judge attached to the 4th Military Zone, 1904–06; tax judge, Veracruz, Veracruz, 1906–09; agent of the Ministerio Público, Monterrey, 1909–10; judge, Piedras Negras, Coahuila, 1911–12; *governor* and military commander of Guanajuato, 1914; *governor* and military commander of Nuevo León, 1915–17; *attorney general* of Mexico, 1918–19. G] None. H] None. I] Son of Albino de la Garza and Leocadia Gutiérrez; married Paula Garza Linares, sister of Colonel Francisco Garza Linares; brother Diódoro substituted for him as governor, 1916. J] Lawyer with military rank, army, 1899–1909; reached rank of auxiliary colonel, 1909, when he resigned; joined the Constitutionalists as a colonel under *Pablo González*; captured Monterrey, 1914; rank of brigadier general, 1914; commander of the 9th Army Brigade, Army of the Northeast, under General *Alvaro Obregón*; military commander of the Southeast, 1920; remained loyal to *Venustiano Carranza*, 1920. K] Went into voluntary exile, 1920–25, returned to Mexico, 1925. L] Enc Mex, V, 225; DP70, 837; QesQ, 236–37; Almanaque of Nuevo León, 101; Covarrubias, II, 107–14.

de la Garza, Emeterio
(Deceased) A] March 3, 1847. B] Marín, Nuevo León. C] Early education unknown; law degree, August 30, 1869. D] Local deputy to the state legislature of Nuevo León, 1871–72, 1877–78; federal deputy from the State of Nuevo León, 1878–80, 1880–82, 1882–84; *federal deputy* from the State of Nuevo León, Dist. 1, 1884–86; *federal deputy* from the State of Guanajuato, Dist. 13, 1886–88. E] None. F] Private secretary to Generals *Gerónimo Treviño* and Francisco Naranjo during the 1871 and 1876 rebellions, and as secretaries of war, 1881–84; *justice* of the Supreme Court, 1904–11. G] None. H] Practicing lawyer; represented many North American companies in Mexico; received government concessions to survey lands in Coahuila, Nuevo León, and Tamaulipas, 1881; owner of many properties; journalist; vice-president and general attorney for the Mexican Gulf-Monterrey Railroad, cofounded with General Gerónimo Treviño, 1878. I] Son of Juan José de la Garza and Manuela Martínez; married Joséfa Martínez; son *Emeterio de la Garza, Jr.*, served as a federal deputy, 1898–16. J] None. K] None. L] Godoy, 98; Peral, Appendix, 140; Hombres prominentes, 397–98; González de Cossío, 8.

de la Garza, Jr. (Martínez), Emeterio
(Deceased) A] 1873. B] Villa de Marín, Monterrey, Nuevo León. C] Preparatory studies, Colegio San Juan de Saltillo, Saltillo, Coahuila; legal studies, National School of Law, 1891–96, graduating, 1896. D] *Federal deputy* from the State of Yucatán, Dist. 6, 1898–1900, 1900–02; *federal deputy* from the State of Hidalgo, Dist. 6, 1902–04, 1904–06, 1906–08, 1908–10; *federal deputy* from the State of Nuevo León, Dist. 4, 1914–15. E] None. F] None. G] None. H] Practicing lawyer. I] Son of *Emeterio de la Garza*, businessman and Supreme Court justice, 1904–11, and Josefa Martínez; brother José, a lawyer. J] None. K] None. L] UNAM, law, 1880–91, 135; C de D, 1914–16.

de la Huerta, Adolfo
(Deceased July 9, 1955) A] May 26, 1881. B] Hermosillo, Sonora. C] Primary studies at the Martínez Calleja Primary School, Guaymas; preparatory studies at the National Preparatory School in accounting; certificate in music, Hermosillo; music teacher, Guaymas. D] Local deputy to the state legislature of Sonora, 1911–12, defeated *Plutarco E. Calles* for the post; *senator* from Sonora, 1918; *governor* of Sonora, 1919–20. E] Representative of the Anti-Reelectionist Club of Guaymas to Central Mexico, 1909; secretary of the Anti-Reelectionist Club, Guaymas, 1910; candidate for president of Mexico, 1923; supported *Lázaro Cárdenas* for president, 1934. F] *Interim governor* of Sonora, 1916–17; oficial mayor of government, 1915–16; consul general of Mexico, New York City, 1918–19; *secretary* of the treasury, 1920–23; inspector general of consulates, United States, 1936–46; director general of civil pensions and retirement, 1946. G] None. H] Worked as a bookkeeper in various businesses, Guaymas, 1900; employee, National Bank of

Mexico, Guaymas; manager, San Germán Tannery, 1909–10; taught piano lessons, Los Angeles, 1924–35. I] Son of Torcuato de la Huerta, an important businessman in Guaymas, and Carmen Marcos; son Adolfo de la Huerta Oriel served as senator; brother Alfonso was a general during the Revolution; nephew of Adrián Marcor, cousin of Governor Celedonio Ortiz; cousin of Alejandro Carrillo Marcos, governor of Sonora, 1975–79, and father of Alejandro Carrillo Castro. J] Joined the Constitutionalists, February 20, 1913, in Monclova, Coahuila; supported the Plan of Agua Prieta, 1920; revolted against *Plutarco Elías Calles*, 1923–24, defeated June 1924. K] Lost his job, 1910, for anti-Díaz activities; exiled to Los Angeles, 1924–25. L] Villa, 85–89; López, 277–78; Enc Mex, VII, 76; Aguilar Camín, 85–86.

de la Lama, Adolfo
(Deceased November 25, 1927) A] June 19, 1870. B] Mexico City. C] Early education unknown; legal studies, National School of Law, 1889–94, law degree, National School of Law. D] Federal deputy from the State of Guanajuato, Dist. 11, 1914–16. E] None. F] Subsecretary of development, 1913; secretary of justice, 1913–14; secretary of the treasury, 1913–14; secretary of government, 1914. G] None. H] Practicing lawyer. I] Son of José de la Lama and Concepción Gómez la Madrid; son Adolfo de la Lama was a career foreign service officer. J] None. K] None. L] Dir social, 1935, 285; UNAM, law, 1891–96, 15; Mestre, 279; DP70, 1152.

de la Madrid, Enrique O.
(Deceased 1935) A] 1862. B] Colima, Colima. C] Primary studies in Colima; preparatory studies in Guadalajara; law degree, School of Law, Guadalajara, April 30, 1885. D] Local deputy to the state legislature of Colima; *alternate federal deputy* from the State of Colima, Dist. 1, 1886–88; *alternate federal deputy* from the State of Colima, Dist. 2, 1894–96; *alternate federal deputy* from the State of Colima, Dist 1, 1896–98; *federal deputy* from the State of Colima, Dist. 1, 1898–1900; *governor* of Colima, 1903–11. E] None. F] Oficial mayor of the govern-

ment of the State of Colima, 1885–87; district court judge, Colima, 1887–96; substitute governor of Colima, 1902–03. G] None. H] Owner of El Rosario, Guaracha, Llano Grande, Colomos, Pastores, Santa María and Ticotán, and El Carmen haciendas, Colima, totaling 12,550 hectares; editor, *Revista Literaria*, 1887; editor, Opinión Libre, 1894, 1898. I] Grandfather of President Miguel de la Madrid, 1982–88; related to Miguel de la Madrid, governor of Colima, 1883, 1887, Ignacio de la Madrid, attorney general of the state of Colima, 1857, and Colonel Marino de la Madrid. J] None. K] Opposed by Miguel Alvarez, candidate of the Independent party, for governor, 1903; retired from politics, 1911. L] Romero Aceves; DP70, 1232; Album; Enc Mex, VIII, 199; Moreno, 55–58; Almada, Colima, 123; Holms, 257.

de la Peña, Pragedis
(Deceased) A] Unknown. B] Coahuila. C] Early education unknown; law degree. D] None. E] None. F] *Provisional governor* of Coahuila, 1909; *governor* of Coahuila, 1913–14. G] None. H] Praticing lawyer; businessman; stockholder in and vice-president of Compañía Industrial Jabonera de la Laguna; primary investor in Compañía Industrial de Hilados y Tejidos La Fe, Laguna; stockholder in the San Patricio Mine, Chihuahua; vice-president of the Banco de la Laguna; owner of El Pilar hacienda, 3,600 hectares; cotton grower in Nuevo León and Coahuila; director general of the Bank of Coahuila; director of *El Coahuilense*. I] Married Concepción Valdés; cousin of *Ernesto Madero*, secretary of the treasury, 1911–13, and uncle of *Francisco I. Madero*; in business with his brothers Emilio and Mauro de la Peña; Madero family favored him over *Venustiano Carranza* for the governorship of Coahuila. J] None. K] None. L] Album; Cuéllar Valdés, 207; Langston, 72.

de la Vega, José María
(Deceased April 28, 1917) A] June 18, 1856. B] Oaxaca, Oaxaca. C] Early education unknown; engineering degree, National Military College, 1872. D] *Federal deputy* from the State of Tamaulipas, Dist. 4, 1902–04; *federal deputy* from the State of México, Dist. 1, 1904–06, 1906–

08; *federal deputy* from the State of Guanajuato, Dist. 9, 1912–14. E] None. F] Director, Naval Department, 1900–01. G] None. H] None. I] Student with *Victoriano Huerta* and *Joaquín Maas*. J] Career naval officer; rank of rear admiral, August 16, 1892; rank of admiral, December 27, 1911. K] None. L] Sec of War, 1900, 297; Sec of War, 1914, 18; Sec of War, 1902; Cuevas, 349; Mestre, 257–58.

del Castillo, Porfirio
(Deceased January 8, 1957) A] February 26, 1884. B] Cuayuca, Puebla. C] Primary studies in Acatlán, Puebla; normal studies, Normal Institute of Puebla; teacher. D] *Constitutional deputy* from the State of Puebla, Dist. 12, 1916–17; *federal deputy* from the State of Puebla, Dist. 1, 1917–18; *federal deputy* from the State of Puebla, Dist. 9, 1920–22; *federal deputy* from the State of Puebla, Dist. 3, 1922–24. E] Secretary of the Anti-Reelectionist party, Tlaxcala. F] Secretary general of the State of Tlaxcala, 1914–15; *substitute governor* of Tlaxcala, 1915; inspector general of police, Puebla, 1920; treasurer of Pachuca, Hidalgo; director, Department of Government, Hidalgo, 1941. G] None. H] Employee, private firm; journalist. I] Son of Pascual Alejandro del Castillo and Elena Gobón Márquez. J] Joined the revolutionaries, 1910, with the rank of colonel; joined the Constitutionalists, 1913, with the rank of captain, rose to colonel; resigned from the army to protest against *Plutarco Elías Calles*, 1924. K] None. L] CyT, 163; C de D, 1916–17, 1917–18, 1920–22, 1922–24.

Delgadillo, Antonio
(Deceased December 30, 1914) A] 1881. B] Tepic, Nayarit. C] Early education unknown; enrolled in the National Military College, December 31, 1898, graduated as a 2nd lieutenant of cavalry, June 24, 1901; professor of fencing, Military Aspirants School, 1904–12. D] None. E] None. F] *Governor* and military commander of Colima, 1914. G] None. H] None. I] Unknown. J] Career military officer; joined the 13th Regiment, 1901; officer, machine gun company, 7th Regiment; staff officer, 10th Military Zone; fought in the Yucatán campaign, 1902–03; rank of

1st lieutenant, May 5, 1904; fought in the Yaqui campaign, 1904–08; rank of 2nd captain, 1909; supported Díaz against Madero, 1910–11; rank of 1st captain, September 11, 1911; second-in-command of the Mariano Escobedo Regiment, 1911–12, fought against the *Pascual Orozco* rebellion; rank of major, February 26, 1913; supported *Venustiano Carranza* a few days before switching back to *Victoriano Huerta*, 1913; rank of lt. colonel, April 4, 1913; rank of brigadier general, October 13, 1913; rank of brigade general, March 5, 1914. K] Captured and executed by the Constitutionalists, Poncitlán, Jalisco, December 30, 1914. L] Almada, Colima, 73; DP70, 629; Sec of War, 1914, 26; Peral, Appendix, 102; Mestre, 252.

Delgado, J. Jesús
(Deceased) A] February 3, 1890. B] Villa García, Zacatecas. C] Primary studies in the public school of Villa García; no degree. D] Mayor of Villa García, Zacatecas, 1918; *federal deputy* from the State of Zacatecas, Dist. 5, 1924–26, 1926–28; *federal deputy* from the State of Zacatecas, Dist. 4, 1930–32; *senator* from the State of Zacatecas, 1932–34, 1934–37. E] Member of the Mexican Liberal party. F] Interim governor of Zacatecas, 1929; official mayor of the Senate, 1937. G] None. H] Textile worker. I] Unknown. J] Unknown. K] None. L] C de D, 1924–26, 1926–28, 1930–32.

Delgado, José
(Deceased December 20, 1915) A] 1851. B] Tepic, Nayarit. C] Early education unknown; graduated as a construction engineer, National Military College, 1877. D] None. E] None. F] *Interim governor* of Zacatecas, 1912–13. G] None. H] None. I] Student with *Victoriano Huerta* at the National Military College. J] Career army officer; lieutenant, engineering staff, 1877; member, U.S.-Mexico Boundary Commission; inspector of telephones, secretariat of war; rank of major, 1891; assigned to the parade ground of Mexico, 1891–92; rejoined the army as a brigadier general, 1911; chief of arms in Chiapas, Oaxaca, and Sinaloa; supported *Francisco I. Madero*, 1911–13; rank of brigade general in the engineers, July 30,

1912; supported Huerta, 1913–14; fought in the battle of Zacatecas against the Constitutionalists, 1914; rank of division general, March 6, 1914; supported the Convention of Aguascalientes, 1914–15; supported *Francisco Villa*, 1915. K] Killed by Villistas trying to leave Mexico for the United States. L] Cuevas, 349; DP70, 630; Sec of War, 1914, 19; Mestre, 254.

Delhumeau, Eduardo
(Deceased 1926) A] 1866. B] Chihuahua, Chihuahua. C] Early education unknown; law degree, Scientific and Literary Institute of Chihuahua, 1888; prefect, Scientific and Literary Institute of Chihuahua. D] Local deputy to the state legislature of Chihuahua, 1904–05; *federal deputy* from the State of Jalisco, Dist. 10, 1908–10, 1910–12; *federal deputy* from the Federal District, Dist. 13, 1924–26. E] None. F] Clerk, Secretariat of Government, State of Chihuahua, 1882; public defender; secretary, civil and criminal court district; secretary, Higher Board of Public Education; interim judge, Federal Circuit Court, 1897–1901; private secretary to governor *Luis Terrazas*, 1903–04; secretary general of government of the State of Chihuahua, 1905–08; judge of the Superior Tribunal of Justice of Chihuahua; consulting lawyer to *Benjamín Hill*, secretary of war, 1920; attorney general of Mexico, 1922–24. G] None. H] Practicing lawyer; author. I] Son of Eduardo Delhumeau, lt. colonel and secretary of government of the state of Chihuahua; son *Enrique Delhumeau* served as secretary general of the government of the Federal District, 1923–26. J] None. K] None. L] DP70, 631; López, 285; Almada, 1960, 162; Quirós, 353–55.

Delhumeau, Enrique
(Deceased 1952) A] February 12, 1896. B] Early education unknown; preparatory studies from the National Preparatory School; legal studies, National School of Law, UNAM, 1914–19, graduating with a degree in law, September 25, 1919; professor of Spanish, National Preparatory School; professor of public law, National School of Law, UNAM. D] Mayor of Mixcoac, Federal District; member of the City

Council of Mixcoac, Federal District. E] Member of the Mexican Labor party. F] Lawyer, Secretariat of Industry, Commerce, and Labor; agent of the Ministerio Público; public defender; director, Department of Legal Affairs, Secretariat of Industry and Commerce; oficial mayor of the Department of the Federal District, 1923; secretary general of the Department of the Federal District, 1923–26. G] None. H] Author of many books; edited various newspapers and magazines. I] Son of *Eduardo Delhumeau*, attorney general of Mexico, 1922–24; grandson of Eduardo Delhumeau, secretary general of government of the State of Chihuahua; married Francisca Porras. J] None. K] None. L] Almada, 1960, 162; Dir social, 1935, 78; Quirós, 405–08; UNAM, law, 1912–16, 75.

Delorme y Campos, Jorge
(Deceased January 13, 1926) A] March 22, 1867. B] Guadalajara, Jalisco. C] Primary studies in Mexico City; preparatory studies in Guadalajara; law degree, School of Law, Guadalajara, December 5, 1891; teacher, Liceo for boys, Guadalajara; professor of logic, National Preparatory School. D] Local deputy to the state legislature of Jalisco; *federal deputy* from the State of Jalisco, Dist. 15, 1912–13. E] None. F] Director, Public Library of Jalisco, Guadalajara; chief of diplomatic affairs, Secretariat of Foreign Relations; oficial mayor of the Secretariat of Foreign Relations; *secretary* of foreign relations, 1913–14; consulting lawyer, Mexico–United States General Claims Committee, 1925–26. G] None. H] Journalist; active intellectual in French letters. I] Son of French and Mexican parents. J] None. K] None. L] Villaseñor, 313–14; C de D, 1912–13.

del Valle, Jesús
(Deceased January 3, 1938) A] July 7, 1853. B] Saltillo, Coahuila. C] Primary studies in Saltillo; preparatory studies in the Ateneo Fuente; law degree, Scientific and Literary Institute of Coahuila, 1879. D] *Governor* of Coahuila, 1909–11. E] Founded a party to oppose the candidate of *Miguel Cárdenas* for reelection as governor, including his friend *Pragedis de la*

Peña. r] Syndic, City Council of Saltillo, 1877; judge of the Viesca District, Coahuila, under Governor Evaristo Madero, 1879; judge, civil and criminal courts, Saltillo; attorney of the Superior Tribunal of Justice of Coahuila; justice of the Superior Tribunal of Justice of Coahuila; political boss of the Central District, Coahuila, 1884–88; interim governor of Coahuila for Governor *José María Garza Galán*, 1888, 1890. G] None. H] Practicing lawyer. I] Parents were wealthy and socially prominent in Coahuila; intimate friend of *José María Garza Galán*; defeated *Venustiano Carranza* for governor of Coahuila, 1909. J] None. K] None. L] Album; Mestre, 293; DP70, 2221.

de Negri, Ramón P.
(Deceased 1955) A] August, 1887. B] Hermosillo, Sonora. C] Early education unknown. D] None. E] Supported the Liberal movement under the Flores Magón brothers, 1906; supported *Francisco I. Madero*, 1909. F] Executive secretary, Agrarian Commission of Sonora, 1912; ambassador to Turkey; chargé d'affaires, Washington, D.C.; consul to San Francisco; consul to New York City; subsecretary of agriculture in charge of the secretariat, 1922; *secretary* of agriculture, 1922–24; ambassador to Germany and Austria, 1926–27; *secretary* of industry, 1929–30; ambassador to Belgium, 1930–32; ambassador to Chile, 1936; ambassador to Valencia, Spain, 1936–37. G] None. H] Unknown. I] Brother Manuel served in the foreign service, including as ambassador to Italy, 1932; son Carlos Denegri, a well-known journalist and author. J] None. K] None. L] Enc Mex, III, 426–27; Dir social, 1935, 271.

Díaz Dufoo, Carlos
(Deceased September 5, 1941) A] December 4, 1861. B] Veracruz, Veracruz. C] Primary studies in the Veracruz Institute of Esteban Morales; self-educated in Madrid, Spain; founder and chair of the second-year course in political economy, Free Law School, 1912; professor of political economy, National School of Law, UNAM. D] *Alternate federal deputy* from the State of Michoacán, Dist. 1, and from the State of Jalisco, Dist. 6, 1894–96;

alternate federal deputy from the State of Hidalgo, Dist. 9, 1896–98; *federal deputy* from the State of Hidalgo, Dist. 1, 1900–02, 1902–04; *federal deputy* from the State of Guerrero, Dist. 3, 1904–06, 1906–08, 1908–10, 1910–12. E] None. F] None. G] Member of the Mexican Academy of Language. H] Journalist, 1884– ; wrote for *El Globo*; founded *El Imparcial* with *Rafael Spíndola*, 1896; editor, 1896–1912; wrote for *La Prensa*, 1884; wrote for *El Nacional*, 1885; director of *El Ferrocarril* of Veracruz, 1887; cofounder and editor of *Revista Azul*, 1894–96, with *Manuel Gutiérrez Nájera*, leading intellectual and federal deputy; editorial writer for *Excélsior*, 1917–41, and *El Demócrata*; editor of *El Economista Mexicano*, 1910–11; dramatist; author of numerous books on politics, biography, and economics. I] Son of Pedro Díaz Fernández, a nationalized Spanish physician who served in the Mexican navy; married María A. Romo; son Carlos, Jr., a distinguished dramatist. J] None. K] None. L] UNAM, law, 1906–12, 120; DP70, 648; López, 290; Pasquel, Jalapa, 193–94; WWM35, 123; Carreño, 349; Illescas, 220–21; Mestre, 297; Enc Mex, III, 443–44; María y Campos, 296–97; Pasquel, 79–80.

Díaz Lombardo, Miguel
(Deceased September 13, 1924) A] 1866. B] Mexico City. C] Early education unknown; law degree, National School of Law, Mexico City, 1883–87; professor of law, National School of Law, Mexico City. D] None. E] Founded the Liberal Board in New York City. F] *Secretary* of public instruction, 1911–12; *ambassador* to France, 1912–13; *secretary* of foreign affairs, 1914–15. G] None. H] Practicing lawyer; in practice with *Emilio Pardo*. I] Son of Isidro Díaz, wealthy lawyer and alternate federal deputy from México, 1904–96, and Merced Lombardo; nephew of Concha Lombardo, wife of General Miramón; brother Francisco was a Supreme Court justice, 1930s; brother José, a lawyer. J] Supported *Francisco I. Madero*, 1909–10; Villista, 1913–15, served as General *Francisco Villa's* attorney in the United States. K] None. L] Almada, 1968, 167; DP70, 649; López, 291; Peral,

222; Mestre, 274; Puente, 205–09; UNAM, law, 1880–91, 52.

Díaz Mirón, Salvador
(Deceased June 12, 1928) A] December 14, 1853. B] Veracruz, Veracruz. C] Primary studies in Veracruz and Jalapa; secondary studies, Jalapa; no degree; director of the Colegio Preparatorio, Jalapa, 1911–13; taught mathematics in Santander, Spain, and Cuba, 1914; director of the Colegio Preparatorio, Veracruz, 1920–27. D] *Alternate federal deputy* from the State of Veracruz, Dist. 10, 1884–86; *federal deputy* from the State of Veracruz, Dist. 10, 1898–1900, 1900–02, 1902–04, 1904–06, 1906–08, 1908–10, 1910–12; *federal deputy from the State of Veracruz, Dist. 9, 1912–14, 1914–16.* E] None. F] Secretary of the city government of Veracruz, 1892. G] None. H] Journalist; director of *El Veracruzano, El Diario, El Orden,* 1881–86; director of *El Imparcial*; 1913–14; poet. I] Son of Manuel Díaz Mirón, poet, journalist, and governor of Veracruz, and Eufemia Ibáñez, poet; married Genoveva Acea; uncle of José Luis Díaz, intellectual and poet; nephew of Admiral Pedro Díaz Mirón. J] None. K] Exiled to the United States because of articles in *El Pueblo,* 1876–78; killed Federico Woller in a duel, jailed from 1892–96; detained for an altercation with a federal deputy, 1910–11; his violent personality caused him to have many duels. L] Carreño, 177, Puente, 97–160, Covarrubias, 363–70; Enc Mex, III, 447; DP70, 649–50; QesQ, 170–71; Pasquel, 77–78; Illescas, 185–86; López, 292.

Díaz (Mory), Porfirio
(Deceased July 2, 1915) A] September 15, 1830. B] Oaxaca, Oaxaca. C] Primary studies from the Amiga Private School, Oaxaca, and then public school; secondary and preparatory studies from the Conciliar Seminary of Oaxaca, 1843–49; abandoned seminary studies at the point of being ordained; completed law studies, Institute of Arts and Sciences of Oaxaca, 1850–54, but did not receive degree; gave private lessons to the son of lawyer Marcos Pérez, judge in Oaxaca; Benito Juárez helped Díaz remain at the institute after he lost the support of his uncle; librarian, Institute of Arts and Sciences of Oaxaca. D] Federal deputy from the State of Oaxaca, 1861; federal deputy from the State of Oaxaca, 1870–72; president of Mexico, 1877–80; *president* of Mexico, 1884–1911. E] None. F] None. G] Member of the Jockey Club, 1883. H] Supported himself in college with shoemaking and carpentry; practiced law with Marcos Pérez, 1850s; managed the business affairs of Juárez and Pérez, 1853; rancher, 1870. I] Son of José Faustino Díaz, a tinsmith, businessman, and veterinarian, and Petrona Mory; mother operated La Soledad Inn after his father died; first wife, Delfina Ortega, was his niece, the daughter of his sister Manuela and Dr. Manuel Ortega Reyes; second wife, Carmen Romero Castelló, was the daughter of *Manuel Romero Rubio,* his secretary of government; nephew *Félix Díaz, Jr.,* served as a federal deputy; student with *Félix Romero,* justice of the Supreme Court, 1889–1912; close school companion of *Matías Romero,* ambassador to the United States, 1893–98; studied under Benito Juárez. J] Volunteered with a group of friends to fight the North Americans, 1847; rebelled against Antonio López de Santa–Anna, and fought with Liberal guerrillas under Captain Herrera; captain, Oaxaca National Guard, 1857; commander of the Tehuantepec forces, 1858; rank of major, 1858; rank of colonel, 1860; brigade general, August 13, 1861; commander of the Army of the East against the French, 1863–67; rank of division general, October 14, 1863; commander, 2nd Division in Tehuacán, Puebla; led unsuccessful rebellion against Juárez in the Plan of La Noria, 1871; led successful rebellion against Sebastián Lerdo de Tejada, 1876. K] Exiled in Paris, 1911–15. L] QesQ, 172; Album; DP70, 643–44; Pavía, 2–7; Godoy, 20–21; Ramírez, 13–20.

Díaz Soto y Gama, Antonio
(Deceased 1967) A] 1880. B] San Luis Potosí, San Luis Potosí. C] Primary studies in a public school in San Luis Potosí; law degree, Scientific and Literary Institute of San Luis Potosí, 1900; professor of the history of the Mexican Revolution, National Preparatory School, 1933; professor of agrarian law, National School of Law, UNAM, 1930s. D] *Federal deputy*

from the State of San Luis Potosí, Dist. 2, 1920–22, 1922–24; *federal deputy* from the State of San Luis Potosí, Dist. 4, 1924–26; *federal deputy* from the State of San Luis Potosí, Dist. 2, 1928–30. E] Founding member and vice-president of the Liberal Club Ponciano Arriaga; organizer of the first Liberal Congress of Mexico, 1901; active in the Liberal party, 1904–12; cofounder of the National Agrarian party, June 13, 1920; supported *Alvaro Obregón* as a campaign propagandist, 1927–28; supported *Juan Andreu Almazán* for president, 1940; vice-president of the Mexican Democratic party (PDM), which ran Ezequiel Padilla for president, 1946; representative of the PDM to the Federal Electoral Commission, 1946. F] None. G] None. H] Wrote for *Renacimiento* and *El Universal*. I] Related to Valentín Gama, prominent educator at UNAM; son of lawyer Conrado Díaz Soto, a supporter of Sebastián Lerdo de Tejada. J] Joined *Emiliano Zapata*'s forces, 1914–20; represented Zapata at the Convention of Aguascalientes, 1914, and the Convention in Mexico City, January 1915. K] Notable orator during congressional debates in the 1920s; in exile in the United States for opposing the *Porfirio Díaz* regime, 1902–04; named secretary of justice but refused appointment, 1915. L] Letters; Medina, 20, 61; DP70, 2015; Enc Mex, III, 464; Cockcroft, 71; López Escalera, 296.

Díaz (Varela), Félix, Jr.
(Deceased July 9, 1945) A] February 17, 1868. B] Oaxaca, Oaxaca. C] Early education unknown; graduated as a military engineer from the National Military College, 1888. D] *Alternate federal deputy* from the State of Oaxaca, Dist. 12, 1894–96; *alternate federal deputy* from the State of Veracruz, Dist. 1, 1896–98, 1898–1900, under father-in-law *Leandro M. Alcolea*; *federal deputy* from the State of Veracruz, Dist. 6, 1900–02, 1902–04, 1904–06, 1906–08; *federal deputy* from the State of Veracruz, Dist. 7, 1908–10, 1910–12. E] Candidate for governor of Oaxaca, 1902. F] Member of the Exploratory Geographic Commission, 1901; consul general in Chile, 1902–04; inspector of police, Mexico City, 1904; chief of presi-

dential staff, 1909; interim governor of Oaxaca, 1910; ambassador to Japan, 1913. G] None. H] Businessman; in business with Antenor Sala, constitutional deputy, 1916–17. I] Son of Félix Díaz, Sr., governor of Oaxaca, radical Liberal, brigadier general, and brother of *Porfirio Díaz*, and Rafaela Varela; student with *Victoriano Huerta* at the National Military College; married Isabella Alcolea, daughter of Leandro Alcolea, federal deputy from Veracruz. J] Career military officer; rank of captain, 1900; rank of brigadier general of engineers, 1909; separated from the army under President Madero, 1911–13; conspired against Madero in Veracruz, 1912; imprisoned, Santiago Tlatelolco Military Prison and the Federal District Penitentiary, 1912–13; rank of brigade general, February 10, 1913; a chief conspirator with Generals Manuel Mondragón and *Bernardo Reyes* in the uprising against Madero, February 9–19, 1913; fought against the Constitutionalists, 1913; retired from the service, October 27, 1913; supported Obregón against Carranza, 1920. K] Exiled to Havana and New York City, 1914–16; voluntary exile to New Orleans, 1920–37; President Díaz sent him to Chile as a consul to punish him for running for governor of Oaxaca without his permission, 1902. 1-DP70, 641–42; López, 290–91; Sec of War, 1914, 21; Enc Mex, III, 442.

Diéguez, Manuel M.
(Deceased April 20, 1924) A] 1874. B] Guadalajara, Jalisco. C] Only completed part of primary education; no degree. D] Mayor of Cananea, 1912–13; *governor* of Jalisco, 1917. E] None. F] *Governor* and military commander of Jalisco, 1914–16; *governor* of Jalisco, 1916–17. G] Organized a strike with *Esteban Baca Calderón* against the Cananea Consolidated Copper Company, 1906. H] Farm laborer; miner, Green Consolidated Mining Company; employee, company store, and miner, Cananea Consolidated Copper Company. I] Son of Crisanto Diéguez, laborer, and Juana Lara; close friends with Esteban Baca Calderón, *Juan José Ríos*, and *Pablo Quiroga Treviño*, revolutionaries and governors, from mining days in Cananea. J] Joined the navy and worked in the war transport

Oaxaca, out of Mazatlán, 1899; fought against *Pascual Orozco*, 1912; organized 400 men to join General *Alvaro Obregón* against *Victoriano Huerta*, 1913; rank of lt. colonel, 1913; brigade commander, Army of the Northeast, 1913–14; represented Colonel Fermín Carpio at the Convention of Aguascalientes, 1914; chief of military operations in Chihuahua, 1919; remained loyal to *Venustiano Carranza*, 1920; supported the *Adolfo de la Huerta* rebellion, fighting in Guerrero, Oaxaca, and Chiapas, 1923–24. K] Condemned to 15 years in the San Juan Ulloa prison for directing the Cananea strike; imprisoned from 1906–11, until freed by the Revolution; captured and executed as a rebel, April 20, 1924, in Tuxtla Gutiérrez, Chiapas. L] Enc Mex, III, 464–65; DP70, 651; QesQ, 173–74; Bórquez, 145–47; Morales Jiménez, 23–25.

Díez Gutiérrez (y López Portillo), Carlos
(Deceased August 21, 1898) A] May 23, 1843. B] La Pendencia, Valle del Maíz, San Luis Potosí. C] Primary studies, Valle del Maíz, continued in San Luis Potosí; secondary studies, San Luis Potosí, San Luis Potosí; law degree, School of Law, Mexico City, 1869. D] Federal deputy from San Luis Potosí, 1869–71; *senator* from San Luis Potosí, 1884–86; *governor* of San Luis Potosí, 1885–98. E] None. F] Provisional governor of San Luis Potosí, 1877–80; secretary of government, 1880–84. G] Member of the Jockey Club, 1883. H] None. I] Son of Rafael Díez Gutiérrez y Fernández Barragán, landowner, and Agustina López Portillo; brother *Pedro Díez Gutiérrez*, senator from San Luis Potosí; married cousin Juana Díez Gutiérrez y Barajas; grandson of Juana Barragán, wealthy daughter of rich landowner Felipe Barragán; related to Arguinzoniz, Verástegui, and Escontría families; second wife, Mercedes Barajas; related to *Juan F. Barragán* family through marriage; aunt María de Jesús Díez Gutiérrez, is grandmother of *José Rodríguez Cabo*, secretary of communications. J] Interrupted studies to fight the French; joined General *Geronimo Treviño*, 1867; supported *Porfirio Díaz* in the Plan of Tuxtepec, 1876; military commander and gov-

ernor of San Luis Potosí, 1876. K] None. L] Mestre, 202; Ipiña de Corsi, 1956, 65, 80; Godoy, 121; Pavía, 309–11; Covarrubias, I, 379–86; Cockcroft, 38.

Díez Gutiérrez (y López Portillo), Pedro
(Deceased March 5, 1894) A] May 28, 1845. B] Río Verde, San Luis Potosí. C] Early education unknown; studies towards a medical degree, incomplete; law degree. D] Federal deputy from San Luis Potosí, 1877–78, 1878–80; senator from San Luis Potosí, 1880–82; governor of San Luis Potosí, 1880–84; *senator* from San Luis Potosí, 1888–90, 1890–92, 1892–94. E] None. F] None. G] None. H] Practicing lawyer; owner of the Cárdenas hacienda; sold railroad concessions to North American investors; amassed a fortune as a businessman. I] Son of Rafael Díez Gutiérrez y Fernández Barragán, wealthy landowner, and Agustina López Portillo; brother of *Carlos Díez Gutiérrez*, governor of San Luis Potosí; grandson of Pedro Díez Gutiérrez and Juana Barragán, wealthy landowners; married Esther Guzmán, from a wealthy landowning family; aunt, María de Jesús Díez Gutiérrez, grandmother of *José Rodríguez Cabo*, secretary of communications, 1914–15. J] None. K] None. L] Peral, Appendix, 107; Hombres prominentes, 315–16; Ipiña de Corsi, 1956, 65; Cockcroft, 17; Rice, 236; Holms, 330; Mestre, 186.

Dinorín Rivera, Federico
(Deceased September 5, 1944) A] 1879. B] Xochiapulco, Tetela de Ocampo, Puebla. C] No formal education. D] *Constitutional deputy* from the State of Puebla, Dist. 13, 1916–17. E] None. F] None. G] None. H] Unknown. I] Son of Francisco Dinorín and Julia Rivera, peasants; married Felicitas Báez; second wife, Emma Dinorín Orozco. J] Supported *Francisco I. Madero*, rank of sergeant, 1911; joined the Constitutionalists with the rank of 2nd captain, 1913; commander, mountain rifle battalion, 1913–14; rank of lt. colonel in the cavalry, 1914; commander, mountain rifle battalion, 1914–17; rank of colonel, April 1917; commander, 5th of May Battalion, 1917; commander, 37th Battalion, 1917; mili-

tary commander in Puebla; fought the Zapatistas; supported the *Adolfo de la Huerta* Rebellion, 1923; expelled from the army, 1924; reintegrated into the army with the rank of colonel in the cavalry, 1944. K] None. L] CyT, 220–21; C de D, 1916–17.

Domínguez (Palencia), Belisario
(Deceased October 7, 1913) A] April 25, 1863. B] Comitán, Chiapas. C] Primary studies in Comitán; preparatory studies at the Institute of Arts and Sciences, Las Casas, 1879; medical degree, Institute of Arts and Sciences, Las Casas; three years of medical studies in Paris, France, graduating as a surgeon, School of Medicine, Sorbonne, 1889. D] Mayor of Comitán, 1911–12; *alternate senator* in functions from Chiapas, 1912–13. E] None. F] None. G] None. H] Practicing physician, Comitán, 1889–1903, 1904–11; founded *El Vavte*, Comitán, 1904. I] Son of Cleofás Domínguez, businessman, and Pilar Palencia, from Guatemala; married Delina Zebadua. J] None. K] Spoke against *Victoriano Huerta* on the Senate floor; Huerta had him murdered for his public pronouncements; Mexican government created the Belisario Domínguez award in his memory, 1952, for distinguished service to Mexico. L] Gordillo y Ortiz, 68; García Rivas, 252–54; Armijo, 172–74; DP70, 661; QesQ, 177.

Domínguez, Manuel
(Deceased March 16, 1910) A] August 6, 1830. B] Querétaro, Querétaro. C] Primary, secondary, and preparatory studies at San Ildefonso, Mexico City; medical degree, National School of Medicine, Mexico City, 1854; intern, San Hipólito Hospital, 1849 (removed by General Santa–Anna); prefect, National School of Medicine; professor of therapeutics, National School of Medicine; dean, National School of Medicine; director, National School of the Blind. D] President of the City Council of Mexico City; *federal deputy* from the State of México, Dist. 4, 1894–96, 1896–398, 1898–1900, 1900–02; *senator* from the State of Zacatecas, 1906–08, 1908–10. E] None. F] Prefect of San Juan del Río; imperial prefect of Querétaro; *governor* of

the Federal District, 1893; director, Abandoned Girls Home, 1895– ; director, San Andrés Hospital; director, Casa Cuna. G] Director, National Academy of Medicine. H] Author of many scientific works. I] Unknown. J] None. K] None. L] Peña, 369–70.

Domínguez (Salazar), Norberto
(Deceased June 21, 1931) A] 1867. B] Valle de Zaragosa, Chihuahua. C] Primary studies, Hidalgo del Parral, Chihuahua; preparatory studies, Scientific and Literary Institute of Hidalgo, Pachuca; engineering degree, National School of Mines, Mexico City; professor, Juárez Institute, Durango; professor, Colegio Rosales, Culiacán, Sinaloa; professor, National Preparatory School; professor, National School of Mines. D] *Senator* from Sinaloa, 1902–04, 1906–08, 1910–11; *federal deputy* from the State of Chihuahua, Dist. 2, 1920–22. E] Member of the Científico party. F] Director general of the mails, 1903–11; *secretary* of communications and public works, 1911; director of the mint, Culiacán. G] Founder and director of the National Chamber of Mining. H] Engineer; manager of the National Bank of Mexico, Chihuahua; Manager, National Bank of Mexico, Zamora, Michoacán. I] Unknown. J] None. K] None. L] DP70, 663; Mestre, 285; Almada, 1968, 173.

Domínguez Suárez, Luis Felipe
(Deceased December 28, 1928) A] May 5, 1862. B] Hacienda San José del Río, Municipio de Balacán, Tabasco. C] Early education unknown; no degree. D] None. E] Candidate for governor of Tabasco, 1919. F] *Provisional governor* and military commander of Tabasco, 1914; *governor* and military commander of Tabasco, 1916–17. G] None. H] Landowner. I] Son of Luis Felipe Domínguez Abreu, large landowner, and Rosa Suárez Zurita, sister of *José María Pino Suárez*, vice-president of Mexico, 1911–13. J] Supported *Francisco I. Madero*, 1910; accompanied José María Pino Suárez to Guatemala, 1910; joined the Constitutionalists, 1913; commander of the Isthmus of Tehuantepec Military Zone, 1917; op-

posed the Plan of Agua Prieta, 1920; rank of brigadier general. K] Forced to leave Tabasco for political reasons, 1919. L] Bulnes, 163, 138; Almanaque de Tabasco, 150–51.

Dondé, Rafael
(Deceased November 9, 1911) A] September 5, 1832. B] Campeche, Campeche. C] Primary and secondary studies at the Institute of Campeche, Campeche; completed secondary studies in Mexico City; preparatory studies at the Colegio de San Ildefonso, Mexico City; law degree, National School of Law, Mexico City. D] Local deputy to the state legislature of Morelos; local deputy to the state legislature of Hidalgo; president of the Senate, 1876; *alternate senator* from the State of Sonora, 1892–94, 1894–96, 1896–98, 1898–1900, 1900–04; *senator* from the State of Sonora, 1904–06, 1906–08, 1908–10, 1910–11. E] None. F] Chief clerk, Supreme Court; interim secretary of the Supreme Court; oficial mayor of the Supreme Court. G] None. H] Practicing lawyer; practiced law with *Ezequiel Chávez*, federal deputy from Chihuahua, 1906–12. I] Unknown. J] Accompanied Benito Juárez to El Paso during the French Intervention. K] None. L] C de S, 1904–06; C de S, 1900–02, 6; Peral, Appendix, 108; Godoy, 258; DP70, 665; Hombres prominentes, 271–72; Peña, 374.

Dorador, Silvestre
(Deceased November 16, 1930) A] December 31, 1870. B] Aguascalientes, Aguascalientes. C] Early education unknown; no degree. D] Mayor of Durango, 1912, 1913–14; *constitutional deputy* from the State of Durango, Dist. 1, 1916–17; local deputy to the state legislature of Durango, 1917–18; mayor of Durango, 1919; *federal deputy* from the State of Durango, Dist. 1, 1926–28; local deputy to the state legislature of Durango, 1928–30. E] None. F] None. G] Propagandist, Workers and Artisans Mutual. H] Bookbinder in youth, started own business; founded a successful printing business, 1913; journalist. I] Parents were from Durango. J] Supported *Francisco I. Madero*; supported *Venustiano Carranza*;

jailed for revolutionary activities, 1913. K] None. L] DP70, 666; Almanaque de Aguascalientes, 127; Rouaix, 128–29.

Dorantes, Prudenciano
(Deceased August 11, 1907) A] March 19, 1840. B] San Miguel, Temazcaltzingo, México. C] Secondary studies, Colegio de San Nicolás, Morelia, Michoacán; law degree, School of Law, Colegio de San Nicolás, Morelia; professor of international law, School of Law, Colegio de San Nicolás. D] Local deputy to the state legislature of Michoacán; *governor* of Michoacán, 1881–85. E] None. F] Judge, Maravatio, Michoacán; judge, Morelia; oficial mayor of the Secretariat of Government of the State of Michoacán, 1877; *justice* of the Supreme Court, 1884–1907; *president* of the Supreme Court, 1897. G] None. H] Practicing lawyer. I] Unknown. J] None. K] None. L] Dicc mich, 128; Mestre, 228; Blue Book, 1901, 29; González de Cosío, 7.

Dozal, Fortunato
(Deceased 1947) A] 1885. B] Ciudad Guerrero, Chihuahua. C] Primary studies at Professor Mariano Irigoyen's School, Ciudad Guerrero; preparatory studies, Institute of Sciences, Chihuahua, Chihuahua; engineering degree, National School of Engineering, Mexico City, 1910. D] None. E] None. F] Director general of education, State of Chihuahua, 1911–312; subsecretary of agriculture, 1920–21, in charge of the Secretariat, 1921–22. G] None. H] Practicing engineer. I] Related to (probably son or nephew of) Tomás Dozal y Hermosillo, secretary general of government and political boss of the Guerrero District; brother Jesús María, a lawyer; brother of Juan Dozal, revolutionary and governor of Nayarit, 1914–15; married Elena Castro. J] Resigned post after *Pascual Orozco* rebelled, 1912. K] None. L] Dir social, 1935, 79; López, 304; Almada, 1968, 174; DP70, 668.

Dublán, Manuel
(Deceased May 31, 1891) A] April 1, 1830. B] Oaxaca, Oaxaca. C] Primary and secondary studies in Oaxaca; law degree, Literary Institute of Oaxaca, Decem-

ber 2, 1852; director, Institute of Arts and Sciences of Oaxaca; professor, Institute of Arts and Sciences of Oaxaca. D] Member of the City Council of Oaxaca, Oaxaca; local deputy to the state legislature of Oaxaca, 1851–52; federal deputy from the State of Oaxaca, 1861, 1870–72, 1878–80; senator from the Federal District, 1880; *senator* from Oaxaca, 1882–84, 1884–86, 1884–86; *alternate federal deputy* from Oaxaca, Dist. 1, 1884–86. E] Head of the Juarista party faction at the time of Benito Juárez's death, united with Lerdo de Tejada's group. F] Official, Supreme Court, 1852; secretary general of government of the state of Oaxaca under *Porfirio Díaz*, 1858; civil judge; judge of the Superior Tribunal of Justice of Oaxaca (president); justice of the Supreme Court, 1861. G] None. H] None. I] Son of French immigrant father and Oaxacan mother; orphaned at a young age; married Juana Maza, sister of Benito Juárez's wife, Margarita; son *Eduardo Dublán Maza*, federal deputy from San Luis Potosí, 1892–1902; son Juan Dublán Maza, federal deputy from Oaxaca, 1892–1908. J] Accompanied Juárez duing the Reform Wars; served Maximilian's government in Oaxaca. K] None. L] Mestre, 173–74; Velasco, 169ff; González y Cosío, 7; DP70, 669; Pavía, 19:25; Sierra, 91–92; Hombres prominentes, 25–29, 399–400; Armijo, 136–37; UNAM, law, 1886–91, 31.

Dublán Maza, Eduardo
(Deceased) A] Unknown. B] Oaxaca, Oaxaca. C] Early education unknown; university studies, Mexico City. D] Member of the City Council of Mexico City, 1884–85, 1885–86; *federal deputy* from the State of San Luis Potosí, Dist. 5, 1886–88, 1888–90, 1890–92, 1892–94, 1894–96, 1896–98, 1898–1900, 1900–02. E] None. F] None. G] None. H] Businessman; printer and engraver. I] Son of *Manuel Dublán*, secretary of the treasury, 1884–91, and Juana Maza; married Josefa Juárez, his cousin and daughter of Benito Juárez; brother Juan Dublán Maza served as a federal deputy from Oaxaca, 1892–1908. J] None. K] None. L] Hombres prominentes, 399–400.

Duplán (Maldonado), Carlos
(Deceased May 8, 1959) A] April 17, 1890. B] Pichucalco, Chiapas. C] Primary and secondary studies, Model School of Orizaba, Veracruz; preparatory studies at the Colegio de Orizaba and the Colegio del Estado de Puebla; studies, Bliss Electrical School, Washington, D.C., and in accounting. D] *Alternate constitutional deputy* from the Federal District, Dist. 6, in functions, 1916–17. E] Supported *Francisco I. Madero's* presidential campaign, 1909–10. F] Director, Department of Taxes, Secretariat of the Treasury; director, Department of Trade, Secretariat of Industry and Commerce. G] Member of the National Atheneum of Arts and Sciences; member of the Bankers Club. H] Unknown. I] Son of Ernesto Duplán, physician, and Virginia Maldonado; married Asunción Gómez Daza y González, daughter of lawyer Luis Gómez Daza of Puebla; identical twin of *Oscar E. Duplán*, oficial mayor of the Secretariat of Foreign Relations. J] None. K] None. L] Blue Book, 144; Linajes, 92–94; Almanaque de Chiapas, 145.

Duplán (Maldonado), Oscar E.
(Deceased April 23, 1942) A] April 17, 1890. B] Pichucalco, Chiapas. C] Primary and secondary studies in the Model School of Orizaba, Veracruz; preparatory studies at the Colegio de Orizaba and the Colegio del Estado de Puebla; no degree. D] None. E] Joined *Francisco I. Madero's* presidential campaign as a student, 1909. F] Joined the Foreign Service as a secretary of the Mexican embassy, Washington, D.C., 1910; second secretary, Mexican embassy, Washington, D.C., 1917–19; director of correspondence, Secretariat of the Treasury; accountant, confidential agent of Mexico to the United States; consul, Paris, France; tax inspector, Secretariat of the Treasury; customs superintendent, National Railroads of Mexico; oficial mayor, Secretariat of Government; oficial mayor, Secretariat of Agriculture; oficial mayor, Secretariat of Foreign Relations, 1932; ambassador to Colombia, 1933–34. G] Member of the Geographic Society of Washington. H] None. I] Son of Ernesto Duplán, physician, and Virginia

Maldonado; identical twin brother *Carlos Duplán*, constitutional deputy, 1916–17. J] None. K] None. L] Dir soc, 1935, 215; Gordillo y Ortiz, 70; Linajes, 92–94; Almanaque de Chiapas, 145.

E

Eguía Lis, Rafael
(Deceased January 11, 1915) A] 1865. B] Cuautitlán, Mexico. C] Early education unknown; engineering degree, National Military College; professor, School of Military Aspirants, Tlalpan; professor, National Military College, specialist in artillery. D] None. E] None. F] Political boss of Quintana Roo, 1913; *governor* of Quintana Roo, 1913–15. G] None. H] None. I] Related to (probably father or uncle of) Joaquín Eguía Lis, rector of UNAM, 1910–13; brother Felipe, artillery engineer. J] Career military officer; fought against *Francisco I. Madero*'s forces at Casas Grandes, 1910–11; commander of the Military Zone in Chihauhua, 1911; rank of brigadier general, March 6, 1911; left federal army; Constitutionalist, 1913–15; rank of brigade general, January 1, 1914; commander of the Military Zone in Quintana Roo, 1913–15. K] Killed with Jesús Carranza in Xamboan, Oaxaca. L] Sec of War, 1914, 20; Mestre, 258; DP70, 690; Alvarez Corral, 47; Cuevas, 356.

Elguero (Iturbide), Francisco
(Deceased December 17, 1932) A] March 24, 1856. B] Morelia, Michoacán. C] Primary studies at the Ateneo Mexicano of Celso Acevedo, Mexico City; preparatory studies at the Conciliar Seminary of Morelia; law degree, School of Law, Colegio de San Nicolás, Morelia, Michoacán, 1880; professor of forensic eloquence, National School of Law. D] *Federal deputy* from the State of Michoacán, Dist. 14, 1912–13, 1914–15. E] None. F] Judge, Zamora, Michoacán, 1881–83. G] None. H] Practicing lawyer, Zamora, Michoacán, 1884–1911; lawyer, Mexico City, 1911–14, 1919– ; journalist; author of several books. I] Son of Manuel Elguero and Guadalupe Iturbide; brother José a journalist and distinguished historian; disciple of Rafael Angel de la Peña. J] None. K] In

exile, United States, 1914–16, in Cuba, 1916–19; had to move to Mexico City for political reasons, 1911. L] DP70, 696; Mestre, 287; Carreño, 177–78; QesQ, 190–91; WWM45, 36.

Elías, Francisco S.
(Deceased 1963) A] 1882. B] Tecoripa, Sonora. C] Early education unknown; no degree. D] None. E] Candidate for governor of Sonora, 1927. F] Customs inspector and financial agent, New York City, 1915; *governor* of Sonora, 1921–22, 1922–23, 1929–31; *secretary* of agriculture and development, 1931–32, 1932–34. G] None. H] Businessman, Arizona and New York City; rancher; wealthy landowner. I] Cousin of President *Plutarco Elías Calles*. J] Constitutionalist; represented the Constitutionalists as a financial agent in Arizona, 1913; supported the Plan of Agua Prieta, 1920. K] *Alvaro Obregón* disliked him because he would not declare Obregón's friend Carlos Robinson senator-elect when he was interim goveror of Sonora; gave most of his personal fortune to defeat *Victoriano Huerta*, 1913–14; defeated for the governorship by President Obregón's imposition of *Fausto Topete*, 1927. L] DP70, 697; Almanaque de Sonora, 1982, 128; Gruening, 472.

Elías Calles, Plutarco
(Deceased October 19, 1945) A] January 27, 1877. B] Guaymas, Sonora. C] Primary studies at Public School No. 1, Guaymas, Sonora, and at Hermosillo; teaching certificate, Colegio Benigno López y Sierra, 1893; teacher, 1894; taught in Guaymas, Hermosillo, Fronteras; school inspector, Guaymas, 1903; teacher, Colegio de la Moneda. D] Local deputy to the state legislature of Nuevo León; *governor* of Sonora, 1917–19; *president* of Mexico, 1924–28. E] Joined the Anti-Reelectionist party, 1910; candidate for federal deputy, 1910; directed the presidential campaign of General *Alvaro Obregón*, 1920; member Organizing Committee for the National Revolutionary party, December 1928. F] Political boss, Agua Prieta, 1912–13; *provisional governor* and military commander of Sonora, 1915–17; *secretary* of industry, commerce, and labor, 1919–20; *secretary* of war, 1920; *sec-*

retary of government, 1920–23; *secretary* of war, 1929, 1931–32; *secretary* of the treasury, 1933. G] None. H] Rancher, Fronteras, 1903; small businessman; bookkeeper, flour mill, Agua Prieta, 1910–11. I] Illegitimate son of Plutarco Elías Lucero, lawyer and important landowner, and María de Jesús Campuzano; stepfather, Juan B. Calles, owned small bar, raised Plutarco when mother died, 1881; grandson of José Juan Elías, owner of El Leoncito and Santa Rosa haciendas; married Francisca Bernal; second wife, Natalia Chacón; son *Rodolfo Elías Calles*, governor of Sonora, 1931–34; son Plutarco *Elías Calles (Chacón), Jr.*, federal deputy, 1930–32, 1934–37; grandson Fernando Elías Calles Alvarez, subsecretary of government, 1985; daughter Hortensia married to Fernando Torreblanca, subsecretary of foreign relations, 1932–35. J] Supported the Maderistas against *Porfirio Díaz* as a journalist in Hermosillo, 1911; supported *Francisco I. Madero* against the *Pascual Orozco* rebellion, 1912; seconded the Plan of Guadalupe, 1913; joined the Constitutionalists, organized own forces, February 26, 1913; rank of captain, 1913; rank of lt. colonel, 1913; rank of colonel, October 1, 1914; rank of brigadier general, October 18, 1914; organized the Calles Brigade, 1915; rank of brigade general, September 22, 1915; rank of division general, April 14, 1920; left cabinet to proclaim the Plan of Agua Prieta, 1920. K] Forced to emigrate from Guaymas for attacking Díaz in newspaper articles, 1904; in exile, California, 1936–41; reintegrated into the Mexican army, 1942. L] Garrido, 52; DP70, 697–98; Dir social, 1935, 215–16; Almanaque de Nuevo León, 103–04; Moreno, 333–43; Aguilar Camín, 180ff; WWM45, 17.

Elías Calles (Chacón), Jr., Plutarco
A] July 28, 1901. B] Guaymas, Sonora. C] Primary studies in Guaymas; secondary and preparatory studies, military academy, Mt. Tamalpais, California; engineering course, New York. D] Local deputy to the state legislature of Nuevo León; *federal deputy* from the State of Nuevo León, Dist. 1, 1930–32, member of the Great Committee; mayor of Monterrey, 1933; federal deputy from the State of Nuevo

León, Dist. 4, 1934–37, member of the Great Committee. E] Opposed General Fortunato Zuazua for governor of Nuevo León, which led to a bloody confrontation between his supporters and Zuazua's, 1935. F] *Provisional governor* of Nuevo León, 1929, replacing *Aarón Sáenz*. G] None. H] Businessman. I] Son of President *Plutarco Elías Calles* and Natalia Chacón; brother of *Rodolfo Elías Calles*, secretary of communications and public works, 1934–35; brother Alfredo Elías Calles Chacón, rancher; nephew Fernando Elías Calles Alvarez, subsecretary of government, 1985; married Elísa Sáenz Garza, sister of *Aarón Sáenz*, secretary of industry and commerce, with whom he had a business partnership in the El Mante sugar refinery. J] None. K] None. L] Almanaque de Nuevo León, 103–04; DBGM, 1984, 130.

Elías Calles, Rodolfo
(Deceased 1965) A] 1900. B] Guaymas, Sonora. C] Secondary studies, Colegio Guaymense, Guaymas, 1912–13; private accounting studies, Colegio Palmore, El Paso, Texas, 1913–15; studies in New York. D] Mayor of Cajeme. E] None. F] Treasurer general of the State of Sonora, 1923–25; *governor* of Sonora, 1931–34; *secretary* of communications and public works, 1934–35. G] None. H] Rancher in Cajeme; founded first bank in Ciudad Obregón, 1926; founded Mercantile and Agricultural Bank, Hermosillo; general manager, El Mante Sugar Mill, 1920s. I] Son of President *Plutarco Elías Calles* and Natalia Chacón; brother of *Plutarco Elías Calles Chacón, Jr.*, federal deputy, 1930–32; brother Alfredo, a rancher; nephew, Fernando Elías Calles Sáenz, career foreign service officer; nephew Fernando Elías Calles Alvarez, subsecretary of government, 1985; brother-in-law of Elisa Sáenz Garza, sister of *Aarón Sáenz*. J] None. K] None. L] HA, 21 Nov. 1983, 17; DBGM, 1984, 130; HA, 20 Jan. 1987, 34; DP70, 698; Almanaque de Sonora, 1982, 129; de Parodi, 79–85.

Enríquez, Juan de la Luz
(Deceased March 17, 1892) A] May 16, 1836. B] Tlacotalpam, Veracruz. C] Primary studies at a private school in Tlaco-

talpam; cadet, Naval Military College, 1853–55, graduating as a 2nd lieutenant in the engineers. D] *Governor* of Veracruz, 1884–92. E] None. F] None. G] None. H] None. I] Son of Camilo Enríquez and Tranquilina Loera, a middle-class family; brother Félix fought against the French; served in the same cadet company as Sóstenes Rocha and Juan Malpica, under the leadership of Captain Miguel Miramón; met General *Porfirio Díaz* when he was a federal deputy, 1861. J] Career military officer; assigned to an engineering company under Máximo Camacho, 1855; rank of 1st lieutenant, 1859; rank of 2nd captain, 1859; rank of major in the infantry, 1860, serving under Sóstenes Rocha; fought with General Díaz against the French, 1863–65, 1866–67; rank of lt. colonel, October, 1866; commander of mililtary operations in Puebla; commander, 1st Military Zone; commander of the Customshouse, Veracruz, Veracruz, 1876; commander in various states, including Yucatán, Tabasco, Campeche, and Chiapas, 1877; rank of brigade general, July 1877. K] Captured and imprisoned by the French in Puebla, 1865–66, and exchanged for French prisoners, 1866; Díaz lived on his brother-in-law's hacienda after his defeat in 1872; saved Diaz's life by getting him aboard a steamship bound for Oaxaca, 1876. L] Pavía, 383–86; Hombres prominentes, 85–86; Pasquel, 1972, 111–26.

Enríquez (Siqueiros), Ignacio C.
(Deceased) A] August 26, 1889. B] Chihuahua, Chihuahua. C] Primary studies at the Annex to the Normal School of Chihuahua; secondary and preparatory studies at the Private School of Agriculture of Ciudad Juárez; agricultural engineering degree, School of Agriculture, University of Illinois. D] Mayor of Mexico City, 1915; *constitutional deputy* from the State of Chihuahua, Dist. 1, 1916–17, but did not attend; *governor* of Chihuahua, 1920–24. E] Candidate for senator from Chihuahua, 1924, but did not run; candidate for governor of Chihuahua against the National Revolutionary party, 1930. F] Consul general, New York City, 1914; *governor* of Chihuahua, 1915–16; oficial mayor in charge of the Secretariat of War, 1916–17;

governor of Chihuahua, 1918. G] None. H] Experimental farming, Hacienda de Rubio, Municipio Cuauhtémoc, Chihuahua; farmed the Hacienda of Bojayito, Hidalgo, 1930– . I] Son of Ignacio Enríquez, local deputy and political boss of Iturbide District, Chihuahua, and Josefa Siqueiros. J] Joined the Constitutionalists under *Alvaro Obregón* as a 2nd captain, February 1913; wounded, battle for Naco and Santa Rosa, 1913; escorted *Venustiano Carranza* from Sonora to Chihuahua, 1914; battalion commander against *Francisco Villa*'s forces, 1915; served under General *Pablo González*, Army of the East, 1915; rank of colonel, 1915; rank of brigadier general, May 12, 1916; commander of auxiliary troops, Chihuahua, 1919–20; rank of brigade general, 1920; supported Obregón against Carranza, 1920; commander of military operations against *Adolfo de la Huerta*, Chihuahua, 1923; retired from the army, 1928. K] None. L] DP70, 706; Almada, 1968, 180–88; Almada, 525–31.

Escandón (y Barrón), Pablo
(Deceased March 31, 1926) A] 1857. B] Morelos. C] Early education unknown; no degree. D] *Federal deputy* from the State of Guanajuato, Dist. 8, 1894–96, 1896–98; *federal deputy* from Guanajuato, Dist. 7, 1898–1900, 1900–02, 1902–04, 1904–06, 1906–08, 1908–10, 1910–12; *governor* of Morelos, 1909–11. E] None. F] *Interim governor* of Morelos, 1908–09. G] Shareholder in the Jockey Club, 1901. H] Owner of Xochimancas and Atlihuayan haciendas, Morelos. I] Parents were wealthy landowners; related to Eustaquio Escandón, banker; brother of Manuel Escandón y Barrón. J] Career army officer; rank of brigadier general, March 11, 1914; chief of staff for President *Porfirio Díaz*. K] Went into exile to the United States, 1911. L] DP70, 715; Mestre, 277; Blue Book, 1901, 89; WWM45, 37; Album.

Escobar, José Gonzalo
(Deceased 1969) A] 1892. B] Mazatlán, Sinaloa. C] Early education unknown; no degree. D] None. E] None. F] None. G] None. H] Unknown. I] Unknown. J] Joined the Maderistas, April 1911; garrison commander, Parral, Chihuahua; mili-

tary commander, various zones; opposed *Venustiano Carranza* in the Plan of Agua Prieta, 1920; represented President *Adolfo de la Huerta* in the peace negotiations with *Francisco Villa*, 1920; opposed the de la Huerta rebellion, 1923; defeated troops loyal to de la Huerta in the battles of Palo Verde and Ocotlán, 1924; defeated and captured General Arnulfo Gómez, 1927; rank of division general, October 1927; led the last major rebellion, supported by the military, against the government, 1929; reintegrated into the army after returning to Mexico. K] Exiled to the United States and Canada, 1929–43. L] DP70, 716; López, 320.

Escobar (Zerman), Rómulo
(Deceased January 12, 1946) A] February 17, 1872. B] Ciudad Juárez, Chihuahua. C] Primary studies, Ciudad Juárez; agricultural engineering degree, National School of Agriculture, November 16, 1891; cofounder of the Private School of Agriculture, Ciudad Juárez, February 22, 1906; dean, National School of Agriculture, San Jacinto, Federal District, 1907–09. D] *Alternate senator* from Chihuahua, 1920. E] None. F] Member of the Mexican Committee to the International Exposition, Chicago, 1893; subsecretary of agriculture, 1913–14; interim governor of Chihuahua, 1930. G] None. H] Founder of several magazines with brother, including *El Agricultor Mexicano* and *El Hogar*; author of many books on agriculture. I] Son of Jesús Escobar y Armendáriz, teacher, lt. colonel in the national guard, and founder of Colegio Mexicano, and Adelina Zerman; brother Zuma was an agronomist, author, and publisher. J] None. K] None. L] Almada, 1968, 191–92; Almada, 575–76; DP79, 716.

Escobedo (de la Peña), Mariano
(Deceased May 22, 1902) A] January 12, 1827. B] Dos Arroyos, Galeana, Nuevo León. C] Primary studies in Galeana; no degree. D] *Federal deputy* from the State of Guanajuato, Dist. 10, 1886–88; *federal deputy* from the State of Guanajuato, Dist. 3, 1888–90; *federal deputy* from the State of Guanajuato, Dist. 1, 1890–92, 1892–94; *federal deputy* from the State of Aguascalientes, Dist. 1, 1894–96, 1896–

98, 1898–1900, 1900–02, 1902, member of the Great Committee. E] None. F] Governor of Nuevo León, 1865–66; governor of San Luis Potosí, 1867–68; secretary of war, 1876; president, Supreme Military Court, 1892–94. G] None. H] Peasant until 1846; owner of Manulique hacienda, Nuevo León, and ranches in Tamaulipas. I] Son of Manuel de Escobedo and María Rita de la Peña, peasants; son Mariano served as an alternate federal deputy under him, 1896–98. J] Joined the army as a private to fight the North American invasion, 1846, then returned to civilian life; raised a company of soldiers in the Revolution of Ayutla on the Liberal side, 1854–55; rank of colonel, 1859; brigade commander when the French invaded; fought in the battle for Puebla, May 5, 1862; rank of brigadier general, 1864; rank of division general, November 2, 1866; commanded the army which surrounded Maximilian at Querétaro; remained loyal to Sebastián Lerdo de Tejada as secretary of war, and fought *Porfirio Díaz*, 1876; retired from the army, November 26, 1884. K] Captured by the French, 1863, escaped and fought in Oaxaca with Díaz. L] Mestre, 214; Godoy, 207; DP70, 718; QesQ, 196; Covarrubias, II, 19–26; Hombres prominentes, 53–54.

Escontría (Bustamante), Blás
(Deceased January 4, 1906) A] February 5, 1847. B] San Luis Potosí, San Luis Potosí. C] Primary studies in San Luis Potosí; preparatory studies, Seminary of San Luis Potosí; civil engineering degree, National College of Mines, 1868–72; professor of political economy, National School of Law, Mexico City, and at the National Normal School, Mexico City; director, Scientific and Literary Institute of San Luis Potosí, 1886. D] Federal deputy from San Luis Potosí, 1876–78; alternate senator from San Luis Potosí, 1878–80, 1880–82; senator from San Luis Potosí, 1882–84; *senator* from San Luis Potosí, 1884, president of the Senate; *federal deputy* from San Luis Potosí, Dist. 7, 1888–90, 1890–92, 1892–94, 1894–96, 1896–98, 1898–1900; *governor* of San Luis Potosí, 1898–1905; *senator* from Puebla, 1900–02, 1902–04. E] None. F] Director of the public debt, 1888; *in-*

terim governor of San Luis Potosí, 1898; secretary of development, 1905–06. G] None. H] Owned El Naranjo hacienda, Tampico, Tamaulipas; investor in urban real estate, San Luis Potosí; banking interests; business partner of *Carlos Díaz Gutiérrez*. I] Son of Manuel Escontría and Guadalupe Bustamante; grandson of Anastasio Bustamante; son Manuel a prominent physician; married Guadalupe Salin; related to General *Juan Barragán Rodríguez*, presidential chief of staff, 1920, by marriage; related to *Carlos Díez Gutiérrez* by marriage. J] None. K] None. L] Cockcroft, 21, 38; DP70, 719; Mestre, 224; Peral, Appendix, 113; Hombres prominentes, 394; Rice, 238.

Escudero (López Portillo), Francisco
(Deceased 1928) A] 1876. B] Morelia, Michoacán. C] Early education unknown; law degree, 1895. D] *Federal deputy* from the State of Jalisco, Dist. 1, 1912–14; *federal deputy* from the State of Jalisco, Dist. 5, 1922–24. E] None. F] *Secretary* of foreign relations, 1913. G] None. H] Practicing lawyer, 1895–1913, 1920–28. I] Unknown. J] Military adviser in the Yaqui campaign, 1892; joined the Constitutionalists, 1913; supported *Francisco Villa* and *Emiliano Zapata*. K] In exile in Costa Rica and California, 1915–20; nominated for secretary of the treasury by the Convention government, but nomination never acted on, 1915. L] DP70, 720; FSRE, 158; Peral, Appendix, 114.

Escudero (Rebollo), Ignacio M.
(Deceased October 31, 1904) A] 1836. B] Mexico City. C] Early education unknown; no degree. D] Senator from Sinaloa, 1882–84; *senator* from Sinaloa, 1884–86, 1886–88; *federal deputy* from the State of Coahuila, Dist. 2, 1888–90; *federal deputy* from the State of Colima, Dist. 1, 1890–92, 1892–94, 1894–96, 1896–98; *federal deputy* from the State of Colima, Dist. 2, 1900–02; *federal deputy* from the State of Chiapas, Dist. 5, 1902–04, 1904. E] Delegate to the Unión Liberal convention, 1892. F] Oficial mayor of the Secretariat of War, 1891; *subsecretary* and acting secretary of war, 1891–92. G] None. H] Land developer, Lago de Cuitzio, Michoacán, and Mexico City; president, Tres Marías Mining Company, 1892–96. I] Son of Antonio Escudero and María del Carmen Rebollo; married Dolores Revueltas, who died in 1891; married María Vega y Osuma. J] Joined the Lancers Regiment, July, 1853, as a sergeant; served as a lieutenant under General Comonfort, 1856; participated in numerous battles against the French; quartermaster of the Army of the East, 1866; commander of the vanguard, Army of the East, 1866; commander of the Jalisco Division, 1867; commander of the forces supporting the Plan of La Noria, Culiacán, 1872; commander of military forces in Tepic, 1877; commander of the Federal District, 1877; rank of division general, March 8, 1893. K] None. L] Rice, 239; Sec of War, 1901; Mestre, 221.

Espeleta, Rafael
(Deceased January 16, 1940) A] 1856. B] Durango, Durango. C] Primary and preparatory studies in Durango; law degree, 1895. D] *Constitutional deputy* from Durango, Dist. 2, 1916–17. E] None. F] Judge, Durango, Durango; chief of public defenders office, Federal District, 1914; first magistrate, Military Tribunal, 1914; civil judge, 1915; interim attorney general of Mexico, 1915; military attorney general, 1915; consulting lawyer, Secretariat of Government, 1916; director, department of advisers, Secretariat of Government, 1920. G] None. H] Practicing lawyer, 1896–1919, 1920– . I] Unknown. J] None. K] Defended several dozen clients persecuted by the *Porfirio Díaz* administration. L] C de D, 1916–17.

Espinosa Bavara, Juan
(Deceased July 8, 1950) A] March 8, 1876. B] Acaponeta, Tepic (Nayarit). C] Early education unknown; no degree. D] *Constitutional deputy* from the State of Tepic, Dist. 3, 1916–17; *federal deputy* from the State of Nayarit, Dist. 3, 1918–20; *senator* from Nayarit, 1920–22, 1924–26, 1926–28. E] None. F] Section chief, political boss of Tepic, 1902; secretary of the political prefect of San Blas, 1908; municipal treasurer of San Blas, Nayarit; agent of the Ministerio Público; political prefect,

Ixtlán del Río, 1910; director of population, Nogales, Sonora, 1934; director of population, Guadalajara, Agua Prieta, and Manzanillo. G] None. H] Tax collector and manager of properties, Acaponeta; clerk; telegrapher. I] Son of Tomás Espinosa and Rafaela Bavara. J] Joined the Maderistas, 1910. K] None. L] C de D, 1916–17, 1918–20; C de S, 1920–22, 1924–26.

Espinosa (Peñarrieta), Francisco
(Deceased August 31, 1925) A] July 18, 1863. B] Orizaba, Veracruz. C] Early education unknown; law degree, Colegio del Estado, Orizaba, 1884. D] *Alternate constitutional deputy* from the Federal District, Dist. 9, in functions, 1916–17. E] Supported *Francisco I. Madero*, 1909. F] Judge of the first instance, Córdoba, Veracruz, 1911–13; commissioner, Córdoba Canton (District), 1914; secretary general of government, State of Guerrero, 1915; first supernumerary justice, Superior Tribunal of Justice of the Federal District, 1915–16; judge, First Circuit Court, 1916; secretary of the Second Division, Superior Tribunal of Justice of the Federal District, 1916; secretary general of government, State of Guanajuato, 1917–20; interim governor of Guanajuato; private secretary of the secretary of communications and public works, 1922; lawyer for the Consultative Legal Group, Secretariat of communications and public works, 1924–25. G] None. H] Practicing lawyer. I] Son of José Espinosa and Guadalupe Peñarrieta. J] None. K] None. L] C de D, 1916–17.

Espinosa y Cuevas, José María
(Deceased November 8, 1926) A] 1861. B] San Luis Potosí, San Luis Potosí. C] Primary studies in Mexico City; secondary in San Luis Potosí; engineering degree, Scientific and Literary Institute of San Luis Potosí; rector of the Scientific and Literary Institute of San Luis Potosí. D] Member of the City Council of San Luis Potosí, San Luis Potosí; local deputy to the state legislature of San Luis Potosí; *governor* of San Luis Potosí, 1906–11. E] None. F] *Interim governor* of San Luis Potosí, 1905–06. G] None. H] Owner of La Angostura hacienda, covering about a tenth of central San Luis Potosí; industri-

alist; engineer; inherited large amounts of real estate from parents in Tuxpan, Veracruz; president of the Pánuco Petroleum Company. I] Son of Antonio Espinosa y Cervantes and Guadalupe Cuevas y Morán, wealthy landowners. J] None. K] None. L] Cockcroft, 25; Mestre, 277.

Esquivel Obregón, Toribio
(Deceased May 24, 1946) A] September 5, 1864. B] León, Guanajuato. C] Primary studies in León, Guanajuato; preparatory studies, School of Secondary Instruction, León, Guanajuato, 1878–84; law degree, National School of Law, Mexico City, September 8, 1888; professor of Greek roots and philosophy, León, 1887–1900; professor, New York University, 1915–23; professor, Columbia University, 1915–20; professor of mercantile and comparative law, Free Law School, 1932– ; professor, history of Mexican law, National School of Law, 1940. D] Member of the City Council of León, Guanajuato, 1899, 1900–01. E] Vice-president of the Anti-Reelectionist party, 1909–10. F] Consulting lawyer, Military Zone of Guanajuato, 1894–97; secretary of the treasury, 1913. G] Member of the Mexican Academy of History, 1942; member of the Antonio Alzate Scientific Society. H] Landowner; practicing lawyer; editor, *La Prensa*, León, 1890; editor, *El Liceo Mexicano*; contributor to many dailies, 1928–30; author of more than fifty books. I] Son of Dr. Toribio Esquivel Carlín and Rafaela Obregón y Martín del Campo; married Laura Torres Soto. J] Held rank of lt. colonel as a lawyer for the military. K] Exiled in New York, 1913–22; leading critic of *José Yves Limantour's* financial policies. L] Cockcroft, 37; Torres Martínez, 328ff; DP70, 734; Velázquez Bringas, 83–84; Enc Mex, III, 611; WWM 45, 38, WWM40, 176; López, 329–30.

Esteva (y Landero), Adalberto Angel
(Deceased July 30, 1914) A] August 17, 1863. B] Jalapa, Veracruz. C] Secondary and preparatory studies, Colegio Preparatorio de Jalapa; law degree, University of Veracruz. D] *Federal deputy* from the State of Zacatecas, Dist. 2, 1890–92, 1892–94, 1894–96, 1896–98, 1898–1900, 1900–02; *federal deputy* from the State of

Veracruz, Dist. 16, 1902–04, 1904–06, 1906–08, 1908–10, 1910–12; *alternate federal deputy* from the State of Veracruz, Dist. 9, 1912–13. E] None. F] Judge, Jalapa; consul general, Barcelona, Spain, 1914. G] None. H] Writer; author of 14 volumes of legislation; poet; printer; lawyer; in practice with Enrique Jiménez Unda. I] Related to (probably son or nephew of) José María Esteva, Conservative politician, and José Ignacio Esteva, secretary of the treasury; daughter Mercedes Esteva y Cánovas married intellectual Joaquín Felipe Meade; married Mercedes Cánovas y Pasquel; close friend of *Salvador Díaz Mirón*, federal deputy from Veracruz. J] None. K] DP70, 737; Pasquel, Jalapa, 231–32; Linajes, 169–70.

Esteva Ruiz, Roberto A.
(Deceased 1967) A] January 18, 1875. B] Mexico City. C] Early education unknown; law degree, National School of Law, March 14, 1899; doctorate of laws, National School of Law, UNAM; professor of literature and history, National Preparatory School, 1913–14; professor of political economy, constitutional law, and international law, National School of Law, UNAM, 1908–14; interim dean, National School of Law; professor emeritus, National School of Law, 1957. D] *Alternate federal deputy* from the State of México, Dist. 14, 1900–02; *alternate federal deputy* from the State of México, Dist. 13, 1904–06. E] None. F] Assistant attorney general of Mexico; department head, Secretariat of Government; delegate of Mexico to the 4th International Pan American Conference, Buenos Aires, 1910; director, National Musuem of Archeology and History, 1913–14; *subsecretary* of Foreign Relations in charge of the secretariat, 1914; member of the International Tribunal of Justice, The Hague; president, Inter-American Council on Legal Matters, Organization of American States; chairman, tax and rules committee, Petróleos Mexicanos (Pemex), 1967. G] None. H] Practicing lawyer. I] Son of Roberto A. Esteva, Liberal and federal deputy, and Isabel Ruiz; grandson of José María Esteva, secretary of government; great grandson of José Ignacio Esteva, secretary of the treasury and federal deputy;

great nephew of José Ignacio Esteva, secretary of the treasury, 1851; cousin Gonzalo A. Esteva, senator and federal deputy; married Concepción Monroy. J] None. K] In exile in Spain, 1914–20; in exile in Cuba, 1920. L] Mestre, 218; López, 331–32; Justicia, 1966; DP70, 737–38; FSRE, 114; Libro Azul, 152; Peral, Appendix, 116.

Estrada Cajigal, Vicente
A] July 14, 1898. B] Cuernavaca, Morelos. C] Primary and secondary studies in Cuernavaca; preparatory studies, Colegio de San Nicolás de Hidalgo, Morelia; no degree. D] *Governor* of Morelos, 1930–34. E] None. F] Assistant to the governor of Morelos, 1917–20; *head* of the Department of the Federal District, 1932; Mexican representative to the United Nations and the International Labor Organization, 1935–36; ambassador to Poland, 1937–38; ambassador to Panama and Costa Rica, 1938–39; ambassador to El Salvador, 1940. G] None. H] None. I] Son of Enrique Estrada and Juliana Cajigal. J] Captain, Port of Tampico; rank of major, 1920. K] None. L] WWM35, 138.

Estrada (Félix), Genaro
(Deceased September 29, 1937) A] June 2, 1887. B] Mazatlán, Sinaloa. C] Primary studies in Rosario, Sinaloa, 1892–95; secondary studies in the Model School of Culiacán, Sinaloa, 1898; preparatory studies at the Colegio de Rosales, Culiacán, Sinaloa, 1899; secretary of the National Preparatory School, 1913; employee, UNAM, 1914–15; professor of Spanish grammar, National Preparatory School; professor of Mexican literature and history, School of Philosophy and Letters, UNAM; professor of history of Mexico, Graduate School, UNAM, 1921. D] None. E] None. F] Employee in publications department, Secretariat of Industry and Commerce, 1917–18; head, Department of Publications, Secretariat of Industry and Commerce, 1918; head, Administrative Department, Secretariat of Industry and Commerce, 1920; oficial mayor of the Secretariat of Foreign Relations, 1921–23; joined the Foreign Service, 1923; *subsecretary* of foreign relations, 1923–26; *subsecretary* of foreign relations, in charge of the

secretariat, 1927–28, 1928–30; *secretary* of foreign relations, 1930–32; represented Mexico at the League of Nations, 1930–31; ambassdor to Spain, 1932–35; special representative to Turkey, 1933. G] Member of the Mexican Academy of History, Mexican Academy of Language. H] Journalist in Sinaloa; editor, *El Monitor*, 1907; war correspondent, Europe, 1914; author; poet; patron of Jaime Torres Bodet's intellectual circle. I] Son of Genaro Estrada y Haro and Concepción Félix y Osuna; married Consuelo Nieto; originally a political disciple of *Alberto Pani*; nephew of printer Faustino Díaz. J] None. K] None. L] WWLA, 1935, 137–38; Carreño, 351–52; Iguíñiz, 337; Dir social, 1935, 217; Enc Mex, III, 624; López, 383; Velázquez Bringas, 84–85; DP70, 739; Mestre, 293.

Estrada Reynoso, Enrique
(Deceased November 11, 1942) A] 1889. B] Moyahua, Zacatecas. C] Studied in Guadalajara; almost completed studies in civil engineering; no degree. D] Federal deputy from the State of Zacatecas, Dist. 3, 1937–40; senator from the State of Zacatecas, 1940–42. E] None. F] *Governor* of Zacatecas, 1920; *subsecretary* of war, 1921; *secretary* of war, 1922; director general of the National Railroads of Mexico, 1941–42. G] None. H] None. I] Brother of *Roque Estrada Reynoso*, president of the Supreme Court, 1952. J] Joined the Revolution under General Rafael Tapia, 1910; Constitutionalist; chief of operations in Michoacán and Colima, 1923; joined the *Adolfo de la Huerta* Rebellion as a principal leader, 1923, when he was serving as chief of military operations in Jalisco; his forces captured *Lázaro Cárdenas*, but released him unharmed; defeated by General *Alvaro Obregón* in Ocotlán and exiled to the United States; returned to Mexico and supported the Escobar rebellion, 1929; captured General *Manuel Ávila Camacho*, but did not execute him; rank of division general. K] Co-opted back into the political leadership by Cárdenas. L] C de D, 1937–39; C de S, 1946; DP70, 739; Enc Mex, III, 1977, 563; Peral, 255–56; QesQ, 200.

Estrada Reynoso, Roque
(Deceased November 27, 1966) A] August 16, 1883. B] Moyahua, Zacatecas. C] Primary studies in Moyahua; secondary at the Martín Sousa School, Guadalajara; preparatory studies in Guadalajara, Jalisco; attended law school, forced into exile, but later completed his law degree at the University of Guadalajara, 1906. D] *Federal deputy* from the State of Zacatecas, Dist. 17, 1920–22. E] Supported *Ricardo Flores Magón*'s group, 1905–06; member of the Anti-Reelectionist Center, 1909; secretary of press and publicity of the National Executive Committee of PRI, June 19, 1935. F] Provisional secretary to *Francisco Madero*, 1910; general peace delegate of Jalisco, 1911; private secretary to *Venustiano Carranza*, 1914; *provisional governor* of Aguascalientes, 1915; *secretary* of justice, 1915–16; justice of the Supreme Court, 1941–46, 1946–51; president of the Supreme Court, 1952. G] Organized workers in a socialist party, 1904. I] Brother of General *Enrique Estrada Reynoso*, senator from the State of Zacatecas. J] Joined the Constitutionalists, 1913; commanding officer of the 2nd Cavalry Brigade, Western Division, 1914–15; rank of brigadier general; joined brother Enrique in support of the *Adolfo de la Huerta* rebellion, 1923. K] Jailed with Francisco Madero in San Luis Potosí, 1909; turned down candidacy for governor of Jalisco because he did not meet the constitutional age requirement; exiled 1923. L] Enc Mex, III, 564; DP70, 740; D del S, 19 June 1935, 1; DGF51, I, 568; WB48, 1695; Peral, 257; López, 334.

F

Fabela (Alfaro), Isidro
(Deceased August 12, 1964) A] June 28, 1882. B] Atlacomulco, México. C] Primary studies in Mexico City; preparatory at the National Preparatory School, Mexico City; law degree from the National School of Law, Mexico City, 1908; professor of history, National Institute, Chihuahua, 1911–13; professor at the Literary Institute of Chihuahua, 1912–13; professor of international public law, National School of Law, UNAM, 1921. D] *Federal deputy* from the State of México, Dist. 9

1912–13, 1922–23; governor of Mexico, 1942–45; senator from the State of México, 1946, but resigned to accept appointment to the International Court of Justice. E] None. F] Chief public defender for the Federal District, 1911; adviser to and director of the Federal Penitentiary, Federal District, 1911; oficial mayor and secretary general of government of the State of Chihuahua, 1911–13; oficial mayor and secretary general of government of the State of Sonora, 1913; *oficial mayor* in charge of foreign relations, 1914–15; special diplomat to Italy and Spain, 1915; minister to Argentina, Brazil, Chile, and Uruguay, 1916; special ambassador to Argentina, 1918–20; judge for the Italian-Mexican International Arbitration Commission, 1928–32, technical commissioner, Secretariat of Foreign Relations, 1933; legal adviser to the French Legation in Mexico, 1933; president of the First Agricultural Conference, 1938; Mexican delegate to the International Office of Labor, League of Nations, 1937–40; judge of the International Court of Justice, 1946–52. G] None. H] Founded the newspapers *La Verdad*, 1910, and *El Pueblo*, 1914; practicing lawyer, 1921–28; attorney for several private companies, including Cauum Oil Company. I] Established early friendships with *José Vasconcelos*, Alfonso Caso, and *Luis Castillo Ledón*; married Josefina Eisenmann; son of Francisco Trinidad Fabela and Guadalupe Alfaro, members of the upper middle class; daughter Josefina is a historian. J] None. K] One of the founders of the Ateneo de la Juventud, 1901; in exile in Cuba, 1913; in exile in California, 1923; his home has been turned into a public library in San Angel, Federal District. L] DP70, 747; Enc Mex, III, 593; Peral, 258; EBW, 71; WWM45, 38–39; letter, WWLA, 1935, 139.

Fabila (Montes de Oca), Gilberto
(Deceased 1966) A] January 10, 1892. B] Amanalco de Becerra, México. C] Preparatory studies at the Scientific and Literary Institute of Toluca; enrolled, National School of Agriculture, 1908, graduating with a degree in agricultural engineering; rural administration degree, Columbia University; professor of agricultural economics and agricultural credit, Autono-

mous Technological Institute of Mexico; professor of rural economics, rural administration, seminar in agricultural economics, economic theory, and history of economic thought, National School of Agriculture. D] *Federal deputy* from the State of México, Dist. 14, 1922–24; *federal deputy* from the State of México, Dist. 7, 1924–26, 1926–28; *senator* from the State of México, 1930–32; *federal deputy* from the State of México, Dist. 3, 1932–34; local deputy to the state legislature of México, 1936–38, 1938–40. E] None. F] Director, Technical Department, Department of Agriculture, 1931; director of social statistics, Department of National Statistics, Secretariat of Industry and Commerce, 1932–33; director of monetary credit, Division of Pensions, 1935; technical adviser, Bank of Mexico, 1936; director of the Technical Department, National Bank of Foreign Trade, 1937–41; agricultural attaché, Mexican embassy, Washington, D.C.; director of agriculture, State of México, 1966. G] None. H] Author; editor, *El Economista*, 1917–18. I] Son of Andrés Fabila and Luisa Montes de Oca; brother Alonso an educator, author, and ethnologist; brother Manuel a historian. J] None. K] None. L] Aranda Pamplona, 37; WWM45, 39; DP70, 748; Gómez, 178–83; Peral, Appendix, 117.

Fernández, Justino
(Deceased August 19, 1911) A] June 22, 1828. B] Mexico City. C] Early education unknown; law degree, National School of Law, Mexico City, 1853; Dean, National School of Law, 1885–1901. D] Mayor of Mexico City; federal deputy from the Federal District, 1855–57; governor of Hidalgo, 1873–76; *federal deputy* from the State of San Luis Potosí, Dist. 3, 1886–88; *federal deputy* from the State of San Luis Potosí, Dist. 1, 1888–90, 1890–92, 1892–94, 1894–96, 1896–98, 1898–1900, 1900–02; president of the Chamber of Deputies, 1900. E] Member of the Liberal party. F] *Secretary* of justice and public instruction, 1901–05; *secretary* of justice, 1905–11. G] Stockholder in the Jockey Club, 1901; vice-president, Society of Lawyers of Mexico. H] Practicing lawyer. I] Son of Justino Fernández, a so-

cially prominent family; grandfather of Justino Fernández, prominent intellectual; married Francisca Castelló; son Justino, a lawyer; son Alonso, federal deputy from San Luis Potosí, 1900–06. J] None. K] Member of the Group of Notables, 1855; helped write 1857 Constitution. L] Enc Mex, IV, 108; QesQ, 206; López, 348; Godoy, 287; Blue Book, 1901, 89; Mestre, 241.

Fernández, Ramón
(Deceased February 7, 1905) A] 1833. B] San Luis Potosí, San Luis Potosí. C] Early education unknown; medical degree. D] Senator, 1877; *alternate senator* from the State of Tamaulipas, 1894–96, 1896–98; *senator* from the State of Tamaulipas, 1898–1900, 1900–02, 1902–04, 1904–05. E] Opposed Lerdo de Tejada, 1872–76. F] Secretary to General *Manuel González Flores*, 1877–80; ambassador to Spain; *ambassador* to France, 1884–88. G] None. H] Practicing physician. I] Related to President *Manuel González Flores*. J] None. K] None. L] Mestre, 222; Peral, Appendix, 120; Hombres prominentes, 319–20; C de S, 1900–02, 6–7.

Fernández (Imaz), Esteban
(Deceased December 15, 1920) A] 1852. B] Hacienda San Diego Mancha, Municipio Poanas, Nombre de Dios, Durango. C] Primary and preparatory studies at the Seminary of Durango, Durango; law degree, Juárez Institute, Durango, January 17, 1878; professor of 4th- and 6th-year courses, Juárez Institute; rector of the Juárez Institute, 1904. D] Local deputy to the state legislature of Durango, 1880–82; mayor of Durango, Durango, 1883–84; local deputy to the state legislature of Durango, 1884; 1898–1904; *governor* of Durango, 1904–11. E] None. F] Secretary of the Superior Tribunal of Justice of Durango, 1877–79; secretary of the Judicial District of Durango, 1879–80; secretary general of government of Durango under Governor *Juan Manuel Flores*, 1884–98; interim governor of Durango, January 30, 1897. G] None. H] Practicing lawyer. I] Son of José María Fernández Leal and Refugio Imaz, landowning family; brother of *Leandro Fernández Imaz*, secretary of communications and public works, 1907–

11. J] None. K] None. L] Rouaix, 152–53.

Fernández Imaz, Leandro
(Deceased September 10, 1922) A] February 27, 1851. B] Hacienda de San Diego Mancha, Nombre de Dios, Durango. C] Primary studies at the Hacienda de San Diego Mancha and a private school, Durango, Durango; secondary studies at the Conciliar Seminary and Juárez Institute, Durango, Durango; preparatory studies, Mexico City; civil, topographical, and hydrographical engineering degree and assayer, National School of Mines (Engineering), Mexico City, 1873; studies, National Conservatory of Music; studies, National School of Business; special studies in engineering, United States; professor of mathematics, topography, and astronomy, National School of Mines, 1873–91; rector, National School of Mines. D] Member of the City Council of Mexico City. E] None. F] Director of the mint; director of the Central Astronomical Observatory; *governor* of Durango, 1897; *secretary* of communications and public works, 1907–11. G] None. H] Practicing engineer; constructed government buildings. I] Son of José María Fernández Leal and Refugio Imaz, landowners; brother of *Esteban Fernández Imaz*, governor of Durango, 1904–11; married Elorriaga viuda de Zarco. J] None. K] None. L] Godoy, 26; Album; DP70, 755; Mestre, 269; Rouaix, 153–54.

Fernández Leal, Manuel
(Deceased July 2, 1909) A] 1831. B] Jalapa, Veracruz. C] Primary and secondary studies in Puebla; engineering degree, National School of Mines (engineering). D] None. E] None. F] Employee, United States–Mexico Boundary Commission, 1854–56; oficial mayor of the Secretariat of Development; *subsecretary* of development, 1878–92; *secretary* of development, 1891–1903; director of the mint, 1903–09. G] None. H] Practicing engineer. I] Close friend of Francisco Díaz Covarrubias, prominent political figure under President Lerdo de Tejada. J] Hombres prominentes, 329–30; Pasquel, Liberals, 129; Mestre, 236; Godoy, 261; QesQ, 206; DP70, 761; Pasquel, Jalapa, 239–40.

Fernández (Vidaurrázaga), Salvador Diego
(Deceased 1958) A] December 20, 1879.
B] Mexico City. C] Primary studies at the
Colegio Soriano and Colegio Baz; studies
at the Conciliar Pontifical Seminary, Arch-
diocese of Mexico; preparatory studies at
the National Preparatory School and the
Scientific and Literary Institute of San
Luis Potosí; law degree, National School
of Law; professor of international law,
School of Business Administration,
UNAM; professor of Portuguese, Italian,
French, German, and English, Biology Pro-
gram, UNAM. D] None. E] None.
F] Director, Diplomatic Department, Secretariat of Foreign Relations; secretary of
the Legation, Norway, Spain, Portugal,
Austria, and Hungary; director, North
American Section, Secretariat of Foreign Re-
lations; ambassador to Spain, 1911; assistant attorney general of Mexico; district
court judge; oficial mayor in charge of the
Secretariat of Foreign Relations, 1919; *ambassador* to England, 1919–20; chargé
d'affaires, Mexican embassy, Washington,
D.C., 1920. G] None. H] Practicing
lawyer. I] Son of José Diego Fernández
Torres, lawyer, and Dolores de Vidaurrázaga y Vidaurrázaga; married María Man-
cebo y Canedo. J] Constitutionalist.
K] None. L] DP70, 763; FSRE, 171–72;
Dir social, 1935, 215.

Figueroa (Mata), Ambrosio
(Deceased 1913) A] 1869. B] Huitzuco,
Guerrero. C] Primary studies in Quetza-
lapa, Guerrero; no degree. D] None.
E] Joined the Anti-Reelectionist move-
ment, 1910. F] *Provisional governor* of
Morelos, 1911–12. G] None. H] Farmer.
I] Son of Magdaleno Figueroa and Cristina
Mata, farmers; brother of *Francisco A. Fi-
gueroa Mata*, governor of Guerrero,
1918–21, and Rómulo Figueroa Mata,
revolutionary general. J] Joined the 2nd
Military Reserves, 1898; fought Zapatis-
tas; recognized *Victoriano Huerta*, 1913.
K] Brothers opposed Huerta; captured
and executed, Iguala, Guerrero, 1913.
L] None.

Figueroa (Mata), Francisco A.
(Deceased August 22, 1936) A] October
10, 1870. B] Quetzalapa, Guerrero.
C] Primary studies at a private school in

Huitzuco; primary teaching certificate,
Literary Institute of Chilpancingo, Chilpancingo, Guerrero, 1895. D] *Constitutional deputy* from the State of Guerrero,
Dist. 6, 1916–17; *governor* of Guerrero,
1918–21. E] None. F] *Provisional governor* of Guerrero, 1911; secretary general
of the government of Zacatecas, 1915.
G] None. H] Schoolteacher; director and
founder of private schools in Quetzalapa
and Huitzuco, 1905; poet; author. I] Son
of Magdaleno Figueroa and Cristina Mata;
brother of *Ambrosio Figueroa Mata*, provisional governor of Morelos, 1911–12.
J] Supported Madero, 1910–11; joined the
Constitutionalists, 1913; commander,
19th Infantry Regiment, 1914; represented
brother, General Rómulo Figueroa, at the
Convention of Aguacalientes, 1914–15;
rank of brigadier general, January 1, 1914;
executive secretary, Council of War, Zacatecas, 1916; president, Military Council of
Zacatecas, 1916 K] None. L] C de D,
1916–17; Sec of War, 1914, 27.

Flores, Angel
(Deceased March 31, 1926) A] October 2,
1884. B] San Pedro, Municipio de Culiacán, Sinaloa. C] Early education unknown; no degree. D] *Governor* of Sina-
loa, 1920–24. E] Ran for president
against *Plutarco Elías Calles*, 1924.
F] *Interim governor* of Sinaloa, 1916–17.
G] None. H] Agricultural laborer; sailor,
Mazatlán; served as cabin boy aboard the
steamship *Altata*; traveled all over the
world; lived in San Francisco; longshore-
man, Mazatlán; foreman, longshoremen,
Mazatlán. I] Illegitimate son of Bruno
Camacho, peasant, and Juana Flores.
J] Joined the Maderistas, 1910; joined the
Constitutionalists, 1913; fought under
General *Ramón F. Iturbe*, 1914; repre-
sented by Colonel Félix Ortega at the Con-
vention of Aguascalientes, 1914–15; op-
posed *Francisco Villa*, 1915; commander
of the 1st Division of the Army of the
Northeast, under General *Alvaro Obregón*, 1920; supported the Plan of Agua
Prieta, 1920; rank of division general.
K] Apparently died from poison, poor and
disillusioned. L] QesQ, 208; DP70, 778;
González Dávila, 212–13; Nakayama,
251–61.

Flores, Benito
(Deceased 1948) A] March 21, 1868.
B] Villa de Fuentes, Coahuila. C] Secondary studies at the Ateneo Fuentes, Saltillo; law degree. D] Mayor of Torreón, Coahuila, 1906–07. E] None. F] Judge, Mexico City; agent, General Claims Commission between Mexico and the United States; *governor* of the Federal District, 1919; *justice* of the Supreme Court, 1919–22; subsecretary of industry, commerce, and labor, 1930; member of the International Arbitration Tribunal, The Hague. G] None. H] Practicing lawyer; author of legal books. I] Unknown. J] None. K] None. L] DP70, 778; Moreno, 37–39, letter.

Flores, Juan Manuel
(Deceased January 30, 1897) A] May 31, 1831. B] Mineral de Indé, Durango. C] Primary studies in Indé; some studies in agriculture and mining; no degree. D] Governor of Durango, 1877–80; *governor* of Durango, 1884–97. E] Original member of the Conservative party. F] Political boss of Indé, 1861–62; governor and military commander of Durango, 1876; provisional governor of Durango, 1877. G] None. H] Rancher; engaged in mining, Vace Oritz, Durango, 1862–71. I] Married Angela Flores, daughter of Juan Nepomuceno Flores, Conservative, financier, and one of the largest landowners in Mexico, with over a million hectares; father, a businessman, left him property. J] Fought Apaches with troops under his own command; officer, national guard; supported *Porfirio Díaz* in La Noria rebellion, 1871; served as a colonel in the command of Manuel Márquez and Donato Guerra, 1871; supported the Tuxtepec rebellion, 1876, under Generals Treviño and Naranjo; rank of brigadier general, September 28, 1883. K] None. L] DP70, 780; Pavía, 165–68; Hombres prominentes, 443–44; Mestre, 196; Almada, 1968, 210.

Flores, Manuel
(Deceased March 4, 1924) A] June 25, 1853. B] Guanajuato, Guanajuato. C] Primary studies, Mexico City; secondary studies, Colegio de San Ildefonso, Mexico City; medical degree, National School of Medicine, Mexico City, 1880; founding class in legal medicine, Practical Military Medical School; professor of logic, National Preparatory School; teacher, public school, 1875; director, public primary school, Mexico City, 1875; teacher, private girls school, 1875; director, National Preparatory School, 1905. D] *Alternate federal deputy* from the State of Puebla, Dist. 5, 1900–02; *federal deputy* from the Federal District, Dist. 3, 1902–04, 1904–06, 1906–08, 1908–10, 1910–12. E] None. F] Director general of primary and normal instruction; secretary, Council of Higher Public Education; represented the Mexican government, Paris Exposition, 1889. G] None. H] Practicing physician; intern, Military Hospital, 1878; journalist, 1905; contributor to *El Imparcial, Excélsior,* and *El Universal;* author of books on teaching. I] Father a lawyer. J] Rank of lt. colonel, Medical Corps, February 9, 1881. K] None. L] QesQ, 209–10; DP70, 780; Sec of War, 1902.

Flores (Díaz), Jorge
A] August 13, 1896. B] Mazatlán, Sinaloa. C] Preparatory studies, Colegio Civil Rosales, Culiacán, 1910–11; studies, Doctor Mora Business School, Mexico City, 1912–13; studies, Higher School of Business Administration, Mexico City, 1914–16; no degree. D] None. E] None. F] Official, Secretariat of Communications and Public Works, 1917–27; oficial mayor, Department of the Federal District, 1927–34; section chief, Publicity Department, and director of library, Secretariat of Foreign Relations, 1935–36; chief, library and archives, Secretariat of Foreign Relations, 1937–40; assistant director, Department of Information, Secretariat of Foreign Relations, 1941. G] None. H] None. I] Son of Esteban Flores, educator, mayor of Culiacán, and director of the Labor Department, 1922, and Nabora Díaz; married Paz Duque de Estrada. J] None. K] None. L] WWM45, 42.

Flores Magón, Jesús
(Deceased December 7, 1930) A] January 6, 1872. B] San Simón, Teotitlán del Camino, Oaxaca. C] Primary studies in Mexico City; preparatory studies from the

National Preparatory School; law degree, National School of Law. D] *Senator* from Oaxaca, 1912. E] He and his brothers Enrique and *Ricardo Flores Magón* led a movement against *Porfirio Díaz*, beginning as students, 1892. F] Subsecretary of justice, 1911; *secretary* of government, 1912. G] None. H] Founder of *Regeneración*, anti-Díaz magazine which circulated widely throughout México, 1900; practicing lawyer; author. I] Son of Teodoro Flores, Liberal, who rose to rank of lt. colonel during French invasion, and indigenous leader, and Margarita Magón; attended National School of Law with his brother Ricardo, 1890s; brother Ricardo was president of the organizing committee of the Mexican Liberal party, 1905. J] Unknown. K] Exiled to United States. L] Cockcroft, 86; Mestre, 285.

Flores Magón, Ricardo
(Deceased November 20, 1922) A] 1873. B] San Antonio Eloxochitlán, Oaxaca. C] Primary studies in Mexico City; preparatory studies, National Preparatory School, Mexico City; enrolled in the National School of Law, 1893, but never completed degree. D] None. E] Attended the First Congress of Liberal Clubs, San Luis Potosí, 1901; president, organizing committee of the Partido Liberal Mexicano, St. Louis, Missouri, September 28, 1905; coauthor of the Liberal party platform with *Antonio I. Villarreal*, Librado Rivera, Juan Sarabia, and others. F] Journalist, *El Demócrata*, 1893; wrote for opposition newspapers; cofounder with his brother *Jesús Flores Magón* of *Regeneración*, probably the most important opposition newspaper to the future Revolutionary political generations, 1900; reporter, *El Hijo del Ahuizote*, 1902–03; published *Regeneración* in exile, San Antonio, Texas, and St. Louis, Missouri, 1903–05. G] Intellectual leader of the labor movement in Mexico. H] Author of many works. I] Son of Teodoro Flores and Margarita Magón, a poor family; father was a Liberal and lt. colonel during the French invasion; brother of Jesús Flores Magón, secretary of government, 1912; brother Enrique another precursor of the Revolution. J] Directed supporters to oppose *Porfirio Díaz* at the same time as *Francisco I. Madero*, but

would not join Madero's movement or forces; intellectual leader of an insurrection against the government on January 29, 1911, in Baja California. K] Imprisoned and harassed by the Díaz government for his critical writings; forced into exile, United States, 1904; arrested in Los Angeles, California, 1912, for breaking neutrality laws, and imprisoned in McNeil Island, Washington, 1912–14; arrested in Los Angeles, 1916, for violation of neutrality laws, released on probation; arrested, 1918, for publishing an anarchist document, and imprisoned by the United States, 1918, in Washington, then Fort Leavenworth, Kansas, where he died. L] Cockcroft, 86; DP70, 782–83; Enc Mex, IV, 334–36.

Flores (Roseto), Damián
(Deceased December 18, 1927) A] September 27, 1855. B] Tetipac, Alarcón District, Taxco, Guerrero. C] Primary studies in Tetipac and continued in Mexico City, under Agustín Roldán; preparatory studies, National Preparatory School, under Ignacio Altamirano; geographical engineering degree, National School of Mines; professor of political economy, cosmography, and mathematics, National Preparatory School, 1882–1907; professor of financial operations, School of Business; professor of political economy, School of Mines, D] *Federal deputy* from the State of Guanajuato, Dist. 8, 1906–07; *governor* of Guerrero, 1907–11. E] None. F] Head, Department of Banks and Public Credit, Secretariat of the Treasury, 1893–1907; *interim governor* of Guerrero, 1907. G] None. H] Engineer. I] Son of Colonel Juan Flores, companion of Juan Alvarez and Ignacio Altamirano during Liberal wars, and a prominent politician during the Reform, and Luisa Rosete; Ignacio Altamirano obtained a scholarship for him to attend preparatory school. J] None. K] None. L] DP70, 778; Album; Carreño, 5–8; Mestre, 279.

Frías, Heriberto
(Deceased November 12, 1925) A] 1870. B] Querétaro, Querétaro. C] Primary studies, Mexico City; studied preparatory studies at the National Preparatory School until 1884; enrolled in the National Mili-

tary College, 1887, but did not complete course because of financial difficulties. D] None. E] Joined the Anti-Reelectionist party. F] Subsecretary of foreign relations; consul, Cádiz, Spain, 1921–23. G] None. H] Began career as a journalist, 1893; wrote for *El Demócrata*, 1893–95, *El Imparcial*, 1897–99, *Revista Moderna*; editor, *El Correo de la Tarde*, Mazatlán, 1906; editor, *El Constitutional*, Hermosillo; editor, *La Voz de Sonora*, Hermosillo, 1913. I] From a poor family; uncle of poet José D. Frías. J] Joined the 9th Infantry Battalion as a 2nd lieutenant, 1892; fought against the Indians, Tomóchic, Chihuahua, 1892. K] None. L] QesQ, 217; DP70, 792; González Dávila, 215–17.

Fuentes Dávila, Alberto
(Deceased 1954) A] February 18, 1873. B] Saltillo, Coahuila. C] Primary and secondary studies in Saltillo, Coahuila; left school, 1885. D] None. E] President of the Anti-Reelectionist Committee, Aguascalientes. F] Customs official, Ciudad Juárez, 1911; *interim governor of* Aguascalientes, 1912–13; *governor* of Aguascalientes, 1914. G] Treasurer, vice-president, and president, Mutualist Society of Employees. H] Businessman; worked in New York City, 1890–93; employee and later manager, J. H. Simpson, Mexico City; director general, Compañía Maderera de Aguascalientes, S.A. I] Married Anselma Ramos, great-niece of General Mariano Escobedo; school companion of *Francisco I. Madero*. J] Joined the Constitutionalists, 1913; interim chief of staff, General *Pablo González*; represented at the Convention of Aguascalientes by Lt. Colonel David Berlanga, 1914–15. K] None. L] Romero Aceves, 251; Almanaque de Aguascalientes, 101.

Fuero (Unda), Carlos
(Deceased January 11, 1892) A] October 1, 1844. B] Mexico City. C] Early education unknown; tried to enroll at the National Military College, 1854, but refused because of age; no degree. D] *Senator* from San Luis Potosí, 1886–88, 1888–90, 1890–92, 1892–94, but never served. E] None. F] Governor and military commander of Nuevo León, 1875–76; governor and military Commander of Durango,

1976–77; *substitute governor* of Chihuahua, 1884–85. G] None. H] None. I] Son of Colonel Joaquín Fuero and Carlota Unda. J] Joined a rifle battalion as a 2nd lieutenant, January 13, 1858; rank of 1st lieutenant, December 21, 1859; fought for the Liberals during the War of Reform, 1859–62; rank of captain in the 1st National Guard Battalion, Guanajuato, March 24, 1862; commander, 5th National Guard Battalion, San Luis Potosí, 1863, 1866; rank of lt. colonel, army, July 20, 1864; fought under General Sóstenes Rocha, 1869; rank of brigade general, December 12, 1871; commander, 1st Brigade, 3rd Infantry Division, in opposition to the Plan of La Noria, 1871; commander, 3rd Infantry Division, 1873; defeated *Porfirio Díaz* in the Battle of Icamole, May 20, 1876, during the Tuxtepec rebellion; assistant commander, 3rd Infantry Division, 1876; captured during Mariano Escobedo's rebellion against Díaz, 1879; commander, infantry brigade, 1880; chief of arms in Chihuahua and Durango, 1880–81; chief of 2nd Military Zone, 1881–82; commander, 5th Military Zone, 1885–92. K] Díaz saved him from being executed by General Luis Mier y Terán, 1879. L] Almada, 395–402; Mestre, 176.

G

Galván, Pedro A.
(Deceased December 12, 1892) A] 1832. B] Irapuato, Guanajuato. C] Early education unknown; no degree. D] Federal deputy from the State of Jalisco, 1875–77; senator from Colima, 1877–79; *federal deputy* from the State of Jalisco, Dist. 13, 1886–88. 1888–90; *governor* of Jalisco, 1891–92. E] None. F] Provisional governor of Colima, 1880; director of customs, Manzanillo, Colima, 1881–82; governor of the national palace, 1884; *provisional governor* of Jalisco, 1889–91. G] None. H] Unknown. I] Unknown. J] Career army officer; joined the Liberal militia under General Pedro Ogazón as a sergeant, 1854; fought during the War of the Reform and the French Intervention; supported the Plan of La Noria, 1871; supported the Plan of Tuxtepec, 1876; rank of division general, 1885; commander of the Military Zone, Puebla, Puebla, 1886; commander of

the 5th Military Zone, Guadalajara, Jalisco, 1886–89. K] Lost his leg in the Tuxtepec rebellion. L] Enc Mex, V, 72; López, 382–83; DP70, 805; Peral, Appendix, 128; Almada, Colima, 88–89; Mata Torres, 53.

Gálvez, José Manuel
(Deceased 1945) A] 1873. B] Teziutlán, Puebla. C] Early education unknown; teaching certificate, Normal School, State of Puebla, on a scholarship; teacher; director of public schools, Parras de la Fuente, Coahuila; founded the Colegio de Torreón, 1900; founded the Instituto Santiago Lavín; founded the García Condé School for Women, Mexico City; taught indigenous groups. D] *Federal deputy* from the State of Puebla, Dist. 13, 1920–22, president of the Education Committee; *federal deputy* from the State of Puebla, Dist. 13, 1922–24; *federal deputy* from the State of Puebla, Dist. 7, 1943–46. E] None. F] Secretary of the Commission to Reform Education, 1893. G] None. H] Worked in the United States. I] Unknown. J] None. K] None. L] DP70, 806; CyT, 267–68.

Gama (y Cruz), Valentín
(Deceased) A] 1868. B] San Luis Potosí, San Luis Potosí. C] Secondary and preparatory studies, Scientific and Literary Institute of San Luis Potosí; engineering degree, National School of Mines (engineering), 1893; professor, National School of Engineering, UNAM, 1904–42; dean, National School of Engineering; rector of UNAM, 1914, 1915. E] None. F] Member, United States–Mexico International Boundary Commission, 1891–96; subdirector, National Observatory, 1903–10; director, National Observatory, 1910–19; *secretary* of development, colonization, and industry, 1914–15; nominated for secretary of public instruction, but never acted on, 1915. G] President, Mexican Society of Geography and Statistics; vicepresident, Antonio Alzate Academy of Science. H] Engineer. I] Son of Ignacio Gama, physician and career military officer, served as rector of the Scientific and Literary Institute of San Luis Potosí. J] None. K] None. L] Enc Mex, V, 100; DP70, 810.

Gamboa (Iglesias), Federico
(Deceased August 15, 1939) A] December 22, 1864. B] Mexico City. C] Primary studies in New York City and at a private school, Mexico City; preparatory studies at the National Preparatory School, Mexico City; studies in law, National School of Law; professor, School of Philosophy and Letters, UNAM; professor, Free Law School; professor, National Normal School, Mexico City; professor of Spanish, National Preparatory School. D] *Alternate federal deputy* from the Federal District, 1894–96; *alternate federal deputy* from the State of Michoacán, Dist. 11, 1902–04; *federal deputy* from the State of Chihuahua, Dist. 4, 1908–10, 1910–12. E] None. F] Joined the Foreign Service, October 9, 1888; second secretary, Mexican legation, Guatemala, 1888–90; first secretary and chargé d'affaires, Mexican Legation, Argentina, 1890–92; section head, Secretariat of Foreign Relations, 1892; official, Mexican legation, Brazil, 1895–96; first secretary, Mexican embassy, Washington, D.C., 1896; chargé d'affaires, Mexican Legation, Guatemala, 1898–1901; chargé d'affaires, Mexican embassy, Washington, D.C., 1902–05; ambassador to Guatemala, 1905–07; *subsecretary* of foreign relations, 1908–10; ambassador to Holland, 1911–12; *secretary* of foreign relations, 1913. G] President, Mexican Academy of Language, 1923–39. H] Journalist; wrote for numerous papers in Mexico and abroad; translator; novelist; playwright. I] Son of General Manuel Gamboa, governor of Jalisco, 1855, and leading Conservative, and Lugarda Iglesias, sister of Liberal politician José María Iglesias; brother of *José María Gamboa Iglesias*, subsecretary of foreign relations, 1899; uncle of José Joaquín Gamboa, diplomat and dramatist. J] None. K] In exile, 1914–23. 11-QesQ, 224; López, 385; DP70, 810; Godoy, 208; Carreño, 182; Mestre, 295–96; Enc Mex, V, 101; O'Campo, 124–25; WWLA35.

Gamboa (Iglesias), José María
(Deceased September 12, 1911) A] March 22, 1856. B] Mexico City. C] Primary and secondary studies, Mexico City; preparatory studies, Mexico City; law degree, National School of Law. D] *Federal*

deputy from the State of Hidalgo, Dist. 2, 1886–88; *federal deputy* from the Federal District, Dist. 7, 1888–90; *federal deputy* from the Federal District, Dist. 5, 1892–94, 1894–96, 1896–98; *federal deputy* from the Federal District, Dist. 7, 1898–1900, 1900–02; *federal deputy* from the State of Chihuahua, Dist. 3, 1905–06, in a special election; *federal deputy* from the State of Chihuahua, Dist. 3, 1906–08; *federal deputy* from the State of Jalisco, Dist. 4, 1910–12. E] None. F] Subsecretary of foreign relations, 1899; *subsecretary* in charge of foreign relations, 1899–1901; ambassador to South America, 1901; ambassador to Chile, 1902; ambassador to Peru, 1902. G] None. H] None. I] Son of General Manuel Gamboa, Conservative politician and governor of Jalisco, 1855, and Lugarda Iglesias, sister of José María Iglesias, leading Liberal politician; father of José Joaquín Gamboa, dramatist and diplomat; brother *Federico Gamboa Iglesias*, secretary of foreign relations, 1913. J] None. K] None. L] Almada, 1968, 214; Mestre, 241; Enc Mex, V, 106; DP70, 811; Carreño, 353; Peral, Appendix, 124.

Gameros (Ronquillo), Tomás
(Deceased August 26, 1931) A] 1859. B] Villa de Aldama, Morelos, Chihuahua. C] Early education unknown; teaching certificate; schoolteacher, Aldama, 1893–1904; schoolteacher, Chihuahua, Chihuahua; founded and directed own private school in Aldama. D] *Alternate senator* from Chihuahua, 1918–20. E] Joined the Anti-Reelectionist party, 1910. F] Tax collector, Aldama, Chihuahua, 1893; treasurer General of Chihuahua under Governor *Abraham González*, 1911–12; treasurer general of Chihuahua, 1918, 1930; *provisional governor* of Chihuahua, 1920. G] None. H] None. I] Son of Rafael Gameros, political boss of Aldama and local deputy to the state legislature of Chihuahua, and Paz Ronquillo. J] Unknown. K] None. L] Enc Mex, V, 109; DP70, 812; Almada, 551–52; Almada, 1968, 215.

Gamio (Martínez), Manuel
(Deceased 1960) A] March 2, 1883. B] Mexico City. C] Primary studies, Colegio Fournier; secondary studies at the Colegio Colón; preparatory studies at the

National Preparatory School, 1903; B.S. degree, Columbia University, New York City, 1906; enrolled, National School of Mines; studies in archeology under Nicolás León and Jesús Galindo y Villa, National Museum, 1906–08; assistant researcher in history, National Museum, 1906–08; M.A. degree in anthropology, Columbia University, under Franz Boas, 1909–11; Ph.D., Columbia University, 1922; professor, National Academy of Fine Arts, 1913; official, Institute of Social Research, UNAM, 1933; director, Institute of Social Research, UNAM, 1938. D] None. E] None. F] Federal inspector, archeological monuments, 1913–16; director of Anthropology Department, secretariat of agriculture, 1917–24; *subsecretary* of public education, 1925; director, Department of Rural Population, Secretariat of Agriculture, 1934; judge, Supreme Council of Defense and Social Welfare, 1930–32; adviser, Secretariat of Public Education, 1935–37; director, Department of Demography, 1938; director, Inter-American Indigenous Institute, 1942–60. G] President, Mexican Delegation to the Pan American Scientific Congress, 1915–16. H] director, *Ethnos*, 1920–22; leader of major investigation of Teotihuacán, 1918–21. I] Son of Gabriel Gamio and Marina Martínez, wealthy landowners in Santo Domingo, Dominican Republic, Oaxaca, Veracruz, and Puebla; married Margarita León Ortiz; grandson of Lorenzo Gamio de Irurita, Spaniard, and Manuela Otal; grandson of Vicente Martínez and Jesusa Serrano, from Zamora, Michoacán. J] None. K] Parents lost fortune during the Revolution; left engineering program to study Náhuatl on family hacienda; discovered the temple of Quetzalcoatl, Teotihuacán; considered the leader of modern indigenismo in Mexico. L] DP70, 812; WWM45, 43; Enc Mex, V, 109; WWLA, 1940, 203–05.

Gándara (Aguilar), Francisco
(Deceased 1903) A] 1837. B] Ures, Sonora. C] Early education unknown; no degree. D] Mayor of Hermosillo, Sonora, 1879–81; local deputy to the state legislature of Sonora, 1881–1903. E] Political supporter of General *Luis E. Torres*, governor of Sonora, 1899–1903. F] Vice-gover-

nor of Sonora, 1883–87; acting governor of Sonora, 1884, 1885, 1886. G] None. H] Unknown. I] Son of Manuel María Gándara de Gortari, governor of Sonora, 1830s and 1840s, and Dolores Aguilar; grandson of Juan Gándara and Antonia de Gortari, Spaniards who owned the Bamuri and Topahue haciendas, Sonora; nephew of José de Aguilar, governor of Sonora, 1849–51; nephew of Juan B. Gándara, governor of Sonora, 1849. J] Unknown. K] None. L] DP70, 813.

Garay, Eduardo
(Deceased) A] June 12, 1825. B] Mexico City. C] Early education unknown; degree as an assayer, National College of Mines (engineering); professor of physics, history of philosophy, first and second course in mathematics, National Preparatory School; professor of descriptive geometry, analytical, and applied mathematics, School of Engineers, National College of Mines. D] *Alternate senator* from the State of Tlaxcala, 1878–80; senator from the State of Tlaxcala, 1880–82; *senator* from the State of Puebla, 1884–90. E] Led the opposition to Sebastián Lerdo de Tejada. F] Engineer, Department of Public Works, on the Tehuantepec Railroad project; secretary of development, 1876; subsecretary of public works, 1876–77; subsecretary of the treasury, 1877; *subsecretary* of foreign relations, 1885–86; minister to Central America, 1886–87; minister to Italy, 1888. G] Founding member of the Jockey Club, 1883. H] None. I] Grandson of General José María Tornel, oficial mayor of war, 1832; great-nephew of José Julián Tornel, senator from Veracruz. J] Lieutenant of engineers in the forces opposed to the North American invasion, 1846; colonel on the staff of General *Porfirio Díaz*. K] None. L] Hombres prominentes, 191; C de S, 1880–82.

García, Emiliano C.
(Deceased November 9, 1951) A] April 6, 1876. B] Fuerte, Sinaloa. C] Primary studies at Fuerte, Sinaloa; preparatory studies, Colegio Civil Rosales, Culiacán, Sinaloa; medical studies at the Colegio León XIII and the Liceo for Boys, Guadalajara; left medical program to farm in

Sinaloa. D] Mayor of Fuerte, Sinaloa, 1912; mayor of Rosario, Sinaloa, 1916; *constitutional deputy* from the State of Sinaloa, Dist. 5, 1916–17; *senator* from the State of Sinaloa, 1916–18, 1918–20; local deputy to the state legislature of Sinaloa, 1943–47, 1947–51. E] Supported *Ricardo Flores Magón*, 1906; supported *Francisco I. Madero*'s campaign, 1909–10. F] Agent of the Ministerio Público, Mazatlán, 1911; tax collector, 1913; director, Adminstrative Department, Government Printing Office, 1930; inspector, Department of Labor, 1943. G] None. H] Farmer; attorney for a savings bank, Torreón, Coahuila. I] Son of Emiliano García and Refugio Estrella. J] Joined the Constitutionalists, 1913; supported *Alvaro Obregón*, January 4, 1920. K] None. L] C de D, 1916–17; C de S, 1918–20.

García, Francisco H.
(Deceased 1934) A] 1854. B] Hermosillo, Sonora. C] Early education unknown; enrolled in the National Military College, 1875, graduating as a 2nd lieutenant in the cavalry, 1878; professor, National Military College. D] None. E] None. F] Commander, presidential staff, 1887–1911; military attaché to Washington, D.C.; military attaché to London, England; *provisional governor* of Sonora, 1913–14. G] None. H] None. I] Unknown. J] Career military officer; rank of 2nd captain, 1880; rank of 1st captain, 1881; rank of lt. colonel, March 31, 1896; rank of colonel, September 15, 1904; retired from the army, June 1, 1911; rejoined the army, February 22, 1913; rank of brigadier general, May 30, 1913. K] Exiled to the United States, 1914–34. L] Cuevas, 406; DP70, 818; Sec of War, 1914, 25; Almanaque de Sonora, 1982, 126; Peral, Appendix, 133.

García, Julio
(Deceased June 23, 1940) A] December 18, 1858. B] Tacubaya, Federal District. C] Early education unknown; law degree, National School of Law, Mexico City; professor of civil and international law, National School of Law, UNAM. D] *Senator* from the State of Guanajuato, 1912–14; president of the Senate, 1912. E] None. F] *Subsecretary* of public instruction,

1911; *subsecretary* of foreign relations in charge of the secretariat, 1912–13; *president* of the Supreme Court, 1929–32. G] None. H] Practicing lawyer. I] Married Clementina Gómez, sister of María Gómez Luna, second wife of *José López Portillo y Rojas*, secretary of foreign relations, 1914; great-uncle of José López Portillo, president of Mexico, 1976–82; grandfather of Julio Scherer García, intellectual and publisher; professor of *Emilio Portes Gil*, who appointed him president of the Supreme Court; taught many prominent postrevolutionary politicians. J] None. K] None. L] DP70, 819; Almanaque de Guanajuato, 152; Peral, Appendix, 135; Dir social, 1935, 90; letters.

García, Trinidad
(Deceased February 18, 1906) A] May 28, 1831. B] Sombrerete, Zacatecas. C] Early education unknown; teaching certificate; pharmacy studies in Mexico City; professor of liberal arts; director, Deaf-Mute School, Mexico City, 1904. D] Local deputy to the state legislature of Zacatecas, 1867; federal deputy from the State of Zacatecas, 1869–70; *federal deputy* from the Federal District, Dist. 9, 1886–88; *federal deputy* from the Federal District, Dist. 1, 1888–90; *federal deputy* from the Federal District, Dist. 9, 1890–92; *federal deputy* from the Federal District, Dist. 7, 1892–94; *federal deputy* from the Federal District, Dist. 1, 1894–96; *federal deputy* from the Federal District, Dist. 7, 1896–98; *federal deputy* from the State of Oaxaca, Dist. 14, 1898–1900, 1900–02; *federal deputy* from the State of Veracruz, Dist. 14, 1902–04, 1904–06. E] None. F] Political boss, Fresnillo, Zacatecas, 1867–68; secretary general of government of the State of Zacatecas, 1868; justice of the Supreme Court, 1877–78; governor of Zacatecas; secretary of government, 1877–79; secretary of the treasury, 1879–80; director general of the mails, 1880; director, National Pawnshop. G] None. H] Owner of La Esmeralda Mining Company; patented many important copper mining techniques, 1861–65. I] Related to (son or nephew of) Francisco García Salinas, governor of Zacatecas; relative of Trinidad García, mayor of Fresnillo, 1835; married

Luz Valdez; father of Genaro García, prominent historian. J] Joined the national guard, 1856; fought under Ignacio Zaragoza. K] Jailed for supporting *Porfirio Díaz*, 1871. L] Enc Mex, V, 176–77; DP70, 820; Rice, 240, Mestre, 224; Sierra, 88–89.

García Correa, Bartolomé
(Deceased 1978) A] April 2, 1893. B] Uman, Yucatán. C] Primary studies at a private night school; secondary studies from the Literary Institute of Yucatán; primary schoolteacher; professor at the Modelo School. D] Mayor of Uman, Yucatán; mayor of Mérida, Yucatán; local deputy to the state legislature of Yucatán, 1917; *senator* from the State of Yucatán, 1928–30; *governor* of Yucatán, 1930–34; senator from the State of Yucatán, 1934–40. E] Member of the Anti-Reelectionist party, 1910; secretary of the Benito Juárez Political Club, 1913; founder and vice-president of the Socialist party of the Southeast, 1918; member of the organizing committee to establish the National Revolutionary party (PNR), December 1928. F] Interim governor of Yucatán (3 times); private secretary to *Felipe Carrillo Puerto* as mayor of Mérida. G] Founder of the Mutualist Workers Union, 1913. H] Laborer in a harness factory. J] Supported the Constitutionalists, 1913; opposed the *Adolfo de la Huerta* rebellion, 1923. K] Jailed for political activities; retired from politics in Cerro de Ortega, Tecomán, Colima, in 1940. L] C de S, 1928–30; C de S, 1934–40.

García Cuéllar, Samuel
(Deceased August 24, 1923) A] 1867. B] San Fernando, Tamaulipas. C] Early education unknown; enrolled in the National Military College, 1883, graduating as a lieutenant in the engineers, 1887; director, Military Preparatory School; director, National Military College, 1914. D] *Alternate federal deputy* from the State of México, Dist. 14, 1902–04, 1904–06; *alternate federal deputy* from the Federal District, Dist. 8, 1906–08; *alternate federal deputy* from the Federal District, Dist. 6, 1908–10; *federal deputy* from the State of Oaxaca, Dist. 5, 1910–12; *senator* from the State of Tamaulipas,

1914–16. E] None. F] Adviser, International Boundary Commission between Mexico and the United States, 1894–95; inspector of police, 1910; chief of the presidential staff, 1910–11; *governor* of the Federal District, 1911, 1913–14. G] None. H] None. I] Student at the military college with *Alberto Canseco*, interim governor of Zacatecas, 1913–14, *Alberto Robles Gil*, secretary of development, 1913, and David de la Fuente, secretary of communications, 1913. J] Career army officer; aide to General *Felipe Berriozábal*, secretary of war, 1897–1900; rank of 1st captain, March 20, 1900; served in the Tamaulipas Military Zone; rank of colonel, January 14, 1910; fought against the Maderistas, 1910–11, lost his arm in battle, 1911; commander, 6th Battalion, Guerrero District, Chihuahua, 1911; defeated *Francisco I. Madero*'s forces at Casas Grandes, 1911; rank of brigadier general, March 7, 1911; resigned from the army, March 24, 1911; rejoined the army, 1913; rank of brigade general, March 5, 1913; rank of division general, March 5, 1914; retired from the army, 1914. K] None. L] Cuevas, 351; Peral, Appendix, 130–31; DP70, 823; Sec of War, 1914, 19; Mestre, 271.

García de Alba (Larios), Ruperto
(Deceased) A] March 27, 1883. B] Tecolotlán, Jalisco. C] Early education unknown; no degree; professor, Heroic Military College. D] None. E] None. F] Oficial mayor of communications, 1930; *provisional governor* of Jalisco, 1930–31; *governor* of Baja California del Sur, 1931–32. G] None. H] Unknown. I] Son of Esteban García de Alba, physician, and Policarpa Larios; grandson of Rafael García de Alba, physician; brother of Esteban García de Alba, senator from Jalisco, 1940–46. J] Joined the Constitutionalists, 1913; chief of staff for General *Juan Andreu Almazán*; commander of the garrison, Monterrey; commander of the garrison, Laredo; director, Technical Section, staff, Secretariat of War; rank of brigadier general, June 1, 1929. K] None. L] López, 398.

García Granados, Alberto
(Deceased October 8, 1915) A] 1849. B] Puebla, Puebla. C] Early education unknown; law degree, School of Law, Mexico City. D] Federal deputy from the State of Guerrero, Dist. 3, 1882–84; *federal deputy* from the State of Guerrero, Dist. 3, 1884–86. E] Anti-Reelectionist, but opposed *Francisco I. Madero*. F] *Secretary* of government, 1911; *governor* of the Federal District, 1911–12; *secretary* of government, 1913. G] None. H] Practicing lawyer; large landholder, managed own properties. I] Son of General Vicente García Granados, governor of Durango; father of Rafael García, historian and leading intellectual; brother of *Ricardo García Granados*, federal deputy, 1904–12; nephew of Miguel García Granados, president of Guatemala, 1869–78; married Teresa Campero; related by marriage to José Fernando Ramírez, secretary of foreign relations, 1851–52. J] None. K] Executed by *Venustiano Carranza*'s forces, Marksmanship School, San Lázaro, because he was thought to have participated in the murder of Madero. L] Enc Mex, V, 188; DP70, 827; López, 402; Mestre, 253.

García Granados, Ricardo
(Deceased June 8, 1930) A] April 18, 1851. B] Durango, Durango. C] Primary studies at the Hacienda de La Noria, Guanajuato; preparatory studies, Liceo Franco-Mexicano, Mexico City; studies in engineering, Polytechnic Schools, Karlsruhe and Aguisgran, Germany; studies in business, Bremen, Germany. D] *Federal deputy* from the State of Michoacán, Dist. 2, 1904–06, 1906–08, 1908–10, 1910–12. E] None. F] Consul, Hamburg; delegate, Pan American Congress, Rio de Janeiro, 1906; chargé d'affaires, El Salvador and Nicaragua, 1907–08; chargé d'affaires, 1908–09. G] None. H] Author; historian, engineer; helped design the railroad to Puerto Barrios, Guatemala. I] Son of General Vicente García, governor of Durango; brother of *Alberto García Granados*, secretary of government, 1913; nephew of Miguel García Granados, president of Guatemala, 1869–78; uncle of Rafael García Granados, leading intellectual and historian. J] None. K] Exiled by *Porfirio*

Díaz during his third presidential election, 1888; exiled for newspaper articles, 1915–20. L] DP70, 827; López, 402.

García Jurado, Ignacio
(Deceased 1964) A] 1885. B] Palizada, Campeche. C] Early education unknown; engineering degree, Naval College, Veracruz. D] *Senator* from Querétaro, 1930–34. E] None. F] Subdirector, Naval Department, Secretariat of War. G] None. H] None. I] Brother of *Manuel García Jurado*, oficial mayor of foreign relations, 1920. J] Career naval officer; inspector, Department of the Navy; director, national arsenal; director, naval commission to Spain to purchase warships; naval attaché, Washington, D.C.; director general, naval construction, Secretariat of the Navy, 1952–64. K] None. L] DP70, 829; DGF56, 385.

García Jurado, Manuel
(Deceased 1920) A] 1882. B] Palizada, Campeche. C] Early education unknown; law degree; teacher, Veracruz, Veracruz. D] None. E] None. F] Interim secretary of government, State of Veracruz, 1914; secretary of government of the State of Veracruz, under *Cándido Aguilar*, 1914–15; oficial mayor of foreign relations, 1920; in charge of *Venustiano Carranza*'s government in Veracruz, 1920; consul, Havana, Cuba, 1920. G] None. H] Journalist; director, *Alba y Alfa*, Villahermosa, Tabasco; director, *El Dictamen*, Veracruz; writer; lawyer. I] Brother of *Ignacio García Jurado*, naval officer and subdirector of the navy. J] None. K] None. L] DP70, 829; Peral, Appendix, 135.

García Naranjo, Nemesio
(Deceased 1963) A] March 8, 1883. B] Lampazos, Nuevo León. C] Primary studies, El Encinal, Texas, 1888–94; preparatory studies, Colegio Civil of Monterrey, 1897–1902; legal studies, National School of Law, Mexico City, 1903–09, graduating January 4, 1903; lab assistant, national history class, National Preparatory School; professor of Mexican history, National University, 1909–14; professor, National Military College, 1913–14. D] *Federal deputy* from the State of Mi-

choacán, Dist. 1, 1910–12; *alternate federal deputy* from the State of Zacatecas, Dist. 1, 1910–12; *federal deputy* from the State of Nuevo León, Dist. 4, 1912–13, member of the Great Committee. E] None. F] Librarian and secretary, National Museum of Archeology, History, and Ethnology, 1908–10; *subsecretary* of public instruction, in charge of the secretariat, 1913; *secretary* of public instruction, 1913–14. G] Member of the Mexican Academy of Language, 1938. H] Journalist; began writing for *La Tribuna*, 1900; wrote for *Hoy, El Universal*, and other papers; founded *Revista Mexicana*, San Antonio, Texas; wrote for *Excélsior*, 1934; historian. I] Son of Nemesio García y García, successful businessman in Lampazos, and Juana Naranjo; political changes ruined father's business, and had to move to the United States, 1886, where he managed a farm in Encinal, Texas; married Angelina Elizondo. J] None. K] Exiled to New York City, 1914–23, 1926–34; notable orator and member of the "Cuadrilátero group" of *José María Lozano, Querido Moheno* and *Franciso María de Olaguíbel*, who opposed *Francisco I. Madero* in the 1912–13 congress. L] UNAM, law, 1900–06, 149; DP70, WWM45; López, 406; Carreño, 183.

García Peña, Angel
(Deceased November 23, 1928) A] 1856. B] Chihuahua, Chihuahua. C] Early education unknown; enrolled in the National Military College, January 2, 1872, graduating as a 2nd lieutenant in the artillery, December 13, 1877; director, staff officers completing technical courses, 1902. D] None. E] None. F] Director, Geographic Exploratory Commission, 1910; *secretary* of war, 1912–13. G] None. H] None. I] Son of engineer Rodrigo García and Guadalupe Peña; son Rafael a lawyer. J] Career army officer; rank of captain, January 25, 1879; assigned to the National Artillery Foundry; staff officer, 3rd Division; staff, secretariat of war; adjutant; National Observatory; rank of major, December 28, 1880; rank of lt. colonel, July 1, 1884; assistant commander, Scientific Commission, Sonora, 1887; rank of colonel, August 2, 1890; chief of the Sci-

entific Commission, Sonora, 1899; staff inspector, 1st, 2nd and 3rd Military Zones, 1902; battalion commander in the Yaqui campaign, Sonora, 1887–89, 1891–97, 1899–1900, 1900–01; rank of brigadier general, September 15, 1904; rank of brigade general, September 12, 1911; rank of division general, September 11, 1912; retired from the army, March 1, 1913; recalled to active duty to oppose the North American invasion of Veracruz, 1914; military commander in Veracruz, 1914; retired from the army, June 8, 1914. K] Forced into a short exile by *Venustiano Carranza*, 1915. L] Sec of War, 1914, 18; Mestre, 281; Cuevas, 350; Almada, 1968, 220.

García Topete, Miguel
(Deceased May 25, 1928) A] 1856. B] Ameca, Jalisco. C] Early education unknown; law degree, 1903. D] Member of the City Council of Colima, Colima, 1879–80; *alternate federal deputy* from the State of Colima, Dist. 2, 1886–88; local deputy to the state legislature of Colima, 10th, 11th, 13th, and 19th legislatures. E] Member of the Anti-Reelectionist party, 1911. F] Secretary of the 2nd Judicial District of the First Instance, 1880; notary, Superior Tribunal of Justice of Colima; oficial mayor of government of Colima, 1883–87; oficial mayor of the state legislature of Colima, 1887–97; secretary of resolutions, Superior Court of Justice of the State of Colima, 1899; *interim governor* of Colima, 1911; secretary general of the government of Colima, 1912, 1916–17. G] None. H] Practicing lawyer. I] Unknown. J] None. K] None. L] Mestre, 281; Almada, Colima, 91–92; Enc Mex, V, 200; DP70, 833; Moreno, 59–60; Peral, Appendix, 137.

García (Valdez), Genaro
(Deceased November 26, 1920) A] August 17, 1867. B] Fresnillo, Zacatecas. C] Primary studies in San Luis Potosí; preparatory studies, Mexico City; law degree, National School of Law, 1891; professor, National School of Law; director, National Preparatory School. D] *Alternate federal deputy* from the State of Zacatecas, Dist. 4, 1892–94; *federal deputy* from the State

of Zacatecas, Dist. 6, 1894–96, 1896–98, 1898–1900; 1900–02; *governor* of Zacatecas, 1900–04; *federal deputy* from the State of Zacatecas, Dist. 5, 1902–04, 1904–06, 1906–08, 1908–10, 1910–12, president of the chamber, 1910, 1912. E] None. F] Director, National Museum of Archeology, History, and Ethnology. G] None. H] Practiced law briefly; translator; historian; journalist. I] Son of *Trinidad García*, secretary of the treasury, 1879–80, and Luz Valdez; father of José A. García Aguirre, president of Minera Mexicana; father of Trinidad García Aguirre, founder the National Action party; married Concepción Aguirre; guardian at law school was Pedro de Azcué, federal deputy; grandfather of Jaime García Terrés, poet and director of the Fondo de Cultura Económica, 1982–88. J] None. K] None. L] Enc Mex, V, 185; DP70, 818; QesQ, 228; UNAM, law, 1880–91, 9.

García Vigil, Manuel
(Deceased April 19, 1924) A] 1882. B] Oaxaca, Oaxaca. C] Primary studies in Oaxaca, Oaxaca; graduated from the National Military College as a 2nd lieutenant in Artillery, 1902. D] *Constitutional deputy* from the State of Oaxaca, Dist. 1, 1916–17, but did not attend; *federal deputy* from the Federal District, Dist. 10, 1917–18; *federal deputy* from the State of Oaxaca, Dist. 1, 1918–20; *governor* of Oaxaca, 1920–24. E] Supported *Bernardo Reyes*'s group as a student; prominent figure in Constitutional Liberal party, cofounded by *Pablo González*, 1916–22. F] None. G] None. H] Employee, Trolley Car Company of Mexico City; journalist, opposed *Porfirio Díaz*; poet. I] Unknown. J] Joined *Francisco I. Madero*'s forces in the United States; joined the Constitutionalists, 1913; represented General Magdaleno Cedillo, Convention of Aguascalientes, 1914–15; rank of brigadier general; chief of artillery under General *Pablo González*; supported the Plan of Agua Prieta, 1920; supported the *Adolfo de la Huerta* rebellion, 1923. K] Executed, allegedly on orders from *Alvaro Obregón*, for supporting de la Huerta, in Almoloya, Oaxaca. L] DP70, 833; López, 410; Almanaque de Oaxaca, 131; Cuevas, 408.

Garrido Canabal, Tomás
(Deceased 1943) A] September 20, 1890.
B] Catazaja, Chiapas. C] Early education
unknown; legal studies, Campeche, law
degree, Mérida. D] *Governor* of Tabasco, 1923–26; *senator* from the State
of Tabasco, 1926–30; *governor* of Tabasco, 1931–34. E] Founder and leader
of the Bloc of Revolutionary Youth (Red
Shirts), who radicalized politics in Tabasco
and supported *Lázaro Cárdenas* for president, 1934. F] Executive secretary, Revi-
sory Board for Criminal Law, Mérida;
worked for *Salvador Alvarado* in Yucatán,
1915; district court judge, Villahermosa,
Tabasco, 1919; interim governor of Tabasco, 1919; interim governor of Yucatán,
1920; *secretary* of agriculture, 1934–35.
G] None. H] Cattle rancher. I] Parents
were wealthy landowners in Chiapas and
Tabasco; cousin of Manuel Garrido Lacroix, senator from Tabasco, 1930–34;
cousin of Alejandro Lastra Ortiz, governor
of Tabasco, 1935; cousin of *José Domingo
Ramírez Garrido*, federal deputy, 1920–
22; early political mentor of Carlos A.
Madrazo, Red Shirt student leader and
president of PRI, 1964–65. J] None.
K] Left Tabasco because of consequences
of the expedition to Villahermosa under
Rodulfo Brito Foucher, 1935; left cabinet
because of loyalty to *Plutarco Elías Calles*; exiled to Costa Rica, 1935; returned
to Mexico, 1940; remembered for his se-
vere antichurch and antialcohol campaign
and dictatorial control in Tabasco. L] Almanaque de Tabasco, 152; Dulles, 612–
20; Bulnes, 191.

Garza Aldape, Manuel
(Deceased February 28, 1924) A] April 9,
1871. B] Múzquiz, Coahuila. C] Primary and secondary studies, Múzquiz;
preparatory studies at the Ateneo Fuente,
Saltillo, on a scholarship from his home-
town; law degree, National School of Law,
1894. D] *Federal deputy* from the State
of Coahuila, Dist. 4, 1902–04, 1904–06;
federal deputy from the State of Coahuila,
Dist. 3, 1906–08, 1908–10. E] Opposed
the governor of Coahuila, 1893. F] Private secretary to Governor *Miguel Cárdenas*; *secretary* of public instruction, 1913;
secretary of foreign relations, 1913; *secretary* of government, 1913–14; *secretary* of

development, 1913–14; *secretary* of agriculture, 1914. G] None. H] Practicing
lawyer. I] Son of José María Garza and
Catalina Adalpe; brother José María was a
federal deputy from Michoacán, 1914–16;
brother Miguel, a lawyer. J] Civilian supporter of *Félix Díaz* and *Bernardo Reyes's*
rebellion, 1913. K] None. L] Peral, Appendix, 138; Mestre, 272; DP70, 837; Album; Enc Mex, V, 225; FSRE, 155–56;
Carrasco Puente, 51; UNAM, law, 1880–
91, 144.

Garza Ayala, Lázaro
(Deceased May 3, 1913) A] December 17,
1830. B] Monterrey, Nuevo León. C] Pri-
mary studies in Monterrey; secondary
studies at the Conciliar Seminary of Mon-
terrey; law degree, University of Nuevo
León, March 8, 1859. D] *Governor* of
Nuevo León, 1887–89; *senator* from the
State of Nuevo León, 1912–13. E] None.
F] Political boss of the Center, San Luis
Potosí, 1864; interim governor of Nuevo
León, 1869; interim governor and military commander of Nuevo León, 1872;
president, Superior Tribunal of Justice of
the State of Nuevo León. G] None.
H] None. I] Son of Patricio Rodríguez and
Rosalía García, very poor; raised by parish
priest Francisco Garza Ayala, who taught
him primary and paid for his legal studies;
original name was Lázaro Rodríguez García, but changed to the priest's name; married Lilia Bee Martínez, daughter of General Hamilton Bee and Andrea Martínez
Garza; related by marriage to General *Fortunato Maycotte*, provisional governor of
Durango, 1916. J] Drafted into the army,
1846; fought against the North American
invasion, 1846; rank of lieutenant, 1855;
fought under General Vidaurri during the
war of the Reform; fought under General
Zaragoza against the French, 1863; chief of
staff to General Zaragoza, Battle of Puebla;
rank of brigade general, June 18, 1863;
quartermaster general of the army, 1865;
commander of the Fort of Monterrey;
commander general of artillery, Army of
the North; captured by the French and
sent to Martinique, 1864; escaped once
but recaptured; allowed to return by Maximilian; no military post, 1901. K] Broke
with *Bernardo Reyes*, 1889. L] Sec of
War, 1911, 1911, 16; Peral, Appendix,

139–40; Hombres prominentes, 302–04; Enc Mex, V, 226; DP70, 838; Almanaque de Nuevo León, 98; Covarrubias, 4, 115–22; Mestre, 247; González de la Garza, II, 520–22.

Garza Galán, José María
(Deceased December 15, 1902) A] Unknown. B] Villa de Múzquiz, Coahuila. C] Primary studies in Coahuila; no degree. D] *Governor* of Coahuila, 1890–93; *senator* from the State of Zacatecas, 1898–1902. E] None. F] None. G] None. H] Businessman; organized companies to develop the Sierra Mojada; son formed numerous coal companies, 1901–07. I] Son of Andrés Garza and Refugio Galán; related to Múzquiz and Galán families, Villa de Múzquiz; related to María Galán, wife of Alejandro Elquezábal, entrepreneur and senator; introduced to President *Porfirio Díaz* by General *Gerónimo Treviño*; son Andrés, a mining engineer and businessman. J] Joined the national guard to fight Indians; rank of brigadier general in the reserves, October 26, 1893. K] None. L] Sec of War, 1901, 25; Hombres prominentes, 237–38; Mestre, 215; Cuéllar Valdés, 178; Langston, 70, 133.

Garza García, Genaro
(Deceased December 14, 1904) A] 1842. B] Pesquería Grande, Villa García, Nuevo León. C] Primary studies, Villa García; secondary studies Conciliar Seminary of Monterrey; law degree, Conciliar Seminary of Monterrey, May 6, 1864. D] Governor of Nuevo León, 1877–79; supernumerary justice of the Supreme Court, 1878–85; governor of Nuevo León, 1881–83; senator from the State of Nuevo León, 1880–84; *governor* of Nuevo León, 1885. E] None. F] Governor and military commander of Nuevo León, 1871–72; governor of Nuevo León, 1876–77. G] None. H] None. I] Son of Joaquín García, governor of Nuevo León; confidant of General *Gerónimo Treviño*; married Mariana Fernández. J] Supported Maximilian; supported the Plan of La Noria, 1871; supported the Plan of Tuxtepec, 1876. K] Won the election for governor, 1885, but the Senate removed him from office because of intense disputes with the opposition; *Porfirio Díaz* tried to persuade him to run again, but he refused and retired because of disagreements with the president, 1885. L] Enc Mex, V, 226; DP70, 838–39; González Cosío, 9; Covarrubias, II, 131–38.

Garza González, Agustín
(Deceased June 25, 1957) A] February 28, 1873. B] San Isidro hacienda, Pesquería Chica, Nuevo León. C] Primary studies in Villa de Pesquería Chica; preparatory studies at the Colegio Civil de Monterrey; medical degree, surgery and obstetrics, School of Medicine, University of Nuevo León, January 12, 1899. D] *Constitutional deputy* from the State of Nuevo León, Dist. 6, 1916–17; local deputy to the state legislature of Nuevo León, 1918. E] Supported Madero, 1910. F] Consul, Constitutionalists, Brownsville, Texas, 1913–14; customs administrator, Nuevo Laredo, 1915–16; vice-president, Higher Council of Health, State of Nuevo León, 1923; director, Coordinated Health Services, State of Nuevo León, 1935. G] None. H] Physician. I] Son of Francisco Javier de la Garza, small farmer and business partner with León Guzmán, federal deputy, 1867, and María de Jesús González. J] None. K] None. L] Covarrubias, II, 282; C de D, 1916–17.

Garzón Cossa, Gabriel.
A] January 29, 1892. B] Veracruz, Veracruz. C] Primary studies, Alejandro Macías's private school; secondary studies at the Veracruz Institute; enrolled in the National School of Medicine, 1907, but left to serve in the White Cross during the Revolution in Chihuahua, 1911; medical degree, with a thesis on hepatic abscesses, National Medical School, UNAM, 1913; advanced studies, Johns Hopkins University, on a scholarship, 1920; medical assistant in parasitology, Rockefeller Foundation, Veracruz, 1925; rector of the University of Veracruz, 1944. D] Local deputy to the state legislature of Veracruz, 1917–19; president of the state legislature of Veracruz, 1920; *governor* of Veracruz, 1920. E] Ran for mayor of Veracruz, but lost, 1935. F] None. G] None. H] Practicing physician. I] Son of Gabriel Gar-

zón López, musician, and Adela Cossa; son Román is a physician; attended secondary school with President Adolfo Ruiz Cortines. J] Supported the *Adolfo de la Huerta* rebellion, 1923; colonel in de la Huerta's forces in Tabasco, 1924; promoted to brigadier general, 1924. K] In exile in Cuba, physician, 1924–25. L] Pasquel, 134–36; Peral, Appendix, 141.

Gasca, Celestino
(Deceased April 6, 1981) A] May 17, 1893. B] Cuitzeo de Abasolo, Guanajuato. C] Early education unknown; no degree. D] Federal deputy from the State of Guanajuato, Dist. 2, 1937–40; senator from the State of Guanajuato, 1940–46, president of the First National Defense Committee, member of the First Balloting Group, president of the Second Labor Committee, and second secretary of the First Mines Committee. E] Secretary of labor action of the Pro Avila Camacho Committee, 1939–40; supporter of General Miguel Henríquez Guzmán for president, 1951–52. F] *Governor* of the Federal District, 1921–23. G] Joined the House of the Workers of the World, 1913; active in the Red Labor Battalions, which supported General *Alvaro Obregón*; secretary general of the Shoeworkers Union; important leader of Regional Confederation of Mexican Labor (CROM). H] Worked as a saddle maker before the Revolution of 1910; employee of United Shoe Leather. I] Father was a peasant and shoemaker. J] Joined the Revolution, 1910; enlisted in the army, May 2, 1915; fought against *Adolfo de la Huerta's* forces in Tabasco, Veracruz, and Hidalgo, 1923; quartermaster general of the army, 1929; fought against the Escobar rebellion, 1929; rank of brigadier general. K] Founder of the Federal Board of Conciliation and Arbitration as governor of the Federal District; candidate for governor of Guanajuato, but lost to *Agustín Arroyo Ch.*, 1927; precandidate for governor of Guanajuato, 1935; precandidate for secretary general of the Mexican Federation of Labor (CTM); accused by the government of supporting a leftist insurrection against President Adolfo López Mateos, 1962, and briefly imprisoned. L] Peral,

326; C de D, 1937–39, 11; C de S, 1940–46; López, 414; Enc Mex, V, 1977, 277–78; HA, 20 Apr. 1981, 12; Meyer, No. 12, 99.

Gastélum (Izabal), Bernardo J.
(Deceased) A] November 4, 1889. B] Culiacán, Sinaloa. C] Early education unknown; medical degree, University of Guadalajara, 1910; studies, Columbia University, New York City; advanced medical studies, University of Montevideo, Paris, Rome, Vienna, and the United States; professor of gynecology, National Medical School, UNAM; director, Colegio Civil Rosales, Culiacán, Sinaloa; founder and first rector, Universidad de Occidente (University of Sinaloa). D] None. E] None. F] Ambassador to Uruguay, 1923–24; *subsecretary* in charge of public education, 1924; *secretary* of education, 1924; *director*, Department of Health, 1925–28; ambassador to Italy and Hungary, 1929–30; director, Legal Medical Services, Culiacán, Sinaloa, 1935; secretary, Higher Council on Health, 1958–64; adviser, secretary of health, 1971. G] None. H] Practicing physician; director, Carmen Hospital; author of numerous medical works; cofounder of *Contemporáneos*; contributor to *Hoy*. I] Son of Ignacio M. Gastélum Díaz, lawyer, and María del Rosario Izabal y Bátiz; married Ascención Almada. J] Constitutionalist. K] None. L] Dir social, 1935, 222–23; Enc Mex, V, 240; WWM45, 48; López, 414; WNM, 93.

Gaviño (Iglesias), Angel
(Deceased 1921) A] 1855. B] Mexico City. C] Early education unknown; medical degree, National School of Medicine, 1891; lab assistant, hygiene, National School of Medicine, 1884; founded first bacteriology lab in Mexico, 1885–87; professor of bacteriology (founded the course), National School of Medicine, until 1921; professor of hygiene and meteorology, National School of Medicine, studied in Paris under Pasteur, Duclaux, and Roux, and in other European cities, 1891, 1893, 1903, 1904; founder and director, National Bacteriological Institute, UNAM, 1904–14. D] *Alternate senator* from the State of México, 1900–08; *senator* from the State

of Aguascalientes, 1908–10. E] None. F] None. G] Member of the National Academy of Medicine, 1891. H] Physician. I] Unknown. J] Supported *Victoriano Huerta's* presidency. K] Sentenced to death for collaborating with Huerta administration, but not carried out, 1914. L] Enc Mex, V, 247; DP70, 842.

Gavira, Gabriel
(Deceased July 15, 1956) A] March 18, 1867. B] Mexico City. C] Primary studies in the Lancasterian system; studies at the National Vocational School; self-educated in French, English, geometry, chemistry. D] None. E] None. F] President, Higher Tribunal of Military Justice; *interim governor* of San Luis Potosí, 1915; *interim governor* of Durango, 1916–17; governor of Baja California del Norte, 1936. G] Active in the labor movement in Orizaba; cofounder of the Mutualist Liberal Circle, Orizaba, Veracruz, 1892. H] Carpenter for many years. I] Son of Moisés Eduardo Gavira, an accordion player, and Pilar Castro. J] Joined the Revolution under the Maderistas, November 20, 1910; fought under Generals *Manuel Diéguez, Francisco Murguía,* and *Alvaro Obregón,* in San Luis Potosí and Durango; commander of expeditionary forces in Sinaloa and Sonora; attended the Convention of Aguascalientes, 1914–15; military commander of San Luis Potosí, 1915; military commander of Durango, 1916–17; supported General Obregón in 1920; chief of staff, secretariat of war, 1925–27; reached rank of brigade general. K] Led a rebellion against the authorities of Veracruz before the Revolution; imprisoned in San Juan de Ulloa; losing candidate for the governorship of the State of Veracruz; president of the Council of War which sentenced *Felipe Angeles* to death. L] López, 414; letter; Enc. Mex., V, 247.

Gaxiola (del Castillo Negrete), Francisco Javier
(Deceased November 18, 1933) A] January 31, 1870. B] Villa de Sinaloa, Sinaloa. C] Primary and secondary studies, Colegio de Rosales, Culiacán, Sinaloa; began medical studies, but switched to law, National Medical School, Mexico City; law de-

gree, National School of Law, 1894; professor, National School of Law. D] Local deputy to the state legislature of Mexico; *alternate federal deputy* from the State of México, Dist. 16, 1894–96, 1896–98; *alternate federal deputy* from the State of México, Dist. 12, 1900–02, 1906–08. E] None. F] *Interim governor* of México, 1919–20. G] None. H] Intellectual; author of several historical volumes; founder of Gaxiola law firm, Mexico City. I] Son of Celso Gaxiola, engineer and director of the mint, Mexico City, and Victoria del Castillo Negrete; grandson of José Antonio Gaxiola, miner, and Francisca Alcalde; nephew of Jesús Gaxiola Alcalde, deputy and governor of Sinaloa; father of Francisco Javier Gaxiola, secretary of industry and commerce, 1940–44; fellow students included *Jorge Vera Estañol,* secretary of public instruction, 1913, and *Jesús Urueta,* secretary of foreign relations, 1914; married Blanca Zendejas, daughter of career officer Joaquín Zendejas. J] None. K] None. L] Linajes, 113–16; Mestre, 288; UNAM, law, 1891–96, 31; Martínez Torres, 552; DP70, 843; Enc Mex, V, 248; López, 414; letters.

Gayol (y Soto), Roberto
(Deceased 1936) A] 1857. B] Tulancingo, Hidalgo. C] Primary studies in Tulancingo; engineering degree, College of Mines, Mexico City, February 1880; professor of engineering, College of Mines; advanced studies in engineering, United States. D] *Federal deputy* from the State of Puebla, Dist. 3, 1894–96; *federal deputy* from the State of Puebla, Dist. 4, 1896–98, 1898–1900, 1900–02, 1902–04, 1904–06. E] None. F] Subdirector of public works, Mexico City, 1885–88; director, drainage works, Mexico City, 1888–97. G] None. H] Began engineering practice with Eleuterio Méndez, Cuautitlán–El Salto Railroad, 1879–80; engineer, Dolores Hidalgo and San Luis Potosí highway, 1881–82; engineer, Inter-Oceanic Railroad Road project, Jalapa to Veracruz, 1883; chief engineer, Jalapa, Perote and Veracruz Railroad project, 1882–85; stockholder, Central Railroad and National Railroad of Mexico. I] Unknown. J] None. K] None. L] Hombres promi-

nentes, 305–06; Enc Mex, V, 249; DP70, 843; Pérez López, 161–62; QesQ, 239; Peral, Appendix, 141; López, 415.

Gochicoa, Francisco de Paula
(Deceased August 4, 1908) A] 1825. B] Mexico City. C] Early education unknown; no degree; founding member of Lancasterian Society (peer education). D] *Federal deputy* from the State of México, Dist. 14, 1886–88, 1888–90, 1890–92; *federal deputy* from the State of México, Dist. 16, 1892–94; *federal deputy* from the State of México, Dist. 6, 1894–96, 1896–98; *federal deputy* from the State of Guanajuato, Dist. 13, 1898–1900, 1902–04, 1904–06, 1906–08; 1908. E] None. F] Comptroller general and acting secretary of the treasury, 1861; director general, National Pawnshop, 1877–78; director general of mails, 1879–89. G] None. H] Unknown. I] Unknown. J] Accompanied Benito Juárez to the frontier during the French invasion. K] None. L] Mestre, 232; Enc Mex, V, 421; López, 422; DP70, 878; Sierra, 75–76.

Gómez, Arturo
(Deceased) A] 1879. B] Colima, Colima. C] Preparatory studies, National Preparatory School; law degree, National School of Law, Mexico City, 1906. D] Member of the City Council, Coyoacán, Federal District; *federal deputy* from the State of Colima, Dist. 1, 1912–13, member of the Great Committee; *senator* from the State of Colima, 1920–22; federal deputy from the State of Colima, Dist. 2, 1934–37. E] Candidate for senator, but his opponent was imposed, 1918; member of the Colima Liberal party, 1934. F] President of the Superior Tribunal of Justice; chief of political control, State of Colima, 1911–12; secretary of government of the State of Colima, 1915; director, official paper of the State of Jalisco; agent of the Ministerio Público, Guadalajara, Jalisco; agent of the Military Ministerio Público, Jalisco; chief of lawyers, Federal Board of Conciliation and Arbitration. G] None. H] Director and owner, *Cultura*; editor, *La Gaceta de Guadalajara*; practicing lawyer. I] Son of *Gildardo Gómez*, governor of Colima. J] Constitutionalist, 1913; rank of major.

K] None. L] Colliman, 112—13; C de S, 1920–22.

Gómez, Gildardo
(Deceased August 9, 1907) A] June 1851. B] Ciudad Guzmán, Jalisco. C] Primary studies in Ciudad Guzmán and Colima; no degree. D] Member of the City Council of Colima, 1876–77; *alternate senator* from the State of Colima, 1884–88; *governor* of Colima, 1887–91, 1891–93; *alternate federal deputy* from the State of Guanajuato, Dist. 1, 1894–96, 1896–98; *alternate federal deputy* from the State of Guanajuato, Dist. 11, 1898–1900, 1900–02, 1902–04, 1904–06. E] None. F] Director of printing, State of Colima, 1877–79; political boss of Colima, 1879–80; oficial mayor of the government of Colima, 1880–81; secretary general of government of the State of Colima, 1881–82; editor, official paper, State of Colima, 1881. G] None. H] Began working as a printer in youth; journalist; published *La Sociedad Católica, El Boletin Municipal*, 1875. I] Parents were poor, orphaned at a young age, raised by relatives; son *Arturo Gómez*, senator from Colima, 1922–24. J] None. K] Resigned as governor, November 29, 1893. L] Godoy, 152; Enc Mex, V, 438; DP70, 880; Pavía, 109–11; Peral, Appendix, 143–44; Mestre, 228; Moreno, 47–50; Hombres prominentes, 265–66.

Gómez (Díaz), Abundio
(Deceased) A] Unknown. B] Hacienda Nueva, Tetipac Municipio, Guerrero and México state frontier. C] Early education unknown; no degree. D] *Governor* of the State of México, 1921–25. E] Founder of the Socialist Workers party, 1925. F] *Governor* of México , 1920–21; oficial mayor of war, 1928–29; *subsecretary* of war, 1929. G] None. H] Cattle broker with brother Filiberto; treasurer, Cía. Minera Rey de Plata, S.A. I] Son of Antonio Gómez and Rita Díaz, peasants employed on the Hacienda Nueva in Tetipac; married Carlota Martínez; brother *Filiberto Gómez Díaz*, governor of México, 1929–33; brother Telésforo died fighting in the Revolution. J] Constitutionalist in the Obregón Brigade; opposed *Francisco Villa*

at Celaya, 1914–15; supported the Plan of
Agua Prieta, 1920; rank of brigade general,
July 20, 1920; commander of the Valley of
México military zone; commander of the
Mexico City garrison, 1935; retired from
the army because of blindness. K| None.
L| Dir social, 1935, 92, 223; Sánchez Gar-
cía, 287–89.

Gómez (Díaz), Filiberto
(Deceased June 20, 1934) A| August 22,
1884. B| Hacienda Nueva, Tetipac Muni-
cipio, Guerrero and México state frontier.
C| Primary studies, Ixcapuzalco, Guerrero;
no degree. D| Local deputy to the state
legislature of México; *federal deputy* from
the State of México, Dist. 10, 1922–24,
1924–26, president of the Great Committee; *senator* from the State of México,
1926–30; *governor* of México, 1929–33.
E| President of the Organizing Committee
of the National Revolutionary party, 1929.
F| None. G| None. H| Miner; owned
a mine in Guerrero; cattle broker with
brother *Abundio Gómez*. I| Son of Anto-
nio Gómez and Rita Díaz, peasants employed on the Hacienda Nueva in Tetipac;
brother Telésforo died in the Revolution;
brother Abundio Gómez subsecretary of
war, 1929; married Eleazar Hernández.
J| Constitutionalist, fought under *Joaquín
Amaro*; opposed *Francisco Villa* at Celaya,
1914–15, as an officer in the Obregón Brigade; supported the Plan of Agua Prieta,
1920. K| None. L| Enc Mex, V, 437–38;
Sánchez García, 287–88; Siliceo, 94–99.

Gómez Morín, Manuel
(Deceased April 19, 1972) A| February 27,
1897. B| Batopilas, Chihuahua. C| Pri-
mary studies at the Colegio del Sagrado
Corazón in León, Guanajuato, 1906–10;
started preparatory studies at the Instituto
María Inmaculada, León, Guanajuato,
1910–13, and completed at the National
Preparatory School in Mexico City, 1913–
15; law degree from the National Law
School, UNAM, 1918; member of the generation of the National Preparatory School
known as the Seven Sages, which included
Narciso Bassols, Vicente Lombardo Toledano, Alfonso Caso, Octavio Medellín Ostos, and Teófilo Olea; courses in economics, Columbia University, New York, 1921;

secretary of the National Law School,
UNAM, 1918–19, dean of the National
Law, School, UNAM, 1922–24; professor
of law, UNAM, 1919–38; rector of the National Autonomous University of Mexico,
1933–34; member of the Governing Coun-
cil of UNAM. D| None. E| Supporter of
José Vasconcelos, 1929; founder and president of the National Executive Committee of the National Action party (PAN),
1939–49; candidate for federal deputy on
the PAN ticket, 1946, 1958. F| Clerk of
the 4th Correctional Court, Mexico City,
1915; official of the Department of Statistics, secretariat of development, 1916; oficial mayor of the Secretariat of the Treasury, 1919–20; *subsecretary* in charge of
the Secretariat of the Treasury, 1920–21;
financial agent for the federal government
in New York City, 1921–22; founder and
first chairman of the board of the Bank of
Mexico, 1925. G| President of the Stu-
dent Society of the National Law School.
H| Editor of *La Vanguardia*, 1915; practic-
ing lawyer, 1918–19, 1921–72; lawyer,
Soviet trade delegation, Mexico City,
1928; author of legislation creating the
Bank of Mexico; author of the first reform
of credit institutions 1931; major investor
in the Bank of London and Mexico, 1941,
and Cervecería Modelo, 1943; author of
several books. I| Longtime personal
friendships maintained with Alfonso Caso
and Vicente Lombardo Toledano despite
different political views; married Lydia
Torres; father a miner; father-in-law of
Juan Landerreche Obregón, leader of PAN;
son, Juan Manuel Gómez Morín, served
as secretary general of PAN, 1969–72.
J| None. K| Considered by some scholars
to have been a secret supporter of *Adolfo
de la Huerta*, 1923. L| WWM45, 50;
WB48, 2014–15; DBM68, 292; HA, 24
April 1972, 21; letters.

Gómez (Segura), Marte Rodolfo
(Deceased December 16, 1973) A| July 4,
1896. B| Ciudad Reynoso, Tamaulipas.
C| Primary studies in Aguascalientes and
at the Escuela Anexa a la Normal de Maes-
tros, Mexico City; no secondary or preparatory studies; agricultural engineering
studies from the National School of Agriculture, San Jacinto, 1909–14, agricultural

engineering degree, September 1917; helped organize the Escuela Libre Ateneo Ceres; attended the Free Social Science School, Paris, 1916–17; professor of rural economy, National School of Agriculture; director of the National School of Agriculture, 1923–24. D] Local deputy to the state legislature of Tamaulipas, 1927; *federal deputy* from the State of Tamaulipas, Dist. 2, 1928–30, president of the Chamber of Deputies, 1928; *senator* from the State of Tamaulipas, 1930–32, president of the Senate, 1932; governor of Tamaulipas, 1937–40. E] None. F] Topographer for the Agrarian Commission of Yautepec, Morelos, 1915; director of the Department of Ejido Improvements, 1917–22; auxiliary director of the National Agrarian Commission, 1917–22; assistant manager of the National Agrarian Credit Bank, 1926–28; *secretary* of agriculture, 1928–30; *subsecretary* of the treasury, 1933–34; *secretary* of the treasury, 1934; general manager of the National Railroads of Mexico, 1934; ambassador to France, 1935–36; secretary of agriculture, 1940–46; ambassador to the League of Nations, 1935–36; president of the Council of Development and Coordination of National Productivity, 1954–56. G] President of the local Agrarian Commission of Tamaulipas, 1925, appointed by *Emilio Portes Gil.* H] President of Worthington de México, S.A., 1950–66; author of many books on Mexican agriculture. I] Political associate of Emilio Portes Gil since 1920; close friend of General Jesús M. Garza, who graduated from the National School of Agriculture; father, Rodolfo Vidal Gómez, was a colonel and graduate of the National Military College; mother was a teacher in a private school; son a physician; close friend of Jaime Torres Bodet since 1935, when he served under Gómez in France; married Hilda Leal. J] Joined the Revolution in Morelos, 1915, served in the forces of *Emiliano Zapata.* K] Important leader of the *Plutarco Elías Calles* bloc in the Chamber of Deputies, 1928–30. L] WWM45, 50; EBW, 189; DBM68, 290; Brandenburg, 80; Peral, 338; WB48, 2015; HA, 8 Sept. 1944, 27; Enc Mex, V, 438–39; letter; HA, 24 Dec. 1973, 8; Medina, No. 20, 11; Meyer, No. 12, 27.

Gómez y Villavicencio, Ramón
(Deceased) A] August 1840. B] Ciudad de Bravos, Chihuahua. C] Primary studies in Bravos; no degree. D] Federal deputy from the State of Tamaulipas, 1880–82; federal deputy from the State of Querétaro, 1882–84; *senator* from the State of Aguascalientes, 1884–88; *federal deputy* from the State of México, Dist. 10, 1886–88, 1888–90, 1890–92; *federal deputy* from the State of México, Dist. 8, 1892–94; *alternate federal deputy* from the State of Tamaulipas, Dist. 1, 1894–96. E] None. F] None. G] None. H] Unknown. I] Unknown. J] Joined the army, 1853; captured and imprisoned during the French intervention, but released by General Tomás Mejía. K] Saved the life of Colonel Manuel Alas. L] Hombres prominentes, 381–82; C de S, 1886–88, 13; C de S, 1884–86, 9.

Góngora, Víctor Eduardo
(Deceased 1947) A] 1874. B] Ciudad del Carmen, Campeche. C] Secondary studies in Belgium; engineering studies, University of Ghent, 1896; studies at the University of Liege, 1896–97; engineering degree; professor of chemistry and architecture, Liceo Francés, Mexico City. D] *Constitutional deputy* from the State of Veracruz, Dist. 4, 1916–17; *senator* from Veracruz, 1917–18, 1924–28. E] Supported Madero, 1910; member of the Anti-Reelectionist party; opposed the re-election of Obregón, 1928. F] Inspector, ports and navigable rivers; oficial mayor of the government of Veracruz; treasurer, Veracruz, Veracruz; employee of the Secretariat of Public Works, 1935; represented Mexico at the Interplanetary Congress, Geneva, 1936. G] Union organizer. H] Civil engineer; journalist; directed the installation of streetcars from Mexico City to Villa de Guadalupe, 1898; engineer, Hydroelectric and Irrigation Company of Hidalgo. I] Wealthy parents. J] None. K] None. L] DP70, 889; C de D, 1916–17.

González, Martín
(Deceased July 27, 1908) A] 1832. B] Oaxaca, Oaxaca. C] Early education unknown, no degree. D] Federal deputy,

1872–74, 1878–80, 1880–82, 1882–84; *federal deputy* from the State of Jalisco, Dist. 13, 1884–86; *federal deputy* from the State of Oaxaca, Dist. 3, 1886–88, 1888–90, 1890–92; *federal deputy* from the State of Jalisco, Dist. 4, 1886–88, 1888–90; *federal deputy* from the State of Jalisco, Dist. 8, 1890–92, 1892–94; *federal deputy* from the State of Chihuahua, Dist. 4, 1894–96; *governor* of Oaxaca, 1894–1902; *senator* from the State of Guanajuato, 1902–04, 1904–06, 1906–08. E] None. F] Official, tax department, State of Oaxaca; chief of staff for President *Porfirio Díaz*, 1884–88. G] None. H] Founder and owner of many companies, including firms producing beer, soap, and cigarettes. I] Unknown. J] Career army officer; joined the National Guard as an ordinary soldier during the Ayutla Revolution, August 12, 1856; rank of Corporal, 1st Battalion, national guard of Oaxaca, 1858; rank of sergeant, 1st Morelos Battalion, October 10, 1859; rank of 2nd lieutenant, Mixed Brigade, Isthmus of Tehuantepec, 1860; adjutant to General *Porfirio Díaz* as commander of the Mountain Division, 1860; fought in the Bravos Battalion under General Rosas Londa, 1860; rank of captain (paymaster), October 10, 1862; paymaster, Guerrero Battalion, Oaxaca, 1862; captured, siege of Puebla, but escaped and fought in Oaxaca 1863; rank of captain (paymaster), Morelos Battalion, 1863–65; captured by General Bazaine, February 9, 1865, in Oaxaca; commander, First Division, 1866; captured a second time in Tecomatlán, 1866; rank of major, national guard, Oaxaca, February 12, 1867; rank of lt. colonel, February 28, 1876; chief of staff to General Díaz, 1877–80; rank of colonel in the reserves, June 30, 1877; rank of colonel, January 25, 1883; rank of brigadier general, September 21, 1887; rank of brigade general, 1903. K] Elected federal deputy from Jalisco and Oaxaca both, but served in the Jalisco post. L] Almanaque de Oaxaca, 1982, 130; Peral, 150–51; Mestre, 231; C de D, 1886, 116; Godoy, 208; Enc Mex, V, 452–53; DP70, 893; Sec of War, 1901, 23; Hombres prominentes, 425–26.

González (Alvarez), Aureliano S.
(Deceased August 13, 1915) A] 1869. B] Tepatitlán de Morales, Jalisco. C] Early education unknown; law degree, School of Law, Guadalajara. D] None. E] Joined the Anti-Reelectionist party, 1909; founder and first president, Central Club Benito Juárez, 1909. F] Judge, Judicial District of Mina, 1897–98; judge of the first instance, Iturbide District, 1898–1900; judge of the first instance, Ciudad Juárez, 1900–01; judge, Superior Tribunal of Justice of Chihuahua, 1901–07; judge, Bravo District, 1911; judge, Superior Tribunal of Justice of Sonora, 1913; interim governor of Chihuahua, 1911–12; secretary general of government of Chihuahua, 1912–13; secretary general of government of the State of Nuevo León under Governor Raúl Madero, 1914; advisory lawyer, Department of Government, State of Nuevo León, 1914. G] Secretary of the Press Association of Chihuahua. H] Stockholder and partner, La Gloria Mining Company. I] Son of Víctor González and Carmen Alvarez; married Carmen Vargas; close personal friend and confidant of *Abraham González*, governor of Chihuahua. J] Member of the Constitutionalist Revolutionary Board, El Paso, Texas, 1913; represented General Francisco Urbalejo, Convention of Aguascalientes, 1914. K] Executed on orders from *Francisco Villa*. L] DP70, 890; Almada, 462–64.

González (Casavantes), Abraham
(Deceased March 7, 1913) A] July 4, 1864. B] Ciudad Guerrero, Chihuahua. C] Primary studies, Chihuahua Institute, under Mariano Irigoyen, Ciudad Guerrero; preparatory studies, Scientific and Literary Institute of Chihuahua and the National Preparatory School, Mexico City; business studies, Notre Dame University, 1886, and Indiana University. D] *Governor* of Chihuahua, 1912–13. E] Cofounder, treasurer, and president of the Benito Juárez Central Club, 1909; president of the assembly of the Anti-Reelectionist Club, 1909; delegate to the Anti-Reelectionist Convention, Mexico City, 1910; proposed *Francisco I. Madero* as presidential candidate of the Anti-Reelectionist party, 1910.

F] *Provisional governor* of Chihuahua, 1911–12; *secretary* of government, 1911–12. G] None. H] Merchant, mining business, 1886; small mining business, Chorreras, Municipio of Aldama, Chihuahua, 1906; agent of the Hereford Breeding Company of Kansas City, introduced the Hereford to Chihuahua; translator, *El Padre Padilla*; teller, Bank of Chihuahua; traffic inspector, Chihuahua; administrator, streetcar company, Chihuahua, Chihuahua. I] Son of Abraham González and Dolores Casavantes, daughter of Colonel Jesús José Casavantes, governor of Chihuahua; nephew of Cruz González, governor of Chihuahua; close friend of Francisco I. Madero. J] Commander of the Maderista revolution in Chihuahua, 1910–11; provisonal governor and commander, 2nd Military Zone, Chihuahua, under Madero, 1910–11; rank of colonel, 1910. K] Assassinated by agents of *Victoriano Huerta*. L] QesQ, 247–48; López, 433; Márquez, 238–40; Serrano, 60–64; Puente, 123–28; Almada, 454; Almada, 1968, 229–30; Mestre, 246; Bojórquez, 159–61.

González de Cosío, Manuel
(Deceased December 14, 1913) A] December 29, 1836. B] Zacatecas, Zacatecas. C] Early education unknown; began engineering studies, National School of Mines, Mexico City, 1852, but left to fight in the Ayutla revolution, 1854. D] Local deputy to the state legislature of Zacatecas; federal deputy from the State of Zacatecas, 1868–70; governor of Zacatecas, 1876; federal deputy from the State of Zacatecas, Dist. 2, 1882–84; *federal deputy* from the State of Zacatecas, Dist. 5, 1884–86, 1886–88; mayor of Mexico City, 1886–89. E] None. F] Section chief, Secretariat of the Treasury; *secretary* of public works, 1891–95; *secretary* of government, 1895–1903; *secretary* of development, 1903–05; *secretary* of war, 1905–11. G] None. H] None. I] Related to (probably son of) Manuel González de Cosío, governor of Zacatecas. J] Joined the army as an adjutant, Guías Battalion, 1854, on the side of the Liberals; fought with the 29th Battalion against the French, 1863; rank of brigadier general, June 29, 1863; captured by the French

and deported to France; reincorporated into the Liberal forces from the United States by General *Francisco Mejía*; remained loyal to President Lerdo de Tejada, 1876–77; rank of division general, December 29, 1905; retired from the army, June 1, 1911. K] None. L] Godoy, 180–81; Album; López, 435; Mestre, 248; DP70, 897; Sec of War, 1911, 15.

González de Cosío (Araus), Francisco
(Deceased February 5, 1914) A] March 5, 1841. B] Querétaro, Querétaro. C] Early education unknown; engineering degree, National School of Mines, 1861. D] Local deputy to the state legislature of Querétaro, 1867–68; member of the City Council of Querétaro, Querétaro, 1877–78; local deputy to the state legislature of Querétaro, 1878–79; governor of Querétaro, 1880–83; *federal deputy* from the State of Puebla, 1884–85; *governor* of Querétaro, 1887–1911. E] None. F] None. G] None. H] Practicing engineer, 1861–67; owned a hacienda in Querétaro. I] Son of José González Cosío and Trinidad Araus. J] None. K] None. L] Mestre, 249; Godoy, 288–89; Enc Mex, V, 461; Hombres prominentes, 253–54; Peral, Appendix, 147–48; Holms, 328; Pavía, 300–03.

González (Esquivel), Celso
(Deceased February 27, 1897) A] July 28, 1834. B] Teocaltiche, Jalisco. C] Early education unknown; no degree. D] Local deputy to the state legislature of Chihuahua, 10th, 16th, 17th, 19th, and 20th legislatures. E] Established the "Papigochi" political group with *Manuel de Herrera*, governor of Chihuahua, and *Lauro Carrillo*, governor of Chihuahua, to oppose Terrazas's control of the governorship. F] Political boss of the Guerrero Canton (District), Chihuahua, 1867; director of taxes, Guerrero Canton, 1872; political boss, Guerrero Canton, 1874; *substitute governor* of Chihuahua, 1884; interim governor of Chihuahua, 1887–88. G] None. H] Owner of the Orientales hacienda; stockholder in the firm of *Jesús E. Valenzuela*; stockholder in a mining firm in La Galera, Chihuahua; business partner with *Manuel de Herrera* and Juan María Salazar in Chihuahua, Chihuahua. I] Son

of Paulino González and Guadalupe Esquivel; nephew of Gerónimo González, Franciscan administrator of the Tarahumara region; married Josefa Casavantes. J] Joined the Liberals and wounded in battle, Manzanillo, 1853; opposed La Noria rebellion, 1871. K] None. L] Almada, 381–84; Almada, 1968, 231.

González (Flores), Manuel del Refugio
(Deceased May 8, 1893) A] June 18, 1833. B] Rancho El Moquete, Municipio Matamoros, Tamaulipas. C] Primary studies only. D] Federal deputy from the State of Oaxaca, 1871–73; president of Mexico, 1880–84; *governor* of Guanajuato, 1885–93. E] None. F] Governor of Michoacán, 1877–78; secretary of war, 1878–79. G] None. H] Started out in business. I] Son of Fernando González Lerma, a landowner who died fighting the North Americans, 1847, and Eusebia Flores Capistrán; married Laura Mantecón; nephew, Marciano González Villarreal, oficial mayor of war, 1939–40; granddaughter, Gloria González, wife of Dr. Gonzalo Septién, cousin of Carlos Septién García, cofounder of the National Action party; grandson Mario González Ulloa, physician. J] Served under the Conservatives during the War of the Reform; joined the 1st Line Battalion as an ordinary soldier, 1853; reinforced San Juan de Ulloa, 1855; rank of lieutenant, 1855; battalion commander, 1859; rank of lt. colonel, March 18, 1860; chief of staff to General *Porfirio Díaz*, 1862; captured by the French, but escaped, 1862; rank of colonel, 1863; commander of the 1st Division, 1865; captured second time by the French, 1865; rank of brigade general, September 7, 1867; lost arm in the siege of Puebla, 1867; supported Díaz in the Plan of La Noria, 1871; supported Díaz during the Tuxtepec rebellion, 1876–77; rank of division general, March 13, 1877. L] QesQ, 249; López, 443; DP70, 892; Pavía, 178–79; Linajes, 116–17; Mestre, 183; García Purón, 211–12.

González Garza, Federico
(Deceased 1951) A] March 7, 1876. B] Saltillo, Coahuila. C] Preparatory studies, Colegio Ateneo Fuente, Saltillo, 1888–93; enrolled in legal studies, National School of Law, 1894, but had to leave school to support family; reenrolled, National School of Law, 1899, graduating with a law degree, March 28, 1906. D] *Senator* from the Federal District, 1922–26. E] Student activist against Governor Garza, expelled from preparatory school, 1893; president of the Executive Committee for *Francisco I. Madero's* presidential campaign, 1910; cofounder, Anti-Reelectionist party, and secretary of the Executive Committee, 1910; vice-president of the Anti-Reelectionist party; editor, *Anti-reelecionista*, 1911. F] Provisional secretary general of government of the State of Coahuila, 1911; subsecretary of justice, 1911; subsecretary of government, 1911–12; *governor* of the Federal District, 1912–13; director, Legal Department, Bank of Mexico, 1932–46. G] None. H] Telegrapher, chief of various offices, 1894–99; chief, Office of Telegrams, Mexico City, 1899; legal internship, Carlos F. Uribe firm, Mexico City, 1905; attorney, Warner, Johnson, and Galston, a firm which employed *José Vasconcelos*, Mexico City, 1906–07; founded firm with Burton W. Wilson, specialized in North American banks, 1907–08; author of Constitutional law books. I] Son of Agustín G. González and Prisciliana Garza; married Carmen Vázquez Tagle; niece married to Jesús Reyes Heroles, president of the Institutional Revolutionary party; brother of *Roque González Garza*, president, Convention government, 1915; met *Francisco I. Madero* as chief of San Pedro de Colonia Telegraph Office, Coahuila. J] Director, Revolutionary Center, San Antonio, Texas, 1910–11; secretary of government, first revolutionary government, Ciudad Juárez, 1911. K] Offered scholarship to study agricultural engineering, but declined. L] UNAM, law, 1891–94, 55; Blue Book, 173; Serrano, 107–17; WWM45, 51–52; López, 438; DP70, 899; EBW, 477.

González (Garza), Pablo
(Deceased March 4, 1950) A] May 5, 1879. B] Lampazos, Nuevo León. C] Primary studies in Nadadores, Coahuila; tried to enter the National Military College, but turned down. D] None. E] Editor of *Revolución*, Liberal party paper,

1907; joined the Anti-Reelectionist party; supported *Francisco I. Madero*, 1910–11; ran for president of Mexico, 1920. F] None. G] None. H] Miller, El Carmen Mill, Lampazos, Nuevo León, 1893; line laborer, Santa Fe Railroad, later foreman, 1902; worked in California, 1903; small businessman. I] Son of Pablo González and Prudencia Garza, but reared by brother (a small storekeeper in Nadadores) after orphaned at five. J] Commander of irregular forces supporting Madero, Coahuila, 1911; chief of Madero's forces in Monclova, Coahuila, 1911; rank of colonel, 1911; commander of the auxiliary forces of Coahuila, 1912; fought against *Pascual Orozco*, 1912; joined the Constitutionalists, 1913; commander-in-chief of the Armies of the Northeast and West; represented at the Convention of Aguascalientes, 1914–15; rank of division general (first Constitutionalist promoted to this rank), June 14, 1914; fought *Emiliano Zapata*, 1916; governor and military commander of Morelos, 1916, 1919; zone commander in Morelos, Puebla, Oaxaca, and Tlaxcala; rebelled against *Alvaro Obregón*, 1920. K] Sentenced to death for leading rebellion in Monterrey, but commuted by *Adolfo de la Huerta*, 1920; considered to be an intellectual author of Zapata's assassination; exiled to San Antonio, Texas, 1920–40. L] Enc Mex, V, 453; Morales Jiménez, 153–57; QesQ, 252–53; DP70, 893.

González Garza, Roque
(Deceased 1962) A] March 23, 1885. B] Saltillo, Coahuila. C] Primary studies in Saltillo; secondary studies in Cadereyta, Coahuila; studies at the Ateneo Fuente, Saltillo, and in Mexico City; law degree. D] *Federal deputy* from the State of Coahuila, Dist. 1, 1912–14; member of the Great Committee; *federal deputy* from the Federal District, Dist. 8, 1922–24. E] Joined the Anti-Reelectionist party, 1909; accompanied *Francisco I. Madero* on presidential campaign, 1910. F] President, Convention government, 1915; coordinator of public works, Vega de Metztitlán, Hidalgo, 1962. G] None. H] White-collar worker; lawyer; author of several historical books. I] Son of Agustín G. González and Prisciliana Garza; married Concepción de Garay; brother

Federico González Garza, governor of the Federal District, 1912–13; daughter Gloria married Jesús Reyes Heroles, president of the Institutional Revolutionary party; personal friend of Francisco I. Madero. J] Commander of the Maderista forces in Coahuila, 1910; Constitutionalist, 1913; commander, Colombia Sector, Coahuila, 1913; fought under *Francisco Villa*, 1914–15; representative of Villa to the Convention of Aguascalientes and Mexico City, 1914–15; president, Legion of Honor; rank of division general; aide to Madero. K] Saved Madero's life in the battle of Casas Grandes; exile, 1915–20. L] Covarrubias, 1952, 109; López, 438–39; DP70, 899; García Purón, 222.

González (González), Alejo G.
(Deceased) A] May 22, 1886. B] Guerrero, Coahuila. C] Primary and secondary studies, public schools in Guerrero; no degree. D] None. E] None. F] *Governor* and military commander of Chiapas, 1920; governor and military commander of Tlaxcala, 1920. G] None. H] Worked for a business, 1902. I] Son of Patricio González and Concepción González. J] Joined the army against *Pascual Orozco*, under Major *Cesáreo Castro*, as a 2nd lieutenant, 1912; signed the Plan of Guadalupe and joined the Constitutionalists, 1913; wounded in the battle for Reynosa, May 22, 1913; brigade commander, October 1914; commander of the Regional Division of Coahuila, 1915; rank of brigade general, April 23, 1915; commander of military operations in the States of México and Chiapas and the Isthmus of Tehuantepec; retired from the army from 1920–29; recalled March 5, 1929, to fight the Escobar rebellion; commander, 6th Military Zone, Coahuila, 1935–37. K] None. L] None.

González (González), Porfirio G.
(Deceased May 28, 1928) A] August 10, 1885. B] Villa de China, Nuevo León. C] Primary studies, Villa de China; abandoned studies after primary to help father farm; no degree. D] *Governor* of Nuevo León, 1923–25. E] None. F] *Provisional governor* and military commander of Nuevo León, 1920–21. G] None. H] Farmed; owned El Mirador hacienda.

I] Son of Máximo González, farmer, and Dolores González; father served in the Revolution as a 1st captain; brother Ramés, a colonel; married Elisa Flores; political mentor to Anacleto Guerrero, senator, 1952–58, and Bonifacio Salinas Leal, who bought El Mirador from his widow, and served as governor of Nuevo León. J] Supported *Francisco I. Madero* as a 2nd lieutenant, 1910; joined the Constitutionalists, 1913; personal escort of general *Pablo González*, 1913; commander, cavalry brigade, under General *Cesáreo Castro*, 1914; rank of colonel, 1914; commander, Nuevo León Brigade, 1915; retired from the army, 1915–20; rank of brigade general, 1920; opposed *Adolfo de la Huerta* rebellion, 1923; director of the Committee to Revise Service Records, 1927–28. K] None. L] Almanaque de Nuevo León, 102; Covarrubias, II, 187–94.

González (Mantecón), Fernando
(Deceased January 25, 1937) A] 1865. B] Oaxaca. C] Early education unknown; enrolled National Military College, 1879, graduating as a 2nd lieutenant of engineers. D] *Federal deputy* from the State of Michoacán, Dist. 4, 1892–94, 1894–96, 1896–98, 1898–1900; *federal deputy* from the State of Michoacán, Dist. 11, 1900–02, 1902–04; *governor* of México, 1905–09. E] None. F] *Interim governor* of México, 1904–05. G] None. H] None. I] Son of President *Manuel González Flores* and Laura Mantecón; grandson of Fernando González Lerma, landowner; cousin Macario González Villarreal, oficial mayor of war, 1939–40. J] Career military officer; staff officer, presidential staff of *Porfirio Díaz*; rank of lt. colonel of engineers, May 4, 1892; rank of brigade general, March 8, 1909; led rebellion against the government in Oaxaca and Puebla, 1926. K] None. L] Peral, Appendix, 149; Mestre, 292; Cuevas, 407.

González Martínez, Enrique
(Deceased February 19, 1952) A] April 13, 1871. B] Guadalajara, Jalisco. C] Primary studies at father's school, Guadalajara; preparatory studies at the Liceo for Boys and the Conciliar Seminary of Guadalajara; medical studies, University of Guadalajara, 1886–93, graduating, April 7,

1893; professor of French literature, School of Philosophy and Letters; professor of general literature, National Teachers College; professor of Spanish literature, National Preparatory School. D] None. E] None. F] Secretary general of government of the State of Sinaloa; secretary general of government of the State of Puebla, 1914; *subsecretary* of public education, 1913–14; ambassador to Chile, 1920–22, ambassador to Argentina, 1922–23; ambassador to Spain, 1924–31. G] Member of the National College, 1943–52; president, Seminar of Mexican Culture, 1942–43; National Prize for Literature, 1944; member of the Mexican Academy of Language. H] Physician, Guadalajara, 1893–95; physician, Sinaloa, 1895–1910; author; poet; distinguished intellectual. I] Son of José María G. González, teacher and principal, and Feliciana Martínez; son Enrique González Rojo, leading intellectual; brother-in-law of Efraín González Luna, founder of the National Action party; uncle of Efraín González Morfín, federal deputy, 1967–70, and leader of the National Action party. J] None. K] None. L] Enc Mex, V, 468–69; WWM45, 52; QesQ, 249–50.

González (Medina), Arnulfo
(Deceased April 10, 1962) A] April 23, 1886. B] Villa de Juárez, Coahuila. C] Primary studies, Villa de Juárez; secondary and preparatory studies, Ateneo Fuente, Saltillo; legal studies, National School of Law; no degree; primary schoolteacher, Piedras Negras and Zaragoza until 1913. D] *Governor* of Coahuila, 1921–23. E] Joined the Democratic party; executive secretary, Democratic party; supported *Francisco I. Madero*, 1910; secretary, Anti-Reelectionist Club, Piedras Negras, Coahuila. F] *Provisional governor* of Durango, 1916; *provisional governor* of Chihuahua, 1916–18; *governor* of the Federal District, 1918–19; director, Cavalry Department, Secretariat of War; director, Justice Department, Secretariat of War; oficial mayor of public works; secretary of Army and Navy Bank. G] None. H] Practiced law without completing degree thesis, 1909. I] Son of Pedro González Ortega and Jerónima Medina; related to General *Francisco Murguía*. J] Sup-

ported Madero's rebellion, 1910; joined the Constitutionalists, 1913; fought under General *Pablo González*, as a 2nd captain; supported *Venustiano Carranza* against *Francisco Villa*, 1914–15; chief of staff, 2nd Division, Army of the Northeast, under General Francisco Murguía, 1915–16; military commander of Coahuila, December 1916; rank of brigadier general, July 1, 1916; chief of staff, various military zones; rank of brigade general, October 16, 1937; commander, Legion of Honor; retired from the army, 1949. K] Forced to leave governorship because of kinship to General Murguía, who was supporting the *Adolfo de la Huerta* rebellion, 1923. L] López, 443–45; DP70, 902; Almada, 534–35.

González Porras, José
(Deceased 1895) A] 1838. B] Chihuahua, Chihuahua. C] Early education unknown; no degree. D] Federal deputy from the State of Chihuahua, 1877–78; *federal deputy* from the State of Tlaxcala, Dist. 1, 1890–92, 1892–94; *federal deputy* from the State of Tamaulipas, Dist. 2, 1894–95. E] None. F] Political boss, Iturbide Canton (District), Chihuahua, 1876, 1877; secretary general of government of the State of Chihuahua, 1877. G] None. H] Unknown. I] Father of General *José González Salas*, secretary of war under *Francisco I. Madero*, who committed suicide after losing the battle of Rellano, 1912; brother Estanislao González Porras, colonel and local deputy; married Luz Salas. J] Unknown. K] None. L] Advocate of free municipalities in Mexico, 1878. L] Almada, 1968, 232–33.

González Salas, José
(Deceased March 25, 1912) A] March 19, 1862. B] Chihuahua, Chihuahua. C] Early education unknown; enrolled in the National Military College, January 9, 1881, graduating as a staff lieutenant in engineering, 1884; professor of engineering. D] None. E] None. F] Director, Department of Infantry, Secretariat of War, 1909–11; *subsecretary* of war in charge of the secretariat, 1911; *secretary* of war and navy, 1911–12. G] None. H] None. I] Son of *José González Porras*, federal deputy, and Luz Salas. J] Career military officer; rank of 2nd captain, October 13,

1884; rank of 1st captain, January 19, 1887; rank of major, May 11, 1889; rank of lt. colonel, July 15, 1898; assigned to the engineering park, 1899; participated in many Yaqui campaigns; fought in the Indian wars in Yucatán, 1898; commander, 2nd Battalion, Yucatán, 1898; rank of colonel, October 15, 1901; fought in the Sierra de Bacatete, 1906–07; commander of military operations in Chihuahua, Coahuila, Durango, and Zacatecas; rank of brigadier general, March 8, 1909; rank of brigade general, July 21, 1911; resigned as secretary of war to fight *Pascual Orozco*; defeated at the battle of Rellano, March 24, 1912. K] Committed suicide after his defeat at Rellano. L] Sec of War, 1900, 273; Sec of War, 1911, 16; Mestre, 242; Cuevas, 407; Enc Mex, V, 474; DP70, 905.

González Torres, Salvador
(Deceased April 5, 1918) A] January 22, 1885. B] Tacambaro, Michoacán. C] Secondary studies at the Colegio de San Nicolás; enrolled, National Military College, 1902, graduated as a 2nd lieutenant of engineers, 1905; studies in engineering, National Military College, as a major, 1910. D] *Constitutional deputy* from the State of Oaxaca, Dist. 1, 1916–17; *federal deputy* from the State of Michoacán, Dist. 8, 1917–18. E] None. F] None. G] None. H] None. I] Son of Manuel González and Salomé Torres. J] Career military officer; joined the Constitutionalist army, 1913; rank of colonel, 1914; chief of staff to General *Jesus Agustín Castro*, commander, 21st Division, Army of the Southeast, 1915; rank of brigadier general, 1915. K] Executed, Zitacuaro, Michoacán. L] DP70, 906; Dicc mich, 174–75; Cuevas, 409; HA, 21 Feb. 1987, 35.

Gordillo León, Reynaldo
(Deceased) A] March 23, 1853. B] Comitán, Chiapas. C] Primary studies in Comitán; preparatory studies at the National Preparatory School; engineering degree, School of Engineering, Mexico City. D] Mayor of Comitán; *governor* of Chiapas, 1913. E] Member of the Liberal Club of Tuxtla Gutiérrez; member of the Democratic party of Tuxtla, Gutiérrez. F] Member, Scientific Commission for the Mexico-Guatemala Boundary; inspec-

tor of monuments, State of Chiapas; director of highways, State of Chiapas; *interim governor* of Chiapas, 1911–12; ambassador to Guatemala, 1911–12. G] None. H] Practicing civil engineer; chief engineer, Cintura Railroad project. I] Unknown. J] None. K] None. L] Gordillo y Ortiz, 105–06.

Gorostieta, Enrique
(Deceased May 8, 1921) A] January 25, 1847. B] Mexico City. C] Early education unknown; law degree, National School of Law, Mexico City, 1880. D] *Senator* from Nuevo León, 1910–12, 1912–14, 1914–16. E] None. F] *Secretary* of the treasury, 1913. G] None. H] Practicing lawyer; formed a lucrative law practice with friends from law school. I] Daughter Eva married Valentín Rivero y Gaja, son of a prominent Monterrey industrialist. J] None. K] None. L] C de S, 1910–12; Mestre. 267.

Grácidas (Moreno), Carlos L.
(Deceased August 18, 1954) A] February 8, 1888. B] Toluca, México. C] Primary studies in Toluca; had to leave to work; no degree. D] *Alternate constitutional deputy* from the State of Veracruz, Dist. 15, 1916–17, in functions for *Cándido Aguilar*. E] None. F] President, Board of Conciliation and Arbitration of Veracruz, under Governor Cándido Aguilar; director, Department of Labor, State of Veracruz, 1915; labor attaché, Mexican Embassy, Buenos Aires, 1926–28. G] Cofounder, National Typographers Union, 1909; member, executive council, National Typographers Union; cofounded the Casa del Obrero Mundial, 1912. H] Typographer, Mexico City, 1903; typographer, *El Popular*; linotypist, *El Imparcial* and *El Universal*, 1928–54. I] Son of Carlos Grácidas, from the working class; married Jovita Vega. J] Supported *Venustiano Carranza*, 1915. K] None. L] DP70, 911; Enc Mex, V, 493; López, 450; Morales Jiménez, 293–95.

Guerrero (Grosso), Julio
(Deceased 1937) A] April 18, 1962. B] Mexico City. C] Early education unknown; law degree, National School of

Law, National University, October 4, 1889; professor of history, National Preparatory School; professor of sociology, Free Law School; dean, National School of Law. D] *Federal deputy* from the State of Jalisco, Dist. 16, 1904–06, 1906–08. E] None. F] Judge, Superior Tribunal of Military Justice, 1914. G] Cofounder of the Academy of Social Sciences with *Ricardo García Granados*. H] Founder, *Revista de Jurisprudencia*; author. I] Son of lawyer José María Guerrero and Luisa Grosso; professor of many prominent political figures in the 1940s and 1950s; good friend of Aquiles Elorduy García, federal deputy, 1912–13. J] Served as a military judge; rank of brigadier general. K] Leading Mexican sociologist and student of crime; author of a classic work on crime in Mexico, 1901. L] Enc Mex, VI, 273; López, 466; DP70, 948; UNAM, law, 1880–91, 51; letters.

Guillén (Ancheyta), Flavio
(Deceased July 16, 1933) A] May 7, 1871. B] Villa Trinitaria, Chiapas. C] Primary studies in Villa Trinitaria; teaching certificate, Guatemala City; professor, National School of Agriculture, San Jacinto, Federal District; professor, women's school, Mexico City; director, School of Arts of Quetzaltenango, Guatemala City; director, Villatoro Institute, Guatemala City; director, School of Agriculture, Guatemala City. D] None. E] Member of the Anti-Reelectionist party; supported *Francisco I. Madero*, 1910 presidential campaign. F] *Interim governor* of Chiapas, 1912–13; named secretary of public education by President Madero, but *Victoriano Huerta* revolt took place before he could hold office, 1913. G] None. H] Teacher; writer; journalist. I] Father of poet and federal deputy Fedro Guillén. J] None. K] Left Mexico for Guatemala City, 1913. L] Velázquez, 126; Gordillo y Ortiz, 109–10; Almanaque de Chiapas, 118; JSH, 188–89; Enc Mex, VI, 300; O'Campo, 161–62.

Guillén Zamora, Fidel
(Deceased 1969) A] April 24, 1890. B] Ometepec, Guerrero. C] Primary studies, Ometepec; secondary and preparatory studies, Colegio del Estado de Puebla;

medical degree, National School of Medicine, UNAM, July 19, 1919. D] *Constitutional deputy* from the State of Guerrero, Dist. 2, 1916–17; *federal deputy* from the State of Guerrero, Dist. 2, 1920–22; mayor of Puebla, 1923, 1929–31, 1931–33. E] Joined the pro-Madero group as a student at the University of Puebla, 1910. F] Director of public welfare, State of Guerrero; director of public welfare, State of Puebla; private secretary to Governor *Juan Andreu Almazán*; physician, Secretariat of Health, 1932–58; director, Health Center, Ometepec, 1935; director, Personnel Department, Secretariat of Health, 1938; director, Civil Registry, Federal District, 1954–58. G] None. H] Practicing physician. I] Son of Ignacio Guillén Polanco and Josefa Zamora Méndez. J] Joined the revolutionaries under Juan Andreu Almazán, 1911; joined the Constitutional army, captain in the medical services, 1914. K] Was still a student when selected as a constitutional deputy. L] DP70, 952; López Barroso, 121–23.

Gutiérrez, Eulalio
(Deceased August 12, 1939) A] 1880. B] Hacienda Santo Domingo, Municipio Ramos Arizpe, Coahuila. C] Early education unknown; no degree. D] Mayor of Concepción del Oro, Zacatecas; *senator* from the State of Coahuila, 1920–22, 1924–28. E] Opposed *Porfirio Díaz*, 1900; joined the Liberal party and supported the Flores Magón brothers, 1906; joined the Anti-Reelectionist movement, 1909. F] *Governor* of San Luis Potosí and military commander, 1914; *president* of the Convention government, 1914–15. G] None. H] Shepherd as a boy; miner, Mazapil Copper Company, Concepción del Oro, Zacatecas. I] Father of Eulalio Gutiérrez Treviño, governor of Coahuila, 1969; brother Luis Gutiérrez, governor of Coahuila, 1920–21. J] Supported the Plan of San Luis Potosí with brother Luis; fought in southern Coahuila, 1911; joined the Constitutionalists, 1913; opposed *Francisco Villa*, 1915; opposed *Venustiano Carranza*, 1915–16; rank of division general; supported the Escobar rebellion, 1929. K] Went into exile to the United States, 1916, 1929. L] García Purón,

220–21; Enc Mex, VI, 329; López, 475; DP70, 955; Moreno, 203–04.

Gutiérrez Nájera, Manuel
(Deceased February 3, 1895) A] December 22, 1859. B] Mexico City. C] Private tutors in Latin, French, and mathematics; self-taught from father's library; no degree. D] *Federal deputy* from the State of México, Dist. 15, 1888–90, 1890–92, 1892–94, 1894–96. E] None. F] None. G] None. H] Journalist, began career 1875, and wrote for numerous major dailies including *El Porvenir*; founded *Revista Azul*, 1894; poet and leading intellectual. I] Parents wealthy; daughter Margarita, poet and great-granddaughter of Francisco Modesto de Olaguíbel, attorney general of Mexico. J] None. K] None. L] Mestre, 190; DP70.

Guzmán, Daniel
(Deceased 1929) A] June 15, 1849. B] Hacienda Santa Cruz, Canton (District) of Jalacingo, Veracruz. C] Primary studies from mother and at the Instituto Perote; secondary studies at the Canton of Jalacingo, 1862–63; enrolled in the Palafoxian Seminary, Puebla, 1864; medical degree, National School of Medicine, Mexico City, 1873. D] Local deputy to the state legislature of Veracruz, 1874, 1880, 1883; member of the City Council of Puebla; *constitutional deputy* from the State of Puebla, Dist. 1, 1916–17; *senator* from the State of Puebla, 1916–18, 1918–20. E] Won election for governorship of Puebla, but not allowed to hold office, 1911. F] None. G] None. H] Physician, Misantla, Veracruz, 1874; worked on the Hacienda Santa Cruz, 1878; physician, Puebla; notable research on infectious diseases. I] Son of landowner José Juan Guzmán, proprietor of the Santa Cruz hacienda, and Manuelita Gómez; son *Salvador Guzmán* replaced father as constitutional deputy, and served as personal secretary to President *Adolfo de la Huerta*, 1920; related to the Aquiles Serdán family. J] Military physician, federal army, 1877; naval physician, corvette *Independence*, 1877–78; president of the first revolutionary junta, Puebla. K] Forced to leave Veracruz for democratic

ideals, 1884; illness prevented him from serving as constitutional deputy. L] CyT, 316–18; C de D, 1916–17.

Guzmán (Esparza), Salvador R.
(Deceased November 5, 1962) A] October 24, 1888. B] Puebla, Puebla. C] Primary and secondary, Lafragua private school, Puebla; preparatory studies at the Colegio del Estado de Puebla; medical degree, Colegio del Estado de Puebla, 1915. D] *Alternate constitutional deputy* from the State of Puebla, Dist. 1, in functions, 1916–17. E] Active against the *Porfirio Díaz* government with Aquiles Serdán, 1909. F] Private secretary to President *Adolfo de la Huerta*, 1920; joined the diplomatic service, first secretary, 1918; first secretary, diplomatic service, 1923; chargé d'affaires, Holland, 1937–38; chargé d'affaires, Venezuela, 1938–39; ambassador to Venezuela, 1939–43; ambassador to El Salvador, 1944–45; ambassador to Poland, 1947–48; ambassador to Sweden, 1949–50; ambassador to Portugal, 1951–52; ambassador to Syria, 1956; ambassador to Switzerland, 1959. G] President, Student Society of the Colegio del Estado de Puebla. H] Physician. I] Grandson of large landholder José Juan Guzmán; son of Dr. Daniel Guzmán, senator from Puebla, 1918–20, and María Esparza. J] Supported *Francisco I. Madero* as a colonel in his forces, 1910–11; joined the Constitutional army as a 1st captain, 1914; major, Medical Corps, 1915; subdirector of the Military Teaching Hospital, 1917; reached rank of colonel, 1918. K] Removed from foreign service post, 1923, because of sympathies for *Adolfo de la Huerta*. L] CyT, 318; López, 483; DP70, 963.

H

Hay (Fortuno), Eduardo
(Deceased December 27, 1941) A] January 29, 1877. B] Federal District. C] Primary, secondary and preparatory studies in Mexico City; engineering degree from the University of Notre Dame, 1901. D] *Federal deputy* from the Federal District, Dist. 4, 1914–16; *federal deputy* from the Federal District, Dist. 1, 1917–18. E] None. F] Inspector general of consulates for Europe, Secretariat of Foreign Relations, 1911–12; inspector general of police, 1912–13; confidential agent to Brazil, Peru, and Colombia, 1914; confidential agent to Venezuela, 1914–15; subsecretary of agriculture and development, 1916; minister to Italy, 1918–23; minister to Japan, 1924–25; subsecretary of commerce and public works, 1927–28; director general of public welfare for the Federal District, 1928–29; ambassador to Guatemala, 1929; director general of customs, 1932–33; consul general, Paris, 1933–34; secretary of foreign relations, 1935–40. G] None. H] Author; chief of the engineering firm of Schonduke and Neubuder. I] Close friend of President *Venustiano Carranza* and General *Alvaro Obregón*; married Angelina Sais; son of engineer Guillermo Hay and Josefina Fortuno. J] Joined the Revolution in January 1911; chief of staff for *Francisco Madero*, 1911; chief of staff under Generals *Antonio Villareal* and *Ramón Iturbe*, 1913; rank of brigadier general, 1913. K] None. L] DP70, 968; Peral, 377; WWLA40, 239; Enc Mex, 1977, VI, 368; López, 486–87.

Hernández (Aguiar), Juan A.
(Deceased November 26, 1925) A] March 30, 1841. B] Ahuacatlán, Jalisco (Nayarit). C] Mother taught him primary studies; no degree. D] *Federal deputy* from the State of Guerrero, Dist. 6, 1904–06, 1906–08, 1908–10, 1910–12. E] None. F] *Governor* of Colima, 1913–14; *governor* of Puebla, 1914. G] None. H] None. I] Son of Rafaela Aguiar. J] Joined the Light Battalion of Tepic as a private under General *Ramón Corona*, June 13, 1859; promoted from sergeant to 2nd lieutenant, battle of San Pedro, 1864; fought under General *Porfirio Díaz*, at the battle of Oaxaca, 1866; rank of major, 1871; supported the Plan of La Noria, 1871; supported the Plan of Tuxtepec under General Donato Guerra, but captured; rank of colonel, November 13, 1876; commander, 1st Troop Regiment; fought in the Yaqui campaign, 1880; rank of brigadier general, April 16, 1886; commander, 5th Regiment, Chihuahua, 1893; commander, 2nd Military Zone, 1893–1903; rank of brigade general, July 13, 1894; member, Council of War,

7th Zone, 1902; commander, 5th Military Zone, 1903; commander, 7th Military Zone; commander, 8th Military Zone, 1910–11, when he fought *Francisco I. Madero's* troops; commander of the military forces in Chihuahua, 1911; retired from active duty, June 20, 1911; recalled to active duty by *Victoriano Huerta*, May 2, 1913; commander, Division of the East, 1914. K] None. L] Peral, Appendix, 162–63; Enc Mex, VI, 402; Sec of War, 1900, 85; Sec of War, 1901, 19; Hombres prominentes, 311–12; Mestre, 276; Almada, Colima, 101; Sec of War, 1914, 17; Almada, 1968, 249; Almanaque de Puebla, 129.

Hernández Cházaro, Eduardo
(Deceased November 23, 1957) A] May 4, 1898. B] Tlacotalpan, Veracruz. C] Early education unknown; no degree. D] Federal deputy from the State of Veracruz, Dist. 12, 1940–43, member of the Great Committee, the First National Defense Committee, and the Second Credentials Committee; secretary of the Political Control Committee. E] Precandidate for governor of Veracruz, 1936; member of the Executive Committee of the National Pre-Electoral Center of Avila Camacho, 1939. F] Attached to the chief of staff, President *Alvaro Obregón*, 1920–24; assistant chief of staff to President *Plutarco Elías Calles*, 1924–28; chief of staff for President *Pascual Ortiz Rubio*, 1928–29; private secretary to President Ortiz Rubio, 1929–30; *head* of the Department of the Federal District, 1930; consul in San Antonio, Texas, 1931–35; inspector of military attachés, 1930–31. G] None. H] None. I] Son Eduardo, an engineer and director of several construction firms; married Sofía Lemus. J] Joined the army, May 23, 1914, as a 2nd lieutenant of cavalry; rank of 2nd captain, 1915; rank of 1st captain, 1920; rank of major, 1924; rank of lt. colonel, 1927; rank of brigadier general, 1944; rank of brigade general, 1949; commander of the 23rd Military Zone, Tlaxcala, Tlaxcala, 1950–51; commander of the 22nd Military Zone, Toluca, Mexico, 1951–57; rank of division general, 1952. K] None. L] DP70, 980; C de D, 1940–42; Peral, 379; letter; Rev de Ejer, 19 Oct. 1957, 52.

Hernández (García), Lamberto
(Deceased 1964) A] 1883. B] Charcas, Río Verde, San Luis Potosí. C] Early education unknown; preparatory studies, San Luis Potosí; studies, School of Business Administration, UNAM. D] *Alternate senator* from the State of San Luis Potosí in functions, 1926–28, 1928–30; *senator* from the State of San Luis Potosí, 1930–32, 1932–34; federal deputy from the State of San Luis Potosí, Dist. 5, 1934–37. E] None. F] *Governor* of the Federal District, 1930–31; adviser, Bank of Mexico. G] President, National Federation of Chambers of Commerce (Concanaco), 1925–27; president, Rotary Club of Mexico City. H] Businessman; worked for a drugstore as a boy, Tacuba, Federal District. I] Son of Flavio Hernández and Delfina García; married Amalia Navarro. J] López, 492; Enc Mex, VI, 403; Dir soc, 1935, 225.

Hernández (González), Lorenzo L.
(Deceased 1970) A] May 9, 1881. B] San Pedro de las Colonias, Coahuila. C] Primary studies, San Pedro School, San Pedro de las Colonias; secondary studies, Literary and Business School of Monterrey, Nuevo León; preparatory studies, Colegio Civil of Monterrey; engineering degree, National School of Engineering, 1907; mining studies, Practical School of Mines, Pachuca, Hidalgo. D] Mayor of Mexico City, 1919. E] None. F] Treasurer general of Mexico, 1923–31, 1932–33; *head* of the Department of the Federal District, 1931–32; founder and director general of the National Finance Bank, 1934–36; secretary, National Banking Commission, 1936–64; director general of the International Boundaries and Waters Commission, Secretariat of Foreign Relations, 1951. G] None. H] Businessman; adviser, Mining and Mercantile Bank, S.A. I] Son of Antonio V. Hernández, director general of the Bank of Nuevo León, and Ana María González Treviño; nephew of Rafaela Hernández, wife of Evaristo Madero; cousin of *Francisco I. Madero*; father of Octavio Andrés Hernández, subsecretary of the Department of the Federal District, 1970–76; married Mercedes González Lafón. J] None. K] None. L] DBM68, 339–40; DGF51, I, 99; WWM45,

56; Peral, 381; DP70, 979; López, 492; Enc Mex, VI, 403; UNAM, law, 1891–96, 157.

Hernández Madero, Rafael
(Deceased 1951) A] 1875. B] Parras de la Fuente, Coahuila. C] Early education unknown; law degree, National School of Law. D] *Alternate federal deputy* from the State of Puebla, Dist. 15, 1900–02; *federal deputy* from the State of Puebla, Dist. 9, 1904–06, 1906–08; *federal deputy* from the State of Puebla, Dist. 11, 1908–10, 1910–12. E] None. F] *Secretary* of justice, 1911; *secretary* of development, 1911; *secretary* of government, 1911; *secretary* of development, 1911–12; *secretary* of government, 1912–13. G] None. H] Practicing lawyer; businessman; member of the board of Cía. Industria de Parras, 1946. I] Cousin of *Francisco I. Madero.* J] Prisoner with President Madero in the National Palace during the Tragic Ten Days, but was released. K] None. L] DP70, 981; Enc Mex, VI, 408–09.

Hidalgo (Téllez), Cutberto
(Deceased 1930) A] March 20, 1880. B] Pachuca, Hidalgo. C] Primary studies, Colegio Mariano Riva Palacio, under Teodomiro Manzano, Pachuca; preparatory studies in Pachuca; enrolled in the National School of Law, 1900, but graduated as a physician, National School of Medicine. D] Senator from Hidalgo, 1817–18. E] Anti-Reelectionist; won the 1921 election for governor of Hidalgo, but the state legislature declared his opponent the winner; candidate for governor of Hidalgo, 1930. F] Consul, Marseilles, France, 1911–13; *subsecretary* in charge of the Secretariat of Foreign Relations, 1920; *secretary* of foreign relations, 1920–21. G] None. H] Physician. I] Son of T. Hidalgo and R. Téllez. J] None. K] Self-exile to Los Angeles, California, 1921. L] Enc Mex, VI, 426; FSRE, 175; DP70, 992; Pérez López, 200–01; UNAM, law, 1900–06, 9.

Hill, Benjamín (Guillermo)
(Deceased December 14, 1920) A] March 31, 1877. B] Rancho San Antonio, Choix, Sinaloa. C] Primary studies, Alamos and Chihuahua; secondary and preparatory studies in Europe; studied in Rome, Berlin, and Bavaria; no degree. D] Member of the City Council, Navojoa, Sinaloa, 1908. E] Cofounder of Anti-Reelectionist clubs in Nogales and Alamos, Sonora, 1906; president, Liberal Constitutionalist party. F] First syndic, City Council of Navojoa, Sinaloa, 1910; political boss of Arizpe, Sonora, 1912–13; political prefect of Hermosillo, 1913; *secretary* of war and navy, 1920. G] None. H] Owner of a 400-hectare ranch near Navojoa, Sinaloa. I] Son of Benjamín Hill Salido, businessman, mine- and landowner; grandson of North American physician William Hill, rancher and ex-Confederate soldier, and Jesús Salido; married an Italian countess, but she died giving birth; second wife Dolores Esquer; first cousin of *Alvaro Obregón*; Hill's aunt, Angelia, married Obregón's brother. J] Supported *Francisco I. Madero*, 1910–11; chief of military operations, Southern Sonora, 1911; joined the Constitutionalists under General Obregón, 1913; rank of brigadier general, April, 1913; chief of military operations, Alamos, Sonora, 1913; rank of brigade general, September, 1913; represented at the Convention of Aguascalientes by Lt. Colonel Julio Madero, 1914; opposed *Francisco Villa*, 1914–15, as Obregón's second-in-command; replaced Obregón as commander-in-chief of the forces fighting Villa when Obregón lost his arm in battle, 1915; chief of military operations in Sonora, 1914–15; rank of division general, 1915; garrison commander, Mexico City, 1916–17; chief of military operations, Valley of Mexico, 1917; commander, Benjamín Hill division, 1917; garrison commander, Mexico City, 1920; garrison commander, Morelos, 1920; supported the Plan of Aguas Prietas, 1920. K] Imprisoned with *Flavio A. Bórquez*, Hermosillo, Sonora, 1911. L] González Dávila, 260–61; Aguilar Camín, 27–29; Morales Jiménez, 169–72; López, 508–09; Enc Mex, VI, 524–25; QesQ, 282; DP70, 1001; Bojórquez, 79–82.

Hinojosa (de la Garza), Pedro
(Deceased March 5, 1903) A] January 31, 1818. B] Matamoros, Tamaulipas. C] Early education unknown; no degree. D] Federal deputy from the State of Chi-

huahua, Dist. 1, 1861–63; senator from Hidalgo, 1882–84. E] None. F] *Governor* of Chihuahua, 1860; governor of Durango, 1861; secretary of war, 1861–62; governor and military commander of Tamaulipas, 1866; *secretary* of war, 1884–96. G] None. H] Owner of Tulapilla hacienda, Papantla, Veracruz, which contained 15,323 hectares. I] Son of Ramón Hinojosa and Mamerta de la Garza y Falcón, from a wealthy landowning family; daughter María married José Ramón Cossío y González, uncle of Roberto Cossío y Cossío, secretary general of the National Action party, 1939–51. J] Joined the Explorer Company, National Guard, Tamaulipas, October 10, 1840, as a private; fought Texas filibusters, 1840–41; fought in the Corpus Christi and Río Nueces campaigns, 1842–44; fought against the North American invasion, 1846; rank of 1st sergeant, 1848; squad commander, 1853; sergeant, national guard, 1849; rank of lieutenant in the cavalry, 1851; rank of captain, 1852; rank of lt. colonel, August 11, 1854; rank of lt. colonel, February, 1854; military commander of Tampico, 1855–56; rank of colonel, regular army, July 1856; rank of brigadier general, November 15, 1858; commander of the military forces in Chihuahua, 1859–61; commander of the 2nd District, State of México, 1862–63; one of the commanders defending Puebla, 1863, but captured by the French; rank of commander of the 3rd Brigade, First Division, Army of the East, under General *Felipe B. Berriozábal*; military commander of Nuevo León, 1864; military commander, Northern Veracruz, 1876–77; military commander of Chihuahua, 1877; commander of the National Battalion of Disabled Soldiers, 1879–80; rank of division general, October 28, 1884; president, Supreme Military Court, 1896–97. K] None. L] Almada, 351–80; Holms, 354; Hombres prominentes, 41–44; Mestre, 216; Pavía, 27–32; QesQ, 283; DP70, 1001–02; López, 511; Enc Mex, VI, 532–33.

Hornedo Bengoa, Francisco G.
(Deceased March 21, 1890) A] 1847. B] Aguascalientes, Aguascalientes. C] Primary studies in Aguascalientes; studies at San Carlos Academy, Mexico City; engi-neering studies, National School of Mines; no degree. D] Federal deputy from the State of Aguascalientes, 1871–73; local deputy to the state legislature of Aguascalientes, 1873–75; federal deputy from the State of Aguascalientes, 1875–77; governor of Aguascalientes, 1877–79; senator from Aguascalientes, 1880–84; *governor* of Aguascalientes, 1883–87; *senator* from Aguascalientes, 1888–90. E] Ran for governor of Aguascalientes, 1877, but lost. F] Interim governor and military commander of Aguascalientes, 1876–77. G] None. H] Businessman; owner of various haciendas, Aguascalientes. I] Son of a wealthy businessman who left him a large estate; son Ricardo served as federal deputy from Michoacán, 1888–98. J] Supported the Plan of Tuxtepec, 1876. K] None. L] Hombres prominentes, 261–62; Mestre, 168; Almanaque de Aguascalientes, 99; DP70, 1005; Enc Mex, VII, 12.

Huerta, Victoriano
(Deceased January 13, 1916) A] March 23, 1845. B] Colotlán, Jalisco. C] Early education unknown; graduated from the National Military College as a construction engineer, 1876. D] None. E] None. F] Director, public works, State of Nuevo León, 1905–09; *secretary* of government, 1913, for 45 minutes; *president* of Mexico, 1913–14. G] None. H] None. I] Son of a cavalry soldier and Huichol Indian; married Emilia Aguila; General Donato Guerra helped him get into the National Military College. J] Career army officer; commander of the 3rd Infantry Battalion, 1894–1901; rank of brigadier general, May 27, 1901; fought Mayas in Yucatán under General *Ignacio A. Bravo*, 1903; fought the Zapatistas in Morelos and Guerrero, 1911; escorted President *Porfirio Díaz* to Veracruz, 1911; defeated the *Pascual Orozco* rebellion, 1912; conspired with *Félix Díaz* and *Bernardo Reyes* to overthrow President *Francisco I. Madero*, 1913; rank of division general, July 30, 1912. K] Responsible for the murder of President Madero and Vice-President *José María Pino Suárez*, February 22, 1913; exiled in London, England, and Barcelona, Spain, 1913–15; arrested by United States agents, June 15, 1915, in Newman, New

Mexico; detained by the United States in Fort Bliss, El Paso, Texas, 1915; died of cirrhosis of the liver, Fort Bliss. K] None. L] DP70, 1035; López, 519; Enc Mex, VII, 78–82; Mestre, 255, 297; Sec of War, 1914, 17; Sec of War, 1901, 24; *Excélsior*, 5 April, 1954; Puente, 293–302; Cuevas, 349; Sec of War, 1900, 289.

Hurtado Suárez, Gerardo
(Deceased 1947) A] November 24, 1876. B] Colima, Colima. C] Studies, Conciliar Tridentine Seminary; medical degree, National Medical School, March 14, 1903. D] Mayor of Colima, Colima, 1914; local deputy to the state legislature of Colima, 1920; *governor* of Colima, 1923–25. E] None. F] None. G] None. H] Practicing physician, Mexico City, 1925–47. I] Son of Dr. Gerardo Hurtado, local deputy, alternate senator, and interim governor of Colima, 1879–80; related to President Miguel de la Madrid. J] Joined the army medical corps as a major, 1903; physician, Military Aspirants School. K] Powers as governor were removed by the local legislature for alleged proclerical sympathies, April 21, 1925; nearly executed in 1920, but saved by General *Francisco R. Serrano*; temporarily removed from the governorship by rebel forces, November 1, 1923–February 23, 1924. L] Almada, Colima, 104; Enc Mex, VII, 105; Moreno, 75–76; Peral, Appendix, 166–67; López, 521.

I

Ibarra (López), Jr., Epigmenio
(Deceased 1947) A] 1880. B] Real del Castillo, Ensenada, Baja California del Norte. C] Early education unknown; no degree. D] None. E] None. F] *Governor* of Baja California del Norte, 1921–22; director, National Pawnshop, 1922–24; subdirector, Monetary Commission, 1924–25; subdirector, Bank of Mexico, 1925–32; treasurer of the Department of the Federal District, 1932. G] President, Mexican Bankers Association, 1937–38. H] Prominent businessman and banker; salesman, Lower California Development Company, 1897–1907; cashier, accountant, subdirector, and director, Mercantile Bank of Cananea, Sonora, 1907–17; manager, Mercantile and Agricultural Bank Company of Sonora, Hermosillo, 1917–20; president, Cía. Hulera El Popo; president, Empresa Industrial Manantiales Garci Crespo; adviser to numerous banks and insurance companies; original shareholder, La Provincial Insurance; member of the board of Banpaís; founder and director general, Banco Mexicano, S.A., 1932–47. I] Son of Epigmenio Ibarra and Natividad López; married Francisca Gándara. J] None. K] None. L] Parodí, 100–04; DP70, 1047; Enc Mex, VII, 107.

Iglesias Calderón, Fernando
(Deceased 1942) A] May 30, 1856. B] Tacubaya, Federal District. C] Primary studies in Mexico City; preparatory studies, National Preparatory School, 1869–74; law degree, National School of Law, 1896; professor of history, National Preparatory School, 1912. D] *Senator* from the Federal District, 1912–13, president; *senator* from the Federal District, 1920–22, 1922–24. E] President of the Liberal party, 1912–15; president, Electoral Center for Obregón for President, 1920. F] High commissioner, with rank of ambassador, to Washington, D.C., 1920–23; chief of arbitration, Mexican-German Claims Commission, 1926–31. G] None. H] Journalist; historian. I] Son of José María Iglesias, leading Liberal politician and secretary of foreign relations under Benito Juárez, 1862–66, and Juana Calderón; cousin of *Federico Gamboa*, secretary of foreign relations, 1913, whose mother was Iglesias's father's sister. J] None. K] Arrested by *Victoriano Huerta* and imprisoned in San Juan de Ulloa, Veracruz, for accusing Huerta of murdering *Francisco I. Madero* and *José María Pino Suárez*, 1913; declined the post of secretary of foreign relations under three presidents, Madero, 1912, *Venustiano Carranza*, 1914, and *Adolfo de la Huerta*, 1920. L] Enc Mex, VII, 145; Cuevas, 93–94; WWLA35, 195; DP70, 1059; Dir social, 1935, 227.

Ipiña (de la Peña), José Encarnación
(Deceased 1913) A] 1836. B] San Luis Potosí, San Luis Potosí. C] Primary and secondary studies, San Luis Potosí; preparatory studies in San Luis Potosí; studies at the Sorbonne, Paris. D] Local

deputy to the state legislature of San Luis Potosí, 1861–63, 1868; member of the City Council, San Luis Potosí, San Luis Potosí, 1865; *alternate senator* from the State of San Luis Potosí, 1900–02, 1902–04; *alternate federal deputy* from the State of San Luis Potosí, Dist. 2, 1908–10, 1910–12. E] None. F] Judge, Superior Tribunal of Justice of San Luis Potosí, 1871; *governor* of San Luis Potosí, 1911. G] None. H] Assisted in the construction of the Santiago Dam, Aguascalientes; mining business; managed large landholdings of his family; refinanced the Potosina Bank, 1870; president of La Lonja, S.A. I] Descendant of Spanish nobility; parents were large landholders; married Luisa de Verástegui Ruiz de Bustamante; daughter Maltilde Ipiña married Octaviano L. Cabrera, engineer; related to the Octaviano B. Cabrera and Barragán families in San Luis Potosí through marriage; brother-in-law of Pablo Verástegui, senator from San Luis Potosí . J] None. K] Won prizes at the Chicago Exposition, 1893, Atlanta Exposition, 1895, Paris Exposition, 1900. L] Ipiña de Corsi, 1956, 123; DP70, 1083–84; C de S, 1900–92, 6; Ipiña de Corsi, 143–44; Cockcroft, 38–39.

Irigoyen (Irigoyen), Ulises
(Deceased 1944) A] February 2, 1894. B] Satevo, Chihuahua. C] Primary studies in Chihuahua; secondary studies at the Colegio Palmore, El Paso, Texas; degree in accounting. D] None. E] None. F] Director of statistics, Secretariat of the National Economy; director, Personnel Department, Secretariat of the Treasury; private secretary to the secretary of the treasury; director, Department of Railroads, Traffic, and Tariffs, National Railroads of Mexico; oficial mayor of the Secretariat of the Treasury, 1934; director of customs. G] Secretary of the Union of Workers of Constitutionalism, 1914; manager, Chamber of Commerce, Ciudad Juárez. H] Accountant, Ciudad Juárez; founder of Cervecería de Ciudad Juárez; developer of the Texas to Gulf of California Railroad; author. I] Son of Dr. David Irigoyen and María de Jesús Irigoyen; nephew of Mariano Irigoyen, federal deputy from Chihuahua, 1924–26, and prominent educator. J] Joined the Consti-

tutionalists, 1913; secretary to Felicitas Villareal, subsecretary in charge of the treasury, the Convention government, 1914. K] None. L] DP70, 1085; Enc Mex, VII, 323–24; Almada, 1968, 285.

Iturbe, Ramón F.
(Deceased 1970) A] November 7, 1889. B] Mazatlán, Sinaloa. C] Primary and secondary studies in Culiacán Seminary, Sinaloa; studies at the California Military School, Los Angeles; studies in civil engineering, United States, 1912–13; no degree. D] Federal deputy from the State of Sinaloa, Dist. 3, 1937–40, President of the Chamber. E] Founder of the Mexican Constitutional Front to support an opposition presidential candidate, 1939. F] *Provisional governor* of Sinaloa, 1917–20; director of Cooperative Development, Secretariat of Industry and Commerce, 1936; military attaché to Japan, 1941–42; commander of the Mexican Legion of Honor, Secretariat of National Defense, 1958–64, 1964–66. G] None. H] Merchant before the Revolution; managed a small general store, Alcoyonque. I] Son of Adolfo Fuentes and Refugio Iturbe; married Mercedes Acosta. J] Career army officer; joined the Revolution in 1910; member of rebel group under Juan Bardes, Culiacán, 1910; fought *Pascual Orozco*, 1912; commander of irregular forces in Sinaloa, 1912; rank of brigadier general, 1912; commander of military operations in Sinaloa, 1913; commander of the 3rd Division, Army of the Northeast, Constitutional army; commander of the forces that captured Culiacán under General *Alvaro Obregón*, 1913; rank of brigade general, October 28, 1913; commander of the forces that captured Mazatlán, 1914; commander of the military zones of Nayarit, Sinaloa, and Sonora, 1914–15; commander of military operations in Jalisco, Colima, 1916; rank of division general. K] Supported the Escobar movement, 1929; in exile in the United States, 1929–33; expelled from the Mexican Revolutionary Party for his early support of General *Juan Almazán's* candidacy for president, 1938–39; later supported the candidacy of Rafael Sánchez Tapia for president; received the Belisario Domínguez Medal from the Mexican Senate, 1966. L] DPE61, 34; C

de D, 1937–39; DP70, 2406; Peral, 407; Enc Mex, VII, 1977, 363; EBW, 1141; González Dávila, 292–95; Nakayama, 223.

Iturralde (y Lara), José María
[Deceased November 4, 1916] A] October 6, 1826. B] Valladolid, Yucatán. C] Early education unknown; no degree. D] Federal deputy from Yucatán; governor of Yucatán, 1877–78. E] Liberal party member. F] Political boss of Vallaldolid, 1859, 1872; *interim governor* of Yucatán, 1897–98; treasurer general of Yucatán. G] None. H] Unknown. I] Son of Patricio de Iturralde y O'Horán, Spanish regidor, and Escolástica de Lara, daughter of Mayor Arastasio de Lara; grandfather of José María Iturralde Traconis, governor of Yucatán, 1924–26; married Severiana Navarrete y Peniche; married second time to Mercedes Rosado y Muñoz; daughter-in-law Joaquina Traconis y Marmolejo is the daughter of General J. B. Traconis, uncle of *Daniel Traconis*, governor of Yucatán, 1890–94. J] Colonel, battalion in Valladolid, and commander of the Eastern line, 1863; supported *Porfirio Díaz's* Plan of Tuxtepec, 1876. K] None. L] Godoy, 236–37; Valdés Acosta, III, 91–93, 196–98; Mestre, 256.

Izabal, Rafael
[Deceased October 4, 1910] A] 1854. B] Culiacán, Sinaloa. C] Early education unknown; no degree; primary school inspector. D] Local deputy to the state legislature of Sonora, 1879–91 (five times); member of the City Council of Hermosillo, Sonora; *federal deputy* from the State of Sonora, Dist. 2, 1888–90, 1890–92; *federal deputy* from the State of Sinaloa, Dist. 2, 1892–94, 1894–96, 1896–98; *governor* of Sonora, 1903–07; *senator* from the State of Guerrero, 1908–10, 1910–12. E] Joined *Luis Torres's* political clique, 1877. F] Vice-governor of Sonora, 1891–95, under Luis Torres; *interim governor* of Sonora, 1900–03. G] None. H] One of the largest landholders in Sonora. I] Son of Dolores Salido and Rafael Izabal; married Dolores Monteverde, daughter of a prominent Hermosillo family; related to Celedonio Ortiz, local deputy; cousin of Bartolomé and Epifanio Salido, local deputies in Sonora;

son married Elvira Corral, *Ramón Corral's* daughter; related by marriage to Luis Torres through the Monteverde family. J] Participated in the expedition against the Yaquis and Seris, 1904. K] Moved to Hermosillo, early 1860s; died on the high seas on a liner from Europe to New York. L] González Dávila, 297–99; Villa, 1951, 416; Balmori, 120; DP70, 1099; Almanaque de Sonora, 123; Aguilar Camín, 92, 104; Mestre, 239.

J

Jara (Rodríguez), Heriberto
[Deceased April 17, 1968] A] July 10, 1884. B] Orizaba, Veracruz. C] Primary and secondary studies, Escuela Modelo, Orizaba; secondary studies at the Scientific and Literary Institute of Hidalgo; attended the Escuela Naval de Antón Lizardo. D] *Federal deputy* from the State of Veracruz, Dist. 13, 1912–13; *constitutional deputy* from the State of Veracruz, Dist. 13, 1916–17; *senator* from the State of Veracruz, 1920–24; *governor* of Veracruz, December 18, 1924–October 31, 1927. E] Member of the Liberal party, 1898; member of the Constitutional party, 1913; president of the National Executive Committee of the Mexican Revolutionary party, 1939–40. F] *Governor* of the Federal District, 1914; *minister* to Cuba, 1917–20; secretary of the navy, 1941–46. G] Participated in the Río Blanco Mill strike, 1907. H] Bookkeeper, Río Blanco Mill, 1907; writer for many magazines and newspapers at the beginning of his career and after his retirement in 1946. I] Married Ana María Avalos; from very humble background. J] Career military officer; joined the Revolution in 1910, fighting under General Camerino Mendoza; rank of colonel, 1913; rank of brigadier general, 1914; directed the cadets against the North American invasion of Veracruz, 1914; rank of brigade general, 1915; rank of division general, 1924; commander of the 26th Military Zone, Veracruz, Veracruz, 1935–37; assistant inspector general of the army, 1935; inspector general of the army, 1935; commander of the 28th Military Zone, Oaxaca, Oaxaca, 1938; director general of military education, Secretariat of National Defense, 1938–39. K] Voted

against the renunciation of *Francisco I. Madero* and *José María Pino Suárez* as a federal deputy, 1913; one of the extreme radicals at the Constitutional Convention; opposed the candidacy of Angel Carvajal for president in an open letter signed by Silviano Barba González and Luis I. Rodríguez, 1958; manager for Avila Camacho's campaign for president, 1940; his appointment as secretary of navy strongly criticized by naval officers who felt a navy rather than an army officer should have been appointed; newspapers were also critical, calling Jara "general of the Ocean Cavalry." L] Peral, 414–15; DP70, 1110; WWM45, 60; Enc Mex, VII, 1977, 450.

Jaramillo, Julián
(Deceased February 13, 1917) A] 1831. B] Mexico City. C] Early education unknown; graduated from the National Military College. D] None. E] None. F] *Governor* and military commander of Colima, 1913. G] None. H] None. I] Unknown. J] Career military; joined the army as a private in the Independence Battalion, 1846; fought the North Americans at Churubusco and Molino del Rey, 1847; rank of 2nd lieutenant, 1862; fought French under General Jesús González Ortega, 1863; captured by the French and imprisoned for a year and a half before escaping and joining the forces of General *Porfirio Díaz*; rank of lt. colonel, 1867; rank of colonel, 1872; supported the Plan of Tuxtepec, 1876; commander of military forces in Miahuatlán, 1881–84; commander of military forces in Salina Cruz, 1884–90; commander of military forces in Tuxtla Gutiérrez, 1894–99; commander, Disabled Soldiers Group, 1900–05; rank of brigadier general, May 27, 1901; commander of military forces along the Guatemalan border, 1906–09; rank of brigade general, March 8, 1909; fought the Zapatistas under *Victoriano Huerta*, 1909–10; fought against the rebellion of *Pascual Orozco*, 1912; supported Huerta, 1913–14; retired from the service, 1914. K] None. L] Peral, Appendix, 171; Almada, Colima, 116; DP70, 1111; Enc Mex, VII, 457; Sec of War, 1901, 24; Mestre, 157; Sec of War, 1914, 19.

Jiménez Domínguez, Enrique
(Deceased 1952) A] March 18, 1891. B] Jalapa, Veracruz. C] Preparatory studies in Orizaba, Veracruz; law degree, School of Law, University of Veracruz, Jalapa, 1914; graduate studies in literature, England; professor of literature, National Preparatory School; professor of language and English literature, School of Philosophy and Letters, UNAM; professor of language and literature, University of Minnesota, 1918; professor of philosophy, School of Philosophy and Literature, UNAM, 1933. D] None. E] None. F] Confidential agent of the Mexican government, Washington, D.C., 1914; employee, Secretariat of Labor; private secretary to the secretary of education, *José M. Puig Casauranc*, 1924–28; private secretary to the secretary of industry and commerce, José M. Puig Casauranc, 1928–29; private secretary to the head of the Department of the Federal District, José M. Puig Casauranc, 1929–30; private secretary to the secretary of education, José M. Puig Casauranc, 1930–31; private secretary to the Mexican ambassador to the United States, José M. Puig Casauranc, 1931–32; oficial mayor in charge of the Secretariat of Foreign Relations, 1932–33; ambassador to the Society of Nations, 1933–34; minister to France. G] None. H] Cofounder of La Razón Publishing House. I] Related to the Marquis Cangas; from a wealthy family. J] None. K] None. L] DP70, 1122; Enc Mex, VII, Dir social, 1935, 227–28.

Jiménez Méndez, Juan
(Deceased 1956) A] April 29, 1886. B] Salamanca, Guanajuato. C] Early education unknown; no degree. D] None. E] None. F] *Governor* and military commander of Oaxaca, 1917–19; chief of staff, Secretariat of National Defense, 1932–34. G] None. H] Unknown. I] Unknown. J] Joined the Maderistas as a private, 1911; joined the Constitutionalists, 1913; member of the Tlalnepantla Garrison under General *Jesús Agustín Castro*, 1913; operated with the 1st Regiment, La Laguna, 21st Rural Group; rank of captain, 1913; rank of brigadier general, 1914; rank of brigade general, March 23, 1917; commander of the 19th Military Zone, Villa Cuauh-

témoc, Veracruz, 1937; rank of division general, January 1, 1939. K] None. L] DP70, 1122; Enc Mex, VII, 493; Dávila, 129; Almanaque de Oaxaca, 131.

Juárez Maza, Benito
(Deceased April 20, 1912) A] October 29, 1847. B] Oaxaca, Oaxaca. C] Early education unknown; law degree. D] *Alternate federal deputy* from the State of México, Dist. 15, 1884–86; *alternate federal deputy* from the State of México, Dist. 4, 1886–88, 1888–90; *alternate federal deputy* from the Territory of Tepic, Dist. 3, 1888–90; *federal deputy* from the State of Oaxaca, Dist. 12, 1890–92, 1892–94, 1894–96, 1896–98, 1898–1900, 1900–02, 1902–04, 1904–06 1906–08, 1908–10; *governor* of Oaxaca, 1911–12. E] Member of the Anti-Reelectionist party; member of the Oaxaca Democratic party. F] Diplomat. G] None. H] Lawyer. I] Son of Benito Juárez, president of Mexico; married María Klerián; brother-in-law of *Ignacio M. Luchichi*, federal deputy from Chihuahua, 1896–1902. J] None. K] None. L] DP70, 2407; Mestre, 242.

K

Kerlegand Flores, Joaquín Zeferino
(Deceased June 22, 1908) A] August 26, 1838. B] Tampico, Tamaulipas. C] Primary studies at the Colegio de París, Paris, France; engineering studies, Paris, France. D] *Governor* of Campeche, 1888–91. E] None. F] *Governor* and military commander of Tabasco, 1892. G] None. H] None. I] Son of Joaquín Kerlegand and Francisca Flores; married Luisa Guzmán; daughter Natalia married lawyer Federico Peraza Rosado, son of General Martín F. Peraza y Cárdenas, governor of Yucatán, 1858. J] Joined the Tampico National Guard as a 2nd lieutenant, 1861; organized the Hidalgo Battalion as a 2nd lieutenant to fight the French, 1861; commander of the Hidalgo Battalion, Central Division, siege of Puebla; fought in the battle of Altamira, 1864; fought in the siege of Matamoros, 1865; commander of the Santiago Military Prison, 1880; rank of brigadier general, August 29, 1884; commission to Yucatán, 1886, Sonora, 1887, and Campe-

che, 1888; military commander of Tabasco, 1891; rank of brigade general, May 27, 1901; commander, 6th Military Zone, 1901. K] None. L] Valdés Acosta, 3, 252; Almanaque de Tabasco, 149; Pavía, 86–88; Sec of War, 1901, 19; Hombres prominentes, 331–32; Mestre, 231.

L

Lagos Cházaro, Francisco
(Deceased November 13, 1932) A] September 30, 1878. B] Tlacotalpan, Veracruz. C] Early education unknown; law degree. D] Member of the City Council of Orizaba, 1911; *governor* of Veracruz, 1912. E] Anti-reelectionist, 1909. F] President of the Superior Tribunal of Justice of Coahuila, 1913; private secretary to the president of the Convention government, *Roque González Garza*, 1915; *president* of the Convention government, 1915–16; agent of the Ministerio Público, Criminal Court, Belén; public defender. G] None. H] Lawyer; Director, *Vida Nueva*, Chihuahua, Chihuahua, 1915. I] Son of Francisco R. Lagos Jiménez and Francisca Cházaro. J] Supported *Francisco I. Madero*, 1910; joined the Constitutionalists, 1913; supported *Francisco Villa*, 1915; represented General *Fidel Avila*, Convention government, Mexico City, 1915. K] Nominated for secretary of government, but did not serve, March 1915; voluntary exile in Costa Rica, Honduras, and Nicaragua, 1916–20. L] Covarrubias, 120; Enc Mex, VII, 575; Mestre, 287; García Purón, 223.

Lancaster Jones, Alfonso
(Deceased August 9, 1903) A] August 22, 1841. B] Guadalajara, Jalisco. C] Early education unknown; law degree, 1863. D] *Federal deputy* from the State of Jalisco, Dist. 5, 1886–88; *senator* from the State of Jalisco, 1900–02; *ambassador* to England, 1902–03. E] None. F] Secretary of government of the State of Jalisco, 1872; secretary of justice and public instruction, 1876–77. G] Member of the Royal Academy of Legislature and Jurisprudence of Madrid. H] Large landholder; owner of the Santa Cruz and El Cortijo haciendas; poet; author; lawyer. I] Son of Adolfo Lancaster Jones, physician; father

of Alberto Lancaster Jones y Mijares, scientist and businessman. J] Fought the French. K] None. L] C de S, 1900–02, 6; Agraz, 1958, 230–32; DP70, 1154; Enc Mex, VII, 586; Mestre, 217; García de Alba, 1958, 177.

Landa y Escandón, Guillermo de
(Deceased 1927) A] 1848. B] Mexico City. C] Early education unknown; preparatory studies at Stoneyhurst College, England; professional studies, Europe. D] Alternate senator from the State of Morelos, 1878–80; senator from the State of Morelos, 1880–82; *senator* from the State of Morelos, 1886–90; *senator* from the State of Chihuahua, 1890–94, 1894–1900, 1900–04, 1904–06; president of the City Council of Mexico City, 1900. E] None. F] *Governor* of the Federal District, 1900, 1903–11. G] Founding member of the Jockey Club, 1883. H] Cofounder of an insurance company with *Eduardo Liceaga* and *José Castellot*; leader of a literary group which exalted President *Porfirio Díaz*. I] From an aristocratic and wealthy family; married Blanca Macía; nephew of Manuel Escandón, capitalist and financier of the Mexico City–Veracruz railroad; brother José was federal deputy from San Luis Potosí, 1896–98. J] None. K] Left Mexico for Europe, 1910. J] Album; DP70, 1155; Enc Mex, VII, 587; Hombres prominentes, 377–78.

Landázuri, Pedro
(Deceased November 29, 1905) A] January 28, 1832. B] Guadalajara, Jalisco. C] Preparatory studies at the Colegio de San Gregorio, Mexico City; math and engineering studies, College of Mines, Mexico City; continued engineering studies at the School of Mines, Freiburg, Germany, 1849, graduating with an engineering degree. D] Local deputy to the state legislature of Jalisco, 1867–68; federal deputy from Jalisco, 1869–71; federal deputy from the State of San Luis Potosí, 1878–80; *federal deputy* from the State of Jalisco, Dist. 12, 1886–88, 1888–90, 1890–92, 1892–94, 1894–96, 1896–98, 1898–1900; *federal deputy* from the State of Jalisco, Dist. 9, 1900–02, 1902–04, 1904–05. E] Member of the Liberal party. F] Joined the Consular Service, 1874; official in Hamburg, Bremen, and Lubeck, Germany, 1874–78; private secretary to President Lerdo de Tejada, 1874; provisional governor of Jalisco, 1882–83; government representative to the Bank of London and Mexico. G] None. H] Unknown. I] Married Isabel Prieto, poet and his cousin; great-uncle of Sotero Prieto, distinguished educator and mathematican. J] Fought against the French; rank of colonel. K] None. L] DP70, 1155; Mestre, 223.

Lanz Duret, Miguel
(Deceased 1940) A] 1878. B] Campeche, Campeche. C] Early education unknown; law degree, National School of Law, Mexico City, 1904; professor of constitutional law, National School of Law. D] *Alternate federal deputy* from the State of Campeche, 1906–08, 1908–10; *federal deputy* from the Federal District, Dist. 5, 1910–12. E] None. F] None. G] President of the Mexican Bar. H] Owner of *El Universal*, and *El Universal Gráfico*, 1922–40. I] Son of Miguel Lanz Duret and Natalia Duret; married Concepción Sierra, daughter of *Justo Sierra*; son Fernando Lanz Duret Sierra, senator from Campeche, 1958–64; son Miguel Lanz Duret Sierra, president of the Bank of Graphic Art, 1946; brother Ramón Lanz Duret served as a Supreme Court justice and alternate senator from Campeche; grandfather Domingo Duret was a physician. J] None. K] None. L] Valdés, 3, 461; Dir social, 1935, 107; UNAM, law, 1896–1900, 156; DP70, 1157.

Lascuráin (Paredes), Pedro
(Deceased July 21, 1952) A] May 12, 1858. B] Mexico City. C] Early education unknown; law degree, National School of Law, Mexico City, July 13, 1880; director, Free Law School, Mexico City; professor of law, Free Law School. D] Mayor of Mexico City, 1896–1911; member of the City Council of Mexico City, 1911. E] None. F] *Secretary* of foreign relations, 1912, 1913; *provisional president* of Mexico (45 minutes), February 18, 1913. G] Member of the Academy of Legislation and Jurisprudence; member of the Mexican Bar. H] Lawyer. I] Son of Francisco Lascuráin and Ana María

Paredes, very wealthy; married María Flores; brother of *Román S. Lascuráin*, federal deputy from Campeche, 1886–96. J] None. K] DP70, 1162; Enc Mex, VII; FSRE, 153–54; Covarrubias, 1952, 121.

Lascuráin (Paredes), Román S.
(Deceased) A] Unknown. B] Veracruz. C] Early education unknown; studies in Germany; director, School of Arts and Trades for Women, Mexico City; director, Academy of Fine Arts, Mexico City, 1888. D] Member of the City Council of Mexico City, 1876, 1883–84; *federal deputy* from the State of Campeche, Dist. 2, 1886–88, 1888–90, 1890–92, 1892–94, 1894–96; *alternate senator* from the State of Aguascalientes, 1896–1900, 1900–04. E] None. F] Director of social welfare, 1867. G] Founding member of the Jockey Club, 1883. H] Businessman; owner of the Tortugas hacienda. I] Son of Francisco Lascuráin and Ana María Paredes, wealthy landowners; brother of *Pedro Lascuráin*, president of Mexico, 1913. J] None. K] None. L] Dir social, 1935, 108; Hombres prominentes, 371–72; C de S, 1900–02, 5; Pasqual, 210–11.

León, Francisco C.
(Deceased) A] October 4, 1844. B] Juchitán, Oaxaca. C] Taught by parents at home in Juchitán; no degree. D] Mayor of Juchitán, Oaxaca, 1888–89; *governor* of Chiapas, 1895–99. E] None. F] Syndic of the City Council of Juchitán, 1876; political boss of Juchitán, 1888–89; general inspector of political bosses in Chiapas, 1890; inspector of public works, Chiapas. G] None. H] Landowner and farmer. I] Parents were landowners. J] Fought the French; career officer; reached the rank of colonel. K] None. L] Godoy, 73–74; Almanaque de Chiapas, 118.

León, Marcelo
(Deceased December 29, 1898) A] February 7, 1846. B] Cosamaloapan, Veracruz. C] Preparatory studies at the Institute of Veracruz; left studies in 1861 to fight the French. D] Federal deputy from the State of Chihuahua, 1878–80, 1880–82; federal deputy from the State of Chihuahua, Dist. 4, 1882–84; *federal deputy* from the State of Chihuahua, Dist. 4, 1884–86; *federal*

deputy from the State of Guerrero, Dist. 3, 1886–88, 1890–92, 1894–96; *federal deputy* from the State of Guerrero, Dist. 2, 1896–98. E] None. F] Prefect and military commander of Cosamaloapan, 1867; prefect of San Andrés Tuxtla, 1876; director, Customshouse, Paso del Norte, 1879–85. G] None. H] None. I] Son Luis L. León secretary of agriculture, 1924–28. J] Joined the National Guard as a 2nd lieutenant, 1861; served in the Libres de la Costa battalion, 1864; rank of captain, 1867; commander, National Guard of Cosamaloapan; rank of lt. colonel, 1876; commander of the 4 cantons (districts) of Sotavento, 1876–77; commander, customs inspectors, Northern Zone, Ciudad Juárez, 1877–78. K] None. L] Hombres prominentes, 437–38; Pasquel, Liberals, 195–96; Almada, 1968, 308.

León de la Barra (y Quijano), Francisco
(Deceased September 23, 1939) A] June 16, 1863. B] Querétaro, Querétaro. C] Primary studies in Querétaro; legal studies, Scientific and Literary Institute of Querétaro; law degree, National School of Law, Mexico City, 1886; professor of mathematics, National Preparatory School, 1884; professor of philosophy, National Preparatory School; professor of mathematics, National School of Law; cofounder of the Free Law School. D] Member of the City Council, Mexico City; *alternate federal deputy* from the State of Tepic, Dist. 3, 1892–94; *federal deputy* from the State of Tepic, 1894–96; *governor* of México, 1913; *senator* from the State of Querétaro, 1913–14. E] None. F] Syndic, Mexico City Council; adviser, secretary of foreign relations, 1898; ambassador to Argentina, 1902–03; ambassador to Belgium, 1904–08; *ambassador* to the United States, 1908–11; *secretary* of foreign relations, 1911; *interim president* of Mexico, 1911; *ambassador* to France, 1913–14. G] None. H] President, International Arbitration Board (England, France, and Belgium), 1939. I] Son of Bernabé León de a Barra, general, consul, and businessman, and Luisa Quijano y Pérez, daughter of General Benito Quijano; uncle of banker Luis León de la Barra Abello; married María Elena Borneque; second wife, Refugio Borneque; brother Ignacio

León de la Barra, director of public works, Mexico City; brother-in-law of Manuela Santacilia y Juárez, grandaughter of Benito Juárez. J] None. K] Resided in France, 1914–39. L] Mestre, 185; García Purón, 215–16; DBM68, 375–76; Godoy, 11; QesQ, 322; Enc Mex, VIII, 52; FSRE, 149; WWM35, 117; Mestre, 296.

Liceaga, Eduardo
(Deceased January 13, 1920) A] October 13, 1839. B] Guanajuato, Guanajuato. C] Secondary and preparatory at the San Gregorio College; studies at the National School of Medicine, 1859–66, graduating with a medical degree, January 8, 1866; gold medal for the best student, 1865; professor of medical operations, National School of Medicine, 1867–90; dean, National School of Medicine; professor of physics and natural history, National School of Law, 1866; professor of acoustics and phonography, National Conservatory of Music, 1868–72. D] *Federal deputy* from the State of Guanajuato, Dist. 1, 1894–96, 1896–98, 1898–1900; *federal deputy* from the State of Guanajuato, Dist. 11, 1900–02; *federal deputy* from the State of Guanajuato, Dist. 1, 1902–04, 1904–06, 1906–08, 1908–10, 1910–12. E] None. F] President, Supreme Council of Health, 1891–98. G] Founder and secretary, Philharmonic Society of Mexico; president, National Academy of Medicine, 1878, 1906. H] Practicing physician; director, Red Cross of Mexico; director, Children's Department, San Andrés Hospital. I] From a poor family; married Dolores Jáuregui; personal physician to Carmen Romero, second wife of *Porfirio Díaz*. J] None. K] Practiced medicine among the poor; originated the idea of building the General Hospital of Mexico City, 1905; founded the Maternity Hospital, Mexico City. L] Godoy, 292–93; Album; letter; QesQ, 330; Hombres prominentes, 247–48; Enc Mex, VIII, 71; UNAM, law, 1891–96, 157; Mestre, 264, 245; Puente, 89–93.

Limantour (Marquet), José Yves
(Deceased 1935) A] December 26, 1854. B] Mexico City. C] Primary and secondary studies in Mexico City; studied French, English, and political economy,

Europe, 1868; preparatory studies, National Preparatory School, Mexico City, 1869–71; legal studies, National School of Law, 1872–75, graduating March 1876; professor of political economy, National School of Business, 1876; interim professor of public and private international law, National School of Business, 1878. D] Member of the City Council of Mexico City, 1881; *alternate federal deputy* from the State of Oaxaca, Dist. 3, 1884–86; *federal deputy* from the Federal District, Dist. 5, 1888–90, 1890–92, president of the Chamber, 1892; *federal deputy* from the Federal District, Dist. 3, 1892–94, 1894–96. E] None. F] Executive secretary of the board of the Drainage System of the Valley of Mexico, 1887–95; *oficial mayor* of the treasury, 1892–93; *interim secretary* of the treasury, 1893; *secretary* of the treasury, 1893–1911. G] Founding member and stockholder, Jockey Club, 1883. H] Co-owner with brother Julio of Orilla del Río Naranjo hacienda, Veracruz, which was 10,460 hectares; editor and owner of *El Foro*, 1877–82, with *Miguel S. Macedo, Justo Sierra*, and *Emilio Pardo, Jr.* I] Son of José Yves Limantour, friend of Benito Juárez, and Adela Marquet, large landholders; married María Cañas de Buch; granddaughter married Bernardo Sepúlveda Amor, secretary of foreign relations, 1982–88; grandson José Yves Limantour Landa, a conductor; brother Julio a banker and federal deputy, 1900–10; a student of *Francisco Díaz Covarrubias, Manuel Fernández Leal*, and Ignacio Ramírez at the National Preparatory School. J] None. K] Considered the leader of the *científico* group. L] Godoy, 157; Enc Mex, VII, 94; Rice, 240–41; DP70, 1184–85; WNM, 130; Wright, 150; Puente, 20–25.

Limón (López), Cristóbal
(Deceased March 11, 1964) A] November 16, 1883. B] Yahualica, Jalisco. C] Primary studies in Yahualica, and at the Colegio de San Francisco Javier, Tepic; studies in logic and philosophy, Conciliar Seminary of Tepic, 1896–1900; no degree. D] *Constitutional deputy* from the State of Tepic, Dist. 1, 1916–17; *federal deputy* from the State of Jalisco, Dist. 3, 1917–18. E] None. F] Clerk, Tepic judicial district,

1906; tax official, Tepic, 1920; agent of the Ministerio Público of the Military Judicial District, Mexicali, Baja California del Norte, 1926–28. G] None. H] Employee, Valadés banking firm, Mazatlán. I] Son of José Limón and María de Jesús López. J] Joined the Constitutionalists under *Benjamín Hill*, 1913; chief of staff of the military commander in Tepic, 1916; commander, Tepic, 1916; commander of the 4th Regiment, Zamora, Michoacán; staff officer, Mazatlán; staff officer, Fort of Michoacán, 1924–26; president, War Council, Guaymas, Sonora, 1928; commander, 2nd Volunteer Battalion, Baja California, 1929; commander, Texcoco Sector, 14th Regiment, 1929; chief of staff, 2nd Military Zone, Tijuana, Baja California del Norte, 1930; commander of the 14th Military Zone, Aguascalientes, Aguascalientes, 1932–33; director, National Armaments Factory, 1935; subdirector, war matériel and artillery warehouses, 1936–40; rank of brigadier general, February 16, 1941. K] None. L] C de D, 1916–17; C de D, 1917–18.

Lizardi, Fernando M.
(Deceased October 7, 1957) A] May 23, 1883. B] Guanajuato, Guanajuato. C] Completed primary studies at the Colegio de la Purísima Concepción, Celaya, 1893; preparatory and first 2 years of legal studies, Colegio del Estado de Guanajuato, 1894–1900; continued legal studies at the National School of Law, Mexico City, 1901, graduating September 11, 1906; interim dean, National School of Law, 1916; director, National Preparatory School. D] *Constitutional deputy* from the State of Guanajuato, Dist. 13, 1916–17. E] None. F] Judge, Celaya, 1911; secretary general of government of the State of Hidalgo, 1915; judge of the Superior Tribunal of Justice of the Federal District, 1915; attorney general of Tamaulipas; chief, Advisory Department, Secretariat of Government, 1935; assistant director, Legal Department, National Railroads of Mexico, 1936; agent of the Ministerio Público, 1946. G] President, local Agrarian Commission, Tamaulipas, 1921. H] Opened law practice with José Natividad Macías; law practice with *Enrique Colunga*, 1908–11. I] Son of Manuel Lizardi, lawyer, and Ana

Santana; related to (probably uncle of) Víctor José Lizardi, governor of Guanajuato, 1911–13. J] Joined the Maderistas, Jaral del Valle, Guanajuato, 1911. K] None. L] UNAM, law, 1900–06, 5; DP70, 1195; Enc Mex, VIII, 124.

López de Lara, César
(Deceased April 11, 1960) A] September 10, 1890. B] Matamoros, Tamaulipas. C] Primary studies at the Colegio Francés (Brothers of Mary), Mexico City; law degree, National School of Law, UNAM. D] *Governor* of Tamaulipas, 1921–23. E] None. F] *Provisional governor* of the Federal District, 1915, 1915–17; *governor of the Federal District, 1917–18.* G] None. H] Journalist; wrote articles against President *Porfirio Díaz* in *México Nuevo*; lawyer. I] Son of Domingo López de Lara, federal deputy from Hidalgo, 1900–02, and treasurer general of Mexico under President Juárez. J] Supported *Francisco I. Madero*, 1910; joined the Constitutionalists as a law student, 1913; rank of brigadier general, October 16, 1914; fought Villistas under General *Jacinto B. Treviño*, 1914–15; supported the *Adolfo de la Huerta* rebellion, 1923; reintegrated into the army, June 6, 1943; rank of brigade general, May 1958. K] Voluntary exile, San Antonio, Texas, 1923–37. L] López, 610; DP70, 1206; Enc Mex, VIII, 140.

López Portillo y Rojas, José
(Deceased May 22, 1923) A] May 26, 1850. B] Guadalajara, Jalisco. C] Early education unknown; law degree, School of Law, University of Guadalajara, 1871; professor of mercantile, penal, and mining law. D] Local deputy to the state legislature of Jalisco; federal deputy, 1875–77; federal deputy from the State of Jalisco, Dist. 9, 1880–82; *alternate federal deputy* from the State of Jalisco, Dist. 13, 1888–90, 1890–92; *federal deputy* from the State of Nuevo León, Dist. 4, 1900–02; *federal deputy* from the State of Nuevo León, Dist. 1, 1902–04, 1904–06, 1906–08; *alternate senator* from the State of Nuevo León, 1908–12; *governor* of Jalisco, 1912–13. E] Supported *Bernardo Reyes* for vice-president, 1908–09. F] Judge, Superior Tribunal of Justice of Jalisco;

subsecretary of public instruction, 1913; *secretary* of foreign relations, 1914. G] Secretary of the Mexican Academy of Language, 1908–16; president of the Mexican Academy of Language, 1916–23. H] Cofounder of *La República Literaria*, 1885–96; journalist; lawyer; important intellectual among Jalisco authors; novelist. I] Son of Jesús López Portillo, lawyer and governor of Jalisco, and María Rojas; grandfather of President José López Portillo Pacheco, 1976–82; father of José López Portillo y Weber, historian and revolutionary; married María Gómez Luna; second wife, Margarita Weber. J] None. K] Imprisoned for supporting Bernardo Reyes; persecuted, 1915–16, for holding post under *Victoriano Huerta*. L] Enc Mex, VIII, 154D–155; López, 620; O'Campo, 198–200.

Lozano, José María
(Deceased August 7, 1933) A] October 28, 1878. B] San Miguel el Alto, Jalisco. C] Primary studies at the Conciliar Seminary of Guadalajara; one year of study, National Military College, Mexico City; law degree, National School of Law; studies in humanities, Jesuit College. D] *Federal deputy* from the State of México, Dist. 2, 1910–12; *federal deputy* from Jalisco, Dist. 7, 1912–13, member of the Great Committee. E] Member of the Anti-Reelectionist party. F] Agent of the Ministerio Público; *secretary* of public instruction, 1913; *secretary* of communications, 1913; *secretary* of communications, 1914. G] None. H] Practicing lawyer; wrote for *El Debate*, 1909; journalist; member of La Horda intellectual group. I] Unknown. J] Supported *Adolfo de la Huerta* rebellion. K] Jailed three months for attacking *José Limantour* in an article in *La Protesta*, 1903; exiled to France and Cuba, 1914–21; notable orator and member of the "cuadrilátero" group of deputies, including *Nemesio García Naranjo* and *Francisco Modesto Olaguíbel*. L] DP70, 1218; Enc Mex, VIII, 168; Mestre, 288; Agraz, 1958, 154.

Lozano (Espinosa), José María
(Deceased March 20, 1893) A] January 5, 1823. B] Texcoco, México. C] Primary studies, Texcoco; preparatory studies, Na-

tional Preparatory School and Colegio de San Gregorio, Mexico City; law degree, National School of Law, Mexico City, 1851; professor of Latin, National School of Law, 1847; professor of philosophy, Colegio de San Gregorio, 1848–51; vice-rector of the Colegio de San Gregorio, 1851; rector and professor of law, Colegio de San Gregorio, 1851–53; professor of comparative law, National School of Law, 1868–76; director, Colegio de la Paz; rector and professor of canon law, Colegio de la Purísima, 1856–58; rector, Colegio de Guanajuato, 1869–62, 1867–68. D] Local deputy to the state legislature of Guanajuato, 1860–62; federal deputy from the State of Guanajuato, 1862, 1882–84; *federal deputy* from the State of Guanajuato, Dist. 4, 1884–86, 1886–88. E] None. F] Agent of the Superior Tribunal of Justice of Guanajuato, 1854; attorney general of Mexico, 1880–82; justice of the Supreme Court, 1873; *justice* of the Supreme Court, 1888–93. G] None. H] Practicing lawyer. I] Son of Hipólito Lozano and Rosa Espinosa, poor family; wrote 47-volume legal work with *Manuel Dublán*; poet. J] Supported Juárez, 1863–67. K] None. L] Mestre, 181–82; Aranda Pamplona, 58; Cruzado, 147–48; González Cosío, 11.

Luchichi, Ignacio M.
(Deceased 1918) A] May 8, 1859. B] Tlacotalpan, Veracruz. C] Early education unknown; no degree. D] *Federal deputy* from the State of Chihuahua, Dist. 4, 1896–98; *federal deputy* from the State of Chihuahua, Dist. 3, 1898–1900, 1900–02; *federal deputy* from the State of Oaxaca, Dist. 3, 1902–04, 1904–06, 1906–08, 1908–10, 1910–12. E] None. F] None. G] None. H] Journalist; poet; collaborated with *Manuel Gutiérrez Nájera* on the *Revista Azul* and *Revista de México*; wrote for newspapers in Veracruz; wrote under the pseudonym of Claudio Frollo. I] Son-in-law of Benito Juárez; brother-in-law of *Benito Juárez Maza*, governor of Oaxaca, 1911–12. J] None. K] None. L] DP70, 1219; C de D, 1896–98.

Lúcido Cambas, Angel
(Deceased November 7, 1898) A] December 24, 1833. B] Jalapa, Veracruz. C] Early education unknown; no degree. D] Mayor of Papantla, Veracruz; *federal deputy* from the State of Sinaloa, Dist. 1, 1896–98, 1898. E] Joined the Liberal party as a youngster. F] Customs official, Nautla, Veracruz; political boss of Papantla, Veracruz, 1882. G] None. H] Unknown. I] Son of Félix Lucido, syndic of the city council of Jalapa, 1847; cousin of historian Manuel Rivera. J] Captain, national guard, Jalapa, 1857; joined the forces of General Ignacio de la Llave, 1858; commander of the Libertad Battalion, 1859; rank of lt. colonel, 1859; defended the Port of Veracruz against the Conservative Army, 1860; fought the French; reached the rank of colonel. K] None. L] Pasquel, Liberals, 233–35; C de D, 1896–98.

Lugo, José Inocencio
(Deceased November 25, 1963) A] December 28, 1874. B] Santa Ana del Aguila, Municipio of Ajuchitlán, Guerrero. C] Primary and secondary studies in Morelia, Michoacán; preparatory studies at the Colegio de San Nicolás, Morelia; law degree from the School of Law, Colegio de San Nicolás, Morelia; professor at the National Military College. D] *Senator* from the State of Guerrero, 1917–18; *federal deputy* from the State of Guerrero, Dist. 8, 1918–20. E] President of the "Nicolaita" Student rebellion at the Colegio de San Nicolás to protest the reelection of Governor *Aristeo Mercado*, 1895; member of the Anti-Reelectionist party, 1909. F] *Governor* of Baja California del Norte, 1922–23; *governor* of Guerrero, 1910–13; *subsecretary* of government, June 1, 1920–August 4, 1920; *secretary* of government, 1920; *subsecretary* of communications and public works, 1921; head of the Department of Justice, Secretariat of War and Navy; interim governor of Guerrero, 1935–36. G] None. H] Practicing lawyer in Coyuca de Catalán, Guerrero. I] Son José Inocente Lugo Lagunas served as federal deputy from Guerrero, Dist. 1, 1955–57, and was president of the Fourth Division of the National Tax Court,

1964–70. J] Coordinated revolutionary activities in Guerrero, 1910; joined the forces of General *Gertrudis Sánchez,* 1910; fought against *Victoriano Huerta* in the forces of General Gertrudis Sánchez; rank of brigadier general, February 16, 1932; rank of division general. K] Imprisoned, 1910; imprisoned by Huerta, 1913. L] DP70, 1219–20; Peral, 468; Enc Mex, VIII, 1977, 170.

Luna y Parra, Pascual
(Deceased November 30, 1938) A] 1876. B] Acatzingo, Puebla. C] Early education unknown; law degree, National School of Law, December 27, 1899; professor in finance and tax law, National School of Law and National School of Business, 1903–38; director, Board of Public Instruction, Federal District. D] *Federal deputy* from the State of Puebla, Dist. 14, 1912–13; *federal deputy* from the State of Puebla, Dist. 3, 1914–16. E] None. F] *Subsecretary* of the treasury, 1913; president, Tax Violation Board, 1925; president, National Highway Commission, 1926–29; director general of the National Railroads of Mexico, 1932–34. G] Director of the Chamber of Commerce of Mexico; director, Federal Chambers of Industries; vice-president, Mexican Bar, 1937. H] Director of the Electric Company of Chapala, S.A., and the Electric Company of Morelia, S.A., 1926–35. I] Son of lawyer Pascual Luna y Parra and Rosario Parra; married Carmen Mariscal y Piña, daughter of engineer Alfonso Mariscal y Fagoaga; father of Jorge Luna y Parra, lawyer; father of José Luna y Parra, director, National Chamber of Industries; granddaughter married Ricardo García Sáinz, secretary of planning and programming, 1977–79. J] None. K] None. L] Linajes, 91–96, 149–51, 188; DP70, 1222; CyT, 383; WWM45, 66–67.

M

Maas Aguila, Joaquín, Jr.
(Deceased 1948) A] 1879. B] Puebla, Puebla. C] Early education unknown; graduated as a 2nd lieutenant in the construction engineers, National Military College, 1901. D] None. E] None.

F] *Governor* of Coahuila, 1913–14.
G] None. H] Practicing engineer, 1920–
48. I] Son of *Joaquín Maas*, governor of
Puebla, 1913–14; nephew of General *Victoriano Huerta*, whose sister was Maas's
mother; father and Huerta were class-
mates at the National Military College.
J] Career army officer; supported *Francisco I. Madero* against the *Pascual
Orozco* rebellion, 1912; commander of the
Bravo Division; rank of brigade general,
October 7, 1913; supported General
Huerta; fought against and defeated by
Francisco Villa, 1914; rank of division
general, 1914. K] None. L] Sec of War,
1914, 20; Cuevas, 355.

Maas Flores, Joaquín
(Deceased January 15, 1914) A] October 9,
1855. B] Mexico City. C] Early educa-
tion unknown; enrolled at the National
Military College, 1868, graduating as
an artillery engineer, 1876. D] None.
E] None. F] *Provisional governor* of Pue-
bla, 1913–14. G] None. H] None.
I] Married sister of General *Victoriano
Huerta*, his classmate at the Military College; son Joaquín Maas, Jr., governor of
Coahuila, 1913–14; brother of Gustavo
Maas Flores, division general. J] Career
army officer; member of the Geographic
Exploratory Commission, 1880; official,
Veracruz–Puebla Boundary Commission,
1884; charged with organizing the Yaqui
and Mayan river populations, 1887; rank
of lt. colonel, engineers, 1891; directed
San Lázaro project, 1892; completed projects in Querétaro, Querétaro, 1893; campaigned against the Yaquis, 1894–99; garrison commander, Mazatlán, Sinaloa,
1901; rank of brigade general, 1911; sent
on a special commission to Europe, 1911–
12; rank of division general, January 1,
1914. K] None. L] Cuevas, 349; Mestre,
249, 288; DP70, 1227; CyT, 393; WNM,
136; Almanaque de Puebla, 129.

Macedo (González de Saravia), Miguel S.
(Deceased July 14, 1929) A] June 8, 1856.
B] Mexico City. C] Preparatory studies at
the National Preparatory School; legal
studies, National School of Law, 1874–79,
graduating October 1, 1879; professor of
criminal law, National School of Law,

1882–1910; dean, National School of
Law; cofounder of the Free Law School.
D] Member of the City Council of Mexico
City, 1896–97; president of the City
Council of Mexico City, 1898–99; *alter-
nate senator* from the State of Puebla,
1900–04; *senator* from the State of
Puebla, 1904–08, 1908–12. E] None.
F] Secretary of the Board to Inspect Jails,
1877–95; vice-president of the Board to
Inspect Jails, 1895–97; secretary of the
Committee to Revise the Civil Codes of
the Federal District, 1884; first syndic of
the City Council of Mexico City, 1895;
president, Committee to Revise the
Criminal Code, 1903–12; *subsecretary* of
government, 1906–11. G] Member of the
Jockey Club; member of the Bankers Club.
H] Lawyer, Mexican Bank of Industry and
Commerce; editor, *La Libertad*, author.
I] Son of Mariano Macedo, lawyer and Supreme Court justice, 1856, and Concepción G. Saravia; brother of *Pablo Macedo*,
federal deputy from the Federal District,
1896–1910; married Concepción Zirión;
grandson of a Portuguese merchant.
J] None. K] None. L] Godoy, 75; Mestre,
283; UNAM, law, 1900–06, 59; Rice, 242;
Enc Mex, VIII, 177–78; DP70, 1227; Puente,
27–30; Velázquez, 158–59; Puente.

Macedo (González de Saravia), Pablo
(Deceased December 25, 1918) A] 1851.
B] Mexico City. C] Preparatory studies at
the Colegio de San Ildefonso; law degree,
National School of Law, 1871; professor of
penal law, UNAM, 1877–86; professor of
political economy, National School of
Law, 1896–1901; dean, National School of
Law, 1901–04. D] Federal deputy from
the Federal District, 1880–82; *federal
deputy* from the Federal District, Dist. 9,
1892–94, 1894–96, 1896–98, 1898–1900;
federal deputy from the Federal District,
Dist. 1, 1900–02; *federal deputy* from the
Federal District, Dist. 2, 1902–04, 1904–
06, 1906–08, president of the Great Committee, 1906–08; *federal deputy* from the
Federal District, Dist. 2, 1908–10, president of the Great Committee, 1908–10;
federal deputy from the Federal District,
Dist. 2, 1910–12. E] None. F] Secretary
of government of the Federal District,
1876–80. G] None. H] Author; editor;

practicing lawyer; founded *Anuario de Legislación y Jurisprudencia* with brother Miguel, 1884; coeditor with *Emilio Pardo, Jr.*, of *El Foro*; director, Fundidora de Fierro y Acero of Monterrey, 1907; president, Banco Mexicano de Comercio y Industria; vice-president and lawyer, Bank of London and Mexico; cofounder of El Boleo Copper Company, Baja California; lawyer, Federal District Railroad Company; lawyer, National Bank of Mexico; owned 3,620,532 hectares of land in Baja California. I] Son of Mariano Macedo, Supreme Court justice and secretary of foreign relations, and Concepción G. Saravia; married Concepción Velázquez; brother of *Miguel S. Macedo*, subsecretary of government, 1906–11; brother-in-law of *Eduardo Velázquez*, federal deputy from Puebla, 1894–97; uncle of *Miguel Palacios Macedo*, subsecretary of industry and commerce, 1923. J] None. K] None. L] Enc Mex, VIII, 178–79; DP70, 1227; Puente, 27–30; Rice, 241–43.

Maceyra (Tavizón), Félix Francisco
(Deceased December 28, 1897) A] May 17, 1832. B] Chihuahua, Chihuahua. C] Primary studies at the Public School of Boys; business studies in Paris, France. D] Local deputy to the state legislature of Chihuahua, 1873–77, 1885–87; *governor* of Chihuahua, 1885–87; *senator* from the State of Guerrero, 1888–92, 1892–96, 1896–97. E] None. F] Secretary, Central Patriotic Council (opposed to the French occupation); political boss of the Iturbide District, 1868–69; political boss of Chihuahua, Chihuahua, 1872. G] None. H] Established a business in Mineral de Ocampo; moved his business to Cusihuiráchic after difficulties with the French authorities, 1864–67; founding stockholder and manager, Banco Mexicano, 1880–97, which joined with the Banco Minero Chihuahuense, 1897; owner of the Hotel Maceyra. I] Son of José Félix Maceyra, important local official in Chihuahua, and Guadalupe Tavizón; brother José Félix, businessman and local deputy; married Guadalupe Bear. J] None. K] None. L] Almada, 403–07; Hombres prominentes, 215–16; Enc Mex, VIII, 179; Mestre, 199; Almada, 1968, 316; Márquez,

251–52; DP70, 1228; Peral, Appendix, 198.

Machorro Narváez, Paulino
(Deceased 1957) A] September 1877. B] Durango, Durango. C] Primary studies in Guadalajara; law degree, School of Law, University of Guadalajara; professor and director, Preparatory School of Guadalajara; professor of constitutional law, National School of Law. D] *Constitutional deputy* from the State of Jalisco, Dist. 18, 1916–17; *federal deputy* from the State of Jalisco, Dist. 1, 1918–20. E] Member of the Liberal party of Jalisco. F] *Attorney general* of the Federal District, 1915–18; oficial mayor of the Secretariat of Government, 1920; subsecretary of government; *justice* of the Supreme Court, 1918–34. G] None. H] Practicing lawyer; consultant to railroad companies; author. I] Related to Paulino Z. Machorro (who was probably his father), prominent Liberal officer. J] Opposed *Victoriano Huerta*, 1914. K] None. L] Enc Mex, VIII, 184; Almada, 1968, 317; Dir social, 1935, 115.

Macías, José Natividad
(Deceased October 19, 1948) A] September 8, 1857. B] Pavileros, Silao, Guanajuato. C] Primary studies in Silao, Guanajuato; preparatory studies in León, Guanajuato, and at the National Preparatory School, Mexico City; law degree, University of Guanajuato, November 24, 1883; law degree, National School of Law, 1894; dean, National School of Law, 1914; rector of UNAM, 1917–20. D] *Federal deputy* from the State of Michoacán, Dist. 14, 1906–08, 1908–10; *federal deputy* from the State of Michoacán, Dist. 10, 1910–12; *federal deputy* from the State of Guanajuato, Dist. 11, 1912–13; *constitutional deputy* from the State of Guanajuato, Dist. 3, 1916–17. E] Member of the Anti-Reelectionist party. F] None. G] None. H] Lawyer, Mexico City; journalist; reporter, San Antonio, Texas, 1910–21; wrote revisions of the 1857 Constitution for president. I] Son of Pedro Macías and Cleofas Castorena; mother possibly related to José de Jesús Castorena, governor of Guanajuato, 1947–48. J] None. K] Imprisoned by *Victo-*

riano Huerta, 113. L] Enc Mex, VIII, 180; DP70, 1228; López, 637.

Madero (Farías), Ernesto
(Deceased February 2, 1958) A] October 12, 1872. B] Parras, Coahuila. C] Early education unknown; no degree. D] None. E] None. F] *Secretary* of the treasury, 1911, 1911–13. G] None. H] Businessman; large landholder. I] Son of Evaristo Madero, entrepreneur and wealthy landholder, and second wife Manuela Farías; married Leonor Olivares Tapia; stepbrother of Francisco Madero Hernández, father of *Francisco I. Madero*. J] None. K] None. L] Enc Mex, VIII, 186–87; Linajes, 159.

Madero (González), Francisco Ignacio
(Deceased February 22, 1913) A] October 30, 1873. B] Hacienda de El Rosario, Parras de la Fuente, Coahuila. C] Primary studies under Albina Maynes and Encarnación Cervantes, Parras, Coahuila; preparatory studies, Jesuit Colegio de San Juan, Saltillo, Coahuila; business studies, Mt. Saint Mary, Baltimore, Maryland, 1886–88; business studies, Liceo de Versailles and the Higher Business School, Paris, France, 1889–91; university studies at the Technical Agricultural School, Berkeley, California, 1893; founded a business school in San Pedro de las Colonias. D] *President* of Mexico, 1911–13. E] Founder, Benito Juárez Anti-Reelectionist Club, 1905; began anti-Díaz campaign, June 10, 1909; president, Democratic Club; founder and vice-president, Anti-Reelectionist Center of Mexico, 1909; candidate for president of the Anti-Reelectionist party, April 15, 1910. F] None. G] None. H] Administered a family business in San Pedro de las Colonias, 1896; practiced homeopathic medicine, 1896; landowner. I] Son of Francisco Madero Hernández, industrialist and businessman, and Mercedes González Treviño; grandson of Evaristo Madero, wealthy landholder; brother of *Gustavo Madero González*, federal deputy from Coahuila, 1912–13; brother-in-law of Carolina Villarreal, daughter of Viviano L. Villarreal, governor of Nuevo León; nephew of *Ernesto Madero*, secretary of the treasury, 1911–13; brother of *Julio*

Madero, oficial mayor of communications; brother Emilio, division general and industrialist, whose son Pablo Emilio Madero Beldén, was president of the National Action party and their presidential candidate, 1982; brother Raúl, governor of Coahuila, 1957–63, whose son Francisco José Madero González was a senator from Coahuila, 1982–88; brother Alfonso, federal deputy from Nuevo León; married Sara Pérez Romero. J] Organized the most significant revolutionary movement against President *Porfirio Díaz*, November 20, 1910. K] Imprisoned for campaign activities, Monterrey and San Luis Potosí, 1910; in exile, United States, 1910; murdered on orders from *Victoriano Huerta*, 1913. L] QesQ, 343–44; DP70, 1230–31; Covarrubias, 3–10; García Purón, 219–20; Morales Jiménez, 67–79.

Madero (González), Gustavo A.
(Deceased February 19, 1913) A] January 16, 1875. B] Hacienda El Rosario, Parras de la Fuente, Coahuila. C] Primary studies in Parras, Coahuila, 1882–86; studies, Buffalo, New York, 1887–92; studies in Berkeley, California, 1893; studies with brother Francisco and uncle Ernesto, Liceo Versailles and the Higher Business School, Paris, France; no degree. D] *Federal deputy*, Dist. 2, 1912–13, and head of the Maderista delegation. E] Directed campaign finances, brother's campaign for president, 1910; founder and leader of the Progressive Constitutional party, 1912. F] Secretary of the treasury of *Francisco I. Madero's* provisional government, Ciudad Juárez, 1911; special ambassador to Japan (but never served), 1913. G] None. H] Employee, La Victoria Thread Factory, Lagos de Moreno, 1895–97; founded a printing and paper firm, El Modelo Typographic Shop, Monterrey, Nuevo León; manager, Industrial Company of Parras, 1897. I] Son of Francisco Madero, businessman and landowner, and Mercedes González Treviño; grandson of Evaristo Madero, wealthy landholder; married Carolina Villarreal, daughter of Viviano Villarreal, governor of Nuevo León; brother Julio, oficial mayor of the Secretariat of Communications; brother Francisco I. Madero, president of Mexico,

1911–13. J] Helped finance brother's revolutionary movement through monies obtained in the United States, 1910–11. K] Forced into exile because of brother's political activities, 1910; murdered by *Félix Díaz's* men in the coup d'état against his brother. L] QesQM, 147; Enc Mex, VII, 196–97; Covarrubias, 11–18; Linajes, 155.

Madero (González), Julio
(Deceased July 5, 1946) A] July 12, 1886. B] Parras de la Fuente, Coahuila. C] Early education unknown; no degree. D] None. E] Candidate for governor of Coahuila, 1933. F] Official, Department of Trade, Secretariat of Agriculture, 1921; ambassador to Italy, 1923–25; ambassador to Sweden, 1922–23; ambassador to Honduras, 1925–26; ambassador to Colombia, 1927. G] None. H] Unknown. I] Son of Francisco Madero Hernández, businessman and landowner, and Mercedes González Treviño; brother of *Gustavo Madero*, federal deputy from Coahuila, 1912–13; brother of *Francisco I. Madero*, president of Mexico, 1911–13; married Carmen García; grandson of Evaristo Madero, wealthy landowner and governor of Coahuila, 1880–84. J] Major, Constitutional army; member of *Alvaro Obregón's* staff; remained loyal to *Venustiano Carranza*, 1920. K] None. L] Peral, Appendix, 479; Linajes, 157.

Madrazo, Antonio
(Deceased April 13, 1941) A] 1885. B] León, Guanajuato. C] Preparatory studies, León, Guanajuato; engineering degree, National Military College. D] Mayor of León, Guanajuato; *constitutional deputy* from the State of Guanajuato, Dist. 8, 1916–17; *federal deputy* from the State of Guanajuato, Dist. 7, 1917–18; *governor* of Guanajuato, 1920–23. E] None. F] President of the board, National Railroads of Mexico; president of the National Highway Commission; *oficial mayor* of the Secretariat of the Treasury, 1916–18; subsecretary of the national economy, 1934–35. G] None. H] Unknown. I] Related to Manuel Madrazo Arcocha and Hortensia Torres Soto (probably his parents); related to *Manuel Madrazo Torres* (probably his brother), director, De-

partment of Health, 1933–34. J] Joined the Constitutionalists, 1913; supported *Adolfo de la Huerta*, 1923. K] None. L] Enc Mex, VIII, 198; Peral, Appendix, 479; DP70, 1232; Almanaque de Guanajuato, 132.

Madrazo (Torres), Manuel
(Deceased November 12, 1890) A] November 12, 1890. B] León, Guanajuato. C] Primary and secondary studies at the Instituto Sollano, León; medical degree in radiology, National School of Medicine, UNAM; postgraduate work, New York; assistant, Hospital for Joint Diseases, New York, 1918–19; professor of clinical medicine, National School of Medicine, UNAM, 1919–30. D] None. E] None. F] Oficial mayor, Department of Health, 1933; *head*, Department of Health, 1933–34; director, Radiology Service, National Railroads of Mexico. G] Member, National Academy of Medicine. H] Practicing physician; director, radiology services, Spanish Hospital, Mexico City; author. I] Son of Manuel Madrazo Arcocha and Hortensia Torres Soto; married Laura Garamendi Alamada; son Manuel is a chemist and served as dean of the National School of Chemistry; uncle of Gonzalo Castellot Madrazo, federal deputy, 1979–82; related to *Antonio Madrazo* (probably brother of). J] None. K] None. L] WWM, 45, 67; Dir social, 1935, 115; Libro de Oro, 152; WNM, 136; Martínez Torres, 323ff.

Magallón, Andrés
(Deceased November 17, 1968) A] November 30, 1882. B] Acaponeta, Jalisco (Tepic). C] Primary studies in Mazatlán, Sinaloa; no degree. D] Secretary of the City Council of Mazatlán, 1911–13; alternate deputy to the state legislature of Sinaloa, 1912–13; *constitutional deputy* from the State of Sinaloa, Dist. 2, 1916–17; *federal deputy* from the State of Sinaloa, Dist. 2, 1917–18; local deputy to the state legislature of Sinaloa, 1918–20; *senator* from the State of Sinaloa, 1920–22, 1922–24; secretary of the City Council of Puebla, Puebla, 1925–26, 1927–29. E] Supported General Miguel Henríquez Guzmán for president, 1951–52. F] Director of political information, Secretariat

of Government, 1914–15; subdirector in charge of the archives, Secretariat of Government, 1915–16; secretary of the Civil Judicial District, 1926–27; justice of the Peace, Tacuba, Federal District, 1929–34; secretary general of government of the State of Puebla, 1941–44. G] President, Group Five, Board of Conciliation and Arbitration, Puebla, 1935. H] Employee, general store; printer; salesman, 1902–07; head, Department of Claims, Naviera del Pacífico Company, 1909–11; journalist. I] Son of Ignacio Magallón Mora Avalos and Micaela Ramírez Llazo. J] Secretary of the general barracks of the Sinaloa Brigade, 1913, 1914. K] None. L] González Dávila, 335; Enc Mex, VIII, 201; DP70, 1233.

Magaña (Cerda), Gildardo
(Deceased December 13, 1939) A] June 8, 1891. B] Zamora, Michoacán. C] Studied at the Colegio de Jacona seminary in Zamora; studied business administration in San Antonio, Texas; studied accounting at Temple College, Philadelphia, completed studies in private accounting, 1908; no degree. D] *Federal deputy* from the State of Michoacán, Dist. 2, 1926–28; *governor* of Michoacán, 1936–39. F] *Governor* of the Federal District, 1915; *secretary* of government, Convention Government, 1914; *governor* of Baja California del Norte, 1934–35. G] Secretary general of the Union of Small Property Owners; organizer of the National Agrarian Federation. H] Practicing accountant, Rojas and Taboada, Mexico City, 1908; author of a major work on Zapata and agrarianism in Mexico. I] Companion and longtime friend of *Saturnino Cedillo* since revolutionary days under *Emiliano Zapata*; precursor of the Revolution in a group which included Camilo Arriaga, *José Vasconcelos*, and *Francisco Múgica*; father, a successful businessman and teacher; brother Octavio Magaña served as a federal deputy from Michoacán, 1924–30. J] Joined the Revolution; instrumental in briefly uniting *Francisco Villa* and Zapata; became chief of staff of the Army of the South on the death of Zapata, 1919; commanding general of the liberating Army of the South, 1919; commander, First Division, Army of the South, 1920;

head of the Agrarian Settlement Program, 1920–24; rank of division general, January 1, 1921; career army officer, without assignment, 1924–34; commander of the 24th Military Zone, Cuernavaca, Morelos; commander of the 2nd Military Zone, Baja California, 1935–36. K] Important intellectual in the Zapatista movement; active in Tacubaya plot against the *Porfirio Díaz* government; imprisoned in Mexico City, 1912–14; the son of General Domingo Arenas accused Magaña of resonsibility in his father's murder; precandidate for president of Mexico, 1939. L] DP70, 1233; Enc Mex, VIII, 1977, 201–02; López González, 123–27.

Malda (Monterde), Gabriel M.
(Deceased 1953) A] March 30, 1876. B] Mexico City. C] Primary and preparatory studies at the Instituto Monasterio; preparatory studies at the National Preparatory School, Mexico City, 1890–94; medical studies, National Medical School, 1895–96; medical degree, Military Medical School, 1896–1900; advanced courses in France, Germany, Belgium, Italy, and Switzerland; professor of anatomy, National School of Medicine, 1911; advanced studies, 1931; professor of legal medicine and pentology, National School of Odontology; chief of topographical anatomy, National School of Medicine, 1902. D] None. E] None. F] *Secretary* of health, 1920; *secretary* of health, 1920–24; chief surgeon, National Railroads of Mexico, 1941–46. G] President, Mexican Academy of Medicine, 1923–24; president, Franco-Mexican Medical Society, 1929–53. H] Practicing physician; director, Juárez Hospital, Mexico City, 1906; author of many medical books. I] Son of José Gabriel Malda, poet and leading intellectual, and Trinidad Monterde, daughter of General Mariano Monterde, director, National Military College. J] None. K] Introduced many new medical practices as director of health. L] Blue Book, 216; Dir social, 1935, 116; Enc Mex, VIII, 229; López, 642–43; DP70, 1240.

Mancera, Gabriel
(Deceased January 25, 1925) A] May 6, 1839. B] Pachuca, Hidalgo. C] Primary studies, private school, Atotonilco de

Chico; preparatory studies, Colegio de San Juan de Letrán, 1851–52; engineering studies, National College of Mines, 1852–57, graduating, 1857. D] Federal deputy from the State of Puebla, 1867; *federal deputy* from the State of Hidalgo, Dist. 3, 1884–86, 1886–88, 1888–90, 1894–96, 1896–98; *federal deputy* from the State of Hidalgo, Dist. 8, 1904–06, 1906–08, 1908–10; *senator* from Hidalgo, 1910–12, 1912–13. E] None. F] Represented the Mexican government at the Philadelphia Exposition, 1876; subsecretary of development, 1878. G] None. H] Director of father's thread factory, Mexico City, 1858–66; director of construction of La Esperanza Thread Factory, Tulancingo, Hidalgo, 1866; primary owner and director of construction of the Hidalgo and Northeast railroads. I] Nephew of Nicolás García de San Vicente, priest and educator; brother Tomás, senator from Puebla, 1906–14; close friend of *Justino Fernández* from childhood; from a wealthy family, father a businessman. J] None. K] Exiled to Puebla by imperial government, 1866. L] Album; Enc Mex, VIII, 239; Armijo, 40–41.

Mancera Ortiz, Rafael
(Deccased September 30, 1968) A] August 22, 1895. B] Federal District. C] Preparatory studies at the National Preparatory School, CPA degree from the National School of Business Administration, UNAM, 1917; professor of accounting at the Graduate School of Business and Administration, UNAM, 1932–36, and the School of Economics and Social Sciences, National Polytechnic School, 1925–36. D] None. E] None. F] Oficial mayor of the comptroller general of Mexico, 1924–27; *oficial mayor* of the Secretariat of the Treasury, 1927–30; *subsecretary* of the treasury, 1930–32; *subsecretary* in charge of the Secretariat of the Treasury, 1932; adviser to Nacional Financiera; subsecretary of credit, Secretariat of the Treasury, 1948–52, 1952–58. G] First president of the National Association of Public Accountants in Mexico, 1929–30, 1959–61. H] Organized a private accounting firm of Mancera and Sons; author of a book on public administration and economic development in Mexico,

1953. I] Son Miguel Mancera was director general of the Bank of Mexico, 1982; son Gabriel is a CPA, managing the firm of Mancera and Sons; married María Luisa Aguayo; brother Alfredo, a CPA, is married to Rosa Aguayo, sister of María Luisa. J] Participated in the Revolution, 1913–20. K] One of the initiators of the certified public accounting system in Mexico. L] DGF56, 161; DP70, 2413; HA, 12 Dec. 1952, 5; WNM, 139; Enc Mex, VIII, 1977, 239; Libro Azul, 217.

Manjárrez (Romano), Froylán C.
(Deceased October 3, 1937) A] October 5, 1894. B] Tochimilco, Puebla. C] Early education unknown; studies in business, no degree. D] *Constitutional deputy* from the State of Puebla, Dist. 6, 1916–17, considered part of the Jacobin group; *federal deputy* from the State of Puebla, Dist. 6, 1917–18; *federal deputy* from the State of Sonora, Dist. 1, 1920–22; *federal deputy* from the Federal District, Dist. 15, 1922–24; *federal deputy* from the State of Puebla, Dist. 3, 1932–34; federal deputy from the State of Puebla, Dist. 3, 1937. E] *Secretary* of publicity for the National Executive Committee of the National Revolutionary party (PNR), 1934; director general of *El Nacional* of the PNR, 1934. F] *Provisional governor* of Puebla, 1922–23. G] Collaborated in the Intellectual Workers Bloc with Adolfo Ruiz Cortines, Gilberto Loyo, and others. H] Began journalistic career, 1910. I] Son of Román C. Manjárrez and María Romano; son Luis C. Manjárrez served as a senator from Puebla, 1952–58; son Héctor was ambassador to Turkey. J] None. K] Exiled to Cuba, France, and Spain, 1920; supported *Adolfo de la Huerta* rebellion, 1923; exiled to Cuba and Spain, 1923–30; *Emilio Portes Gil* brought him back to Mexico; jailed in Madrid for involvement in conspiracy against General Primo de Rivera. L] Enc Mex, VIII, 248; Morales Jiménez, 287; Almanaque de Puebla, 131; C de D, 1937–40.

Manrique de Lara Hernández, Aurelio
(Deceased 1967) A] April 27, 1891. B] San Luis Potosí, San Luis Potosí. C] Primary studies in the Scientific and Literary Institute of San Luis Potosí, San

Luis Potosí; normal teaching certificate from the National Teachers College, Mexico City; completed 4th year of medical studies; professor at the National Preparatory School, 1912–17. D] *Federal deputy* from the State of San Luis Potosí, Dist. 1, 1917–18, member of the Great Committee; *federal deputy* from the State of San Luis Potosí, Dist. 1, 1920–22, secretary of the Great Committee; *federal deputy* from the State of San Luis Potosí, Dist. 1, 1922–23; *governor* of San Luis Potosí, 1923–25; *federal deputy* from the State of San Luis Potosí, Dist. 14, 1928–30. E] Founder of the National Agrarian party, 1920; orator for General *Alvaro Obregón*, 1920; president of the Revolutionary Federation of Independent Parties, 1933. F] Director of information of the Secretariat of Government, 1934–40; director general of the Social Security Institute, 1940–46; ambassador to Sweden, 1946–51, 1952–55; ambassador to Norway, 1946–51; ambassador to Denmark, 1956; director of the National Library, Secretariat of Public Education. G] None. H] Author of numerous articles. I] Active in the precursor movement to the Revolution with *Ricardo Flores Magón*, Juan Sarabia, *Antonio Díaz Soto y Gama, Juan Barragán*, and others; jailed in San Luis Potosí during the Porfiriato; boyhood friend of Jesús Silva Herzog; son of well-known lawyer Aurelio Manrique; uncle Felipe Manrique was mayor of San Luis Potosí. J] Fought under Obregón against *Victoriano Huerta*, 1914. K] Rebuked President *Plutarco Elías Calles* in answer to his State of the Union Message; forced into exile, 1929–33; supported the Escobar rebellion, 1929; known for his dramatic debates with Antonio Díaz Soto y Gama in the Chamber of Deputies. L] DP70, 1248; López, 649; Enc Mex, VIII, 1977, 250; Montejano, 204.

Manterola (Bernal), Ramón
(Deceased November 16, 1914) A] June 1, 1845. B] Tepeji del Río, Hidalgo. C] Primary and preparatory, Colegio de San Juan de Letrán, Mexico City; preparatory studies at Colegio de San Ildefonso; law degree, National School of Law, Mexico City, 1868; studies in anatomy, physics, and physiology, National School of Medicine;

librarian and archivist, National School of Agriculture, 1868–69; founded and operated a private grammar and preparatory school, 1870–79; director of public schools, Tacubaya, Federal District, 1887–96; professor of the second course in pedagogy, Normal School, 1889–1901; director, Normal School, 1890–94. D] Federal deputy, 1869; member of the City Council of the Federal District, 1876–78; *federal deputy* from the State of Puebla, Dist. 14, 1906–08, 1908–10, 1910–12. E] None. F] Prefect of Tlalpan, 1867–68; director of publishing, Chamber of Deputies, 1869–70; chief clerk, Federal District, 1870–76; oficial mayor of the Federal District, 1871–73; civil judge, 1873–78; chief of the First Section, Secretariat of Government, 1879–98. G] Member of the Antonio Alzate Scientific Society. H] Practicing lawyer, 1868–69; Editor, *El Porvenir*, 1876; Editor, *El Publicista*; author. I] Son of Leandro Manterola and Dolores Bernal. J] None. K] Went to Havana during the French Intervention. L] Peral, Appendix, 201–02; Godoy, 37–38; Carreño, 122–42; Enc Mex, VIII, 253–54; Pérez López, 252–52.

Mares Germán, José
(Deceased) A] December 18, 1882. B] Tecolotlán, Jalisco. C] Primary studies at the Public School for Children, Autlán, Jalisco; agricultural engineering studies, on a scholarship from the State of Jalisco, National School of Agriculture, San Jacinto, 1908–13, graduating as a hydraulic and agricultural engineer, July 10, 1913, with a thesis entitled "Infiltration of Water in Soils"; recipient of many medals for scholastic achievement in agricultural studies; chief of students, 1909; 1st sergeant, when National School of Agriculture was militarized, 1912; assistant, National School of Agriculture, 1912–13; dean, National School of Agriculture, 1922–23, 1933–34; professor, National School of Agriculture, 1929–50. D] None. E] None. F] Engineer, various hydraulic projects, Division of Waters, Secretariat of Development, 1913; director, Department of Ejidos, National Agrarian Commission, 1923–24; director, Department of Waters, National Agrarian Commission, 1925–26; executive secretary, National Irrigation

Committee, 1927–28; subsecretary of agriculture, 1930–32; representative, National Urban and Public Works Mortgage Bank, 1935; director general of public works, 1935–38; technical posts, National Ejido Credit Bank, 1938–54; director, National Ejido Credit Bank, Torreón, Coahuila; director, Office of Irrigation, National Ejido Credit Bank. G] None. H] None. I] Son of Bruno Mares and Fermina Germán. J] None. K] None. L] Gómez, 355–57.

Mariscal, Ignacio
(Deceased April 16, 1910) A] July 5, 1829. B] Oaxaca, Oaxaca. C] Early education unknown; preparatory and legal studies, Institute of Arts and Sciences of Oaxaca; philosophy exam, December 23, 1842; logic exam, October 5, 1843; law degree, Institute of Arts and Sciences of Oaxaca, September 18, 1845; law degree, National School of Law, 1849; dean, National School of Law, 1867–68. D] Constitutional deputy from the State of Oaxaca, 1856–57; federal deputy from the State of Oaxaca, 1861–62. E] Joined the Liberal party, 1850. F] Fiscal attorney, State of Oaxaca, 1849; private secretary to Benito Juárez as a justice of the Supreme Court; supernumerary judge of the Superior Tribunal of Justice of Oaxaca, 1857–58; circuit court judge of Veracruz, Puebla, and Oaxaca, 1859–60; justice of the Supreme Court, 1862–63; oficial mayor of foreign relations, 1863; subsecretary of foreign relations, 1863; first secretary of the Mexican legation in Washington, D.C., 1863–67; chargé d'affaires, 1867–68; judge of the Superior Tribunal of Justice of the Federal District, 1868; secretary of justice and public instruction, 1868–69; ambassador to the United States, 1869–71, 1872–76; secretary of foreign relations, 1871–72; president, Superior Tribunal of Justice of the Federal District, 1877–79; secretary of justice and public instruction, 1879–80; justice of the Supreme Court, 1880; secretary of foreign relations, 1880–83; ambassador to Great Britain, 1883–85; *secretary* of foreign relations, 1885–90, 1890–98, 1898–1910. G] President, Mexican Academy of Language. H] Managed a hacienda in Oaxaca; lawyer. I] Family wealthy; daughter, Elena, married Julio Li-

mantour, federal deputy from the Federal District, 1900–10, and brother of *José Yves Limantour*. J] None. K] None. L] Enc Mex, VIII, 285; QesQ, 350–51; DP70, 1260; Carreño, 1945, 150–52; Mestre, 238; Pavía, 33–37; González de Cosío, 11; Velasco, 83ff; FSRE, 115–19; Album de la Paz; Godoy, 214; Ramírez, 90–96; Hombres prominentes, 19–23.

Márquez, Josafat F.
(Deceased December 6, 1964) A] October 4, 1884. B] Jalapa, Veracruz. C] Primary studies at the Rebsamen School, Jalapa; studies in Europe; no degree. D] Local deputy to the state legislature of Veracruz (3 times); *constitutional deputy* from the State of Veracruz, Dist. 8, 1916–17; *federal deputy* from the State of Veracruz, Dist. 9, 1917–18; *alternate federal deputy* (in functions) from the State of Veracruz, Dist. 7, 1928–30. E] None. F] Director, Treasury Department, State of Veracruz, 1915; chief tax administrator, Torreón, Coahuila; treasurer of customs, Port of Veracruz, 1915; director, Treasury Department, Querétaro; inspector general, Secretariat of the Treasury, 1916; administrator, Maritime Customs, Tuxpan, 1918; director, Department of Labor, Veracruz; inspector general of administration, Veracruz; oficial mayor of the legislature of the State of Veracruz. G] None. H] Subdirector, telegraph office, Jalapa; director, telegraph office, Jalacingo and Misantla, Veracruz; postmaster, Jicaltepec, Veracruz. I] Son of Antonio Márquez and Joaquina Carballo. J] Joined the Maderistas, rank of 2nd captain, 1911; joined the Constitutionalists, 1913; retired from the army with a rank of lt. colonel, 1916. K] None. L] Pasquel, Jalapa, 421; C de D, 1916–17.

Márquez Galindo, Ramón
(Deceased) A] Unknown. B] Chignahuapan, Puebla. C] Primary studies in Zacatlán, Puebla; no degree. D] Local deputy to the state legislature of Puebla, 1857; *federal deputy* from the State of México, Dist. 8, 1896–98, 1898–1900, 1900–02, 1902–04, 1904–06, 1906–08, 1908–10; *federal deputy* from the State of México, Dist. 7, 1910–12. E] Joined the Liberal party, 1857. F] None. G] None. H] None. I] Son of General Ramón Már-

quez, important Liberal general and independence leader; father of Ramón Márquez Altamirano, federal deputy; son Ricardo, federal deputy from Puebla, 1920s; brother Manuel, federal deputy from Puebla, 1886–88. J] Career army officer; fought in the War of the Reform; aide to General Miguel Cástulo Alatriste, 1857; commander, Villa de Zacapoaxtla, Puebla, 1859; fought in the battle of Puebla, May 5, 1862; commander, Zacatlán Battalion, national guard, 1876; supported *Porfirio Díaz*, 1876; rank of brigadier general. K] None. L] CyT, 413–14, 418–19; DP70, 1264.

Márquez (Hermosillo), Rosendo
(Deceased April 14, 1899) A] 1836. B] Jalostotitlán, Villa de Jalos, Jalisco. C] Primary studies incomplete for economic reasons; no degree. D] Federal deputy, 1876–78, 1878–80, 1880–82, 1882–84; *federal deputy* from the State of Zacatecas, Dist. 6, 1884–86; *governor* of Puebla, 1885–92; *senator* from the State of Oaxaca, 1892–94, 1894–96, 1896–98, 1898–99. E] None. F] Prefect, various cantons (districts), Jalisco, 1870s. G] None. H] Worked in textile factories, Atemajac, Jalisco, Javja, Tepic, and Bella Vista, Tepic. I] Son of Ignacio Márquez, land surveyor, and María del Refugio Hermosillo; married Enedina Rebollo; son, Rosendo Márquez, federal deputy from the State of Puebla, 1912–14. J] Joined the Liberal army as a 1st sergeant, 1855; rank of lieutenant, national guard, 1857; commander of Bella Vista, Tepic, 1857; rank of captain, September 1861; served in a line battalion, 1861; battalion commander in the defense of Puebla, 1863; fought French in Jalisco and Michoacán under General José María Arteaga; commander, cavalry squadron, 1870; supported *Porfirio Díaz's* rebellion, 1871; retired from the army, November 5, 1871; rank of brigadier general, 1872; supported the Plan of Tuxtepec, 1876; captured and imprisoned in San Miguel de los Alacranes; military commander of Colima, 1877; commander, 9th Military Zone, Puebla, 1882–92; rank of division general, September 28, 1892. K] Sentenced to death, 1876, but saved by wife and Diaz's supporters. L] Peral, Appendix, 204; Almada, 1968, 323; Mestre, 205;

Leight, 230–31; Hombres prominentes, 241–41; Godoy, 239; Enc Mex, VIII, 290; CyT, 413–14; DP70, 1263–64; Pavía, 285–88; Almanaque de Puebla, 128.

Marroquín y Rivera, Manuel
(Deceased March 26, 1927) A] 1865. B] Querétaro, Querétaro. C] Primary studies in Querétaro; engineering degree, National School of Engineering, December 16, 1890. D] None. E] None. F] *Secretary* of development, 1911; member, Agrarian Commission, 1911–12. G] None. H] Practicing engineer; directed water pipeline project, Xochimilco to Mexico City, 1903–14. I] Father of Carlos Francisco Marroquín, prominent engineer; married Ana Molina. J] None. K] Prominent member of the Knights of Columbus. L] WWM45, 71; DP70, 2368; QesQ, 354; Mestre, 278; Enc Mex, VIII, 60.

Martí Atalay, Rubén
(Deceased 1970) A] July 25, 1877. B] Matanzas, Cuba. C] Primary studies in Costa Rica; correspondence courses, Serantan, New York; no degree. D] *Constitutional deputy* from the State of Mexico, Dist. 16, 1916–17. E] None. F] Director, Department of Utilization, Secretariat of Industry and Commerce; employee, Division of Properties, 1918. G] None. H] Employee, drugstore; owner, Cosmopolitan Pharmacy, Mexico City; partner of *Félix Palavicini* in many business enterprises; cofounder of many newspapers, including *El Universal*; owned a large lumber business, Tepic, Nayarit. I] Son of Hildebrando Martí and Ana María Artalay, Cubans; naturalized Mexican; nephew of Cuban independence figure and intellectual José Martí. J] Joined the Maderistas, 1910–11; administrator, Health Service, Army of the Northeast, under General *Alvaro Obregón*, 1915; organized sappers sanitation battalion, 1915; chief of staff, 14th Brigade, 4th Division, Army of the East; director of purchasing, military hospitals, 1917–18. K] None. L] Enc Mex, VIII, 296–97; C de D, 1916–17.

Martín del Campo, Francisco
(Deceased December 3, 1951) A] October 10, 1886. B] Lagos de Moreno, Jalisco. C] Primary and secondary studies in Lagos

de Moreno; preparatory studies, Institute of Science of Aguascalientes; law degree, School of Law, San Luis Potosí, 1911. D] *Constitutional deputy* from Jalisco, Dist. 5, 1916–17; *federal deputy* from the State of Jalisco, Dist. 5, 1917–18, 1918–20. E] Supported *Bernardo Reyes*, 1908; supported *Francisco I. Madero*, 1910–11. F] Consulting lawyer to the secretary of government, *Manuel Aguirre Berlanga*, 1916. G] None. H] Practicing lawyer. I] Son of Alejandro Martín del Campo, physician, and María Dolores González. J] Commissions for Generals *Manuel M. Diéguez* and Manuel Aguirre Berlanga, Jalisco, 1914–15. K] None. L] C de D, 1916–17; C de D, 1917–18.

Martínez, Angel
(Deceased May 22, 1904) A] July 1837. B] Arandas, Ayo el Chico, Jalisco. C] Early education unknown; no degree. D] Federal deputy from the State of Colima, 1873–75; senator from the State of Colima, 1875, 1880–84; *senator* from the State of Colima, 1884–88, 1888–92, 1892–96, 1896–1900, 1900–04. E] Candidate for governor of Sinaloa, 1868. F] Interim governor of San Luis Potosí, 1876. G] None. H] Purchased the Hacienda Paso del Río, Colima, 1872. I] Unknown. J] Career army officer; enlisted in the national guard under General *Ramón Corona*, September 2, 1856; fought during the Three Years' War, 1858–60; organized guerrillas to fight the French, 1862; commander, 3rd Brigade of the West; defeated French in Sinaloa, 1865; rank of·brigade general, May 25, 1866; chief of arms, Sinaloa, 1867–68; fought in France against Germany, 1870–71; rejoined army, 1876; supported Lerdo de Tejada against the Plan of Tuxtepec, 1876; accompanied José María Iglesias to the United States, 1876–78; military commander of troops against the Yaquis, Sonora, 1885–87; military commander, Matamoros, Tamaulipas, 1888–89. K] Imprisoned but amnestied, 1872, on return from France. L] Enc Mex, VIII, 300–01; DP70, 1267; Sec of War, 1901, 21; Mestre, 220; Almada, Colima, 129–30.

Martínez, Rafael
(Deceased April 22, 1949) A] October 24, 1881. B] Mexico City. C] Primary studies Mexico City; seminary studies, Mexico City; preparatory studies, National Preparatory School; no degree. D] *Constitutional deputy* from the Federal District, Dist. 6, 1916–17; *federal deputy* from the Federal District, Dist. 6, 1917–18; *senator* from the Federal District, 1918–20, 1920–22; mayor of Dolores Hidalgo, Guanajuato, 1944. E] Member, Anti-Reelectionist party, 1909; collaborated with *Francisco I. Madero* on *El Demócrata*, Parras, Coahuila. F] Consul, Barcelona, Spain. G] None. H] Typesetter; journalist; wrote for *Sucesos*, *La Prensa*; director, *Policromía*; director, *El Constitucional*, 1909–10; director, *El Demócrata*, 1914–26. I] Unknown. J] Joined the Constitutionalists, 1913. K] Left Mexico, 1920. L] DP70, 1270; Enc Mex, VIII, 306; CyT, 426.

Martínez, Rosalino
(Deceased October 26, 1907) A] 1847. B] Juchitán, Oaxaca. C] Early education unknown; no degree. D] *Federal deputy* from the State of Jalisco, Dist. 9, 1888–90, 1890–92, 1892–94, 1894–96; *federal deputy* from the State of Tabasco, Dist. 3, 1902–04, 1904–06; *federal deputy* from the State of Sonora, Dist 3, 1906–07. E] None. F] *Subsecretary* of war, 1904–07. G] None. H] Unknown. I] Unknown. J] Career army officer; joined the army as a 2nd lieutenant, 1865; fought French at the Battle of Tehuantepec, 1866; fought under *Porfirio Díaz*, Fort of Oaxaca, Oaxaca, October 6, 1866; fought under Díaz, battle of Puebla, April 2, 1867; commander of the Mayan campaign, Yucatán, 1868; fought the Mayas, Yucatán, 1889–90; rank of brigadier general, November 29, 1893; rank of brigade general, February 1, 1901; commander of military forces in Veracruz, 1901; commander, 12th Infantry Regiment, Sonora, 1906. K] Put down strikes under direct orders from Díaz, January 7, 1906, at factories in Santa Rosa, Nogales, and El Yute. L] Enc Mex, VIII, 307; Sec of War, 1901, 20; Mestre, 229; Sec of War, 1900, 85.

Martínez de Arredondo (y Peraza), Francisco
(Deceased) A] February 1, 1829. B] Mérida, Yucatán. C] Studies, Seminary of Mérida; law degree, National School of Law, Mexico City, 1854; secretary, Literary University of Mérida, 1855–60. D] Federal deputy from Yucatán, 1861–62, 1875–76; *senator* from Yucatán, 1904–06, 1906–08, 1908–10, 1910–12. E] None. F] Secretary, Superior Tribunal of Justice of Yucatán, 1860; civil judge, Yucatán, 1873–74; supernumerary judge of the Circuit Court, 1874; judge of the first instance; judge of the Circuit Court in Yucatán, Campeche, Tabasco, and Chiapas, 1877–86; *justice* of the Supreme Court, 1886–1904. G] None. H] Lawyer. I] Son of Francisco Martínez de Arredondo y Valleto, independence leader and governor of Yucatán, and Tomasa Peraza y Cárdenas, daughter of a military officer; Dr. Manuel José Delgado, rector of the Colegio de San Ildefonso in Yucatán, became his guardian when his parents died, 1854; daughter Concepción married Manuel F. Villaseñor, federal deputy from Puebla and father of Víctor Manuel Villaseñor, prominent intellectual and political figure, 1960s and 1970s; married Gertrudis Castro y Lara, daughter of the founder of Progreso, Yucatán; godson of General Pedro del Castillo, treasurer general of Mexico. J] None. K] None. L] Godoy, 158–59; Valdés Acosta, 240–44; Blue Book, 1901, 29; González Cosío, 11; Pavía, Judges, 37–46.

Martínez de Castro, Mariano
(Deceased December 19, 1901) A] 1841. B] Culiacán, Sinaloa. C] Early education unknown; topographical engineering degree, National School of Mines, Mexico City. D] Member of the City Council of Culiacán; governor of Sinaloa, 1880–84; *alternate senator* from the State of Durango, 1884–88; *governor* of Sinaloa, 1888–92; *alternate senator* from the State of Sonora, 1894–98; *senator* from the State of Chiapas, 1892–96, 1896–1900, 1900–01. E] None. F] Political prefect of Culiacán. G] None. H] Practicing engineer, Sinaloa; businessman; economic interests in agriculture and mining.

I] Son of Agustín Martínez de Castro, governor of Sinaloa, 1844; from a wealthy family; brother Ricardo an engineer and senator from Sinaloa, 1892–94; great-uncle of Ricardo J. Zevada, director general of the National Foreign Trade Bank, 1952–65. J] Associate of *Francisco Cañedo* during La Noria rebellion, 1871–72. K] None. L] C de S, 1900–02, 6; González Dávila, 339–40; Peral, Appendix, 206; Pavía, 320; Hombres prominentes, 201–02; Mestre, 212; Godoy, 239–40; Enc Mex, VIII, 310–11; DP70, 1271–72.

Martínez de Escobar, Rafael
(Deceased October 3, 1927) A] April 12, 1889. B] Huimanguillo, Tabasco. C] Primary studies in Huimanguillo; legal studies at the Institute of Villahermosa, Tabasco; law degree, National School of Law, UNAM, 1912. D] *Constitutional deputy* from the State of Tabasco, Dist. 1, 1916–17; *federal deputy* from the State of Tabasco, Dist. 1, 1917–18, member of the Great Committee; *federal deputy* from the Federal District, Dist. 2, 1918–20, 1920–22; president and local deputy to the Constitutional Convention of Tabasco, 1919; *federal deputy* from the Federal District, Dist. 5, 1924–26. E] Delegate to the national convention of the Constitutional Progressive party, 1911; president, Liberal Constitutionalist party; leader of the Anti-Reelectionist party, in support of the presidential candidacy of General *Francisco R. Serrano*, 1927. F] Employee, State of Coahuila, 1913; private secretary to General Pedro C. Colorado, 1913; appointed secretary general of the State of Tabasco, but did not serve, 1915; secretary general of the State of Tabasco, 1916; consulting lawyer, Secretariat of Foreign Relations, 1918. G] None. H] Practicing lawyer. I] Unknown. J] Maderista as a student, 1911; joined the Constitutionalists, 1913; supported the Plan of Agua Prieta, 1920. K] Executed on orders from President *Alvaro Obregón* with General Francisco R. Serrano, Huitzilac, Morelos, October 3, 1927. L] Almanaque de Tabasco, 163; Enc Mex, VIII, 311; DP70, 1272.

Martínez del Río, Pablo
(Deceased November 14, 1907) A] Unknown. B] Unknown. C] Preparatory Studies, Jesuit College, Stoneyhurst, England, and Eton; law degree, National School of Law, Mexico City, 1887; studies at Oxford University, England. D] *Federal deputy* from the State of Puebla, Dist. 14, 1894–96; *federal deputy* from the State of Puebla, Dist. 15, 1896–98; *federal deputy* from the State of Puebla, Dist. 14, 1898–1900, 1900–02; *federal deputy* from the State of Durango, Dist. 1, 1902–04; *federal deputy* from the Federal District, Dist. 4, 1904–06, 1906–07. E] None. F] None. G] Stockholder, Jockey Club. H] Lawyer for major mining and railroad companies; financier; wealthy landowner in Durango; owner of the Guadalupe hacienda. I] Son of Dr. José Pablo Martínez del Campo, Conservative, distinguished scientist, landowner, and professor; grandson of a wealthy landowner and banker; married Barbara Vinent; friend of *José Limantour*; father of Pablo Martínez del Río, distinguished intellectual and educator. J] None. K] Served as federal deputy through the intervention of his childhood friend Adelaida Pani de Darqui, who asked President *Porfirio Díaz*'s wife, Carmen, for the post. L] López, 664; Puente, 109–12; Holms, 260; Mestre, 229; Blue Book 1901, 89; Almada, 1968, 324; Peral, Appendix, 207.

Martínez (González), Mucio Práxedis
(Deceased October 26, 1920) A] May 13, 1841. B] Galeana, Nuevo León. C] Primary studies in Galeana; no degree. D] *Federal deputy* from the State of Puebla, Dist. 6, 1886–88; *federal deputy* from the State of Puebla, Dist. 8, 1888–90; *governor* of Puebla, 1893–11. E] None. F] None. G] None. H] Owner of the Santa Débora hacienda, Puebla. I] Son of Leandro Martínez de la Fuentes and Josefa González, working-class family; married Soledad Peregrina Cabrera; great-uncle of Elena Flores, mother of Román Cepeda, governor of Coahuila; daughter Debóra Martínez married lawyer Eduardo Mestre Ghigliazza, son of *Manuel Mestre Ghigliazza*, governor of Tabasco, 1911–13; longtime companion of General *Porfirio*

Díaz. J] Career army officer; joined the national guard as a sergeant, 1861; rank of lieutenant in the cavalry, 1863; fought against the French in the battles of Tlalpan and San Nicolás, Federal District, 1863; fought with Díaz in the battle for the Fort of Oaxaca, October 6, 1866; fought with Díaz in the assault on Puebla, April 2, 1867; supported Díaz in the Plan of Tuxtepec, 1876; rank of brigadier general in the cavalry, May 26, 1884; rank of brigade general, April 22, 1890; retired from active duty, June 3, 1911. K] Accused of supporting *Félix Díaz*, 1912, but exonerated; imprisoned, 1914, but freed by Zapatistas, December, 1914. L] Wright, 294; Album; Enc Mex, VIII, 306; Sec of War, 1901, 19; Sec of War, 1914, 20; Sec of War, 1911, 17; Almanaque of Puebla, 128; Holms, 326; Leight, 232; Mestre, 265; Sec of War, 1900, 85, 89; Peral, Appendix, 209.

Martínez (González), Pedro
(Deceased November 16, 1891) A] April 29, 1835. B] Galeana, Nuevo León. C] Primary studies in Galeana, Nuevo León; no degree. D] *Senator* from Nuevo León, 1888–91. E] None. F] None. G] None. H] Began working as an agricultural laborer, 1855. I] Son of Leandro Martínez de la Fuentes and Josefa González, working-class family; brother of General *Mucio P. Martínez*, governor of Puebla; brother Andrés, a colonel; great uncle of Elena Flores, mother of Román Cepeda, governor of Coahuila; niece, Débora Martínez, married son of *Manuel Mestre Ghigliazza*, governor of Tabasco, 1911–13. J] Joined the army as a private in Tanquecillos, Galeana, under Captain *Mariano Escobedo*; rank of corporal, 1855; rank of sergeant, 1855; fought under General Ignacio Zaragoza, 1859; commander, Advanced Scouting Squadron, Army of the East, against the French, 1861; commander, 2nd Brigade, Cavalry Division, 1866; rank of brigadier general, September 5, 1867; commander of the parade ground of San Luis Potosí, 1869; fought under *Gerónimo Treviño*, who supported the Plan of La Noria rebellion, 1871; amnestied by President Lerdo de Tejada, 1872. K] None. L] Enc Mex, VIII, 306.

Martínez (Pérez), Miguel F.
(Deceased February 2, 1919) A] July 5,
1850. B] Monterrey, Nuevo León. C] Primary studies in Monterrey, 1854–62; secondary and preparatory studies, Colegio de Monterrey, 1863–68; topographical engineering degree, October 30, 1871; director, public school; director, Public School of Lampazos de Naranjo, 1875–76; founded a private school in Monterrey, 1876, which failed; founded a secondary school, 1877; director, Normal School of Nuevo León, 1881–84; inspector, primary schools, Monterrey, 1881–84; professor of geography, Colegio Civil of Nuevo León, 1885; rector of the Colegio Civil of Nuevo León, 1900; director, Professional Academy for Women, 1896; director of the National Normal School of Mexico, 1911–14; organized extension courses for UNAM, 1911; director, Normal School of Teachers, Monterrey, Nuevo León, 1915–18. D] Member of the City Council of Monterrey, 1880, 1899–1901; alternate local deputy to the state legislature of Nuevo León, 1881–83; *senator* from Durango, 1902–06, 1906–10. E] None. F] City engineer, Monterrey, 1872–74; representative of the State of Nuevo León to the National Congress on Education, 1889–90; director general of public instruction, State of Nuevo León, 1801–93; director general of primary instruction for the Federal District and Federal Territories, 1901–11. G] None. H] Editor, *Flores y Frutos*, 1879–81; editor, *La Revista*, 1881–86. I] Son of Antonio Martínez, painter and violinist, and Francisca Pérez; father of *Miguel Martínez Rendón*, federal deputy from Nuevo León, 1920–24. J] Lieutenant of engineers and aide to General *Gerónimo Treviño*, during rebellion of the Plan of La Noria, 1871–72; left the army, 1872. K] First prize for the best preparatory student. L] C de S, 102–04; Album; Enc Mex, VIII, 305; DP70, 1269–70; Covarrúbias, 59–66.

Martínez Rendón, Miguel
(Deceased 1966) A] May 12, 1891.
B] Monterrey, Nuevo León. C] Primary studies in Monterrey; preparatory studies in Monterrey; no degree; professor, Normal School of Nuevo León, 1915–20. D] *Federal deputy* from the State of

Nuevo León, Dist. 1, 1920–22, 1922–24. E] None. F] Director, public library, Nuevo León, 1917–20; private secretary to *Juan de Dios Bojórquez*, secretary of government, 1934–35; oficial mayor, Department of National Statistics; director, Department of Labor Inspectors, Secretariat of Labor. G] Cofounder and secretary, Intellectual Workers Bloc. H] Librarian; teacher; author; journalist; manager, *La Ilustración*, Monterrey, 1917–19; manager, *El Constitucional*, 1917–20; director, *Crisol*, 1929–39; director, *El Universal*, 1936. I] Son of *Miguel F. Martínez*, senator from Durango, and Josefa Rendón; married Josefina Lavalle; grandson of Antonio Martínez, painter and violinist, and Francisca Pérez. J] None. K] None. L] WWM45, 73; DP70, 1276.

Martínez Rojas (Rosales), Federico
(Deceased July 16, 1959) A] August 30, 1890. B] San Cristóbal de las Casas, Chiapas. C] Early education unknown; legal studies, School of Law, San Cristóbal; completed law degree, October 28, 1914, with a thesis entitled "The Law of Retention"; founding student of the Free Law School, July 24, 1912. D] *Senator* from the State of Tamaulipas, 1926–27, 1928–30; *alternate senator* from the State of Tamaulipas, 1930–34. E] None. F] Judge, Superior Tribunal of Justice, Tamaulipas; consulting lawyer, Office of National Properties, Secretariat of the Treasury, Tampico; secretary general of the government of Tamaulipas; agent of the Ministerio Público, Tampico; judge of the first instance, Torreón; *governor* of Chiapas, 1927–28. G] None. H] Notary public, Tampico; practicing lawyer, Tampico, 1922. I] Son of Jesús Martínez Rojas, federal deputy from Chiapas, 1912–13, and Rosaura Rosales; related to Jesús Martínez Rojas, federal deputy, 1912–13. J] Joined the Constitutionalists, 1913; judge and military adviser, Division of the North. K] None. L] Almanaque de Chiapas, 119; ELD, 60.

Mascareñas (Navarro), Alberto
(Deceased 1944) A] March 10, 1876.
B] Guaymas, Sonora. C] Business studies, Hermosillo, Sonora; studies in economics, Los Angeles, California, and the Univer-

sity of Santa Clara, California; founder of the first school of banking in Mexico. D] None. E] None. F] Secretary, City Council of Hermosillo, Sonora, 1911; consul general, San Francisco, California, 1920; consul general, Havana, Cuba; consul general, Liverpool, England; consul general, New York City; *subsecretary* of the treasury, 1924; director general (first) of the Bank of Mexico, 1926–32; *ambassador* to Great Britain, 1932–34; director, Monetary Commission. G] Cofounder, Mexican Association of Bankers, 1928. H] Subdirector, Banco de Sonora, Chihuahua, Chihuahua; director, Bank of Sonora, Nogales, Sonora; president, Golden Girl Mining Company, 1940. I] Son of Manuel Mascareñas and Luisa Navarro; grandson of Cayetano Mascareñas, governor of Durango; great-grandson of Ramón Mascareñas, assayer; brother of Manuel Mascareñas, governor of Chihuahua, 1927. J] None. K] Founder of the first department of tourism. L] Enc Mex, VIII, 325–26; DP70, 1279.

Mata, Filomeno
(Deceased 1967) A] October 24, 1889. B] Mexico City. C] Early education unknown; studied singing and opera; no degree. D] *Federal deputy* from the Federal District, Dist. 3, 1917–18. E] Secretary, Liberal Constitutional party, 1916–17; oficial mayor of the Federation of Independent Revolutionary Parties. F] Consul, Boston, 1919–25; official, Secretariat of Foreign Relations, 1925–29; director, Conciliation Section, Department of Labor, Secretariat of Industry and Commerce; employee, Federal District Department. G] None. H] Journalist; founder *El Nuevo Régimen*, to support General Villarreal for president, 1933; founder of *El Liberal*. I] Son of Filomeno Mata, teacher, journalist, and federal deputy who founded the Liberal Reform group, 1891; grandson of Casiano Mata and Josefa Ramírez. J] Private secretary to General *Jacinto B. Treviño*; accompanied General *Antonio Villarreal*, 1915. K] Accused of social dissolution and imprisoned in Lecumberi, 1960–64. L] Mestre, 241; Enc Mex, VIII, 334; QesQ, 364; DP70, 1281; Morales Jiménez, 27.

Mateos (Lozada), Juan A.
(Deceased December 29, 1913) A] June 24, 1831. B] Mexico City. C] Primary studies under José María Rico; preparatory studies at the Colegio de San Gregorio and the Scientific and Literary Institute of México, Toluca, 1847, where he studied under Ignacio Ramírez; legal studies, Colegio de San Juan de Letrán, Mexico City, 1853–57. D] Federal deputy, 1867–68; *federal deputy* from the State of Hidalgo, Dist. 8, 1886–88; *federal deputy* from the State of Hidalgo, Dist. 11, 1888–90, 1890–92; *federal deputy* from the State of Jalisco, Dist. 3, 1892–94, 1894–96, 1896–98, 1898–1900, 1900–02, 1902–04; *federal deputy* from the State of Hidalgo, Dist. 10, 1904–06, 1906–08, 1908–10, 1910–12. E] None. F] Secretary, Supreme Court, 1868; director, Library of the Chamber of Deputies. G] None. H] Novelist; prolific author; editor, *La Orquesta*. I] Son of Remegio Mateos, important Reform leader, and María Lozada; brother José Perfecto, judge of the Superior Tribunal of Justice of the Federal District. J] Interrupted legal studies to fight the Conservatives in Puebla under General Comonfort, 1856; fought in the Three Years' War under *Felipe Berriozábal*, 1858–60; secretary to General José María Arteaga; fought the French, but captured and amnestied; rejoined *Porfirio Díaz* forces, 1867. K] Imprisoned for article, 1865. L] Enc Mex, 8, 342–43; DP70, 1284; Hombres prominentes, 410–12; Pavía, Judges, 188–92.

Maycotte (Cameros), Fortunato
(Deceased 1924) A] Unknown. B] Múzquiz, Coahuila. C] Early education unknown; no degree. D] None. E] None. F] *Interim governor* of Hidalgo, 1915; *provisional governor* of Durango, 1916. G] None. H] Unknown. I] Son of Apuleyo Maycotte and Juana Cameros Martínez; grandson of Teresa Martínez Garza and Santiago Cameros; uncle of the director El Indio Fernández; grandmother is the sister of Andreas Martínez Garza, wife of General Hamilton Bee and mother-in-law of General *Lázaro Garza Ayala*, governor of Nuevo León, 1887–89. J] Supported *Francisco I. Madero*, 1910–11; joined the Constitutionalists, 1913; fought under

Generals *Pablo González, Francisco Mur-guía*, and *Cesáreo Castro*; represented at the Convention of Aguascalientes, 1914; fought *Francisco Villa* at Celaya with the Maycotte Brigade, 1915; rank of division general; commander of military operations, various states; supported *Alvaro Obregón* as chief of arms, Chilpancingo, Guerrero, 1920; supported the *Adolfo de la Huerta* rebellion as chief of military operations, Oaxaca, 1923–24. K] Captured and executed, Ayutla, Oaxaca, 1924. L] Rouaix, 251; Enc Mex, VIII, 367; Pérez López, 266; DP70, 1290.

Maytorena (Tapia), José Maria
(Deceased January 18, 1948) A] July 18, 1867. B] Guaymas, Sonora. C] Primary studies Guaymas, Sonora; studies in Europe, and at the University of Santa Clara, San Jose, California. D] *Governor* of Sonora, 1911–13, 1914. E] Supported *Bernardo Reyes* for president, 1909; joined the Anti-Reelectionist party, 1909; founded the first Reyista Club in Sonora, Guaymas. F] None. G] None. H] Administered father's property, De la Misa hacienda, the most valuable in Guaymas. I] Son of José María Maytorena, a wealthy landowner active in state politics as a candidate for governor, and Santos Tapia; father a good friend of *Bernardo Reyes*; José grew up with *Adolfo de la Huerta*; related to *Roberto Pesqueira*. J] Established headquarters for the revolutionary junta in Nogales, Sonora, to support *Francisco I. Madero*, 1910; joined Madero in Ciudad Juárez, May, 1911; supported Convention Government, 1914; represented at the Convention of Aguascalientes; supported *Francisco Villa* against *Venustiano Carranza*, 1915; reintegrated into the army, April 3, 1943, as a division general. K] Lived in Los Angeles, California, 1915–38. L] Enc Mex, VIII, 369–70; Moreno, 119–25; Aguilar Camín, 77; Villa, 101–07; Serrano, 65–75.

Meade Fierro, Ernesto
(Deceased April 22, 1962) A] March 7, 1888. B] Parras (San Pedro de la Colinas), Coahuila. C] Primary studies, Parras; no degree. D] Local deputy to the state of legislature of Coahuila; *constitutional*

deputy from the State of Coahuila, Dist. 2, 1916–17; *federal deputy* from the State of Coahuila, Dist. 1, 1918–20. E] None. F] Joined anti-Diaz political clubs in Coahuila; supported *Francisco I. Madero* in San Pedro de las Colinias, 1910; founded *El Coahuilense* to support *Venustiano Carranza* for the presidency, 1916. G] Official mayor, state legislature of Coahuila, 1911; private secretary to Venustiano Carranza, 1912; consul, United States; official, Secretariat of the Treasury; chief of the Office of Stamps and Money Orders, Post Office Department, 1941; subdirector general of the Post Office, 1941. H] None. I] Journalist; editor of *La Raza*, San Antonio, Texas; founded *El Demócrata*, Piedras Negras. J] Unknown. K] Joined the Constitutionalists, 1913; served under Lucio Blanco; rank of colonel; president, Council of War, general under Pablo González. L] HA, 21 Feb. 1987, 361; C de D, 1916–17.

Medellín Ostos, Roberto
(Deceased March 5, 1941) A] April 29, 1881. B] Finca Repartidero, Tantoyuca, Veracruz. C] Primary studies in Tantoyuca; preparatory studies at the National Preparatory School; engineering degree, National School of Engineering, UNAM, 1908; professor of chemistry, National Preparatory School; professor at the National School of Medicine, UNAM; secretary of the National University; professor of graduate studies, UNAM; director of natural sciences at the National Preparatory School; director of technical instruction, School of Chemical Sciences, UNAM; prosector of botany, National Preparatory School; head of the Chemistry Department, National Medical Institute; secretary general and rector, National Autonomous University of Mexico, September 12, 1932–October 15, 1933; director general of the National Polytechnic Institute, 1937. D] None. E] Supporter of *José Vasconcelos*'s presidential campaign, 1928–29. F] Oficial mayor of the Secretariat of Public Education, 1934–35, under *Eduardo Vasconcelos*; secretary general of the Department of Public Health, 1935–37. G] None. H] Author of numerous works on botany. I] Brother of Octavio

Medellín Ostos, leader of José Vasconcelos's campaign, 1929; father of Jorge Medellín León, subsecretary of government properties, 1964–70. J] None. K] Organizer of the school breakfast program. L] WWLA40, 316; Gruening, 535; López, 678; Enc Mex, VIII, 1977, 395; WWLA35, 244; Illescas, 383–84.

Medina Barrón, Luis
(Deceased April 27, 1937) A] September 30, 1873. B] Jerez, Zacatecas. C] Early education unknown; no degree. D] None. E] None. F] *Governor* of Zacatecas; served in the consular service; consul general, Toronto; consul general, Havana, 1924–25; minor official, Department of the Federal District, 1930s; judge, 8th Police Delegation, 1937. G] None. H] None. I] Unknown. J] Career army officer; joined the auxiliary forces as a 2nd lieutenant, Sonora, 1890; major, 11th Rural Group; fought Indians under Governor Izabal; fought against the Maderistas in the mountains of Chihuahua and Sonora, 1910–11; rank of brigade general in the infantry, July 21, 1913; fought the Constitutionalist forces in San Rosa, 1913; commander of an infantry brigade, Yaqui division, 1913; supported *Félix Díaz* in Veracruz, 1917–20; rank of division general, June 14, 1914; supported the Plan of Agua Prieta, 1920; chief, Department of Reserves, army, 1921–24. K] None. L] Enc Mex, VIII, 415; Peral, 512; DP70, 1300; Mestre, 2929; Sec of War, 1914, 19.

Medina (Gaona), Hilario
(Deceased July 24, 1964) A] June 26, 1891. B] León, Guanajuato. C] Primary studies at the Porfirio Díaz Model School, León; preparatory studies from the Preparatory School of León and the National Preparatory School, 1918; law degree from the National School of Law, UNAM; professor of history at the National Preparatory School; professor of constitutional law, National School of Law, UNAM, 1930. D] *Constitutional deputy* from the State of Guanajuato, Dist. 8, 1916–17, considered a Jacobin; senator from the Federal District, 1958–64, member of the Great Committee, the Committee on the Department of the Federal District,

the Rules Committee; president of the Second Justice Committee; member of the First Committee on Government, and the First Constitutional Affairs Committee. E] None. F] *Subsecretary* in charge of the Secretariat of Foreign Relations, 1919–20; justice of the Supreme Court, 1941–57; chief justice of the Supreme Court, 1953, 1957–58. G] None. H] Librarian during last year in law school to earn money to finish degree. I] Son of Romualdo Medina, a businessman, and Leovigilda Gaona García; brother Francisco, a professor at UNAM; married Raquel Meléndez. J] Active in the Revolution. K] Important member of the *Venustiano Carranza* administration; his public career suffered after Carranza was murdered in 1920. L] C de S, 1961–64, 61; Enc Mex, V, 36; Peral, 513; DP70, 1299; WWM45, 75; Func., 174; Enc Mex, VIII, 1977, 414; Linajes, 173–74.

Médiz Bolio (Cantarell), Antonio
(Deceased September 15, 1957) A] October 13, 1884. B] Mérida, Yucatán. C] Primary studies in Mérida; secondary studies at the Seminario Conciliar Universitario de Mérida and the Colegio Católico de San Ildefonso; law degree from the School of Law, University of Yucatán, 1907, with a thesis on strikes. D] *Federal deputy* from the State of San Luis Potosí, Dist. 4, 1912–14; *federal deputy* from the State of Yucatán, Dist. 1, 1928–30; *senator* from the State of Yucatán, 1952–57, member of the Indigenous Affairs Committee, the First Public Education Committee, the First Foreign Relations Committee, the First Balloting Committee, and substitute member of the National Properties Committee; president of the First Instructive Committee for the Grand Jury. E] Director of popular culture, National Revolutionary party, 1936. F] Private secretary to the governor of Yucatán, 1903; secretary to the 2nd Civil Court of Mérida, 1905; director of the Bulletin of the Secretariat of Public Education and Bellas Artes of Yucatán, 1912–13, 1915–18; director general of fine arts, State of Yucatán, 1918–19; second secretary of the Mexican legation in Spain, 1919; chargé d'affaires, Mexican legation in Spain, 1920; second

secretary and chargé d'affaires, Colombia, 1921; first secretary and chargé d'affaires, Argentina, 1921–22; first secretary, Sweden, 1923–24; ambassador to Costa Rica and Nicaragua, 1925–32; director of the Department of Civic Action, 1932–34; director of the Archeology Department, National Museum, 1937–39. G] None. H] Important figure in the development of Yucatán theater. I] Married Lucrecia Cuartas; son of Tomás Médiz and María Bolio y Cantarell; uncle of *Carlos Loret de Mola*; grandson of lawyer Antonio Médiz y Chacón, justice of the Supreme Court, and lawyer Rafael Bolío Rivas. J] Supported *Francisco I. Madero* during the Revolution. K] Exiled by *Victoriano Huerta* and lived in Havana, 1914–15. L] DP70, 130; WWM45, 75; Peral, 514–15; C de S, 1952–58; Novo, 543; López, 688; Enc Mex, VIII, 1977, 416; Valdés, 3, 230–31.

Medrano (Valdivia), Federico
(Deceased 1959) A] March 2, 1896. B] Unión de San Antonio, Jalisco. C] Primary studies in San Francisco del Rincón; preparatory studies at the Colegio de León, 1913–17; law degree from the National School of Law, UNAM, 1918–22; taught at the Studies Center, University of Guanajuato, 1917. D] *Federal deputy* from the State of Guanajuato, Dist. 9, 1922–24, 1924–26, 1928–30; *federal deputy* from the State of Guanajuato, Dist. 2, 1930–32; *senator* from the State of Guanajuato, 1932–34, 1936–40; federal deputy from the State of Guanajuato, Dist. 3, 1940–43; president of the Chamber of Deputies and party majority leader; senator from the State of Guanajuato, 1946–52; member of the Great Committee, the First Petroleum Committee, the Second Balloting Committee, the Second Labor Committee, the Agricultural and Development Committee; substitute member of the First Committee on National Defense. E] *Secretary* of education of the National Executive Committee of the National Revolutionary party (PNR), 1933; *secretary general* of the National Executive Committee of the PNR, 1933. F] None. G] Student leader during preparatory school days. H] None. I] Close friend of Octavio Véjar Vázquez,

secretary of public education, at law school. J] None. K] Retired from politics in 1952 to raise race horses; political enemy of *Gonzalo N. Santos*, who prevented him from holding his position as federal deputy, 1926–28; precandidate for governor of Guanajuato, 1935; expelled from PNR by *Matías Ramos Santos*, 1935. L] WWM45, 76; DP70, 1301; C de S, 1946–52; DBM70, 376; Peral, 515; DGF51, I, 6, 9, 10,11, 13, 14; HA, 20 Aug. 1943, 7–8.

Mejía (Escalada), Francisco
(Deceased August 15, 1901) A] March 9, 1822. B] Valladolid (Morelia), Michoacán. C] Primary studies in Mexico City, in Agustín Richardet and Luis Octavio Chousal's colegio; student of Francisco Zarco; studied pharmacy, 1840–42; no degree. D] Federal deputy from the State of México, 1867; member of the City Council of Mexico City, 1885–86; *federal deputy* from the State of Puebla, Dist. 3, 1886–88; *federal deputy* from the State of Puebla, Dist. 7, 1890–92; *federal deputy* from the State of Puebla, Dist. 17, 1892–94; *alternate federal deputy* from the State of Guanajuato, Dist. 11, 1896–98; *federal deputy* from the State of Guanajuato, Dist. 10, 1898–1900, 1900–01, member of the Great Committee. E] None. F] Joined the Tax Department, 1842; clerk in Bureau Four, Tax Office, 1842; first clerk, Bureau Two, Tax Office; 4th official, Customs Board, 1846; customs inspector, Tabasco, 1850; director of customs, Mazatlán, 1854–55; treasurer of the Disabled Soldiers Unit, 1855–57; inspector general of maritime customs, 1857; oficial mayor of war, 1869–60; director, Special Office for the Clerical Property, 1861; director, Department of the Treasury, Coahuila, 1864; director, Department of the Treasury, Nuevo León; director of customs, Santo Domingo, 1867; secretary of the treasury, 1872–76; representative of the government to the Michoacán-Pacific Railroad, 1898. G] None. H] Worked for father in the Manzanillo customs office as an accountant, 1835; financier. I] Son of Juan Mejía, customs official; grandson of Octavio Santibáñez Mejía. J] Fought against the North American invasion at the battle of Garita de Belén; fought the

French under General *Porfirio Díaz*, 1867.
K] Imprisoned in Tlatelolco, 1876. L] Godoy, 266–67; Enc Mex, VIII, 419; Sierra,
419; Mestre, 211; Hombres prominentes,
369–70.

Melgar, Rafael E.
(Deceased March 21, 1959) A] March 14,
1887. B] Yanhuitlán, Oaxaca. C] Primary studies in Yanhuitlán and in Seminary School, Oaxaca, Oaxaca; no degree.
D] *Federal deputy* from the State of Oaxaca, Dist. 8, 1924–26, 1926–28, president of the Balloting Committee; *federal
deputy* from the State of Oaxaca, Dist. 8,
1928–30, president of the Administrative
Committee; *federal deputy* from the State
of Oaxaca, Dist. 10, 1930–32; president of
the Obregonista bloc and *federal deputy*
from the State of Oaxaca, Dist. 7, 1932–34;
local deputy to the state legislature of Oaxaca; senator from the State of Oaxaca,
1952–58, member of the First Committee
on National Defense, the Second Foreign
Relations Committee, and the First Balloting Committee. E] Founding member of
the National Revolutionary party (PNR),
1929; *secretary* of press of the National
Executive Committee of the PNR, 1931.
F] Governor of Quintana Roo, 1935–
40; ambassador to Holland, 1946–48.
G] None. H] Administrator, *El Economista Mexicano*, 1907; second paymaster,
Secretariat of Development, 1911–12; special mission to the United States, 1918;
president, Naviera Mexicana Company.
J] Joined the Revolution, 1913; career
army officer; reached the rank of brigade
general, 1916. K] Head of the Nationalist
Campaign, 1930. L] DGF56, 7, 10, 12–
14; Peral, 517; DP70, 1304; C de S, 1952–
58; López, 683; Ind Biog. 171–74; Alvarez
Coral, 129.

Melo, Gastón
(Deceased October 26, 1933) A] December 7, 1887. B] Huejutla, Hidalgo. C] Primary studies in Huejutla; preparatory
studies in Jalapa; medical degree, National
School of Medicine, UNAM, 1916; assistant in histology, National School of Medicine; professor of clinical medicine and
gastrology, National School of Medicine.
D] None. E] None. F] Director, Department of Health, 1932, 1932–33. G]

None. H] Practicing physician. I] Son of
Macario Melo y Téllez and Clarinda Andrade; personal physician to *Plutarco
Elías Calles*; brother Eduardo Melo, lawyer and poet; married María Zamora; mentor of Salvador Zubirán, rector of UNAM.
J] None. K] None. L] Dir social, 1935,
119; CyT, 271; Peral, 517; DP70, 1304; Pérez López, 271.

Mena, Francisco Zacarias
(Deceased January 10, 1908) A] September 6, 1841. B] León, Guanajuato.
C] Primary studies; no degree. D] Federal
deputy, 1867; governor of Guanajuato,
1876–80. E] None. F] Ambassador to
England; ambassador to Germany; tax official, Guanajuato, 1876; *secretary* of public works, 1895–1907; *secretary* of war,
1903–05. G] None. H] Went into mining in his youth; stockholder, Jockey
Club. I] Unknown. J] Joined the Liberal
Forces as a 2nd lieutenant in the national
guard, March 1, 1857; fought the French in
Puebla, 1862; captured and deported by
the French, 1863–65; staff officer, General
Porfirio Díaz, 1865–67; fought under Díaz
in the battle for Puebla, April 2, 1867;
chief of staff, Plan of La Noria Rebellion,
General Diaz, 1871; captured and amnestied by the government, Ciudad Camargo,
Coahuila, 1872; supported the Plan of
Tuxtepec, 1876; rank of brigade general,
January 5, 1877; rank of division general,
April 9, 1902. K] None. L] Almanaque
de Guanajuato, 130; Mestre, 230; Sec
of War, 1900, 89; Blue Book, 1901, 89;
Godoy, 185; Enc Mex, VIII, 423; Peral,
517–18; DP70, 1305; Hombres prominentes, 227–28; Sec of War, 1901, 19.

Méndez (Sánchez), Juan Nepomuceno
(Deceased November 29, 1894) A] July 2,
1824. B] Tetela del Oro (Tetela de
Ocampo), Puebla. C] Primary studies
only; no degree. D] Local deputy to the
state legislature of Puebla, 1857, 1861–63;
senator from the State of Puebla, 1878–80;
governor of Puebla, 1880–85. E] None.
F] Prefect, Zacatlán District, Puebla, 1858;
treasurer general of Puebla, 1858; secretary general of government of the State
of Puebla, 1861–62; governor and military commander of Puebla, 1867–68;
provisional president of Mexico, 1876–

77; president of the Supreme Court of Military Justice, 1885–94. G| None. H| Went into business as a youth. I| Son of José Mariano Méndez and María de Jesús Sánchez. J| Joined the national guard as a volunteer to fight against the North American invasion, 1846; served under Colonel *Ramón Márquez Galindo*, commander, national guard, Puebla, 1854; rank of colonel in the infantry, 1857; captured by the Conservatives, but escaped, 1858; military commander of Zacapoaxtla, Puebla, 1859–61; rank of brigade general, July 27, 1863; badly wounded in an engagement with the French; commander, 2nd Infantry Division, Army of the East, under General *Porfirio Díaz*, 1867; military commander of Puebla, 1867–68; supported the Plan of La Noria, 1871; rank of division general, December 8, 1872; supported the Plan of Tuxtepec, 1876. K| None. L| Covarrubias, 1952, 127; Covarrubias, II, 123–30; Hombres prominentes, 71–72; Márquez, Puebla, 326–27; Ríos, 428; Mestre, 189; García Purón, 209–10.

Méndez (Villegas), Luis
(Deceased September 13, 1935) A| June 30, 1884. B| Zamora, Michoacán. C| Primary studies, seminary, Zamora; abandoned seminary studies to work. D| Local deputy to the state legislature of Michoacán, 1925; *federal deputy* from the State of Michoacán, Dist. 8, 1928–30; federal deputy from the State of Michoacán, Dist. 1, 1934–35. E| Helped *Antonio Díaz y Soto y Gama* found the National Agrarian party, 1920. F| Head, Department of Labor, Secretariat of Industry and Commerce, 1923–24; *interim governor* of Michoacán, 1928–32. G| Labor leader; helped established the Casa del Obrero Mundial; director, Agrarian Commission of Michoacán, 1924. H| Began working in uncle's tailor shop; moved to Mexico City and opened own shop; tailor; business was used as a meeting place by revolutionaries. I| Son of Carmen Villegas. J| Supplied *Emiliano Zapata* during the Revolution, 1910–15; delegate of the Zapatistas to the Convention of Aguascalientes, 1914. K| Imprisoned by *Victoriano Huerta*, 1913–14; imprisoned again, 1915; removed from the Chamber of Deputies for

supporting *Gilberto Valenzuela* for president, 1929; killed in an exchange of gunfire in the Senate. L| DP70, 1306; Morales Jiménez, 235–38.

Mendizábal, Gregorio
(Deceased 1932) A| 1846. B| Orizaba, Veracruz. C| Primary and preparatory studies, José Miguel Sánchez Oropeza's school, Orizaba; won first prize for academic performance, primary and preparatory studies; medical degree, National School of Medicine, Mexico City, 1869; professor of physics and chemistry, Colegio de Orizaba, 1869–94; professor of clinical medicine, National School of Medicine, 1907. D| *Federal deputy* from the State of Puebla, Dist. 8, 1894–96, 1896–98, 1898–1900, 1900–02; *federal deputy* from the State of Veracruz, Dist. 12, 1902–04, 1904–06, 1906–08 1908–10, 1910–12. E| None. F| None. G| Member, National Academy of Medicine, 1895–1932. H| Practicing physician, Orizaba, 1869–94; physician, Juárez Hospital, 1895–98; director, Juárez Hospital, Mexico City, 1898–1911; author of numerous books. I| Unknown. J| None. K| None. L| DP70, 1310; C de D, 1894–96.

Mendoza González, Octavio
A| December 1, 1900. B| León, Guanajuato. C| Primary and secondary studies in León, Guanajuato; preparatory studies at the University of Guanajuato, 1913–18; law degree, National School of Law, 1918–22, with a thesis on administration and administrators, August 29, 1923; assistant to the secretary of the preparatory school, León, Guanajuato, 1916. D| *Federal deputy* from the State of Guanajuato, Dist. 1, 1928–29. E| None. F| Secretary of the justice of the peace, Dist. 8; commissioner of the first justice of the Peace, 1917–19; secretary of the first cooperative founded by President *Alvaro Obregón*, 1920; consulting lawyer to the Secretariat of the Government, 1924; secretary general of government of the State of Guanajuato, 1926; interim governor of Guanajuato, 1927; *subsecretary* of government, 1929–30, in charge of the Secretariat of Government, 1931; ambassador to Germany and Austria, 1931–32; oficial mayor of the Secretariat of Foreign

Relations, 1932–34; secretary of the Board of Private Welfare, 1934–36; director of the Legal Department, Department of the Federal District, 1936–38; justice of the Supreme Court, 1941–46, 1947–52, 1953–58, 1959–64, 1965–68. G] None. H] None. I] Great-grandfather served as a federal deputy under President Juárez; married Magdalena Causier. J] None. K] None. L] *Justicia*; letter.

Mercado, Manuel Antonio

(Deceased 1909) A] 1838. B] La Piedad de Cabadas, Michoacán. C] Studies at the Seminary of Morelia, Michoacán; preparatory studies at the Colegio de San Ildefonso, Mexico City; law degree, Colegio de San Juan de Letrán, Mexico City, 1861. D] Federal deputy from the State of Michoacán, 1869–70, 1870–72, 1872–74, 1874–76, 1876–78, 1878–80, 1880–82; *federal deputy* from the State of Michoacán, Dist. 6, 1886–88; *federal deputy* from the State of Michoacán, Dist. 10, 1888–90, 1890–92, 1892–94; *federal deputy* from the State of Michoacán, Dist. 9, 1894–96; *federal deputy* from the State of Michoacán, Dist. 12, 1896–98. E] Positions in Liberal party during French intervention. F] Judge, Ario de Rosales, Michoacán, 1861; judge of the first instance, Morelia; civil judge, Mexico City; secretary general of government of Michoacán, 1864; oficial mayor of government of Michoacán, under *Felipe Berriozábal*, 1863; secretary of government of the Federal District, 1874–76; *subsecretary* of government, 1882–1900. G] None. H] Practicing lawyer, 1876–82. I] Close personal friend of José Marti, Cuban independence leader; son Manuel Mercado, Jr., alternate federal deputy from Michoacán, 1898–1902; related to *Aristeo Mercado Salto* (probably brother of), governor of Michoacán, 1892–1911. J] None. K] None. L] Godoy, 296; Enc Mex, VIII, 452; Hombres prominentes, 317–18; Peral, Appendix, 217.

Mercado, Salvador R.

(Deceased November 25, 1936) A] 1864. B] Morelia, Michoacán. C] Early education unknown; no degree. D] None. E] None. F] *Provisional governor* of Chihuahua, 1913. G] None. H] Farmed in

Canutillo and El Paso, Texas, after 1914. I] Unknown. J] Career army officer; 2nd lieutenant, 16th Infantry Battalion, April 14, 1884–87; rank of 1st lieutenant, December 28, 1886; served in the 15th Battalion, under General Pablo Yáñez, 1887–1902; rank of 2nd captain, April 23, 1891; rank of captain, June 29, 1894; rank of major, July 1, 1902; instructor, army reservists, 1902–03; returned to the 15th Infantry Battalion, to fight Indian rebels in Quintana Roo, 1903; rank of lt. colonel, October 22, 1906; commander, 21st Infantry Battalion, Veracruz, Veracruz, 1906–10; agent of the military Ministerio Público, Veracruz, Veracruz, 1906–09; military judge, Veracruz, Veracruz, 1909–10; assistant commander, 12th Battalion, Chihuahua, fought against the Maderistas, 1910–11; joined the 6th Battalion, July 21, 1911; commander, 6th Battalion, Division of the North, April 5, 1912, under General *Victoriano Huerta*; rank of colonel, April 5, 1912; commander of the federal garrison, Hidalgo del Parral, Chihuahua, 1913; rank of brigadier general, February 10, 1913; fought against *Francisco Villa*, 1913–14; rank of brigade general, August 23, 1913. K] Left Mexico for the United States, interned in Ft. Bliss, Texas, 1914. L] Mestre, 292; Almada, 1968, 332; Peral, Appendix, 217; DP70, 1316; Almada, 473–77; Sec of War, 1914, 20.

Mercado (Salto), Aristeo

(Deceased April 4, 1913) A] 1836. B] Hacienda de Villachuato, Purandiro, Michoacán. C] Primary studies, seminary in Morelia; continued studies in Mexico City; engineering studies, National College of Mines, Mexico City, but left because of War of the Reform. D] Mayor, Uruapan, Michoacán, 1876–80; federal deputy from the State of Michoacán, 1880–82, president of the Chamber of Deputies; local deputy to the state legislature of Michoacán, 1890; *governor* of Michoacán, 1892–1911. E] Member of the Liberal party. F] Editor, *Diario Oficial*, Michoacán; oficial mayor of the Secretariat of Government of Michoacán under Governor Justo Mendoza; official, Secretariat of the Treasury, 1863; secretary of government of the State of Michoacán, under Governor Manuel Carrillo, 1875; in-

terim governor of Michoacán, 1875–76.
G] None. H] Worked in a printing firm in
college to help family after father died;
journalist. I] Son of Antonio Mercado
and Dolores Salto; educated by uncle Florentino Mercado, a lawyer; grandson of
Antonio Florentino Mercado, lawyer; related to *Manuel Antonio Mercado*, subsecretary of government. J] Commander and
staff officer, Army of the East, during the
Reform Wars; fought the French under
General Justo Mendoza; captured and imprisoned by the French. K] None. L] Godoy, 240; DP70, 1316; Enc Mex, VIII, 451;
Mestre, 247; Dicc mich, 268; Album.

Merino Jiménez, Calixto
(Deceased December 4, 1915) A] January
24, 1836. B] Tacotalpa, Tabasco. C] Early
education unknown; law degree. D] Member of the City Council of Tacotalpa, Tabasco, 1854–60; *alternate senator* from
Tabasco, 1890–94, 1894–98. E] None.
F] Prefect of Tacotalpa; judge of the first instance, Tabasco, 1860; *interim governor* of
Tabasco, 1888–89, 1890, 1891. G] None.
H] Landowner. I] Son of José María Merino and Trinidad Jiménez; married Dolores Quintero. J] Fought the French.
K] None. L] Hombres prominentes,
453–54; Mestre, 254; Ghigliazza, 128–34.

Mestre Ghigliazza, Manuel
(Deceased 1954) A] November 15, 1870.
B] Villahermosa, Tabasco. C] Studies at
the Instituto Campechano and in Mexico
City, 1889; graduated from the National
School of Medicine, Mexico City, September 20, 1898. D] *Governor* of Tabasco, 1911–13. E] Member of the Anti-
Reelectionist party. F] *Interim governor*
of Tabasco, 1911; director, National
Library. G] None. H] Founder and director, *La Revista de Tabasco*; author of archival work on Tabasco; journalist; contributor to *El Universal*, 1913. I] Son of
Manuel Mestre Gorgoll, physician, and
governor of Tabasco, 1883–84, and Dolores Ghigliazzi; grandson of Angel Ghigliazza and Josefa García Poblaciones;
brother Eduardo, lawyer, and federal
deputy from Puebla, 1910–12; brother-in-
law of the daughter of General *Mucio
Práxedis Martínez*; uncle of Manuel
Mestre Martínez, director general of

Spicer, S.A. J] Supported *Francisco I. Madero*, 1910–11. K] None. L] UNAM,
law, 1896–1900, 179; Almanaque de Tabasco, 150; Enc Mex, VIII, 484; Ghigliazza,
157–58.

Meza (Llorente), Enrique
(Deceased) A] March 16, 1890. B] Villa
de Ixhuatlán, Chicontepec, Veracruz.
C] Early education unknown; enrolled in
the Free Law School, April 1913, graduating with a law degree, May 5, 1919, with a
thesis on the law of family relations.
D] *Alternate constitutional deputy* from
the State of Veracruz, Dist. 3, 1916–17;
federal deputy from the State of Veracruz,
Dist. 3, 1918–20; *federal deputy* from the
State of Veracruz, Dist. 12, 1920–22; *federal deputy* from the State of Veracruz,
Dist. 2, 1922–24; *federal deputy* from
the State of Veracruz, Dist. 3, 1928–30.
E] None. F] Consul general, Buenos Aires,
1925; lawyer, Secretariat of Communications and Public Works; lawyer, Secretariat of Government, 1935. G] None.
H] Practicing lawyer. I] Son of Emilio
Meza and Concepción Llorente. J] None.
K] None. L] ELD, 103; C de D, 1916–17.

Mier (de los Santos), José María
(Deceased July 8, 1914) A] 1847. B] Cadereyta Jiménez, Nuevo León. C] Primary and secondary studies in Monterrey;
preparatory studies in Monterrey; law
degree, School of Law, Monterrey, 1869.
D] *Governor* of Nuevo León, 1910.
E] None. F] Director, Department of Cavalry, Secretariat of War; oficial mayor of
war and navy, 1907; *subsecretary* of war
and navy, 1907–09; *provisional governor*
of Nuevo León, 1909–10; *governor* of Jalisco, 1914. G] None. H] Practicing
lawyer. I] Son of Francisco de Mier and
Teresa de los Santos; great-nephew of Father Servando. J] Supported the Plan of
Tuxtepec under Generals *Porfirio Díaz*
and *Gerónimo Treviño*, 1876; rank of brigade general, May 12, 1884; director, Department of Special Services, Secretariat of
War, 1901; rank of division general of cavalry, December 27, 1911; commander of
the 3rd Military Zone, 1912–13; commander, Division of the West, 1914.
K] Died fighting against the Constitutionalists in the Battle of Castillo. L] Rev de

Ejer, Dec. 1968, 11; Mestre, 251; Alamanaque de Nuevo León, 100; Sec of War, 1901, 19; Sec of War, 1914, 17.

Mier y Terán, Luis
(Deceased August 19, 1891) A] March 5, 1835. B] Guanajuato, Guanajuato. C] Early education unknown; graduated from the National Military College, 2nd lieutenant of engineers, 1853. D] Senator from Morelos, 1882–84; *senator* from Morelos, 1884–86; *governor* of Oaxaca, 1884–86, 1886–87. E] None. F] Governor and military commander of Veracruz. G] None. H] Unknown. I] Student at the National Military College with *José Montesinos*, senator from Guanajuato, 1884–95. J] Career army officer; fought in the Reform wars; companion of General *Porfirio Díaz*; fought the French, 1862–67, supported the Plan of La Noria, 1871; supported the Plan of Tuxtepec, 1876; rank of division general, March 19, 1876. K] None. L] Cuevas, 425; Almanaque de Sonora, 129; Mestre, 174; Almanaque de Oaxaca, 129.

Mijares Palencia, José
(Deceased 1965) A] March 1, 1895. B] Villahermosa, Tabasco. C] Primary studies at the Colegio Ayala and the Colegio San Bernardo, Puebla, 1902–07; secondary studies at the Colegio San Pedro and the Colegio San Pablo, and at the La Salle Christian School, Puebla, 1907–10; cadet at the National Military College, Chapultepec, 1910–11; graduated, 1912, as a 2nd lieutenant of infantry; founder and director of the Ignacio Zaragoza School, Puebla, Puebla, which later became a military academy. D] *Governor* of Puebla, 1933–37. E] Campaign manager for General *Juan Almazán's* presidential campaign, 1940. F] Chief of mounted police for the Federal District, 1929–31; director general of agricultural education, Secretariat of Public Education, 1946–52. G] None. H] Director of a private military academy, 1946; author of an organizational manual for the federal government, 1936, and other works. J] Joined the Revolution as a 2nd lieutenant, 1912; rank of captain, 1914; rank of brigadier general, 1927; rank of brigade general, 1931; commander of the 17th Military Zone, Queré-

taro, Querétaro; commander of the 27th Military Zone, Acapulco, Guerrero. K] Founder of the first private military academy in Mexico. L] EBW 1136; CyT, 444–45; Enc Mex, IX, 1977, 68; NYT, 21 Aug. 1940, 8; Almanaque de Tabasco, 163.

Millán, Agustín
(Deceased May 18, 1920) A] July 24, 1879. B] Texcaltitlán, México. C] Some primary studies; no degree. D] *Governor* of Veracruz, 1915–16. E] None. F] *Governor* of México, 1917–18, 1919. G] None. H] Worked as an agricultural laborer; artisan; railroad worker; policeman in Veracruz; carpenter, Orizaba, Veracruz. I] Son of Jesús Millán and Damiana Vivero, very poor family. J] Joined Daniel Herrera with a small guerrilla band, 1911; joined *Cándido Aguilar*, 1911; rank of 2nd lieutenant, June 1911; rank of 2nd captain, October, 1911; rank of major, 1912; rank of lt. colonel, 1913; chief of arms, Veracruz, Veracruz, 1914; rank of brigadier general, May 20, 1914; represented at the Convention of Aguascalientes, 1914, by José Muñoz Infante; military commander of Puebla, 1914; commander of the parade ground of Mexico City, 1916; accompanied *Venustiano Carranza*, 1920. K] Imprisoned for anti-Díaz activities with *Diódoro Batalla*, Veracruz, 1910–11; recruited prisoners to the anti-reelection movement as a policeman; died defending Carranza in Aljibes. L] DP70, 1348; Sánchez García, 283–84; Siliceo, 126–31.

Moctezuma, Mariano
(Deceased July 28, 1942) A] February 15, 1877. B] Ciudad del Maíz, San Luis Potosí. C] Early education unknown; engineering degree in geology, School of Mines, August 23, 1905; professor at the National School of Engineering, UNAM, 1936–42; director of the School of Engineering, UNAM, 1915–23, 1929–33, 1938–42. D] None. E] None. F] *Subsecretary* of public works, 1932–34, in charge of the Secretariat, November 1934; *subsecretary* of public education, 1934–36; subsecretary of industry and commerce, 1936–38; director of the National Observatory, Tacubaya, Federal District. G] None. H] None. I] Brother Fernando Moctezuma served as a senator from San

Luis Potosí, 1946–52; brother-in-law of General *Juan Barragán*; married Rosa Barragán; grandfather of Pedro Moctezuma Díaz Infante, subsecretary of government properties, 1970–76. J] None. K] None. L] DP70, 1372; Peral, 537; HA, 7 Aug. 1942, 40; López, 714.

Moheno (y Tabares), Querido
(Deceased April 12, 1933) A] December 3, 1873. B] Pichucalco, Chiapas. C] Primary studies in a public school, Pichucalco; secondary and preparatory studies, Instituto Juárez, Villahermosa, Tabasco, on a scholarship from the state government; law degree, National School of Law, Mexico City, 1897. D] *Alternate federal deputy* from the State of Jalisco, Dist. 18, 1900–02, 1902–04, 1904–06; *alternate federal deputy* from the State of Jalisco, Dist. 17, 1908–10, 1910–12; *federal deputy* from the State of Chiapas, Dist. 6, 1912–13; *senator* from the State of Chiapas, 1914. E] Led anti-Díaz movements as a student; attacked the government as a journalist; opposed *Francisco I. Madero* as a journalist. F] *Subsecretary* of foreign relations, 1913; *secretary* of foreign relations, 1913–14; *secretary* of development, 1914; *governor* of Chiapas, 1914. G] None. H] Journalist; lawyer; secretary, Credit Bank, Havana, Cuba. I] Father of Querido Moheno, Jr., lawyer and journalist. J] None. K] Named interim governor of Chiapas by state legislature but never served, 1911; member of the Cuadrilátero group in the 1912–13 legislature; exiled to San Antonio, Texas, and Havana, Cuba; returned to Mexico, 1920; imprisoned (under *Porfirio Díaz*) in Belén prison many times. L] Almanaque de Chiapas, 149; Enc Mex, VIII, 109; Gordillo y Ortiz, 162–63; DP70, 1373; FSRE, 157–58; Illescas, 593; Mestre, 287.

Molina y Solís, Manuel
(Deceased April 21, 1904) A] Unknown. B] Bolonchenticul, Yucatán (Campeche). C] Primary and secondary studies from the Colegio de Enseñanza; preparatory studies, Literary Institute of Yucatán; law degree, Literary Institute of Yucatán. D] Local deputy to the state legislature of Tabasco; local deputy to the state legislature of Yucatán; *alternate senator* from

the State of Oaxaca, 1904. E] None. F] *Interim governor* of Yucatán, 1903–04. G] None. H] Practicing lawyer; businessman. I] Son of Juan Francisco Molina y Esquivel, farmer and small businessman, and Cecilia Solís Rosales; brother of *Olegario Molina*, secretary of development, 1907–11; brother of Juan Francisco Molina Solís, local politician and attorney; brother of Audormaro Molina, linguist and planter; grandson of Julián Molina y Bastante, small farmer; uncle of Ricardo Molina Hubbe, federal deputy, 1910–12. J] None. K] None. L] Valdés, II, 26–27; Mestre 220.

Molina (y Solís), Olegario
(Deceased April 28, 1925) A] 1843. B] Bolonchenticul, Yucatán (Campeche). C] Primary studies Bolonchenticul; secondary studies at the Seminary of San Ildefonso and Colegio de José María González, Mérida; law degree, School of Law, Mérida, Yucatán, 1886; founder and first director, Literary Institute of Yucatán, Mérida, 1867. D] Federal deputy, 1869–71, 1873–75; *senator* from the State of Oaxaca, 1900–02; *governor* of Yucatán, 1890–1907. E] None. F] Attorney, Superior Tribunal of Justice of Yucatán, 1874; secretary general of government of Yucatán under Governor Cepeda, 1872; *governor* of Quintana Roo, 1902–11. G] None. H] Owner of six henequen plantations; one of the wealthiest families in Yucatán; economic interests tied to the International Harvester Company; founded a construction company; began working for Mérida-Progreso Railroad Company as director of projects, 1877–81; superintendent, Mérida-Progreso Railroad, 1881–87; member of the board, Mérida-Progreso Railroad, 1887–90; partner, Renón Peniche Import-Export Company. I] Son of Juan Francisco Molina y Esquivel, farmer and small businessman, and Cecilia Sánchez Rosales; brother of *Manuel Molina y Solís*, interim governor of Yucatán, 1903–04; brother of Audomaro Molina, linguist and planter; brother of Juan Francisco Molina Solís, attorney in his firm and local politician; uncle of Ricardo Molina Hubbe, publisher and federal deputy, 1910–12; married Dolores Figueroa y Milán; grandson of Julián Molina y Bas-

tante, small farmer. J] Private secretary to General Manuel Cepeda Peraza in the fighting against the French, 1866. K] Fled to Havana, Cuba, 1911. L] Enc Mex, VIII, 113–14; Carreño, 143–56; Valdés Acosta, II, 9–17; DP70, 1375; Holms, 364.

Mondragón, Manuel
(Deceased September 28, 1922) A] October 15, 1859. B] Ixtlahuaca, México. C] Early education unknown; enrolled in the National Military College, December 20, 1876, graduating as a 2nd lieutenant in artillery; professor, National Military College. D] None. E] None. F] Military attaché to the Mexican Delegation, Paris, France, 1900–01; director of the military foundries, secretariat of war, 1901; chief, Department of Artillery, secretariat of war; *secretary* of war, 1913. G] None. H] None. I] Married Mercedes Balseca. J] Career army officer; rank of colonel, June 28, 1899; fought against the Maderistas, 1910–11; retired from the army, 1912–13; rejoined the army after leading the revolt against President *Francisco I. Madero* during the Decena Trágica, with *Bernardo Reyes* and *Félix Díaz*, 1913; rank of division general, February 10, 1913. K] Arrested for attempting to free Félix Díaz, 1912; exiled, Europe, 1913–22. L] Sec of War, 1901, 27; Sec of War, 1914, 17; Mestre, 269; Aranda Pamplona, 64; Enc Mex, VIII, 123; QesQ, 386–87; DP70, 1379–80.

Montaño, Otilio E.
(Deceased May 18, 1917) A] December 13, 1877. B] Villa de Ayala, Morelos. C] Primary studies under Celso Hormigo, Guillermo Prieto School, Cuautla, Morelos; teacher, Tepalcingo and Jonacatepec, Morelos; director, Villa de Ayala Public School, Tepalcingo. D] None. E] None. F] *Secretary* of public instruction, Convention government, 1915. G] None. H] Schoolteacher. I] Son of Esteban Montaño and Guadalupe Sánchez, peasants. J] Joined the Zapatistas under Torres Burgos, Ayala, Morelos, March 11, 1911; wrote the Plan of Ayala, November 25, 1911; represented self at the Convention of Aguascalientes, 1914; defected from the Zapatistas after the promulgation of the Constitution, 1917. K] Executed as a trai-

tor by the Zapatistas, 1917. L] Moreno, 155–56; Carrasco Puente, 69; Enc Mex, VIII, 134; QesQ, 390; DP70, 1389; López González, 153–56.

Montero Villar, Mariano
(Deceased) A] October 18, 1883. B] Mexico City. C] Early education unknown; no degree; instructor, School of Military Aspirants, 1906. D] *Federal deputy* from the State of Morelos, Dist. 2, 1920–22, member of the Great Committee; *federal deputy* from the State of Morelos, Dist. 1, 1922–24, member of the Great Committee. E] Secretary of publicity of the Pro de la Huerta Committee, 1923. F] None. G] None. H] Typographer; businessman. I] Unknown. J] Joined the army reserves as a 2nd sergeant, 1902; joined the regular army as a 2nd lieutenant in the 26th Battalion, under the command of General Lauro Villar; joined the Constitutionalists under Emilio Madero with the rank of captain; fought under General Guadalupe Sánchez; rank of brigadier general; chief of staff to General *Salvador Alvarado*; chief of staff to General *Cándido Aguilar*; supported the *Adolfo de la Huerta* rebellion, 1923; consul, New York, representing de la Huerta, 1923; supported the Escobar rebellion, 1929. K] Exiled to New York, 1923–35. L] Peral; C de D, 1920–22, 1922–24.

Montes de Oca, Luis
(Deceased December 4, 1958) A] 1894. B] Federal District. C] Early education unknown; accounting degree; CPA; Superior School of Business, Administration, and Consular Affairs, Mexico City; professor of public accounting, School of Business, UNAM, 1916–21. D] None. E] Campaigned for General *Juan Andreu Almazán*, 1940. F] Consul general to El Paso, Texas, Hamburg, Germany, Paris, France, 1914–20; comptroller general of Mexico, 1924–27; *secretary* of the treasury, 1927–28, 1928–30, 1930–32; director general of the Bank of Mexico, 1935–40; presidential adviser to the National Banking Council. G] None. H] First employment as a public accountant for the federal government; financial agent to the United States for *Venustiano Carranza*; author of the important 1931 monetary re-

form; founder and president of the International Bank of Mexico, 1958; founder with Eduardo Suárez, secretary of the treasury, of the National Bank of Foreign Commerce. J] Served in civilian posts as a consul during the Revolution. K] Opposed General *Victoriano Huerta* as a student; initiator of the use of CPA's in the comptroller's office; resigned from the directorship of the Bank of Mexico to support General Almazán, September 7, 1940. L] HA, 15 Dec. 1958, 10; Peral, 545; DP70, 1398; WWM45, 80; DBM68, 545; Enc Mex, IX, 1977, 171; NYT, 8 Sept. 1940, 28.

Montesinos, José
(Deceased September 14, 1895) A] 1839. B] Veracruz, Veracruz. C] Early education unknown; graduated as a 2nd lieutenant in the engineers, National Military College, 1853. D] *Senator* from the State of Guanajuato, 1884–88, 1888–92, 1892–95. E] None. F] Oficial mayor of war, 1880, 1883–85. G] None. H] None. I] Unknown. J] Career army officer; opposed the Constitution of 1857; battalion commander, Conservative forces, 1858; rank of lt. colonel, 1860; defeated by Liberal forces and captured, battle of Guadalajara, October 30, 1860; joined the Republican forces, December 22, 1860; captured by the French at Puebla, 1863, and deported to Loreau, France, after refusing to recognize the French empire, 1863; helped by Spanish General Prim to go to Spain, where he worked on La Mota Castle as a laborer until 1866; returned to Mexico, June 1866, and appointed commander of Republican forces, Matamoros; commander of the 6th Battalion of Guanajuato under General *Sóstenes Rocha*; commander of the 1st Brigade, siege of Querétaro, 1867; rank of brigade general. K] None. L] QesQ, 392; DP70, 1398–99; Cuevas, 425.

Monzón (Teyatzin), Luis G.
(Deceased June 6, 1942) A] November 15, 1872. B] Hacienda de Santiago, San Luis Potosí, San Luis Potosí. C] Primary and secondary studies, Hacienda de Santiago; primary teaching certificate, Normal School, San Luis Potosí, 1893; teacher, San Luis Potosí; director of schools in Hermosillo, Nogales, Moctezuma, Estación Torres, and Nacozari de García, Sonora;

director, Benito Juárez School, Cerritos, San Luis Potosí, 1909; director, Primary School of Cumpas, Sonora; zone inspector, Alamos, Sonora, 1911–13; founder and director, Normal School of Sonora, 1915–16. D] *Constitutional deputy* from the State of Sonora, Dist. 1, 1916–17; *senator* from the State of Sonora, 1917–18, 1918–20; *senator* from the State of San Luis Potosí, 1922–24, 1924–26. E] Joined the Liberal party to support the Flores Magón brothers; joined the Green Club, Hermosillo, in opposition to local government candidates, 1900; director, Office of Political Information and Revolutionary Reform, Hermosillo, Sonora, 1916. F] Technical school inspector, Federal District, 1918. G] None. H] Journalist; wrote for *El Diario del Hogar*, Mexico City, 1909–10; director, *La Reforma Social*, 1916; director, *La Vanguardia*, Hermosillo, 1919; director of *El Tiempo*, Cananea, Sonora, 1920. I] Married María de Jesús Aragón; grandmother, an Indian. J] Joined the Constitutionalists, 1913, and tried to take the Alamos fort, 1913; supported and signed the Plan of Agua Prieta, 1920. K] Had to leave San Luis Potosí because of his attacks on a local political boss and his anarchist ideas in the classroom, 1899; imprisoned in Douglas, Arizona, and Agua Prieta, Sonora, for attempted revolt under the Magonistas, September 1906; imprisoned by Huertistas in Alamos, Sonora, 1913. L] QesQ, 393; DP70, 1402; Morales Jiménez, 257–61; Montesinos, 259; Aguilar Camín, 123.

Mora (Hernández), Agustín
(Deceased) A] August 28, 1888. B] Uruapan, Michoacán. C] Preparatory studies at the Colegio de San Nicolás, Morelia, Michoacán, 1900–04; cadet, Military Aspirants School, Mexico City, 1905–08. D] None. E] None. F] Director, Infantry Department, Secretariat of War, 1926–27; chief of staff, President *Pascual Ortiz Rubio*, 1930–32. G] None. H] None. I] Son of Jesús Mora and Genoveva Hernández; married Josefina Lerma. J] Career army officer; commander, various infantry battalions, 1915–25; joined the Constitutionalists, 1913; chief of military operations, various states; rank of brigade general, November 21, 1927; commander,

parade ground of Mexico City, 1928–29; commander, 21st Military Zone, Morelia, Michoacán, 1944; commander, 10th Military Zone, Durango, Durango. K] None. L] WWM45, 80.

Morales, Miguel N.
(Deceased July 7, 1936) A] 1846. B] Jalapa, Veracruz. C] Early education unknown; no degree. D] None. E] None. F] Political chief and military commander of Tepic; oficial mayor of war, 1910–11; *interim governor* of Colima, 1913. G] None. H] None. I] Unknown. J] Career army officer; joined the army as a private, Scouting Squadron of Puebla, December 1, 1861; fought the French, 1861–67; rank of captain, 1867; escorted Benito Juárez to San Luis Potosí, Chihuahua, and El Paso, Texas; opposed the Plan of La Noria, 1871; opposed the Plan of Tuxtepec, 1876; rank of colonel in the infantry, 1882; commander, 27th Infantry Battalion, 1901; rank of brigadier general, May 27, 1901; rank of brigade general, March 8, 1909; retired from active duty, 1912, but returned after Huerta rebellion, 1913. K] None. L] Sec of War, 1901, 24; Sec of War, 1914, 20; Mestre, 291; Almada, Colima, 134; Peral, Appendix, 227–28.

Morelos Zaragoza, Ignacio
(Deceased December 19, 1927) A] 1853. B] Monterrey, Nuevo León. C] Primary studies in Monterrey; preparatory studies in Mexico City; law degree, School of Law, Mexico City. D] *Federal deputy* from the State of Nuevo León, Dist. 5, 1913–14. E] None. F] Provisional governor of Tamaulipas, 1914. G] Leader, Masonic lodges, Monterrey. H] Author; novelist. I] Son of José María Morelos, career military officer, and Genoveva Zaragoza, sister of General Ignacio Zaragoza; grandson of Miguel G. Zaragoza, military officer, and María de Jesús Seguín. J] Career military officer; chief of staff to General *Gerónimo Treviño*, during Indian campaigns; inspector of police, Monterrey, Nuevo León, under Governor *Bernardo Reyes*; rank of brigade general, December 31, 1913; rank of division general, June 4, 1914. K] None. L] DP70, 2337; Sec of War, 1914, 20; Mestre, 280.

Moreno Cora, Silvestre
(Deceased September 14, 1922) A] December 31, 1837. B] Mexico City. C] Secondary and preparatory studies, Colegio Nacional, Orizaba, Veracruz; law degree, School of Law, Jalapa, Veracruz, 1861; professor of philosophy, civil law, and literature, Orizaba Preparatory School, Orizaba, 1861; director, Orizaba Preparatory School, Orizaba; professor, preparatory school, Córdoba, Veracruz; teacher, Orizaba, 1912–22. D] Member, City Council of Orizaba (various times). E] None. F] Prosecutor, Superior Tribunal of Justice of Veracruz, Jalapa; *justice* of the Supreme Court, 1898–1902, president, 1900; secretary general of government of the State of Veracruz. G] Member, Mexican Academy of Language; founder of the intellectual center, Sánchez Oropeza Society, Orizaba. H] Author of numerous books; practicing lawyer in Orizaba, 1861. I] Son of lawyer Manuel Moreno Cora and Manuela Castillo of Orizaba, Veracruz. J] None. K] None. L] González Cosío, 12; Illescas, 132–33; Mestre, 269; Blue Book, 1901, 29; Enc Mex, VIII, 260; DP70, 1416; Carreño, 197–98.

Morones, Luis N.
(Deceased 1964) A] 1890. B] Tlalpan, Federal District. C] Primary studies, Mexico City; no degree. D] *Federal deputy* from the Federal District, Dist. 12, 1922–24, 1924–26. E] Founder of the Mexican Labor party, 1922; opposed the re-election of General *Alvaro Obregón*, 1928. F] Director of factories, Secretariat of War; secretary of Industry, Trade, and Labor, 1924–28. G] Organized union of electricians and workers, Mexican Telephone Company; first secretary general, Mexican Telephone Company Workers Union; member, Casa del Obrero Mundial, 1912; leader, first and second National Workers Congress, 1916, 1917; presided over the constitutional assembly of the Regional Confederation of Mexican Workers (CROM), 1918; secretary general of CROM; permanent adviser to CROM. H] Typographer; worked in a local electric company, Mexico City; mechanic, Mexican Light and Power, Mexico City; foreman, repair shop, Mexican Light and

Power; founded *El Sol*, labor newspaper, 1922. I] From a working-class family. J] None. K] Expelled from Mexico by President *Lázaro Cárdenas*, 1935; wounded in a gun battle in the Chamber of Deputies. L] Enc Mex, VIII, 262; WWM45, 81; DP70, 1418–19.

Mucel Acereto, Joaquín
(Deceased March 2, 1970) A] 1889. B] Ciudad Carmen, Campeche. C] Early education unknown; engineering studies; director, Heroic Military College, Mexico City, 1920. D] None. E] None. F] *Governor* of Campeche, 1914–17, 1917–19. G] None. H] Unknown. I] Son of engineer Joaquín Mucel Ceballos and Juana Acereto Pérez. J] Joined the Constitutionalists as 1st captain of engineers, July 14, 1913, under General *Lucio Blanco*; participated in 18 battles in Tamaulipas, Campeche, and Tabasco, 1913–18; rank of major, November 18, 1913; served under Lucio Blanco and *Luis Caballero*, 1913–17; rank of lt. colonel, March 14, 1914; rank of colonel, August 17, 1914; rank of brigadier general, March 28, 1915; defended President *Venustiano Carranza* with the military cadets, 1920; rank of brigade general; requested unlimited leave from army, October 1927. K] Decorated for loyalty to President Carranza, 1939. L] Rev de Ejer., Sept. 1976, 117; Dec. 1976, 46–47; DP70, 1425.

Múgica, Francisco José
(Deceased April 12, 1954) A] September 2, 1884. B] Tinguindín, Michoacán. C] Primary and secondary studies at the Seminary of Zamora, Michoacán; schoolteacher; no degree. D] *Constitutional deputy* from the State of Michoacán, Dist. 16, 1916–17; *governor* of Michoacán, 1920–22. E] Leader of the *Lázaro Cárdenas* campaign for president, 1934; director of the Constitutional party, 1952. F] Head of the port of Tampico, 1914; president of the Superior Tribunal of Justice, 1915; *governor* and military commander of the State of Tabasco, 1916; director of the Department of General Provisions, 1918–20; director of the federal prison on Islas Marías, 1927–33; head of the Administrative Department, Secre-

tariat of National Defense, May 1933; *secretary* of industry and commerce, 1934–35; secretary of public works, 1935–1939; governor of Baja California del Sur, 1940–46. G] None. H] Tax collector, Chauinda, Michoacán, 1906; postal employee, Zamora, Michoacán; journalist; member of *Luis Cabrera's* law firm, 1924. I] Longtime enemy of General *Alvaro Obregón* and *Melchor Ortega*; close friend and supporter of Lázaro Cárdenas, 1925–39; father, a schoolteacher; married Doctor Matilde Rodríguez Cabo; brother Carlos Múgica was oficial mayor of the Secretariat of War, 1920; members of his political group included Luis Mora Tovar, Jesús Romero Flores, and *Agustín Arroyo Ch.*; son Janítzio Múgica Rodríguez Cabo was director of forests and ejidos, Secretariat of Agrarian Reform, 1979. J] Joined the Revolution under *Francisco I. Madero*, November 20, 1910, as a 2nd lieutenant; rank of 1st captain, 1911; captain of the Constitutional forces under General *Lucio Blanco*; rank of 2nd captain, 1911; aide to *Venustiano Carranza*, 1911–13; rank of colonel in the cavalry, 1914; rank of brigadier general, 1914; chief of military operations of various states; rank of brigade general, 1932; commander of the 32nd Military Zone, Mérida, Yucatán, 1933; commander of the 21st Military Zone, Morelia, Michoacán, 1939; commander of the 3rd Military Zone, La Paz, Baja California del Sur, 1939–40; rank of division general, 1939; without assignment, 1940–49; retired, 1949. K] Precandidate for president of Mexico, 1939; considered too radical; identified with Leon Trotsky, whom he helped bring to Mexico; Gruening states that Múgica was imposed over other candidates as governor of Michoacán, 1920; supported the candidacy of Miguel Henríquez Guzmán for president, 1952. L] WWM45, 81–82; DP70, 1425–26; Peral, 560–61; Gruening, 461; Enc Mex, IX, 1977, 273; QesQ, 401–02.

Muñoz Arístegui, Enrique
(Deceased April 23, 1936) A] July 1854. B] Mérida, Yucatán. C] Primary studies at a private school in Mérida under Juan González Arfían and Mariano Correa; studies at the Seminary of San Ildefonso,

Mérida, until 1871; no degree. D] Member of the City Council of Mérida, 1890–92, 1894–96. E] None. F] Political boss of Mérida, Yucatán, 1902–06; *interim governor* of Yucatán, 1907, 1909–11. G] None. H] Successful furrier; director, Banco Yucateco, 1895–97; adviser, Banco Yucateco and various other banks, 1898–1903; treasurer of the board, Mérida Hospital, 1902–06. I] Son of José Trinidad Muñoz and Ursula Arístegui. J] None. K] None. L] Album; Mestre, 291.

Murguía, Francisco
(Deceased October 31, 1922) A] 1873. B] Hacienda de la Gruñidora, Zacatecas. C] Early education unknown; no degree. D] None. E] None. F] *Governor* of México, 1914. G] None. H] Herdsman as a boy; photographer, Monclova, Coahuila. I] From a poor family; married Aurora González; brother José was commander of the 4th Brigade, Army of the Northeast; related to General *Arnulfo González Medina*, governor of Coahuila, 1921–23. J] Joined the Maderistas, 1910; joined a rifle company to fight the *Pascual Orozco* rebellion, 1912, under Gregorio Osuna; joined the Constitutionalists as a captain in the irregulars under *Pablo González*; rank of major, Army of the Northeast, 1913; rank of colonel, August 1913; rank of brigade general, August 27, 1914; military commander of México, 1914; represented at the Convention of Aguascalientes by Carlos S. Fierros, 1914; fought against *Francisco Villa*, 1914–15; chief of military operations, Durango, 1915–16; commander of the Chihuahua campaign, 1916–18; chief of military operations, Laguna region, 1918; rank of division general, 1918; remained loyal to *Venustiano Carranza*, 1920; initiated rebellion against President *Alvaro Obregón*, 1922, but captured in Tepehuanes, Durango. K] Imprisoned in Mexico City, but escaped, 1913; imprisoned in Santiago Tlatelolco, 1920, but escaped with the help of General Helidoro T. Pérez and went into exile in Texas, 1920–22; executed by a council of war. L] Covarrubias, 203–10; 335; Almada, 534–35; Rev de Ejer, Nov. 1957, 42; Almada, 1968, 354; Enc Mex, VIII, 280–81; DP70, 1433–34.

Murrieta Murrieta, Marcelino
(Deceased June 17, 1938) A] June 2, 1880. B] Xalalcingo, Veracruz. C] Early education unknown; teaching certificate; director, Heroic Military College, 1920–21; founded the Agricultural Industrial School, Cajeme, Sonora, 1926; director, School of Industrial Arts, Teziutlán, Puebla, 1927; established schools for army dependents for the Secretariat of Public Education; teacher, Normal School of Veracruz, 1932. D] None. E] Candidate for governor of Veracruz. F] Customs administrator, Salina Cruz, Oaxaca; customs administrator, Ciudad Juárez; chief of staff of the Secretariat of National Defense, 1924; director, Agricultural Experiment Station, La Aurora, Guatemala; inspector general, army; governor of the Islas Marías Prison, 1937–38. G] Organized agricultural colonies, Veracruz, 1925. H] Unknown. I] Son of Francisco Murrieta Velázquez and Claudia Murrieta Matus. J] Joined the Constitutionalists as a 1st captain under the command of colonel Benito Vargas Barranco; commander, 31st Battalion; rank of colonel of the cavalry, January 16, 1915; rank of brigadier general, April 28, 1915; commander of the Carranza Brigade; defended Ciudad Juárez, June 14–16, 1919; fought against the *Adolfo de La Huerta* rebellion, 1923; commander of the garrison, Chihuahua, Chihuahua; supported the Escobar rebellion, 1929. K] Exiled to the United States, Cuba, and Guatemala, 1929–32. L] Rev de Ejer, Sept. 1976, 118; DP70, 1435; Cuevas, 344.

N

Nájera, Enrique R.
(Deceased July 3, 1945) A] 1884. B] Topia, Durango. C] Early education unknown; no degree. D] Mayor of Durango, Durango; *senator* from the State of Durango, 1922–24; *governor* of Durango, 1924–28. E] None. F] Inspector general of Police, Durango, Durango, 1911–12; director, military factories, Secretariat of War, 1914; *substitute governor* of Durango, 1920, 1921. G] None. H] Peasant. I] From a poor rural family; intimate friend of *Jesús A. Castro*, governor of Durango. J] Supported *Francisco I. Ma-*

dero, 1911, with a rank of major; fought under *Domingo Arrieta*, 1911; joined the Constitutionalists, 1913; supported the Escobar rebellion in Durango, 1929. K] None. L] Gruening, 423–25; Enc Mex, IX, 303; DP70, 1447; Rouaix, 275–76.

Naranjo (García), Francisco
(Deceased 1915) A] 1867. B] Lampazos, Nuevo León. C] Early education unknown; engineering degree. D] None. E] Member of the first Liberal Club, Lampazos, Nuevo León, 1902; early supporter of *Francisco I. Madero* and member of the Anti-Reelectionist party. F] Provisional governor of Morelos, 1912. G] None. H] Journalist; engineer. I] Son of General Francisco Naranjo, secretary of war, 1882–84, who distanced himself from *Porfirio Díaz* after 1884, and Dolores García; father of Francisco Naranjo, newspaper editor and professor. J] Formed irregular company of riflemen, Nuevo León, 1911, to support Madero. K] Persecuted by Díaz's government for newspaper articles critical of the administration. L] DP70, 1449; QesQ, 405–06; Enc Mex, IX, 314; Covarrubias, 219–26; Mestre, 231.

Navarro, Juan
(Deceased October 25, 1934) A] May 19, 1843. B] Alamos, Sonora. C] Early education unknown; no degree. D] *Senator* from Oaxaca, 1913–14. E] None. F] Political boss, 4th Canton (District), Jalisco, 1885–87; political boss, 5th Canton (Ameca), Jalisco, 1890–91. G] None. H] None. I] Son of Pedro Navarro and Bibiana Rochis, working-class family. J] Career army officer; joined the national guard as a private, October 23, 1859; rank of corporal, November 1, 1861; fought the French under General Rosas; rank of 2nd sergeant, August 1, 1862; rank of 1st sergeant, December 22, 1864; rank of 2nd lieutenant, auxiliary army battalion, March 16, 1865; rank of 1st lieutenant, January 7, 1866; rank of captain, February 16, 1867; opposed the Plan of La Noria in San Luis Potosí, 1872; opposed the Plan of Tuxtepec, 1876; rank of major, April 4, 1879; fought the Yaquis in Sonora, 1899–1908; commander, 20th Infantry Battalion, Chihuahua, 1910–12; defeated at Ciudad Juárez by *Francisco Villa* and *Pascual*

Orozco, May 1911; commander of military forces, Colima, 1912–13; rank of brigade general, September 11, 1913; retired from the army, 1914. K] *Francisco I. Madero* prevented his forces from executing Navarro after he surrendered Ciudad Juárez, 1911. L] Sec of War, 1914, 20; Almnaque de Sonora, 154; Almada, 1968, 359; Enc Mex, IX, 323; DP70, 1453; Villa, 116–19.

Navarro, Luis T.
(Deceased 1961) A] 1881. B] Puebla, Puebla. C] Primary and preparatory studies in Puebla; engineering degree, School of Mines, Mexico City. D] *Federal deputy* from the State of Puebla, Dist. 11, 1912–13; *constitutional deputy* from the State of Puebla, Dist. 11, 1916–17, president of the Credentials Committee. E] None. F] None. G] None. H] Practicing engineer. I] Unknown. J] Joined the Maderistas under *Cándido Aguilar* in Veracruz, 1910; supported *Emiliano Zapata*, 1913; rank of lt. colonel in the engineers. K] Persecuted by *Victoriano Huerta* government for authoring critical newspaper articles. L] CyT, 848; DP70, 1454.

Neri (Lacumza), Rodolfo
(Deceased) A] Unknown. B] Chilpancingo, Guerrero. C] Primary studies at private schools; preparatory studies Guerrero; law degree, National School of Law, 1904. D] *Alternate senator* from the State of Guerrero, 1916–18; *governor* of Guerrero, 1921–23, 1924–25. E] None. F] Local judge; district court judge. G] None. H] Practicing lawyer. I] Son of General Canuto A. Neri, who participated in the war against the French, and Virginia Lacumza; cousin of Eduardo Neri, attorney general of Mexico, 1920. J] Joined the Constitutionalists, 1913; rank of brigadier general; supported *Alvaro Obregón*, 1920; supported *Adolfo de la Huerta*, 1923. K] None. L] Gruening, 431–32; UNAM, law, 1906–12, 74.

Nieto, Rafael
(Deceased April 11, 1926) A] October 24, 1883. B] Cerritos, San Luis Potosí. C] Primary studies in Cerritos; self-educated; no degree. D] *Federal deputy*

from the State of San Luis Potosí, Dist. 4, 1912–13; *constitutional deputy* from the State of San Luis Potosí, Dist. 4, 1916–17; *governor* of San Luis Potosí, 1919–23. E] None. F] Director, National Railroads of Mexico; *oficial mayor* in charge of the Secretariat of the Treasury, 1914; *subsecretary* of the treasury, 1914–19; ambassador to Sweden, 1923–25; ambassador to Italy, 1925–26. G] None. H] Worked for several stores in youth; opened own business in Cerritos; wrote for *El Chisgarabis*; author; journalist. I] Possibly related (son of) to Rafael Nieto del Castillo, ambassador. J] Joined the Constitutionalists, 1913. K] Gave women in San Luis Potosí the vote before any other state in Mexico, January 8, 1923. L] Enc Mex, IX, 389–90; Montejano, 269; JSH, 269–70; DP70, 1468.

Noris, Ignacio
(Deceased) A] September 22, 1878. B] Mazatlán, Sinaloa. C] Early education unknown; law degree, 1899; professor, Colegio Civil Rosales, Culiacán, Sinaloa, 1900–01. D] *Alternate federal deputy* from the State of Sinaloa, Dist. 3, 1912–13. E] None. F] Agent of the Ministerio Público, Culiacán, 1899; judge of the first instance, Cosalá, Sinaloa, 1899–1900; Second judge of the first instance, Culiacán, Sinaloa, 1900–01; judge of the first instance, Mazatlán, Sinaloa, 1901; Judge of the Superior Tribunal of Justice of Sinaloa, 1901–08; minor judge, San Angel, Federal District, 1911–12; secretary general of government of Sinaloa, 1912–13; secretary, First Division, Superior Tribunal of Military Justice, 1914–15; director, Department of Justice, Secretariat of War, 1915; attorney general for military justice, 1915–16; judge of the Superior Tribunal of Justice of the Federal District, 1916–19; *justice* of the Supreme Court, 1919–23; president, Superior Tribunal of Military Justice, 1924; judge, Federal Circuit Court, Monterrey, Nuevo León, 1926; director, Public Registry, 1926–28. G] None. H] None. I] Probably son of Teófilo Noris, military officer and surviving cadet from the North American attack on Chapultepec Castle. J] None. K] None. L] González Dávila, 395–96.

Novelo, José Inés
(Deceased 1956) A] January 21, 1868. B] Valladolid, Yucatán. C] Teaching certificate; law degree, School of Law, Literary Institute of Mérida; professor of rhetoric and poetry, Normal School, Mérida; director, Literary Institute of Mérida, 1902. D] *Federal deputy* from the State of Yucatán, Dist. 6, 1912–13, member of the Great Committee and president of the Renovation Bloc; *alternate senator* from the Federal District, 1916–18; *federal deputy* from the Federal District, Dist. 3, 1920–22; *senator* from the State of Yucatán, 1922–24. E] Supported *Francisco I. Madero*, 1910; president, Liberal Constitutional party. F] Oficial mayor of government; private secretary to Vice-President *José María Pino Suárez*, 1911–12; director, *Diario Oficial*, Secretariat of government, 1937. G] None. H] Poet; journalist; author; director of *El Pueblo*. I] Related to (probably uncle of) Ernesto Novelo Torres, senator from Yucatán, 1946–52. J] None. K] Imprisoned by the *Victoriano Huerta* administration, 1913; exiled to New York and Havana, late 1920s, returned to Mexico, 1932. L] Enc Mex, IX, 408; DP70, 1478.

Núñez (Castañares), Roberto
(Deceased December 27, 1912) A] December 1, 1859. B] Mexico City. C] Early education unknown; preparatory studies in Tlaxcala, Tlaxcala, 1870–73, and at the National Preparatory School, 1874; law degree, National School of Law, April 26, 1878. D] Member of the City Council of Mexico City, 1886–88; *federal deputy* from the Federal District, Dist. 6, 1886–88, 1888–90; *federal deputy* from the Federal District, Dist. 2, 1890–92; *federal deputy* from the Federal District, Dist. 4, 1892–94, 1894–96; *federal deputy* from the State of Puebla, Dist. 18, 1896–98, 1898–1900, 1900–1902; *federal deputy* from the Federal District, Dist. 1, 1902–04, 1904–06, 1906–08, 1908–10, 1910–11. E] Delegate, Unión Liberal Convention, 1892. F] Tax judge, Hidalgo, 1878–79; district court judge, San Luis Potosí, 1879–80; judge, Second Correctional District, Mexico City, 1880–81; director, Welfare Department, Secretariat of Gov-

ernment, 1881; ambassador to El Salvador; oficial mayor of the treasury, 1893–1900; *subsecretary* of the treasury, 1900–04, 1905–11. G] Member of the Jockey Club. H] None. I] Son of José Higinio Núñez, lawyer, and Juana Castañares; married Josefina Prida y Arteaga, daughter of industrialist and banker Francisco Macario de Prida Palacios; son Roberto served as his alternate federal deputy, 1908–10; grandson of Francisco Núñez, colonel, and Filomena Góngora. J] None. K] Accompanied *Porfirio Díaz* to Paris, 1911. L] Album; Enc Mex, IX, 459; Linajes, 186–88; Mestre, 245; Rice, 244–45.

Núñez y Domínguez, José de J.
(Deceased March 31, 1959) A] April 27, 1887. B] Papantla, Veracruz. C] Primary studies in Papantla; secondary studies in Puebla; preparatory studies at the National Preparatory School, Mexico City; legal studies, National School of Law; no degree; professor of literature and history, National Preparatory School, National Normal School, National Museum, and the National University. D] *Federal deputy* from the State of Veracruz, Dist. 5, 1912–13. E] None. F] Secretary, National Library, 1914; secretary, National Museum of Anthropology and History, 1924–44; director, National Museum of Anthropology and History, 1944–45; ambassador to Belgium, 1946–48; ambassador to the Dominican Republic, 1949–50; ambassador to Honduras, 1951–52; ambassador to Chile, 1953–59. G] President, Press Association of Mexico, 1912; permanent secretary, Mexican Academy of History; member, Mexican Academy of Language. H] Journalist; founded *El Mercurio Ilustrado*, and *La Semana*; cofounder of *Excélsior*, 1918; director, *Revista de Revistas*, 1915–24; editor, *El Imparcial*; author of numerous historical works. I] Son of José de Jesús Núñez, physician, and Zenaida Domínguez; married Altagracia Córdova; brother Roberto, journalist and director of congressional library. J] None. K] None. L] DBM68, 460; WWM45, 84; Enc Mex, IX, 461; DP70, 1489; Illescas, 426–27; López, 777–78; O'Campo, 258–59; Estrada, 199–201.

O

Obregón González, Joaquín
(Deceased February 12, 1923) A] November 17, 1843. B] San Miguel de Allende, Guanajuato. C] Early education unknown; law degree, University of Guanajuato, 1864. D] *Federal deputy* from the State of Zacatecas, Dist. 6, 1890–92, 1892–94; *governor* of Guanajuato, 1893–1911. E] None. F] *Interim governor* of Guanajuato, 1893. G] Founding member of the Jockey Club, 1881; stockholder, Jockey Club, 1883. H] Successful lawyer. I] Brother of Alberto Obregón González, lawyer; uncle of Teresa Obregón Katholl, wife of lawyer Salvador Reynoso Híjar. J] None. K] None. L] Torres Martínez, 363ff; DP70, 1496; Almanaque de Guanajuato, 131; Mestre, 270; Blue Book, 1901, 89.

Obregón (Salido), Alvaro
(Deceased July 17, 1928) A] February 19, 1880. B] Hacienda de Siquisiva, Navojoa, Sonora. C] Primary studies from older sisters in Huatabampo and Alamos, Sonora; no degree. D] *President* of Mexico, 1920–24. E] President-elect of Mexico, 1928. F] Chief of War Section, Secretariat of Government, State of Sonora, 1913; *secretary* of war, 1916–17. G] None. H] Worked in a flour mill on the Hacienda de Tres Hermanos, Huatabampo, Sonora, 1898–1902, where he eventually became manager; primary schoolteacher, Moroncarit, 1900; employee, flour mill, Navolato, Sinaloa, 1902–06; employee, Valderráin family, Río Maya, 1906–08; purchased own ranch, Quinta Chilla, Río Maya, 1908; farmed chick-peas, Navojoa, 1917–19. I] Son of Francisco Obregón, farmer, and Cenobia Salido; father lost investments after French Intervention because his partner supported the Conservatives; nephew of Bartolomé Salido, prefect of Alamos; brother José, mayor of Huatabampo, 1911; married Refugio Urrea; son Humberto Obregón Urrea was federal deputy from Sonora, 1937–40; daughter María del Refugia married aviator Rafael Ponce de León; second wife, María Tapia; son Alvaro Obregón Tapia was governor of Sonora; nephew of General *Benjamín Hill.*

J] Organized and commanded the 4th Irregular Battalion of Sonora under General Agustín Sanginés against the *Pascual Orozco* rebellion, 1912; rank of lt. colonel, 1912; commander of the garrison, Hermosillo, Sonora, 1913; rank of colonel, February 26, 1913; defeated *Victoriano Huerta's* forces in the battles of Nogales, Cananea, and Naco, 1913; rank of brigadier general, May 13, 1913; rank of brigade general, July 1913; commander of the Army of the Northeast, September 20, 1913; defeated Huerta's forces in the battle of Orendáin, Jalisco, July, 1914; commander-in-chief of operations against the Conventionists, 1914–15; rank of division general, June 29, 1914; defeated *Francisco Villa's* forces in two major battles in Celaya, 1915; attended the convention of Aguascalientes, 1914; supported the Plan of Agua Prieta against *Venustiano Carranza*, 1920. K] Assassinated, Bombilla Restaurant, Mexico City, by José de León Toral. L] DP70, 1495–96; Covarrubias, 267–74; Morales Jiménez, 183–91; Enc Mex, IX, 528; Aguilar Camín, 221.

Olachea Avilés, Agustín
(Deceased April 13, 1974) A] September 3, 1892. B] Todos Santos, San Venancio, Baja California del Sur. C] No formal education. D] None. E] President of the National Executive Committee of PRI, April 26–December 3, 1958. F] *Governor* of Baja California del Sur, 1929–31; *governor* of Baja California del Norte, 1931–35; governor of Baja California del Sur, 1946–52, 1952–56; secretary of national defense, 1958–64. G] Participated in the Cananea mining strike as a teenager, 1906. H] Before the Revolution, worked as a miner. I] Parents were rural laborers; son Agustín Olachea Borbón was director of the Department of Tourism, 1970–73; married Ana María Borbón. J] Joined the Revolution as a private, 1913, under the forces of General *Manuel Diéguez*; head of military operations in Yucatán and Quintana Roo, 1925–26; fought the Yaquis in Sonora, 1926; rank of brigadier general, May 16, 1929; fought against the Escobar rebellion, 1929; commander of the 13th Military Zone, Tepic, Nayarit, 1940–45; commander of the 15th Military Zone, Guadalajara, Jalisco, 1945–46; rank of division general. K] Supported General *Lázaro Cárdenas* for President in 1934. L] HA, 8 Dec. 1958, 25; Peral, 584; Enc Mex, IX, 1977, 569; *Excélsior*, 14 Apr. 1974, 4; HA, 22 Apr. 1974, 19; López, 787.

Olaguíbel y Arista, Carlos de
(Deceased May 3, 1907) A] 1847. B] Puebla. C] Primary studies in Puebla, Puebla; preparatory studies, Colegio San Juan Letrán, Mexico City. D] *Federal deputy* from the State of Guanajuato, Dist. 8, 1886–88; *federal deputy* from the State of Guanajuato, Dist. 4, 1888–90; *federal deputy* from the State of Guanajuato, Dist. 8, 1890–92; *federal deputy* from the State of Guanajuato, Dist. 7, 1892–94; *federal deputy* from the State of Guerrero, Dist. 6, 1894–96; *federal deputy* from the State of Guanajuato, Dist. 6, and the State of Guerrero, Dist. 5, 1896–98; *federal deputy* from the State of Guerrero, Dist. 4, 1900–02; *federal deputy* from the State of Guerrero, Dist. 3, 1902–04; *federal deputy* from the State of Hidalgo, Dist. 1, 1904–06, 1906–07. E] None. F] Tax collector, State of Guanajuato; inspector of maritime and border customshouses; customs official, Matamoros; second official, Secretariat of the Treasury, 1877–78; second official, Secretariat of Foreign Relations; private secretary to Sebastián Lerdo de Tejada. G] None. H] Journalist; co-founder with Trinidad Sánchez Santos of *El País*, 1899. I] Son of Manuel de Olaguíbel, lawyer and judge of the Superior Tribunal of Justice of Mexico; grandson of Francisco Modesto de Olaguíbel, lawyer, senator, and attorney general of Mexico; great-grandson of Hilario de Olaguíbel y Santelices, from Spain; related to *Manuel Gutiérrez Nájera*, poet and federal deputy. J] Joined father briefly in war against French. K] None. L] DP70, 1510; Hombres prominentes, 387–88; Mestre, 228.

Olaguíbel y Arista, Francisco Modesto de
(Deceased December 14, 1924) A] November 6, 1874. B] Mexico City. C] Preparatory studies at the Scientific and Literary Institute of Mexico, Toluca; law degree, Scientific and Literary Institute of Mexico, Toluca, 1900; professor, Scientific and Literary Institute of Mexico, Toluca;

professor of Spanish, Western history, and Mexican history, Normal School for Girls, Toluca; professor, National Preparatory School; professor, School of business Administration, UNAM. D] Local deputy to the state legislature of México; *alternate federal deputy* from the State of México, Dist. 10, and from the State of Michoacán, Dist. 9, 1904–06; *alternate federal deputy* from the State of México, Dist. 3, and the State of Hidalgo, Dist. 7, 1906–08; *federal deputy* from the Federal District, Dist. 6, 1908–10, 1910–12; *federal deputy* from the State of México, Dist. 2, 1912–13; *federal deputy* from the State of México, Dist. 8, 1914–16. E] None. F] Attorney general of Mexico; *subsecretary* of foreign relations, 1913–14. G] None. H] Practicing lawyer, Toluca; journalist; wrote for *El Tribuna, El Clarín, La Gaceta del Gobierno, El Imparcial, El Universal,* and *El Mañana.* I] Son of Manuel de Olaguíbel, lawyer and judge of the Superior Tribunal of Justice of Mexico; grandson of Francisco Modesto de Olagubel, attorney general of Mexico and senator; related to Margarita Gutiérrez Nájera, poet; related to *Manuel Gutiérrez Nájera,* poet and federal deputy. J] None. K] Member of the distinguished group of orators critical of *Francisco I. Madero* in the 1912–13 legislature. L] DP70, 960, 1509–10; Enc Mex, IX, 569; QesQ, 425; María Carreño, 199–200.

Olavarría y Ferrari, Enrique
(Deceased August 10, 1918) A] July 13, 1844. B] Madrid, Spain. C] Preparatory studies in the arts, University of Madrid; professor, National Normal School, Mexico City, 1871–74; professor, National Conservatory, Mexico City. D] *Alternate federal deputy* from the State of Morelos, Dist. 3, 1896–98; *federal deputy* from the Federal District, Dist. 10, 1898–1900, 1900–02; *federal deputy* from the State of Michoacán, Dist. 12, 1902–04, 1904–06, 1906–08; *federal deputy* from the State of Michoacán, Dist. 11, 1908–10; *senator* from Michoacán, 1910–13. E] None. F] None. G] None. H] Moved to Mexico, 1865, and became a journalist; returned to Europe, 1874–78; journalist, Mexico City, 1878– ; novelist; historian. I] Unknown. J] None. K] Member of the

Rebirth literary movement with *Ireneo Paz* and Vicente Riva Palacio, 1869. L] Mestre, 260; Enc Mex, IX, 570; Godoy, 43; Carreño, 251–54.

Olivares, Bonifacio
(Deceased) A] June 5, 1864. B] Irapuato, Guanajuato. C] Primary studies in Guanajuato, Guanajuato; law degree, School of Law, University of Guanajuato; professor of the 5th year, School of Law, University of Guanajuato. D] Local deputy and president, state legislature of Guanajuato; *federal deputy* from the State of Guanajuato, Dist. 3, 1908–10, 1910–12; *federal deputy* from the State of Guanajuato, Dist. 14, 1914–16, member of the Great Committee. E] Director, Corralista party, Guanajuato. F] Syndic, City Council of Guanajuato, 1894–95; adviser, City Council of Guanajuato; supernumerary judge of the Superior Tribunal of Justice of Guanajuato; alternate district court judge. G] None. H] Practicing lawyer; joined the firm of *Joaquín Chico Obregón,* federal deputy from Guanajuato, 1880s. I] Son of Benito Olivares and Juana Ruiz y Blanquete; adopted by *Joaquín Chico Obregón;* related to (probably father of) Francisco Olivares, federal deputy from Guanajuato, 1922–24. J] None. K] None. L] Album.

Orozco, Pascual
(Deceased August 30, 1915) A] January 28, 1882. B] Rancho de San Pascual, San Isidro, Municipio de Guerrero, Chihuahua. C] Primary studies only. D] None. E] None. F] Appointed governor of Chihuahua by *Victoriano Huerta,* but never held post, 1913. G] None. H] Farmed, San Isidro, Chihuahua; employee, father's store, San Isidro; muleteer, Mineral del Río Plata to Sánchez Station and Chihuahua City. I] Son of Pascual Orozco, small businessman, local deputy, and revolutionary; married Refugio Frías. J] Joined *Francisco I. Madero,* November 19, 1910; he and *Francisco Villa* defeated General *Juan N. Navarro,* commander of the federal forces in Ciudad Juárez, 1911; first revolutionary promoted to brigadier general by Madero, 1911; commander of rural forces in Chihuahua, 1911–12; rebelled against Madero, March 3, 1912; defeated

by General Huerta, 1912; recognized Huerta's government, 1913; rank of brigadier general, March 17, 1913; rank of brigade general, November 11, 1913; fought the Constitutionalists in the Nazas Division with General *Salvador R. Mercado*; rank of division general, May 1914. K] In exile in El Paso, Texas, 1914–15; killed by Texas Rangers crossing the Río Bravo near Van Horn, Texas. L] DP70, 1528; Márquez, 220–26; Sec of War, 1914, 20; Almada, 1968, 381–82; Morales Jiménez, 109–12.

Ortega, Melchor
A] January 16, 1896. B] Comonfort, Guanajuato. C] Primary studies in Comonfort; no degree. D] *Federal deputy* from the State of Michoacán, Dist. 11, 1924–26, 1926–28, 1928–30, member of the Great Committee, 1926–28, 1928–30; *federal deputy* from the State of Guanajuato, Dist. 2, 1932–34; *governor* of Guanajuato, 1932–35. E] Secretary of organization of the National Revolutionary party, 1929; special secretary of the National Revolutionary party, 1929–30; secretary of press of the National Revolutionary party, 1930; *president* of the National Executive Committee of the National Revolutionary party, 1933. F] Director, Department of Statistics; general manager, Agricultural and Ejido Banks; manager, National Bank of Cooperative Development; subsecretary of agriculture, 1930. G] None. H] Employee, National Railroads of Mexico; director of repairs, telegraph lines, Bajío. I] From a working-class family; had to leave school for economic reasons; part of *Plutarco Calles's* political group and career ended with Calles's downfall. J] Joined the Constitutionalists, 1914; rejoined the army, 1923, to fight *Adolfo de la Huerta*; rejoined the army, 1929, to oppose Escobar; retired from the army with the rank of colonel, 1929. K] None. L] C de D, 1924–26, 1926–28, 1928–30.

Ortega, Miguel F.
(Deceased) A] October 4, 1887. B] Chilapa (Chilpancingo), Guerrero. C] Preparatory studies in Chilpancingo; law degree, National School of Law, Mexico City, July 19, 1911; professor of business law,

Colegio de San Nicolás, Morelia. D] *Federal deputy* from the State of Guerrero, Dist. 4, 1920–22, member of the Great Committee; *senator* from the State of Guerrero, 1922–24, 1924–26, 1926–28, 1928–30, 1934–40. E] None. F] Judge of the first instance, Iguala, Guerrero; secretary general of government of Tlaxcala; director of the Patent Office, Secretariat of Industry and Commerce; director of the Legal Department, Secretariat of Government. G] None. H] Practicing lawyer. I] Son of Miguel Ortega and Francisca Nava. J] Joined the Constitutionalists; legal adviser, Division of the South; represented at the Convention of Aguascalientes by Fernando Castro, 1914; supported *Alvaro Obregón*, 1920. K] None. L] UNAM, laws, 1906–12, 126.

Ortega Reyes, Manuel
(Deceased November 13, 1908) A] July 1, 1819. B] Oaxaca, Oaxaca. C] Early education unknown; medical degree, School of Medicine, Oaxaca, 1846; rector, Institute of Arts and Sciences of Oaxaca; professor, Military Hospital. D] *Federal deputy* from the State of Chiapas, Dist. 4, 1886–88; local deputy to the state legislature of Chiapas; *alternate senator* from the Federal District, 1890; *senator* from the Federal District, 1900–04, 1904–08, 1908. E] None. F] Director of the Mint, Oaxaca. G] Member, National Academy of Medicine. H] Practicing physician; author. I] Father of Manuel Ortega Reyes, physician. J] Director, Military Hospital. K] None. L] DP70, 1534; C de S, 1900–02, 6; UNAM, law, 1880–91, 144.

Ortiz (Arriola), Andrés
(Deceased February 5, 1945) A] November 2, 1890. B] Chihuahua, Chihuahua. C] Primary and preparatory studies in Chihuahua; engineering degree in the field of hydraulics and topography, National School of Engineering, National University of Mexico, November 1913. D] Local deputy in Chihuahua, 1917–18; *federal deputy* from the State of Chihuahua, Dist. 1, 1918; *provisional governor* of Chihuahua, 1918–20; *governor* of Chihuahua, 1930–31. E] None. F] Chief and founder of the Department of Bridges and Highways, Secretariat of Communication,

1916–17; director of the Trolley Company of Mexico City, 1918; director general of the National Railroads of Mexico, 1944–45; member of the Committee for the Administration and Inspection of Foreign Properties, 1941–44. G] None. H] Author of the National Highway Law. I] Son of journalist Pablo Ortiz and Regina Arriola; grandson of Dr. Guillermo Ortiz, imperial prefect of the Department of Jiménez, Chihuahua. J] Remained loyal to *Venustiano Carranza*, 1920. K] In exile in the United States, 1920; as provisional governor of Chihuahua put a price of 50,000 pesos for the capture of *Francisco Villa*; originally supported by *Luis León* for governor of Chihuahua, 1930, but betrayed León's political program. L] DP70, 1534; Peral, 596; HA, 10 Mar. 1944; López, 802; Enc Mex, X, 1977, 10; Almada, 539; Almada, 1968, 383–84.

Ortiz Garza, Nazario S.
A] December 31, 1893. B] Saltillo, Coahuila. C] Primary studies in Public School No. 2, Saltillo (completed 4th year); preparatory studies at the Ateneo Fuente, Saltillo; no degree. D] Councilman of Torreón, 1920, 1921–22; mayor of Torreón, 1922; mayor of Torreón, 1927–28; local deputy to the state legislature of Coahuila, 1925; president of the state legislature; mayor of Torreón, Coahuila, 1927–28; *governor* of Coahuila, 1930–34; senator from the State of Coahuila, 1934–40. E] Campaign director for General *Manuel Pérez Treviño* for governor of Coahuila, 1924. F] Appointed mayor of Saltillo, Coahuila, 1928; appointed mayor of Torreón, 1926; director general of the National Foodstuffs Program (CONASUPO), 1943–46; secretary of agriculture, 1946–52. G] President of the National Association of Vintners, 1954–63, 1969–71. H] Began working at age 14; businessman. I] Protégé of Manuel Pérez Treviño, president of the National Revolutionary Party; father a small businessman; married Rebeca Rodríguez. J] Fought with General *Francisco Murguía* without military rank, 1915–17; purveyor of military trains, Chihuahua, Chihuahua, 1917. K] Won election as federal deputy, 1923, but did not hold office; the *New York Times* claimed that the government expro-

priated his landholdings in Tampico in 1953 in a move against former Alemanistas. L] HA, 5 Nov. 1943, 34; HA, 6 Dec. 1946, 5; HA, 26 Jan. 1951; Peral, 598; NYT, 25 June 1953, 17; letter; Enc Mex, X, 1977, 14–15; López, 804.

Ortiz Hernán, Gustavo
A] 1901. B] San Luis Potosí, San Luis Potosí. C] Early education unknown; public accounting degree, School of Business and Administration, UNAM. D] None. E] *Secretary* of press of the National Executive Committee of the National Revolutionary party, 1934–35. F] Director, Government Printing Office, 1935–39; consul, Philadelphia, 1939–45; consul, San Antonio, 1945–47; chargé d'affaires, Austria, 1951–52; director general of tourism, 1953–56; minister to Israel, 1956–58; ambassador to Chile, 1959–64. G] None. H] Journalist; founder and director of *Gaceta Cultural de México*, 1925; editorial staff, *La Batalla*, 1926; editorial staff, *La Prensa*, 1927; editorialist and columnist, *El Nacional*, 1927–29; editor-in-chief, *El Nacional*, 1929–35; founder and publisher, *México Nuevo*, 1936; director general of *Novedades*, 1947; director general of *La Prensa*, 1948; subdirector, *El Nacional*, 1969–71; director, *El Universal Gráfico*, 1972–74; director of *Hoy*, 1974–. I] Unknown. J] None. K] Awarded the National Prize in Journalism, 1935. L] Enc Mex, X, 15–16.

Ortiz Monasterio e Yrisarri, Angel
(Deceased 1922) A] January 15, 1849. B] Mexico City. C] Primary studies in Spain; graduated from the San Fernando Military College, Cádiz, Spain; founded the naval colleges at Campeche and Mazatlán. D] *Alternate federal deputy* from the State of Guanajuato, Dist. 5, 1886–88; *federal deputy* from the State of Guanajuato, Dist. 16, 1888–90; *federal deputy* from the State of Guanajuato, Dist. 15, 1890–92, 1892–94; *federal deputy* from the State of México, Dist. 16, 1894–96; *federal deputy* from the State of Aguascalientes, Dist. 4, 1900–02; *alternate federal deputy* from the State of Guanajuato, Dist. 13, 1902–04; *federal deputy* from the State of Oaxaca, Dist. 7, 1904–06, 1906–08. E] None. F] Director, Naval

Department, Secretariat of War, 1885; presidential chief of staff, 1895–96, 1899; consul to Belize, 1898; naval attaché, Washington, D.C. G] None. H] Founded the Trans-Atlantic-Mexican Company. I] Father of Juan Ortiz Monasterio Popham, prominent banker; married Marie Popham; father of Francisco Ortiz Monasterio Popham, diplomat. J] Joined the Spanish navy as a 2nd marine guard, 1864; rank of 1st marine guard, 1868; fought in Spain under General Juan Prim, 1868; rank of sergeant, 1870; in Cuban campaign, 1870–73; sent to Guinea, 1874; participated in the Carlist War, 1875; rank of lieutenant, 1876; moved to Mexico and joined the navy, 1878; commander of the corvette *Zaragoza*; commander of the *Liberty*, *Zaragoza*, *Independence*, and *Mexico*; commander of the first Mexican vessel to sail around the world, 1896–97; rank of brigadier general in the navy, March 23, 1896. K] Saved President *Porfiro Díaz* from an assassination attempt, September 16, 1897. L] DP70, 15439; Dir social, 1935, 275–76; Godoy, 134–35; Enc Mex, X, 17; Sec of War, 1900, 297.

Ortiz Rubio, Pascual
(Deceased November 4, 1963) A] March 10, 1877. B] Morelia, Michoacán. C] Preparatory studies at the Colegio de San Nicolás; topographical engineering degree, National School of Mines, Mexico City, 1902; postgraduate work, Columbia University, New York City. D] Local deputy to the state legislature of Michoacán; *federal deputy* from the State of Michoacán, 1912–13; *governor* of Michoacán, 1917–20; *president* of Mexico, 1930–32. E] Opposed the re-election of President *Porfirio Díaz* with *José Inocencio Lugo*, 1896; supported *Miguel Silva* for governor of Michoacán, 1911–12. F] Director, Government Stamp Bureau, 1914; director of enemy properties, 1914; director, engineer supply depot, Mexico City, 1916; director, Department of Military Engineers, Secretariat of War, 1917; *secretary* of communications and public works, 1920, 1920–21; ambassador to Germany, 1924; ambassador to Brazil, 1926; *secretary* of government, 1928. G] None. H] Manager, Mexican Oil Company, 1935. I] Son of Pascual Ortiz de Ayala y Huerta, judge, al-

ternate senator, and rector of the Colegio de San Nicolás, and Leonor Rubio; son Pascual married María de Lourdes Downy, daughter of the director general of Nicaragua Light and Power, whose daughter married the son of President José López y Portillo; married Josefina Ortiz y Ortiz Roa, daughter of a lawyer and large landholder. J] Joined *Francisco I. Madero* as a 1st captain, 1911; joined the Constitutionalists as a military engineer, 1913–14; rank of brigadier general, April 30, 1915; supported the Plan of Agua Prieta, 1920; rank of brigade general, 1920; commander, Western Division, 1920. K] Imprisoned by *Victoriano Huerta's* government, 1913; resigned from the presidency because of *Plutarco Elías Calles's* interference. L] Enc Mex, X, 19; WWM45, 88, Moreno, 345–49; Romero Flores, 40–41; Dicc mich, 321.

Osuna (Hinojosa), Andrés
(Deceased 1957) A] June 27, 1872. B] Ciudad Mier, Tamaulipas. C] Primary studies under his mother on La Meca ranch; completed primary in Monterrey; teaching certificate, Night Normal School, Monterrey; teaching certificate, Normal School of Nuevo León, Monterrey, October 6, 1892; teacher, Methodist mission, Monterrey, 1892; professor, Normal School of Saltillo, 1894–98; director, Normal School of Saltillo, 1898–1909; graduated from Bridgewater State Normal School, Bridgewater, Massachusetts; M.A. degree, Vanderbilt University, 1912–15; assistant professor of Spanish, Vanderbilt University and Peabody College for Teachers, Nashville, Tennessee, 1912–15. D] None. E] None. F] Director general of primary education, Saltillo, Coahuila, 1899–1909; director general of education, Federal District, 1915–18; *provisional governor* of Tamaulipas, 1918–19; director general of education, Nuevo León, 1927–32. G] None. H] Official translator, Methodist Episcopal Church South, Nashville, Tennessee, 1909–15; manager, publishing firm, Mexico City, 1920–26; managed property, 1945; textbook author. I] Son of Félix Osuna, rancher, and Matilde Hinojosa, a teacher; father of Eugenio E. Osuna Treviño, teacher and landowner, and Miguel Osuna Treviño, public works

engineer. J] Joined the Constitutionalists, 1913. K] Deposed as provisional governor by Congress. L] Enc Mex, X, 26; WWM45, 89; DP70, 1544; QesQ, 1952, 190.

P

Pacheco (Villalobos), Carlos
(Deceased September 15, 1891) A] October 16, 1839. B] San Nicolás del Guerrero, Municipio de Balleza, Chihuahua. C] Primary studies in Hidalgo de Parral; no degree. D] Federal deputy from the State of Puebla, 1870–72; senator from Chihuahua, 1882; *governor* of Chihuahua, 1884; *senator* from the State of Chihuahua, 1888–91. E] None. F] Director of mails, Puebla, 1867; tax administrator of Puebla, Puebla, 1867–70; governor and military commander of Puebla, 1876–77; governor and military commander of Morelos, 1878–79; secretary of war and navy, 1879–80; governor of the Federal District, 1880–81; *secretary* of development, 1881–91. G] None. H] Went into business after completing primary studies; worked for Juan Cordero's firm, Chihuahua, 1855; businessman, 1856–57; self-employed, 1872–76. I] Son of Carlos Pacheco, lawyer, and Altagracia Villalobos; brother Gustavo died fighting for the Liberals. J] Joined the Liberal forces in Chihuahua under Colonel José Esteban Coronado, January 15, 1855; fought under General *Ignacio Pesqueira* in the Three Years' War; joined the Liberal forces as a 2nd lieutenant, national guard, January 13, 1858; 2nd lieutenant, national guard, Sinaloa, 1861; promoted to 1st lieutenant by *Porfirio Díaz*, September 1, 1863, after opposing the French in Oaxaca; rank of captain, March 21, 1864; captured by French forces under General Bazaine, 1865–66; rank of lt. colonel, April 2, 1867; supported the Plan of La Noria, 1871; supported the Plan of Tuxtepec, 1876; rank of colonel, July 1, 1877; rank of brigadier general, November 10, 1879; rank of brigade general, May 8, 1881; rank of division general, March 31, 1891. K] Arrested for supporting revolutionary activities, 1858; lost arm and leg in the Battle of Puebla, April 2, 1867. L] Almada, 1968, 387; Almanaque de Puebla, 127; Márquez,

241–45; Pavía, 39–46; Enc Mex, X, 41–42; Almada, 385–93; Hombres prominentes, 31–35; Mestre, 175; Armijo, 455–57.

Padilla, Angel M.
(Deceased 1905) A] 1837. B] Morelia, Michoacán. C] Early education unknown; law degree, Colegio de San Nicolás, Morelia; professor, Colegio de San Nicolás. D] *Alternate federal deputy* from the State of Querétaro, Dist. 3, 1886–88; *federal deputy* from the State of Michoacán, Dist. 4, 1888–90; *federal deputy* from the State of Michoacán, Dist. 3, 1890–92; *federal deputy* from the State of Michoacán, Dist. 9, 1892–94; *federal deputy* from the State of Michoacán, Dist. 10, 1894–96, 1896–98, 1898–1900; *federal deputy* from the State of Michoacán, Dist. 2, 1900–02. E] None. F] Judge of the Superior Tribunal of Justice of Michoacán, 1867; interim governor of Michoacán, 1889. G] None. H] Practicing lawyer; newspaper publisher. I] Married Violante Valdovinos; father of *Manuel Padilla Valdovinos*, justice of the Supreme Court, 1923–26. J] Persecuted by the Conservatives and nearly executed during the French Intervention; opposed the Plan of Tuxtepec, supporting Lerdo de Tejada, 1876. K] Opposed *Porfirio Díaz* in his newspaper *El Renacimiento*. L] Dicc mich., 325.

Padilla (Peñalosa), Ezequiel
(Deceased September 6, 1971) A] December 31, 1890. B] Coyuca de Catalán, Guerrero. C] Secondary schooling at the Normal School, Chilpancingo, Guerrero; teaching certificate; preparatory studies at the National Preparatory School, Mexico City; legal studies, National School of Law, National University of Mexico, on a government scholarship; law degree, 1912; founding member of a group of students who formed the Escuela Libre de Derecho; studies at the Sorbonne, Paris, on a scholarship from the Secretariat of Education, 1913–14; advanced studies, Columbia University, New York, 1916; professor of constitutional law, UNAM, 1928. D] *Federal deputy* from the State of Guerrero, Dist. 8, 1922–24; *federal deputy* from the State of Guerrero, Dist. 4, 1924–26; *fed-*

eral deputy from the State of Guerrero, Dist. 1, 1932–34; senator from the Federal District, 1934–40; senator from the State of Guerrero, 1964–70. E] State delegate of the Mexican Revolutionary party in Guerrero; candidate for president of Mexico of the Mexican Democratic party, 1946. F] Attorney general of Mexico, 1928; *secretary* of public education, 1928–30; minister to Hungary and to Italy, 1930–32; secretary of foreign relations, 1940–45. G] None. H] Author of several books. I] Knew Francisco Gaxiola and Ernesto Enríquez Coyro in preparatory school and at the Escuela Libre de Derecho; student companion of *Emilio Portes Gil* at the Escuela Libre de Derecho; father, Mariano Padilla, an impoverished lawyer in Coyuca de Catalán; mother, Evarista Peñalosa, was a schoolteacher; married María G. Couttolenc; son Ezequiel was director general of Banca Confía, 1982. J] Joined the Revolution; served under *Emiliano Zapata* as a common soldier; served as a secretary to several generals fighting under *Francisco Villa*; fled Mexico in 1916 after Villa's defeat. K] Padilla received government scholarships for all of his professional education, beginning with a scholarship to study at normal school, Chilpancingo, Guerrero; answered President *Plutarco Elías Calles*'s State of the Union address, 1925; precandidate for the PRI nomination for president, 1945; self-exile in Cuba and the United States until 1922; Padilla's family accused of owning illegal amounts of land in Guerrero by the secretary general of the state National Peasant Federation, August 1972. L] WWM45, 89; DBM68, 474; EBW, 14; HA, 13 Sept. 1971, 21; letters; *Excélsior,* 29 Aug. 1972, 27; Peral, 607; Enc Mex, X, 1977, 73; López, 817; HA, 8 Dec. 1944, 5.

Padilla (Valdovinos), Manuel

(Deceased 1951) A] February 2, 1880. B] Morelia, Michoacán. C] Primary studies under Joaquín Campos and Timoteo Carrasco, 1885–90; second year of preparatory studies at the Institute of Toluca; remainder of preparatory studies at the Colegio de San Nicolás; law degree, School of Law, Colegio de San Nicolás, 1904; cofounder of the School of Law, Colegio de San Nicolás, 1901. D] *Federal*

deputy from the State of Michoacán, Dist. 7, 1912–13, member of the Renovation Bloc and the Great Committee; *federal deputy* from the State of Michoacán, Dist. 2, 1920–22, 1922–24. E] None. F] *Secretary* of the treasury, Convention government, 1915; president, Superior Tribunal of Justice of the Federal District, 1920–23; *justice* of the Supreme Court, 1923–25, 1933–34; *president* of the Supreme Court, 1925–26; head, Department of the Federal District, 1932; director, Legal Department, Public Health, 1934–38. G] None. H] Opened a law practice in Mexico City, 1905; editor, *El Bohemio,* as a student; journalist; practicing lawyer. I] Son of *Angel Padilla,* federal deputy and interim governor of Michoacán, and Violante Valdovinos; married María Bamery. J] Dir social, 131; Andrade, 431–32; Dicc mich, 325.

Palacios Macedo, Miguel

A] 1898. B] Tulancingo, Hidalgo. C] Early education unknown; law degree, National School of Law, UNAM; professor of American history, Free Preparatory School, 1917; studies in political economy, Sorbonne, Paris, 1924–28; professor, National Preparatory School; professor, National School of Law. D] None. E] Remained loyal to *Adolfo de la Huerta,* accompanied him to New York, served as treasury secretary to his movement, 1923–24; leading figure in *José Vasconcelos*'s presidential campaign, 1929; led a protest movement from Bellas Artes to Chapultepec Park in support of Vasconcelos, 1929. F] Private secretary to the subsecretary of the treasury, 1920–21; chief, Department of Legislation, Secretariat of the Treasury, 1921; subsecretary of industry and commerce, 1923. G] President of the Federation of University Students, 1919–20; secretary general of the Student Society of the Law School with *Narciso Bassols.* H] In law practice with *Manuel Gómez Morín,* founder of the National Action party, 1939. I] Grandson of Colonel Miguel Palacios, liberal officer; son of General José María Palacios, physician, and chief of medical services for the Division of the North; mother was sister of *Miguel Macedo,* subsecretary of government, 1904–11; brother of José Palacios Macedo, dean of the National School of

Medicine, 1934. J] None. K] Exile in France, 1924–28, returning to support Vasconcelos; credited with preventing police violence in the Bellas Artes protest march by singing the national anthem, 1929. L] Letters.

Palafox, Manuel
(Deceased) A] 1876. B] Morelos. C] Early education unknown; teaching certificate as a primary school teacher; no degree. D] None. E] None. F] *Secretary* of agriculture, Convention government, 1915. G] None. H] Employee, Santa Clara hacienda sugar mill, owned by *Joaquín García Pimentel.* I] Close to his employer, Joaquín García Pimentel. J] Supported *Emiliano Zapata,* 1912–14; supported *Alvaro Obregón,* 1920; rank of brigadier general; remained in army until death. K] Prisoner of the government, 1911; tried to get his employer to donate money to Zapata's cause. L] López González, 189–90.

Palavicini, Félix P.
(Deceased February 10, 1952) A] March 31, 1881. B] Teapa, Tabasco. C] Completed primary studies, 1892; topographical engineering degree, Juárez Institute, Villahermosa, 1901; studies, Conservatory of Arts Metiers, Paris; normal school teacher, 1906; scholarship from *Justo P. Sierra* to study in Europe, 1906–07; in charge of organizing industrial schools, 1907; director, Industrial School for Orphans, 1911. D] *Federal deputy* from the State of Tabasco, Dist. 1, 1912–13; *constitutional deputy* from the Federal District, Dist. 5, 1916–17. E] Founder and director of Anti-Reelectionist newspaper and secretary of the party, Mexico City, 1909–10. F] Oficial mayor in charge of the Secretariat of Public Education, 1914; *secretary* of public education, 1914–16; special ambassador, Europe, 1920; ambassador to Argentina, 1938–42. G] None. H] Journalist; author; founder of *El Precursor,* Villahermosa, Tabasco, 1903; editor, *El Partido Republicano,* Mexico City, 1908; founder and director of *El Universal Ilustrado;* founder and director of *El Universal Gráfico;* founder of *Todo,* Mexico City; founder of *El Día,* Mexico City; founder of

El Universal, 1916–23. I] Son of Juan Vicente Palavicini and Beatriz Loría; mother supported family by sewing after father died; married Belina Hernández; daughter Julieta, an artist; daughter Laura, a poet; son Manuel, lawyer and successful businessman, married to Berta Viezca. J] None. K] Jailed by *Victoriano Huerta,* 1913–14; resided in the United States, 1918. L] Almanaque de Tabasco, 163; Santamaría, 109–10; Morales Jiménez, 281–86; WWM45, 90–91; Enc Mex, X, 89–90; López, 820; DP70, 1562; Dir social, 238–39.

Palazuelos Léycegui, Pedro
A] October 15, 1891. B] Veracruz, Veracruz. C] Secondary studies, Business Academy, Jalapa; preparatory studies, Preparatory School of Veracruz, with an emphasis on business; no degree. D] Mayor of Veracruz, 1923–24, 1926; *federal deputy* from the State of Veracruz, Dist. 17, 1926–28, 1928–30; federal deputy from the State of Veracruz, Dist. 13, 1934–37. E] None. F] Chief of the Immigration Service, Veracruz, 1926; director of the *Diario Oficial,* 1931; secretary general of government of Baja California del Norte, 1932. G] None. H] Unknown. I] Unknown. J] Unknown. K] None. L] C de D, 1926–28, 1928–30.

Paliza, Ruperto L.
(Deceased June 23, 1939) A] March 27, 1857. B] Mexico City. C] Primary studies, Reforma School; preparatory studies, National Preparatory School, Mexico City; medical degree, National School of Medicine, UNAM, July 10, 1880; reorganized the Colegio Civil of Sinaloa for Governor *Mariano Martínez de Castro;* rector, Colegio Civil of Sinaloa, 1893; professor, Colegio Civil of Sinaloa. D] Member of the City Council of Culiacán, Sinaloa (seven years); local deputy to the state legislature of Sinaloa. E] None. F] Supernumerary judge of the Superior Tribunal of Justice of Sinaloa; *governor* of Sinaloa, 1911, 1912. G] None. H] Physician, Juárez Hospital, Mexico City; physician to the poor. I] Father of Juan L. Paliza, engineer and professor at the National Politechnic Institute. J] None. K] None. L] None.

Palomino, Guillermo
(Deceased May 12, 1889) A] November 16, 1834. B] Veracruz, Veracruz. C] Early education unknown; no degree. D] Federal deputy from Yucatán; federal deputy from Veracruz; federal deputy from Sinaloa; senator from Tabasco, 1882–84; *governor* of Yucatán, 1886–89. E] None. F] None. G] None. H] None. I] Unknown. J] Career army officer; naval aide, March 1, 1853–54; joined the infantry, Liberal forces, as a 2nd lieutenant, December 5, 1854; officer, infantry battalion, Acayucán, Veracruz, 1854–55; rank of 1st lieutenant, artillery, 1856; participated in the attack on San Juan de Ulloa, 1856; commander, line artillery unit, Veracruz, 1858–60; rank of 2nd captain, January 1, 1860; fought in the siege of Veracruz, 1860; rank of 1st captain, March 29, 1860; commander, Perote Artillery, 1861; second-in-command, artillery, Army of the East, 1862–63; captured in Puebla by the French, May 17, 1863, but escaped in Orizaba; commander of the Jalapa Artillery, 1863; staff officer, Costa de Sotavento, 1863–64; rank of lt. colonel, March 19, 1864; commanding general of artillery under General *Porfirio Díaz*, May 19, 1864–February 9, 1865; fought in the siege of Oaxaca, 1865; captured by the French with Porfirio Díaz, whom he helped escape, 1865; exchanged for French prisoners, with *Juan de la Luz Enríquez*, 1866; adjutant to General Díaz, March, 1866; commander of artillery in the east, 1866–67; commander of the Army of the East, 1867; rank of colonel, January 31, 1870; rank of brigadier general, September 14, 1872; fought against rebels, Peto, Yucatán, 1873; commander of federal forces, Yucatán. K] None. L] Hombres prominentes, 221–22; Pasquel, liberals, 285–88; Mestre, 165.

Pani (Arteaga), Alberto J.
(Deceased 1955) A] June 12, 1878. B] Aguascalientes, Aguascalientes. C] Primary studies, French Women's School, Aguascalientes; preparatory studies, Institute of Sciences, Aguascalientes, Aguascalientes; engineering degree, National School of Engineering, 1902; fellowship, state government of Aguascalientes, to study in Mexico City; professor, water

routes and hydraulic works, National School of Engineering; rector of the Popular University of Mexico, 1912–22. D] None. E] Candidate for federal deputy from the 1st Dist. of Aguascalientes, from the Liberal party, 1912, but lost; founded the Student Democratic Education Group to support *Francisco I. Madero* for president, 1911. F] *Subsecretary* of public education and fine arts, 1911–12; director general of public works, Federal District, 1912–13; treasurer general of Mexico, 1915; director general, National Railroads of Mexico, 1915; *secretary* of industry and commerce, 1917–18; *ambassador* to France, 1918–20; *secretary* of foreign relations, 1921–23; *secretary* of the treasury, 1923–27; ambassador to Spain and Portugal, 1931–32; *secretary* of the treasury, 1932–33. G] None. H] Practicing engineer; in practice with José R. Calderón, uncle of *José Vasconcelos*; engineer, Valley of México; chief construction engineer, Legislative Palace, Mexico City; managing director of the Hotel Construction Company, 1933–34. I] Son of Julio Pani, engineer and federal deputy, and Paz Arteaga, who inherited large landholdings; married Esther de Alba, granddaughter of President Manuel de la Peña y Peña; brother of Arturo Pani, consul general, France, 1924 and architect; uncle of prominent businessman and winner of the National Prize in Fine Arts, Mario Pani; grandson of Ricardo Pani, physician, from Florence, Italy, and Mónica Letechipia; maternal grandson of Camilo Arteaga, physician and cabinet minister in the administrations of Comonfort and Juárez; mother related to Gabino Barreda; daughter Consuelo married Diego Covarrubias, nephew of mathematician Francisco Díaz Covarrubias; mentor to many prominent intellectuals and politicians, including Martín Luis Guzmán, *Genaro Estrada*, and *Marte R. Gómez*. J] None. K] One of three names presented by *Plutarco Elías Calles* to congress for president after *Pascual Ortiz Rubio* resigned, 1932. L] WWM45, 91; Enc Mex, X, 116; López, 824.

Pankhurst (Cuéllar), Eduardo G.
(Deceased July 5, 1908) A] April 10, 1840. B] Zacatecas, Zacatecas. C] Primary studies in Zacatecas; secondary and pre-

paratory studies, Concillar Seminary of Guadalajara, Jalisco; law degree, National School of Law, Mexico City, 1861, left school to fight in the War of the Reform, 1858–59; professor of logic, Institute of Sciences, Zacatecas; professor of law, National School of Law, 1876. D] Member of the City Council, Zacatecas, 1861; local deputy to the state legislature of Zacatecas; federal deputy from the State of Zacatecas, 1867, 1875–77; *alternate federal deputy* from the State of Sinaloa, Dist. 4, 1890–92; *senator* from the State of Zacatecas, 1902–04; *governor* of Zacatecas, 1904–08. E] None. F] Editor, official paper, State of Zacatecas, 1862; tax agent, treasury of the State of Zacatecas, 1862–64; adviser to the treasurer of the State of Zacatecas; judge of the Superior Tribunal of Justice of the Federal District, 1867, 1876–79; secretary general of government of the State of Zacatecas, 1875; secretary of government, 1879–80; justice of the Supreme Court, 1880. G] None. H] Practicing lawyer; published *Album Zacateno*, against the French Intervention, 1864. I] Son of Jaime Guillermo Pankhurst, engineer and naturalized Mexican, and Margarita Cuéllar. J] Fought in the War of Reform, 1858–59, under Liberal colonel Miguel Cruz Aedo; supported Plan of Tuxtepec as a federal deputy, 1876. K] Imprisoned and almost executed for opposing the empire, 1865. L] Album; Enc Mex, X, 118; Mestre, 232.

Pardo (Sabariego), Emilio
(Deceased January 9, 1911) A] 1850. B] Mexico City. C] Early education unknown; law degree, National School of Law, 1871; fellowship, 5th year of law school, 1868–69; professor, National School of Law, Mexico City; professor of business law, School of Business, 1899. D] *Alternate federal deputy* from the Federal District, Dist. 2, 1888–90, under *José Y. Limantour; federal deputy* from the State of Hidalgo, Dist. 4, 1890–92; *federal deputy* from the State of Hidalgo, Dist. 10, 1892–94, 1894–96, and from the State of México, Dist. 11; *federal deputy* from the Federal District, Dist. 11, 1896–98; *federal deputy* from the Federal District, Dist. 2, 1898–1900, 1900–02; *federal deputy* from the Federal District,

Dist. 4, 1902–04; *senator* from Tlaxcala, 1904–06, 1906–08, 1910–12. E] Unión Liberal delegate. F] Judge, 2nd and 5th divisions, District Court, Mexico City, 1891; ambassador to Belgium and Low Countries, 1902; ambassador to Guatemala and El Salvador, 1909. G] None. H] Director, International and Mortgage Bank of Mexico, 1909–11. I] Son of Manuel Pardo and Rosaura Sabariega; brother Rafael, federal deputy from the State of México, 1900–04; father of Emilio Pardo y Aspe, justice of the Supreme Court, 1941–47; son-in-law of *Francisco de P. Aspe*, senator from Veracruz, 1890–1914; married Enriqueta Aspe. J] None. K] None. L] UNAM, law, 1869, 29–30; 1906–12, 43; Rice, 245; Mestre, 239.

Parra, Porfirio
(Deceased July 5, 1912) A] February 26, 1854. B] Chihuahua, Chihuahua. C] Primary studies in Chihuahua; secondary and preparatory studies, Literary Institute of Chihuahua, 1864–71; completed preparatory studies on a scholarship from the state government at the National Preparatory School, 1870–72, where he placed first in all his classes; medical studies, National School of Medicine, 1873–77, graduating February 9, 1878; professor by opposition in world history and Mexican history, Secondary School for Girls, Mexico City, 1871; professor of hygiene and medicine, National Conservatory, 1877; professor of logic, National Preparatory School, 1878–80; professor of the second course in mathematics, National School of Agriculture, 1881; professor by opposition in physiology, National School of Medicine, 1879; professor of external pathology, National School of Medicine, 1882–86; professor of descriptive anatomy, National School of Medicine, 1887–98; director, National Preparatory School, 1912. D] Alternate federal deputy from the State of Chihuahua, in functions, 1882–84; *federal deputy* from the State of Chihuahua, Dist. 2, 1886–88; *alternate federal deputy* from the State of Chihuahua, Dist. 16, 1888–90; *alternate federal deputy* from the State of Chihuahua, Dist. 1, 1894–96; *alternate federal deputy* from the State of Chihuahua, Dist. 2, 1896–98; *federal deputy* from the State

of Hidalgo, Dist. 12, 1900–02; *federal deputy* from the State of Chihuahua, Dist. 6, 1902–04, 1904–06, 1906–08; *federal deputy* from the State of Chihuahua, Dist. 8, 1908–10; *senator* from Aguascalientes, 1910–12. E] None. F] None. G] None. H] Intern, San Andrés Hospital, under Rafael Lavista, 1874; poet; journalist; wrote for *El Universal*; founded *El Método* and *El Positivismo*; novelist; surgeon, Juárez Hospital, Mexico City, 1880–88. I] Disciple of leading 19th-century educator, Gabino Barreda. J] None. K] None. L] Almada, 1968, 396; Mestre, 243; Godoy, 244; Enc Mex, X, 148; Puente, 59–62; Márquez, 124–30; Carreño, 204–05; Armijo, 143–44.

Parres Guerrero, José G.
(Deceased July 5, 1949) A] December 15, 1889. B] Real Mineral del Monte, Hidalgo. C] Primary studies in Real Mineral del Monte; secondary studies at Real Mineral del Monte and the Liceo Hidalgo, Pachuca, Hidalgo; preparatory studies at the Scientific and Literary Institute of Hidalgo, Pachuca; medical degree, National School of Medicine, National University of Mexico, internship as a Zapatista, 1911–14; director general of rural agricultural schools. D] *Governor* of Morelos, 1920–23. E] None. F] Oficial mayor of agriculture, 1924; subsecretary of agriculture, 1924–27; *subsecretary* in charge of the Secretariat of Agriculture, 1927–28; subsecretary of agriculture and livestock, 1933–34; subsecretary of agriculture and livestock, 1934–37; secretary of agriculture and livestock, August 16, 1937–November 30, 1940; adviser to the National Agrarian Council, 1932; president of the National Irrigation Commission; executive member of the National Irrigation Commission, 1940–46; adviser to President *Manuel Avila Camacho*, 1940–46. G] Secretary general of the Zapatista Front. H] Practicing physician, 1914. I] Son of Adrián Parres and Concepción Guerrero. J] Joined *Emiliano Zapata's* forces 1911; head of a brigade in the Army of the South, 1916; head of sanitary services for the Army of the South, 1916–18. K] Removed from the governorship of Morelos by a leading Zapatista, General De la O; resigned from post as subsecretary of agriculture to run for the governorship of Hidalgo, 1928, but not selected as the candidate; investigators from the Secretariat of Government considered Parres an honest governor of Morelos. L] EBW, 186; Peral, 617; Enc Mex, V, 44; DP70, 1088; Gruening, 659; QesQ; Enc Mex, X, 1977, 148–49; Pérez López, 341–42; López González, 195–96.

Pastrana Jaimes, David
(Deceased April 7, 1953) A] December 29, 1884. B] Mayanalan, Municipio de Tepecoacuilco, Guerrero. C] Early education unknown; legal studies, Colegio de San Nicolás, Morelia, Michoacán, graduating April 6, 1908. D] *Constitutional deputy* from the State of Puebla, Dist. 5, 1916–17; *federal deputy* from the State of Guerrero, Dist. 7, 1918–20. E] None. F] Secretary of the Committee to Reform the Civil Code, Morelia, Michoacán, 1909; judge of the first instance, Chilpancingo, Guerrero, 1910; public defender and agent of the Ministerio Público, Mexico City, 1911; secretary, 1st and 2nd judicial districts, Mexico City, 1912–13; private secretary to the secretary of justice, Eduardo Preciat Castillo, 1914; oficial mayor, Department of Justice of the secretary general of government of the State of Puebla, 1916; oficial mayor of the Supreme Court, 1919; district and circuit court judge, 1925–36; director, Legal Department, Secretariat of Health, 1936; judge of the first instance, 1942; judge, Tax Court, 1953. G] Executive secretary, National Agrarian Commission, 1918; director, Legal Section, National Agrarian Commisson, 1920. H] Practicing lawyer. I] Unknown. J] Military adviser to General Juan Lechuga; rank of colonel, Constitutionalist forces, 1915; supported *Pablo González*, 1920. K] None. L] C de D, 1918–20.

Patoni, Carlos
(Deceased) A] September 15, 1853. B] Mineral de Guanacevi, Durango. C] Early education unknown; engineering degree, United States. D] *Governor* of Durango, 1912–13. E] None. F] *Secretary* of development, Convention government, 1915. G] None. H] Topographical engineer, Durango; coauthored a map of Durango with *Pastor Rouaix*, 1905; bota-

nist. I] Son of General José María Patoni, governor of Durango; grandson of Juan B. Patoni, Spanish miner and geologist, and Mercedes Sánchez; daughter Guadalupe Patoni de Rueda, director of the Normal School of Durango. J] None. K] In the United States, 1913–14. L] Rouaix, 310–11.

Paz, Ireneo
(Deceased November 4, 1924) A] July 3, 1836. B] Guadalajara, Jalisco. C] Preparatory studies, Conciliar Seminary of Guadalajara, 1849–51, under Antonio Alcocer; law degree, National School of Law, Mexico City, 1861. D] Member of the City Council of Mexico City; senator from the State of México, 1876–78; *federal deputy* from the State of Jalisco, Dist. 16, 1886–88, 1888–90, 1890–92, 1892–94, 1894–96, 1896–98; *federal deputy* from the State of Jalisco, 1900–02, 1902–04, 1904–06, 1906–08, 1908–10. E] None. F] Syndic, City Council of Guadalajara; judge, Colima; secretary general of government, Colima, Sinaloa, Jalisco, and San Luis Potosí. G] President, Associated Press of Mexico. H] Founder and editor of *La Patria*; poet; novelist; historian. I] Father died when he was a boy; had to work as a laborer to put himself through school; father of Octavio Paz Solórzano, Zapatista, lawyer, and federal deputy, 1920–22; grandfather of leading poet and intellectual Octavio Paz. J] Fought the French; joined the Liberals as a sergeant, 1863; reached the rank of brigadier general, 1876; supported the Plan of Tuxtepec, 1876. K] None. L] DP70, 1592; Godoy, 135–36; Album; Mestre, 274; QesQ, 448; Enc Mex, X, 189; López, 835; O'Campo, 277–78; Godoy, 135–36; Carrasco Puente, 181; Romo, 121.

Peña y Reyes, Antonio
(Deceased June 24, 1928) A] May 30, 1869. B] Mexico City. C] Early education unknown; no degree; professor of Spanish language. D] Local deputy to the state legislature of Mexico; *federal deputy* from the State of México, Dist. 10, 1900–02, 1902–04, 1904–06, 1906–08, 1908–10; *federal deputy* from the State of México, Dist. 9, 1910–12. E] None. F] Private secretary to President *Francisco*

León de la Barra, 1911; *subsecretary* in charge of the Secretariat of Foreign Relations, 1913; member of the Morelos–Federal District Boundary Commission. G] Member of the Mexican Academy of Language; member of the Liceo Mexicano literary group. H] Journalist. I] Son of eminent philologist Rafael Angel de la Peña and Guadalupe Reyes. J] None. K] None. L] Carreño, 207; Enc Mex, X, 200.

Peralta (Rodríguez), Alberto
(Deceased September 1, 1950) A] 1890. B] Hermosillo, Sonora. C] Early education unknown; no degree. D] Constitutional deputy from the State of Michoacán, Dist. 2, 1916–17; *federal deputy* from the State of Guanajuato, Dist. 13, 1922–24. E] Propagandist for *Francisco I. Madero*, 1909. F] Administrator of property with absent owners, State of Sonora, 1913; oficial mayor of the comptroller general; president of the Committee to Reorganize the Secretariat of Government; subchief of police, Federal District, 1930–32; official, License and Inspectors Office, Department of the Federal District, 1932. G] None. H] Manager of the liquidation of the national railroads of Mexico, Tehuantepec; technical adviser to private firms. I] Son of Teodoro Peralta and Josefina Rodríguez; father lost property; had to support family as a boy by becoming the chief clerk in a large Guaymas, Sonora, firm. J] Joined the Constitutionalists, 1913; fought *Francisco Villa*, 1914; chief of staff of the military commander of Guanajuato. K] None. L] C de D, 1916–17.

Peralta, Miguel Angel
(Deceased October 3, 1927) A] September 9, 1889. B] Chilpancingo, Guerrero. C] Studies at the Presbyterian Theological Seminary, Coyoacán, Federal District; director, National Military College, 1923–25. D] *Federal deputy* from the Federal District, Dist. 12, 1917–18. E] Supported General *Francisco R. Serrano* for president, 1927. F] Interim governor of Guanajuato, 1915; oficial mayor of war, 1919–20; minister to Peru, 1922. G] None. H] Evangelical minister before the Revolution. I] Unknown. J] Joined the Constitutionalists as a 2nd captain in the

forces of General Daniel Cerecedo Estrada, 1914; chief of staff to General *Benjamín Hill*; represented at the Convention of Aguascalientes by General de la Luz Romero, 1914; fought at Celaya, 1915; commander of a cavalry brigade, Benjamín Hill Division, 1920; rank of brigadier general, May 29, 1920; commander of the 34th Regiment, May 19, 1920; supported the Plan of Agua Prieta as commander, rural defense forces, Aldama, Guanajuato, 1920. K] Executed by the forces of General Fox at Huitzilac with other supporters of General Francisco R. Serrano, October 3, 1927. L] Enc Mex, X, 26; Rev de Ejer, Sept. 1976, 121.

Pereyra, Orestes
(Deceased 1915) A] 1861. B] El Oro, Durango. C] Early education unknown; no degree. D] None. E] Member, Anti-Reelectionist party, 1910. F] *Governor* of Coahuila, 1915. G] None. H] Laborer; tinsmith by profession. I] Sons Gabriel and Orestes fought with him during the Revolution. J] Joined the Revolution in Gómez Palacio, Durango, with *Jesús A. Castro*, November 20, 1910; rank of colonel, 1911; commander of the 22nd Rural Group against *Pascual Orozco's* rebellion, 1911; joined the Constitutionalists, 1913, fought under *Francisco Villa*; commander, Division of the North; rank of brigadier general; represented at the Convention of Aguascalientes by Francisco Encinas, 1914; commander, First Brigade, Durango; captured by *Alvaro Obregón's* forces, Sinaloa, 1915. K] Executed by Obregón's forces. L] Enc Mex, X, 210; Rouaix, 318–19.

Pereyra (Gómez), Carlos
(Deceased July 1, 1942) A] November 3, 1871. B] Saltillo, Coahuila. C] Primary studies at the Colegio de San Juan, Saltillo; secondary and preparatory at the Ateneo Fuente, Saltillo; law degree, National School of Law, Mexico City, 1895; professor of history and sociology, National Preparatory School and the National University; professor of Spanish, National Preparatory School, 1905. D] *Federal deputy* from the State of Coahuila, Dist. 5, 1910–11. E] None. F] Agent of the Ministerio Público; public defender, Federal

District; second secretary to the Mexican embassy, Washington, D.C., 1909–10; chargé d'affaires, Havana, Cuba, 1910–11; first secretary, Washington, D.C., 1911; *subsecretary* of foreign relations in charge of the Secretariat, 1913; ambassador to Belgium and the Low Countries, 1913–14. G] None. H] Founder of *El Pueblo Coahuilense*, 1897; director of *El Espectador*, Monterrey, 1887; contributor to *El Imparcial* and *El Mundo Ilustrado*; author of numerous books. I] Son of Miguel Pereyra Bosque, engineer, and María de Jesús Gómez Méndez; married Enriqueta Camarillo, author and poet. J] None. K] Went into exile, 1914; invited back by *Venustiano Carranza*, 1916, but stayed in Spain and Switzerland rest of life. L] DP70, 1607; FSRE, 155; UNAM, law, 1891–96, 7; QesQ, 453; Enc Mex, X, 209–10; Carreño, 209; López, 841.

Pérez Taylor, Rafael
(Deceased) A] August 1, 1890. B] Popotla, Federal District. C] Early education unknown; no degree. D] *Alternate federal deputy* from the Federal District, Dist. 6, 1912–13; *federal deputy* from the Federal District, Dist. 4, 1922–24. E] Official orator, *Pascual Ortiz Rubio's* presidential campaign, 1929. F] Director, Fine Arts Department, Secretariat of Public Education, 1924–28; director, National Museum, 1930; director, Department of Libraries, Secretariat of Public Education, 1930–31; oficial mayor of the Secretariat of Government, 1932; chief, Department of Tourism, 1933–34; director of publications, Secretariat of Public Education, 1935. G] Cofounder, Casa del Obrero Mundial, 1911; member, Press Editors Union. H] Wrote theatrical works for the Department of the Federal District, 1929; editor of *México Nuevo, Nueva Era*, and *Excélsior*; director of *El Monitor, El Norte, and El Universal*. I] Son of Víctor Pérez Valenzuela and Lía Taylor. J] None. K] None. L] Dir social, 1935, 241–42.

Pérez Treviño, Manuel
(Deceased 1945) A] June 5, 1890. B] Guerrero, Coahuila. C] Early education unknown; engineering studies, National School of Engineering, UNAM, but left studies to join the Revolution.

D] *Governor* of Coahuila, 1925–29; *sena-tor* from the State of Coahuila, 1932–34. E] *Treasurer*, Organizing Committee of the National Revolutionary party, 1928–29; *president* of the first National Executive Committee of the National Revolutionary party, 1929–30, 1931–33, 1933. F] Chief of staff, Secretariat of National Defense, 1920; *secretary* of industry, commerce, and labor, 1923–24; *secretary* of agriculture, 1930–31; ambassador to Spain, 1935; ambassador to Chile, 1937–38. G] None. H] Unknown. I] Unknown. J] Joined the forces of *Pablo González* as a 2nd captain, 1913; supported the Plan of Agua Prieta, 1920; military attaché to Argentina and Uruguay, 1921; rank of brigade general, November 1, 1924. K] Forced out of political life because of ties with *Plutarco Elías Calles*. L] Enc Mex, X, 220; Dávila, 137.

Pérez Verdía, Luis
(Deceased August 15, 1914) A] April 13, 1857. B] Guadalajara, Jalisco. C] Primary studies at the School for Boys, Guadalajara; secondary studies at the Conciliar Seminary, Guadalajara; law degree, School of Law, Guadalajara, 1877; professor of history, School for Boys, Guadalajara, 1877–89; professor of international law, School of Law, Guadalajara, 1889–98; secretary, School for Boys, Guadalajara, 1877–81; director, School for Boys, Guadalajara, 1882, 1912–13. D] Local deputy to the state legislature of Jalisco, 1889–90; *federal deputy* from the State of Jalisco, Dist. 3, 1890–92; *federal deputy* from the State of Hidalgo, Dist. 11, 1892–94; *federal deputy* from the State of Jalisco, Dist. 18, 1894–96, 1896–98; *federal deputy* from the State of Jalisco, Dist. 13, 1900–02; *federal deputy* from the State of Jalisco, Dist. 12, 1902–04, president of the Chamber; *federal deputy* from the State of Jalisco, Dist. 2, 1904–06, 1906–08, 1908–10; *federal deputy* from the State of Jalisco, Dist. 1, 1910–12. E] None. F] Judge of the Superior Tribunal of Justice, 1884–89; director general of public instruction, State of Jalisco, 1887–90, 1912–13. G] None. H] Practicing lawyer; represented many railroad and mining companies. I] Related to (probably son of) Antonio Pérez Verdía, lawyer; married

Beatriz Calderón. J] None. K] None. L] WNM, 175; Dir social, 133; Blue Book, 254; Godoy, 105–06; Enc Mex, X, 220–21; Rice, 246–47; Mestre, 251; Agraz, 1958, 184–86.

Perusquía, Ernesto
(Deceased June 15, 1946) A] March 10, 1877. B] San Juan del Río, Querétaro. C] Completed primary and preparatory studies only. D] *Constitutional deputy* from the State of Querétaro, Dist. 2, 1916–17; *senator* from the State of Querétaro, 1917–18, 1918–20; *governor* of Querétaro, 1917–19. E] None. F] Director general of taxes, Secretariat of the Treasury, 1919–20; tax administrator, State of Coahuila. G] None. H] Accountant; bookkeeper. I] Son of Manuel Perusquía and Ramona Layseca. J] Joined the Constitutionalists, 1913; remained loyal to *Venustiano Carranza*, 1920. K] Voluntary exile to the United States, 1920–23. L] C de D, 1916–17.

Pesqueira, Ignacio L.
(Deceased October 18, 1940) A] March 13, 1867. B] Huepec, Arizpe, Sonora. C] Early education unknown; advanced education unknown. D] Member of the City Council of Cananea, 1907–08; local deputy to the state legislature of Sonora, 1911–13; *constitutional deputy* from the Federal District, Dist. 1, 1916–17. E] Joined the Anti-Reelectionist movement, 1909. F] *Provisional governor* of Sonora, 1913; *subsecretary* of war, in charge of the secretariat, 1914–15, 1915–16; president, Superior Tribunal of Military Justice, 1916, 1934; *provisional governor* of Sinaloa, 1917; director, artillery warehouse, Secretariat of War; director of military factories, Secretariat of War, 1917–20; appointed governor of Sonora, but never took office, 1920. G] None. H] Owner of the Tetoachi hacienda, Arizpe, Sonora. I] Nephew of General Ignacio Pesqueira, governor of Sonora; related to *Roberto V. Pesqueira*, federal deputy from Sonora, 1912–13, 1917–18; married María Quinta. J] Joined the Constitutionalists as commander of the Sonoran forces under *Alvaro Obregón*, 1913; rank of division general. K] None. L] Holms, 336; Mestre, 155; Villa, 137

-44; Villa, 1937, 305–07; Enc Mex, X, 277; Almanaque de Sonora, 124; Dir social, 1935, 134.

Pesqueira (Gallegos), Roberto V.
(Deceased 1966) A] 1882. B] Cuchuta Ranch, Ures, Sonora. C] Early education unknown; no degree. D] *Federal deputy* from the State of Sonora, Dist. 1, 1912–13, 1917–18. E] Supported *Francisco I. Madero*, 1910. F] Roving ambassador, Washington, D.C., for President *Venustiano Carranza*; financial agent, Mexican government, New York City and Washington, D.C. G] None. H] Co-author with *Ramón P. Denegri* of a radical agrarian reform law in Veracruz, 1914. I] Son of Agustín Pesqueira, military commander, governor of Sonora, and rancher, and Guadalupe Gallegos; related to *Ignacio Pesqueira*, subsecretary of war, 1914–16; father of Roberto Pesqueira Rebeil, assistant director general of Union Carbide of Mexico. J] Joined the Constitutionalists under *Adolfo de la Huerta*, 1913; used family cattle to trade for guns to support the Constitutionalists. K] None. L] Bojórquez, 150–54; Holms, 336; Dir social, 1935, 134.

Peza, Juan de Dios
(Deceased March 15, 1910) A] June 29, 1852. B] Mexico City. C] Primary and secondary studies, Mexico City; enrolled at the National Preparatory School, 1867, as a disciple of Gabino Barreda and Ignacio Ramírez; medical studies, National School of Medicine, Mexico City, but had to leave for financial reasons. D] *Federal deputy* from the State of Oaxaca, Dist. 14, 1888–90; *federal deputy* from the State of Yucatán, Dist. 5, 1890–92, 1892–94, 1894–96; *alternate federal deputy* from the State of Guanajuato, Dist. 1, 1896–98, 1898–1900, 1900–02, 1902–04, 1904–06, 1906–08, 1908–10. E] None. F] First secretary to Spain, 1878–88; private secretary to the secretary of public works, *Francisco Z. Mena*, 1898. G] None. H] Prolific author; poet; founded *El Lunes*, Mexico City. I] Son of Juan de Dios Peza y Fernández de Córdova, Liberal and colonel who served in Maximilian's cabinet, 1864–66; intimate friend of Manuel Acuña, poet, and member of the Liceo Hidalgo group at medical school; political disciple of General Vicente Riva Palacio and Ignacio Ramírez. J] None. K] None. L] Carreño, 209–10; Mestre, 238; Covarrubias, 347–54; Enc Mex, X, 300–01; Godoy, 161.

Pimentel (Velasco), Emilio
(Deceased March 10, 1926) A] 1857. B] Tlaxiaco, Oaxaca. C] Primary studies, public school, Oaxaca; preparatory studies, Institute of Arts and Sciences of Oaxaca; law degree, Institute of Arts and Sciences of Oaxaca; professor of administration and constitutional law, National School of Business, Mexico City, 1899. D] Mayor of Mexico City; *federal deputy* from the State of Oaxaca, Dist. 13, 1886–88; *federal deputy* from the State of Oaxaca, Dist. 7, 1888–90, 1890–92, 1892–94; *federal deputy* from the State of Oaxaca, Dist. 9, 1894–96, 1896–98, 1898–1900, 1900–02, 1902–04; *governor* of Oaxaca, 1902–11. E] Member of the Científico party. F] Special missions to Latin America and Europe for President *Porfirio Díaz*; minister to Argentina; secretary general of government of the State of Oaxaca, under General *Luis Mier y Terán*. G] None. H] Practiced law, Mexico City. I] Son of Gabriel Pimentel and María Velasco; married to Amparo Jordan (one year); part of political group closely tied to *Rosendo Pineda*; guardian of brother Rafael's son, Guillermo; brother *Rafael Pimentel*, governor of Chiapas, 1899–1905. J] None. K] None. L] Wright, 349; Enc Mex, X, 310; Rice, 247; Mestre, 277.

Pimentel (Velasco), Rafael
(Deceased July 31, 1929) A] 1855. B] Oaxaca, Oaxaca. C] Early education unknown; law degree, School of Arts and Sciences of Oaxaca. D] Local deputy to the state legislature of Oaxaca; *governor* of Chiapas, 1899–1905; *senator* from the State of Colima, 1906–10, 1910–13. E] None. F] Oficial mayor of the State of Chihuahua, 1887–88; secretary general of government of the State of Chihuahua, 1888–93; interim governor of Chihuahua, 1890–91; *substitute governor* of Chihuahua, 1892; judge, Supreme Court of Military Justice, 1892–93; secretary general of

government of the State of Oaxaca under General *Martín González*, 1895–96. G] None. H] Practicing lawyer. I] Son of Gabriel Pimentel and María Velasco; brother of *Emilio Pimentel Velasco*, governor of Oaxaca, 1902–11; married Dolores Cajiga; son Guillermo, a lawyer. J] Colonel, army reserves; chief of staff, 11th Military Zone, 1897; military adviser to the States of Guerrero and Jalisco. K] Involved in intrigues to bring down *Francisco I. Madero*, 1913. L] UNAM, law, 1906–12, 174; Almada, 1968, 414; Enc Mex, X, 310; Almada, 419–22; Almanaque de Chiapas, 118.

Pineda, Rosendo
(Deceased September 13, 1914) A] March 3, 1855. B] Juchitán, Oaxaca. C] Preparatory studies, Institute of Arts and Sciences of Oaxaca; legal studies, School of Law, Institute of Arts and Sciences of Oaxaca, 1874–82, graduating 1882, with the highest grades in his class. D] *Federal deputy* from the State of Oaxaca, Dist. 16, 1884–86, 1886–88, 1888–90, 1890–92, 1892–94; *federal deputy* from the State of Guanajuato, Dist. 7, 1894–96; *federal deputy* from the State of Oaxaca, Dist. 16, 1896–98, 1898–1900, 1900–02, 1902–04, 1904–06, 1906–08, 1908–10, 1910–12. E] Leader of the Científico party; supported *Ramón Corral* as a successor to *Porfirio Díaz*. F] Private secretary to the secretary of government, *Manuel Romero Rubio*. G] None. H] Practicing lawyer; legal counsel to the Bank of London and Mexico. I] Illegitimate, some sources believe he was the son of Father Pablo Pineda of Juchitán, who was killed by *Félix Díaz*, brother of Porfirio Díaz; son-in-law of *Manuel Romero Rubio*; reared by a French engineer. J] None. K] None. L] Enc Mex, X, 314; Rice, 247; Mestre, 251; Puente, 115–20.

Pino Suárez, José María
(Deceased February 22, 1913) A] September 8, 1869. B] Primary studies Tenosique, Tabasco, and Progreso, Yucatán; preparatory studies, Colegio Católico de San Ildefonso, Mérida, Yucatán, 1881–91; legal studies, School of Law, Literary Institute of Yucatán, 1891–94, graduating September 12, 1894. D] *Governor of*

Yucatán, 1911; vice-president of Mexico, 1911–13. E] Joined journalist *Filomeno Mata* to oppose *Porfirio Díaz*; organized groups to support *Francisco I. Madero* in Yucatán and Tabasco during his presidential campaign, 1909; candidate for governor of Yucatán, but forced to abandon the state, 1909; president, National Independent Convention of the Anti-Reelectionist and National Democratic parties, 1910; candidate for governor of Tabasco, 1911. F] Secretary of justice, Madero's government in Ciudad Juárez, 1911; *provisional governor* of Yucatán, 1911; *secretary* of public education, 1912–13. G] None. H] Worked with father-in-law, Raymundo Cámara, 1894–1904; founder of *El Peninsular*, 1904–06; poet; lawyer. I] Son of José María Pino, businessman, and Josefa Juliana Suárez; grandson of Tomás Pino and Perfecta Salvatiel; great-grandson of Pedro Sáinz de Baranda, naval commander and political boss, Yucatán; nephew of *Joaquín Baranda y Quijano*, secretary of justice, 1884–1901; married María Cámara Vales, teacher; nephew of General Pedro Baranda, governor of Campeche; brother-in-law of *Nicolás Cámara Vales*, governor of Yucatán, 1912–13. J] None. K] Fled to Guatemala, Havana, New Orleans, and San Antonio, Texas, 1910–11; murdered with Madero on *Victoriano Huerta*'s orders. L] Enc Mex, X, 319; Morales Jiménez, 117–20; HA, 11 Nov. 1986, 38–45; Almanaque de Tabasco, 164; Covarrubias, 355–62.

Plank, Carlos
(Deceased September 7, 1927) A] 1876. B] Bayoreca, Sonora. C] Early education unknown; no degree. D] Local deputy to the state legislature of Sonora, 1911; *federal deputy* from the State of Sonora, Dist. 2, 1917–18; *alternate senator* from the State of Sonora under *Adolfo de la Huerta*, 1918–20, in functions, 1919–20; *senator* from the State of Sonora, 1920–22. E] Member of the Anti-Reelectionist party, 1910. F] Director of the federal penitentiary, Federal District, 1914; commander of the tax police, Sonora; *provisional governor* of Zacatecas, 1916; *interim governor* of Quintana Roo, 1916. G] None. H] Miner, Real de Colorado, 1910; small businessman in mining and commercial

activities. I] Unknown. J] Joined the Constitutionalists; rank of major; fought under Generals *Plutarco Elías Calles* and *Alvaro Obregón*; fought against General *José María Maytorena* in Sonora; signed the Plan of Agua Prieta, 1920. K] None. L] Enc Mex, X, 375; Alvarez Coral, 53; Aguilar Camín, 177.

Plata, Manuel M.
(Deceased December 14, 1926) A] December 24, 1855. B] Toluca, México. C] Primary studies in Toluca; secondary and preparatory studies, National Military College, graduating as a 2nd lieutenant in the engineers, January 1876. D] *Federal deputy* from the State of México, Dist. 3, 1896–98; *federal deputy* from the State of Jalisco, Dist. 18, 1900–02, 1902–04, 1904–06, 1906–08. E] None. F] *Subsecretary* of war in charge of the secretariat, 1911; *subsecretary* of war, 1911–13. G] None. H] None. I] Student with *Victoriano Huerta* at the National Military College. J] Career army officer; fought *Porfirio Diaz's* supporters in Puebla and Morelos as an officer in an engineering battalion, 1876–77; assigned to the military engineers, Federal District, 1878–81; officer, geographical explorations, 1881–85; commander of military parades, National Military College, 1885; chief of staff, 2nd Military Zone, Chihuahua, 1886; commander of the garrison, Ciudad Juárez; commander, sappers battalion, 1892; rank of colonel of engineers, January 15, 1892; rank of brigadier general, September 2, 1902; commander of the Puebla Military Zone; commander of León, Guanajuato, Military Zone; commander of the 2nd Military Zone, Chihuahua, 1908–10; rank of brigade general, March 8, 1909; rank of division general, October 26, 1912; retired March 1, 1913. K] None. L] Enc Mex, X, 376; Sec of War, 1914, 18; Mestre, 278; Cuevas, 442.

Pliego y Pérez, Antonio
(Deceased) A] 1854. B] México. C] Early education unknown; no degree. D] *Federal deputy* from Tepic, Dist. 2, 1886–88, 1888–90, 1890–92, 1892–94, 1894–96, 1896–98, 1898–1900, 1900–02, 1902–04; *federal deputy* from the State of Zacatecas, Dist. 3, 1904–06, 1906–08;

federal deputy from the State of Zacatecas, Dist. 2, 1908–10, 1910–12, member of the Great Committee; *alternate federal deputy* from the State of México, Dist. 14, 1913–14. E] None. F] Accountant, Bank of the State of México. G] None. H] Businessman; founder of La Latina Americana Insurance Company; loan officer, 1909–10. I] Parents were large landholders in México; married Amparo Villalava. J] None. K] None. L] C de D, 1900–02.

Pombo, Ignacio
(Deceased) A] Unknown. B] San Martín Tilcajete, Ocotlán, Oaxaca. C] Secondary and preparatory studies in Latin and philosophy, Seminary of Oaxaca; studies in French and drawing, Institute of Arts and Sciences of Oaxaca; medical studies, National School of Medicine, Mexico City, graduating 1854; director, Military Hospital, 1856; professor of practical medicine and obstetrics, Institute of Arts and Sciences, 1862; director, Central School, 1862. D] Alternate federal deputy from the State of Oaxaca, 1858; federal deputy from the State of Oaxaca, 1862, secretary of the Permanent Committee; federal deputy from the State of Oaxaca, 1878–80; senator from Oaxaca, 1878–80, 1880–82; *federal deputy* from the State of Veracruz, 1882–84; *federal deputy* from the State of Veracruz, Dist. 8, 1886–88; *federal deputy* from the State of Veracruz, Dist. 7, 1888–90; *senator* from the State of Oaxaca, 1894–1900, 1900–02. E] None. F] Chief clerk, State of Oaxaca; director, Sanitary Committee of Veracruz, 1867–77; director, Medical Department, Secretariat of War, 1877. G] None. H] Practicing physician; physician, San Andrés Hospital. I] Unknown. J] None. K] None. L] Hombres prominentes, 401–02; C de S, 1900–02, 6.

Pombo, Luis
(Deceased) A] 1838. B] Oaxaca, Oaxaca. C] Primary and secondary studies in Oaxaca; preparatory studies in Oaxaca; law degree, School of Law, Institute of Arts and Sciences of Oaxaca, 1861; professor of logic, anthropology, morals, and civil law, Institute of Arts and Sciences of Oaxaca. D] Local deputy to the state legislature of Oaxaca; *federal deputy* from the State of

Jalisco, Dist. 7, 1884–86; *federal deputy* from the State of Jalisco, Dist. 3, 1886–88; *federal deputy* from the State of Jalisco, Dist. 18, 1888–90, 1890–92; *federal deputy* from the State of Oaxaca, Dist. 15, 1892–94; *federal deputy* from the State of Oaxaca, Dist. 11, 1894–96; *federal deputy* from the State of Oaxaca, Dist. 15, 1896–98, 1898–1900, 1900–02, 1902–04, 1904–05. E| None. F| Founder of the Ministerio Público system in Mexico; director, Office of Mortgages; oficial mayor of the State of Oaxaca; judge of the first instance, Oaxaca. G| None. H| Practicing lawyer. I| Studied under Benito Juárez and *Manuel Dublán* at the Institute of Arts and Sciences. J| None. K| Hombres prominentes, 323–24; Godoy, 189; Peral.

Portes Gil, Emilio
(Deceased December 10, 1978) A| October 3, 1890. B| Ciudad Victoria, Tamaulipas. C| Primary studies in Ciudad Victoria; secondary studies at the Normal School, Ciudad Victoria, 1906–10; law studies, Escuela Libre de Derecho, 1912–14, degree in 1915; professor of primary schools, Ciudad Victoria, 1910–12; professor of agrarian legislation, School of Law, UNAM, 1930. D| *Federal deputy* from the State of Tamaulipas, Dist. 4, 1916–17, 1921–22; *federal deputy* from the State of Tamaulipas, Dist. 3, 1924–25; *governor* of Tamaulipas, 1925–28. E| *President* of the National Executive Committee (CEN) of the National Revolutionary party (PNR), 1930; president of the CEN of PNR, 1935–36; founder of the Partido Socialista Fronterizo, Tamaulipas. F| First official of the Department of War and Navy, 1914; subchief of the Department of Military Justice, Department of War and Navy, 1915; judge of the first instance, Civil Section, Hermosillo, Sonora; judge of the Superior Tribunal of Justice of Sonora, 1916; consulting lawyer to the secretary of war, 1917; secretary general of government of the State of Tamaulipas, 1918–19; *provisional governor* of Tamaulipas, 1920; general lawyer for the national railroads of Mexico, 1921–22; *president* of Mexico, December 1, 1928–February 4, 1930; *secretary* of government, 1928, 1930; *minister* to France, 1931–32; delegate to the League of Nations, 1931–32; attorney gen-

eral of Mexico, 1932–34; *secretary* of foreign relations, 1934–35; special ambassador to the Dominican Republic, 1944; special ambassador to Ecuador, 1946; first ambassador from Mexico to India, 1951; president of the National Securities Committee, 1959; adviser to the Constructora Nacional de Carros de Ferrocarril, S.A., 1966; president of the Advisory Technical Committee, National Banking Commission, 1970. G| None. H| Author of books on the church, labor, and politics in Mexico. I| Attended the Escuela Libre de Derecho with Francisco Javier Gaxiola and *Ezequiel Padilla*; son of Domingo Portes and Adela Gil; married Carmen García. J| Administrative positions during the Revolution. K| One of the founders of the Escuela Libre de Derecho. L| Letter; DBM68, 495–96; Peral, 648; WWM45, 94; DP70, 1663–64; Enc Mex, X, 405–06; Justicia, Aug. 1970; HA, 18 Dec. 1978, 17–18.

Pous, Guillermo
(Deceased 1936) A| 1847. B| Tlacotalpan, Veracruz. C| Early education unknown; no degree; director of secondary school of Tlacotalpan; founder of the Higher School for Women. D| Mayor of Tlacotalpan; *federal deputy* from the State of Sinaloa, Dist. 4, 1896–98; *federal deputy* from the State of Sinaloa, Dist. 4, 1898–1900; *federal deputy* from the State of Sinaloa, Dist. 4, 1900–02, 1902–04; *federal deputy* from the State of Puebla, Dist. 17, 1904–06, 1906–08, 1908–10, 1910–12; *alternate federal deputy* from the State of Michoacán, Dist. 2, 1906–08. E| Directed *El Debate*, which opposed the National Democratic party and the Anti-Reelectionists, 1909. F| None. G| Founder of the National Agricultural Union. H| Landowner; journalist. I| From a wealthy landowning family; close friend of *Rosendo Pineda*. J| Fought against the Maderistas. K| None. L| Enc Mex, X, 417.

Pradillo, Agustín
(Deceased March 11, 1910) A| 1839. B| Aguascalientes, Aguascalientes. C| Early education unknown; studies at the National Military College, 1853–57, graduating as a 2nd lieutenant in the infantry. D| Federal deputy from the

State of Puebla, 1880–82; federal deputy from the State of Puebla, Dist. 3, 1882–84; *federal deputy* from the State of Puebla, Dist. 2, 1886–88, 1888–90, 1890–92, 1892–94, 1894–96; *federal deputy* from the State of Oaxaca, Dist. 9, 1886–88, 1890–92; *federal deputy* from the State of Puebla, Dist. 5, 1896–98, 1898–1900, 1900–02; *federal deputy* from the State of San Luis Potosí, Dist. 7, 1904–06, 1906–08, 1908–10. F] Governor of the national palace, 1885–1901; chief of presidential residences, 1910. G] None. H] None. I] Possibly father of General Alfonso Pradillo. J] Career army officer; supported the Liberals; fought in the battle of Ocotlán, Puebla, March 8, 1856; fought in the battle of Salamanca, Guanajuato, March 10, 1858; fought in the siege of Veracruz, 1860; participated in the battle of Calderón Bridge, November 1, 1860; defended the Mexico City barracks, 1871; supported the Plan of La Noria, 1872; supported the Plan of Tuxtepec, 1876; commander of a brigade, Eastern Army, 1877–80; rank of brigade general, May 22, 1885. K] Elected to two districts in 1886 and 1890, chose to serve in the Puebla district. L] C de D, 1886–88, 16; Hombres prominentes, 245–46; Mestre, 237–38; Peral; Sec of War, 1901, 19; Mestre, 264; Cuevas, 441.

Preciado, Jesús H.
(Deceased December 6, 1894) A] 1841. B] Guaymas, Sonora. C] Early education unknown; no degree. D] *Governor* of Morelos, 1887–94. E] None. F] None. G] None. H] Agricultural laborer; merchant sailor on the Guaymas to San Francisco route. I] Son of Víctor Preciado and Loreto Aguayo. J] Joined the national guard in Guaymas as a corporal, 1856, to fight the Yaqui Indians; rose to the rank of sergeant; joined the army as a 2nd lieutenant, 2nd Battalion, Sinaloa, 1860; wounded in battle, June 2, 1860; fought in various battles on the side of the Liberals; captured by the French, 1865, but escaped on the way from Oaxaca to Puebla; rank of major, 1867; fought in the battle of Querétaro, 1867; rank of colonel, 1876; chief of staff to General *Manuel González*, 1876; commander of the 1st Battalion, Juchitán, Oaxaca, 1876; rank of brigade general, July 13, 1894. K] None. L] Mestre, 190; Pa-

vía, 251–54; Enc Mex, X, 421; Hombres prominentes, 189–90.

Prieto, Alejandro
(Deceased June 16, 1921) A] September 14, 1841. B] Hacienda de Chicoy, Southern District, Tamaulipas. C] Primary studies in Tampico, Tamaulipas; began preparatory studies, Colegio de San Gregorio, 1852; topographical engineering degree, School of Agriculture, Chapingo; professor of topography, Guatemala. D] Federal deputy from the State of Tamaulipas; senator from the State of Tamaulipas; *governor* of Tamaulipas, 1888–96. E] None. F] Political boss of Tampico; judge of the civil registry; city engineer, Tampico; secretary of the Mexican legation, Guatemala City, Guatemala, 1876–77; inspector of public works, San José, Costa Rica, 1877; official, Secretariat of Development. G] None. H] Railroad inspector, Esquintla to San José, Costa Rica, line; administrator of family landholdings. I] Son of Ramón Prieto and Rafaela Quintero, large landholders. J] Joined the guerrillas during the French Intervention; captured, imprisoned, and condemned to death by the French, but saved by a Mexican serving in the French forces. K] None. L] Godoy, 270; Pavía, 363; Hombres prominentes, 243–44; Mestre, 267.

Prieto (Pradillo), Guillermo
(Deceased March 2, 1897) A] February 10, 1818. B] Molino del Rey, Federal District. C] Primary studies at Manuel Calderón's school, Mexico City; preparatory studies, Colegio de Letrán, Mexico City; studies, National School of Mines, Mexico City; cofounder of the Academia de San Juan de Letrán, 1836, with Andrés Quintana Roo. D] Federal deputy from the Federal District, 1848–49, 1850–51; senator from the Federal District, 1851; constitutional deputy from the State of Puebla, Dist. 4, 1856–57; federal deputy from the State of Guanajuato, 1864–66, 1866–68; federal deputy from the State of San Luis Potosí, 1868–70; federal deputy from the State of Querétaro, 1870–72, 1872–74; federal deputy from the Federal District, 1874–76, 1876–78; federal deputy from the State of Puebla, Dist. 5, 1880–82, 1882–84; *fed-*

eral deputy from the Federal District, Dist. 8, 1884–86; *federal deputy* from the Federal District, Dist. 2, 1886–88, 1888–90, 1890–92, 1892–94; *federal deputy* from the State of Hidalgo, Dist. 6, 1894–96; *federal deputy* from the Federal District, Dist. 1, 1896–97. E] None. F] Private secretary to President Gómez Farías; private secretary to President Anastasio Bustamante; secretary of the treasury, 1852–53, 1855, 1858–59, 1859, 1861, 1876; secretary of foreign relations, 1876; secretary of government, 1876–77; secretary of justice, 1876; secretary of development, 1876. G] None. H] Journalist; historian, poet; cofounder of *Don Simplicio*, with Ignacio Ramírez, 1845; worked in a clothing store and in customs in youth. I] Grandson of Pedro Prieto; father, a successful businessman, died in 1831, and mother went insane; helped financially in school by Andrés Quintana Roo; friend of President Anastasio Bustamante; married María Caro. J] Accompanied Juárez, 1863–64; opposed *Porfirio Díaz*, 1876–77. K] Exiled by Santa-Anna to Cadereyta, 1854–55; saved Benito Juárez's life in Guadalajara; exiled, United States, 1877–79. L] Armijo, 65–66; Covarrubias, 403–10; Enc Mex, X, 431–32; Sierra, 64.

Pruneda (García), Alfonso
(Deceased 1957) A] August 19, 1879. B] Mexico City. C] Primary studies, Colegio Guadalupe, under father; preparatory studies, National Preparatory School, Mexico City; medical studies, National School of Medicine, Mexico City, 1896–1902, graduating with a medical degree; first-prize student second and third year of medical studies; honorary Ph.D., Marburg University, Germany; professor, School of Philosophy and Letters, UNAM; director, Popular University, 1913–22; director, graduate studies, UNAM, 1912–13; dean, School of Business, UNAM, 1918–20; rector of UNAM, 1924–28; coordinator of humanities, UNAM. D] None. E] None. F] Director, University Department, Secretariat of Public Education, 1905–11; secretary general of the Department of Public Health, 1920–24; director of civic action, Department of the Federal District, 1928–30; director, Department of Fine Arts,

1930–31; adviser, Secretariat of Public Education, 1931–34; member of the advisory board, Secretariat of Public Education, 1932–51; oficial mayor of the Secretariat of Public Education, 1937–38. G] Permanent secretary, National Academy of Medicine. H] Intern, Beístegui Hospital, Mexico City, 1902; practicing physician; gave piano lessons and taught biology to help his family when father died in 1897; author of numerous works on medicine, education, and the social sciences. I] Son of José de Jesús Pruneda, director of the Colegio Guadalupano, and Guadalupe García Navarrete; married Dolores Batres; assistant to José Terres, his mentor; brother Alvaro, constitutional deputy, 1916–17, and cartoonist. J] None. K] None. L] López, 886; UNAM, med, 1897, 99; DP70, 1683; Enc Mex, X, 445; Dir social, 1935, 136.

Puig y Casauranc, José Manuel
(Deceased May 9, 1939) A] January 31, 1888. B] Laguna del Carmen (Ciudad del Carmen), Campeche. C] Primary studies in Minatitlán, Veracruz; secondary studies in Minatitlán, Veracruz; preparatory studies, Colegio de Orizaba, Orizaba, Veracruz, and Jalapa, Veracruz; medical degree, National School of Medicine, UNAM, August 11, 1911. D] *Federal deputy* from the State of Veracruz, Dist. 19, 1912–13, 1922–24; *senator* from the State of Campeche, 1924–26. E] Director, *Plutarco Elías Calles*'s presidential campaign, 1923–24. F] *Secretary* of education, 1924–28; *secretary* of industry, 1928; *head* of the Department of the Federal District, 1929–30, 1930; *secretary* of education, 1930–31; *ambassador* to the United States, 1931–32; *secretary* of foreign relations, 1933–34; ambassador to Argentina, 1935–36; ambassador to Brazil, 1936. G] None. H] Physician, Puerto México, Veracruz, Tampico, Tamaulipas, 1918–21, Albuquerque, New Mexico, 1915–18, and Mexico City; chief surgeon, National Railroads of Mexico, Tehuantepec, 1914; journalist; contributor, *El Universal*, 1919–21; director, *El Demócrata*, 1924. I] Son of José Manuel Puig and Carmen Casauranc; married María Elena Reyes Spíndola; brother of Carlos Puig y Casauranc, federal deputy from Veracruz,

1922–24, 1924–26, 1926–30. J] None. K] None. L] Carreño, 363; Dir social, 1935, 245–46; WWLA35, 321–22.

Q

Quaglia (Zimbrón), Carlos
(Deceased March 3, 1899) A] July 13, 1849. B] Oaxaca, Oaxaca. C] Primary studies in Latin, French, logic, and mathematics, Oaxaca; secondary studies in Oaxaca; legal studies, Institute of Arts and Sciences of Oaxaca; no degree. D] Governor of Morelos, 1880–84; *senator* from the State of México, 1884–88, 1888–92, 1892–96, 1896–99. E] None. F] Prefect of Atlixco, political boss, various districts, Morelos; prefect of Cuernavaca, 1879; interim governor of Morelos, 1879–80. G] None. H] Worked for father in engineering business; businessman. I] Son of Italian Juan B. Quaglia, engineer, and Narcisa Zimbrón; father declined positions with the French; brothers Luis and Juan fought for the Liberals. J] Fought under General *Carlos Pacheco*; fought in the siege of Querétaro against the French; participated in the siege of Mexico City, 1867; supported the Plan of La Noria, 1871; supported the Plan of Tuxtepec, 1876. K] None. L] Godoy, 300–01; Hombres prominentes, 309–10; Mestre, 204.

Quiroga (Escamilla), Pablo
(Deceased 1948) A] 1875. B] Ciénega de Flores, Nuevo León. C] Early education unknown; no degree. D] None. E] None. F] Oficial mayor of war; *subsecretary* of war, 1932; *subsecretary* of war in charge of secretariat, 1932–33; *secretary* of war, 1933–34, 1934–35. G] None. H] Miner; participated in the Cananea Mining Strike. I] Unknown. J] Career army officer; joined the Maderistas, 1910–11; joined the Constitutionalists; fought *Francisco Villa* under *Alvaro Obregón*, 1915; rank of division general, January 1, 1933; assigned to the Subsecretariat of War, 1937. K] None. L] Dávila, 94.

Quiroga Treviño, Pablo
A] January 25, 1903. B] Ciénega de Flores, Nuevo León. C] Secondary studies at the Colegio Civil, Monterrey, Nuevo

León, 1917–22; law degree from the National School of Law, UNAM, June 15, 1928; professor of law, University of Nuevo León, 1930–32. D] Federal deputy from the State of Nuevo León, Dist. 1, 1949–52, member of the first Constitutional Affairs Committee, the Social Welfare Committee, the Consular and Diplomatic Committee, and the Child Welfare Committee. E] None. F] Agent of the Ministerio Público of the Office of the Attorney General; judge of the District Court of Nuevo León, 1929; oficial mayor of the State of Nuevo León, 1930; secretary general of government of the State of Nuevo León, 1930–33; *interim governor* of Nuevo León, 1933–1935; judge of the Superior Tribunal of Justice of Nuevo León, 1943–49; administrator of the Regional Cashier's Office of the Social Security Institute (IMSS), Monterrey, 1952–58. G] None. H] Clerk for the 3rd District Court, Nuevo León; clerk for the Department of Military Justice, Department of the Navy; clerk for the 7th Judicial District, Federal District; Notary public no. 24, Monterrey, Nuevo León, 1953–74. I] Brother Ambrosio was a physician for IMSS. J] None. K] None. L] DBM68, 503–04; WWM45, 96; Peral, 662; C de D, 1949–51, 85; HA, 12 Dec. 1952, 5.

R

Rábago, Antonio
(Deceased March 22, 1915) A] 1861. B] Celaya, Guanajuato. C] Early education unknown; no degree. D] None. E] None. F] *Interim governor* of Chihuahua, 1913; *governor* and military commander of Tamaulipas, 1913. G] None. H] None. I] Son of Domingo Rábago and Francisca Maldonado. J] Joined the Rurales, 1878; sergeant, army reserves, 1880; commissioned as a 2nd lieutenant, 5th Cavalry Regiment, October 4, 1887; rank of captain, December 9, 1887; commander, army police squadron, 1887–1900; rank of major, September 22, 1900; officer, 10th Cavalry Regiment, 1900–05; rank of lt. colonel, August 2, 1905; officer, 13th Cavalry Regiment, 1905–09; commander, 10th Cavalry Regiment, 1909–11; rank of brigadier general, March 13, 1911; fought against the Maderistas, Chihuahua, 1910–

11; director, Department of Cavalry, Secretariat of War, 1911–12; second-in-command, Northern Division, under General *Victoriano Huerta*, against *Pascual Orozco*, 1912; commander of the 4th Military Zone, 1912–13; organized the Northern Division, March 19, 1913; commander of the 2nd Military Zone, 1913; retired from the army, January 24, 1914; captured in Mexico City and sent to Chihuahua as a prisoner. K] Apprehended *Abraham González* on Huerta's orders, 1913. L] Sec of War, 1900, 169; Almada, 1968, 440; Almada, 468–72; Sec of War, 1914, 20; Mestre, 252.

Rabasa (Estebanell), Emilio
(Deceased April 25, 1930) A] May 22, 1856. B] Ocozocoautla, Chiapas. C] Primary studies in home; preparatory studies at the Institute of Arts and Sciences of Oaxaca; law degree, Institute of Arts and Sciences of Oaxaca, April 1878; director, Institute of the State of Chiapas, 1882; rector, Free Law School; professor of law, National School of Law and the Free Law School; professor of economic policy, National School of Business. D] Local deputy to the state legislature of Chiapas, 1881; local deputy to the state legislature of Oaxaca, 1883–85; *alternate federal deputy* from the Federal District, Dist. 2, 1888–90; *alternate federal deputy* from the Federal District, Dist. 3, 1890–92; *governor* of Chiapas, 1891–94; *senator* from the State of Sinaloa, 1894–1900, 1900–04, 1904–08, 1908–12, 1912–14. E] None. F] Civil judge, Oaxaca, 1883–85; private secretary to the governor of Oaxaca, General *Luis Mier y Terán*, 1884–85; public defender, Mexico City; agent of the Ministerio Público, Mexico City; judge, Mexico City. G] Member of the Mexican Academy of Language. H] Practicing lawyer; journalist; notable novelist; contributor to *El Porvenir*, Chiapas, and *Liberal*, Oaxaca; cofounder of *El Universal* with *Rafael Reyes Spíndola*, 1888. I] Son of José Antonio Rabasa, wealthy Spaniard, and Manuela Estebanell; married Mercedes Llanes Santaella; widowed, second wife, María Luisa Massieu; son Oscar a lawyer and ambassador; grandson Emilio Rabasa, secretary of foreign relations, 1971–75; brother Ramón was governor of

Chiapas, 1905–11; taught many future politicians, including *Emilio Portes Gil*, president of Mexico. J] None. K] Supported *Victoriano Huerta*'s designation as president and asked for *Francisco I. Madero*'s resignation; exiled to New York City, 1914–21; considered to be one of Mexico's most knowledgeable constitutional lawyers during his lifetime. L] DP70, 1712–13; Enc Mex, XI, 40; López, 902; O'Campo, 306–08; Carreño, 212.

Ramírez, José María
(Deceased September 10, 1890) A] 1828. B] Ejutla, Oaxaca. C] Early education unknown; no degree. D] *Governor* of Chiapas, 1883–87; *senator* from the State of Chiapas, 1888–90. E] Joined the Liberal party. F] None. G] None. H] Unknown. I] Unknown. J] Joined the national guard as a 2nd lieutenant, March 1852; fought Conservatives in Tehuantepec, 1852; fought in the War of the Reform; rank of 1st lieutenant, August 1856; rank of captain, 1856; commander of a battalion, 1859; defended Veracruz against the French; captured by the French in Oaxaca, but escaped and joined General *Porfirio Díaz*; participated in the siege of Puebla; fought with Díaz in the battle for the fort of Oaxaca, October 6, 1866; rank of lt. colonel of the reserves, 1867; commander of the 10th Infantry Battalion, 1879; rank of brigadier general, 1879; rank of brigade general, November 7, 1883. K] None. L] Hombres prominentes, 337–38; Mestre, 171; Sec of War, 1900, 85, 93.

Ramírez, Rodolfo Rafael
(Deceased October 1, 1954) A] 1874. B] Valle de Santiago, Guanajuato. C] Early education unknown; teaching certificate; medical degree, Colegio de Guanajuato; studied under French physician Alfredo Duges; professor of medicine, Colegio de Guanajuato, 1910; researcher; founded the Casa de Estudiante Indígena; rector of the Colegio de Guanajuato; director of the Normal School of Guanajuato. D] Local deputy to the state legislature of Guanajuato, 1914–16; *senator* from the State of Guanajuato, 1917–18; *federal deputy* from the State of Michoacán, Dist. 18, 1928–30. E] None. F] Director gen-

eral of public education, State of Guanajuato; director, Library of the Supreme Court, Mexico City. G] None. H] Practicing physician; managed various businesses. I] Unknown. J] None. K] None. L] Enc Mex, XI, 52; C de S, 1917–18.

Ramírez (Baños), Alfonso Francisco
(Deceased July 1, 1979) A] November 15, 1896. B] Teposcolula, Oaxaca. C] Primary studies at a parochial school; secondary studies at the Colegio Unión, Oaxaca; preparatory studies at the Institute of Arts and Sciences, Oaxaca; law degree from the Institute of Arts and Sciences, Oaxaca, June 20, 1919; professor of Spanish language and literature at the Institute of Arts and Sciences, Oaxaca; professor at the Superior School of Business Administration, Mexico City; professor of logic and ethics; professor of world history at the National Preparatory School. D] *Federal deputy* from the State of Oaxaca, Dist. 12, 1922–24; *federal deputy* from the State of Oaxaca, Dist. 13, 1924–26; *federal deputy* from the State of Oaxaca, Dist. 16, 1926–28; federal deputy from the State of Oaxaca, Dist. 12, 1930–32; *federal deputy* from the State of Oaxaca, Dist. 8, 1932–34; federal deputy from the State of Oaxaca, Dist. 6, 1937–40. E] Founding member, National Revolutionary party, 1929; orator for *Manuel Avila Camacho*, 1940. F] Judge of the 7th Correctional Court, Federal District, 1924–26; judge of the 8th Correctional Court, 1926; subdirector of the legal department for the Department of Federal Pensions; consulting lawyer to the Secretariat of Government, 1933; justice of the Supreme Court, 1941–46, 1946–52, 1952–58. G] Student leader in Oaxaca, 1916; president of the Alumni Society of the Institute of Arts and Sciences of Oaxaca. H] Author of many works; contributor to *Hoy, Excélsior, El Universal*; poet. I] Son of *Francisco Modesto Ramírez*, a lawyer, Supreme Court justice, and his professor at law school, and Concepción Baños; married Carmen Palacios Almont, daughter of lawyer José Palacios Roji. J] None. K] None. L] WWM45, 97; CdeD, 1937–39, 18; DBM68, 505; EBW, 72; Peral, 665; HA, 25 Dec. 1972, 15; letters; López, 902.

Ramírez (Castañeda), Francisco Modesto
(Deceased June 3, 1955) A] November 2, 1867. B] Ejutla, Oaxaca. C] Primary studies, Ejutla, Oaxaca; preparatory studies, Colegio Católico of Oaxaca; law degree, Institute of Arts and Sciences of Oaxaca, 1891; awarded prizes in eleven courses and disciplines; professor of civil and forensic law, Institute of Arts and Sciences of Oaxaca. D] Local deputy to the state legislature of Oaxaca; *federal deputy* from the State of Nuevo León, Dist. 1, 1890–92, 1892–94, 1894–96, 1896–98, 1898–1900; *federal deputy* from the State of Aguascalientes, Dist. 3, 1900–02; *federal deputy* from the State of Coahuila, Dist. 5, 1902–04; *federal deputy* from the State of Coahuila, Dist. 4, 1906–08; *federal deputy* from the State of Oaxaca, Dist. 6, 1912–13; *federal deputy* from the State of Oaxaca, Dist. 4, 1920–22. E] None. F] Syndic, City Council of Oaxaca; judge of the first instance, Silacoyoapan, Huajuapan de León, Tlaxiaco, and Zimatlán, Oaxaca, 1891–93; justice of the Supreme Court, 1923–28; judge, Federal Tax Court; public defender, Superior Tribunal of Justice of the Federal District; consulting lawyer, Secretariat of the Treasury. G] None. H] Practicing lawyer. I] Son of Cristiano Ramírez, businessman, and Manuela Castañeda; married Concepción Baños, daughter of Lauro Baños, judge; father of *Alfonso Francisco Ramírez*, justice of the Supreme Court, 1941–59. J] None. K] None. L] Dir social, 1935, 139; Linajes, 226–27; letters.

Ramírez Garrido, José Domingo
(Deceased 1958) A] August 2, 1888. B] Hacienda Buena Vista, Macuspana, Tabasco. C] Primary studies, Colegio Santa María de Guadalupe, San Juan Bautista, Tabasco; bookkeeping studies, Tehuacán; enrolled normal school, Mexico City; studied riding and gymnastics, Instructors Military School. D] Local deputy to the Constitutional Convention of Tabasco; *federal deputy* from the State of Yucatán, Dist. 12, 1917–18; *federal deputy* from the State of Tabasco, Dist. 2, 1920–22. E] Member of the Anti-Reelectionist party; wrote for *Regeneración*; supported the Flores Magón brothers as a teenager. F] Private secretary to the

secretary of government, *Jesus Flores Mugón*, 1912; director of education, State of Yucatán, under General *Salvador Alvarado*; subsecretary of government of the State of Tabasco under General *Francisco Múgica*; secretary of government of Tabasco; inspector general of police, Federal District; ambassador to Colombia, 1937; director of archives, Secretariat of National Defense, 1958. G] None. H] Journalist; bookkeeper. I] Son of Calixto N. Ramírez, ox-driver, and Carlota Garrido Lacroix; father of General Graco Ramírez Garrido, commander 3rd Air Group, 1974; father of José Domingo Ramírez Garrido, chief of adjutants, 1986; great-uncle of General José Domínguez Ramírez Garrido Abreu, chief of police of the Federal District, 1988; related to General *Tomás Garrido Canabal*, secretary of agriculture, 1934–35; brother-in-law of Manuel Garrido Lacroix, senator from Tabasco, 1930–34. J] Supported Maderistas, 1910–11; joined the Constitutionalists, 1913; captain, 45th Rural Forces; inspector general of police, Yucatán; interim commander, 4th Brigade, 21st Division, Oaxaca; chief of staff, 4th Brigade, 31st Division; commander of military forces in Yucatán; interim commander, 2nd Division, Army of the Northeast; supported the Plan of Agua Prieta, 1920; rank of brigadier general, June 6, 1920; supported the *Adolfo de la Huerta* rebellion, 1923; chief of staff, General *Enrique Estrada*, 1923–24; reintegrated into the army, 1935; commander of the 9th Regiment, 1945; commander of the 30th Military Zone, Tabasco, 1949–51; commander of the 33rd Military Zone, Campeche, Campeche, 1951–57. K] Exiled, 1924. L] DP70, 1720; Enc Mex, XI, 56; Rev de Ejer, Sept. 1976, 120; Santamaría, 125–29; Bulnes, 665.

Ramírez Villarreal, Francisco
(Deceased January 16, 1982) A] February 23, 1890. B] Saltillo, Coahuila. C] Early education unknown; law degree. D] *Constitutional deputy* from the State of Colima, Dist. 1, 1916–17. E] None. F] Secretary general of government of Colima, under General *Juan José Ríos*, 1916; interim governor of Colima, 1916, 1920; president, Superior Tribunal of Justice of

Tamaulipas, 1921; oficial mayor of the State of Nuevo León; director general of the *Diario Oficial*, Mexico City; director, Department of Government, Secretariat of Government, 1934; oficial mayor, Secretariat of government, 1934–35; subsecretary of government, 1935. G] None. H] Practicing lawyer. I] Unknown. J] None. K] None. L] Peral, 671; Almada, Colima, 156; *Excélsior*, 17 January 1982, 5; HA, 25 January 1982, 14.

Ramos, Ramón
(Deceased 1937) A] March 13, 1894. B] Villa de Chinipas, Chihuahua. C] Agricultural engineering degree, National School of Agriculture, 1910–14. D] *Federal deputy* from the State of Sonora, Dist. 4, 1924–26, member of the Great Committee; *federal deputy* from the State of Chihuahua, Dist. 5, 1926–27; *senator* from the State of Sonora, 1930–34; governor of Sonora, 1935. F] Secretary general of government of Sonora, under *Rodolfo Elías Calles*, 1931–32. G] None. H] Unknown. I] Unknown. K] Removed from the Chamber of Deputies for opposing the constitutional reform allowing *Alvaro Obregón* to be re-elected, 1927; removed from the governorship because of loyalties to Calles. L] DP70, 1723; Dulles, 661; Almanaque de Sonora, 129; Almada, 1968, 443.

Ramos Arceo, José
(Deceased February 26, 1909) A] August 18, 1857. B] San Luis Potosí, San Luis Potosí. C] Primary studies, Conciliar Seminary, San Luis Potosí; preparatory studies, National Preparatory School, 1871–76; medical studies, with first prize for the highest grades in every subject, National School of Medicine, 1876–81, graduating February 12, 1881; professor, Scientific and Literary Institute of Mexico, Toluca, 1881–85; advanced studies, Sorbonne, Paris, 1885–87, where he served as chief clinician; professor of internal pathology, by opposition, National Medicial School, until 1909; founder, class in clinical opthamology, National School of Medicine; degree in ocular medicine, Harvard University. D] *Alternate senator* from the State of San Luis Potosí, 1892–94; *senator* from the State of San Luis Potosí,

1894–98, president of the Senate; *alternate senator* from San Luis Potosí, 1898–1902; *senator* from San Luis Potosí, 1902–06, 1906–09. E] None. F] None. G] None. H] Practicing physician. I] Disciple of Gabino Barreda at the National Preparatory School. J] None. K] None. L] Puente, 103–05; QesQ, 486–87; Mestre, 234; Montejano, 330.

Ramos Pedrueza, Antonio
(Deceased November 1930) A] 1860. B] Chihuahua, Chihuahua. C] Primary studies in Chihuahua; law degree, National School of Law, Mexico City; professor, National School of Law, (forty years). D] *Federal deputy* from the State of Oaxaca, Dist. 5, 1886–88; *alternate federal deputy* from the State of Oaxaca, Dist. 16, 1898–1900; *alternate federal deputy* from the State of Guanajuato, Dist. 3, 1900–02, 1902–04; *alternate federal deputy* from the State of Oaxaca, Dist. 16, 1900–02; *federal deputy* from the State of Chihuahua, Dist. 4, 1904–06, 1906–08; *federal deputy* from the State of Chihuahua, Dist. 5, 1908–10, 1910–12. E] None. F] None. G] None. H] Practicing lawyer. I] Brother Rafael, federal deputy from the Federal District. J] None. K] None. L] Enc Mex, XI, 61; Dir social, 1935, 140; Almada, 1968, 443.

Ramos Praslow, Ignacio
(Deceased) A] February 1, 1886. B] Culiacán, Sinaloa. C] Primary studies in Culiacán; preparatory studies, University of Guadalajara; law degree, School of Law, University of Guadalajara. D] *Constitutional deputy* from the State of Jalisco, Dist. 13, 1916–17. E] Propagandist for *Francisco I. Madero*, 1910. F] Director, legal department, Secretariat of the Treasury; *subsecretary* of justice, 1916; *governor* of Jalisco, 1920; adviser to President *Alvaro Obregón*, 1920–24. G] None. H] Lawyer; lawyer for the Bank of London and Mexico, 1942. I] Son of Guillermo Ramos Urrea, lawyer, and Amelia Praslow; married Francisca Márquez Vilar. J] Joined the Constitutionalists under General *Enrique Estrada*; chief of staff to general Enrique Estrada; fought against *Francisco Villa*, 1914–15; supported the

Plan of Agua Prieta, 1920; rank of colonel. K] None. L] Blue Book, 266.

Ramos Santos, Matías
(Deceased March 4, 1962) A] February 24, 1891. B] San Salvador, Zacatecas. C] Primary and secondary studies in Concepción del Oro, Zacatecas; no degree. D] *Federal deputy* from the State of Zacatecas, Dist. 8, 1918–20; *Governor* of Zacatecas, 1932–34, 1935–36. E] *President* of the National Executive Committee of PRI, December 14, 1934–June 15, 1935. F] Inspector of railroads, Secretariat of Public Works, 1917; oficial mayor of the Secretariat of War, 1928–29; *subsecretary* of war, 1929–30; *secretary* of national defense, 1952–58. G] None. I] Friend of Generals Marcelino García Barragán and *Francisco Urquizo*; son Ismael Ramos served as 1st captain of the chief of staff of the secretary of national defense, 1952; son of Ezequiel Ramos, major in the federal army, and María Santos; married Dolores Arteaga. J] Joined the Revolution on March 18, 1911, as a private; rank of corporal, May 13, 1911; rank of 2nd sergeant, December 15, 1911; fought under Captain *Gertrudis Sánchez*, March 18–August 20, 1911; rank of 1st sergeant in the cavalry, April 15, 1912; fought under Major *Eulalio Gutiérrez*, August 21, 1911–February 17, 1913; rank of 2nd lieutenant, June 10, 1912; rank of lieutenant, August 30, 1912; rank of 2nd captain, February 18, 1913; rank of 1st captain, April 25, 1913; fought under Eulalio Gutiérrez, Division of the Center, against *Victoriano Huerta*, February 18, 1913–14; rank of major, September 3, 1913; rank of lt. colonel, December 31, 1913; rank of colonel, March 7, 1914; rank of brigadier general, December 31, 1915; commander of the El Rayo Brigade, 3rd Division of the Army of the Northeast, 1915, against *Francisco Villa*; wounded commanding the El Rayo and Félix Gómez brigades, 1916; fought under General *Jacinto B. Treviño*; rank of brigade general, May 20, 1915; ordered retired from the army, 1921–23; reactivated December 18, 1923, to fight against the *Adolfo de la Huerta* revolt; commander of military operations, 11th Military Zone, Zacatecas, Zacatecas, 1923; commander of opera-

tions, 26th Military Zone, Tepic, Nayarit, 1923–24; commander of operations, 17th Military Zone, Querétaro, Querétaro, 1924–26; commander of operations, 22nd Military Zone, Oaxaca, Oaxaca, 1926–27; commander of military operations, 9th Military Zone, Tampico, Tamaulipas, 1927–28; fought against Escobar rebellion in the defense of Ciudad Juárez, 1929; commander of military operations, 5th Military Zone, Chihuahua, Chihuahua, 1929; rank of division general, May 16, 1929; commander of military operations, 5th Military Zone, Chihuahua, Chihuahua, 1930–32; commander of the 10th Military Zone, Durango, Durango, 1938–40; commander of the 22nd Military Zone, Toluca, Mexico, 1940–41; commander of the 18th Military Zone, Pachuca, Hidalgo, 1941–43; commander of the 27th Military Zone, Acapulco, Guerrero, 1943–45; commander of the 12th Military Zone, San Luis Potosí, San Luis Potosí, 1945–46; commander of the 7th Military Zone, Monterrey, Nuevo León, 1946–51. K] Retired from active service, 1959; one of a few officers to have commanded more than ten military zones in a career from 1923 to 1951. L] Peral, 673; D de Y, 3 Dec. 1952, 12; QesQ, 487–88; Dulles, 635; López, 913–14; Enc Mex, XI, 1977, 61; Rev de Ejer, Apr. 1962, 50–52.

Ramos (y Magaña), Samuel
(Deceased June 20, 1959) A] June 8, 1897. B] Zitácuaro, Michoacán. C] Primary studies at Carlos Treviño's school, Morelia, Michoacán, 1907–09; preparatory studies, Colegio de San Nicolas, Morelia; medical studies, Colegio de San Nicloas, 1916–17, and Medicial Military College, Mexico City, 1918–19; left medical studies third year and enrolled full-time in philosophy, National University, 1919–22; professor, introduction to philosophy, National Preparatory School, 1922; professor of logic, National Normal School, Mexico City; studies, Sorbonne, University of Rome. D] None. E] None. F] Oficial mayor of the Secretariat of Public Education, 1931–32, under friend *Narciso Bassols*; technical adviser, Secretariat of Public Education, 1932–34. G] Member of the National College, 1952–59. H] Lead-

ing intellectual; author; directed *Antorcha*; founder and editor of *Ulises*; philosopher. I] Son of Samuel Ramos Cortés, physician and professor, Colegio de San Nicolás; married Adela Palacios, author and granddaughter of *Lauro Carrillo*, governor of Chihuahua, 1888–92, and niece of General *Jacinto B. Treviño*; disciple of Antonio Caso and *José Vasconcelos*. J] None. K] Author of a classic work entitled *Profile of Man and Culture in Mexico*. L] JSH, 323; Romero Aceves, 642–43; Enc Mex, XI, 119; López, 913; DP70, 1723.

Randall (Bazozabal), Carlos E.
(Deceased 1929) A] May 23, 1860. B] Guaymas, Sonora. C] Early education unknown; no degree. D] Mayor of Guaymas; *federal deputy* from the State of Sonora, Dist. 2, 1912–13. E] Joined the political group of Governor Carlos L. Ortiz, 1883; member of the first Reyista Club, Sonora; joined the Anti-Reelectionist party, 1910. F] *Governor* of Sonora, 1911; treasurer general of Sonora; *interim governor* of Sonora, 1914–15; *governor* of Sonora, 1915, under *Francisco Villa*; treasurer of Guaymas, 1929. G] None. H] Assayer; bookkeeper; miner; businessman; small orange grower in Guaymas; journalist; printing business, Guaymas; founded opposition paper to General Vicente Mariscal, 1880. I] Son of Guillermo Randall, an English sea captain and follower of General *Ignacio Pesqueira*, and Mercedes Bazozabal. J] Executive secretary, revolutionary junta, Nogales, Arizona. K] Exiled from Sonora with Carlos L. Ortiz, 1884–94; exiled to the United States, 1914, and in 1915–20; imprisoned by the state government, 1880s. L] Enc Mex, XI, 63; Almanaque de Sonora, 1982, 125–26; Serrano, 78–81.

Real (Félix), Carlos
(Deceased January 27, 1982) A] November 17, 1892. B] Tamazula, Durango. C] Primary studies in Durango, Durango; studies at the National Military College; no degree. D] *Governor* of Durango, 1932–35; senator from the State of Durango, 1958–64, president of the Second Committee for National Defense, member

of the Committee on the Electric Industry, the War Matériel Committee, the Special Livestock Committee, the Second Balloting Committee, and the Second Instructive Committee for the Grand Jury. E] Founding member of the National Revolutionary party, 1929; oficial mayor of the National Executive Committee of PRI, 1956. F] Director, Telegraph Office, Agiabampo, Sinaloa, 1913; oficial mayor of the Chamber of Deputies, 1946–49; gerente of the national lottery, 1949–52. G] None. H] Rancher, 1936–46. I] Son Carlos Real served twice as a federal deputy from Durango; son Roberto, president of Diteza, S.A., Robespierre, S.A., Turbotex, S.A., and Atoyac Textil, S.A. J] Joined the Revolution as a 2nd lieutenant, 1913; career army officer; imprisoned by rebels, 1927, but escaped; chief of staff to General *Ramón F. Iturbe*; commander of Santiago Tlatelolco Prison, 1927; rank of brigadier general, 1932; commander of the 7th Military Zone, Monterrey, Nuevo León; reached the rank of division general. K] Political boss of Durango during the early 1930s; removed from the governorship because of loyalty to *Plutarco Elías Calles*. L] Dulles; C de S, 1961–64, 67; *Siempre*, 14 Jan. 1959, 6; D del S, 3 Dec. 1946, 1; Func., 199; NYT, 17 Dec. 1935, 1; HA, 8 Feb. 1982, 17; *Excélsior*, 28 Jan. 1982.

Rebollar, Rafael
(Deceased May 9, 1915) A] August 25, 1847. B] Mexico City. C] Primary studies in Mexico City; law degree, National School of Law, Mexico City, 1871; professor, School of Law, National School of Law; prefect, National School of Law. D] *Senator* from the State of San Luis Potosí, 1898–1900. E] None. F] Criminal judge; director, *Diario Oficial*, Mexico City; oficial mayor of the Federal District, 1878; secretary of the Federal District, 1878–96; delegate of Mexico to the Ibero-American Congress, Madrid, 1892; *governor* of the Federal District, 1896–1900; attorney general of Mexico, 1900–11. G] None. H] Practicing lawyer; author of numerous books. I] Married Guadalupe Cordero. J] None. K] None. L] UNAM, law, 1891–96, 167; Enc Mex, XI, 74; QesQ, 490; Mestre, 253; HA, 5 Aug 1986, 48.

Rebolledo, Efrén
(Deceased December 11, 1929) A] July 8, 1877. B] Actopan, Hidalgo. C] Primary and secondary studies with great financial difficulty, under David Noble, Actopan; preparatory studies, on a scholarship, Scientific and Literary Institute of Hidalgo and the National Preparatory School; enrolled in legal studies, National School of Law, 1895, graduating with a law degree; professor, National Preparatory School. D] *Federal deputy* from the State of Hidalgo, Dist. 1, 1917–18, 1918–20. E] None. F] Secretary of the Mexican Legation, Tokyo, Japan; minister to Japan; minister to Spain; director of protocol, Secretariat of Foreign Relations, 1920; adviser, Mexican Legation in Spain, 1929. G] Member of the *Revista Moderna* literary group. H] Poet; author; founded *Nosotros* review, 1912–14. I] Son of Petronilo Flores and Petra Rebolledo; abandoned by father and took mother's name; Antonio Robert was his guardian in law school. J] None. K] None. L] Enc Mex, XI, 75; QesQ, 490; Pérez López, 378; Estrada, 251; UNAM, law, 1891–96, 150.

Redo, Joaquín
(Deceased 1906 or 1907) A] Unknown. B] Durango, Durango. C] Early education unknown; no degree. D] *Alternate senator* from the State of Sinaloa, 1884–86, 1886–88; *senator* from the State of Sonora, 1888–90; *senator* from the State of Colima, 1890–94, 1894–98, 1898–1900; *senator* from the State of Chihuahua, 1900–04. E] None. F] None. G] None. H] Went into business in youth; owned a cotton factory in Culiacán, Sinaloa; owned many businesses in Sinaloa, Sonora, and Durango; owned El Dorado sugar hacienda, Mazatlán; mining investments; owned sugar factory; founded an iron and machinery foundry, 1878. I] Married Alejandra Vega, from a wealthy Culiacán family; good friend of General *Francisco Canedo*, governor of Sinaloa, 1892–1909; father of Diego Redo Vega, governor of Sinaloa, 1909; father of Joaquín Redo Vega, federal deputy from Jalisco, 1906–12. J] None. K] None. L] Godoy, 301; C de S, 1900–02, 6; Album; González Dávila, 520; Dir social, 1935, 140.

Rendón (y Alcocer), Serapio
(Deceased August 22, 1913) A] September 3, 1867. B] Ciudad del Carmen, Campeche. C] Preparatory studies, Literary Institute of Yucatán, Mérida; law degree, School of Law, Mérida, 1886; secretary, National School of Law. D] *Federal deputy* from the State of Yucatán, Dist. 1, 1912–13. E] Notable orator in *Francisco I. Madero's* presidential campaign, 1911; member of the Anti-Reelectionist party; director, *Nueva Era*, official paper of the Constitutional Progressive party. F] Public defender, Mérida, 1886. G] None. H] Practicing lawyer; journalist; wrote under the pseudonym León Roch; contributor to *La Revista de Mérida*. I] Son of Víctor Rendón Buendía, lawyer and notary, and Catalina Alcocer; married Pilar Ponce y Cámara, daughter of José María Ponce y Solís; close friend of *José María Pino Suárez*. J] None. K] Denounced the murder of Madero and Pino Suárez in the Chamber of Deputies, 1913; briefly exiled to Havana, before returning to denounce assassination, 1913; kidnapped on the orders of *Victoriano Huerta* and *Aureliano Blanquet* and murdered, Tlalnepantla, Mexico. L] Enc Mex, XI, 111; QesQ, 494; Valdés Acosta, II, 225–30.

Reyes (Ochoa), Alfonso
(Deceased 1959) A] May 17, 1889. B] Monterrey, Nuevo León. C] Primary studies in a private school, Monterrey, and at the Lycée Français, Mexico City; preparatory studies, Colegio Civil de Nuevo León and the National Preparatory School, Mexico City; enrolled in the National School of Law, UNAM, graduating July 16, 1913; secretary of the National School of Higher Studies, UNAM, 1912–13; Center of Historical Studies, Madrid, 1913; founding professor of history of the Spanish language and Spanish literature, 1914; honorary doctorate, Harvard University, 1942; professor, School of Philosophy and Letters, UNAM, 1941; president, Colegio de México, 1939–59. D] None. E] None. F] Second secretary, Mexican legation to France, 1913–14; secretary, Mexican Historical Commission, Spain, 1919–20; first secretary, Mexican Legation to Spain, 1921; chargé d'affaires, Spain, 1921–24; *minister* to France, 1924; minister to Ar-

gentina, 1924; minister to Spain, 1926; minister to Argentina, 1927–29; ambassador to Brazil, 1930–36; ambassador to Argentina, 1936–37; special ambassador, Brazil, 1938–39. G] Member, National College; president, Mexican Academy of Language, 1957–59. H] Leading intellectual; translator; author; contributor to *El Imparcial* and *El Sol*, Madrid. I] Son of General *Bernardo Reyes*, governor of Nuevo León, 1889–1900, and Aurelia Ochoa; married Manuela Mota; son, Alfonso Reyes Mota, a physician; granddaughter Alicia Reyes, a poet; brother of *Rodolfo Reyes*, secretary of justice, 1913; great-uncle of Bernardo Reyes Morales, ambassador and career foreign service officer. J] None. K] National Prize of Arts and Sciences, 1945; candidate for the Nobel Prize in Literature. L] JSH, 329–30; DP70, 1755; WWM45, 100–01; WWLA40, 427.

Reyes (Ochoa), Rodolfo
(Deceased 1954) A] April 16, 1878. B] Guadalajara, Jalisco. C] Early education unknown; law degree, National School of Law, Mexico City; professor of constitutional law, National School of Law. D] *Federal deputy* from the State of Jalisco, Dist. 10, 1912–13, member of the Committee on Constitutional Affairs. E] Attacked President *Porfirio Díaz* in *La Protesta*, as a student. F] *Secretary* of justice, 1913. G] Member of the Royal Academy of Law, Madrid. H] Practicing lawyer, Spain, 1914–54. I] Son of General *Bernardo Reyes*, governor of Nuevo León, 1889–1900, and Aurelia Ochoa; brother of notable intellectual *Alfonso Reyes*, minister to France, 1924; father of Bernardo Reyes Morales, career foreign service officer and ambassador. J] Conspired with *Félix Díaz* and *Victoriano Huerta* against *Francisco I. Madero*, 1913. K] Imprisoned 4 months, condemned to death, but sentence commuted to exile, 1914. L] Enc Mex, XI, 130; DP70, 1758; WNM, 188; UNAM, law, 1891–96, 117.

Reyes (Ogazón), Bernardo
(Deceased February 9, 1913) A] August 20, 1850. B] Guadalajara, Jalisco. C] Primary studies, public school, Guadalajara; secondary school, Liceo for Boys, Guadala-

jara; enrolled, legal studies, 1864–65, abandoned to fight against the French, 1865. D] *Federal deputy* from the State of San Luis Potosí, Dist. 9, 1884–86; *governor* of Nuevo León, 1885–87, 1889–1900, 1902–09. E] Candidate for president of Mexico, 1909. F] Oficial mayor of war, 1896; *subsecretary* of war, 1902; *secretary* of war, 1902. G] None. H] None. I] Son of Domingo Reyes, colonel from Central America, and Juana Ogazón Vallarte, from an old Jalisco family; father of *Alfonso Reyes*, distinguished intellectual and foreign service officer; father of *Rodolfo Reyes*, secretary of justice, 1913; grandfather of Bernardo Reyes, foreign service officer. J] Joined the Liberals in 1865 under General *Ramón Corona*, serving as his aide; captured in first battle, 1865, and returned home; rejoined the service as a sergeant, under General *Francisco Tolentino*, 1866; rank of lieutenant, October 8, 1866; commander in the 4th Division, 1868; rank of lt. colonel, 1876; commander, 6th Regiment, 1877; remained loyal to Lerdo de Tejada, 1877; rank of colonel, 1878; commander of arms, San Luis Potosí, 1883; commander of military operations, Nuevo León, 1885; rank of division general, February 2, 1900; retired from the army, September 2, 1911; killed attacking the national palace, 1913. K] Imprisoned briefly, 1877; voluntary exile because of presidential candidacy, Paris, 1909–11; imprisoned by *Francisco I. Madero* for conspiring against his government with *Félix Díaz*, 1912–13; freed by son Rodolfo, 1913. L] López, 927–28; DP70, 1755; Album; Almanaque de Nuevo León, 100; Pavía, 263–65; Sec of War, 1911, 15.

Reyes Spíndola, Rafael
(Deceased January 13, 1922) A] October 24, 1860. B] Tlaxiaco, Oaxaca. C] Primary studies in Oaxaca, Oaxaca; preparatory studies at the Seminario de Oaxaca; law degree, Institute of Arts and Sciences of Oaxaca. D] *Alternate federal deputy* from the State of Michoacán, Dist. 6, 1888–90, under *Angel Padilla*; *federal deputy* from the State of Michoacán, Dist. 6, 1890–92, 1892–94; *federal deputy* from the State of Michoacán, Dist. 5, 1896–98; *federal deputy* from the State of

Michoacán, Dist. 2, 1898–1900, 1900–02; *federal deputy* from the State of Michoacán, Dist. 9, 1902–04, 1904–06, 1906–08; *federal deputy* from the State of Michoacán, Dist. 8, 1908–10; *federal deputy* from the State of Michoacán, Dist. 7, 1910–12. E] None. F] Private secretary to the governor of Michoacán, 1885. G] None. H] Publisher; journalist; founded *El Universal*, 1888; publisher of *El Mundo Ilustrado*, Puebla; founded *El Imparcial*, September 12, 1896; pianist and composer. I] Father of Rafael Reyes Spíndola, federal deputy and diplomat; brother of Octavio Reyes Spíndola, federal deputy from Oaxaca, 1892–94. J] None. K] None. L] Enc Mex, XI, 130; QesQ, 495; Mestre, 268.

Reynoso, José J.
(Deceased May 23, 1945) A] May 23, 1868. B] Guanajuato, Guanajuato. C] Early education unknown; preparatory studies, Colegio de Guanajuato; engineering degree, specializing in mining geology and metallurgy, Colegio de Guanajuato, 1892; professor of mechanics and mathematics, Colegio de Guanajuato, 1894. D] *Federal deputy* from the State of México, Dist. 8, 1912–13; *constitutional deputy* from the State of México, Dist. 8, 1916–17; *senator* from México, 1917–18, 1920–24, 1924–28, 1928–32. E] None. F] *Subsecretary* of the treasury, 1914; *subsecretary* in charge of the Secretariat of the treasury, 1914; *provisional governor* of Guanajuato, 1932. G] None. H] Mining engineer; director, many large mines, Jalisco; manager, Dos Estrellas Mining Company; manager, El Buen Tono Cigar Company. I] Son of Luis Gonzaga Reynoso and María López; married María Gilgan. J] Joined the Constitutionalists, 1913. K] None. L] Almanaque de Guanajuato, 132; Dir soc, 1935, 250–51; WWLA35, 336–37.

Reynoso Díaz, Leopoldo
(Deceased May 4, 1957) A] July 9, 1878. B] Zacualpan, México. C] Early education unknown; no degree. D] *Federal deputy* from the State of Morelos, Dist. 1, 1920–22; *federal deputy* from the State of Morelos, Dist. 2, 1922–24; *federal deputy*

from the State of Guerrero, Dist. 6, 1930 - 32. F] President of the Mexican Revolutionary party, State of Morelos, 1940; candidate for federal deputy from Morelos, 1940. F] None. G] None. H] Farmer, Xochitepec, Morelos. I] Son of Andrés Delabra and Francisca Díaz Ronces. J] Joined the Zapatistas under *Lorenzo Vázquez*, 1911; represented Lorenzo Vázquez at the Convention in Mexico City, 1915; rank of brigadier general; captured by the Carrancistas, 1919, but amnestied. K] None. L] López González, 211–12.

Rincón Gallardo (Romero de Terreros), Carlos
(Deceased June 7, 1950) A] July 31, 1874. B] Mexico City. C] Educated at Stoneyhurst College, Lancashire, England. D] None. E] None. F] *Secretary* of agriculture, 1914. G] Member of the Jockey Club. H] Landowner; author of books on horses; leading charro. I] Son of *Eduardo Rincón Gallardo y Rosso*, senator from San Luis Potosí, 1896–1902, and businessman, and María del Refugio Romero de Terreros, niece of Manuel Pedro Ramón Romero de Terreros, governor of the Federal District; nephew of *Pedro Rincón Gallardo y Rosso*, governor of the Federal District, 1893–96; grandson of General José María Rincón Gallardo. J] Career army officer; inspector general of the Rurales; rank of brigadier general, army reserves, November 3, 1913. K] None. L] Enc Mex, XI, 133; QesQ, 496; Sec of War, 1914, 29; Dir social, 1935, 251; Linajes, 231–33.

Rincón Gallardo y Rosso, Eduardo
(Deceased January 1, 1906) A] December 1, 1848. B] Mexico City. C] Early education unknown; no degree. D] *Federal deputy* from the State of Jalisco, Dist. 6, 1888–90; *alternate senator* from the State of San Luis Potosí, 1892–96; *senator* from the State of San Luis Potosí, 1896–1900, 1900–02. E] None. F] Founding member and stockholder, Jockey Club, 1883. H] Landowner. I] Son of José María Rincón Gallardo, brigadier general, and Ana María Rosso Delgado; married María del Refugio Romero de Terreros, 5th Countess of Regla; daughter Carmen mar-

ried Rafael Ortiz de la Huerta, landowner and son of president of the National Bank of Mexico; son *Carlos Rincón Gallardo*, secretary of agriculture, 1914; brother *Pedro Rincón Gallardo y Ross*, governor of the Federal District, 1893–96. J] None. K] None. L] Linajes, 231–33; C de S, 1900–02, 6; Blue Book, 1901, 89.

Rincón Gallardo (y Rosso), Pedro
(Deceased September 1, 1909) A] June 29, 1836. B] Hacienda de Ciénega de la Mata, Jalisco. C] Early education unknown; no degree. D] Mayor of Mexico City, 1881–82, 1885; *federal deputy* from the Federal District, Dist. 1, 1886–88;1888–90, 1890–92. E] None. F] President of the Committee to Drain the Valley of Mexico, 1888; ambassador to Russia, 1892–93; governor of the Federal District, 1893–96; ambassador to Germany, 1900–03; *ambassador* to the United Kingdom, 1903–05. G] Founding member and stockholder, Jockey Club, 1883. H] Landowner; businessman. I] Son of General José María Rincón Gallardo, who joined the Liberal army as a brigade general to fight the French, and Ana María Rosso; brother of *Eduardo Rincón Gallardo*, senator from San Luis Potosí, and married to his wife's sister; uncle of *Carlos Rincón Gallardo*, secretary of agriculture, 1914; married Paz Romero de Terreros y Gómez, daughter of Manuel Pedro Ramón Romero de Terreros, governor of the Federal District; second wife, María de los Dolores Barrón; daughter Paz married Alfredo Barrón, diplomat. J] Fought against the French; rank of lt. colonel, 1863; auxiliary brigadier general, army reserves, February 4, 1891. K] None. L] Mestre, 236; Blue Book, 1901, 89; Godoy, 246; Linajes, 231–33; Sec of War, 1901, 25; QesQ, 496–97.

Ríos Ríos, Juan José
(Deceased April 18, 1955) A] December 27, 1882. B] San Luis del Mezquital, Zacatecas. C] Early education unknown; no degree; director, Heroic Military College, 1927–28. D] None. E] Propagandist against President *Porfirio Díaz*, early 1900s. F] *Governor* of Colima, 1915–17; oficial mayor of war, 1918; *subsecretary* of war in charge of the secretariat, 1918–

20; director general of military industry; chief of staff, Secretariat of National Defense; *secretary* of government, 1932. G] Coleader of the Cananea mining strike, 1906. H] Miner. I] Son of Anacleto Ríos and Francisca Ríos. J] Joined the Constitutionalists as a major in the Army of the Northeast, September 10, 1913; commander of the 2nd Battalion at Cananea; military commander of Colima and Jalisco, 1914–15; fought under *Alvaro Obregón* against *Francisco Villa*, 1915; commander of the expeditionary column to Michoacán; rank of brigade general, May 22, 1916; remained loyal to *Venustiano Carranza*, 1920; commander of the 12th Military Zone; commander of the 9th Military Zone; commander of the 1st Military Zone, Mexico City; commander of the 17th Military Zone, Querétaro, Querétaro; commander of the 27th Military Zone, Iguala, Guerrero; commander of the 11th Military Zone, Zacatecas, Zacatecas, 1937; rank of division general, October 16, 1937. K] None. L] Rev de Ejer, Sept 1976, 125; Dávila, 135; Almada, Colima, 162; Rev de Ejer, April 1958, 66; DP70, 1767; Enc Mex, XI, 141; Moreno, 67; González Dávila, 527–28.

Riva Palacio, Carlos
(Deceased 1936) A] October 4, 1892. B] Chalco, México. C] Primary studies in Chalco; preparatory studies, Mexico City; no degree. D] *Federal deputy* from the State of Michoacán, Dist. 6, 1924–26; *governor* of México, 1925–29; *senator* from the Federal District, 1932–33. E] *President* of the National Executive Committee of the National Revolutionary party, 1933–34. F] *Secretary* of government, 1929–30; ambassador to Chile, 1934–35; ambassador to Costa Rica, 1935–36; appointed ambassador to Guatemala, but never held post, 1936. G] None. H] Businessman. I] Son of Agustín Riva Palacio and Luz Carrillo; parents were from the working class; brother of Manuel Riva Palacio, senator and federal deputy from México; influenced politically by *Filiberto* and *Abundio Gómez Díaz*, prominent figures from the State of México. J] Joined the Constitutionalists under General *Agustín Millán*, 1913. K] None. L] Enc Mex, XI, 141–42; Dir social, 1935, 251.

Rivas (Gómez), Carlos
(Deceased January 21, 1908) A] 1844. B] Guaymas, Sonora. C] Primary studies at the Liceo Franco Mexicano of Fournier, Mexico City, and the Conciliar Seminaries of Tepic and Guadalajara; law degree, National School of Law, Mexico City, 1865. D] Federal deputy from the State of Tepic, 1868–70, 1870–72, 1872–74, 1880–82; *senator* from the State of Hidalgo, 1884–88, 1888–92, 1892–96, 1896–1900, 1900–04, 1904–08. E] None. F] Private secretary to the president of Mexico, General *Manuel González*, 1880–83; special mission to England to settle debts, 1883; private secretary to the president of Mexico, 1883–84; governor of the Federal District, 1884. G] Member and stockholder, Jockey Club. H] Landowner and businessman; poet; owner of the El Peñón de los Baños hacienda; owned La Constancia Mexicana textile factory, Puebla; manager, La Sociedad de Terrenos, Tepic, 1891. I] Son of Carlos Rivas Góngora and Domilita Gómez, landowners; married his cousin Leonor Rivas de Rivas; brother Francisco, large landowner and federal deputy from Tepic, 1898–1912. J] Accompanied General *Ramón Corona* on a campaign; accompanied General González on his campaign to the Alica Mountains, Tepic, 1879–80. K] None. L] Godoy, 81–82; Rice, 249; Hombres prominentes, 236–37; Mestre, 230; Blue Book, 1901, 89.

Rivera Cabrera, Crisóforo
(Deceased July 2, 1955) A] Unknown. B] Tehuantepec, Oaxaca. C] Primary studies, Oaxaca, Oaxaca; law degree, Institute of Arts and Sciences, Oaxaca. D] *Federal deputy* from the State of Oaxaca, Dist. 15, 1912–13; *constitutional deputy* from the State of Oaxaca, Dist. 15, 1916–17; *federal deputy* from the State of Oaxaca, Dist. 16, 1917–18, 1920–22. E] Wrote articles against *Porfirio Díaz* as a student. F] Tax administrator, Isthmus of Tehuantepec, 1913; official, Secretariat of the Treasury, 1915; customs administrator, Piedras Negras, 1916; substitute president, Board of Conciliation and Arbitration; auxiliary lawyer, Board of Conciliation and Arbitration, Federal District, 1937–39. G] None. H] Practicing lawyer. I] Father of Octavio Rivera Sánchez,

director general in the Secretariat of Communications, 1982; married Guadalupe Sánchez Ugalde. J] Joined the Constitutionalists, 1913; chief of staff to General Jesús Carranza, 1913; military commander of the Isthmus of Tehuantepec, 1916. K] None. L] C de D, 1916–17.

Robles, José Isabel
(Deceased April 2, 1917) A] December 25, 1891. B] Jalpa, Zacatecas. C] Primary studies in Zacatecas; primary teaching certificate; elementary school teacher, Zacatecas. D] None. E] None. F] *Governor* of Coahuila, 1914; *secretary* of war for the Convention government, 1914–15. G] None. H] None. I] Unknown. J] Organized the Robles Brigade, and joined the Constitutionalists under the Division of the North, 1913; represented at the Convention of Aguascalientes, 1914; represented by Santiago Winfiel, Convention of Mexico City, 1915; rank of brigadier general; supported *Francisco Villa*, switched support to *Venustiano Carranza*, and then back to Villa, 1915; rebelled against the government, 1917; captured, 1917. K] Executed by government forces, Sierra de Juárez, Oaxaca, 1917. L] Enc Mex, XI, 157; Almada, 1968, 463; Rouaix, 365.

Robles Domínguez, Alfredo
(Deceased August 28, 1928) A] July 31, 1876. B] Guanajuato, Guanajuato. C] Primary studies, Pruneda private school, Guanajuato; preparatory studies, National Preparatory School, Mexico City; architectural engineering degree, United States. D] *Constitutional deputy* from the State of Guanajuato, Dist. 12, 1916–17; *federal deputy* from the State of Guanajuato, Dist. 12, 1917–18. E] Activist in *Francisco I. Madero*'s Anti-Reelectionist campaign, 1908–10; vice-president, Anti-Reelectionist Convention, 1910; leader, Anti-Reelectionist Center of Mexico City; lent his building in Mexico City for meetings of the Democratic party, the Mexico City Reyista Club, the National Democratic party, and the Anti-Reelectionist Club of Mexico City; candidate for president of Mexico of the Catholic party, 1920. F] *Governor* of the Federal District, Convention government, 1914; director of public works, 1915. G] None. H] Engi-

neer; constructed and designed large buildings; designed La Palestina and La Mexicana buildings, Mexico City. I] From a middle–class family. J] Joined the Constitutionalists, 1913; commander-in-chief, Division of the South, Acapulco, Guerrero, 1914. K] Experimented with airplanes. L] Enc Mex, XI, 157–58; QesQ, 505.

Robles Gil, Alberto
(Deceased March 6, 1936) A] December 16, 1865. B] Guadalajara, Jalisco. C] Early education unknown; graduated from the National Military College as a 2nd lieutenant of engineers, 1889. D] *Governor* of Jalisco, 1911–12. E] None. F] *Secretary* of development, 1913. G] None. H] Engineer. I] Related to Emeterio Robles Gil (father or uncle), lawyer and governor of Jalisco; married María Luisa Souza; son Alberto, Jr., an engineer, married Consuelo Maza, related to Benito Juárez; student with *Samuel García Cuéllar, Alberto Canseco,* and *David de la Fuente.* J] Career army officer. K] None. L] Enc Mex, XI, 158; Cuevas, 351; Mestre, 225; Dir social, 1935, 142; Mestre, 291.

Rocha, Sóstenes
(Deceased March 31, 1897) A] November, 1831. B] Mineral de Marfil, Municipio de Guanajuato, Guanajuato. C] Early education unknown; graduated from the National Military College as a 2nd lieutenant in the engineers, 1853; military studies in Europe, 1876–80; director, National Military College, 1880–86. D] *Federal deputy* from the State of Puebla, Dist 11, 1888–90, 1890–92, 1892–94. E] None. F] None. G] None. H] Journalist; director, *El Combate,* Liberal paper. I] Military mentor to numerous high-ranking officers and politicians in *Porfirio Díaz*'s administrations. J] Career army officer; opposed the Revolution of Ayutla, 1854–55, and then supported it, 1855; defected to the Conservatives, 1856; joined the Hidalgo Battalion, national guard, to fight the Conservatives, 1856–57; fought against the Conservatives, 1857–61; captured by the French, but escaped in Veracruz; rank of brigade general, 1867; opposed the Plan of La Noria, 1871, and defeated the rebels; rank of division general, June 11, 1871. K] None. L] Mestre,

197; DP70, 1781–82; Almanaque de Guanajuato, 162.

Rocha y Portú, Pablo
(Deceased November 18, 1908) A] March 1, 1840. B] Celaya, Guanajuato. C] Preparatory studies, Colegio de la Purísima, Guanajuato; mining engineering degree, Guanajuato, 1856; medical studies, National Medical School, 1858–60, left school to join the Liberal forces. D] *Governor* of Guanajuato, 1884–85. E] None. F] Judge of the Supreme Military Court; *political boss* of Tepic (governor of Nayarit), 1897–1904. G] None. H] None. I] Unknown. J] Career army officer; joined the Liberals, 1860, during the War of the Reform; fought the French; captured and deported to France as a prisoner of war; officer, sappers battalion; inspector, 8th Regiment; rank of brigadier general, November 6, 1882; rank of brigade general, December 18, 1891; chief of arms in Tepic, 1901. K] Worked in Spain in great poverty as a prisoner of war. L] Godoy, 108; Sec of War, 1901, 19; Almanaque de Guanajuato, 130; Mestre, 233.

Rodiles, Saúl
(Deceased 1951) A] 1885. B] Atlixco, Puebla. C] Primary studies, private schools in Atlixco and Zacapoaxtla, Puebla; enrolled, National Military College, but left because of an accident; teaching certificate, Normal School of Jalapa; studies, University of Puebla; professor of logic and ethics, Normal School, Jalisco; professor of sociology, philosophic doctrine, history of education in Mexico, and literature, Preparatory School of Jalisco; teacher, Tlacotepec, Puebla; founder and director of the Night School for Workers, Jalisco; director, Normal School of Jalisco, 1934. D] Member of the City Council of Puebla; mayor of Puebla; *constitutional deputy* from the State of Veracruz, Dist. 2, 1916–17. E] None. F] Director, Department of Labor, 1918; president, Educational Advisory Board, Veracruz. G] None. H] Founder of *Ultimas Noticias*, Jalapa, Veracruz. I] Unknown. J] None. K] None. L] CyT, II, 573.

Rodríguez, Abel S.
(Deceased March 24, 1955) A] 1874. B] Jalapa, Veracruz. C] Teaching certificate, Rébsamen Normal School, Jalapa, 1895; professor in Chihuahua, 1895–96; teacher, Veracruz, Veracruz; subdirector, Primary School Annex to the Normal, Jalapa, 1894–95; director of Escuelas Filomáticas, for wealthy children, 1895–1911. D] *Senator* from the State of Chihuahua, 1916–20, 1922–26; *senator* from the State of Veracruz, 1930–34. E] Editor of *La Voz de Coronado*, paper of the political club which supported *Enrique Creel* for governor, 1907; president of the Regional Committee, Mexican Revolutionary party, Jalapa. F] Director general of primary education, Chihuahua, 1912–13, 1916, 1918; secretary general of government of Chihuahua, 1920; provisional governor of Chihuahua, 1920; *head*, Department of the Federal District, 1923–26; *interim governor* of Veracruz, 1927–28; president, National Pension Funds, Mexico City. G] None. H] None. I] Son of a wealthy coffee hacienda owner. J] Joined the Constitutionalists; supported *Alvaro Obregón*, 1920. K] None. L] Pasquel, Jalapa, 605–06; Almada, 549–50; Almada, 1968, 646; Dir social, 1935, 143.

Rodríguez, José María
(Deceased January 17, 1946) A] October 15, 1870. B] Saltillo, Coahuila. C] Primary studies, public school, Saltillo; secondary and preparatory studies, Ateneo Fuente, Saltillo; medical degree, National Medical School, 1895; professor by opposition of topographical anatomy, National Medical School, 1893. D] *Constitutional deputy* from the State of Coahuila, Dist. 3, 1916–17. E] Student leader against the government of *José María Garza Galán*, Coahuila, 1892; founded *El Pueblo Coahuilense* as a medical student, 1893. F] Consul for the Constitutionalists, San Antonio, Texas, 1913; president, Board of Health for Mexico, 1914–16; *head*, Department of Health, 1917–19; *governor* of Morelos, 1920; president, Supreme Council of Health, Coahuila, 1934. G] None. H] Practicing physician. I] Son of Jesús María Rodríguez and Melquíades Rodríguez y Rodríguez. J] Major, army Medical

Corps, 1895; *Francisco I. Madero* and Anti-Reelectionist leaders met in his home, Torreón, Coahuila, 1909; supported the Maderistas in Torreón, 1911; physician in the Battle of Gómez Palacio, Durango, 1912; rank of brigadier general. K] Organized health services in Coahuila, 1921–34. L] Moreno, 57–58.

Rodríguez de la Fuente, Jesús
(Deceased 1967) A] 1894. B] Nadadores, Coahuila. C] Preparatory studies from the National Preparatory School; enrolled, National School of Law, April 22, 1912, graduating with a law degree, 1916. D] *Federal deputy* from the State of Coahuila, Dist. 4, 1918–20; mayor of Tacubaya, Federal District, 1923–24. E] None. F] Secretary general of government of Puebla, 1917; secretary general of government of Querétaro, 1917; director of the Legal Office of the City of Mexico, 1918; secretary general of government of the Federal District; oficial mayor of industry, 1920; treasurer general of the State of Nuevo León; lawyer, Secretariat of Agriculture; lawyer, Department of Health, 1941–43; secretary general of government of Coahuila, 1948; oficial mayor of the Popular Foodstuffs Program (Conasupo); subdirector of military pensions, 1956–67. G] None. H] Lawyer, Telephone and Telegraph Company of Mexico, 1924–35. I] Son of Francisco Rodríguez Cantú and Domitila de la Fuente. J] Staff officer, army of the East, under General *Pablo González.* K] None. L] C de D, 1918–20; UNAM, law, 1912–16, 4.

Rodríguez (Ladislao), Pedro L.
(Deceased August 30, 1918) A] June 27, 1841. B] San Pedro Apóstol Etla, Oaxaca. C] Some primary studies only. D] Local deputy to the state legislature of Hidalgo; federal deputy from the State of Hidalgo, 1878–80, 1880–82, 1882–84; *federal deputy* from the State of Hidalgo, Dist. 9, 1886–88, 1888–90, 1890–92, 1892–94, 1894–96; *federal deputy* from the State of Hidalgo, Dist. 7, 1896–98; *governor* of Hidalgo, 1897–1911; *senator* from the State of Hidalgo, 1914–16. E] Joined the Liberal party, December 1857. F] *Substitute governor* of Hidalgo, 1896–97. G] None.

H] Began working as an agricultural laborer at nine; small farmer; telegrapher; constructed a telegraph line from Mexico City to Cuernavaca, 1868; director, telegraph office, Pachuca, Hidalgo, 1872–96. I] Parents from the upper middle class, but died without an estate when he was eight; distant relative of *Porfirio Díaz.* J] Joined the Liberals under Valentín Palacios, December 20, 1857; fought the Conservatives during the War of the Reform, 1858–59; fought the French; constructed a telegraph line from Oaxaca to Mexico City for Díaz; supported the Tuxtepec rebellion, 1876. K] None. L] Wright, 318; Album; Pérez López, 395–96; Godoy, 163–64; Mestre, 260.

Rodríguez (Luján), Abelardo L.
(Deceased February 13, 1967) A] May 12, 1889. B] San José de Guaymas, Sonora. C] Primary education in Nogales, Sonora; no degree. D] *President* of Mexico, 1932–34; governor of Sonora, 1943–48. E] None. F] Police chief of Nogales, Sonora, 1912; *governor* and military commander of Baja California del Norte, 1923–29; *governor* of Baja California del Norte, 1929–30; *subsecretary* of war and navy, 1931–32; *secretary* of war and navy, August 2, 1932–September 2, 1932; *secretary* of industry and commerce, January 20, 1932–August 2, 1932; president of the Advisory Fishing Council, Secretariat of Industry and Commerce, 1961; general coordinator of national production, 1942–43. G] None. H] Wealthy businessman in the States of Sonora and Baja California del Norte; began investments in the 1920s; important shareholder in Banco Mexicano; cofounder of Empacadora del Norte, Navajoa, 1927; cofounder of Nacional de Productos Marinos, 1927; shareholder in National Portland Cement Company; coinvestor with Francisco Javier Gaxiola, Jr., in La Suiza; invested in Pesquera del Pacífico, 1937. I] Father Nicolás Rodríguez went bankrupt running several mule trains; worked in a hardware store with brother Fernando; employed at Cananea copper mines; professional baseball player. J] Joined the Revolution, lieutenant, 1913; rank of 1st captain, 1914; fought against *Victoriano Huerta*, 1913–14; rank of ma-

jor, 1914; rank of lt. colonel, 1915; commander of the 53rd Battalion under General *Alvaro Obregón* against *Francisco Villa*, 1915; rank of colonel, 1916; rank of brigadier general, 1920; military commander of Baja California del Norte, 1921; chief of military operations in Oaxaca, 1923; rank of brigade general, 1924; rank of division general, June 11, 1928; commander of the Military Zone of the Gulf, 1942. K] Resigned from the governorship of Sonora, April 1948, giving health as a reason. L] HA, 11 Dec. 1961, 3; NYT, 14 Feb. 1967, 43; QesQ, 508; WWM45, 103; DP70, 1783; Covarrubias, 156; NYT, 26 Mar. 1943, 2; *Justicia*, July 1970.

Rodríguez Malpica, Hilario
(Deceased) A] January 14, 1858. B] Veracruz, Veracruz. C] Primary studies at the Veracruz Institute, Veracruz; graduated from the Naval School of Campeche, March 1876. D] None. E] None. F] Chief of staff to President *Francisco I. Madero*, 1911–13; naval attaché, Brazil and Argentina, 1914. G] None. H] None. I] Son of José Rodríguez Malpica and Florentina Segovia; married Margarita Saliba. J] Career naval officer; commander of the Mexican fleet; director, Naval Department, Secretariat of war. K] None. L] Dir social, 1935, 252–53.

Rodríguez (Melgarejo), Matías
(Deceased November 11, 1945) A] February 24, 1876. B] Tetepango, Hidalgo. C] Completed the 4th grade only. D] *Constitutional deputy* from the State of Hidalgo, Dist. 8, 1916–17; *federal deputy* from the State of Hidalgo, Dist. 8, 1918–20, 1922–24; *governor* of Hidalgo, 1925–29; *senator* from the State of Hidalgo, 1930–34. E] Member of the Anti-Reelectionist party, 1910; *secretary general* of the National Executive Committee of the National Revolutionary party, 1930; *secretary* of the National Executive Committee of the National Revolutionary party, 1931; *secretary* of agrarian action, National Revolutionary party, 1933. F] None. G] Founder of the Agrarian League of Hidalgo; president, Agrarian Commission of Hidalgo, 1919–20. H] Worked as a peon on father's farm; worked in a lime oven; founded *El Voto*,

in Mexico City. I] Parents were peasants. J] Joined the Maderistas, 1910–11; joined the Constitutionalists under General Antonio Medina, 1913–14; rank of lt. colonel; member of the Liberty Brigade; fought with the Hidalgo Loyalists Brigade under General Vicente Segura; fought under General Nicolás Flores, 1914–15; reached the rank of colonel. K] Imprisoned for anti-Díaz attacks, January 11, 1911. L] Pérez López, 403–04; Gruening, 438–39.

Rodríguez Rivera, Ramón
(Deceased September 29, 1889) A] May 22, 1850. B] Córdoba, Veracruz. C] Preparatory studies, Colegio Carolina of Puebla, 1865–68; completed preparatory studies, as one of the first students, at the National Preparatory School, 1868; medical degree, National School of Medicine, 1875; professor of world history and literature, Preparatory School of Córdoba; professor of literature and hygiene, Girls' High School; student of Ignacio Ramírez and Gabino Barreda at the National Preparatory School. D] Local deputy to the state legislature of Veracruz; *federal deputy* from the State of Jalisco, Dist. 17, 1886–88, 1888–89; member of the City Council of Mexico City, 1888. E] None. F] Secretary general of government under *Apolinar Castillo Ramírez*, 1880–83. G] Member of many intellectual societies. H] Physician, Córdoba, 1875–82; physician, San Andrés Hospital, Mexico City, 1888. I] Son of Ramón Rodríguez, from Pontevedra, Spain, and Trinidad Rivera; friend of *Gustavo Baz* and Manuel Acuña in youth; father of Ramón Rodríguez Rivera, senator from Veracruz, 1918–22. J] None. K] None. L] Illescas, 154–55; Peral; Hombres prominentes, 343–44.

Rojas, Máximo
(Deceased 1924) A] May 11, 1881. B] San Francisco Papalotla, Tlaxcala. C] Early education unknown; no degree. D] Mayor of Papalotla, 1912–13; *governor* of Tlaxcala, 1918–21; local deputy to the state legislature of Tlaxcala, 1923. E] None. F] *Governor* and military commander of Tlaxcala, 1914–15. G] None. H] Peasant; laborer, thread factory. I] From a working-class family.

J] Joined the Maderista rebels under General Juan Cuamatzi, 1910–11; fought under General Francisco A. García, 1911–12; joined the Constitutionalists as a colonel, San Agustín Tlaxco, Tlaxcala, February, 1913; rank of brigadier general, 1914; represented at the Convention of Aguascalientes by Colonel Pedro Morales; supported *Alvaro Obregón*, 1920; fought against the *Adolfo de la Huerta* rebellion, 1923–24. K] Killed in battle against the de la Huerta forces, San Juan de los Llanos, Puebla. L] QesQ, 513–14.

Rojas (Arreola), Luis Manuel
(Deceased February 27, 1949) A] September 21, 1870. B] Ahualulco, Jalisco. C] Preparatory studies from the Liceo for Boys, Guadalajara; law degree, School of Law, Guadalajara, 1897; professor of constitutional law, National School of Law. D] *Federal deputy* from the State of Jalisco, Dist. 11, 1912–13; *constitutional deputy* from the State of Jalisco, Dist. 1, 1916–17, president of the Constitutional Convention, 1917. E] None. F] Ambassador to Guatemala; director, National Library of Mexico, 1914–17; director, Department of Fine Arts, 1918. G] None. H] Practicing lawyer; journalist; publisher; founder and director, *Gaceta de Guadalajara*, 1902–06; founder and director, *Revista de Revistas*, 1910–12; director, *El Universal*. I] Son of Anastasio Rojas Topete, one of the leading lawyers in Jalisco, and Antonia Arreola O'Campos; married Elodia Ramírez García. J] Joined the Maderistas, 1909–11; joined the Constitutionalists, 1913; judge of the Supreme Military Court, with the rank of division general, 1916–17. K] One of the few deputies to vote against *Francisco I. Madero's* forced resignation, 1913; imprisoned by *Victoriano Huerta*, 1913. L] Enc Mex, XI, 172–73; WWM45, 104; DP70, 1793; Morales Jiménez, 263–66; Moreno, 248–50.

Rojas (Martínez), Rafael R.
(Deceased September 5, 1926) A] Unknown. B] Los Reyes, Cholula, Puebla. C] Primary studies at the Annex to the Normal School; secondary studies, Normal School; studies in accounting, Colegio de Puebla, Puebla. D] *Federal deputy*

from the State of Puebla, Dist. 5, 1917–18, 1918–20. E] Treasurer, Aquiles Serdán Revolutionary Junta. F] *Provisional governor* of Puebla, 1920. G] None. H] Unknown. I] Son of Sebastián Rojas and Nazaría Martínez Toxtle, a wealthy family; married Elena Bonilla de Huerta. J] Joined *Francisco I. Madero's* forces as a captain, December 19, 1910; rank of major, February 25, 1911; rank of lt. colonel, March 25, 1911; left the army, 1911–14; joined the Constitutionalists, under the 2nd Division of the East, August 25, 1914; commander of military operations in Cholula, 1914–15; rank of colonel, February 5, 1915; commander of a brigade, Cholula, 1915–16; rank of brigadier general, January 4, 1916; commander of the 4th Brigade, 2nd Division, Army of the East, 1916; supported *Alvaro Obregón*, 1920; rank of brigade general, May 2, 1920. K] Murdered at the Hacienda Santo Domingo, Atoyatempan, Atlixco, Puebla. L] Almanaque de Puebla, 130; CyT, II, 592.

Romero, Félix
(Deceased September 2, 1912) A] March 31, 1831. B] Oaxaca, Oaxaca. C] Primary studies at the Conciliar Seminary of Oaxaca; preparatory studies at the Institute of Arts and Sciences of Oaxaca, 1840; law degree, Institute of Arts and Sciences of Oaxaca, July 8, 1852; director, Institute of Arts and Sciences of Oaxaca, 1865; professor of Spanish grammar, Institute of Arts and Sciences of Oaxaca; professor of Roman law, Institute of Arts and Sciences of Oaxaca. D] Constitutional deputy from the State of Tehuantepec, 1856–57; constitutional deputy to the State Convention of Oaxaca, 1857; federal deputy from the State of Oaxaca, 1862, 1878–80, 1880–82. E] Joined the Liberal party. F] Court reporter, Oaxaca; governor of Oaxaca, 1857; secretary of government of the State of Oaxaca, 1860, vice-governor of Oaxaca, 1871–72; secretary general of government of Oaxaca, 1865; president of the Superior Tribunal of Justice of Oaxaca, 1871; district judge, Puebla, 1871–74; attaché, Mexican Legation, Paris, France; *justice* of the Supreme Court, 1889–1912. G] Vice-president of the Mexican Society of Geography and Statistics. H] Practicing law-

yer; founded *El Azote de los Tiranos*, 1856. I] Early political disciple of Benito Juárez and his student at the Institute of Arts and Sciences; student with *Porfirio Díaz*. J] Journalist during the Reform War and the French Intervention; opposed the Plan of la Noria, 1871; supported the Plan of Tuxtepec, 1876. K] Jailed for opposing the Conservatives in *La Bandera Amarilla*. L] Iturribaría, 233–42; Pavía, 18–28; Godoy, 221; QesQ, 516; Hombres prominentes, 259–60; Almanaque de Oaxaca, 128–29; Mestre, 243; Blue Book, 1901, 29.

Romero, Matías
(Deceased December 30, 1898) A] February 24, 1837. B] Oaxaca, Oaxaca. C] Primary studies, Clemente Ramírez School; secondary studies at the Conciliar Seminary of Santa Cruz of Oaxaca; preparatory studies, Institute of Arts and Sciences of Oaxaca; legal studies, Institute of Arts and Sciences of Oaxaca, until 1855; completed law degree, National School of Law, Mexico City, October 12, 1857; studied under Benito Juárez in Oaxaca. D] Alternate senator from the State of Chiapas, 1875–76; federal deputy from the State of Oaxaca, 1876. E] None. F] Joined the Secretariat of Foreign Relations, 1855; secretary to Melchor Ocampo, Veracruz, 1857; first secretary of the Mexican Legation in Washington, D.C., 1859–60; chargé d'affaires, Mexican Legation, Washington, D.C., 1860–62, 1862–63; ambassador to the United States, 1863–67, for Benito Juárez; secretary of the treasury, 1868, 1869–72; postmaster general of Mexico; secretary of the treasury, 1877–79; *ambassador* to the United States, 1882–92; *secretary* of the treasury, 1892–93; *ambassador* to the United States, 1893–98. G] None. H] Managed own landholdings, Soconusco, Veracruz, 1872–75; manager, Isthmus of Tehuantepec Railroad, 1879–82. I] Political disciple of Benito Juárez. J] Fought the French as chief of staff to General *Porfirio Díaz*, 1863; rank of colonel. K] None. L] Godoy, 222; Sierra, 80–83; Enc Mex, XI, 179; QesQ, 516–17; Ramírez, 77–83; Iturribarría, 221–27.

Romero (y Andrade), Francisco
(Deceased January 4, 1930) A] August 18, 1853. B] Tulancingo, Hidalgo. C] Early education unknown; enrolled National Military College, 1870, graduating as a 2nd lieutenant in the engineers, 1876; professor of astronomy, navigation, and cosmography, National Military College, 1885. D] Federal deputy from the State of Yucatán; federal deputy from the State of Sonora; federal deputy from the State of Hidalgo; *federal deputy* from the State of Jalisco, Dist. 11, 1886–88, 1888–90, 1890–92, 1892–94, 1894–96; *federal deputy* from the State of Guerrero, Dist. 8, 1896–98; *federal deputy* from the State of Guerrero, Dist. 6, 1900–02; *federal deputy* from the State of Guerrero, Dist. 5, 1902–04; *federal deputy* from the State of Hidalgo, Dist. 4, 1904–06, 1906–08, 1908–10, 1910–12; *federal deputy* from the State of Hidalgo, Dist. 8, 1912–14. E] None. F] *Governor* of San Luis Potosí, 1913–14. G] None. H] None. I] Son of José María Romero, lawyer, and Ana Andrade. J] Career army officer; joined the 4th Artillery Brigade, 1876; attached to the staff, secretary of war; rank of colonel, May 11, 1889; rank of division general, January 2, 1914. K] Killed José Verástegui in a duel. L] Pérez López, 410; Hombres prominentes, 213–14; Mestre, 283; Sec of War, 1902; Sec of War, 1914, 17; Cuevas, 349.

Romero Courtade, Enrique
(Deceased May 12, 1940) A] August 26, 1894. B] Silao, Guanajuato. C] Early education unknown; law degree, Colegio de Guanajuato. D] Local deputy to the state legislature of Guanajuato; *federal deputy* from the State of Guanajuato, Dist. 5, 1928–30, 1930–32; *federal deputy* from the State of Guanajuato, Dist. 4, 1934–37. E] *Secretary* of organization of the National Executive Committee of the National Revolutionary party, 1933–35. F] Agent of the Ministerio Público; judge, Superior Tribunal of Justice of Guanajuato; president, Superior Tribunal of Justice of Guanajuato; interim governor of Guanajuato; head, Department of the Federal District, 1931; secretary general of the Department of the Federal District, 1932. G] None. H] Practicing lawyer. I] Un-

known. J] Unknown. K] None. L] Peral; C de D, 1928 30.

Romero Flores, Jesús
(Deceased) A] April 28, 1885. B] La Piedad, Michoacán. C] Teaching certificate from the Colegio de San Nicolás, Morelia, October 7, 1905; director of the Normal School for the State of Michoacán, 1915; director of Primary Schools, Valle de Santiago, Guanajuato; director, private school, Piedad Cabados; director of secondary schools, Piedad, Morelia; director of the School of Tangancicuaro de Artista, Zamora, Michoacán, 1910; inspector general of public and private schools, 1913–14; director of El Pensador Mexicano Primary School, Mexico City, 1920. D] *Constitutional deputy* from the State of Michoacán, Dist. 16, 1916–17; local deputy to the state legislature of Michoacán, 1922; *federal deputy* from the State of Michoacán, Dist. 17, 1922–24; senator from the State of Michoacán, 1964–70. E] None. F] Director of primary education, Michoacán, 1930; director of public education for the State of Michoacán, 1915–16; director of normal schools, Morelia, 1925; section chief, Department of Primary Education, Department of the Federal District, 1918; private secretary to General *Francisco Múgica*, 1918; director of the Public Library of Morelia, 1928; historian for the National Museum of Mexico, 1935–45. G] None. H] Author of many works. I] Married Refugio Pérez; widowed, married María Pureco Rasso. J] None. K] None. L] C de S, 1964–70; WWM45, 106; HA, 27 Nov. 1972, 11.

Romero Rubio, Manuel
(Deceased October 3, 1895) A] 1828. B] Atzcapotzalco, Mexico City. C] Primary studies, Colegio de San Gregorio; secondary studies, Conciliar Seminary of Mexico City; law degree, Colegio de San Gregorio, Mexico City, under Juan Rodríguez Puebla, 1854. D] Constitutional deputy from Puebla, 1856–57; federal deputy from the State of Puebla, 1867–68; *senator* from the State of Tabasco, 1880–84, 1884–88, 1888–92, 1892–95. e–Propagandist for Benito Juárez, 1857. F] Judge, Tulancingo, Hidalgo, 1855; secretary, Supreme Court, 1855; secretary to

General Agustín Alcérreca, 1857; governor of Mexico City, 1857; official, Liberal government in Veracruz, 1858; secretary of foreign relations, 1876; *secretary* of government, 1884–95. G] Founding member and stockholder, Jockey Club, 1883. H] Practicing lawyer, 1854–55; traveled in the United States, 1877–80; founded opposition paper in Mexico, 1880. I] Son of Luis Romero, businessman; married Agustina Castello; father-in-law of *Porfirio Díaz*; father-in-law of *Rosendo Pineda*, federal deputy from the State of Oaxaca, 1884–1912; father-in-law of prominent banker José de Teresa. J] Joined the Liberals during the Revolution of Ayutla, 1855–56; imprisoned in Santiago Tlatelolco, Federal District, 1858; chief of staff to General Garza; captured by the French and exiled to Europe, 1863; opposed the Plan of Tuxtepec, 1876. K] Exiled to New York City, 1877–80. L] Velasco, 99ff; Pavía, 47–55; FSRE, 120–21; Enc Mex, XI, 182; QesQ, 518; Hombres prominentes, 13–18; Mestre, 192; Blue Book, 1901, 89.

Romero Vargas, Ignacio
(Deceased August 9, 1895) A] 1835. B] Acatzingo, Puebla. C] Primary studies in Puebla; preparatory studies in Puebla; had to leave school in the 1850s; no degree. D] Local deputy to the state legislature of Puebla; governor of Puebla; senator from Puebla, 1880–84; *senator* from Yucatán, 1894–95. E] None. F] Interim governor of Puebla; ambassador to Germany, 1888. G] None. H] Unknown. I] Son of José Manuel Romero, lawyer. J] Formed a band of fifty soldiers to oppose General Haro y Tamáriz, 1855; defended Matamoros Izúcar from the Conservatives; fought against the French in the defense of Puebla, May 5, 1862; second-in-command of the Loreto Brigade of Jalisco, under General *Pedro Hinojosa*; secretary to General Santiago Tapia; captured by the French in Teziutlán, Puebla. K] None. L] Hombres prominentes, 183–84; C de S, 1894–96.

Romo de Vivar y González, Luis Arturo
A] April 16, 1894. B] Unknown. C] Primary studies, Public School No. 6, Aguascalientes, Aguascalientes; enrolled in the National School of Agriculture, San Ja-

cinto, 1908, on a scholarship from the federal government, graduating with an agricultural engineering degree, 1914. D] None. E] None. F] Director of hunting and fishing, Secretariat of Agriculture; director of waters, Secretariat of Agriculture; oficial mayor of agriculture, 1928; subsecretary of agriculture, 1928–30. G] None. H] Practicing engineer; represented International Harvester, Sonora, 1930. I] Son of José de Jesús Romo de Vivar, pharmacist; grandson of José María Romo de Vivar y Gallardo, lawyer and political boss; brother of Jesús María Romo de Vivar, pilot and air force commander. J] Unknown. K] None. L] Linajes, 235–41; Gómez, 464.

Rosales (Rodríguez), Ramón
(Deceased April 30, 1928) A] August 15, 1872. B] Pachuca, Hidalgo. C] Primary studies at the Scientific and Literary Institute of Hidalgo; preparatory studies at the National Preparatory School, 1890–91; studies, National School of Business and Administration, Mexico City, 1891–92; sociology and philosophy degree, Institute of Sciences, New York City, 1905. D] *Governor* of Hidalgo, 1913. E] Formed No-Reelection Group, 1901; founded the Anti-Reelectionist Club with Jesús Silva, Pachuca, 1909; candidate of the Anti-Reelectionist Club for federal deputy, 1910; delegate to the National Anti-Reelectionist Convention, Mexico City, 1910. F] Agent, mining and lands, Secretariat of Development, 1901–09; *interim governor* of Hidalgo, 1911–12. G] President of the Student Society, National School of Business and Administration, 1892; Degree 33 in the Masonic Lodge. H] Inherited substantial wealth; businessman. I] Father a lawyer and agent of the Secretariat of Development. J] Bought supplies and planned an armed uprising with *Cándido Aguilar* in the Rancho de San Ricardo, Veracruz, 1910; offered *Francisco I. Madero* his fortune to oppose *Porfirio Díaz*, 1910; Maderista, 1910–11; rank of brigadier general. K] Imprisoned in Belén Prison for student activities against Díaz, 1892. L] Pérez López, 416–17; Mestre, 280.

Ross, Ramón
(Deceased January 24, 1934) A] July 24, 1864. B] Alamos, Sonora. C] Primary studies in Alamos; agricultural engineering degree, National School of Agriculture. D] Mayor of Huatabampo, Sonora, 1905; mayor of Navojoa, Sonora; *constitutional deputy* from the State of Sonora, Dist. 3, 1916–17. E] None. F] Director of public welfare, Mexico City; delegate of Mexico to the Bucareli Conferences, 1923; *head*, Department of the Federal District, 1923, 1924–26; *secretary* of communications and public works, 1926–28. G] None. H] Businessman. I] Unknown. J] Unknown. K] None. L] C de D, 1916–17.

Rouaix, Pastor
(Deceased December 31, 1949) A] April 15, 1875. B] Tehuacán, Puebla. C] Preparatory studies, National Preparatory School, Mexico City, 1889–93; topographical engineering degree, National School of Mines, Mexico City, 1894–98. D] Local deputy to the state legislature of Durango, 1912; *constitutional deputy* from the State of Puebla, Dist. 10, 1916–17; *federal deputy* from the State of Puebla, Dist. 2, 1924–26, 1926–28; *alternate senator* from Durango, in functions, 1926–28; *senator* from the State of Durango, 1930–31. E] *Secretary* of acts, National Executive Committee of the National Revolutionary party, 1930. F] Political boss of Durango, Durango, 1911–12; political boss of Durango, 1913; *provisional governor* of Durango, 1913–14; oficial mayor in charge of the Secretariat of Development, 1914–17; *secretary* of agriculture and colonization, 1917–20; director general of Waterworks for irrigation, Durango, 1926; secretary of government of the State of Durango, 1928–30; *provisional governor* of Durango, 1931–32; director of geography, Secretariat of Agriculture, 1934. G] Founder, National Agrarian Commission. H] Agricultural engineer, Durango, 1898–1911; author of numerous historical and geographical books. I] Son of Narcisco Rouaix and Benigna Méndez; grandson of Ildefonso Rouaix, pharmacist, and Rosario Castro; lived with aunts who were fashion models; married Rosa Villarreal; son Alfonso, an engineer. J] Joined *Fran-*

cisco I. Madero, 1910–11; joined the Constitutionalists, 1913; fought with the Division of the North, 1914; accompanied *Venustiano Carranza* to Tlaxcalantongo, 1920. K] Promulgated the first agrarian law of Durango, 1913; promulgated the Agrarian Law of 1915, written by *Luis Cabrera*; one of the initiators of Articles 27 and 123 at the Constitutional Convention. L] DP70, 1809–10; Morales Jiménez, 252–55; Rouaix, 369; Enc Mex, XI, 196–97; CyT, 603–04; Moreno, 249–67; López, 965–66; WWM45, 106–07; Bojórquez, 119–21.

Rueda Magro, Manuel
(Deceased) A] October 15, 1887. B] Oaxaca, Oaxaca. C] Early education unknown; secondary and preparatory studies, Institute of Arts and Sciences of Oaxaca; law degree, Institute of Arts and Sciences of Oaxaca; professor of law, School of Law, Institute of Arts and Sciences of Oaxaca. D] *Federal deputy* from the State of Oaxaca, Dist. 5, 1917–18, member of the Great Committee; *federal deputy* from the State of Oaxaca, Dist. 5, 1924–26; *federal deputy* from the State of Oaxaca, Dist. 6, 1932–34, member of the Great Committee; federal deputy from the State of Oaxaca, Dist. 2, 1940–43. E] Joined the Anti-Reelectionist movement as a student, 1902. F] *Governor* of the Federal District, 1919–20. G] None. H] Practicing lawyer. I] Married María Chapital, from an important Oaxaca political family. J] Joined the Constitutionalists, 1913; accompanied *Venustiano Carranza* when he left Mexico City, 1920. K] None. L] C de D, 1917–18; Dir social, 1935, 145.

Ruiz, Eduardo
(Deceased November 1, 1907) A] May 22, 1838. B] Paracho, Uruapan, Michoacán. C] Primary studies in Pátzcuaro, 1848–49, and under father, 1850–51; preparatory studies, Colegio de San Nicolás, Morelia, Michoacán, 1852; scholarship student, state of Michoacán, 1953; notary public degree, Colegio de San Nicolás, 1863; law degree, Colegio de San Nicolás, January 1864; professor of constitutional and administrative law, National School of Law,

Mexico City; professor of literature, public and canon law, Colegio de San Nicolás. D] Local deputy to the state legislature of Michoacán; mayor of Uruapan, Michoacán; member of the City Council of Mexico City. E] None. F] Syndic, Mexico City; subsecretary of government of Michoacán; editor, *Diario Official*, State of Michoacán; private secretary to the governor of Michoacán, Justo Mendoza; private secretary to Vicente Riva Palacio; secretary of the Federal District; judge, Michoacán, 1872; prefect of Guadalupe, Mexico City; section head, staff, Secretariat of War, 1881–82; attorney general of Mexico, 1882–1900; *justice* of the Supreme Court, 1900–07. G] None. H] Leading intellectual; held gatherings of poets Luis Urbina, *Ezequiel Chavez*, and *Carlos Díaz Dufoo* in his home; owner of the coffee finca La Quinta, Uruapan, 1876–81; editor of *Siglo XIX, La República*, and *La Tribuna*. I] Son of Toribio Ruiz, prefect of Uruapan; father of Daniel Ruiz, engineer; sister married Jesús Rodríguez, federal deputy. J] Fought during the War of the Reform in the Michoacán Battalion, under General *Mariano Escobedo*; fought against the French under Vicente Riva Palacio and Nicolás de Regules; rank of colonel in the cavalry. K] None. L] Dicc mich, 390–91; Mestre, 215; Pavía, judges, 79–90; Hombres prominentes, 471–72; Romero Flores, 59–62; Godoy, 47–48; Andrade, 157–58.

Ruiz, Mariano
(Deceased December 1, 1932) A] January 26, 1843. B] Texcoco, México. C] Early education unknown; no degree. D] *Alternate federal deputy* from the State of Jalisco, Dist. 18, 1886–88; *federal deputy* from the State of Jalisco, Dist. 18, 1888–90; *federal deputy* from the State of Hidalgo, Dist. 8, 1900–02; *federal deputy* from the State of Hidalgo, Dist. 7, 1902–04; *federal deputy* from Quintana Roo, Dist. 1, 1904–06, 1906–08; *federal deputy* from the State of Hidalgo, Dist. 2, 1908–10, 1910–12. E] None. F] *Political boss* of Tepic, 1904; *governor* of Nayarit, 1904–11. G] None. H] Unknown. I] Unknown. J] Career army officer, infantry; rank of brigadier general, Septem-

ber 28, 1883; commander, 13th Infantry Battalion, 1901; rank of division general, May 1914; commander of the 1st Infantry Brigade, West Division, 1914. K] None. L] Sec of War, 1914, 19; Sec of War, 1901, 23; Mestre, 287.

Ruiz Sobredo, Santiago
(Deceased January 6, 1958) A] July 25, 1885. B] Teapa, Tabasco. C] Early education unknown; law degree. D] Constitutional deputy to the State Convention of Tabasco, 1918–19; local deputy to the state legislature of Tabasco, 1926. E] Member of the Radical Tabasco party; represented this party at the state constitutional convention, 1918–19. F] Interim governor of Tabasco, 1922; *interim governor* of Tabasco, 1924–25; *substitute governor* of Tabasco, 1926. G] None. H] Businessman; attorney; general attorney for the Southern Banana Company, 1912; owner, Hotel Toma, Mexico City. I] Brother Tacilo, colonel; grandfather of David Gutiérrez Ruiz, governor of Quintana Roo, 1971–75. J] Joined the Constitutionalists under General Carlos Greene, 1913. K] None. L] Bulnes, 391–99.

S

Sada Muguerza, Francisco G.
(Deceased March 31, 1945) A] 1856. B] Monterrey, Nuevo León. C] Primary studies, Monterrey; no degree. D] None. E] None. F] *Subsecretary* of the treasury, 1920. G] President of the National Chambers of Commerce, 1917–18. H] Worked for Francisco Armendáriz Firm, Matamoros, 1873–78; worked for González Treviño brothers, Chihuahua, 1878–80; operated own business, Saltillo, Coahuila, 1880–90; purchased stock in Cervecería Cuauhtémoc, 1891; manager, Cervecería Cuauhtémoc, Monterrey, 1892; cofounder of the Mercantile Bank of Monterrey, 1899; cofounder of the Fundidora de Fierro y Acero. I] Son of José Francisco Sada González, lawyer and businessman, and María del Carmen Muguerza Crespo; niece, Dora González Sada, married Raúl Madero, brother of *Francisco I. Madero*; daughter married Roberto Garza Sada and is mother of Bernardo Garza Sada, who di-

rected Alfa group; married Mercedes García Fuentes; son Luis G. Sada García, industrialist; son Camilo G. Sada García was president of Hojalata y Lámina; son Andrés G. Sada García was head of Fomento de Industrias and father of Andrés Marcelo Sada Zambrano, prominent industrialist; father-in-law of Ana Gorostieta, daughter of *Enrique Gorostieta*, secretary of the treasury, 1913. J] None. K] None. L] Linajes, 242–45; QesQM, 1952, 221–23; DP70, 1827.

Sáenz (Garza), Aarón
A] June 1, 1891. B] Monterrey, Nuevo León. C] Secondary studies, Colegio Civil of Monterrey; preparatory studies, Normal Preparatory of Monterrey and the Ateneo Fuente, Saltillo, Coahuila; began legal studies, School of Law, Coahuila, 1910–12; received state fellowship to continue legal studies at the National School of Law, 1912–13; law degree, National School of Law. D] *Federal deputy* from the State of Coahuila, Dist. 3, 1917–18; *senator* from the State of Nuevo León, 1932–34. E] Member of the Organizing Committee of the National Revolutionary party, 1928; precandidate for the National Revolutionary party presidential nomination, 1928. F] Private secretary to the secretary of war, General *Alvaro Obregón*, 1916; minister to Brazil, 1918–20; *subsecretary* of foreign relations, 1920–24; *secretary* of foreign relations, 1924–27; special mission to Cuba, 1925; *secretary* of public education, 1930; secretary of commerce and industry, 1930–32; *head* of the Department of the Federal District, 1932–35. G] Director general, National Sugarcane Producers; president, Mexican Bankers Association, 1942–43. H] Prominent businessman; stockholder, many banks and businesses; established a construction firm with *Plutarco Elías Calles*; built El Mante sugar refinery; president, Bank of Industry and Commerce, 1932–74. I] Son of Juan Sáenz Garza and Concepción Garza, a middle-class family; father of Aarón Sáenz Couret, member of the board of his father's firms; married Margarita Couret; brother of *Moisés Sáenz*, secretary of public education, 1928; brother of Josué Sáenz, treasury official, econo-

mist, and author; sister Elisa Saenz married *Plutarco Elías Calles, Jr.*, federal deputy from Nuevo León; daughter Dora Sáenz Couret married industrialist Julio Hirshfield Almada. J] Joined the Constitutionalists, 1913; member of General *Alvaro Obregón's* staff; chief of staff to General *Manuel Diéguez*; rank of brigade general, November 1, 1925. K] None. L] Dávila, 97–98; WWM45, 109; Almanaque de Nuevo León, 103; Enc Mex XI, 222; FSRE, 177; QesQ, 528.

Sáenz (Garza), Moisés
(Deceased October 24, 1941) A] February 16, 1888. B] El Mezquital, Apodaca, Nuevo León. C] Secondary studies at the Colegio Civil of Monterrey; preparatory studies, Presbyterian School of Coyoacán, 1912, and the Washington and Jefferson Institute, New York City; M.A. degree, 1920; Ph.D., magna cum laude, Columbia University, New York, 1920–22; studies, Sorbonne, 1922; professor of elementary and superior primary, Normal School of Jalapa, 1909; director general of the National Preparatory School, 1920; professor of philosophy, National Teachers School; director of the summer school, the National University. D] None. E] None. F] Director of education, State of Guanajuato, 1915–16; director, Department of Exchanges, Secretariat of Public Education; inspector general, Secretariat of Public Education; oficial mayor of public education, 1924–25; *subsecretary* of public education, 1925–28, 1928–30; *secretary* of public education, 1928; director general of public welfare; ambassador to Denmark, 1935–36; director, Inter–American Indigenist Institute; ambassador to Peru, 1936–41. G] None. H] None. I] Son of Juan Sáenz Garza and Concepción Garza, a middle-class family; married Herlinda Treviño; brother of *Aarón Sáenz*, secretary of foreign relations, 1924–27. J] None. K] None. L] DP70, 1827; QesQ, 529–30; López, 977; Enc Mex, XI, 222; QesQM, 529–30.

Salado Alvarez, Victoriano
(Deceased October 13, 1931) A] September 30, 1867. B] Teocaltiche, Jalisco. C] Primary studies in Teocaltiche; prepara-

tory studies, School for Boys, Guadalajara; law degree, School of Law, Guadalajara, 1890; professor by opposition of Spanish language, National Preparatory School, Mexico City. D] *Federal deputy* from the State of Sonora, Dist. 4, 1902–04; *federal deputy* from the State of Sonora, Dist. 3, 1904–06, member of the Great Committee; *federal deputy* from the State of Tabasco, Dist. 3, 1906–08, 1908–10; *senator* from the State of Tabasco, 1910–12, 1912–13. E] None. F] Agent of the Ministerio Público; public defender; secretary general of government, State of Chihuahua, under Governor *Enrique Creel*, 1906; first secretary, Mexican Embassy, Washington, D.C., 1908–09; chargé d'affaires, Mexican Embassy, Washington, D.C.; president of the Mexican Delegation to the 4th Pan-American Conference, 1910; *subsecretary* of foreign relations, 1910–11, in charge of the secretariat, 1911; minister to Guatemala, 1911–12; minister to Brazil, 1912–13. G] Secretary, Mexican Academy of Language, 1908; member of the Jalisco literary group, which included *José López Portillo y Rojas*, and *Luis Pérez Verdía*. H] Practicing lawyer; journalist; began writing for the *Diario de Jalisco*, 1888; editor, *El Imparcial*; editor, *El Mundo Ilustrado*; historian; author of more than one thousand articles. I] Political disciple of Enrique Creel. J] None. K] Exiled in Spain, 1915–31. L] Carreño, 219; Enc Mex, XI, 228–29; DP70, 1832; Mestre, 286; FSRE, 145; QesQ, 532.

Salas, Ismael
(Deceased August 28, 1901) A] February 6, 1836. B] Saltillo, Coahuila. C] Primary studies in Monterrey, Nuevo León; preparatory studies, Colegio de San Ildefonso, Mexico City; medical degree, Paris, France; ophthalmology studies, London, England. D] *Federal deputy* from the State of Veracruz, Dist. 3, 1888–90; *federal deputy* from the State of Hidalgo, Dist. 8, 1890–92, 1892–94; *federal deputy* from the State of Guanajuato, Dist. 18, 1894–96; *alternate senator* from the State of San Luis Potosí, 1894–96; *federal deputy* from the State of Guanajuato, Dist. 18, 1896–98; *federal deputy* from the State of Guanajuato, Dist. 15, 1898–1900.

E] None. F] Governor and military commander of Coahuila, 1872. G] None. H] Practicing ophthalmologist. I] Unknown. J] Joined the Liberals, rank of colonel; inspector, Military Medical Corps, 1867–69; rejoined the army, 1870. K] None. L] Montejano.

Salgado, Jesús H.
(Deceased 1919) A] 1872. B] Las Sauces, Municipio de Teloloapa, Guerrero. C] Early education unknown; no degree. D] None. E] None. F] *Governor* of Guerrero, 1914, appointed by Zapatista forces. G] None. H] Rancher; owned transportation business, Balsas, Guerrero. I] Unknown. J] Supported *Francisco I. Madero*, 1911–12; fought in Apaxtla, Guerrero, 1911; joined *Emiliano Zapata*, 1912; fought against *Victoriano Huerta*'s forces, 1913–14; captured in Chilpancingo, 1914; represented at the Convention of Mexico City, February 1915, by Antonio Mezo Salinas; opposed *Venustiano Carranza*, 1915–19; rank of division general. K] Died fighting near Tecpan de Galeana, Guerrero. L] DP70, 1838; López González, 241–42.

Salido (Zayas), Felipe
(Deceased October 6, 1939) A] 1863. B] Alamos, Sonora. C] Enrolled in the National Military College as a cadet, 1878; graduated as a 2nd lieutenant in the engineers; founded a primary and secondary school, Alamos, 1888–1900; director of the Colegio de Sonora, Hermosillo, 1900–11. D] *Senator* from the State of Sonora, 1920–24, president of the Claims Committee, 1920–22. E] None. F] Inspector general of primary schools, Sonora, 1900–11. G] None. H] Practicing engineer, 1911. I] Son of Francisco Salido and Carmen Zayas y Almada; father of Francisco Roberto Salido Verdugo, Mexican consul and government official, who married Julia Torres, daughter of lawyer Octavio Torres; grandfather of Felipe Arturo Salido Torres, architect; married Rafaela Verdugo Perrón; cousin of *Alvaro Obregón*. J] Member of staff, 1st Military Zone, Sonora, 1884–87, serving under Generals José Guillermo Carbó, Marcos Carrillo, and *Angel Martí*; requested permanent leave to found his own school, 1887. K] None. L] DP70, 1839; Linajes, 248; Villa, 24–26; Cuevas, 457.

Salinas, Emilio
(Deceased 1927) A] 1859. B] Cuatro Ciénegas, Coahuila. C] Early education unknown; no degree. D] *Senator* from the State of Coahuila, 1918–20. E] Joined the Anti-Reelectionist party, 1910. F] Interim governor and military commander of Coahuila, 1912, under *Venustiano Carranza*; *governor* and military commander of Querétaro, 1917; consul, San Antonio, Texas; director, military industries, Secretariat of War; director, Department of Cavalry, Secretariat of War, 1920; *governor* of Chihuahua, 1920. G] None. H] Unknown. I] Related to Venustiano Carranza. J] Took up arms against the reelection of *José María Garza Galán* as governor of Coahuila, 1893; joined the Maderistas in Chihuahua, April 1911; joined the auxiliary forces to oppose General *Pascual Orozco* under General Fernando Trucy, 1912; rank of captain, 1912; rank of major, February 1913; joined the Constitutionalists, 1913; rank of colonel, September 1913; rank of brigadier general, 1914; defeated by *Francisco Villa*, Ramos Arizpe, Coahuila, 1915; commander, 2nd Red Battalion, Veracruz, 1915. K] None. L] DP70, 1839; Almada, 545; Almada, 1968, 478.

Sánchez, Gertrudis G.
(Deceased April 25, 1915) A] August 15, 1882. B] Saltillo, Coahuila. C] Primary studies under aunt, Victoria Sánchez; studies, Annex to the Normal; did not complete teaching certificate for financial reasons. D] None. E] None. F] *Provisional governor* and military commander of Michoacán, 1914–15. G] None. H] Peasant; began work on the Hacienda de Agua Nueva, Coahuila. I] Son of Tomás García and Francisca Sánchez, but father died when he was four; took aunt's name. J] Supported *Francisco I. Madero*'s Plan de San Luis, 1911; commander of twenty-eight rurales in Guerrero, 1911–12; commander of rurales against *Victoriano Huerta*'s forces, 1913–14; represented at the Convention of Aguascalientes by

Sabas Valladares, 1914; supported *Venustiano Carranza*, 1915; fought with José Rentería Luviano in Michoacán. K] Killed in battle by Alejo Mastache's troops, Huetamo, Michoacán. L] Enc Mex, XII, 334–35; DP70, 1907; Dicc mich, 399–400.

Sánchez Azcona (Díaz), Juan
(Deceased May 18, 1938) A] January 13, 1876. B] Mexico City. C] Primary studies, Mexico City; secondary studies, Royal Gymnasium, Stuttgart; studies in sociology and political science, Polytechnic School, Paris, with a diploma from the Sorbonne, 1892; legal studies, National School of Law, 1893–94; degree in philosophy and letters, University of Heidelberg; professor of languages, School of Business Administration, UNAM. D] *Federal deputy* from the Federal District, Dist. 12, 1912–13; *senator* from the Federal District, 1917–18. E] Founder, Democratic party, 1908; member, Anti-Reelectionist party; president, Liberal Constitutional party, 1917; member, Democratic League, 1920; vice-president, National Anti-Reelectionist party, 1917. F] Private secretary to *Francisco Madero*, 1911–13; special agent of Madero, Washington, D.C.; secretary general of government of Sonora, 1914; special mission, Spain, 1914–16; minister to Italy, 1916; minister to France, 1916, minister to Belgium, 1916; minister to Spain and Portugal, 1916; *secretary* of foreign relations, 1920; minister to Germany, 1921; adviser, secretary of foreign relations, 1921–24. G] Member of the National Rite Masons, 33rd degree. H] Journalist, 1894; director, *México Nuevo*, 1910; secretary of the board, Rafael Dondé Foundation, 1935–38. I] Son of Juan Sánchez Azcona, ambassador, judge, and senator, and Leoncia Díaz Covarrubias, sister of Francisco Díaz Covarrubias, distinguished mathematician and professor; grandfather Sánchez Roca was the mentor of *Joaquín D. Casasús*; met Madero in Paris while studying; uncle José Díaz Covarrubias, secretary of public education under Benito Juárez. J] Joined the Maderista Revolutionary Junta, San Antonio, Texas; helped write the Plan of San Luis, 1911. K] Exiled, San Antonio,

Texas; exiled, Havana, Cuba, 1927–30. L] Enc Mex, XI, 337–38; Bojórquez, 75–78; FSRE, 174; Puente, 347; Mestre, 294; DP70, 1909–10; QesQ, 539; Dir social, 1935, 148.

Sánchez Mármol, Manuel
(Deceased March 6, 1912) A] May 25, 1839. B] Cunduacán, Tabasco. C] Primary studies, private school, Cunduacán, Tabasco; preparatory studies, Conciliar Seminary of San Ildefonso, Mérida, Yucatán, on a scholarship from the bishop of Tabasco; law studies, School of Law, Chiapas, 1860–64, graduating November 13, 1865; professor of Spanish literature and history, National Preparatory School, Mexico City; director, Juárez Institute, Tabasco, 1878. D] Member of the City Council of Mérida, Yucatán; *federal deputy* from the State of Tabasco, 1871–72, 1872–74, 1874–76; *federal deputy* from the State of Hidalgo, Dist. 4, 1892–94; *federal deputy* from the State of México, Dist. 12, 1894–96, 1896–98, 1898–1900, 1900–02, 1902–04; *federal deputy* from the State of Michoacán, Dist. 13, 1904–06; *senator* from the State of Chihuahua, 1906–10, 1910–13. E] None. F] Secretary general of government of Tabasco, 1862; oficial mayor of justice, 1867; judge, Superior Tribunal of Justice, Tabasco, 1878. G] Member of the Mexican Academy of Language, 1906. H] Journalist; founded *La Burla* as a student in Mérida with José Peón Contreras; leading literary figure; founder of *La Concordia* literary circle; founder of *El Aguila Azteca*, Tabasco; founder of *El Radical*, Mexico City. I] Son of Ceferino Sánchez and Josefa Mármol; nephew of José Evaristo Sánchez, political boss. J] Joined the Liberals under Colonel Gregorio Méndez, 1862–67. K] None. L] Palavicini, 93–105; Carreño, 200; Enc Mex, XI, 339; DP70, 1912; Mestre, 242.

Sánchez Mejorada, Javier
(Deceased May 20, 1941) A] February 24, 1886. B] Pachuca, Hidalgo. C] Early education unknown; engineering degree, National School of Engineering, Mexico City. D] None. E] None. F] Ambassador to Italy; *secretary* of communications

and public works, 1928–30; ambassador to Germany, 1933; *ambassador* to Great Britain, 1934. G] None. H] Practicing engineer; author; president of the National Railroads of Mexico. I] Brother of Carlos Sánchez Mejorada, attorney and federal deputy from Hidalgo, 1914–16; uncle of Pedro Sánchez Mejorada Rodríguez, director general of Industrias Peñoles, 1978; uncle of Jorge Sánchez Mejorada Canedo, president of the Council of Mexican Entrepreneurs. J] None. K] None. L] Pérez López, 438; DP70, 1912.

Sánchez Pontón, Luis
(Deceased June 19, 1969) A] August 5, 1889. B] Puebla, Puebla. C] Primary and secondary education in public and private schools in Puebla; preparatory studies at the National Preparatory School; law degree, National School of Law, National University of Mexico, 1912; professor of law and economics, UNAM, 12 years; founder and president of the Council of Primary Education, 1932–40. D] *Federal deputy* from the State of Puebla, Dist. 2, 1917–18. E] Member of the Constitutional Liberal party, 1916, but opposed *Venustiano Carranza* for president. F] Secretary general of government of the Federal District, 1914; secretary general of government of Veracruz, 1915; *interim governor* of Puebla, 1920–21; *oficial mayor* of the Secretariat of the Treasury, 1930–31; director, Budget Department, Secretariat of the Treasury, 1928–29; secretary of public education, 1940–41; minister to Ecuador, 1942; ambassador to the Soviet Union, 1946–47; Mexican delegate to the 7th Pan-American Conference; ambassador to Canada; ambassador to Switzerland. G] Member of the First Congress of Students, 1910. H] Author of education books; president of Financiera Hispano-Mexicana, S.A.; member of the National Council of Higher Education. I] Carlos Madrazo and Germán Parra were close collaborators when he served as secretary of education; attended school with *Juan Andreu Almazán*; married Ana María Garfías. J] None. K] A distinguished student at law school; as a student leader asked for the resignation of *Porfirio Díaz*,

1910; one of the first of the radical holdovers from the Lázaro Cárdenas period to be forced out of a cabinet position. L] EBW, 516; DP70, 1914; WWM45, 111; Enc Mex, XI, 1977, 340; López, 996.

Sánchez (Rojas), José María
(Deceased 1959) A] 1890. B] Chachapa, Puebla. C] Early education unknown; no degree. D] *Federal deputy* from the State of Puebla, Dist. 3, 1917–18, 1918–20; *federal deputy* from the State of Puebla, Dist. 1, 1920–22; *governor* of Puebla, 1921–22; *federal deputy* from the State of Puebla, Dist. 3, 1924–26. E] President, Social Democratic party. F] *Provisional governor* of Puebla, 1924. G] None. H] Unknown. I] Unknown. J] Maderista, 1910–11; joined the Constitutionalists, 1913; rank of brigadier general; supported *Álvaro Obregón*, 1920; organized agrarian groups against the *Adolfo de la Huerta* rebellion, 1923. K] None. L] DP70, 1907, 1914; CyT, II, 620, 627–28; Almanaque de Puebla, 130–31.

Sánchez y González, José María
(Deceased January 13, 1940) A] 1850. B] San Buenaventura, Coahuila. C] Primary studies only, San Buenaventura. D] Member of the City Council of Chihuahua, 1880–81; local deputy to the state legislature of Chihuahua, 1883–87. E] None. F] Treasurer general of Chihuahua, 1903–07; interim governor of Chihuahua, 1906, 1907, 1908, 1909, 1910; *substitute governor* of Chihuahua, 1910. G] Organized the National Chamber of Commerce, Chihuahua, 1887; treasurer, Central Catholic Board. H] Worked in youth for the González Treviño firm, and from 1867 to 1873; moved to Chihuahua with branch of the firm, 1873; later opened own firm in Chihuahua; became one of the most successful businessmen in Chihuahua; stockholder, Cía. Harinera de Chihuahua. I] Son of Santos Sánchez and Dolores González; married Concepción Olivares. J] Joined the national guard in Nuevo León during the French Intervention; 2nd lieutenant, mobile battalion; fought in Matamoros, 1866. K] None. L] DP70, 1911–12; Almada, 1968, 689.

Sangines (Calvillo), Agustín
(Deceased September 15, 1924) A] September 24, 1852. B] Boca de los Ríos, Teotitlán, Oaxaca. C] Early education unknown; no degree. D] None. E] None. F] Political boss, Iturbide District, 1890, 1892; political boss, Bravo District, Chihuahua, 1892; *governor* and military commander, Baja California del Norte, 1894–1902; *governor* of Baja California del Sur, 1902–11; *interim governor* and chief of military operations in Hidalgo, 1913–14. G] None. H] Worker in a bakery, La Paz, Baja California del Sur. I] Son of José María Sangines and Pascuala Calvillo; married Teresa Vallalca. J] Career army officer; rank of 2nd lieutenant, January 4, 1872; rank of captain in the cavalry, May 11, 1872; commander of a cavalry squadron, March 5, 1876; chief of auxiliary cavalry, June 20, 1877; rank of lt. colonel, auxiliary cavalry, July 25, 1884; rank of lt. colonel, regular cavalry, December 7, 1885; military judge, Chihuahua, 1886–88; rank of colonel, December 13, 1889; judge, Higher Military Court; attached to the 2nd Military Zone, 1894; rank of brigadier general, March 8, 1909; rank of brigade general, February 10, 1913; rank of division general, January 1, 1914. K] None. L] Sec of War, 1914, 17; Sec of War, 1902; Pérez López, 441; Rice, 250–51; Mestre, 274; Almada, 1968, 491.

Santa Cruz, Francisco
(Deceased May 8, 1902) A] October 4, 1836. B] Guaymas, Sonora. C] Early education unknown; no degree. D] Member of the City Council of Colima; mayor of Colima; local deputy to the state legislature of Colima; governor of Colima, 1871–72; governor of Colima, 1880–83; *senator* from the State of Colima, 1884–88; *governor* of Jalisco, 1891–93; *governor* of Colima, 1893–1902; *alternate federal deputy* from the State of Colima, Dist. 1, 1900–02. E] None. F] Political prefect of Colima, Colima, 1867; governor of Colima, 1869–71. G] None. H] Sailor. I] Father of Francisco Santa Cruz Ceballos, senator from the State of Colima, 1912–13. J] Colonel, auxiliary forces, August 16, 1892. K] None. L] DP70, 1927–28; Moreno, 54–55; Almada, Colima, 167.

Santa Marina, Juan
(Deceased March 31, 1944) A] July 1, 1855. B] Santiago Papasquiaro, Durango. C] Primary studies, Santiago Papasquiaro, Durango; preparatory studies, Juárez Institute, Durango; law degree, Juárez Institute, Durango, 1878; professor of Law, Juárez Institute, 1888. D] Member of the City Council of Durango, Durango, 1881–82; local deputy to the state legislature of Durango, 1882–84; *governor* of Durango, 1900–04. E] None. F] Judge, District Court, Durango, 1878–79; secretary general of government of Durango, 1897–98; *interim governor* of Durango, 1898. G] None. H] Practicing lawyer, Durango, 1879–97, 1904–41; practicing lawyer, Mexico City, 1941–44. I] Son of Carlos Santa Marina, physician and federal deputy; related to Manuel Santa Marina, governor of Durango. J] None. K] None. L] DP70, 1933; Mestre, 301; Rouaix, 421–22.

Santos, Samuel M.
(Deceased March 19, 1959) A] June 10, 1886. B] Tampamolón Corona, San Luis Potosí. C] Primary studies, Ciudad Santos, San Luis Potosí; preparatory studies, Scientific and Literary Institute of San Luis Potosí; two years of legal studies; Scientific and Literary Institute of San Luis Potosí; no degree. D] *Federal deputy* from the State of San Luis Potosí, Dist. 9, 1912–13; *constitutional deputy* from the State of San Luis Potosí, Dist. 1, 1916–17. E] None. F] Tax official; director of customs, Tampico; director of the Fishing and Hunting Department, Secretariat of Agriculture; member of the board, National Lottery, 1958–59. G] None. H] None. I] Son of Pedro Antonio Santos and Isabel Rivera de Santos. J] Joined the Constitutionalists, 1913; director, Practical Military School, Guadalajara, 1913; represented at the Convention of Aguascalientes by *Jacinto B. Treviño*, 1914; first secretary, Aguascalientes Convention, 1914; rank of brigade general, June 1, 1920; supported the Plan of Agua Prieta, 1920; supported the *Adolfo de la Huerta* rebellion, 1923; rank of division general. K] None. L] DP70, 1952.

Santos (Rivera), Gonzalo N.
(Deceased October 17, 1978) A] January 10, 1897. B] Tampamolón, Corona, Villa Guerrero, San Luis Potosí. C] Primary studies, public school, Tampamolón, 1905–11; no degree. D] *Federal deputy* from the State of San Luis Potosí, Dist. 10, 1924–26, member of the Great Committee; *federal deputy* from the State of San Luis Potosí, 1926–28, answered the presidential State of the Union address, 1926, and served as majority leader as head of the Alliance of Socialist Parties; *federal deputy* from the State of San Luis Potosí, Dist. 10, 1928–30, member of the Great Committee; *federal deputy* from the State of San Luis Potosí, Dist. 3, 1930–32, member of the Great Committee; *federal deputy* from the State of San Luis Potosí, Dist. 6, 1932–34, member of the Great Committee; senator from the State of San Luis Potosí, 1934–40; governor of San Luis Potosí, 1943–49. E] Secretary of affairs for the Federal District, National Executive Committee of the National Revolutionary party, 1929; *secretary general* of the National Executive Committee of the National Revolutionary party, 1931. F] Customs agent, 1917; minister to Belgium, 1940; director of fishing, Secretariat of Industry and Commerce, 1959–61. G] None. H] None. I] Son Gastón Santos involved in San Luis Potosí politics; son of Pedro Antonio Santos, owner of Tantuité hacienda, and Isabel Rivera; political enemy of *Federico Medrano*. J] Fought with the Constitutionalists during the Revolution; rank of brigadier general. K] Regional caudillo in San Luis Potosí; his power in San Luis Potosí declined after the middle 1950s; accused of large-scale illegal landholdings in San Luis Potosí; important Callista congressional leader and member of the "Reds" in Congress. L] HA, 7 Oct. 1949, xxii; Peral, 755; HA, 28 Sept. 1944, VIII; DP70, 1581; HA, 8 Oct. 1943, 13; HA, 28 Aug. 1978, 20; HA, 23 Oct. 1978, 18; *Excélsior*, 26 June 1975, 4; NYT, 7 Jan. 1959, ll; *Excélsior* 28 Sept. 1976; *Excélsior* 2 Sept. 1972, 11; NYT, 18 May 1958, 7; NYT, 4 Dec. 1958, 13; *Excélsior* 23 Aug. 1978.

Sarabia, Juan
(Deceased October 28, 1920) A] June 24, 1882. B] San Luis Potosí, San Luis Potosí. C] Primary and preparatory studies, Scientific and Literary Institute of San Luis Potosí; legal studies, Scientific and Literary Institute of San Luis Potosí, had to leave when parents died. D] *Federal deputy* from the State of San Luis Potosí, Dist. 1, 1912–13; *senator* from the State of San Luis Potosí, 1920. E] Secretary of the Liberal Club Ponciano Arriaga, 1902–03; reestablished the Liberal Club Ponciano Arriaga in Mexico City, 1903; member of the Organizing Group for the Mexican Liberal party, 1905–08; vice-president of the Mexican Liberal party, 1905; signer of the Liberal Party Plan, 1906. F] None. G] None. H] Worked in the Morales Foundry, weighing freight cars; worked in the El Cabezón mine; worked in a library, San Luis Potosí; journalist; wrote for *El Diario del Hogar* and *El Hijo del Ahuizote*; learned printing from father in Mexico City, 1895; published *El Demócrata*, 1899–1900. I] Son of a musician and conductor of the San Luis Potosí military band; childhood friend of *Antonio Díaz Soto y Gama*; cousin of Manuel Sarabia, Magonista and journalist. J] Active in the Mexican Liberal party revolts with the Flores Magón brothers, 1906, 1908. K] Imprisoned for establishing Liberal Club Ponciano Arriaga, 1903; imprisoned with the staff of *El Hijo del Ahuizote*, 1905; in exile in St. Louis and Toronto, 1905–06; imprisoned in San Juan de Ulloa, Veracruz, 1908–11. L] Enc Mex, XI, 352; Morales Jiménez, 45–49; QesQ, 547; DP70, 1954.

Saravia y Murúa, Emiliano G.
(Deceased November 10, 1920) A] May 3, 1857. B] Hacienda de San Pedro Mártir, Durango. C] Early education unknown; law degree, Juárez Institute, Durango. D] Federal deputy from the State of Durango; *governor* of Durango, 1911–12. E] None. F] *Provisional governor* of Durango, 1914–15; *governor* of San Luis Potosí, 1915. G] None. H] Large landowner; owned the Atotonilco and

Esten Yerbanis haciendas, Durango, with brother; practicing lawyer; editor, Durango newspapers. I] Son of Buenaventura Saravia González, prefect for Maximilian; father of Emiliano Saravia y Ríos, provisional governor of San Luis Potosí, 1914; brother of *Ventura G. Saravia y Murúa*, governor of Durango, 1911; direct descendant of the captain general of Guatemala, Antonio González de Saravia. J] Maderista; fought in the Revolution under *Francisco Villa*, 1913–15; represented at the Convention of Mexico City by Genaro Palacios Moreno, 1915. K] None. L] Rice, 251; Holms, 258, Rouaix, 425–26.

Saravia y Murúa, Ventura G.
(Deceased August 1, 1917) A] May 15, 1854. B] Durango, Durango. C] Early education unknown; no degree. D] None. E] None. F] Governor of Durango, 1911. G] None. H] Rancher; large landowner; cattleman. I] Son of Buenaventura Saravia González, prefect for Maximilian; uncle of Emiliano Saravia y Ríos, provisional governor of San Luis Potosí, 1914; brother of *Emiliano G. Saravia y Murúa*, governor of Durango, 1911–12; direct descendant of the captain general of Guatemala, Antonio González de Saravia. J] None. K] None. L] DP70, 1955; Rouaix, 425.

Sarlat (Nova), Simón
(Deceased April 14, 1906) A] December 13, 1839. B] Tabasco, Villahermosa. C] Primary studies in Mérida, Yucatán; medical degree, National School of Medicine, Mexico City. D] Governor of Tabasco, 1872–76; senator from the State of Tabasco, 1876–78; governor of Tabasco, 1878–82; *federal deputy* from the State of Zacatecas, Dist. 7, 1884–86; *governor* of Tabasco, 1889–90, 1890–91, 1891–92, 1892–94, 1894–95; *senator* from the State of México, 1900–04, 1904–08. E] None. F] None. G] None. H] Practicing lawyer. I] Son of Simón Sarlat, physician, and María de Jesús Nova; married Amada Dueñas Magdonel. J] None. K] None. L] Mestre, 225; Pavía, 342–44; Hombres prominentes, 423–24; Ghigliazza, 132–36.

Saucedo (Pérez), Salvador
(Deceased March 1963) A] November 9, 1890. B] Colima, Colima. C] Early education unknown; no degree. D] *Federal deputy* from the State of Colima, Dist. 1, 1917–18, member of the Great Committee; *federal deputy* from the State of Colima, Dist. 1, 1918–20, member of the Great Committee; *federal deputy* from the State of Colima, Dist. 1, 1920–22, member of the Great Committee; *governor* of Colima, 1931–35. E] Organizer and member of the Colima Liberal party. F] Director of government printing, 1914, under Governor *J. Trinidad Alamillo*, State of Colima; director of the Federal Treasury Office, Tuxtla Gutiérrez, Chiapas; Tuxpan, Veracruz, and the Federal District; director of the Federal Treasury Office, Colima, 1961–63; director of the Federal Treasury Office, Zacatecas, Zacatecas, 1956. G] None. H] Became a printer in his youth; writer for the newspaper *La Revancha*; published the newspaper *El Popular*, 1909; founded *Colima Libre*, 1917; newspaper editor in Guadalajara. I] Brother Miguel was interim governor of Colima, 1935, and a local deputy; defeated General Miguel Santa Ana and *Higinio Alvarez* for governor, 1931. J] Maderista during the Revolution. K] Removed from the governorship because of friendship with *Plutarco Elías Calles*. L] Peral, 759; letter; DP70, 1958; DGF56, 168; Moreno, 83–85.

Serrano, Francisco R.
(Deceased October 3, 1927) A] August 16, 1889. B] Choix, Quilá, Sinaloa. C] Primary studies, Huatabampo; business studies; no degree. D] *Federal deputy* from the State of Sonora, Dist. 3, 1918–20. E] Campaigned for José Ferrel, anti-Porfirista candidate for governor, 1909; joined the Anti-Reelectionist party, 1910; candidate for president of Mexico, 1927. F] Private secretary to Governor *José María Maytorena*, 1911–13; chief of the treasury, Nogales, Sonora, 1913; *subsecretary* of war, 1920–21; *secretary* of war, 1921–24; *head* of the Federal District, 1926–27. G] None. H] Worked in the office of Fortunato Vega, El Fuerte, Sinaloa, 1903;

bookkeeper, Angel Almada's store, Navojoa, Sinaloa; journalist, 1907; laborer, construction project for Southern Pacific Railroad of Mexico, 1908; bookkeeper, Lauro Quiroz's store, Navojoa, Sinaloa, 1909–10; circus clown, 1911.   I] Son of Rufino Serrano and Micaela Berbeytia Gambusino, middle-class family; related to *Alvaro Obregón* through Francisco's sister Amalia, who married Obregón's older brother Lamberto; married Amada Bernal; second wife, Josefina Méndez.   J] Joined the Maderistas under *Benjamín Hill*, 1911; chief of staff to General Obregón, 1913; fought *Victoriano Huerta* under Obregón, 1913–14; fought Villistas, 1914–15; remained loyal to Obregón, 1920; rank of division general.   K] Murdered by General Fox on direct orders from Obregón, Huitzilac, October 3, 1927.   L] Bulnes, 177, 178; Enc Mex, XI, 384; Bojórquez, 113–18; Puente, 219–25; QesQ, 555–56; González Dávila, 564–65; DP70, 1981.

Serrano (Daza), Miguel
(Deceased 1916)   A] 1842.   B] Puebla, Puebla.   C] Primary studies, public school, Puebla; preparatory studies, Palafoxian Conciliar Seminary, Puebla; legal studies, Palafoxian Conciliar Seminary, Puebla, but degree issued from the Colegio de San Nicolás, Morelia; director of the Colegio de Puebla, 1884; professor, Colegio de Puebla, 1884; director and cofounder, Normal School of Mexico, 1884–1901; director, Normal School of Puebla, 1912; professor at the Normal School of Puebla.   D] *Federal deputy* from the State of Puebla, Dist. 7, 1886–88, 1888–90, 1890–92, 1892–94, 1894–96; *federal deputy* from the State of Puebla, Dist. 2, 1896–98, 1898–1900; 1900–02, 1902–04, 1904–06, 1906–08, 1908–10, 1910–12.   E] None.
F] Secretary general of government, Puebla, 1879–80; secretary of development, Puebla, 1880.   G] None.   H] Practicing lawyer.   I] Son of Epifano Serrano and Soledad Daza; brother Rafael, leading intellectual and poet.   J] None.   K] None.
L] DP70, 1981; CyT, II, 640–42.

Serratos (Amador), Alfredo
(Deceased 1955)   A] October 27, 1870.
B] Mexico City.   C] Early education unknown; no degree.   D] None.   E] None.
F] Consul, United States; director, Department of Fish and Game, Secretariat of Agriculture; director, Federal Highway Police; *secretary* of war, Convention government, 1915.   G] None.   H] Unknown.
I] Married María Mayagoitia; father of Cristina Nami Serratos Mayagoitia, married to René Oswald Alex Benoit, businessman.   J] Involved with the Flores Magón brothers and *Antonio Díaz Soto y Gama* before the Revolution; Maderista, 1910–11; joined *Emiliano Zapata*; represented at the Convention of Mexico City by Julio Ramírez Vieye, 1915; commander, 26th Cavalry Regiment; member, Legion of Honor.   K] None.   L] DP70, 1981; Linajes, 39–40.

Sierra Méndez, Justo
(Deceased September 13, 1912)   A] January 26, 1848.   B] Campeche, Campeche.
C] Primary studies, Colegio San Miguel Estrada, where he studied with *Francisco Sosa*, a close childhood friend; completed primary at the Colegio San Ildefonso, Mérida, Yucatán; preparatory studies, Colegio de San Ildefonso, Mérida, 1861–62, and the Liceo Franco Mexicano, Mexico City, 1862–64; law degree, Colegio San Ildefonso, Mexico City, 1871; professor, National Conservatory of Music; professor of history, National Preparatory School, 1878–98.   D] Federal Deputy, 1882; *federal deputy* from the State of Sinaloa, Dist. 1, 1888–90, 1890–92, 1892–94.
E] None.   F] Secretary of the Supreme Court, 1872–81; *justice* of the Supreme Court, 1893–1901; *subsecretary* of justice and public instruction, 1902–05; *secretary* of justice and public instruction, 1905–11; ambassador to Spain, 1912.
G] Cofounder with Ignacio M. Altamirano of the Society of Free Thinkers, 1868.
H] Leading intellectual; political essayist; contributor to *El Renacimiento, El Domingo,* and *El Universal*; founder of *La*

Libertad with José María Iglesias, 1876–77. I] Son of Justo Sierra O'Reilly, lawyer, judge, and distinguished intellectual, and Concepción Méndez y Echazarreta, daughter of Governor Santiago Méndez; brother of Santiago, journalist, intellectual, and diplomat, who was killed in a duel by *Ireneo Paz*, grandfather of Octavio Paz, leading poet and intellectual; uncle of Tarcila Sierra González, wife of *Jesús Urueta*, subsecretary of foreign relations, 1914–15; brother of *Manuel Sierra Méndez*, federal deputy from various states, 1886–1912; married Luz Mayarola, granddaughter of poet Manuel Carpio; father of Manuel J. Sierra Mayarola, oficial mayor of foreign relations, 1935–36, married to Margarita Casasús, daughter of *Joaquín Casasús González*, ambassador to Washington, 1905–06; father-in-law of *Miguel Lanz Duret*, federal deputy and publisher, who married his daughter María Concepción; father of Justo Sierra Mayarola, federal deputy, married to Evangelina Casasús, daughter of Carlos Casasús González, federal deputy, 1894–1912. J] None. K] None. L] López, 1023–25; Godoy, 139; QesQ, 558; letter; Valdés Acosta, III, 200–03; O'Campo, 363–64; Mestre, 244.

Sierra Méndez, Manuel
(Deceased April 2, 1924) A] 1852. B] Campeche, Yucatán. C] Primary studies in Mexico City; preparatory studies in Mexico City. D] *Alternate federal deputy* from the State of Zacatecas, Dist. 8, 1886–88; *alternate federal deputy* from Tepic, Dist. 2 and 10, 1888–90; *alternate federal deputy* from Tepic, Dist. 2, 1890–92; *federal deputy* from Jalisco, Dist. 5, 1894–96, 1896–98, 1898–1900; *federal deputy* from Yucatán, Dist. 3, 1902–04, 1904–06, 1906–08, 1910–12; mayor of Mexico City. E] None. F] None. G] Member and stockholder of the Jockey Club. H] Unknown. I] Son of Justo Sierra O'Reilly, lawyer, judge, and intellectual, and Concepción Méndez y Echazarreta, daughter of Governor Santiago Méndez; brother of journalist and diplomat Santiago Sierra Méndez, killed in a duel with *Ireneo Paz*; brother of *Justo Sierra Méndez*, secretary of justice, 1905–11; uncle of María Concepción Sierra, married

to publisher and federal deputy *Miguel Lanz Duret*; uncle of Manuel J. Sierra, oficial mayor of foreign relations, 1935–36; uncle of Justo Sierra, Jr., federal deputy. J] None. K] None. L] Blue Book, 1901, 89; López, 1025–27; Valdés Acosta, 203–06; O'Campo, 364–65; DP70, 1986–88; QesQ, 558.

Silva, Jesús
(Deceased December 3, 1961) A] June 6, 1862. B] Molango, Hidalgo. C] Primary studies in Molango under Arcadio Castro; studied with notary Gabriel Ormaechea, Tulancingo; law degree, Scientific and Literary Institute of Hidalgo, September 26, 1886. D] *Federal deputy* from the State of Hidalgo, Dist. 6, 1917–18. E] President of the Benito Juárez Club, 1910; cofounder of the private Patriotic Club to support *Francisco I. Madero*, 1910. F] Named governor of Hidalgo by Madero, but did not take office, 1910; *governor* of Hidalgo, 1911. G] None. H] Assistant to Refugio Rojas, notary, Tulancingo, Hidalgo, 1880; opened own law firm in Pachuca, Hidalgo, 1887; practicing notary public. I] Unknown. J] Maderista, 1910–11. K] Imprisoned in Mexico City because of activities in support of Madero's movement, 1910. L] Pérez López, 453–54.

Silva, Rafael
(Deceased April 17, 1944) A] October 3, 1876. B] Mexico City. C] Preparatory studies at the Colegio de San Ildefonso, Mexico City; medical degree, National School of Medicine, 1898, under Doctor Carmona y Valle, 1893–98; special studies in ophthamology, Military Hospital, under Doctor Fernando López; professor of ophthamology, National School of Medicine; studies in ophthamology, Europe, 1904; studied in ophthamology clinics, Europe, for the Secretariat of Public Instruction, 1910. F] *Director*, Department of Health, 1930–32. G] President, National Academy of Medicine, 1928. H] Director, Ophthamology Hospital Señorita de la Luz. I] Married Elena Villarreal. J] None. K] None. L] DP70, 1992; Dir social, 1935, 151.

Silva (González), Miguel
(Deceased August 20, 1916) A] September 29, 1857. B] Morelia, Michoacán.
C] Primary studies at the Francisco Brena School, Morelia; preparatory studies, Colegio de San Nicolás, Morelia; medical degree, National Medical School, 1883, on a scholarship from the State of Michoacán; advanced studies, United States and France, 1894, 1905; professor of operations, School of Medicine, Colegio de San Nicolás, Morelia. D] *Alternate federal deputy* from the State of Michoacán, Dist. 7, 1900–02; *alternate senator* from the State of Michoacán, 1910–12; *governor* of Michoacán, 1911–13. E] None. F] None. G] None. H] Practicing physician; director, operating room, General Hospital, Mexico City. I] Son of Miguel Silva Macías and María González Gutiérrez, grandson of José María Silva, large landholder, federal deputy, and governor of Michoacán; grandson of Juan Manuel González Urueña, governor of Michoacán; godson of General Miguel Zincúnegui, interim governor of Michoacán; father, Miguel Silva Macías, was a physician and governor of Michoacán, 1857; mother received a pension from the state government when his father died, 1860. J] Maderista, 1910–11; joined the Constitutionalists under *Francisco Villa*, 1913; chief surgeon, Division of the North, 1913–14. K] Exiled to Havana, Cuba, 1915–16. L] Flores Romero, 63–66; Mestre, 256; DP70, 1992; QesQ, 558–59; Puente, 361–65; Enc Mex, XI, 393–95.

Simón (Jalife), Neguib
(Deceased February 13, 1950) A] March 20, 1895. B] Mérida, Yucatán. C] Early education unknown; law degree, Literary Institute of Mérida and the National School of Law, UNAM. D] *Federal deputy* from the State of Yucatán, Dist. 4, 1924–26; *federal deputy* from the State of Yucatán, Dist. 1, 1930–32; *alternate senator* from the State of Yucatán, 1930–34; federal deputy from the State of Yucatán, Dist. 2, 1934–37, president of the Great Committee, but ousted from the Chamber, September 1935, for being loyal to *Plutarco Elías Calles*. E] None. F] Private secretary to the governor of Yucatán, *Felipe Carrillo Puerto*, 1922–23. G] None.

H] Industrialist; banker; financier; built the Plaza de Toros, Mexico City; built the Olympic Stadium, Mexico City. I] Son of Nicolás Simón, businessman, and Julia Jalife. J] None. K] None. L] UNAM, law, 1912–16, 172.

Siurob Ramírez, José
(Deceased November 5, 1965) A] November 11, 1886. B] Querétaro, Querétaro. C] Began studies in Querétaro; medical degree, National School of Medicine, National University of Mexico, 1912. D] *Constitutional deputy* from the State of Guanajuato, Dist. 13, 1916–17; *federal deputy* from the State of Querétaro, Dist. 3, 1918–20; *federal deputy* from the State of Querétaro, Dist. 1, 1920–22; *federal deputy* from the State of Querétaro, 1922–24; *federal deputy* from the State of Querétaro, Dist. 3, 1924–26, secretary of the Great Committee; president of the Congress (twice). E] Campaigned for *Francisco I. Madero*, 1909. F] *Governor* of Querétaro, 1914–15; *governor* of Guanajuato, 1915–16; *governor* of Quintana Roo, 1928–31; director of military health, Secretariat of National Defense, 1934–35; secretary of the Department of Public Health, June 19, 1935–January 4, 1938; head of the Department of the Federal District, 1938–39; secretary of health, August 5, 1939–November 30, 1940. G] None. H] Author of books on medicine and health in Mexico. I] Distant relative of Father Hidalgo. J] Joined the Revolution as a medical student in support of Madero, 1910; physician in the Northeast Medical Corps; career army officer; rank of brigadier general, 1915; rank of division general; director of military health, Secretariat of National Defense, 1945; retired from the army, 1945; commander of the 17th Military Zone, Querétaro, Querétaro; inspector general of the army, 1932–34. K] One of the founders of the Army Bank. L] Peral, 771; DP70, 1996, 2022; López, 1035; Enc Mex, XI, 1977, 442; Alvarez Coral, 109–10.

Sodi (Candiani), Demetrio
(Deceased October 29, 1934) A] October 18, 1866. B] Oaxaca, Oaxaca. C] Primary and preparatory studies, Oaxaca, Oaxaca; law degree, Institute of Arts and

Sciences of Oaxaca, 1890; professor, philosophy of law, National School of Law, Mexico City, 1890; professor of the synthesis of Law, elocution, and international law, National School of Law, UNAM, 1911; professor of ethics, National Preparatory School; professor of civil law, mercantile law, and criminal law, Free Law School. D] *Alternate federal deputy* from the State of Guerrero, Dist. 6, 1900–02. E] None. F] Civil judge, Oaxaca; agent of the Ministerio Público, Mexico City, 1895; judge, 5th Civil District, Mexico City; judge, Superior Tribunal of Justice of the Federal District and Federal Territories; *justice* of the Supreme Court, 1906–11; *secretary* of justice, 1911. G] Member of the Mexican Academy of Legislation and Jurisprudence. H] Editor, *El Foro Colimense*; law firm with *Genaro García*, 1912; author of numerous legal codes. I] Son of Carlos Sodi Candiani, large landholder and owner of the Candiana hacienda, and Dolores Guigué Antuñaño; married to Carmen Pallares, daughter of Jacinto Pallares, distinguished lawyer and professor, and political opponent of *Porfirio Díaz*; brother of Carlos Sodi Candiani, senator from the State of Michoacán, 1900–08; father of Ernesto Sodi Pallares, scientific researcher; uncle of Federico Sodi Romero, novelist; father of Demetrio Sodi Pallares, recipient of the Carnot Prize in medicine. J] None. K] Offered a post by *Francisco I. Madero* but declined, 1911; defended José de León Toral, assassin of president-elect *Alvaro Obregón*, 1929. L] López, 1035; DP70, 2002–03; Enc Mex, XI, 448; Mestre, 289.

Solórzano Béjar, Francisco
A] May 14, 1895. B] Colima, Colima. C] Primary studies in Colima; secondary and preparatory studies, Guadalajara, Jalisco; law degree, School of Law, Guadalajara, 1919. D] *Federal deputy* from the State of Colima, Dist. 1, 1922–24, 1924–26; *governor* of Colima, 1925–27; *senator* from the State of Colima, 1928–29. E] None. F] Civil judge, Colima, 1919; consulting lawyer to President *Adolfo de la Huerta*, 1920; judge and president, Superior Tribunal of Justice of Durango, 1932; lawyer for the National Railroads of Mexico, 1930s. G] None. H] Practicing law-

yer, Mexico City; notary public; raised sugarcane, El Mante. I] Political enemy of Governor *Francisco Santa Cruz*. J] Joined the Constitutionalists; served with the rank of colonel in Sonora; supported Escobar, 1929. K] Involved in many political intrigues in Colima, including an attempt to depose Governor Cervantes, which failed, 1930. L] Moreno, 77–80; Almada, Colima, 171.

Sosa, Francisco de Paula
(Deceased April 9, 1925) A] April 2, 1848. B] Campeche, Campeche. C] Primary studies, Seminario de San Ildefonso, Mérida, under Ildefonso Barreda; secondary studies, Seminario de San Ildefonso, Mérida; preparatory studies and law degree, Mérida, Yucatán. D] *Federal deputy* from the Federal District, Dist. 3, 1898–1900, 1900–02; *federal deputy* from the Federal District, Dist. 7, 1902–04, 1904–06; *senator* from the State of Guerrero, 1906–10, 1910–13. E] None. F] Director of archives, Secretariat of Development, 1877; private secretary to the oficial mayor of the Secretariat of Development; private secretary to the secretary of development, *Manuel Fernández Leal*; director, national library, 1909–11. G] None. H] Journalist; historian; wrote for *El Renacimiento*, *La Revista Universal*, and *La Vida de México*; editor, *La Libertad*, 1883; founder of *El Radical* with Vicente Riva Palacio. I] Son of José Domingo Sosa, prefect of Yucatán, and Petrona Castillo; childhood friend of *Justo Sierra Méndez*. J] None. K] Jailed in San Juan de Ulúa on the orders of General Manuel Zepeda Peraza, who hated his father, for criticizing a Yucatecan governor . L] Hombres prominentes, 255–56; Enc Mex, XI, 499; QesQ, 56; DP70, 2013; Rice, 251.

Sosa Cisneros, Porfirio
(Deceased 1970) A] September 1, 1879. B] Tezoatlán, Municipio de Huajuapan, Oaxaca. C] Primary studies in Oaxaca, Oaxaca; preparatory studies, Oaxaca, Oaxaca; law degree, Institute of Arts and Sciences of Oaxaca, 1913; director, Juárez Institute, Villahermosa, Tabasco, 1920–21. D] *Constitutional deputy* from the State of Oaxaca, Dist. 12, 1916–17. E] Vice-

president, Constitutional party of Oaxaca, 1917. F] First civil judge, Oaxaca, 1916; agent of the Ministerio Público, Tabasco, Veracruz, Nayarit, Chihuahua, Guerrero, Morelos, Campeche, and Yucatán, 1920–23; adviser, Pension Department, 1934; public notary, First Criminal Judicial District, Federal District, 1935–41; official, subdirector of income tax, Secretariat of the Treasury, 1958–70. G] None. H] Lawyer. I] Son of Donaciono Sosa and Aniceta Cisneros, working-class family. J] Maderista, 1910–11; joined the Constitutionalists; adviser, war council, Oaxaca, 1915; rank of lt. colonel, 1917; rank of colonel, 1918; agent of the military Ministerio Público, Secretariat of War, Puebla, 1918; rank of brigadier general, 1918; accompanied *Venustiano Carranza* to Tlaxcalantongo, 1920. K] Imprisoned under *Victoriano Huerta.* L] DP70, 2444.

T

Tamariz (y Sánchez), Eduardo
(Deceased March 13, 1957) A] January 21, 1880. B] Puebla, Puebla. C] Primary and secondary studies in Puebla; preparatory studies, National Preparatory School, Mexico City; law degree, National School of Law, 1905; professor, National School of Law, UNAM, 1920; teacher, Rafael Dondé Center. D] *Federal deputy* from the State of Tlaxcala, Dist. 3, 1912–13, member of the Great Committee; *federal deputy* from the State of Puebla, Dist. 18, 1914–16. E] None. F] *Secretary* of public education, 1913; *secretary* of development, 1914. G] None. H] Practicing lawyer. I] Son of Eduardo Tamariz Almendaro, architect; married Magdalena Maurer. J] None. K] None. L] UNAM, law, 1896–1900, 153; Enc Mex, XI, 546–47; CyT, II, 661–62; Blue Book, 294; DP70, 2034; Peral, 784; Carrasco, 55.

Tapia Freyding, José María
(Deceased 1969) A] May 16, 1896. B] Nogales, Sonora. C] Early education unknown; technical military studies, New York; no degree. D] *Federal deputy* from the State of Baja California del Norte, Dist. 1, 1926–28, member of the Great Committee; senator from the State of Baja

California del Norte, 1958–64; president of the Mail and Telegraph Committee and of the First National Defense Committee, member of the Committee on Taxes, the Military Justice Committee, and the War Materiél Committee; vice-president of the Senate, September 1961. E] None. F] Chief of staff of the Secretariat of National Defense, 1928; chief of staff of President *Emilio Portes Gil,* 1929; *governor* and military commander of Baja California del Norte, 1929–30; director general of federal retirement and pensions; director general of public charities, 1932–35; consul general, New York City; director general of the mails, 1944; chief of staff, Secretariat of National Defense, 1952; director general of customs; director general of the National Army-Navy Bank, 1964–69. G] None. H] None. J] Joined the expeditionary column, Baja California, Constitutionalist forces, 1913; career army officer; rank of major, 1920; member of the staff of General *Abelardo Rodríguez,* 1920; fought against *Adolfo de la Huerta,* 1923; rank of brigadier general, May 16, 1929; reached rank of division general; chief of staff for Baja California del Norte, Nayarit, and Sinaloa; commander of the 25th Military Zone, Puebla, Puebla, 1952; commander of the 1st Infantry Regiment; commander of the 6th Military Region, Tijuana, 1956. K] None. L] C de S, 1961–64, 70; Peral, 785; DP70, 2045; Func., 122; Rev de Ejer, Apr.–June 1952, 134.

Teja Zabre, Alfonso
(Deceased March 1962) A] December 23, 1888. B] San Luis de la Paz, Guanajuato. C] Primary studies in Pachuca, Hidalgo; preparatory studies, Scientific and Literary Institute of Hidalgo, Pachuca, 1898–1903, and at the National Preparatory School; law degree, National School of Law, Mexico City, 1904–09; special studies in the history of Mexico, National Museum of History, 1909–11; professor of penal law and history, National School of Law, UNAM, 1925. D] *Federal deputy* from the State of Guanajuato, Dist. 8, 1913–14. E] None. F] Secretary, National Museum, 1910–11; attorney general in criminal matters and public defender, 1911–13;

judge of the Superior Tribunal of Justice of the Federal District, 1928–34; president of the Committee to Revise the Penal Code, 1931; director of information, Secretariat of Foreign Relations, 1934–36; judge, Federal Tax Court, 1937; president of the Board of Pipsa; ambassador to Honduras, 1947–50; ambassador to the Dominican Republic, 1951–52; ambassador to Cuba. G] Member of the Mexican Academy of History. H] Author; historian; novelist; lawyer; journalist; wrote for *El Universal*, 1922; wrote for *Demócrata*, 1933–34. I] Son of Manuel A. Teja and Isabel Zabre. J] None. K] None. L] WWM45, 115–16; López, 1058; Pérez López, 466–67; Peral, 786; MAH, 21, 1962, 105–06; Enc Mex, XII, 33–34; DP70, 2064; UNAM, law, 1900–06, 163.

Tejeda (Olivares), Adalberto
(Deceased September 8, 1960) A] March 28, 1883. B] Chicontepec, Veracruz. C] Primary studies in the Cantonal School, Chicontepec; preparatory studies at the National Preparatory School, Mexico City; engineering studies, National School of Engineering; no degree. D] *Constitutional deputy* from the State of Veracruz, Dist. 4, 1916–17; *senator* from the State of Veracruz, 1918–20; *governor* of Veracruz, 1920–24, 1928–32. E] Candidate for president of Mexico, 1934. F] *Secretary* of communications and public works, 1924–25; *secretary* of government, 1925–28; ambassador to France, 1936–37; ambassador to Guatemala, 1937–38; ambassador to Spain, 1938–39, 1940–41; ambassador to Peru, 1942–48. G] None. H] None. I] Son Luis Tejeda Tejeda served under his father in Spain and became a consul in the Mexican Consular Service, 1961; mentor to *Manlio Fabio Altamirano*; son of Entiquia Olivares. J] Maderista during the Revolution; chief of staff of the Eastern Division under General *Cándido Aguilar*; fought against *Victoriano Huerta*'s forces; commander of military operations in northern Veracruz; rank of brigadier general, 1948. K] Did not attend the Constitutional Congress because of military activities and personal affairs; caudillo of the State of Veracruz during the 1920s; considered an inner circle

favorite of President *Plutarco Elías Calles*, 1924–28. L] DP70, 2064; Peral, 787; DBM68, 595; López, 1058; Enc Mex, XII, 1977, 34.

Téllez, Manuel C.
(Deceased May 23, 1937) A] February 16, 1885. B] Zacatecas, Zacatecas. C] Early education unknown; no degree. D] None. E] None. F] Career foreign service officer; official, Bureau of Public Works, 1903–06; chancellor, Mexican Consulate, San Antonio, Texas, 1909; consul, Kobe, Japan, 1911–13; consul general, Yokohama, Japan, 1914; director of archives, Mexican Legation, Japan, 1914–15; chargé d'affaires ad interim, Tokyo, Japan, 1915; secretary, Special Mission, Tokyo, Japan, 1915; first secretary, Tokyo, Japan, 1916–18; counselor, Mexican Embassy, Washington, D.C., 1918; chargé d'affaires ad interim, China, 1919; consul, Vancouver, British Columbia, 1919; first secretary, Mexican Embassy, Washington, D.C., 1920; chargé d'affaires ad interim, Mexican Embassy, Washington, D.C., 1920–24; special ambassador to China and Venezuela, 1924; *ambassador* to the United States, 1924–31; *secretary* of government, 1931–32; *secretary* of foreign relations, 1932; ambassador to Italy, 1933–34. G] None. H] None. I] Son of José María Téllez and Jobita Acosta; married Emilia Benoit; father of Emilia María Téllez Benoit, subsecretary of the Secretariat of Foreign Relations, 1976–82. J] None. K] None. L] WWLA35, 395; Enc Mex, XII, 50–51; DP70, 2069; López, 1059; Dir social, 1935, 259–60.

Teresa y Miranda, José de
(Deceased January 11, 1902) A] 1850. B] Mexico City. C] Primary and preparatory studies in Mexico City; no degree. D] Member of the City Council of Mexico; *alternate senator* from the State of Sinaloa, 1888–92, 1892–96; *senator* from the State of Yucatán, 1898–1902. E] None. F] Ambassador (first) to Austria, 1902. G] None. H] Businessman; constructed El Centro Mercantil, Mexico City; owner of the Contreras Textile companies, San Angel, Federal District; stockholder, Jockey Club; president, Mexican Mortgage

Bank. I] Son of a wealthy Spaniard; inherited a fortune from his parents. J] None. K] None. L] Godoy, 272–73; QesQ, 168; DP70, 2097; Blue Book, 1901, 89; Peral, 789; López, 1064.

Terrazas, Luis
(Deceased June 15, 1923) A] July 24, 1829. B] Chihuahua, Chihuahua. C] Primary studies under Bernardo Vignot and Father Luis Rubio, Chihuahua; began studies for the priesthood, Literary Institute of Chihuahua, but left school, 1849, after father's death. D] Member of the City Council of Chihuahua, 1854–55; alternate local deputy to the state legislature of Chihuahua, 1859–61; governor of Chihuahua, 1861–64; governor of Chihuahua, 1869–73; local deputy to the state legislature of Chihuahua, 1875–76; governor of Chihuahua, 1880–84; *senator* from the State of Chihuahua, 1886–90; *governor* of Chihuahua, 1903–07. E] None. F] Tax guard, Chihuahua, 1851; syndic of the City Council of Chihuahua, 1859–60; political boss of the Iturbide District, Chihuahua, 1859–60; substitute governor of Chihuahua, 1860–61; governor and military commander of Chihuahua, 1865–69. G] None. H] Coowner of the del Sauz y Encinillas haciendas, 1860; eventually owned 2,580,000 hectares in (one-ninth of) Chihuahua; largest rancher in Mexico; businessman; president, Mining Bank of Chihuahua; owned *La República*, 1871. I] Son of Juan Terrazas and Petra Fuentes; married Carolina Cuilty, aunt of *Enrique Creel*, and daughter of Colonel Gabino Cuilty; father-in-law of Enrique Creel, who married Angela Terrazas; Terrazas's wife is Creel's mother's sister; grandson of Gabriel Terrazas; great-grandson of Lucas Terrazas; father of Juan Terrazas Cuilty, federal deputy from Chihuahua, 1882–84; father of *Alberto Terrazas Cuilty*, governor of Chihuahua, 1910–11; father of Luis Terrazas Cuilty, federal deputy. J] Organized the 1st Battalion of Chihuahua to fight the French; rank of colonel, 1860; member of the Council of War against the Apaches, 1860; rank of brigadier general, 1865; defeated Porfirista forces, 1876. K] Exiled, El Paso, Texas, 1913–20; *Alvaro Obregón*'s government bought his prop-

erty for 13 million pesos. L] Album; Márquez, 266–72; Enc Mex, XII, 146–47; Almada, 219–73; Mestre, 271; DP70, 2095–99; Hombres prominentes, 203–04; Almada, 1968, 523–26.

Terrazas (Cuilty), Alberto
(Deceased August 14, 1926) A] August 1, 1869. B] Chihuahua, Chihuahua. C] Primary studies in Chihuahua; no degree. D] *Governor* of Chihuahua, 1910–11. E] None. F] None. G] None. H] Businessman; owner of the Palos Prietos and Monte Marqueño haciendas; owned the Ciudad Juárez racetrack; manager, Mining Bank of Chihuahua; industrialist; in business with father. I] Son of *Luis Terrazas*, wealthy landowner and dominant political figure in Chihuahua, and Carolina Cuilty, daughter of Colonel Gabino Cuilty, cousin of *Enrique Creel*, whose mother was his mother's sister; brother of Luis Terrazas Cuilty, federal deputy. J] Colonel in the state reserves, 1913; supported *Victoriano Huerta*, 1913–14. K] Exiled, United States, 1914–20; lived in Chihuahua, 1920–23, then returned to El Paso, Texas, 1923. L] Almada, 451–53; DP70, 2098; Almada, 1968, 522.

Terrones Benítez, Alberto
(Deceased December 28, 1981) A] June 3, 1887. B] Villa de Nombre de Dios, Durango. C] Primary studies in Nazas, Topia, and Durango, Durango, under his father; preparatory studies at the Juárez Institute, Durango, 1900; preparatory studies in engineering, National Preparatory School; studies toward a degree in mining engineering, National School of Engineering, UNAM; law degree, Juárez Institute, December 10, 1910, with a specialty in mining labor law. D] *Constitutional deputy* from the State of Durango, Dist. 6, 1916–17; *alternate federal deputy* from the State of Durango, Dist. 4, 1920–22, 1922–24; *federal deputy* from the State of Durango, Dist. 6, 1924; *senator* from the State of Durango, 1924–26; senator from the State of Durango, 1952–58, member of the Indigenous Affairs Committee, the Special Legislative Studies Committee; president of the Special Committee on Small Agricultural Property;

president of the First Mines Committee, and first secretary of the Military Justice Committee; senator from the State of Durango, 1964–70. E] None. F] Lawyer, Attorney General's Office; official of the Department of Agrarian Affairs; *provisional governor* of Durango, 1929–30. G] Organized the Agrarian Union of Durango, 1917. H] Practicing lawyer, Mexico City. I] Father was a schoolteacher; brother of General Adolfo Terrones Benítez, director of the infantry, Secretariat of National Defense, 1956; married María Lanone; son José served as president of Canacintra. K] Removed as provisional governor of Durango after attempting to implement stronger proagrarian reforms. L] C de D, 1922–24, 34; C de D, 1920–22, 34; C de D, 1924–26, 35; C de S, 1924–26; Ind Biog, 155; DGF56, 6, 8, 9, 11, 12, 14; *Excélsior*, 29 Dec. 1981, 10; Rouaix, 456.

Tolentino, Francisco
(Deceased March 12, 1903) A] 1838. B] Tepic, Nayarit. C] Early education unknown; no degree. D] *Governor* of Jalisco, 1883–87. E] None. F] None. G] None. H] Barber, Tepic. I] Served under Colonel José de Landero y Cos in the "Degollado" Battalion. J] Career army officer; joined the Liberal forces, 1855; rank of 2nd lieutenant, 1862; fought in Tepic, 1862; rank of 1st lieutenant, 1862; rank of captain, 1864; rank of brevet major, 1865; rank of colonel, 1867; rank of brigadier general, 1867; supported *Porfirio Díaz* in the Tuxtepec rebellion in the crucial battle of Tecoac, Puebla, November 16, 1876; rank of division general, 1877; president, Supreme Court of Military Justice, 1903. J] None. K] None. L] Hombres prominentes, 421–22; Mestre, 216; Mata Torres, 47.

Topete, Bonifacio
(Deceased April 7, 1896) A] 1835. B] Guadalajara, Jalisco. C] Primary studies in Guadalajara; no degree. D] None. E] None. F] Political boss and military commander of Baja California del Sur, 1890; appointed oficial mayor of the Secretariat of War, 1896, but died before serving. G] None. H] Unknown. I] Unknown. J] Joined the national guard as a

teenager; supported the Liberals in the War of the Reform; rank of 2nd lieutenant in the Prisciliano Sánchez Brigade, January 1857; fought at the siege of Puebla, 1863; captured by the French and held prisoner in France; escaped to Spain and returned to Mexico, where he joined *Porfirio Díaz* in Oaxaca; rank of colonel, 1867; commander of the 19th Infantry Battalion, 1871; fought the Yaqui Indians in Sonora; rank of brigade general, February 26, 1876; fought in the Sierra campaign in Puebla, 1875–76; commander, 11th Military Zone, 1888; rank of brigade general, 1894. K] None. L] Pavía, 74–80; DP70, 2144; Hombres prominentes, 291–92; Mata Torres, 99.

Topete (Almada), Fausto
(Deceased 1954) A] 1890. B] Alamos, Sonora. C] Early education unknown; no degree. D] None. E] None. F] *Governor* of Sonora, 1927–29. G] None. H] Businessman. I] Brother of Ricardo Topete, federal deputy from Sonora, 1926–28, and revolutionary. J] Joined the Constitutionalists, 1913, as a 2nd lieutenant; member of the staff of General *Benjamín Hill*, 1913–15; rank of brigadier general, 1920; supported the Plan of Agua Prieta, 1920; opposed the *Adolfo de la Huerta* rebellion, 1923; commander of the military district of Alamos, Sonora; leader of the Plan of Hermosillo with *Gilberto Valenzuela* against *Plutarco Elías Calles*, 1929; commander of the 2nd Army of the Northeast against the government, 1929; interned and exiled to the United States, April 29, 1929. K] None. L] Peral, 793; Almanaque de Sonora, 129; DP70, 2144–45; López, 1073.

Torre Díaz, Alvaro
A] 1899. B] Mérida, Yucatán. C] Primary and secondary studies at the Benito Ruz y Ruz Institute; medical degree, University of the Southeast, Mérida, Yucatán; postgraduate studies, Paris, France. D] Local deputy to the state legislature of Yucatán, 1915; *governor* of Yucatán, 1926–30. E] None. F] Commercial attaché to Washington, D.C.; oficial mayor of government of the State of Yucatán, under *Salvador Alvarado*; secretary general

of government of the State of Yucatán, 1918; consul to New York City, 1922; ambassador to Brazil, 1922. G] None. H] Founded *El Ateneo Peninsular* with Calixto Maldonado; head, editorial page, *El Diario Yucateco.* I] Son of Gregorio Torre y Medir and Prisciliana Díaz y Piña; grandson of Gregorio de la Torre y Rendón; married Mercedes Palma y Medina. J] None. K] None. L] DP70, 2149; Peral, 796; Valdés Acosta, 2, 73–85.

Torres, Lorenzo
(Deceased November 24, 1912) A] 1836. B] Mochiacahui, Fuerte District, Sinaloa. C] Early education unknown; enrolled at the National Military College, 1857, but left without completing studies. D] Local deputy to the state legislature of Sonora, 1878–80; *governor* of Sonora, 1887 (elected for 1887–91, but only served four months); *senator* from the State of Sonora, 1898–1912 (alternate, Alejandro Prieto, always in functions). E] None. F] None. G] None. H] Unknown. I] Father a miner. J] Career military officer, joined the army, 1857; joined the Liberal forces as a major, 1863, under General *Ramón Corona*; fought the French, 1863–67; fought in the battle of Alamos, under General Angel Martínez, January 1866; rank of colonel, 1871; supported the Plan of La Noria, 1871; commander of El Fuerte, Sinaloa; fought against the Yaquis and Apaches; commander of the 1st Military Zone, Sonora; revolted against Governor *Ignacio Pesqueira*, 1876; assistant inspector of military colonies, 1880; rank of brigadier general, February 2, 1893; chief of arms, Sonora; rank of brigade general, February 24, 1895; retired from the army, June 17, 1911. K] In exile, Los Angeles, California, 1911–12. L] Almanaque de Sonora, 122–23; DP70, 2152–53; Mestre, 245; Almada, 1968, 533–34; González Dávila, 625–26.

Torres, Luis Emeterio
(Deceased September 9, 1935) A] 1844. B] Guadalupe y Calvo (mining camp), Chihuahua. C] Early education unknown; no degree. D] Local deputy to the state legislature of Sonora; federal deputy from the State of Sonora, president of the Chamber, 1875; governor of Sonora,

1879–81; *governor* of Sonora, 1883–87, 1891–95, 1903, 1907–11; *senator* from the State of Sinaloa, 1890–92; *senator* from the State of Morelos, 1904–12. E] None. F] Political boss, El Fuerte District, Sinaloa; *political boss* of Baja California del Norte, 1888–94. G] None. H] Businessman; large landowner; inspector, Atcheson, Topeka, & Santa Fe Railroad, Los Angeles, California. I] Son of José del Rayo Torres, a miner, and Francisca Meléndez; formed a powerful political group in 1879, whose members included *Ramón Corral*, Carlos Ortiz, and Rafael Izabal. J] Joined the "Guerrero" Battalion, June 15, 1862, as a corporal, to fight the French; rank of captain, January 4, 1866; rank of major, May 16, 1866; commander of the Legion of Honor under Adolfo Palacio, 1866; adjutant to General Angel Martínez, Sonora, 1866; rank of lt. colonel, January 20, 1868; led revolt against General Domingo Rubí, governor of Sinaloa, 1868; supported the Plan of La Noria, 1871; rank of colonel, 1876; supported the Tuxtepec Plan, 1876; rank of brigade general, December 3, 1887; military commander of Baja California del Norte, 1888–94; commander of the 11th Military Zone, 1893; fought against the Yaquis, 1899; commander of the 1st Military Zone, Sonora, 1901; reintegrated into the army, 1913, but never returned to Mexico. K] Self–exile to Los Angeles, California, 1912–35. L] Album; Pavía, 72; Almanaque de Sonora, 21–22; Sec of War, 1901, 19; Sec of War, 914, 19; Enc Mex, XII, 192; DP70, 2153; López, 1080; Peral, 800; Aguilar Camín, 104; Mestre 290; Almada, 1968, 534.

Torres Ortiz, Pedro
(Deceased) A] May 13, 1887. B] Colima, Colima. C] Primary studies in Colima; no degree. D] Mayor of Zamora, Michoacán; mayor of Puruándiro, Michoacán; mayor of Ciudad Guzmán, Michoacán; senator from the State of Colima, 1934–39; governor of Colima, November 1, 1939–October 31, 1940. E] Candidate of Cooperative party for governor of Colima, 1923; formed own political party, Only Revolutionary Front of Colima, 1939, to oppose General Miguel Santa Ana; supported General Miguel Henríquez Guz-

mán for president, 1945, 1951. F] *Provisional governor* of Colima, 1931. G] None. H] None. J] Career army officer; commander of the 57th Cavalry Regiment; joined the Revolution, 1914; initially opposed *Venustiano Carranza*; supported Carranza, 1920; supported General Maycotte in Oaxaca against *Alvaro Obregón*, 1923; rank of brigadier general, October 1, 1942. K] Political opponent of Miguel G. Santa Ana; in exile in the United States, 1923. L] Letter; Peral, 800–01; López, 1081; Moreno, 84.

Torri (Máynes), Julio
(Deceased 1970) A] June 27, 1889. B] Saltillo, Coahuila. C] Primary studies, Colegio Torreón, Saltillo; preparatory studies, Ateneo Fuente, Saltillo, 1904–07; law studies, National School of Law, UNAM, 1908–13, graduating October 25, 1913; Ph.D. in philosophy and letters, UNAM, 1933; professor of Spanish and French literature, National Preparatory School; professor of literature and advanced Spanish, School of Philosophy and Letters, UNAM, 1913–64; dean of the faculty, UNAM; professor at the National Preparatory School, 1913–49; professor emeritus of UNAM, 1953–70. D] None. E] None. F] Oficial mayor of the Federal District, 1919–20; founder and director of the Publishing Department, Secretariat of Public Education, 1921–25. G] Member of the Ateneo de la Juventud, with *Alfonso Reyes, José Vasconcelos* and other leading intellectual figures; member of the Mexican Academy of Language, 1942. H] Codirector of Editorial Cultura with *Agustín Loera Chávez*, 1916–23. I] Son of Julio S. Torri and Sofía Máynez; studied at the Ateneo Fuente with *Aarón Sáenz, Manuel Aguirre Berlanga* , and *Miguel Alessio Robles*. J] None. K] None. L] Enc Mex, XII, 196; Carreño, 369–70; López, 1083; DP70, 2156; WWM45, 117–18.

Torroella (Romaguera), Enrique
(Deceased January 15, 1928) A] August 6, 1852. B] Havana, Cuba. C] Early education unknown; graduated as a 2nd lieutenant in the engineers, National Military College, 1878; director of studies, National Military College; subdirector, National Military College, 1896–1909; in-

terim director, National Military College, 1906. D] None. E] None. F] Military attaché to Guatemala; chief of staff, Secretariat of War, 1909–11; chief of staff, President *Francisco León de la Barra*, 1911. G] None. I] Father of Julio Torroella y Estrada, public accountant; brother of Alfredo Torroella, poet; married Emelina de Estrada y Zenea; son-in-law of Ildefonso de Estrada, doctor of philosophy; father of Mario A. Torroella, president of the National Academy of Medicine, 1943; brother of Alfredo Torroella, poet and dramatist. J] Career army officer; in charge of coastal planning in Tamaulipas as a military engineer; rank of lt. colonel, June 28, 1899; rank of brigadier general, March 8, 1909; retired from the army to protest *Francisco I. Madero*'s assassination, April 1, 1913. K] None. L] Sec of War, 1914, 28; Mestre, 280; QesQ, 584–85; DP70, 2156; López, 1083; Peral, 802; Linajes, 266–67; Sec of War, 1901, 26; Cuevas, 342.

Traconis, Daniel
(Deceased October 24, 1912) A] January 3, 1836. B] Mérida, Yucatán. C] Primary studies in Mérida; preparatory studies at the San Ildefonso Seminary, Mexico City, graduating 1852; enrolled at the National Military College, 1852, graduating as a 2nd lieutenant, 1854. D] *Governor* of Yucatán, 1890–94. E] None. F] None. G] None. H] Owner, Muchucux Hacienda, Valladolid, Yucatán. I] Son of Demetrio Traconis and Guadalupe García; nephew of Juan Bautista, brigade general; uncle of Joaquina Traconis, mother of José María Iturralde Traconis, governor of Yucatán, 1924–26; father of Juan Bautista Traconis, political boss and mayor of Valladolid; married Luisa Traconis. J] Career military officer; joined a line battalion under Colonel Silverio Núñez, Aguascalientes, 1854; captain, line battalion, Guadalajara; battalion commander, Sierra Gorda campaign; imprisoned in Puebla, 1857; fought in the battle of Tacubaya, 1859, captured and condemned to death, but saved by Archbishop de la Garza; escaped from military prison Santiago Tlatelolco, 1859; fought in campaigns against the Mayas; commander of the military colonies

of the east, 1888; rank of brigadier general, infantry reserves, December 5, 1893. K] None. L] Sec of War, 1901, 25; Hombres prominentes, 389–90; Mestre, 244; Album; Pavía, 412–18; Peral, 803; Holms, 365.

Trejo y Lerdo de Tejada, Carlos
(Deceased December 3, 1941) A] November 5, 1879. B] Mexico City. C] Primary studies in Mexico City; law degree, School of Law, Mexico City; professor of civil law and forensic speaking, National School of Law, National University. D] *Federal deputy* from the Federal District, Dist. 1, 1912–13, member of the Great Committee; *federal deputy* from the Federal District, Dist. 9, 1913–14. E] None. F] Agent of the criminal Ministerio Público; agent of the military Ministerio Público; public defender; attorney general of the Federal District and Federal Territories, 1912; ambassador to Chile, 1922–24; ambassador to Argentina, 1924–27; *ambassador* to Cuba, 1927–29; *subsecretary* of public education, 1930; *subsecretary* in charge, Secretariat of Public Education, 1930; *governor* of Baja California, 1930–31; consulting lawyer to President *Pascual Ortiz Rubio*; consulting lawyer to the secretary of development; consulting lawyer to the Federal District. G] None. H] Practicing lawyer. I] Unknown; related to President Lerdo de Tejada. J] None. K] None. L] Dir social, 1935, 361; Enc Mex, XII, 215–16; DP70, 2169, Peral, 804; Carrasco Puente, 81.

Treviño (Flores), José
(Deceased August 28, 1927) A] January 6, 1886. B] Monterrey, Nuevo León. C] Primary studies, Monterrey Public Schools; completed sixth grade; no degree. D] Member of the City Council of Monterrey, 1912–16; *constitutional deputy* from the State of Nuevo León, Dist. 2, 1916–17; local deputy to the state legislature of Nuevo León, 1918–19. E] Supported *Francisco I. Madero*, 1911. F] None. G] None. H] Apprentice mechanic, National Railroads of Mexico; mechanic; owner, bicycle repair shop. I] Son of Santiago Treviño and Joaquina Flores; married Abigail Martínez; son Abel Eli, a

businessman, Monterrey J] None. K] None. L] C de D, 1916–17.

Treviño (González), Francisco L.
(Deceased June 22, 1937) A] June 21, 1881. B] Villa Guerrero, Coahuila. C] Primary studies in Villa Guerrero, Coahuila; no degree. D] *Federal deputy* from the State of Coahuila, Dist. 5, 1918–20. E] None. F] Customs administrator, Piedras Negras, Coahuila, 1915; treasurer general of Chihuahua, 1916; *provisional governor* of Coahuila, 1916. G] None. H] Employee, Mining Bank of Chihuahua. I] Son of Colonel Francisco Z. Treviño, farmer, rancher, and colonel in the National Guard, and Trinidad González; brother of General *Jacinto B. Treviño*; brother-in-law of María Carrillo Gutiérrez, daughter of Colonel *Lauro Carrillo*, governor of Chihuahua, 1887–92; nephew, Salvador, director of mines, Secretariat of Industry and Commerce, 1957–58. J] Joined the Constitutionalists as part of *Venustiano Carranza's* escort, 1913; rank of colonel, 1915; supported general *Pablo González* for president, 1920; supported the Plan of Agua Prieta, 1920; rank of brigadier general, May 1921; chief of staff, military operations, Torreón, Coahuila, 1937. k–None. l–Almada, 532–33; DP70, 2170; Peral, 805; Almada, 1968, 538–39; Moreno, 195–200.

Treviño (González), Jacinto B.
(Deceased November 6, 1971) A] September 11, 1883. B] Ciudad Guerrero, Coahuila. C] Primary studies in Ciudad Guerrero and in the Colegio Hidalgo and Colegio Bolívar, Monterrey; preparatory studies at the Colegio Civil of Monterrey, enrolled in the National Military College, December 26, 1901, graduated as an industrial engineer with the rank of artillery lieutenant, December 6, 1908. D] *Federal deputy* from the State of Coahuila, Dist. 5, 1917–18; senator from the State of Coahuila, 1952–58, member of the Second Foreign Relations Committee, the Public Welfare Committee, and the Great Committee. E] Supporter and organizer of the pro-Almazán Revolutionary Committee for National Reconstruction, 1939–40; founder and president of the Au-

thentic Party of the Mexican Revolution (PARM), 1957–65; precandidate for governor of Coahuila, 1957. F] Oficial mayor of the Secretariat of War, 1914; *secretary* of industry, commerce, and labor, 1920; director of Mexican Free Ports, 1957–66. G] None. H] None. I] Son-in-law of Colonel *Lauro Carrillo*, governor of Chihuahua, 1887–92; son of Francisco Z. Treviño, colonel in the national guard, and Trinidad González; married María Carrillo Gutiérrez; father of Salvador F. Treviño, a mining engineer; brother of *Francisco L. Treviño*, provisional governor of Coahuila, 1916. J] Rank of 2nd captain, 1910; member of *Francisco I. Madero's* staff, 1911; organized the 25th Irregular Regiment, Saltillo, Coahuila, 1912; fought General *Victoriano Huerta*, 1913; rank of major; chief of staff for *Venustiano Carranza*, 1913; rank of colonel, June 8, 1913; brigadier general, June 5, 1914; commander of the 1st Brigade of the 1st division of the Army of the Center, 1914; rank of brigade general, 1915; rank of division general, December 22, 1915; general-in-chief of the forces against *Francisco Villa*, 1916; military commander of Chihuahua, 1916; supported *Alvaro Obregón* against Carranza, 1920; supported the *Adolfo de la Huerta* rebellion, 1923; supported the Escobar rebellion, 1929. K] First signer of the Plan of Guadalupe, March 26, 1913; imprisoned, 1923–25; opposed Obregón's reelection, 1927; supported Escobar rebellion, 1929; in exile, 1929–36; rejoined the army at the rank of division general, 1941. L] HA, 15 Nov. 1971; Peral, 806; Enc Mex, Annual, 1977, 597–98; Moreno, 195–200; WNM, 228.

Treviño (Leal), Gerónimo
(Deceased November 13, 1914) A] November 22, 1836. B] Hacienda La Escondida, Municipio of Cadereyta, Jimenez, Nuevo León. D] Primary studies in Cadereyta; secondary studies, Conciliar Seminary, Monterrey, Nuevo León. E] None. F] Governor of Nuevo León, 1867–69, 1869–71, 1871–73; secretary of war, 1880–81; *governor* of Nuevo León, 1913. G] None. H] Cattle rancher, Nuevo León and Coahuila, 1885; cofounder of the Cía. Ferrocarrilera de Monterrey al Golfo, 1887,

with *Emeterio de la Garza*, justice of the Supreme Court, 1904–11. I] Son of Francisco Treviño and Antonia Leal, small ranchers; married Elena Barragán, daughter of General Miguel Barragán, president of Mexico, 1836; second wife, Berta Ord, daughter of North American general; third wife; Guadalupe Zambrano, daughter of Eduardo Zambrano, large landholder; son Gerónimo Treviño Ord baptized by *Porfirio Díaz*; close friend of General Francisco Naranjo, father of *Francisco Naranjo*, governor of Morelos, 1912. J] Joined the Liberal forces in the defense of Monterrey, 1856; sergeant, war of Reform, 1858–69; rank of major, Legion of the North, 1860; fought in 35 battles during the French intervention, 1861–67; fought in the battle of Puebla, May 5, 1862; won the battle of Santa Isabel, Coahuila, March 1, 1866; commander of the 2nd and 3rd military zones, 1867; commander of the 1st Division, under General Díaz, siege of Querétaro, 1867; commander, Parade Ground of Mexico City, 1867; supported the Plan of la Noria, 1871; supported the Plan of Tuxtepec, 1876; rank of division general of cavalry, March 13, 1877; commander of the 3rd Military Zone, Monterrey, Nuevo León, 1909–12; commander of the Military Zone, Coahuila, 1913; offered leadership of the Constitutionalists by *Venustiano Carranza*, 1913, but refused; president, Supreme Military Tribunal, 1913. K] In exile, 1913–14, Laredo, Texas. L] Enc Mex, XII, 217; Langston, 45; DP70, 2171; Peral, 806; Sec of War, 1911, 15; Rev de Ejer, 13 Dec. 1968, 3; Mestre, 252.

Troncoso, Francisco Villa de Paula
(Deceased December 29, 1919) A] October 20, 1839. B] Veracruz, Veracruz. C] Early education unknown; enrolled in the National Military College, 1853; professor in strategy and military transportation, National Military College. D] Federal deputy of the State of Guanajuato; *senator* from the State of Michoacán, 1914. E] None. F] Department head, Secretariat of War, 1899; chief of staff, Secretariat of War, 1914. G] None. H] Unknown. I] Son of Francisco de P. Troncoso and Ana Josefa Pancardo; descendant

of the Counts of Troncoso from Veracruz; attended the National Military College with *Juan de la Luz Enríquez*; possibly brother of Pedro, brigade general. J] Fought as a 2nd lieutenant, 1858; fought with the Liberals under General Santos Degollado; battalion commander; commander of the national guard, State of México, 1861; rank of 1st captain, engineers, Mexico City, 1862; fought against the French in the siege of Puebla,1863; captured and sent to France, 1863; rank of colonel, 1865; rank of brigadier general, 1868; supported the Tuxtepec Rebellion, 1876; rank of brigade general, July 10, 1884; president, Inspection Committee for Artillery Factories; rank of division general, May 15, 1913. K] None. L] Peral, 807; Pasquel, 1972, 341–43; Mestre, 263; Illescas, 199–200; Sec of War, 1901, 23; Sec of War, 1914, 17, 19; Sec of War, 1900, 289.

U

Urbina y Frías, Salvador
(Deceased September 12, 1961) A] June 4, 1885. B] Federal District. C] Primary studies at a private school and Public School No. 5, Mexico City; secondary studies, Colegio de Joaquín Noreña; preparatory studies, National Preparatory School; law degree, National School of Law, National University of Mexico, 1902–07, with a thesis on the conflict of administrative laws in international law; professor of political economy, National School of Law, UNAM, 1912; professor of civil proceedings, National School of Law, UNAM. D] Senator from the Federal District, 1952–58. E] None. F] Agent of the Ministerio Público of the District Court of Durango, 1909; oficial mayor of the Supreme Court of Mexico, 1910–12; first agent of the Ministerio Público, 1913; first agent of the Ministerio Público, Office of the Attorney General of Mexico, 1914; presidential negotiator to *Venustiano Carranza*, 1914; director of the Advisory Department, Secretariat of the Treasury, 1915–16; oficial mayor of the Secretariat of the Treasury; *subsecretary of the treasury*, 1922, interim secretary of the treasury, 1922; attorney general of Mexico;

justice of the Supreme Court of Mexico, 1923–35; *president* of the Supreme Court, 1929–34; justice of the Supreme Court, 1940; president of the Supreme Court, 1941–46, 1946–51; director of the national lottery, 1958. G] None. H] Delegate to the Pan-American Conference, 1928; private law practice, 1914–15, 1935–40; founder and principal author of *Revista Mexicana de Petróleos*, 1915. I] Son of Manuel Urbina, a physician; married Leticia Bolland. J] None. K] Gruening considered him completely honest as a public official in the 1920s. L] Gruening, 504; WWM45, 119; DGF56, 6; Peral, 811; EBW, 411; DP70, 2201; HA, 14 Dec. 1951, 6; Ind biog., 160–61; Enc Mex, XII, 1977, 277.

Urquizo (Benavides), Francisco L.
(Deceased April 6, 1969) A] October 4, 1891. B] San Pedro de las Colonias, Coahuila. C] Primary education in Torreón, Coahuila; secondary education at the Liceo Fournier, Federal District; no degree. D] None. E] None. F] Oficial mayor of the Secretariat of War; *subsecretary* of war (in charge of the ministry), 1920; director of the Federal Office of the Treasury, Pachuca, Hidalgo; bureau director, Secretariat of the Treasury, 1930–34; chief of staff, Secretariat of National Defense; subsecretary of national defense, 1940–45; secretary of national defense, 1945–46; director of the Military Industry Department, 1952–58. G] None. H] Author of many books and articles on the history of the Revolution. I] Parents were campesinos; he was forced into the federal army for disobeying a landowner; friend of *Matías Ramos Santos* and General Marcelino García Barragán, secretary of national defense. J] 2nd lieutenant in the federal army, 1911; joined Constitutionalists, 1913; chief of military operations in Veracruz, 1918; rank of brigadier general, 1920; military zone commander, 1938–40; member of the Presidential Council for National Defense, 1959–69. K] Retired from the army but later rejoined, reaching the rank of division general. L] WWM45, 119; DBM68, 612; DGF56, 529; DP70, 1104–05; Peral, 814; EBW, 1148; *Siempre*, 4 Feb. 1959, 6; Enc Mex, XII, 1977, 279–80.

Urrutia, Aurelliano
(Deceased) A] 1880. B] Xochimilco, Federal District. C] Early education unknown; medical degree, National School of Medicine; professor, National Medical School; dean, National Medical School; professor, Military Medical College. D] *Senator* from the Federal District, 1913–16. E] None. F] *Secretary* of government, 1913. G] None. H] Director, General Hospital, Mexico City, 1913–14; founded a medical clinic in San Antonio, Texas; famous surgeon. I] From Tarascan Indian parents; became compadre of *Victoriano Huerta* after he saved his life when Huerta's own battalion revolted and tried to murder him. J] Major, Medical Corps, 3rd Battalion; medical officer, Quintana Roo. K] Ordered shot by *Victoriano Huerta*, 1913, but *Aureliano Blanquet* let him escape, 1913; went into exile, 1914, where he remained until his death; refused amnesty from Presidents *Emilio Portes Gil* and *Lázaro Cárdenas*. L] López, 1104–05; DP70, 2448; Puente, 165–70; DP70, 2448.

Uruchurtu, Alfredo P.
(Deceased) A] March 10, 1884. B] Hermosillo, Sonora. C] Teaching certificate, Normal School, Mexico City, in elementary and higher primary; postgraduate studies in Switzerland and Germany, on a scholarship from the State of Sonora; director, Higher Primary School; director, Primary Elementary School; director, National Teachers School; subdirector, National Teachers School; director, Normal School of San Luis Potosí. D] None. E] None. F] Director, Department of Normal and Primary Teaching, Secretariat of Public Education; director, Primary Education, Northern District of Baja California; oficial mayor of Public Education, 1928–30. G] None. H] Author of many books on teaching. I] Son of Dr. Gustavo Alfredo Uruchurtu, federal deputy from the Federal District, 1928–30; brother of Ernesto P. Uruchurtu, head of the Federal District Department, 1952–66; brother-in-law of María Luis Peralta, sister of Francisco Martínez Peralta, senator from the State of Sonora, 1940–46; related to Manuel R. Uruchurtu, federal deputy from

the State of Sinaloa, 1908–12. J] None. K] None. L] Peral, 814; QesQ, 592–94; López, 1105.

Urueta (Siqueiros), Jesús
(Deceased December 8, 1920) A] February 9, 1868. B] Chihuahua, Chihuahua. C] Primary studies in Chihuahua; law degree, National School of Law, Mexico City; librarian, National School of Law; professor, National School of Law; professor of literature, National Preparatory School. D] *Alternate federal deputy* from the State of México, Dist. 15, 1900–02; local deputy to the state legislature of México, 1902–04; *federal deputy* from the State of Chihuahua, Dist. 4, 1902–04; *federal deputy* from the State of Guerrero, Dist. 5, 1904–06, 1906–08; *federal deputy* from the Federal District, Dist. 3, 1912–14, leader of the Revolutionary Bloc; *federal deputy* from the Federal District, Dist. 4, 1917–18, member of the Great Committee. E] Member of the Reyista party; joined the National Anti-Reelectionist party, 1908. F] *Subsecretary* of foreign relations, 1914–15, in charge of the secretariat, 1915–16; ambassador to Argentina and Uruguay, 1919–20. G] None. H] Author of numerous books; journalist; wrote for *El Universal*, *Revista Moderna*, and *México Nuevo*; poet. I] Son of Dr. Eduardo Urueta, Liberal politician and senator, 1875, and Refugio Siqueiros; father close to the Creel and Terrazas families; married Tarcila Sierra González, daughter of *Santiago Sierra Méndez* and niece of *Justo Sierra Méndez*. J] Joined the Constitutionalists, 1913; remained loyal to *Venustiano Carranza*, 1920. K] None. L] Márquez, 160–62; FSRE, 165; Enc Mex, XII, 283; Mestre, 266; Puente, 64–68; QesQ, 593; Almada, 1968, 555; UNAM, law, 1880–91, 127, 1891–96, 54.

Utrilla Trujillo, Miguel
(Deceased October 7, 1917) A] September 29, 1830. B] San Cristóbal de la Casas, Chiapas. C] Primary studies in San Cristóbal de la Casas; preparatory studies in philosophy and letters, Seminary of San Cristóbal de las Casas; began law studies, but never completed. D] Governor of

Chiapas, 1879–83; *alternate senator* from the State of Veracruz, 1884–86; *alternate senator* from the State of Colima, 1886–90; *federal deputy* from the State of Chiapas, Dist. 1, 1890–92, 1892–94, 1894–96, 1896–98, 1898–1900. E] None. F] Political boss of San Cristóbal de las Casas, 1864. G] None. H] Unknown. I] Son of Juan Manuel Utrilla and Candelaria Trujillo. J] Joined the national guard as a 1st Sergeant, December 3, 1857; rank of 2nd lieutenant, 1857; fought against the French; commander of the 2nd Company, Chiapas Battalion, siege of Puebla, 1863; commander, 2nd Company, Chiapas Battalion, Jonuta; military commander of Tapachula, Chiapas, 1858; rank of captain, May 6, 1859; military commander of San Cristobal de la Casas, 1864; rank of lt. colonel, 1864; commander, national guard, Chiapas; rank of colonel, September 13, 1877; rank of brigadier general, July 1, 1900. K] None. L] López, 1106; Mestre, 259; Dicc biog de Chiapas, 253; Almanaque de Chiapas, 117.

V

Vaca, Francisco
(Deceased) A] April 20, 1824. B] Chilchota, Zamora, Michoacán. C] Primary studies under Francisco Alvarez Cuesta; enrolled in the Seminary of Morelia, 1839; legal studies under Clemente de Jesús Munguía, graduating from the Superior Tribunal of Justice of Michoacán, August 20, 1850. D] Federal deputy from the State of Michoacán, 1852, secretary of the Chamber; constitutional deputy from the State of Michoacán, 1857; local deputy to the state legislature of Michoacán, 1861; federal deputy from the State of Colima, Dist. 1, 1867–69; federal deputy from the State of Michoacán, 1869–71, 1873–75, 1880–82; senator from the State of Michoacán, 1882–83, president of the Chamber. E] None. F] Third secretary of government, State of Michoacán, 1850; first alternate, district judge, Michoacán, 1851; special treasury judge, 1853–55; judge of the first instance, Colima, 1855; judge, Superior Tribunal of Justice of Michoacán, 1855; district judge, Jalisco, 1856; judge, 6th Civil District, Mexico City, 1857; circuit court judge, Guadala-

jara, 1861–62; judge, 3rd Civil District, Mexico City, 1867; president and judge, Superior Tribunal of Justice of Michoacán, 1877–79; *justice* of the Supreme Court, 1883–93. G] None. H] Lawyer, 1858–61. I] Son of Vicente Vaca y Orejel and Gertrudis Herrera y Cuesta. J] None. K] Refused nomination for governor of Michoacán, 1861, 1879. L] Pavía, judges, 60–70.

Valentí, Rubén
(Deceased 1915) A] 1879. B] Comitán, Chiapas. C] Primary studies, Comitán; preparatory studies, Tuxtla Gutiérrez, Chiapas; teaching certificate, Tuxtla Gutiérrez; law degree, National School of Law, Mexico City, 1902. D] *Federal deputy* from the State of Chiapas, Dist. 4, 1913–14. E] None. F] Agent of the Ministerio Público; *subsecretary* of public instruction, 1914; *secretary* of public instruction, 1914. G] Member of the Ateneo de la Juventud. H] Author; poet; practicing lawyer. I] Unknown. J] None. K] None. L] DP70, 2217; Gordillo y Ortiz, 257–58; Carrasco Puente, 59.

Valenzuela (Galindo), Gilberto
(Deceased February 9, 1978) A] April 27, 1891. B] Sahuaripa, Sonora. C] Primary studies in Sonora under Epifanio Vieyra; preparatory studies at the Boys Liceo, Guadalajara, Jalisco; law studies, National School of Law, UNAM, 1910–14, law degree; director, Bacanora Elementary School, 1906. D] Local deputy to the state legislature of Sonora, 1916. E] Candidate for president of Mexico, 1928; supported General *Juan Andreu Almazán* for president, 1940. F] *Governor* of Sonora, 1916–17; *subsecretary* in charge of government, 1920; *subsecretary* of government, 1922–23; *secretary* of government, 1925; *minister* to the United Kingdom, 1925–28; justice of the Supreme Court, 1953–60. G] President of the Literary Center of the Fiat Lux Preparatory School, Guadalajara; founded the Student Anti-Reelectionist Union, 1910. H] None. I] Father of Gilberto Valenzuela Esquerro, secretary of public works, 1964–70; son of Federico Valenzuela and Eustaquia Galindo; married Olga Esquerro. J] Joined the Constitutionalists under *Venustiano Carranza* in Veracruz, 1914; chief military

instructor, Jalapa, Veracruz; agent of the Ministerio Público, military attorney general; opposed Carranza, 1920; supported the Escobar movement, 1929. K] In exile, Mesa, Arizona, 1929; offered post of justice of the Supreme Court, 1928, but broke ties with President *Plutarco Elías Calles*; offered post of secretary of foreign relations by *Emilio Portes Gil*, 1929, but refused. L] López, 1111–12; *Excélsior*, 10 Feb. 1978, 5; Meyer, No. 12, 93.

Valenzuela (González), Jesús E.
(Deceased May 20, 1911) A] December 24, 1856. B] Guanaceví, Durango. C] Primary studies, Alamos, Sonora; secondary studies, Scientific and Literary Institute of Chihuahua; preparatory studies at the National Preparatory School, Mexico City; law degree, National School of Law, Mexico City, 1877. D] Federal deputy from the State of Chihuahua, Dist. 3, 1880–82, 1882–84, 1884–86, 1886–88, 1888–90, 1890–92, 1892–94, 1894–96, 1896–98, 1898–1900; *federal deputy* from the State of Chihuahua, Dist. 4, 1900–02, 1902–04. E] None. F] None. G] None. H] Partner in many business ventures; partner with brother José in real estate firm; partner with brother in the Trolley Car Company of Chihuahua; one of the largest landholders in Mexico; owner of 6,954,626 hectares in Chihuahua; owner of the Minas Nuevas hacienda; business partner with *Lauro Carrillo*, governor of Chihuahua, 1887–92; founder and director, *Revista Moderna*, with *Luis Urbina* and *Manuel Gutiérrez Nájera*. I] Son of Jesús Valenzuela and Juana González; brother of José, secretary general of government of Chihuahua. J] None. K] None. L] Holms, 250; DP70, 2217; Mestre, 240; Almada, 1958, 557; Márquez, 85–91; Enc Mex, XII, 293; Rice, 252.

Valenzuela (Yera), Policarpo
(Deceased January 4, 1914) A] January 26, 1831. B] San Antonio de los Naranjo, Cárdenas, Tabasco. C] Early education unknown; no degree. D] *Alternate senator* from the State of Tabasco, 1898–1902. E] None. F] *Governor* of Tabasco, 1911. G] None. H] Landowner; owned eleven haciendas in Tabasco. I] Son of Valentín Valenzuela García, peasant, and María

Yera López, peasant; nephew Nicolás, director of the Bank of Tabasco; married Clara Ramos. J] Commander of the national guard and chief of the 1st Military Line, La Chontalpa, Tabasco, 1863; rank of colonel, December 29, 1867. K] None. L] Bulnes, 19; Ghigliazza, 156–57; Rice, 253; Holms, 341; Mestre, 249.

Valle, José Felipe
(Deceased July 2, 1928) A] 1890. B] Colima, Colima. C] Primary studies in Colima; secondary studies at the Conciliar Tridentine Seminary, Colima; no degree; founded the Colegio Mazatlán, Mazatlán, Sinaloa, 1902; professor, San Luis Gonzaga Preschool; school inspector, Colima, 1914. D] *Federal deputy* from the State of Sinaloa, Dist. 2, 1912–13; *governor* of Colima, 1917–19. E] None. F] Oficial mayor of the state legislature of Colima, 1914; customs inspector, Acapulco, 1919–28. G] None. H] Journalist; wrote for *El Correo de la Tarde*. I] Intimate friend of *Heriberto Frías*. J] None. K] Jailed in Mazatlán for supporting an opposition candidate, 1909, but released. L] González Dávila, 644; Romero Aceves, 190–92; Moreno, 71–72; DP70, 2221; López, 1116.

Valles, Adolfo
(Deceased 1937) A] 1873. B] Santa Rosalia, Chihuahua. C] Preparatory studies at the National Preparatory School; enrolled, National School of Law, January 27, 1894; law degree, National School of Law, Mexico; professor of fencing, National Preparatory School; professor of penal law, National School of Law, UNAM, 1920–35. D] None. E] None. F] Agent of the Ministerio Público; penal judge; attorney general of Mexico, 1912. G] None. H] Practicing lawyer; author. I] Son of Trinidad Baca and Merced Valles. J] None. K] Dueled with José Gaona. L] UNAM, law, 1891–96, 111; Enc Mex, XII, 298; DP70, 2226.

Vargas Lugo, Bartolomé
(Deceased June 19, 1972) A] 1890. B] Tulancingo, Hidalgo. C] Early education unknown; agricultural engineering degree, National School of Agriculture, San Jacinto, on a fellowship from the State of Hidalgo; substitute professor, National

School of Agriculture, 1914. D] *Federal deputy* from the State of Hidalgo, Dist. 7, 1928–29; *governor* of Hidalgo, 1929–33. E] *Secretary general* of the National Executive Committee of PRI, 1933; supported *Juan A. Almazán* for president, 1940; president, Federation of Parties of the Mexican People, Hidalgo, which supported General Henríquez Guzmán for president, 1951–52. F] Delegate of the federal government to set aside land for *Francisco Villa* and his men in the Hacienda Canutillo, Parral, Chihuahua, 1920, 1922; director, Secretariat of Agriculture office, Monterrey, Nuevo León, 1923–24; first engineer, National Agrarian Commission, 1924; subdirector, Advisory Body, National Agrarian Commission, 1925–28; manager, National Agricultural Credit Bank, 1933–35; adviser, National Agricultural Credit Bank, 1940–46; member, Advisory Council, Department of Agrarian Affairs and Colonization, 1964–70. G] Oficial mayor, National Agrarian Commission. H] None. I] Unknown. J] Fought with *Emiliano Zapata*'s troops, 1914. K] Member of the Pachuca soccer team, national champions, 1917–18. L] Gómez, 492–98; Pérez López, 487–88; López, 1123.

Vasconcelos (Calderón), José
(Deceased) A] February 28, 1882. B] Oaxaca, Oaxaca. C] Primary studies, Eagle Pass, Texas, Piedras Negras, Coahuila, the Annex to the Institute of Sciences and Literature of Toluca, and at the Campeche Institute; preparatory studies, National Preparatory School, Mexico City; enrolled in the National School of Law, 1900, graduating with a law degree, 1905; rector of UNAM, 1920–21; visiting professor, University of Chicago, 1928; visiting professor, School of Social Sciences, University of La Plata, 1934; president, University of Sonora. D] None. E] Campaigned for *Francisco I. Madero*, 1910–11; vice-president, Constitutional Progressive party; leader of the Anti-Reelectionist Center of Mexico City, 1909; candidate for governor of Oaxaca, 1924; candidate for president of Mexico, 1929. F] Fiscal agent, Secretariat of the Treasury, Durango, 1906; offered subsecretary of justice and public instruction by Madero, 1911, but refused; secre-

tary to Madero's confidential agent in Washington, D.C., *Francisco Vázquez Gómez*, 1911; head, Department of the University and Fine Arts, 1920–21; *secretary of public education*, 1921–24; director of the National Library. G] Member of the Ateneo de la Juventud. H] Author; essayist; philosopher; founded *Antorcha* in opposition to *Plutarco Elías Calles*'s regime, 1924. H] Practicing lawyer; lawyer for Warner, Johnson, and Galston, Mexico City; ran own law firm. I] Son of Ignacio Vasconcelos, customs official, and Carmen Calderón; grandson of Joaquín Vasconcelos, prosperous businessman from Oaxaca, who was *Porfirio Díaz*'s first employer, and Perfecta Varela; grandson of Dr. Esteban Calderón, personal physician to Porfirio Díaz, whom Calderón kept at his home in 1857, and senator from the State of Oaxaca; father-in-law of Herminio Ahumada, federal deputy from the State of Sonora; nephew of José R. Calderón, president of the National Railroad Board, 1930s; good friend of *Manuel Gómez Morín*, who supported him in exile and during his 1929 presidential campaign; produced a generation of political disciples, including President Adolfo López Mateos. J] Maderista, 1910–11; supported the Constitutionalists, 1913–14; supported *Alvaro Obregón* against *Venustiano Carranza*, 1920. K] Self-exile, 1924–28, 1929. L] WWM45, 122; Enc Mex, XII, 302–03; López 1124; UNAM, law, 1900–06, 47; letters.

Vázquez, Lorenzo
(Deceased May 5, 1917) A] August 10, 1879. B] Los Hornos, Tlaquiltenango, Morelos. C] Primary studies in Los Hornos; no further education. D] None. E] None. F] *Governor* of Morelos, 1915–16. G] None. H] Laborer, Tenextepango Hacienda, Morelos. I] Son of José Vázquez and Juana Herrera, peasants. J] Joined the Revolution as a Zapatista, March 1911; rank of division general, 1914; represented at the Convention of Mexico City by Leopoldo Reynoso, 1915; changed affiliation to *Venustiano Carranza*, 1916–17; reversed to supporting the Zapatistas, 1917. K] Killed by troops loyal to Carranza. L] López González, 225–26; López, 1129.

Vázquez del Mercado, Alberto
(Deceased July 1980) A] 1893. B] Chilpancingo, Guerrero. C] Primary studies at a public school, Chilpancingo; preparatory studies in Chilpancingo, Guerrero; completed preparatory studies at the National Preparatory School, 1912–14; legal studies, National School of Law, UNAM, 1915–18, graduating August 16, 1919; won the first prize for a 5th-year law student, 1919; professor, National Preparatory School, 1914–15. D] *Federal deputy* from the State of Guerrero, 1924–26. E] Candidate for federal deputy from the State of Guerrero, Dist. 5, 1918; active supporter of *José Vasconcelos* for president, 1928–29; supported the Almazán campaign actively, 1939–40. F] Head, Department of Publications, Museum of History, 1915; secretary of government of the Federal District, 1921–22; subsecretary of industry, commerce, and labor, 1922–23; *justice* of the Supreme Court, 1929–31. G] None. H] Opened a law office in Acapulco, 1919; practiced law with *Manuel Gómez Morín*, 1927–28; practicing lawyer, Mexico City, 1931–80; founded the CVLTVRA publishing company, 1916. I] Son of lawyer Jesús Vázquez del Mercado, Liberal supporter and loyal to President Lerdo de Tejada, who served as secretary of the Chilpancingo court, and Nicolosa Manquina; close friend of Manuel Gómez Morín, Antonio Castro Leal, Pedro Henríquez Ureña, and Manuel Toussaint. J] None. K] Resigned from the Supreme Court to protest the illegal expulsion of *Luis Cabrera* from Mexico; never returned to public life. L] Letters.

Vázquez del Mercado, Alejandro
(Deceased May 5, 1923) A] April 24, 1841. B] Sombrerete, Zacatecas. C] Primary studies in Sombrerete; secondary studies in Aguascalientes; had to leave studies to work; no degree. D] Local deputy to the state legislature of Aguascalientes, 1867; *federal deputy* from the State of Aguascalientes, Dist. 1, 1886–88; *governor* of Aguascalientes, 1887–91, 1891–95, 1903–07, 1907–11; *senator* from the State of Durango, 1900–03. E] None. F] Political boss of Aguascalientes, Aguascalientes, 1882–83; political

boss of Rincón de Romos District, Aguascalientes. G] None. H] Worked in a clothing store, 1850s; businessman. I] Unknown. J] Fought against the French; battalion commander. K] None. L] Pavía, 57–63; Enc Mex, XI; López, 1127; DP70, 2232.

Vázquez Gómez, Emilio
(Deceased February 24, 1926) A] May 22, 1858. B] Rancho El Carmen, Tula, Tamaulipas. C] Began primary in Rancho El Carmen, at a poor public school, and completed in Tula; preparatory studies at the Ateneo Fuente, Saltillo, beginning 1875, on a scholarship from Manuel Godoy, prefect of Saltillo; law degree, National School of Law, Mexico City, October 5, 1883. D] None. E] Opposed the reelection of *Porfirio Díaz*, 1888, 1892; president, Anti-Reelectionist Club, Mexico City, 1909; co-organizer of the national Anti-Reelectionist party, 1909; precandidate for presidential candidacy of the Anti-Reelectionist party, but defeated by *Francisco I. Madero*, 1910. F] Syndic, City Council, Saltillo, 1880; *secretary* of government, 1911. G] None. H] Began working in a store in Tula after primary studies; worked as a porter in Práxedis Charles's store, Saltillo, Coahuila, 1874; tutored in mathematics and geography to support himself; lawyer, firm of Luis Gutiérrez Otero, 1883. I] Son of Ignacio Vázquez, poor cattle rancher, and Juana Gómez; brother of *Francisco Vázquez Gómez*, secretary of public education, 1911. J] Supported *Pascual Orozco* rebellion in Chihuahua, 1912. K] In exile, 1911, San Antonio, Texas; in exile, 1913. L] DP70, 2232; López, 1128; Mestre, 276–77; Morales Jiménez, 85–89; Moreno, 68–77; Enc Mex, XII, 309.

Vázquez Gómez, Francisco
(Deceased August 16, 1934) A] September 23, 1860. B] Rancho El Carmen, Tula, Tamaulipas. C] Primary studies in Rancho El Carmen, at a public school; preparatory studies, Ateneo Fuente, Saltillo, Coahuila; medical degree, National School of Medicine, Mexico City; professor, National School of Medicine; studies in Europe. D] None. E] Supported *Bernardo Reyes*, 1908; vice-presidential can-

didate of the National Anti-Reelectionist and the National Democratic parties, 1910; lost the vice-presidential nomination of the Progressive Constitutional party to *José María Pino Suárez*, 1911. F] Secretary of foreign relations in the *Francisco I. Madero* cabinet in exile, 1911; *secretary* of public education, 1911. G] None. H] Supported self as a student working as a night watchman; physician in Jalapa, Veracruz, for many years; very successful physician. I] Son of Ignacio Vázquez, poor cattle rancher, and Juana Gómez; personal physician to President *Porfirio Díaz*'s family; good friend of Porfirio Díaz, Jr.; brother of *Emilio Vázquez Gómez*, secretary of government, 1911; married Guadalupe Norma; son Francisco, Jr., a lawyer. J] Briefly supported *Pascual Orozco* against Madero, 1912; briefly supported *Emiliano Zapata*, 1912. K] In exile, 1913. L] Enc Mex, XII, 310; DP70, 2232–33; López, 1128; Mestre, 280; Morales Jiménez, 103–07; Moreno, 68–77; Puente, 137–42.

Vázquez Schiaffino, José
(Deceased) A] May 8, 1881. B] Sayula, Jalisco. C] Early education unknown; engineering degree, National School of Mines, Mexico City; professor of analytical mechanics, National School of Agriculture, San Jacinto, and the National Veterinary School, UNAM; professor of geography and carpentry, National School of Engineering, UNAM. D] None. E] None. F] Director, Tax Office; engineer, Technical Petroleum Committee; engineer, Hydraulic Commission; *oficial mayor* in charge of the Secretariat of Communications, 1915; official representative of the Mexican government to the International Exposition, Brazil, 1922; subsecretary of industry and commerce, 1924–25; *subsecretary* of the treasury, 1925; ambassador to Japan and China, 1925–29; ambassador to Brazil, 1929–30; *subsecretary* of foreign relations, 1930; minister to Honduras, 1934–35; minister to Haiti, 1936. G] None. H] Practicing engineer. I] Unknown. J] Unknown. K] None. L] García de Alba, 1958, 136.

Vázquez Vela, Gonzalo
(Deceased September 28, 1963) A] November 7, 1894. B] Jalapa, Veracruz. C] Primary studies in Veracruz; preparatory studies at the University of Veracruz, Jalapa; law degree, National School of Law, National University of Mexico. D] *Governor* of Veracruz, 1932–35. E] Member of the League of Professionals and Intellectuals of the Mexican Revolutionary party. F] Subsecretary general of government of the State of Veracruz, 1920; secretary general of government of the State of Veracruz, 1920, under *Cándido Aguilar*; secretary general of government of the State of Veracruz, 1928–32, under *Adalberto Tejeda*; oficial mayor of the Secretariat of Government, 1929–32; secretary of public education, June 17, 1935–November 30, 1940. G] None. H] Adviser to various businesses; adviser to the president of Mexico; adviser to the National Mortgage Bank; manager of Aseguradora Mexicana. I] Protégé of Adalberto Tejeda; son of lawyer Manuel Vázquez. J] None. K] None. L] DP70, 2234; *Excélsior*, 18 June 1935; Dulles, 629; Meyer, 13, 280; Pasquel, Jalapa, 667–68.

Vega Limón, José M.
(Deceased) A] 1846. B] Valladolid, Michoacán. C] Preparatory studies at the Colegio de San Ildefonso, Mexico City; law degree, National School of Law, Mexico City. D] *Federal deputy* from the State of Jalisco, Dist. 17, 1910–12. E] None. F] Local judge; judge of the first instance, Guadalupe Hidalgo, Federal District; private secretary to President *Porfirio Díaz*, 1877–80; secretary of the Superior Tribunal of Justice of the Federal District; *justice* of the Supreme Court, 1893–90; consul general in France, 1896; justice of the Superior Tribunal of Justice of the Federal District. G] None. H] Practicing lawyer. I] Knew *Porfirio Díaz* since youth; probably brother of Salvador Vega Limón, federal deputy from the State of Michoacán, 1908–10. J] Oficial mayor of the barracks, Díaz's troops, Tuxtepec rebellion, 1876. K] None. L] Godoy, 140; Pavía, judges, 333, 344.

Vega Sánchez, Rafael
(Deceased February 13, 1946) A] 1888.
B] Huichapán, Hidalgo. C] Primary studies in Huichapán; secondary and preparatory studies, Scientific and Literary Institute of Hidalgo, Pachuca; no degree;
professor of literature and grammar, Scientific and Literary Institute of Hidalgo,
Pachuca. D] *Constitutional deputy* from
the State of Hidalgo, Dist. 5, 1916–17;
federal deputy from the State of Hidalgo,
Dist. 5, 1917–18; secretary of the Great
Committee. E] Cofounder of the Benito
Juárez Anti-Reelectionist Club, Pachuca,
Hidalgo, 1910. F] Served in the state government of Hidalgo. G] None. H] Journalist; author; editor, *El Constituyente*,
1916; publisher of *La Reforma*, 1915;
publisher, *El Voto*. I] Unknown. J] Organized supporters in Pachuca for *Francisco I. Madero*, 1910; joined the Constitutionalists, 1913; fought under General
Nicolás Flores; rank of major. K] Coini-
tiator of paragraph 4, Article 79, of the
Constitution of 1917. L] Pérez López,
492–93; DP70; C de D, 1916–17.

Vela, Eulalio
(Deceased February 2, 1890) A] February
12, 1838. B] Veracruz, Veracruz. C] Educated by his uncle, José María Blanco; enrolled in the National Military College,
1880. D] *Federal deputy* from the State
of Querétaro, Dist. 3, 1886–88. E] None.
F] Political boss of Minatitlán, Veracruz,
1866; governor of Veracruz, 1879–80.
G] None. H] None. I] Parents died
when he was very young; lived with uncle.
J] Joined the national guard under Colonel Manuel Gutiérrez Zamora, 1856, as
a sergeant; fought with the Liberals;
fought against the French, 1861–67; supported La Noria rebellion, 1871; rank of
colonel, 1876; commander of Sotavento
Zone, 1876; supported the Tuxtepec rebellion, 1876; rank of brigade general, August
2, 1877; pacified the Papaloapan region,
1879; commander of the Fort of Veracruz,
1880; defeated indigenous rebellion in Tamaulipas, 1886; commander of the 2nd
Military Zone, 1890. K] Lost left forearm
from battle wounds. L] Pasquel, liberals,
345–47; Mestre, 168; Cuevas, 467.

Velasco, José Refugio
(Deceased March 27, 1919) A] 1851.
B] Aguascalientes, Aguascalientes.
C] Early education unknown; graduated
from the National Military College.
D] *Federal deputy* from the State of
México, Dist. 12, 1913–14. E] None.
F] *Governor* of Coahuila, 1913; governor
of México, 1913; *governor* of San Luis
Potosí, 1914; *secretary* of war, 1914.
G] None. H] None. I] Unknown.
J] Career army officer; commander of the
19th Battalion during the Yaqui campaign,
1901; commander of the Military Zones of
Sonora and Sinaloa, 1911; commander, 1st
Military Zone, Mexico City, 1911; rank of
brigade general, September 12, 1911; supported *Victoriano Huerta*, 1913; commander of the Veracruz Military Zone,
1913; rank of division general, June 27,
1913; commander of the Nazas Division,
1914. K] None. L] Sec of War, 1914, 17;
DP70, 2238; López, 1136; Mestre, 262.

Velázquez (Estrada), Eduardo
(Deceased September 24, 1897) A] 1863.
B] Villa de Guadalupe Hidalgo, Mexico
City. C] Early education unknown; no
degree. D] *Alternate federal deputy* from
the State of Puebla, Dist. 11, 1892–94,
1894–96, under *Sóstenes Rocha*; *federal
deputy* from the State of Puebla, Dist. 11,
1896–97. E] None. F] Prefect of Guadalupe Hidalgo, Mexico City; police chief
of Mexico City, 1895–97. G] None.
H] Financier; owner of ranches in Villa de
Guadalupe and urban real estate in Mexico City; journalist. I] Son of Francisco
Velázquez and Clementina Estrada; married Carlota Ricoy, daughter of Carlos Ricoy and Modesta Pardo; sister Concepción
Velázquez married to *Pablo Macedo*.
J] None. K] Died from a gunshot wound.
L] Rice, 252.

Vélez (y Gallardo), Francisco A.
(Deceased February 25, 1919) A] July 24,
1830. B] Jalapa, Veracruz. C] Early education unknown; graduated from the National Military College as a 2nd lieutenant. D] *Federal deputy* from the State of
Michoacán, Dist. 10, 1886–88; *federal
deputy* from the State of Michoacán, Dist.
3, 1888–90, 1890–92, 1892–94, 1894–96,

1896–98, 1898–1900; *federal deputy* from the State of Michoacán, Dist. 10, 1900–02, 1902–04, 1904–06, 1906–08; *federal deputy* from the State of Michoacán, Dist. 9, 1908–10; *federal deputy* from the State of Michoacán, Dist. 8, 1910–12. E] None. F] Governor and military commander of Guanajuato, 1859; governor and military commander of San Luis Potosí, 1860; governor of the Federal District, 1869–71. G] None. H] Owned a sugarcane hacienda near Cuautla, Morelos. I] Father of Daniel Vélez, leading ophthalmologist and professor; son Francisco de Asis Vélez, Jr., served as his alternate federal deputy, 1890–1912; married María Carlota Ruiz Canizo. J] Career army officer; joined the national guard, Orizaba, 1846; fought in the battle of Santa Bárbara against the North Americans, 1847; supported the Conservatives during the War of the Reform, 1858–61; left the Conservatives and retired from the army, 1861; fought the French, 1866–67; rank of division general, February 2, 1900; military commander of the Federal District 1900–01; retired from the army, July 26, 1912. K] None. L] QesQ, 606–07; Pasquel, liberals, 357–58; Mestre, 262; Sec of War, 1914, 18; Sec of War, 1901, 16; Sec of War, 1911, 15; Almanaque, 129; DP70, 22443; López, 1140.

Vera Estañol, Jorge
(Deceased 1958) A] November 19, 1873. B] Mexico City. C] Early education unknown; legal studies, National School of Law, Mexico City, 1888–93, graduating with a law degree; cofounder of the Free Law School, Mexico City, 1812. D] *Federal deputy* from the Federal District, Dist. 5, 1912–13. E] Founder of the Evolutionary Political Club, 1911. F] Interim secretary of government, 1911; *secretary* of public instruction, 1911, 1913. G] None. H] Practicing lawyer; lawyer to President *Porfirio Díaz*; author of many history books. I] Son of José Vera Estañol and Rafaela Pérez; son Jorge, Jr., married Caridad Arellano; longtime friend of *Javier Gaxiola* and *Miguel Callero* J] None. K] Exiled in Europe, 1914–16; exiled in the United States, 1916–31. L] UNAM, law, 1891–96, 72; Enc Mex, XII, 328;

WWM45, 124; Dir social, 1935, 162; DP70, 2247; López, 1142.

Vidal (Sánchez), J. Amilcar
(Deceased April 17, 1958) A] March 19, 1890. B] Pichucalco, Chiapas. C] Primary studies, Hidalgo Institute, Pichucalco; preparatory studies, Peekskill Military Academy, United States; civil engineering degree, Rensselaer Polytechnic Institute, Troy, New York, 1914. D] Local deputy to the state legislature of Chiapas, 1926; *constitutional deputy* from the State of Chiapas, Dist. 6, 1916–17. E] Supported General *Francisco Serrano* for president, 1927. F] Chief of the Agrarian Commission of Tabasco, 1915–16; director, 4th Zone of Ports, Lighthouses, and the Merchant Marine, Secretariat of Communications and Public Works, 1917–26; interim governor of Chiapas, 1926; chief of the Machinery Department, Secretariat of Communications and Public Works, 1932–35. G] None. H] Construction engineer, 1935–58. I] Son of Pomposo Vidal, wealthy landowner, and Encarnación Sánchez; brother of General *Carlos Vidal*, governor of Chiapas, 1925–27; brother of General Luis Vidal. J] Served in the army; reached rank of colonel. K] Imprisoned briefly for supporting Serrano, 1927; exiled in Central America, 1927. L] C de D, 1916–17; Gordillo y Ortiz, 265.

Vidal (Sánchez), Carlos A.
(Deceased October 3, 1927) A] March 4, 1885. B] Pichucalco, Chiapas. C] Primary studies in Pichucalco; secondary studies at the Juárez Institute, Villahermosa, Tabasco; no degree. D] *Governor* of Chiapas, 1925–27. E] Supported General *Francisco Serrano* for president, 1927. F] *Governor* and military commander of Quintana Roo, 1916–17; *governor* and military commander of Tabasco, 1919; oficial mayor of the Secretariat of War, 1924. G] None. H] Owner of La Mercedes hacienda. I] Son of Pomposo Vidal, large landholder, and Encarnación Sánchez; brother of General Luis F. Vidal, governor of Chiapas; brother of *J. Amilcar Vidal*, constitutional deputy; married Debora Rojas Ortiz, daughter of Ponciano Rojas. J] Joined the Constitutionalist forces un-

der General Pedro Colorado, April 1, 1913; aide to General Colorado, 1913; rank of captain, 1913; rank of brigadier general, July 1915; supported the Plan of Agua Prieta, 1920; opposed the *Adolfo de la Huerta* rebellion, 1923–24; rank of brigade general, January 1, 1924. K] Left the governorship to support Serrano for president, 1927; murdered by General Fox with Serrano and other supporters, Huitzilac, Morelos. L] Almanaque de Chiapas, 119; QesQ, 611–12; Gordillo y Ortiz, 266; López, 1155; Almanaque de Tabasco, 152; Alvarez Coral, 65–66; Bulnes, 161–66.

Villa, Francisco
(Deceased July 20, 1923) A] June 5, 1878. B] Rancho Río Grande, San Juan del Río, Durango. C] Some primary education; taught to read in prison as an adult. D] None. E] Supported *Francisco I. Madero*, 1909. F] *Provisional governor* of Chihuahua, 1913–14. G] None. H] Worked as a woodcutter as a boy; worked in El Verde Mine, Chihuahua; bricklayer, Chihuahua, Chihuahua; worked on the Gogojito hacienda, 1894; joined a bandit group under Ignacio Parra, 1895; took over the band in the name of one of the leaders, Francisco Villa, when Parra and Villa were killed; cattle rustler, 1905–10; cattle rancher, 1910–11; rancher, 1920–23. I] Son of Agustín Arango and Micaela Arambula; real name was Doroteo Arango; orphaned at a young age; grandson of Antonio Arango and Faustina Vela; grandson of Trinidad Arambula and María de Jesús Alvarez; married Luz Corral, Juana Torres, Soledad Seañez, and Austreberta Rentería without divorcing. J] Force drafted into the 14th Cavalry Regiment, 1903; deserted and recaptured; joined the revolutionary forces, 1910; originally fought under Cástulo Herrera, 1910–11; key leader in capturing Ciudad Juárez, 1911; honorary brigadier general, 1912; defeated *Pascual Orozco*'s forces at the battle of Rellano, 1912; rejoined the army to help *Victoriano Huerta* defeat Orozco, 1912; formed the Division of the North, Constitutionalists, 1913; Constitutionalist, 1913–14; defeated federal army in the decisive battles of Torreón, September 30, 1913, and March–April 1914;

supported the Convention governments, 1914–15; chief of operations, Convention forces, 1914; defeated decisively by *Alvaro Obregón*, 1915; recognized the Plan of Agua Prieta, 1920. K] Captured by authorities and imprisoned in San Juan del Río, 1903; recaptured and imprisoned in Durango penitentiary; escaped, 1905; imprisoned by President *Francisco I. Madero* in the Federal District military prison for disobeying orders, 1912; sentenced to death by General Huerta, 1912, but saved by *Raúl Madero* and Emilio Madero; escaped from prison and went to the United States, 1912; his troops provoked Pershing's Punitive Expedition after attacking Columbus, New Mexico, March 9, 1916; ambushed and killed by Jesús Salas Barranza and Melitón Lozoya, near Parral, Chihuahua. L] QesQ, 613–14; DP70, 2261; López, 1158–59; Marquez, 227–36; Almada, 478–518; Morales Jiménez, 145–51; Enc Mex, XII, 400–01; Almada, 1968, 564–66.

Villada, José Vicente
(Deceased May 6, 1904) A] December 15, 1843. B] Mexico City. C] Early education unknown; no degree. D] Federal deputy from the State of México, 1870–72, 1872–74; *senator* from the State of México, 1886–90; *governor* of México, 1889–1904. E] None. F] None. G] None. H] Topographer; businessman; printer; left business to become active in the Liberal party; founder of *La Revista Universal* and director, *El Partido Liberal*, 1885. I] Son of General Manuel María Villada, but orphaned at a young age and had to support self; possibly brother of Eduardo Villada, governor of México, 1895–97, and Manuel Villada, naturalist and intellectual. J] Joined the Liberal forces as a 2nd lieutenant, 3rd Light Battalion, under Colonel Arteaga; joined the Legion of Honor, with rank of captain, under General Doblado, to fight the French, 1861; adjutant and private secretary to General Hinojosa, 3rd Jalisco Brigade; fought in the siege of Puebla, 1863; captured by the French, but escaped, 1863; saved the Mexican flag at the battle of Morelia, December 18, 1863, for which he was promoted to major by General *Berriozábal*; commander, scout

battalion; rank of lt. colonel, 1867; brigade commander, 1867; captured by the French and released, 1867; rank of brigadier general, March 8, 1893. K] None. L] López, 1159; Hombres prominentes, 193–94; Mestre, 220; Pavía, 228–31; Sec of War, 1901, 24; Enc Mex, XII, 405; Godoy, 168; QesQ, 614–15; DP70, 2268.

Villa Michel, Primo
(Deceased August 22, 1970) A] November 7, 1893. B] Ciudad Carranza, Jalisco. C] Primary and secondary studies at the Colegio de la Inmaculada, Zapopan, Jalisco; preparatory studies at the Instituto San José, Guadalajara, Jalisco; law studies, School of Law, University of Guadalajara; law degree, National School of Law, UNAM. D] None. E] None. F] Judge of the lower court of Sonora, 1915; public defender, Nogales, Sonora, 1917; federal public defender for the State of Sonora, 1920; director of records, Secretariat of Government, 1923; oficial mayor, Secretariat of Industry and Commerce, 1923–24; *subsecretary* of government, 1925; secretary general of the Department of the Federal District, 1925–26; *head* of the Department of the Federal District, 1927–28; ambassador to Germany, 1929; subsecretary of industry and commerce, 1930–32; *secretary* of industry and commerce, 1932–34; ambassador to Uruguay, 1935; ambassador to Great Britain, 1937–38; ambassador to Japan, 1939–41; first secretary of the Mexican Embassy, Washington, D.C., 1941–43; oficial mayor of the Secretariat of Government, 1944–45; secretary of government, 1945–46; ambassador to Canada, 1947–51; ambassador to Guatemala, 1952–53; ambassador to Syria, 1956–57; ambassador to Luxemburg, 1959–60; ambassador to Belgium, 1960–64. G] Secretary, National Chamber of Commerce. H] Delegate to many international conferences; manager, Petróleos Mexicanos; director, National Institute of Housing; director of the Bulletin of Federal Statutes, Secretariat of Government, 1923. I] Son, Primo, Jr., was director of the Department of Primary Statistics, Investment Commission, 1956; married María Dávila. J] None. K] None. L] WWM45, 125; DP70, 2266; EBW, 128; Peral, 859; López, 1162; NYT, 15 May 1938, 36; NYT, 27

July 1954, 10; NYT, 24 Dec. 1941, 3; NYT, 3 Dec. 1942; HA, 5 July 1946, 4; Enc Mex, XII, 1977, 404–05; Medina, No. 20, 48.

Villanueva, Aquilino
(Deceased) A] Unknown. B] Unknown. C] Early education unknown; medical degree, National School of Medicine, Mexico City, founding professor of Urology, National School of Medicine; emeritus professor, National School of Medicine. D] None. E] None. F] *Director*, Department of Health, 1938–30; secretary general of the Department of Health, 1935. G] None. H] Practicing physician; chief of medical interns, Ward Four, General Hospital, Mexico City, 1924; founder, Urology Service, General Hospital, 1930; founder, Infant Hygiene Service, Department of Health; director of the General Hospital, 1940–45; director, Institute of Urology, 1951; chief of Urology Unit, General Hospital, 1957; personal adviser to the secretary of health, 1965; coeditor, *Urologia Internacionalis*. I] Son of Francisco A. Villanueva, mayor of Torreón, 1895–97, and local public official; married Blanca Lazaga. J] None. K] None. L] Dir social, 1935, 163.

Villarello, Juan de Dios
(Deceased August 1945) A]1869. B] Mexico City. C] Primary studies at Rode's English Boarding School; topographical engineering degree, School of Mines (National School of Engineering), 1888; mining and metallurgy degree, National School of Engineering, 1891; disciple of José Guadalupe Aguilera; professor of geology, mineralogy, paleontology, National School of Engineering. D] None. E] None. F] Subsecretary of development, 1911–13; director, National Geological Institute, 1914–29; director, Department of Explorations and Geology, 1923–29. G] None. H] Author of many works. I] Unknown. J] None. K] Considered a pioneer in petroleum geology in Mexico. L] Enc Mex, XII, 406–07; DP70, 2273–74.

Villarreal, Antonio I.
(Deceased December 16, 1944) A] July 3, 1879. B] Lampazos, Nuevo León. C] Secondary education at the Normal School of San Luis Potosí and Monterrey; primary

teaching certificate, Normal School of Monterrey; teacher in Monterrey normal schools. D] None. E] Three-time candidate for the presidency of Mexico, the last time in 1934; secretary of the Organizing Committee for the Mexican Liberal party, Saint Louis, Missouri, 1906. F] Consul general for President *Francisco I. Madero* in Barcelona, Spain, 1912–13; *governor* and military commander of Nuevo León, 1914–15; *secretary* of agriculture, June 1, 1920–November 26, 1921. G] Reopened the Casa del Obrero Mundial, 1914. H] Writer for *Regeneración*, published by *Juan Sarabia* and *Ricardo Flores Magón*, 1904. I] Relative of General Zuazua, commander of the Northern Armies during the War of the Reform; good friend of *José Vasconcelos* during the Revolution; married Blanca Sordo; son of Próspero Villarreal and Ignacia González. J] Leader of a revolt in Las Vacas, Coahuila, 1908; joined the Revolution, 1910; rank of colonel, 1910; rank of brigade general, 1913, supported the Plan of Guadalupe; first president of the Convention of Aguascalientes, 1914; supported *Venustiano Carranza* until 1920; supported *Adolfo de la Huerta*, 1923; supported General *Francisco Serrano* and Arnulfo Gómez, 1927; supported General *José G. Escobar*, 1929; rank of division general, November 16, 1940. K] Imprisoned for publishing *El Liberal* in Nuevo León, 1906; went into exile, 1920, 1923, 1929; imprisoned several times. L] DP70, 2274; Peral, 863; López, 1163; Enc Mex, XII, 1977, 407; Almanaque de Nuevo León, 100–01; Morales Jiménez, 19–22.

Villarreal, Julián
(Deceased 1934) A] 1869. B] Saltillo, Coahuila. C] Preparatory studies, Colegio Civil de Monterrey; lab assistant in physics, Colegio Civil de Monterrey; enrolled in the National School of Medicine, Mexico City, 1888, graduating as a surgeon, 1893, with a thesis on encephalic craniums; advanced studies in ophthalmology, New York, Berlin, Vienna, and London; assistant anatomical dissector, National School of Medicine, 1891; director of the observatory, Colegio Civil de Monterrey; director, Anatomical Works, National School of Medicine, 1894; profes-

sor by opposition of anatomical topography, National School of Medicine, 1895–1935; dean, National School of Medicine, 1911. D] *Federal deputy* from the State of Michoacán, Dist. 7, 1900–02, 1902–04; *federal deputy* from the State of México, Dist. 15, 1904–06, 1906–08; *federal deputy* from the State of México, Dist. 16, 1908–10; *federal deputy* from the State of México, Dist. 15, 1910–12. E] None. F] None. G] President, Mexican Academy of Medicine, 1910. H] Physician; physician, Morelos Hospital, 1897; director, Red Cross Hospital; author of medical works; introduced asepsia technique in Mexico; introduced radium therapy in Mexico. I] Unknown. J] None. K] None. L] DP70, 2274.

Villarreal, Viviano L.
(Deceased) A] 1838. B] San Nicolas Hidalgo, Nuevo León. C] Early education unknown; law degree, 1863. D] Federal deputy from the State of Nuevo León, 1867; senator from the State of Nuevo León, 1877; *governor* of Nuevo León, 1911–13. E] None. F] Secretary general of government of the State of Nuevo León, 1868–72; governor of Nuevo León, 1879–81; judge, 1909. G] None. H] Stockholder in many industrial and mining firms; practicing lawyer; served as an attorney for Evaristo Madero, governor of Coahuila. I] Parents were large landholders; married Carolina Madero Hernández, daughter of Evaristo Madero, grandfather of President *Francisco I. Madero*; brother of Felícitos Villarreal, secretary of the treasury under the Convention government, 1914–15; brother Melchor married to Victoriana Madero. J] None. K] None. L] Almanaque de Nuevo León, 100; DP70, 2275.

Villegas, Juan
(Deceased April 11, 1906) A] 1855. B] Villa Guerrero, México. C] Studies at the School of Arts and Trades, Toluca, México; enrolled in the National Military College, March 4, 1869, graduating December 1, 1875, as a lieutenant of engineers; subdirector, National Military College, 1883–84; director, National Military College, 1884–1900, 1903–06. D] *Federal deputy* from the State of México,

Dist. 14, 1896–98. E] None. F] Director, Department of Artillery, Secretariat of War, 1900–02; *subsecretary* of war, 1902–03. G] None. H] None. I] Student with *Victoriano Huerta*, Flaviano Paliza, and *Joaquín Maas*. J] Career army officer; joined the Engineering Corps, 1875; participated in the pacification campaigns in Jalisco and Sinaloa, 1876; defended President Lerdo de Tejada against the Tuxtepec rebellion, 1876; built the National Military College in Chapultepec Castle under orders from General *Sóstenes Rocha*, 1884; rank of colonel, January 19, 1892; rank of brigade general, September 4, 1902. K] None. L] QesQ, 619–20; DP70, 2278; Mestre, 225; Sec of War, 1900, 272; Cuevas, 466.

Villers (Muñoz), Moisés E.
(Deceased 1950) A] July 21, 1883.
B] Chiapa de Corzo, Chiapas. C] Primary and secondary studies, Higher School No. 1, Chiapa de Corzo; enrolled in the National School of Agriculture, San Jacinto, 1909; on a fellowship until 1911; abandoned studies, 1913. D] None.
E] None. F] *Governor* of Chiapas, 1930–31. G] None. H] None. I] Unknown.
J] Joined the Constitutionalists as a 2nd lieutenant in the Vicente Guerrero Battalion, 1913; 2nd lieutenant, Benito Juárez Battalion, 6th Brigade, Army of the Northeast; commander, 7th Company; rank of major, García Brigade, 1914; fought against *Francisco Villa* and *Emiliano Zapata*, 1915; rank of lt. colonel, 1915; served under General *Pablo González* in the Army of the East, 1915; rank of colonel, 1917; served under General *Salvador Alvarado*, 1917; commander of the Pachuca Battalion, 2nd Division, Army of the Northeast; commander, Mexico City garrison, 1917; battalion commander, infantry, 1917–25; fought in a campaign in Tabasco, 1918–19; commander of the 34th Battalion against the *Adolfo de la Huerta* rebellion, 1923; zone commander, Jiquipilas and Cintalapa valleys, Chiapas; rank of brigadier general, May 1, 1925; rank of brigade general, 1945; retired from active duty, 1948. K] None. L] Gómez, 518–19; Gordillo y Ortiz, 268.

Y

Yarza Gutiérrez, Alberto
(Deceased February 28, 1933) A] October 21, 1857. B] Mexico City. C] Early education unknown; enrolled at the National Military college, 1871. D] None.
E] None. F] Governor of the Federal District, 1913; governor of Michoacán, 1913; governor of Tlaxcala, 1913; *governor* of Tabasco, 1913–14. G] None. H] None.
I] Son of colonel Remegio Yarza and Concepción Gutiérrez; married Luz Barona; student with *Victoriano Huerta* at the National Military College. J] Career military officer; rank of colonel in the artillery, October 11, 1897; commander, 1st Artillery Battalion, 1899–1901; rank of brigade general, February 10, 1913; military commander of Tabasco, 1913; rank of division general, March 6, 1914. K] None.
L] Sec of War, 1900, 255; Sec of War, 1914, 18; DP70, 2309; López, 1173; Mestre, 270; Almanaque de Tabasco, 150; Ghigliazza, 164; Sec of War, 1901, 27; Cuevas, 471.

Z

Zamacona y Murphy, Manuel María de
(Deceased May 29, 1904) A] September 13, 1826. B] Puebla, Puebla. C] Primary studies, Colegio Carolino and Palafoxian Seminary, Puebla; law degree; director, School of Arts and Trades for Women.
D] Federal deputy from the State of Puebla, 1862. E] As a journalist opposed Juárez, 1867; precandidate for president of Mexico, 1890. F] Secretary of foreign relations, 1861; member of the Mexico–United States Claims Commission; ambassador to the United States, 1880; *justice* of the Supreme Court, 1892–04.
G] None. H] Practicing lawyer; poet; director, *El Siglo XIX*, Mexico City. I] Parents were an important landowning family in Puebla; father of Manuel Zamacona e Inclán, federal deputy, 1904–10; related to Pablo M. Zamacona, brigade general.
J] None. K] None. L] Rice, 253; Mestre, 254; Márquez, 234; DP70, 2328; López, 1177–78; Pavía, judges, 70–78; Blue Book, 1901, 29.

Zambrano, Nicéforo
(Deceased September 21, 1940) A] February 22, 1862. B] Monterrey, Nuevo León.
C] Early education unknown; no degree.
D] Member of the City Council of Monterrey, 1912–13; mayor of Monterrey, 1913–14; *constitutional deputy* from the State of Nuevo León, Dist. 2, 1916–17; *governor* of Nuevo León, 1917–19.
E] Joined the Anti-Reelectionist party, 1909. F] Treasurer general of Mexico, 1915; consul general in San Francisco, 1917–19. G] None. H] Wealthy businessman. I] Parents were poor; probably related to Adolfo Zambrano, alternate federal deputy from Nuevo León, 1902–06.
J] Joined the Constitutionalists, 1913.
K] Imprisoned by *Victoriano Huerta*, 1913.
L] Almanaque de Nuevo León, 102; DP70, 2329; López, 1178.

Zapata, Emiliano
(Deceased April 10, 1919) A] August 8, 1879. B] Anenecuilco, Villa de Ayala, Morelos. C] Studied under Emilio Vara for primary; no degree. D] None. E] Supported the candidacy of Patricio Leyva for governor of Morelos. F] None. G] President, Board of Defense of Anenecuilco Lands, 1909. H] Peasant; worked on various haciendas; horsebreaker, 9th Cavalry Regiment, under Fernando Gámez, 1908–09. I] Son of Gabriel Zapata y Cleofas and Cristina Robles, peasants; brother Eufemio, revolutionary. J] Joined the revolutionaries under Pablo Torres Burgos, March 10, 1911, Villa de Ayala, with 72 peasants, and assumed command after Torres was killed; commander of the Liberation Army of the Center and South, 1914; represented at the Convention of Aguascalientes by *Antonio Díaz Soto y Gama*, 1914; continued resistance against the federal government until his death.
K] Forced to serve as Pablo Escandón's horsebreaker as punishment for his antiregime activities, 1908–09, in the 9th Cavalry Regiment; jailed by the political boss of Cuautla; launched the Plan of Ayala, November 25, 1911, a landmark document for agrarian reform; assassinated by Jesús Guajardo on authorization from *Venustiano Carranza*'s administration.
L] López, 1179; Enc Mex, XII, 556–57; QesQ, 634–36; DP70, 2331–32.

Zárate, Julio
(Deceased November 18, 1917) A] April 12, 1844. B] Jalapa, Veracruz. C] Early education unknown; law degree, Colegio Carolino, Puebla; professor of history, National Teachers School, 1883. D] Federal deputy from the State of Puebla, 1862; federal deputy, 1880–82, 1882–84; *federal deputy* from the State of Aguascalientes, Dist. 2, 1884–86; *federal deputy* from the State of Hidalgo, Dist. 6, 1886–88; *federal deputy* from the State of Hidalgo, Dist. 8, 1888–90; *federal deputy* from the State of Veracruz, Dist. 3, 1890–92, 1892–94, 1894–96; *senator* from the State of Campeche, 1908–10, 1910–12. E] Joined Liberal party in youth. F] Section chief, Secretariat of Foreign Relations, 1879; oficial mayor in charge of the Secretariat of Foreign Relations, 1879–80; secretary general of government of the State of Veracruz, 1884–86; *justice* of the Supreme Court, 1897–1906. G] None. H] Practicing lawyer; historian; journalist; opposed Maximilian in his *El Eco del País*, Atlixco, Puebla. I] Son of Manuel Zárate, lawyer, Liberal, and intimate friend of President Lerdo de Tejada; sister Clotilde, writer and poet; sister Leonor, poet; grandfather a large landholder from Jalapa, Veracruz; brother of Eduardo Emilio Zárate, lawyer, professor, and attorney general of military justice. J] None. K] None. L] Pasquel, 1972, 361, 363–64; Mestre, 257; Blue Book, 1902, 29; FSRE, 134; Enc Mex, XII, 566; Rice, 254; López, 1182; Godoy, 195–96; Pasquel, Jalapa, 689–90; Illescas, 147.

Zayas Enríquez, Rafael de
(Deceased June 9, 1932) A] 1848. B] Veracruz, Veracruz. C] Primary, secondary and preparatory studies in Germany, Canada, and the United States, 1853–67; law degree, Campeche. D] *Federal deputy* from the State of Jalisco, Dist. 14, 1892–94, 1894–96; *federal deputy* from the State of Jalisco, Dist. 15, 1896–98; *federal deputy* from the State of Jalisco, Dist. 16, 1898–1900, 1900–02; *federal deputy* from the State of Sinaloa, Dist. 3, 1900–02 (at same time); *federal deputy* from the State of Jalisco, Dist. 16, 1902–04; *federal deputy* from the State of México, Dist. 14, 1906–08. E] Supported *Félix Díaz* against *Francisco Madero*, 1913. F] Po-

litical boss of Veracruz; public defender. G] Member of the Liceo Hidalgo. H] Practicing lawyer; journalist; wrote for *Revista Azul* and *El Mundo Ilustrado*; worked in the United States for various publishers; consul, San Francisco, California. I] Father, editor of *El Ferrocarril*, Veracruz; father banned to United States by Santa-Anna, 1853. J] None. K] Exiled to Peru, 1873. L] Enc Mex, XII, 570; DP70, 2341; Pasquel, 416–17.

Zenteno, Cástulo
(Deceased) A] May 22, 1837. B] Matamoros, Tamaulipas. C] Primary studies in Matamoros; preparatory studies in Guadalajara, 1846–51; no degree. d–Federal deputy from the State of Yucatán, 1876–78; *senator* from the State of Yucatán, 1884–88; *federal deputy* from the State of Yucatán, Dist. 1, 1896–98, 1898–1900. E] None. F] Represented the Mexican government on Oriental, International, and Interoceanic Railroads, 1881; comptroller, National Bank of Mexico, 1882–84; chief tax collector, Federal District, 1884. G] None. H] Owner of the El Cristo coal mine, Tempoal, Veracruz; began own business, 1862. I] Son of Juan Zenteno, assistant treasurer, federal treasury, Baja California. J] Special messenger for General *Porfirio Díaz*, 1876; rank of colonel, November 9, 1878. K] None. L] Hombres prominentes, 469–70.

Zertuche, Albino
(Deceased May 4, 1890) A] March 1, 1837. B] Villa de García, Nuevo León. C] Early education unknown; no degree. D] *Federal deputy* from the State of Oaxaca, Dist. 6, 1886–88, 1888–90; *governor* of Oaxaca, 1888–90. E] Member of the Liberal party. F] Prefect, Oaxaca, 1871. G] None. H] Unknown. I] Son of Manuel Zertuche and Juana María Garza; father of Albino Zertuche, graduate of the National Military College. J] Career army officer; joined the Oaxaca national guard as a private, May 13, 1855; fought in the War of the Reform, 1857–59; fought the French, 1861–67; captured by the French in Oaxaca, February 9, 1865; participated in the siege of Puebla, April 2, 1867; commander, 10th Military Zone; rank of brigade general, April 9, 1885.

K] None. L] López, 1190; Hombres prominentes, 185; Almanaque de Sonora, 130; QesQ, 639; DP70, 2343; Mestre, 169; Cuevas, 472.

Zincúnegui Tercero, Leopoldo
A] February 23, 1895. B] Zinapécuaro, Michoacán. C] Secondary studies at the Scientific and Literary Institute of Toluca, México; preparatory studies at the National Preparatory School, Mexico City; law degree, National School of Law, UNAM. D] *Federal deputy* from the State of Michoacán, Dist. 4, 1918–20; *federal deputy* from the State of Michoacán, Dist. 4, 1920–22; *federal deputy* from the Federal District, Dist. 1, 1924–26; *federal deputy* from the State of Michoacán, Dist. 4, 1926–28, 1928–30; alternate federal deputy from the State of Michoacán, Dist. 11, 1937–40; federal deputy from the State of Michoacán, Dist. 11, 1940–43, member of the Permanent Commission, 1940, member of the Protocol Committee, the First Balloting Committee, the Rules Committee, and the First Instructive Section of the Grand Jury. E] None. F] Judge of the Civil Registry, Mexico City; federal inspector for the Secretariat of the Treasury; subdirector of the Technical Industrial Department, Secretariat of Public Education. G] None. H] Author of several works. I] Grandson of General Miguel Zincúnegui, governor of Michoacán in the 1850s; Governor *Miguel Silva González* was his political mentor. J] None. K] None. L] Peral, 886–87; DP70, 2345; C de D, 1937–39; C de D, 1940–42, 47, 53, 55, 59; López, 1190–91; C de D, 1918–20; C de D, 1920–22; C de D, 1924–26; C de D, 1926–28; C de D, 1928–30; Dicc mich., 492.

Zubarán (Capmany), Juan
(Deceased 1932) A] 1872. B] Campeche. C] Early education unknown; law degree, Campeche Institute. D] *Federal deputy* from the State of Campeche, Dist. 2, 1912–13; *constitutional deputy* from the State of Campeche, Dist. 1, 1916–17, 1917–18, 1920–22; member of the Great Committee; president of the Chamber, 1921. E] Joined the Constitutional Liberal party, 1916. F] None. G] None. H] Practicing lawyer. I] Brother of *Rafael*

Zubarán Capmany, secretary of industry and commerce, 1920–21; son of Francisco Zubarán and Josefa Capmany. J] Unknown. K] Captured in Mérida and imprisoned in Mexico City on orders from *Victoriano Huerta*, 1913; exiled to Havana, Cuba, 1914–15; almost fought a duel with *Querido Moheno* after legislative debate. L] Enc Mex, XII, 594; DP70, 2350.

Zubarán Capmany, Rafael
(Deceased 1948) A] 1875. B] Campeche, Campeche. C] Early education unknown; law degree, National School of Law, Mexico City, 1901. D] Mayor of Mexico City; *federal deputy* from the State of Jalisco, Dist. 1, 1908–10; *senator* from the Federal District, 1917–18. E] None. F] Agent of the Ministerio Público; public defender; confidential agent of the Constitutionalists, Washington, D.C.; *secretary* of government, 1914; *secretary* of industry and commerce, 1920–21. G] None. H] Practicing lawyer; journalist; wrote for *El Universal*, 1937–48. I] Son of Francisco Zubarán and Josefa Capmany; brother *Juan Zubarán Capmany*, constitutional deputy, 1916–17. J] Jailed for opposing *José Limantour*; leader of the *Adolfo de la Huerta* rebellion, 1923–24. K] Exiled to the United States, 1924–37. l–Enc Mex, XII, 594; López, 1194; UNAM, law, 1900–06, 38.

Zubieta (y Estanillo), José
(Deceased May 14, 1912) A] March 20, 1830. B] Havana, Cuba. C] Early education unknown; law degree, National School of Law, Mexico City. D] *Governor* of the State of México, 1881–85; *senator* from the State of Morelos, 1884–88; *governor* of the State of México, 1886–89; *senator* from the State of Durango, 1910–12, 1912. E] None. F] Judge of the first instance, State of México; assistant to governor Juan Mirafuentes; judge of the Su-

perior Tribunal of Justice of the Federal District and Federal Territories, 1890–93; *justice* of the Supreme Court, 1904–07, president, 1906. G] None. H] Practicing lawyer. I] Unknown. J] Unknown. K] None. L] Hombres prominentes, 199–200; Mestre, 243; Pavía, judges, 247–52.

Zuno Hernández, José G.
A] April 18, 1891. B] Hacienda San Agustín de Gauica, La Barca, Municipio de Jamay, Jalisco. C] Primary studies in Guadalajara; preparatory studies, Liceo de Guadalajara; founder of the University of Guadalajara, 1925; law degree, University of Guadalajara, 1931; professor, National Teachers School; director, University Extension, University of Guadalajara; professor of economics and sociology, Preparatory School of Jalisco, 1931–32; professor of industrial and labor law, School of Law, University of Guadalajara. D] *Federal deputy* from the State of Jalisco, Dist. 1, 1920–22; *federal deputy* from the State of Jalisco, Dist 10, 1922–24; mayor of Guadalajara, 1922–23; *governor* of Jalisco, 1923–26; adviser to the president of Mexico; attorney general of the National Railroads of Mexico, 1932–36; president, Federal Board of Conciliation and Arbitration, 1936–47; director, Regional Museum of Guadalajara, 1948. G] None. H] Journalist at age 14; cartoonist, 1908; wrote for *El Constitucionalista*, Mexico City, 1909–10; founder of various newspapers in Jalisco; editor, *Mexican Herald, El Antireelecionista*, and *El Demócrata*, Mexico City. I] Son of Vicente Zuno Estrada and María Trinidad Hernández Gómez; brother of Alberto, director of the Cavalry Department, 1941; married Carmen Archy Tomathy; daughter María Esther married President Luis Echeverría. J] None. K] None. L] DP70, 2352; López, 1198; HA, 9 Sept 1974, 43; WNM, 250; Enc Mex, XII, 596; EBW, 433.

APPENDIXES

Italicized names in the appendixes have biographical entries in the text.

APPENDIX A

Supreme Court Justices, 1884–1934

1884
President: Miguel Auza
Members: *Francisco Vaca*, Carlos González Ureña, Guillermo Valle, Manuel Saavedra, Jesús M. Vázquez Palacios, Manuel Contreras, T. Melesio Alcántara, Juan Simeón Arteaga, Vacant
Supernumeraries: Fernando J. Corona, Miguel Villalobos, Moisés Rojas, Joaquín M. Escoto, Manuel M. Seoane

1885
President: *Miguel Auza*
Members: *Francisco Vaca, Prudenciano Dorantes*, Carlos González Ureña, Miguel Sagaseta, Guillermo Valle, Manuel Saavedra, Jesús M. Vázquez Palacios, Manuel Contreras, T. Melesio Alcántara, Vacant
Supernumeraries: Fernando J. Corona, Miguel Villalobos, Moisés Rojas, Manuel María Seoane, Joaquín M. Escoto

1886
President: Jesús H. Vázquez Palacios
Members: *Francisco Vaca, Prudenciano Dorantes*, Carlos González Ureña, Miguel Sagaseta, Guillermo Valle, Manuel Saavedra, Miguel Auza, Manuel Contreras, T. Melesio Alcántara, Vacant
Supernumeraries: Fernando J. Corona, Miguel Villalobos, Moisés Rojas, Manuel María Seoane, Joaquín M. Escoto

1887
President: Manuel Saavedra
Members: *Francisco Martínez de Arredondo, Prudenciano Dorantes*, Miguel Sagaseta, *Eustaquio Buelna*, José María Aguirre de la Barrera, Carlos González Ureña, Miguel Auza, *Francisco Vaca*, T. Melesio Alcántara, Manuel Saavedra
Supernumeraries: Fernando J. Corona, Miguel Villalobos, Moisés Rojas, Manuel María Seoane, Joaquín M. Escoto

1888
President: Miguel Auza
Members: *Félix Romero, Francisco M. de Arredondo, Prudenciano Dorantes, José María Lozano*, Miguel Sagaseta, José María Aguirre de la Barrera, *Eustaquio Buelna, Francisco Vaca*, Manuel Saavedra
Supernumeraries: Aurelio Melgarejo, Antonio Falcón, Miguel Sandoval, Manuel María Seoane

1889
President: Miguel Auza
Members: *Félix Romero, Francisco M. de Arredondo, Prudenciano Dorantes, José María Lozano*, Miguel Sagaseta, Manuel Saavedra, *Francisco Vaca*, José María Aguirre de la Barrera, *Eustaquio Buelna*, Manuel Castilla Portugal
Supernumeraries: Aurelio Melgarejo, Antonio Falcón, Miguel Sandoval, Manuel María Seoane, Miguel Villalobos

1890

President: Miguel Auza
Members: *Félix Romero, Francisco M. de Arredondo, Prudenciano Dorantes, Jose María Lozano,* Manuel Saavedra, *Francisco Vaca,* José María Aguirre de la Barrera, *Eustaquio Buelna,* Manuel Castilla Portugal, Vacant
Supernumeraries: *José María Vega Limón,* Antonio Falcón, Miguel Sandoval, Eduardo Novoa, Miguel Villalobos

1891

President: *Félix Romero*
Members: Miguel Auza, *Francisco M. de Arredondo, Prudenciano Dorantes, Jose María Lozano,* Manuel Saavedra, *Francisco Vaca,* José María Aguirre de la Barrera, *Eustaquio Buelna,* Manuel Castilla Portugal, Vacant
Supernumeraries: *José María Vega Limón,* Antonio Falcón, Miguel Sandoval, Eduardo Novoa, Miguel Villalobos

1892

President: *Félix Romero*
Members: *Francisco M. de Arredondo, Prudenciano Dorantes, José María Lozano,* Manuel Saavedra, *Francisco Vaca,* José María Aguirre de la Barrera, *Eustaquio Buelna,* Manuel Castilla Portugal, *Manuel María de Zamacona, Eligio Ancona*
Supernumeraries: *José María Vega Limón,* Antonio Falcón, Miguel Sandoval, Eduardo Novoa, Miguel Villalobos

1893

President: *Félix Romero*
Members: *Francisco Martínez de Arredondo, Prudenciano Dorantes, José María Lozano, Manuel M. de Zamacona, Francisco Vaca,* José María Aguirre de la Barrera, *Eustaquio Buelna,* Manuel Castilla Portugal, Manuel Saavedra, *Eligio Ancona*
Supernumeraries: *José María Vega Limón,* Antonio Falcón, Miguel Sandoval, Eduardo Novoa, Miguel Villalobos

1894

President: *Eustaquio Buelna*
Members: Alberto García, Modesto Herrera, *Francisco Vaca, Félix Romero, Francisco Martínez de Arredondo,* Manuel

M. Zamacona, Prudenciano Dorantes, Justo Sierra, Manuel Castilla Portugal
Supernumeraries: Eduardo Novoa, *José María Vega Limón*

1895

President: *Francisco Vaca*
Members: Alberto García, *Francisco Vaca, Félix Romero, Francisco Martínez de Arredondo, Manuel M. Zamacona, Eustaquio Buelna, Prudenciano Dorantes, Justo Sierra,* Manuel Castilla Portugal
Supernumeraries: *José María Vega Limón,* Eduardo Novoa

1896

President: Unknown
Members: Alberto García, *Félix Romero, Francisco Martínez de Arredondo, Manuel M. Zamacona, Eustaquio Buelna, Prudenciano Dorantes, Justo Sierra,* Manuel Castilla Portugal
Supernumeraries: *José María Vega Limón,* Eduardo Novoa

1897

President: *Prudenciano Dorantes*
Members: *Francisco Martínez de Arredondo, Félix Romero, Manuel M. Zamacona, Justo Sierra, Ignacio Mariscal,* Vacant, *Eustaquio Buelna,* Manuel Castilla Portugal
Supernumeraries: Manuel García Méndez, *Julio Zárate,* Andrés Horcasitas, Eduardo Novoa, Macedonio Gómez

1898

President: Manuel Castilla Portugal
Members: *Francisco Martínez de Arredondo, Félix Romero, Manuel M. Zamacona, Justo Sierra, Ignacio Mariscal, Silvestre Moreno Cora, Eustaquio Buelna, Prudenciano Dorantes,* Vacant
Supernumeraries: Manuel García Méndez, *Julio Zárate,* Andrés Horcasitas, Eduardo Novoa, Macedonio Gómez

1899

President: *Félix Romero*
Members: *Francisco Martínez de Arredondo, Prudenciano Dorantes, Manuel M. Zamacona, Justo Sierra, Ignacio Mariscal, Silvestre Moreno Cora,* Vacant, *Eustaquio Buelna,* Eduardo Castañeda, Vacant

Supernumeraries: Manuel García Méndez, *Julio Zárate,* Andrés Horcasitas, Eduardo Novoa, Macedonio Gómez

1900
President: *Félix Romero*
Members: *Francisco Martínez de Arredondo, Prudenciano Dorantes, Manuel M. Zamacona, Justo Sierra, Ignacio Mariscal, Silvestre Moreno Cora,* Vacant, *Eustaquio Buelna,* Eduardo Castañeda, Francisco de P. Segura
Supernumeraries: Manuel García Méndez, *Julio Zárate,* Eduardo Novoa, Macedonio Gómez

1901
President: Eduardo Castañeda
Members: *Francisco Martínez de Arredondo, Prudenciano Dorantes, Manuel M. Zamacona, Ignacio Mariscal, Silvestre Moreno Cora, Félix Romero, Eustaquio Buelna,* Macedonio Gómez, *Eduardo Ruiz, Julio Zárate,* Francisco de P. Segura
Supernumeraries: Manuel García Méndez, *Justo Sierra* (on leave), Andrés Horcasitas, Eduardo Novoa (on leave), Juan García Peña

1902
President: Eduardo Castañeda
Members: *Francisco Martínez de Arredondo, Prudenciano Dorantes, Manuel M. Zamacona, Félix Romero,* Macedonio Gómez, *Silvestre Moreno Cora, Eduardo Ruiz, Eustaquio Buelna,* Francisco P. de Segura, *Julio Zárate*
Supernumeraries: Eduardo Novoa (on leave), *Justo Sierra* (on leave), Manuel García Méndez, Andrés Horcasitas, Juan García Peña

1903
President: *Félix Romero*
Members: *Francisco Martínez de Arredondo, Prudenciano Dorantes, Manuel M. Zamacona,* Macedonio Gómez, Manuel García Méndez, *Eduardo Ruiz, Eustaquio Buelna,* Eduardo Castañeda, *Julio Zárate,* Andrés Horcasitas
Supernumeraries: *Justo Sierra* (on leave), Juan García Peña, Nicolás López Garrido, Manuel Osio

1904
President: Eduardo Castañeda
Members: *Francisco Martínez de Arredondo, Prudenciano Dorantes, Manuel M. Zamacona,* Macedonio Gómez, Manuel García Méndez, Manuel Osio, *Eustaquio Buelna,* Andrés Horcasitas, Juan N. García, *Félix Romero*
Supernumeraries: *Justo Sierra* (on leave), *Julio Zárate , José Zubieta*

1905
President: *Félix Romero*
Members: *Julio Zárate,* Eduardo Castañeda, *Prudenciano Dorantes,* Macedonio Gómez, Nicolás López Garrido, Manuel García Méndez, Manuel Osio, Cristóbal Chapital, Juan N. García, Manuel Olivera Toro
Supernumeraries: *Justo Sierra* (on leave), *José Zubieta,* Miguel Bolaños Calero, *Emeterio de la Garza*

1906
President: *José Zubieta*
Members: *Julio Zárate,* Eduardo Castañeda, *Prudenciano Dorantes,* Macedonio Gómez, Manuel García Méndez, Cristóbal Chapital, *Demetrio Sodi,* Manuel Olivera Toro, *Félix Romero,* Ricardo Rodríguez
Supernumeraries: *Justo Sierra* (on leave), Miguel Bolaños Calero, *Emeterio de la Garza*

1907
President: *Félix Romero*
Members: Eduardo Castañeda, *Prudenciano Dorantes,* Macedonio Gómez, Manuel García Méndez, Cristóbal Chapital, Manuel Olivera Toro, Ricardo Rodríguez, *José Zubieta,* Martín Mayora, *Demetrio Sodi*
Supernumeraries: *Justo Sierra* (on leave), *Emeterio de la Garza,* Nicolás López Garrido

1908
President: *Félix Romero*
Members: Eduardo Castañeda, Martín Mayora, Macedonio Gómez, Manuel García Méndez, Cristóbal Chapital, *Francisco S. Carvajal,* Manuel Olivera Toro, *Emeterio de la Garza,* Ricardo

Rodríguez, *Demetrio Sodi*
Supernumeraries: Francisco Belmar,
Alonso Rodríguez Miramón, Carlos Flores

1909
President: *Félix Romero*
Members: Eduardo Castañeda, Martín
Mayora, Macedonio Gómez, Manuel
García Méndez, Cristóbal Chapital,
Manuel Olivera Toro, *Demetrio Sodi,
Emeterio de la Garza*, Ricardo Rodríguez,
Francisco S. Carvajal
Supernumeraries: Carlos Flores, Alonso
Rodríguez Miramón, Francisco Belmar

1910
President: *Félix Romero*
Members: Eduardo Castañeda, Martín
Mayora, Macedonio Gómez, Manuel
García Méndez, Cristóbal Chapital,
Ricardo Rodríguez, Manuel Olivera Toro,
*Francisco S. Carvajal, Demetrio Sodi,
Emeterio de la Garza*
Supernumeraries: Carlos Flores, Alonso
Rodríguez Miramón, Emilio Bulli Goyri,
Emilio Alvarez

1911
President: *Félix Romero*
Members: Eduardo Castañeda, Martín
Mayora, Macedonio Gómez, Manuel
García Méndez, Cristóbal Chapital,
Ricardo Rodríguez, Manuel Olivera Toro,
*Emeterio de la Garza, Demetrio Sodi,
Francisco S. Carvajal*
Supernumeraries: Carlos Flores, Alonso
Rodríguez Miramón, Emilio Bulli Goyri,
Emilio Alvarez

1912
President: *Félix Romero*
Members: Eduardo Castañeda, Martín
Mayora, Macedonio Gómez, Cristóbal
Chapital, Manuel Olivera Toro, *Emeterio
de la Garza*, Ricardo Rodríguez, Francisco
Belmar, *Francisco S. Carvajal*, Emilio
Bulli Goyri, David Gutiérrez Allende,
Jesús L. González
Supernumeraries: Carlos Flores, Alonso
Rodríguez Miramón, Emilio Alvarez

1913
President: *Francisco S. Carvajal*
Members: Eduardo Castañeda, Martín
Mayora, Macedonio Gómez, Cristóbal

Chapital, Manuel Olivera Toro, *Emeterio
de la Garza*, Ricardo Rodríguez, Francisco
Belmar, *Félix Romero*, Emilio Bulli Goyri
Supernumeraries: Carlos Flores, Alonso
Rodríguez Miramón, Emilio Alvarez

1914–16
Supreme Court not in functions

1917
President: Enrique M. de los Ríos
Members: *José María Truchuelo*, Alberto
M. Gonzalez, Enrique Moreno, *Manuel E.
Cruz*, Agustín Urdapilleta, Enrique García
Parra, *Enrique Colunga*, Victoriano
Pimentel, Agustín de Valle, Santiago
Martínez Alomía

1918
President: Enrique M. de los Ríos
Members: *José María Truchuelo*, Alberto
M. González, Enrique Moreno, *Manuel E.
Cruz*, Agustín Urdapilleta, Enrique García
Parra, *Enrique Colunga*, Victoriano
Pimentel, Agustín de Valle, Santiago
Martínez Alomía

1919
President: Ernesto Garza Pérez
Members: Adolfo Arias, Alberto M.
González, *Benito Flores*, Gustavo A.
Vicencio, Patricio Sabido, Agustín
Urdapilleta, *Ignacio Noris*, José María
Mena, *Enrique Moreno*, Antonio Alcocer

1920
President: Ernesto Garza Pérez
Members: Adolfo Arias, Alberto M.
González, *Benito Flores*, Gustavo A.
Vicencio, Patricio Sabido, Agustín
Urdapilleta, *Ignacio Noris*, José María
Mena, *Enrique Moreno*, Antonio Alcocer

1921
President: Ernesto Garza Pérez
Members: Adolfo Arias, Alberto M.
González, *Benito Flores*, Gustavo A.
Vicencio, Patricio Sabido, Agustín
Urdapilleta, *Ignacio Noris*, José María
Mena, *Enrique Moreno*, Antonio Alcocer

1922
President: Ernesto Garza Pérez
Members: Adolfo Arias, Alberto M.
González, *Benito Flores*, Gustavo A.

Vicencio, Patricio Sabido, Agustín Urdapilleta, *Ignacio Noris,* José María Mena,
Enrique Moreno, Antonio Alcocer

1923
President: *Francisco Modesto Ramírez*
Members: *Manuel Padilla, Sabino M.
Olea,* Leopoldo Estrada, Ricardo B. Castro,
Jesús Guzmán Vaca, Ernesto Garza Pérez,
Gustavo A. Vicencio, Francisco Díaz
Lombardo, *Salvador Urbina,* Victoriano
Pimentel

1924
President: *Francisco Modesto Ramírez*
Members: *Manuel Padilla, Sabino M.
Olea,* Leopoldo Estrada, Ricardo B. Castro,
Jesús Guzmán Vaca, Ernesto Garza Pérez,
Gustavo A. Vicencio, Francisco Díaz
Lombardo, *Salvador Urbina,* Victoriano
Pimentel

1925
President: Gustavo A. Vicencio
Members: *Manuel Padilla, Sabino M.
Olea, Salvador Urbina,* Leopoldo Estrada,
Ricardo B. Castro, Jesús Guzmán Vaca,
Ernesto Garza Pérez, *Francisco Modesto
Ramírez,* Francisco Díaz Lombardo,
Teófilo H. Orantes

1926
President: *Manuel Padilla*
Members: Jesús Guzmán Vaca, *Sabino M.
Olea,* Gustavo A. Vicencio, Ricardo B.
Castro, Ernesto Garza Pérez, *Francisco
Modesto Ramírez,* Francisco Díaz
Lombardo, *Teófilo H. Orantes,* Leopoldo
Estrada, *Salvador Urbina*

1927
President: *Manuel Padilla*
Members: Jesús Guzmán Vaca, *Sabino M.
Olea,* Gustavo A. Vicencio, Ricardo B.
Castro, Francisco Díaz Lombardo,
*Francisco Modesto Ramírez, Teófilo H.
Orantes,* Leopoldo Estrada, Elías Monges
López, *Salvador Urbina*

1928
President: Francisco Díaz Lombardo
Members: Jesús Guzmán Vaca, *Sabino M.
Olea,* Gustavo A. Vicencio, *Manuel
Padilla, Francisco Modesto Ramírez,
Teófilo H. Orantes,* Arturo Cisneros

Canto, Ricardo B. Castro, Leopoldo
Estrada

1929
President: *Julio García Pimentel*
Members: Carlos Salcedo, *Paulino
Machorro Narváez,* Francisco Barba,
Fernando de la Fuente, Salvador Urbina,
Luis M. Calderón, Arturo Cisneros Canto,
Jesús Guzmán Vaca, Daniel L. Valencia,
Francisco Díaz Lombardo, *Alberto
Vázquez del Mercado, Francisco H. Ruiz,*
Joaquín Ortega, Juan José Sánchez

1930
President: *Julio García Pimentel*
Members: Carlos Salcedo, *Paulino
Machorro Narváez,* Francisco Barba,
Fernando de la Fuente, Salvador Urbina,
Luis M. Calderón, Arturo Cisneros Canto,
Jesús Guzmán Vaca, Daniel L. Valencia,
Francisco Díaz Lombardo, *Alberto
Vázquez del Mercado, Francisco H. Ruiz,*
Joaquín Ortega, Juan José Sánchez

1931
President: *Julio García Pimentel*
Members: Carlos Salcedo, *Paulino
Machorro Narváez,* Francisco Barba,
Fernando de la Fuente, Salvador Urbina,
Luis M. Calderón, Arturo Cisneros Canto,
Jesús Guzmán Vaca, Daniel L. Valencia,
Francisco Díaz Lombardo, *Alberto
Vázquez del Mercado, Francisco H. Ruiz,*
Joaquín Ortega, Juan José Sánchez

1932
President: *Julio García Pimentel*
Members: *Fernando de la Fuente,* Daniel
V. Valencia, Jesús Guzmán Vaca, Ricardo
Couto, Enrique Osornio Aguilar, *Salvador
Urbina,* Luis M. Calderón, Francisco Díaz
Lombardo, *Paulino Machorro Narváez,*
Manuel Padilla, Arturo Cisneros Canto,
Francisco Barba, *Francisco H. Ruiz,*
Joaquín Ortega

1933
President: *Salvador Urbina*
Members: *Fernando de la Fuente,* Daniel
V. Valencia, Jesús Guzmán Vaca, Ricardo
Couto, Enrique Osornio Aguilar, *Salvador
Urbina,* Luis M. Calderón, Francisco Díaz
Lombardo, *Paulino Machorro Narvaez,*
Manuel Padilla, Arturo Cisneros Canto,

Francisco Barba, *Francisco H. Ruiz,* Joaquín Ortega, Jose López Lira

1934
President: *Salvador Urbina*
Members: *Fernando de la Fuente,* Daniel V. Valencia, Jesús Guzmán Vaca, Ricardo

Couto, Enrique Osornio Aguilar, *Salvador Urbina,* Luis M. Calderón, Francisco Díaz Lombardo, *Paulino Machorro Narváez, Manuel Padilla,* Arturo Cisneros Canto, Francisco Barba, *Francisco H. Ruiz,* Joaquín Ortega, José López Lira

APPENDIX B

Senators, 1884–1934

1884–86 (12th Legislature)

State	Senator	Alternate
Aguascalientes	*Ramón Gómez Villavicencio* Agustín R. González *Ignacio T. Chávez*	Miguel Rul
Campeche	Pedro Montalvo Pedro Baranda	Salvador Dondé *Ignacio T. Chávez*
Chiapas	Federico Méndez Rivas Francisco Loaeza	Eduardo Esparza
Chihuahua	*Felipe Arellano* Gustavo Ruiz Sandoval	*Lauro Carrillo* Eduardo Urueta
Coahuila	Ismael Salas	Roque J. Rodríguez José S. Aguayo
Colima	*Francisco Santa Cruz* Pedro Galván	*Gildardo Gómez* Miguel Utrilla
Distrito Federal	*Joaquín Baranda*	*Manuel Dublán* Manuel Medina
Durango	*Manuel Fernández Leal*	*Mariano Martínez de Castro* Pedro Sánchez Castro
Guanajuato	*José Montesinos* *José Ceballos*	Alberto Escobar
Guerrero	Joaquín Díaz *Pedro Landazuri*	Agustín D. Bonilla

State	Senator	Alternate
Hidalgo	*Carlos Rivas* Pedro Hinojosa	Epifanio Reyes José Justo Alvarez
Jalisco	Francisco Rincón Gallardo Darío Balandrano	Maximino Valdovinos
México	*Carlos Quaglia* Jesús Lalanne	Angel Martínez José Mijares Añgora
Michoacán	Octaviano Fernández	Ricardo Rodríguez
Morelos	*José Maria Zubieta* *Luis Mier y Terán*	Miguel Castellanos Sánchez *Guillermo de Landa Escandón*
Nuevo León	*Genaro Garza García* Canuto García	Atenógenes Ballesteros
Oaxaca	Juan de Mata Vázquez *Manuel Dublán*	Francisco Meixueiro Carlos Sodi
Puebla	José María Couttolene *Eduardo Garay*	Miguel R. Méndez Miguel Serrano
Querétaro	*Pedro Díez Gutiérrez* Enrique M. Rubio	Fernando Rubio
San Luis Potosí	Juan Francisco Gavino *Blas Escontría*	Juan Flores Ayala Antonio Arguinzonis
Sinaloa	José G. Carbo *Ignacio M. Escudero*	*Joaquín Redo*
Sonora	Francisco Montes de Oca José T. Otero	Mariano Espejo Jesús Castañeda
Tabasco	*Manuel Romero Rubio* Guillermo Palomino	Miguel Castellanos Sánchez Luis Rojas
Tamaulipas	Antonio Canale Domingo López de Lara	Pedro Argüelles
Tlaxcala	Agustín del Río Francisco Poceros	
Veracruz	Miguel de la Peña *Carlos Díez Gutiérrez*	*Miguel Utrilla* Ignacio P. Chávez
Yucatán	*Cástulo Zenteño* Francisco Maldonado J.	José Peón y Contreras
Zacatecas	Andrés Piñón Jesús Loera	Pedro Molina

1886–88 (13th Legislature)

State	Senator	Alternate
Aguascalientes	Agustín R. González	José Carballeda
	Ramón Gómez Villavicencio	Miguel Rul
Campeche	*Pedro Baranda*	*Ignacio T. Chávez*
	Pedro Montalvo	Salvador Dondé
Chiapas	Benigno Arriaga	Magín Llaven
	Federico Méndez Rivas	Eduardo Esparza
Chihuahua	*Luis Terrazas*	Eduardo Urueta
	Felipe Arellano	*Lauro Carrillo*
Coahuila	*Julio M. Cervantes*	*Andrés S. Viesca*
	Roque J. Rodríguez	Victoriano Zepeda
		Gustavo Ruiz Sandoval
Colima	*Angel Martínez*	*Miguel Utrilla*
	Francisco Santa Cruz	*Gildardo Gómez*
Distrito Federal	Genaro Raigosa	Manuel Medina
	Joaquín Baranda	
Durango	*José Ceballos*	Pedro Sánchez Castro
	Manuel Fernández Leal	*Mariano Martínez de Castro*
Guanajuato	Gumersindo Enríquez	Agustín Obregón
	José Montesinos	Alberto Escobar
Guerrero	Hermenegildo Carrillo	José G. Ney
	Joaquín Díaz	Agustín D. Bonilla
Hidalgo	*Rafael Cravioto*	Gabriel Islas
	Carlos Rivas	Epifanio Reyes
Jalisco	Sabás Lomelí	Esteban Calderón
	Francisco Rincón Gallardo	Maximino Valdovinos
México	*José Vicente Villada*	Jesús Alberto García
	Carlos Quaglia	Angel Martínez
Michoacán	*Manuel González Cosío*	Epifanio Reyes
	Ramón Fernández	Ricardo Rodríguez
Morelos	*Guillermo de Landa y Escandón*	Teodoro Zúñiga
	José Zubieta	Miguel Castellanos Sánchez
Nuevo León	Narciso Dávila	Jesús M. Benítez y Pinillos
	Genaro Garza García	Atenógenes Ballesteros
Oaxaca	*Manuel Dublán*	*Félix Romero*
	Juan de M. Vázquez	Francisco Meixueiro

State	Senator	Alternate
Puebla	*Eduardo Garay* Nicolás Islas y Bustamante	Fernando G. Mendizábal Miguel R. Méndez
Querétaro	Enrique M. Rubio *Pedro Díez Gutiérrez*	Manuel Domínguez Fernando Rubio
San Luis Potosí	*Carlos Fuero* Juan Francisco Gaviño	Ignacio López Portillo Juan Flores Ayala
Sinaloa	*Juan Sánchez Azcona* Jesús Castañeda (1888) José G. Carbo	Ricardo Martínez de Castro *Joaquín Redo*
Sonora	José T. Otero *Joaquín Redo* (1888) Francisco Montes de Oca	Francisco Leyva Mariano Espejo
Tabasco	*Simón Sarlat* *Manuel Romero Rubio*	José Luis Rojas
Tamaulipas	Emilio Velasco Antonio Canale	Francisco Vargas Pedro Argüelles
Tlaxcala	Agustín del Río Mariano Rivadeneyra y Lemus	José Luis Rojas
Veracruz	*Teodoro A. Dehesa* Miguel de la Peña	*Francisco de P. Aspe*
Yucatán	Octavio Rosado *Cástulo Zenteño*	José Trinidad Ferrer José Peón y Contreras
Zacatecas	Jesús Aréchiga Andrés Piñón	Jesús Loera Pedro Molina

1888–90 (14th Legislature)

State	Senator	Alternate
Aguascalientes	*Francisco G. Hornedo* Agustín R. González	Julio Serafín Azcué
Campeche	Pedro Montalvo *Pedro Baranda*	Juan Montalvo *Ignacio T. Chávez*
Chiapas	*José M. Ramírez* Benigno Arriaga	Sebastián Escobar Magín Llaven
Chihuahua	*Carlos Pacheco* *Luis Terrazas*	Antonio Mora Eduardo Urueta
Coahuila	Enrique Baz *Julio M. Cervantes*	Victoriano Zepeda *Andrés S. Viesca*

Colima	*Joaquín Redo* *Angel Martínez*	Anastasio T. Cañedo *Miguel Utrilla*
Distrito Federal	Genaro Raigosa *Joaquín Baranda*	Manuel Ortega Reyes
Durango	*Manuel Fernández Leal* *José Ceballos*	Felipe Arellano Pedro Sánchez Castro
Guanajuato	*José Montesinos* Gumersindo Enríquez	Alberto Escobar Agustín Obregón
Guerrero	*Félix Francisco Maceyra* Hermenegildo Carrillo	Ricardo Rodríguez José G. Ney
Hidalgo	*Carlos Rivas* *Rafael Cravioto*	Epifanio Reyes Gabriel Islas
Jalisco	*Alfonso Lancaster Jones* Sabás Lomelí	*Sebastián Camacho* Esteban Calderón
México	*Carlos Quaglia* *José Vicente Villada*	Eufemio M. Rojas Jesús Alberto García
Michoacán	Marcelino Morfín Chávez *Manuel González Cosío*	José C. Téllez Epifanio Reyes
Morelos	Miguel Castellanos Sánchez *Guillermo de Landa y Escandón*	Cristóbal Sarmina Teodoro Zúñiga
Nuevo León	*Pedro Martínez* Narciso Dávila	*Apolinar Castillo* Jesús M. Benítez y Pinillos
Oaxaca	Francisco Meixueiro *Manuel Dublán*	Roberto Maqueo *Félix Romero*
Puebla	José Maria Couttolene *Eduardo Garay*	Eufemio M. Rojas Fernando G. Mendizábal
Querétaro	*Bernardo Reyes* Enrique M. Rubio	Antonio Arguinzoniz Manuel Domínguez
San Luis Potosí	*Pedro Díez Gutiérrez* *Carlos Fuero*	Antonio Espinosa Cervantes Ignacio López Portillo
Sinaloa	*Luis E. Torres* *Juan Sánchez Azcona* Jesús Castañeda (1888)	*José de Teresa y Miranda* Ricardo Martínez de Castro
Sonora	*Francisco Cañedo* José T. Otero *Joaquín Redo* (1888)	Adolfo Castañares Francisco Leyva
Tabasco	*Manuel Romero Rubio* *Simón Sarlat*	Jesús Castañeda José Luis Rojas

State	Senator	Alternate
Tamaulipas	*Rómulo Cuéllar* Emilio Velasco	Francisco Estrada Francisco Vargas
Tlaxcala	Francisco Ibarra Ramos Agustín del Río	Agustín Picazo Cuevas José Luis Rojas
Veracruz	Julián Herrera *Teodoro A. Dehesa*	Vicente Vila *Francisco de P. Aspe*
Yucatán	José Peón y Contreras Octavio Rosado	Eufemio M. Rojas José Trinidad Ferrer
Zacatecas	*Agustín Canseco* *Jesús Aréchiga*	Manuel Aspe Jesús Loera

1890–92 (15th Legislature)

State	Senator	Alternate
Aguascalientes	*Ignacio T. Chávez* *Francisco G. Hornedo*	Rodrigo Rincón Gallardo Julio Serafín Azcué
Campeche	*Pedro Baranda* Pedro Montalvo	Agustín R. González Juan Montalvo
Chiapas	*Mariano Bárcena* *José M. Ramírez*	Patricio L. León Sebastián Escobar
Chihuahua	*Guillermo de Landa y Escandón* *Carlos Pacheco*	Buenaventura Becerra Antonio Mora
Coahuila	José T. Otero Enrique Baz	Jesús de la Vega Victoriano Zepeda
Colima	*Angel Martínez* *Joaquín Redo*	José Antonio Puebla Anastasio T. Cañedo
Distrito Federal		*Manuel Ortega Reyes* *Ignacio Pombo*
Durango	*José Ceballos* *Manuel Fernández Leal*	Pedro Sánchez Castro Felipe Arellano
Guanajuato	Gumersindo Enríquez *José Montesinos*	Alberto Escobar
Guerrero	Eufemio M. Rojas *Félix Francisco Maceyra*	Manuel Parra Ricardo Rodríguez
Hidalgo	Bernabé Loyola *Carlos Rivas*	Manuel F. Soto Epifanio Reyes
Jalisco	Sabás Lomelí *Alfonso Lancaster Jones*	Eduardo Rincón Gallardo *Sebastián Camacho*

México	Jesús Alberto García *Carlos Quaglia*	Ignacio Mañón y Valle
Michoacán	*Manuel González Cosío* Marcelino Morfín Chávez	Epifanio Reyes José C. Téllez
Morelos	*Lauro Carrillo* Miguel Castellanos Sánchez	*Manuel de Herrera* Cristóbal Sarmina
Nuevo León	Narciso Dávila *Pedro Martínez*	Jesús M. Benítez y Pinillos *Apolinar Castillo*
Oaxaca	Esteban Calderón *Benito Gómez Farías (1892)* Francisco Meixueiro	Miguel Castro Joaquín M. Ruiz (1892) Roberto Maqueo
Puebla	*Vidal de Castañeda y Nájera* José María Couttolene	Fernando G. Mendizábal Eufemio M. Rojas
Querétaro	Enrique M. Rubio *Bernardo Reyes*	Manuel Domínguez Antonio Arguinzoniz
San Luis Potosí	*Carlos Fuero* *Pedro Díez Gutiérrez*	Ignacio López Portillo Antonio Espinosa Cervantes
Sinaloa	Ricardo Martínez de Castro *Luis E. Torres*	Cleofas Salmón *José de Teresa y Miranda*
Sonora	*Julio M. Cervantes*	Melesio Alcántara
Tabasco	Adolfo Castañares *Manuel Romero Rubio*	*Calixto Merino* Jesús Castañeda
Tamaulipas	*Rafael Cravioto* *Rómulo Cuéllar*	Francisco Estrada
Tlaxcala	Agustín del Río Francisco Ibarra Ramos	Domingo León Agustín Picazo Cuevas
Veracruz	*Teodoro A. Dehesa* Julián Herrera	*Francisco de P. Aspe* Vicente Vila
Yucatán	Octavio Rosado	Pomposo Verdugo Eufemio Rojas
Zacatecas	Jesús Loera *Agustín Canseco*	Manuel J. Aguilar Manuel Aspe

1892–94 (16th Legislature)

State	Senator	Alternate
Aguascalientes	*Francisco O. Arce* *Ignacio T. Chávez*	Julio S. Azcué Rodrigo Rincón Gallardo

State	Senator	Alternate
Campeche	Maríano Ortiz de Montellano *Pedro Baranda*	Juan Montalvo Agustín R. González
Chiapas	*Maríano Martínez de Castro* *Mariano Bárcena*	Sebastián Escobar Patricio L. León
Chihuahua	*Lauro Carrillo* *Guillermo de Landa y Escandón*	Genaro Raigosa Buenaventura Becerra
Coahuila	Enrique Baz José T. Otero	Victoriano Zepeda Jesús de la Vega
Colima	*Joaquín Redo* *Angel Martínez*	Genaro Raigosa
Distrito Federal		*Manuel Ortega Reyes* Ignacio Pombo
Durango	*Manuel Fernández Leal* *José Ceballos*	José A. Gamboa Pedro Sánchez Castro
Guanajuato	*José Montesinos* Gumersindo Enríquez	Alberto Escobar
Guerrero	*Félix Francisco Maceyra* Eufemio M. Rojas	Manuel Carrascosa Manuel Parra
Hidalgo	*Carlos Rivas* *Bernabé Loyola*	Epifanio Reyes Manuel F. Soto
Jalisco	*Alfonso Lancaster Jones* Sabás Lomelí	*Sebastián Camacho* Eduardo Rincón Gallardo
México	*Carlos Quaglia* Jesús Alberto García	Eufemio M. Rojas Ignacio Mañón y Valle
Michoacán	Ramón Corral *Manuel González Cosío*	Manuel de Estrada Epifanio Reyes
Morelos	Miguel Castellanos Sánchez *Lauro Carrillo*	Cristóbal Sarmina *Manuel de Herrera*
Nuevo León	Carlos Bernardi Narciso Dávila	José Peón y Contreras Jesús M. Benítez y Pinillos
Oaxaca	*Rosendo Márquez* *Benito Gómez Farías* (1892)	Miguel Castro Joaquín M. Ruiz
Puebla	José M. Couttolene *Vidal de Castañeda y Nájera*	Vicente Gutiérrez Palacios Fernando G. Mendizábal
Querétaro	*Bernardo Reyes* Enrique M. Rubio	Antonio Arguinzoniz Manuel Domínguez

San Luis Potosí	*Juan Bustamante* (1894)	*Eduardo Rincón Gallardo*
	Pedro Diez Gutiérrez	*José Ramos*
	Carlos Fuero	
Sinaloa	*Luis Torres*	*José de Teresa y Miranda*
	Ricardo Martínez de Castro	Cleofas Salmón
Sonora	*Francisco Cañedo*	*Rafael Dondé*
	Julio M. Cervantes	Melesio Alcántara
Tabasco	*Manuel Romero Rubio*	Jesús Castañeda
	Adolfo Castañares	*Calixto Merino*
Tamaulipas	*Rómulo Cuéllar*	Francisco Estrada
	Rafael Cravioto	
Tlaxcala	Francisco Ibarra Ramos	Genaro Raigosa
	Agustín del Río	Domingo León
Veracruz	Julián F. Herrera	Vicente Vila
	Teodoro A. Dehesa	*Francisco de P. Aspe*
Yucatán	*Apolinar Castillo*	*Manuel Dondé Cámara*
	Octavio Rosado	Pomposo Verdugo
Zacatecas	*Agustín Canseco*	Manuel S. Aspe
	Jesús Loera	Manuel J. Aguila

1894–96 (17th Legislature)

State	Senator	Alternate
Aguascalientes	*Ignacio T. Chávez*	Rodrigo Rincón Gallardo
	Francisco O. Arce	Julio S. Azcué
Campeche	Agustín R. González	Miguel Utrilla
	Maríano Ortiz de Montellano	Juan Montalvo
Chiapas	*Maríano Bárcena*	Patricio L. León
		Serapio Baqueiro (1896)
	Maríano Martínez de Castro	Sebastián Escobar
Chihuahua	*Guillermo de Landa y Escandón*	Buenaventura Becerra
	Lauro Carrillo	Genaro Raigosa
Coahuila		José María Múzquiz
	Enrique Baz	Victoriano Zepeda
Colima	*Angel Martínez*	José Antonio Puebla
	Joaquín Redo	Genaro Raigosa
Distrito Federal	Manuel Payno	*Manuel Ortega Reyes*
Durango	José María Garza Galán	Pedro Miranda
	Manuel Fernández Leal	José A. Gamboa

State	Senator	Alternate
Guanajuato	Francisco de P. Castañeda *José Montesinos*	Enrique María Rubio Alberto Escobar
Guerrero	Diego Alvarez *Félix Francisco Maceyra*	Manuel Parra Manuel Carrascosa
Hidalgo	Gumersindo Enríquez *Carlos Rivas*	Manuel Fernando Soto Epifanio Reyes
Jalisco	Sabás Lomelí *Alfonso Lancaster Jones*	Jesús de la Vega *Sebastián Camacho*
México	Juan Hijar y Haro *Carlos Quaglia*	
Michoacán	*Manuel González Cosío* Ramón Corral	Carlos Sodi Eduardo Cañas (1896) Manuel de Estrada
Morelos	*Manuel de Herrera* Miguel Castellanos Sánchez	Tomás de la Torre Cristóbal Sarmina
Nuevo León	Narciso Dávila Carlos Berardi	Jesús Benítez y Pinillos José Peón y Contreras
Oaxaca	*Ignacio Pombo* *Rosendo Márquez*	Joaquín María Ruiz
Puebla	*Vidal de Castañeda y Nájera* José M. Couttolene	Fernando G. Mendizábal Vicente Gutiérrez Palacios
Querétaro	Bernabé Loyola Bernardo Reyes	Antonio Alvarez Rul Antonio Arguinzoniz
San Luis Potosí	*José Ramos* *Juan Bustamante*	*Ismael Salas* *Eduardo Rincón Gallardo*
Sinaloa	*Emilio Rabasa* *Luis Torres*	Cleofas Salmón *José de Teresa y Miranda*
Sonora	*Julio María Cervantes* *Francisco Cañedo*	*Maríano Martínez de Castro* *Rafael Dondé*
Tabasco	Adolfo Castañares *Manuel Romero Rubio*	*Calixto Merino* Jesús Castañeda
Tamaulipas	*Rafael Cravioto* *Rómulo Cuéllar*	*Ramón Fernández* Francisco Estrada
Tlaxcala	Agustín del Río Francisco Ibarra Ramos	Joaquín María Ruiz Genaro Raigosa

Veracruz	*Francisco de P. Aspe*	Pedro del Paso y Troncoso
	Julián F. Herrera	Vicente Vila
Yucatán	*Ignacio Romero Vargas*	Pomposo Verdugo
	Apolinar Castillo Ramírez	Manuel Dondé Cámara
Zacatecas	Jesús Loera	Pedro G. Nafarrate
	Agustín Canseco	Manuel S. Aspe

1896–98 (18th Legislature)

State	Senator	Alternate
Aguascalientes	Patricio L. León	*Román S. Lascuráin*
	Ignacio T. Chávez	Rodrigo Rincón Gallardo
Campeche	Genaro Raigosa	*Francisco O. Acre*
	Agustín R. González	Miguel Utrilla
Chiapas	*Maríano Martínez de Castro*	Manuel Lacroix
	Maríano Bárcena	Patricio L. León
Chihuahua	Antonio Falcón	José Domínguez Peón
	Guillermo de Landa y Escandón	Buenaventura Becerra
Coahuila	Francisco Arispe Ramos	Maríano Ortiz de Montellano
		José María Múzquiz
Colima	*Joaquín Redo*	Pedro del Valle
	Angel Martínez	José Antonio Puebla
Distrito Federal		Benito Gómez Farías
		Manuel Ortega Reyes
Durango	*Manuel Fernández Leal*	*Alejandro Vázquez del M.*
	José María Garza Galán	Pedro Miranda
Guanajuato	Francisco de P. del Río (1898)	
	Francisco Z. Mena	Francisco de C. Segura
	Francisco de P. Castañeda	Enrique María Rubio
Guerrero	*Félix Francisco Maceyra*	*Jesús Aréchiga*
	Diego Alvarez	Manuel Parra
Hidalgo	*Carlos Rivas*	Epifanio Reyes
	Gumersindo Enríquez	Manuel Fernando Soto
Jalisco	*Alfonso Lancaster Jones*	*Sebastián Camacho*
	Sabás Lomelí	Jesús de la Vega
México	*Carlos Quaglia*	Tomás de la Torre
	Juan Hijar y Haro	

State	Senator	Alternate
Michoacán	Eduardo Cañas *Manuel González Cosío*	*Pascual Ortiz* Carlos Sodi Eduardo Cañas (1896)
Morelos	Miguel Castellanos Sánchez *Manuel de Herrera*	Luis Flores Tomás de la Torre
Nuevo León	Carlos Berardi Narciso Dávila	José Peón y Contreras Jesús M. Benítez y Pinillos
Oaxaca	*Rosendo Márquez* *Ignacio Pombo*	Joaquín María Ruiz
Puebla	José María Couttolene *Vidal de Castañeda y Nájera*	Rafael Aguilar Fernando G. Mendizábal
Querétaro	Bernardo Reyes Bernabé Loyola	Antonio Arguinzoniz Antonio Alvarez Rul
San Luis Potosí	*Eduardo Rincón Gallardo* *José Ramos*	Francisco Bustamante *Ismael Salas*
Sinaloa	*José Yves Limantour* *Emilio Rabasa*	Francisco Estrada Cleofas Salmón
Sonora	*Francisco Cañedo* *Julio María Cervantes*	*Rafael Dondé* *Maríano Martínez de Castro*
Tabasco	Jesús Castañeda Adolfo Castañares	Pedro Miranda *Calixto Merino*
Tamaulipas	*Rómulo Cuéllar* *Rafael Cravioto*	Francisco Martínez y Calleja *Ramón Fernández*
Tlaxcala	Manuel M. Contreras Agustín del Río	Bernardo González Joaquín María Ruiz
Veracruz	Julián F. Flores *Francisco de P. Aspe*	Guillermo Valleto Pedro del Paso y Troncoso
Yucatán	*Apolinar Castillo Ramírez* *José de Teresa y Miranda* (1898)	Manuel Dondé Cámara Pomposo Verdugo
Zacatecas	*Agustín Canseco* Jesús Loera	Pedro G. Nafarrate

1898–1900 (18th Legislature)

State	Senator	Alternate
Aguascalientes	*Ignacio T. Chávez* Patricio L. León	Rodrigo Rincón Gallardo *Román S. Lascuráin*

Campeche	*Manuel González Cosío*	*Jesús Aréchiga*
	Genaro Raigosa	*Francisco O. Acre*
Chiapas	*Mariano Bárcena*	Patricio L. León
	Maríano Martínez de Castro	Manuel Lacroix
Chihuahua	Guillermo de Landa y Escandón	Buenaventura Becerra
	Antonio Falcón	José Domínguez Peón
Coahuila	Benito Gómez Farías	Gregorio Mendizábal
	Francisco Arispe Ramos	Maríano Ortiz de Montellano
Colima	*Angel Martínez*	José Antonio Puebla
	Joaquín Redo	Pedro del Valle
Distrito Federal	*Sebastián Camacho*	*Manuel Ortega Reyes*
Durango	Faustino Michel	Miguel Sánchez Aguirre
	Manuel Fernández Leal	*Alejandro Vázquez del M.*
Guanajuato	*Francisco de P. Castañeda*	Francisco de P. del Río
	Francisco de P. del Río (1898)	
	Francisco Z. Mena	Francisco de C. Segura
Guerrero	*Diego Alvarez*	Juan Cházaro Soler
	Jesús Aréchiga	
Hidalgo	Gumersindo Enríquez	José María Múzquiz
	Carlos Rivas	Epifanio Reyes
Jalisco	Sabás Lomelí	Jesús de la Vega
	Alfonso Lancaster Jones	*Sebastián Camacho*
México		Francisco Díez Barroso
	Carlos Quaglia	Tomás de la Torre
Michoacán	Carlos Sodi	Primitivo Ortiz
		Pascual Ortiz
Morelos	Manuel de Herrera	*Pedro Martínez López*
	Miguel Castellanos Sánchez	Luis Flores
Nuevo León	Carlos Félix Ayala	Jesús M. Benítez y Pinillos
	Carlos Berardi	
Oaxaca	*Ignacio Pombo*	Andrés Ruiz
	Rosendo Márquez	Joaquín María Ruiz
Puebla	*Vidal de Castañeda y Nájera*	Juan Quintana
	José María Couttolene	Rafael Aguilar
Querétaro	Bernabé Loyola	Carlos G. de Cosío
	Benardo Reyes	Antonio Arguinzoniz

State	Senator	Alternate
San Luis Potosí	Rafael Rebollar *Eduardo Rincón Gallardo*	José Ramos Francisco Bustamante
Sinaloa	*Emilio Rabasa* *José Yves Limantour*	Cleofas Salmón Francisco Estrada
Sonora	*Lorenzo Torres* *Francisco Cañedo*	Alejandro Prieto *Rafael Dondé*
Tabasco	Adolfo Castañares Jesús Castañeda	*Policarpo Valenzuela* Pedro Miranda
Tamaulipas	*Ramón Fernández* *Rómulo Cuéllar*	Francisco Estrada Francisco Martínez y C.
Tlaxcala	· Agustín del Río Manuel M. Contreras	Manuel Peniche Bernardo González
Veracruz	*Francisco de P. Aspe* Julián F. Flores	Pedro del Paso y Troncoso Guillermo Valleto
Yucatán	*José de Teresa y Miranda* *Apolinar Castillo Ramírez*	Joaquín Patrón Peniche Manuel Dondé Cámara
Zacatecas	*José M. Garza Galán* *Agustín Canseco*	 Pedro F. Nafarrete

1900–02 (20th Legislature)

State	Senator	Alternate
Aguascalientes	Patricio L. León *Ignacio T. Chávez*	*Ramón S. Lascuráin* Rodrigo Rincón Gallardo
Campeche	Genaro Raigosa *Manuel González Cosío*	Eduardo Castillo Lavalle *Jesús Aréchiga*
Chiapas	*Maríano Martínez de Castro*	Abraham A. López Patricio L. León
Chihuahua	*Joaquín Redo* Guillermo de Landa y Escandón	José Domínguez Peón Buenaventura Becerra
Coahuila	Maríano Ortiz de Montellano Benito Gómez Farías	*Venustiano Carranza* Gregorio Mendizábal
Colima	Antonio Mercenario *Angel Martínez*	Trinidad García José Antonio Puebla
Distrito Federal	*Sebastián Camacho* *Manuel Ortega Reyes*	
Durango	*Alejandro Vásquez del Mercado* Faustino Michel	Manuel F. de la Hoz Miguel Sánchez Aguirre

Guanajuato	*Francisco Albístegui*	Manuel Arizmendi
	Francisco de P. Castañeda	Francisco de P. del Río
Guerrero	Jesús Aréchiga	Tomás Reyes Retana
		Juan Cházaro Soler
Hidalgo	*Carlos Rivas*	Vicente Vila
	Gumersindo Enríquez	José María Múzquiz
Jalisco	*Alfonso Lancaster Jones*	Felipe Robleda
	Sabás Lomelí	Jesús de la Vega
México	*Simón Sarlat*	*Angel Gavino*
	Carlos Quaglia	*Francisco Díez Barroso*
Michoacán	Eduardo Cañas	Vicente Maciel
	Carlos Sodi	Primitivo Ortiz
Morelos	Miguel Castellanos Sánchez	Luis Flores
	Manuel de Herrera	Pedro Martínez López
Nuevo León	Ramón G. Chávarri	José Peón y Contreras
	Carlos Félix Ayala	Jesús M. Benítez y P.
Oaxaca	*Olegario Molina Solís*	Manuel Molina Solís
	Ignacio Pombo	Andrés Ruiz
Puebla	*Blas Escontría*	*Miguel S. Macedo*
	Vidal de Castañeda y Nájera	Juan Quintana
Querétaro	Antonio Arguinzoniz	Agustín Ruiz Olloqui
	Bernabé Loyola	Carlos G. de Cosío
San Luis Potosí	*Eduardo Rincón Gallardo*	José Encarnación Ipiña
	Rafael Rebollar	*José Ramos*
Sinaloa	*Emilio Rabasa*	Leopoldo Ortega
	Ramón Alcázar	Cleofas Salmón
Sonora	*Francisco Cañedo*	*Rafael Dondé*
	Lorenzo Torres	Alejandro Prieto
Tabasco	Jesús Castañeda	Manuel Domínguez Elizalde
	Adolfo Castañares	*Policarpo Valenzuela*
Tamaulipas	*Rómulo Cuéllar*	Francisco Martínez Calleja
	Ramón Fernández	Francisco Estrada
Tlaxcala	Manuel M. Contreras	José M. Macías
	Agustín del Río	Manuel Peniche
Veracruz	Mauro S. Herrera	Efrén M. Reyna
	Francisco de P. Aspe	Pedro A. del Paso y T.

State	Senator	Alternate
Yucatán	Lorenzo García *José de Teresa y Miranda*	*Apolinar Castillo* Joaquín Patrón Peniche
Zacatecas	Alonso Mariscal *José María Garza Galán*	Ramón Romero Pedro F. Nafarrete

1902–04 (21st Legislature)

State	Senator	Alternate
Aguascalientes	Patricio León *Ignacio T. Chávez*	*Román S. Lascuráin*
Campeche	Genaro Raigosa *Tomás Aznar Cano*	Eduardo Castillo Lavalle Francisco S. Carbajal
Chiapas	*José Castellot* *Maríano Martínez de Castro*	Abraham A. López
Chihuahua	*Joaquín Redo* Guillermo de Landa y Escandón	
Coahuila	Benito Gómez Farías Mariano Ortiz de Montellano	*Venustiano Carranza*
Colima	Antonio Mercenario *Angel Martínez*	José Antonio Puebla
Distrito Federal	*Sebastián Camacho* *Manuel Ortega Reyes*	
Durango	*Alejandro Vásquez del Mercado* *Miguel F. Martínez*	Manuel F. de la Hoz
Guanajuato	*Francisco Albístegui* *Martín González*	Manuel Arizmendi
Guerrero	*Jesús Aréchiga*	Tomás Reyes Retana
Hidalgo	*Carlos Rivas* *Francisco Díez Barroso*	Vicente Vila Francisco P. del Río
Jalisco	*Alfonso Lancaster Jones* *Jesús de la Vega*	Felipe Robleda Agustín R. González
México	*Simón Sarlat* Gumersindo Enríquez	*Angel Gaviño*
Michoacán	Eduardo Cañas Carlos Sodi	Vicente Maciel
Morelos	Miguel Castellanos Sánchez José María Romero	Luis Flores

Nuevo León	Carlos F. Ayala Ramón G. Chavarri	José Peón y Contreras
Oaxaca	*Ignacio Pombo* *Olegario Molina Solís*	Manuel Molina Solís
Puebla	*Vidal Castañeda y Nájera* *Blas Escontría*	*Miguel S. Macedo* Tomás Mancera
Querétaro	Antonio Arguinzoniz Bernabé Loyola	Agustín Ruiz Olloqui
San Luis Potosí	*Eduardo Rincón Gallardo* *José Ramos*	*José Encarnación Ipiña*
Sinaloa	*Emilio Rabasa* Ramón Alcázar	Leopoldo Ortega
Sonora	*Francisco Cañedo* *Lorenzo Torres*	*Rafael Dondé* Alejandro Prieto
Tabasco	Jesús Castañeda Adolfo Castañares	Manuel Domínguez Elizalde
Tamaulipas	*Ramón Fernández* *Rómulo Cuéllar*	Francisco Martínez C. José de Jesús Peña
Tlaxcala	Agustín del Río Manuel M. Contreras	José N. Macías Jesús F. Uriarte
Veracruz	Mauro S. Herrera *Francisco de P. Aspe*	Efrén M. Reyna
Yucatán	*Luis C. Curiel* Lorenzo García	Manuel Irigoyen Lara Carlos Flores
Zacatecas	Alonso Mariscal *Eduardo G. Pankhurst*	José María Gamboa Ramón Romero

1904–06 (22nd Legislature)

State	Senator	Alternate
Aguascalientes	*Ignacio T. Chávez* Patricio L. León	*Román S. Lascuráin* Rafael J. Gutiérrez
Campeche	*Tomás Aznar Cano* Genaro Raigosa	Francisco S. Carbajal
Chiapas	*José Castellot* Antonio Hernández	Abraham A. López Manuel F. de la Hoz
Chihuahua	Guillermo Landa y Escandón Eduardo Villada	

State	Senator	Alternate
Coahuila	Benito Gómez Farías *Venustiano Carranza*	
Colima	Antonio Mercenario	José Antonio Puebla
Distrito Federal	*Sebastián Camacho* *Manuel Ortega Reyes*	
Durango	*Manuel F. Martínez* Miguel A. Mercado	
Guanajuato	*Martín González* *Francisco Albístegui*	
Guerrero	Juan Chávez Solcr *Jesús Aréchiga*	Pedro Landázuri Tomás Reyes Retana
Hidalgo	Francisco de P. del Río *Carlos Rivas*	
Jalisco	Carlos Flores *Jesús de la Vega*	Agustín R. González
México	Gumersindo Enríquez *Simón Sarlat*	*Angel Gaviño*
Michoacán	Carlos Sodi Eduardo Cañas	José de Landcro y Cos
Morelos	José María Romero *Luis E. Torres*	*Román S. Lascuráin*
Nuevo León	Carlos F. Ayala	José Peón y Contreras
Oaxaca	Aurelio Valdivieso *Ignacio Pombo*	Francisco González Mena *Manuel Molina Solís*
Puebla	*Miguel S. Macedo* *Vidal Castañeda y Nájera*	Feliciano García Tomás Mancera
Querétaro	*Bernabé Loyola* Antonio Arguinzoniz	
San Luis Potosí	*José Ramos* *Eduardo Rincón Gallardo*	
Sinaloa	*Emilio Rabasa* Ramón Alcázar	
Sonora	*Rafael Dondé* *Lorenzo Torres*	Alejandro Prieto
Tabasco	Adolfo Castañares Jesús Castañeda	

Tamaulipas	*Ramón Fernández*	
	Rómulo Cuéllar	José de Jesús Peña
Tlaxcala	*Emilio Pardo*	Rafael Angel Peña
	Agustín del Río	Jesús F. Uriarte
Veracruz	Mauro S. Herrera	
	Francisco de P. Aspe	
Yucatán	*Luis C. Curiel*	Manuel Irigoyen Lara
	Francisco Martínez Arredondo	
Zacatecas	Rafael Angel Peña	
	Marcos Simoni Castelvi	
	Alonso Mariscal	

1906–08 (23rd Legislature)

State	Senator	Alternate
Aguascalientes	Patricio L. León	Rafael Gutiérrez
	Ignacio T. Chávez	
Campeche	Genaro Raigosa	Juan Terrazas
	Francisco S. Carbajal	
Chiapas	Antonio V. Hernández	Manuel F. de la Hoz
	José Castellot	Abraham A. López
Chihuahua	Eduardo Villada	
	Manuel Sánchez Mármol	
Coahuila	Benito Gómez Farías	
	Venustiano Carranza	
Colima	Antonio Mercenario	
	Rafael Pimentel	
Distrito Federal	*Manuel Ortega Reyes*	
	Sebastián Camacho	
Durango	Manuel A. Mercado	
	Miguel F. Martínez	
Guanajuato	*Francisco Albístegui*	
	Martín González	
Guerrero	Juan Chávez Soler	Tomás Reyes Retana
	Francisco Sosa	
Hidalgo	*Carlos Rivas*	
	Francisco Díez Borroso	Francisco de P. del Río
Jalisco	Carlos Flores	
	Agustín R. González	

State	Senator	Alternate
México	*Simón Sarlat* Gumersindo Enríquez	*Angel Gaviño*
Michoacán	Eduardo Cañas Carlos Sodi	José de Landero y Cos
Morelos	*Luis E. Torres* José María Romero	*Román S. Lascuráin*
Nuevo León	Carlos F. Ayala	José Peón y Contreras
Oaxaca	Aurelio Valdivieso	Francisco González Mena
Puebla	*Miguel S. Macedo* Tomás Mancera	Feliciano García
Querétaro	Antonio Arguinzoniz Bernabé Loyola	
San Luis Potosí	*Eduardo Rincón Gallardo* *José Ramos*	
Sinaloa	Ramón Alcázar *Emilio Rabasa*	
Sonora	*Rafael Dondé* *Lorenzo Torres*	Alejandro Prieto
Tabasco	Jesús Castañeda Adolfo Castañares	
Tamaulipas	*Rómulo Cuéllar* *Miguel Bolaños Cacho*	José de Jesús Peña
Tlaxcala	*Emilio Pardo* Jesús F. Uriarte	
Veracruz	Mauro S. Herrera *Francisco de P. Aspe*	
Yucatán	*Francisco Martínez Arredondo* *Luis C. Curiel*	
Zacatecas	Alonso Mariscal *Manuel Domínguez*	Genaro G. García

1908–10 (24th Legislature)

State	Senator	Alternate
Aguascalientes	*Angel Gaviño* Juan García Peña	Wenceslao Briseño

Campeche	*Francisco S. Carbajal* *Julio Zárate*	Ramón Lanz Duret
Chiapas	*José Castellot* Antonio V. Hernández	Abraham A. López
Chihuahua	*Manuel Sánchez Mármol* Eduardo Villada	
Coahuila	Benito Gómez Farías *Venustiano Carranza*	Encarnación Dávila
Colima	*Rafael Pimentel* Antonio Mercenario	Gregorio Mendizábal
Distrito Federal	*Sebastián Camacho* *Manuel Ortega Reyes*	Manuel Zamacona e Inclán
Durango	*Miguel F. Martínez* Manuel A. Mercado	Fernando Pimentel y Fagoaga
Guanajuato	Mauro S. Herrera *Francisco Albístegui*	
Guerrero	*Francisco Sosa* *Rafael Izábal*	Prisciliano Martínez
Hidalgo	Francisco Díez Borroso Nicolás López Garrido	Francisco de P. del Río
Jalisco	Enrique Pazos *Esteban Maqueo Castellanos*	
México	Gumersindo Enríquez *Joaquín Baranda*	Carlos Castillo
Michoacán	Carlos Sodi Serapión Fernández	Francisco C. García
Morelos	José María Romero *Luis E. Torres*	*Román S. Lascuráin*
Nuevo León	Carlos F. Ayala José María Garza Ramos	*José López Portillo y R.*
Oaxaca	Aurelio Valdivieso *Guillermo Landa y Escandón*	Francisco González Mena
Puebla	Tomás Mancera *Miguel S. Macedo*	Feliciano García
Querétaro	Bernabé Loyola Antonio Arguinzoniz	

State	Senator	Alternate
San Luis Potosí	*José Ramos* Tomás Reyes Retana	
Sinaloa	*Emilio Rabasa* Ramón Alcázar	
Sonora	*Lorenzo Torres* *Rafael Dondé*	Alejandro Prieto
Tabasco	Adolfo Castañares Jesús Castañeda	
Tamaulipas	*Miguel Bolaños Cacho* José de Jesús Peña	
Tlaxcala	Jesús Uriarte *Emilio Pardo*	
Veracruz	*Francisco de P. Aspe* *Joaquín D. Casasús*	Efrén M. Reyna
Yucatán	*Luis C. Curiel* *Francisco Martínez de Arredondo*	
Zacatecas	*Manuel Domínguez* Alonso Mariscal	Genaro G. García

1910–12 (25th Legislature)

State	Senator	Alternate
Aguascalientes	Juan García Peña *Porfirio Parra*	Wenceslao Briseño
Campeche	*Julio Zárate* *Víctor Manuel Castillo*	Ramón Lanz Duret
Chiapas	Antonio V. Hernández *José Castellot*	
Chihuahua	Eduardo Villada *Manuel Sánchez Mármol*	
Coahuila	*Venustiano Carranza* Benito Gómez Farías	Encarnación Dávila
Colima	Antonio Mercenario *Ràfael Pimental*	Gregorio Mendizábal
Distrito Federal	*Francisco Alfaro* *Sebastián Camacho*	

| Durango | Manuel A. Mercado | Fernando Pimental y Fagoaga |
| | *José Zubieta* | Carlos Aquirre |

| Guanajuato | *Francisco Albístegui* | |
| | Mauro S. Herrera | |

| Guerrero | *Rafael Izábal* | Prisciliano Martínez |
| | *Francisco Sosa* | Rafael Martínez Freg |

| Hidalgo | Nicolás López Garrido | |
| | *Gabriel Mancera* | |

| Jalisco | Esteban Maqueo Castellanos | |
| | Ricardo Guzmán | |

| México | Gumersindo Enríquez | Manuel Medina Garduño |
| | | Carlos Castillo |

| Michoacán | Serapión Fernández | Francisco C. García |
| | *Enrique Olavarría y Ferrari* | |

| Morelos | José María Romero | Jesús Urías |
| | | Manuel Zapata Vera |

| Nuevo León | José María Garza Ramos | *José López Portillo y R.* |
| | *Enrique Gorostieta* | Nicolás Berazaluce |

| Oaxaca | *Guillermo Landa y Escandón* | Francisco González Mena |
| | Aurelio Valdivieso | |

| Puebla | *Miguel S. Macedo* | Feliciano García |
| | Tomás Mancera | Rafael Martínez Carrillo |

| Querétaro | Antonio Arguinzoniz | |
| | Tomás Macmanus | Antonio Alvarez Rul |

| San Luis Potosí | Tomás Retana Reyes | |
| | Modesto R. Martínez | |

| Sinaloa | Ramón Alcázar | |
| | *Emilio Rabasa* | |

| Sonora | *Rafael Dondé* | |
| | *Lorenzo Torres* | Alejandro Prieto |

| Tabasco | Jesús Castañeda | |
| | *Víctoriano Salado Alvarez* | Nicandro L. Melo |

| Tamaulipas | *Rómulo Cuéllar* | José de Jesús Peña |
| | Alejandro Pezo | *Miguel Bolaños Cacho* |

| Tlaxcala | *Emilio Pardo* | |
| | Jesús F. Uriarte | |

State	Senator	Alternate
Veracruz	*Joaquín D. Casasús*	Efrén M. Reyna
	Francisco de P. Aspe	
Yucatán	*Francisco Martínez de Arredondo*	
	Luis C. Curiel	Juan R. Zavala
Zacatecas	Alfonso Mariscal	
	Heriberto Zazueta	Antonio Juambeltz y Redo

1912–13, 1913–14 (26th Legislature)

State	Senator	Alternate
Aguascalientes	Carlos García Hidalgo	Francisco Macías
	Antonio Morfín Vargas	Wenceslao Briseño
Campeche	*Víctor Manuel Castillo (1912–14)*	
	Carlos Martínez Mac Gregor	Ramón Lanz Duret
	Manuel Rojas Moreno	
	Manuel Gutiérrez Zamora	
Chiapas	*José Castellot (1912–14)*	*Belisario Domínguez*
	Querido Moheno, Sr. (1913–14)	
	Leopoldo Gout (1912–13)	
Chihuahua	Manuel Balbás	
Coahuila	*Ignacio Alcocer (1913–14)*	Ignacio Michel
	Benito Gómez Farías (1912–13)	
	José María Garza Elizondo	
	Reginaldo Cepeda	
Colima	*Rafael Pimentel (1912–13)*	Ignacio Padilla
	Francisco Santa Cruz Ceballos	
	Carlos J. Margani	
Distrito Federal	*Sebastián Camacho (1912–14)*	Arturo Alvaradejo
	Aureliano Urrutia (1913–14)	
	Fernando Iglesias Calderón (1912–13)	
Durango	*José Zubieta (1912)*	Carlos Aguirre
Guanajuato	Mauro S. Herrera (1912–13)	Antonio Alcocer
	Emilio Lojero (1913–14)	*Nicéforo Guerrero*
	José de Jesús Peña (1913–14)	
	Julio García (1912–13)	
Guerrero	Nicolás Pinzón	Rafael Martínez Freg
	Francisco Sosa (1912–13)	
	Enrique C. Gudiño	

Hidalgo	*Gabriel Mancera* (1912–13) *Pedro L. Rodríguez* (1913–14) Ignacio Durán Francisco Bracho	Carlos Sánchez de Tagle
Jalisco	Ricardo Guzmán Clemente Villaseñor Salvador Gómez (1912–13)	
México	Gumersindo Enríquez (1912–13) Benito Sánchez Valadez Felipe Mier *Manuel Calero Sierra* (1912–13)	Manuel Medina Garduño Miguel V. Avalos
Michoacán	*Enrique Olavarría y Ferrari* (1912–13) *Francisco de P. Troncoso* (1913–14) Eduardo N. Iturbide (1912–14)	Salvador Cortés Rubio
Morelos	Manuel Araoz José Diego Fernández *Francisco Bulnes* (1913–14)	José Urías
Nuevo León	*Enrique Gorostieta* (1912–14) Francisco de P. Morales (1913–14) *Lázaro Garza Ayala* (1912–13)	Nicolás Berazaluce Víctor Rivero Juan C. Fernández
Oaxaca	Ignacio Salamanca Aurelio Valdivieso Jesús Flores Magón	Ramón Pardo
Puebla	Tomás Mancera (1912–?) Luis C. Valle (1913–14) *Rafael Cañete* (1912–13)	Rafael Martínez Carrillo Alfonso Mariscal y Piña Eduardo Novoa
Querétaro	Manuel Gutiérrez Závala Tomás Macmanus (1912–13) *Francisco León de la Barra* (1913–14)	Antonio Alvarez Rul
San Luis Potosí	Antonio Alonso Carlos Aguirre *Jesús Aréchiga* (1913–14) Modesto R. Martínez (1912–13)	Antonio Arguinzoniz
Sinaloa	Luis Martínez de Castro (1913–14) *Emilio Rabasa* (1912–13) Luis A. Martínez (1913–14) *Manuel Bonilla* (1912)	Rosendo Verdugo
Sonora	Alberto Morales	Alejandro Prieto

State	Senator	Alternate
Tabasco	José Segundo Gómez Cabral *Víctoriano Salado Alvarez* (1912–13) Rómulo Becerra Fabre (1912–13)	Adolfo Aguirre Nicolás L. Melo
Tamaulipas	*Othón P. Blanco* (1912–13) Guillermo Obregón (1913–14) *Samuel García Cuéllar* (1913–14) Alejandro Pezo (1912–13)	*Miguel Bolaños Cacho* Alfredo M. Guerra
Tlaxcala	Ignacio Torres Adalid Jesús F. Uriartc (1912–14) *Próspero Cahuantzi* (1913–14)	Rafael Avila Vicente Sánchez Gavito
Veracruz	*Francisco de P. Aspe* (1912–14) José María del Toro Julio J. Gutiérrez	
Yucatán	*Luis C. Curiel* (1912–13) Ignacio Magaloni (1913–14) *José Castellot* (1912–14)	Vicente Vidaurrazaga
Zacatecas	Daniel García (1913–14) Heriberto Zazueta (1912–13) *Miguel Ruelas* (1913–14) Rodolfo J. Elorduy (1912–13)	Antonio Juambeltz y Redo Juan R. Zavala

1916–18 (27th Legislature)

State	Senator	Alternate
Aguascalientes	Francisco L. Jiménez Federico Ramos Barrera	
Campeche	Alfonso Quintana Pérez	Herminio Pérez Abreu
Chiapas	Cristóbal Ll. Castillo Teófilo H. Orantes	
Chihuahua	Julio Ornelas *Abel S. Rodríguez*	
Coahuila	Juan Manuel García Rafael Zepeda	Epigmenio Rodríguez
Colima	J. Concepción Rivera Ramón de la Vega	
Distrito Federal	*Juan Sánchez Azcona* *Rafael Zubarán Capmany*	*José Inés Novelo*
Durango	Leónardo Pescador Fernando Gómez Palacio	

Guanajuato	Francisco S. Mancilla Rodolfo Ramírez	
Guerrero	*José Inocente Lugo*	Teófilo Cervantes *Rodolfo Neri*
Hidalgo	*Cutberto Hidalgo* Antonio Guerrero	
Jalisco	*Amado Aguirre* Francisco Labastida Izquierdo	Bernardino Germán
México	*José J. Reynoso* Pascual Morales y Molina	
Michoacán	Jesús Silva Rosendo Toledo	Rafael Reyes
Morelos	None	
Nayarit	Bernardo L. Martínez Quirino Ordaz	Jerónimo Mesa
Nuevo León	Ildefonso Vázquez Gerónimo Elizondo	Fernando Cantú Cárdenas
Oaxaca	Juan Sánchez	Francisco Eustacio Vázquez
Puebla	Enrique Contreras *Daniel Guzmán*	Juan Ramírez Ramos
Querétaro	Juan N. Frías *Ernesto Perusquía*	Lamberto Retana
San Luis Potosí	Antonio F. Alonso Arturo Méndez	
Sinaloa	Guillermo Laveaga *Emiliano C. García*	
Sonora	*Flavio A. Bórquez* *Luis G. Monzón*	
Tabasco	*Aureliano Colorado* Joaquín Pedrero	
Tamaulipas	Emiliano P. Nafarrete Francisco M. González	Albino Hernández Alberto Villasana Ortiz
Tlaxcala	Antonio Hidalgo Pedro Corona	
Veracruz	Adalberto Tejeda *Víctor E. Góngora*	León Villamil

State	Senator	Alternate
Yucatán	Patricio Sabido	
	Bautista Pastor	Florencio Avila y Castillo
Zacatecas	Trinidad Cervantes	Enrique García
	Luis J. Zalce	Narciso González

1918–20 (28th Legislature)

State	Senator	Alternate
Aguascalientes	Federico Ramos Barrera	
	Angel Nájera	
Campeche	Alfonso Quintana Pérez	Herminio Pérez Abreu
	Francisco Field Jurado	Pablo Emilio Sotelo Regil
Chiapas	Teófilo H. Orantes	
	Cristóbal Ll. Castillo	
Chihuahua	Julio Ornelas	*Tomás Gameros*
	Abel S. Rodríguez	
Coahuila	Rafael Zepeda	
	Manuel Cepeda Medrano	Emilio Salinas
Colima	Ramón de la Vega	
	Elías Arias	
Distrito Federal	*Rafael Zubarán Capmany*	
	Rafael Martínez	Rosendo Amor
Durango	Fernando Gómez Palacio	
	Adalberto Ríos	
Guanajuato	Francisco S. Mancilla	
	Juan Barrón Vázquez	
Guerrero	Martín Vicario	Teófilo Cervantes
Hidalgo	Antonio Guerrero	
	Alfonso Cravioto	
Jalisco	Francisco Labastida Izquierdo	
	Esteban B. Calderón	Fernando Banda
México	Pascual Morales y Molina	
	Darío López	José Guzmán
Michoacán	Rosendo Toledo	
	Porfirio García de León	
Morelos	None	

Nayarit	Quirino Ordaz	Jerónimo Mesa
	Roberto Valadez	
Nuevo León	Gerónimo Elizondo	
	Jonás García	Fernando Cantú Cárdenas
Oaxaca	Juan Sánchez	
Puebla	*Daniel Guzmán*	Juan Ramírez Ramos
	Carlos B. Zetina	Sabino Palacios
Querétaro	*Ernesto Perusquía*	Lamberto Retana
	Benito Reynoso	
San Luis Potosí	*Rafael Cepeda*	
	Juan F. Barragán	Arturo Guzmán
Sinaloa	*Emiliano C. García*	
	Mariano Rivas	
Sonora	*Luis G. Monzón*	
	Adolfo de la Huerta	*Carlos Plank*
Tabasco	Joaquín Pedrero	
	Aquileo Juárez	Ruperto Jiménez Mérito
Tamaulipas	Francisco M. González	Alberto Villasana Ortiz
	José Morante	
Tlaxcala	Pedro Corona	
	Gerzayn Ugarte	Anastacio Meneses
Veracruz	*Víctor E. Góngora*	León Villamil
	Ramón Rodríguez Rivera	Juan de Dios Bonilla
Yucatán	Bautista Pastor	Florencio Avila y Castillo
	Antonio Ancona Albertos	José Cleofas Echeverría
Zacatecas	Luis J. Zalce	Narciso González
	Trinidad Cervantes	

1920–22 (29th Legislature)

State	Senator	Alternate
Aguascalientes	Alejandro Martínez Ugarte	
	Angel Nájera	José B. Villegas
Campeche	Francisco Field Jurado	*Joaquín Lanz Galera*
Chiapas	Cristóbal Ll. Castillo	
	Teófilo H. Orantes	
Chihuahua	Jesús J. Corral	Angel J. Lagarda
	Abel S. Rodríguez	

State	Senator	Alternate
Coahuila	*Eulalio Gutiérrez* Manuel Cepeda Medrano	
Colima	Arturo Gómez Elías Arias	
Distrito Federal	*Fernando Iglesias Calderón* *Rafael Martínez*	Rosendo Amor
Durango	*Severino Ceniceros* Adalberto Ríos	
Guanajuato	Manuel Gutiérrez de Velasco Juan Barrón Vázquez	
Guerrero	*Héctor F. López* Martín Vicario	
Hidalgo	Antonio Guerrero *Alfonso Cravioto*	
Jalisco	Camilo E. Pani *Esteban B. Calderón*	Fernando Banda
México	*José J. Reynoso* Darío López	
Michoacán	*José Ortiz Rodríguez* Porfirio García de León	
Morelos	Benito A. Tajonar Vicente Aranda	
Nayarit	*Juan Espinosa Bavara* Antonio Zuazo	
Nuevo León	Ildefonso Vázquez Jonás García	
Oaxaca	Juan Sánchez Guillermo Meixueiro	Eleazar del Valle
Puebla	Jesús Zafra Carlos B. Zetina	
Querétaro	Juan N. Frías Benito Reynoso	
San Luis Potosí	*Juan Sarabia* *Juan F. Barragán*	Arturo Guzmán
Sinaloa	*Andrés Magallón* Maríano Rivas	

Sonora	Felipe Salido *Carlos Plank*	
Tabasco	*Aureliano Colorado* Aquileo Juárez	Ruperto Jiménez Mérito
Tamaulipas	Joaquín Argüelles José Morante	Francisco Villarreal
Tlaxcala	Anastacio Meneses Gerzayn Ugarte	
Veracruz	*Heriberto Jara* Ramón Rodríguez Rivera	Juan de Dios Bonilla
Yucatán	*José Inés Novelo* *Antonio Ancona Albertos*	José Cleofas Echeverría
Zacatecas	Antonio Acuña Navarro Luis J. Zalce	

1922–24 (30th Legislature)

State	Senator	Alternate
Aguascalientes	Angel Nájera *Pedro de Alba*	José B. Villegas
Campeche	Francisco Field Jurado	Pablo Emilio Sotelo Regil
Chiapas	Teófilo H. Orantes Cristóbal Ll. Castillo	José H. Ruiz
Chihuahua	Jesús J. Corral *Abel S. Rodríguez*	Angel J. Lagarda
Coahuila	*Manuel Cepeda Medrano* *Vito Alessio Robles*	José Guadalupe Güitrón
Colima	*Arturo Gómez* José D. Aguayo	
Distrito Federal	Federico González Garza *Fernando Iglesias Calderón*	Rosendo Amor
Durango	Enrique R. Nájera *Severino Ceniceros*	
Guanajuato	*Enrique Colunga* Juan Barrón Vázquez	Manuel Hernandez Galván
Guerrero	*Héctor F. López* *Miguel F. Ortega*	

State	Senator	Alternate
Hidalgo	*Alfonso Cravioto* *Antonio Guerrero*	Eduardo J. Santander
Jalisco	Francisco Labastida Izquierdo Camilo E. Pani	Fernando Banda
México	Darío López *José J. Reynoso*	Enrique del Castillo
Michoacán	Porfirio García de León José María Mora	
Morelos	*León Salinas* Vicente Aranda	José María Muñoz
Nayarit	Francisco Trejo Antonio Zuazo	
Nuevo León	Atanacio Carrillo Jonás García	
Oaxaca	Juan Sánchez Isaac M. Ibarra	Eleazar del Valle José Maqueo Castellanos
Puebla	Claudio N. Tirado Jesús Zafra	Ricardo Reyes Márquez
Querétaro	J. Manuel Truchuelo Benito Reynoso	
San Luis Potosí	*Luis G. Monzón*	Arturo Guzmán
Sinaloa	José H. Heredia *Andrés Magallón*	
Sonora	*Flavio A. Bórquez* *Felipe Salido*	Tomás A. Robinson
Tabasco	Ricardo B. Castro *Aureliano Colorado*	Epafrodito Hernández C. Ruperto Jiménez Mérito
Tamaulipas	José Morante Joaquín Argüelles	Francisco Villarreal
Tlaxcala	Gerzayn Ugarte Anastacio Meneses	
Veracruz	Ramón Rodríguez Rivera Alberto Z. Palacios	Juan de Dios Bonilla Benigno E. Mata
Yucatán	*Antonio Ancona Albertos* *José Inés Novelo*	José Cleofas Echeverría

Zacatecas   José María Ruvalcaba
                   Luis J. Zalce

1924–26 (31st Legislature)

State	Senator	Alternate
Aguascalientes	Alejandro Martínez Ugarte *Pedro de Alba*	Vidal Roldán y Avila
Campeche	*J. Manuel Puig Casauranc* *Joaquín Lanz Galera*	*Adalberto Galeana Sierra* Pablo Emilio Sotelo Regil
Chiapas	Tiburicio Fernández Ruiz Teófilo H. Orantes	Alfredo Aguilar José H. Ruiz
Chihuahua	Manuel M. Prieto *Abel S. Rodríguez*	Emilio Zamora
Coahuila	*Eulalio Gutiérrez* *Vito Alessio Robles*	Candor Guajardo José Guadalupe Guitrón
Colima	*Higinio Alvarez* José D. Aguayo	José Padilla Gómez
Distrito Federal	Manuel M. Méndez *Federico González Garza*	
Durango	*Jesús Agustín Castro* *Enrique R. Nájera*	*Alberto Terrones Benítez* Antonio Gutiérrez
Guanajuato	Manuel Gutiérrez de Velasco *Enrique Colunga*	Manuel Hernández Galván
Guerrero	Eduardo Neri Miguel J. Ortega	
Hidalgo	Jesús F. Azuara *Alfonso Cravioto*	Eduardo J. Santander
Jalisco	Juan de Dios Robledo Francisco Labastida Izquierdo	
México	*José J. Reynoso*	Julio Pomposo Gorostieta
Michoacán	*José Ortiz Rodríguez* José María Mora	
Morelos	Fernando López *León Salinas*	José María Muñoz
Nayarit	*Juan Espinosa Bavara* Francisco Trejo	

State	Senator	Alternate
Nuevo León	Francisco González y González	
	Atanacio Carrillo	
Oaxaca	Eleazar del Valle	
	Isaac M. Ibarra	José Maqueo Castellanos
Puebla	Lauro Camarillo	
	Claudio N. Tirado	Ricardo Reyes Márquez
Querétaro	Abraham Araujo	
	J. Manuel Truchuelo	
San Luis Potosí	*José C. Cruz*	
	Luis G. Monzón	
Sinaloa	Manuel Rivas	
	José H. Heredia	
Sonora	Ventura G. Tena	
	Flavio A. Bórquez	Tomás A. Robinson
Tabasco	Demófilo Pedrero	
	Ricardo B. Castro	Epafrodito Hernández C.
Tamaulipas	Pedro González	Epigmenio García
	José Morante	
Tlaxcala	Anastacio Meneses	
Veracruz	*Víctor E. Góngora*	Francisco Riveros
	Alberto Z. Palacios	Benigno E. Mata
Yucatán	Arturo Cisneros Canto	
	Antonio Ancona Albertos	
Zacatecas	Fernando Rodarte	Manuel Méndez Muñoz
	José María Ruvalcaba	

1926–28 (32nd Legislature)

State	Senator	Alternate
Aguascalientes	*Manuel Carpio*	
	Alejandro Martínez Ugarte	Vidal Roldán y Avila
Campeche	Pablo Emilio Sotelo Regil	
	Adalberto Galeana Sierra	
Chiapas	Luis Espinosa	Benigno Cal y Mayor
	Tiburcio Fernández Ruiz	Alfredo Aguilar
Chihuahua	Luis Esther Estrada	
	Manuel M. Prieto	Emilio Zamora

Coahuila	Carlos Garza Castro *Eulalio Gutiérrez*	Leobardo P. Castro Candor Guajardo
Colima	José D. Aguayo *Higinio Alvarez*	José Padilla Gómez
Distrito Federal	Ezequiel Salcedo Manuel M. Méndez	
Durango	Antonio Gutiérrez *Jesús Agustín Castro*	*Pastor Rouaix*
Guanajuato	 Manuel Gutiérrez de Velasco	Juan B. Castelazo
Guerrero	*Miguel F. Ortega* Eduardo Neri	
Hidalgo	*José Rivera* Jesús J. Azuara	
Jalisco	Antonio Valadez Ramírez Juan de Dios Robledo	
México	*Filiberto Gómez* *José J. Reynoso*	Gilberto Dávila Julio Pomposo Gorostieta
Michoacán	Rafael Alvarez y Alvarez *José Ortiz Rodríguez*	Jesús Cuevas B.
Morelos	Manuel E. Acosta Fernando López	
Nayarit	José María Aguilar *Juan Espinosa Bavara*	Pedro López S.
Nuevo León	Federico Rocha Francisco González y González	
Oaxaca	José Maqueo Castellanos Eleazar del Valle	
Puebla	Ricardo Reyes Márquez Lauro Camarillo	
Querétaro	Juan J. Bermúdez Abraham Araujo	Agustín Casas
San Luis Potosí	Enrique Henshaw *José C. Cruz*	*Lamberto Hernández*
Sinaloa	José E. Heredia Manuel Rivas	

State	Senator	Alternate
Sonora	Manuel Montoya Ventura G. Tena	
Tabasco	*Tomás Garrido Canabal* Demófilo Pedrero	Homero Margalli G.
Tamaulipas	Federico Martínez Rojas Pedro González	Epigmenio García
Tlaxcala	Rafael Apango Anastacio Meneses	
Veracruz	*Arturo Campillo Seyde* *Víctorio E. Góngora*	Francisco Riveros
Yucatán	*José Castillo Torre* Arturo Cisneros Canto	
Zacatecas	Pedro Belauzarán Fernando Rodarte	Manuel Méndez Muñoz

1928–30 (33rd Legislature)

State	Senator	Alternate
Aguascalientes	Isaac Díaz de León *Manuel Carpio*	
Campeche	José C. Prieto Anguiano Pablo Emilio Sotelo Regil	
Chiapas	Tiburcio Fernández Ruiz Benigno Cal y Mayor	
Chihuahua	Nicolás Pérez Luis Esther Estrada	
Coahuila	Pablo Valdez Carlos Garza Castro	Lobardo P. Castro
Colima	*Francisco Solórzano Béjar* José D. Aguayo	Francisco J. Silva
Distrito Federal	Tomás Jonas Bay Ezequiel Salcedo	Tomás A. Robinson
Durango	*Pastor Rouaix* Antonio Gutiérrez	
Guanajuato	Juan G. Abascal Juan B. Castelazo	
Guerrero	Eduardo Neri *Miguel J. Ortega*	

Hidalgo	Arcadio Cornejo José Rivera	
Jalisco	Juan de Dios Robledo Antonio Valadez Ramírez	
México	José J. Reynoso *Filiberto Gómez*	Gilberto Dávila
Michoacán	*Enrique Ramírez* *Rafael Alvarez y Alvarez*	Jesús Cuevas B.
Morelos	Fernando López Manuel E. Acosta	Pedro López S.
Nayarit	Francisco Anguiano José María Aguilar	
Nuevo León	Jerónimo Siller Federico Rocha	
Oaxaca	Eleazar del Valle José Maqueo Castellanos	
Puebla	José M. González *Rodrigo Gómez*	
Querétaro	*Enrique Osornio Camarena* Juan J. Bermúdez	Agustín Casas
San Luis Potosí	Valentin Aguilar *Lamberto Hernández*	
Sinaloa	José María Valenzuela José E. Heredia	Ignacio Bermúdez
Sonora	Alejo Bay Manuel Montoya	
Tabasco	Alcides Caparroso *Tomás Carrido Canabal*	Homero Margalli G.
Tamaulipas	Pedro González *Federico Martínez Rojas*	
Tlaxcala	Moisés Huerta Rafael Apango	
Veracruz	*Manlio Fabio Altamirano* *Arturo Campillo Seyde*	
Yucatán	Bartolomé García Correa *José Castillo Torre*	Enrique Castillo

State	Senator	Alternate
Zacatecas	*Lauro C. Caloca* Pedro Belaunzarán	

1930–32 (34th Legislature)

State	Senator	Alternate
Aguascalientes	Miguel Ramos Isaac Díaz de León	
Campeche	Pablo Emilio Sótelo Regil José C. Prieto Anguiano	
Chiapas	Benigno Cal y Mayor Tiburcio Fernández Ruiz	
Chihuahua	Luis Esther Estrada Práxedes Giner Durán	
Coahuila	Carlos Garza Castro Pablo Valdez	
Colima	José D. Aguayo Francisco J. Silva	
Distrito Federal	*Gonzalo N. Santos* Tomás Jonás Bay	David Montes de Oca Tomás A. Robinson
Durango	Antonio Gutiérrez *Pastor Rouaix*	
Guanajuato	Juan B. Castelazo Juan G. Abascal	
Guerrero	Eduardo Neri	Desiderio Borja
Hidalgo	*Matías Rodríguez* Arcadio Cornejo	
Jalisco	Antonio Ramírez Valadez Juan de Dios Robledo	
México	Zenón Suárez *José J. Reynoso*	
Michoacán	Silvestre Guerrero *Enrique Ramírez*	
Morelos	Ambrosio Puente Fernando López	
Nayarit	Gustavo R. Cristo Francisco Anguiano	

Nuevo León	Carlos F. Osuna Jerónimo Siller	
Oaxaca	Genaro V. Vázquez Eleazar del Valle	
Puebla	Miguel Andreu Almazán José M. González	
Querétaro	*Ignacio García Jurado* Enrique Osornio Camarena	
San Luis Potosí	*Lamberto Hernández* Valentín Aguilar	
Sinaloa	Rodolfo T. Loaiza José María Valenzuela	Ignacio Bermúdez
Sonora	*Ramón Ramos* Alejo Bay	Leobardo Tellechea
Tabasco	Manuel Garrido Lacroix Alcides Caparroso	
Tamaulipas	*Marte R. Gómez* Pedro González	Federico Martínez Rojas
Tlaxcala	Ignacio Mendoza Moisés Huerta	
Veracruz	*Abel S. Rodríguez* *Manlio Fabio Altamirano*	
Yucatán	César Olayola Becerra Bartolomé García Correa	*Neguib Simón* Enrique Castillo
Zacatecas	Pedro Belaunzarán *Lauro C. Caloca*	

1932–34 (35th Legislature)

State	Senator	Alternate
Aguascalientes	Rafael Quevedo Miguel Ramos	Alberto del Valle
Campeche	Javier Illescas A. Pablo Emilio Sótelo Regil	
Chiapas	Benigno Cal y Mayor	Alberto Domínguez R.
Chihuahua	Gustavo L. Talamantes Luis Esther Estrada	

State	Senator	Alternate
Coahuila	*Manuel Pérez Treviño* Carlos Garza Castro	Elpidio Rodríguez
Colima	José Campero José D. Aguayo	
Distrito Federal	*Carlos Riva Palacio* *Gonzalo N. Santos*	David Montes de Oca
Durango	Severino Ceniceros Antonio Gutiérrez	Alfonso Breceda Mercado
Guanajuato	*Federico Medrano V.* Juan B. Castelazo	
Guerrero	Alfredo Guillén	Desiderio Borja
Hidalgo	Juan Cruz O. *Matías Rodríguez*	
Jalisco	Margarito Ramírez Antonio Ramírez Valadez	
México	Wenceslao Labra Zenón Suárez	
Michoacán	Dámaso Cárdenas Silvestre Guerrero	
Morelos	J. Guadalupe Pineda Ambrosio Puente	
Nayarit	*Esteban B. Calderón* Gustavo R. Cristo	
Nuevo León	*Aarón Sáenz* Carlos F. Osuna	David Alberto Cossío
Oaxaca	Francisco Arlanzón Genaro V. Vázquez	
Puebla	Rubén Ortiz Miguel Andreu Almazán	
Querétaro	Severiano Montes *Ignacio García Jurado*	
San Luis Potosí	Valentín Aguilar *Lamberto Hernández*	Josué Escobedo
Sinaloa	*Juan de Dios Bátiz* Rodolfo T. Loaiza	

Sonora	Emiliano M. Corella	
	Ramón Ramos	Leobardo Tellechea
Tabasco	*Ausencio C. Cruz*	Alcides Caparroso
	Manuel Garrido Lacroix	
Tamaulipas	Manuel Tarrega	
	Marte R. Gómez	Federico Martínez Rojas
Tlaxcala	Moisés Huerta	
	Ignacio Mendoza	
Veracruz	Manuel Almanza	
	Abel S. Rodríguez	
Yucatán	Max Peniche Vallado	José C. Conde Perera
	César Olayola Becerra	*Neguib Simón*
Zacatecas	*J. Jesús Delgado*	
	Pedro Belaunzarán	

APPENDIX C

Federal Deputies, 1884–1934
(Numbers refer to legislative districts)

1884–86 (12th Legislature)

State	Deputy	Alternate
Aguascalientes	1. Agapito Silva	Julio Pani
	2. *Julio Zárate*	*Alejandro Vázquez Mercado*
	3. Diego Pérez Ortigosa	Mateo Guerrero
	4. *Jesús Aréchiga*	*Alejandro Vázquez Mercado*
Baja California	1. Antonio Gómez	Rodolfo Gilbert
Campeche	1. José Gómez	José Trinidad Ferrer
	2. Fernando Duret	Luis Miranda e Iturbe
Chiapas	1. Martín Morales	Eduardo Esparza
	2. Jesús Oliver	Emilio Pimentel
	3. Román Pino	Bernardo M. Vaca
	4. Manuel Ortega Reyes	Jesús A. Velasco
	5. *Manuel Carrascosa*	*José J. Rivas*
Chihuahua	1. Ignacio Gómez del Campo	Emigdio Rodríguez
	2. Ramón Guerrero	Antonio Mena
	3. *Jesús E. Valenzuela*	Manuel Gutiérrez Nájera
	4. *Marcelo León*	*Porfirio Parra*
Coahuila	1. Antonio Ramos Cadena	
	2. Arnulfo García	Ignacio García Lozano
Colima	1. Manuel Cortés	Francisco C. Palmira
	2. Ignacio Alcalá	Severo Campero
Distrito Federal	1. José Simeón Orteaga	Mauro F. Arteaga
	2. Eugenio Barreiro	Ignacio Bejarano
	3. Francisco Rincón	Manuel Rincón

	4. Gregorio Ruiz	*Ireneo Paz*
	5. Enrique Mackintosh	Enrique Landa
	6. *Roberto Núñez*	Carlos López
	7. *Pedro Rincón Gallardo*	Juan Pérez de León
	8. *Guillermo Prieto*	Hermenegildo Dávila
	9. José Mena	Francisco Vázquez
	10. Hilario S. Gabilondo	Rafael G. Martínez
Durango	1. Alberto Sante Fe	Francisco Flores
	2. Rafael Salcido	Manuel Valenzuela
	3. Francisco Escobar y V.	Faustino Michel
	4. Ignacio Michel	Julio H. González
Guanajuato	1. *Sóstenes Rocha*	Francisco C. Troncoso
	2. Mariano Robles	Antonio Gutiérrez
	3. Jacinto García	Manuel Anaya
	4. *José María Lozano*	Pedro Collantes y Buenrostro
	5. Alberto Malo	Nicolás del Moral
	6. Diego de A. Berea	Francisco Paul
	7. Pablo Chávez	Andrés Treviño
	8. Francisco Cosmes	Mariano Leal
	9. Vicente A. Fernández	Manuel Rincón Gallardo
	10. Nicolás Tuñón Cañedo	Joaquín Robles Rocha
	11. Jesús Morales	Emiliano Bustos
	12. Luis Olivo	José Guadalupe Lobato
	13. Manuel García Ramírez	Juan Argumedo
	14. Rafael Pérez Gallardo	Miguel José Malo
	15. Antonio Vázquez	Manuel M. Abasola
	16. Francisco Soní	Francisco López Gutiérrez
	17. Francisco Araujo	Manuel Espinosa
	18. José Manuel Jaúregui	Manuel Rubio
Guerrero	1. Sixto Moncada	José E. Celada
	2. Manuel Guillén	Amado Berdeja
	3. *Alberto García Granados*	Mariano Ortiz de Montellano
	4. José Epigmenio Pineda	Cirilo R. Heredia
	5. Julio T. Alvarez	José María Arce
	6. Julián Deloya	Juan Hidalgo
	7. Juan Pablo de los Ríos	José Ramón Tamayo
	8. Juan Gutiérrez	Carlos Ferrer y Crespo
Hidalgo	1. Carmen de Ita	Manuel Garrido
	2. Luis Rivas Góngora	Juan Rivas Mercado
	3. *Gabriel Mancera*	Francisco Portilla
	4. Agustín Ruiz Olloqui	José María Delgado
	5. José M. Prieto	Francisco Olvera
	6. Juan José Baz	Francisco Treviño Canales
	7. *Francisco Romero*	Manuel Inda
	8. *Juan A. Mateos*	Rafael David
	9. *Pedro Rodríguez*	Manuel Mirus
	10. *Juan Castelló*	Nabor Chávez
	11. Emilio Islas	Gabriel Islas
Jalisco	1. Francisco Sepúlveda	Clemente Muñoz
	2. Mariano Coronado	Jesús Flores

State	Deputy	Alternate
	3. Francisco Besares	Carlos Villegas
	4. Javier Torres Adalid	José Torres Rivas
	5. José María Vigil	Daniel Palacios
	6. Antonio Z. Balandrano	Ventura Gómez Alatorre
	7. *Luis Pombo*	Apolonio Casillas
	8. Joaquín Castaños	Antonio Riba y Echeverría
	9. Manuel García Granados	Francisco José Závala
	10. Julio Arancivia	Cipriano Covarrubias
	11. *Rosendo Márquez*	Florencio Riestra
	12. Guillermo Rivera y Río	Jacobo Carrera
	13. *Martín González*	Antonio Gil Ochoa
	14. Justiniano Figueroa	Ignacio L. Montenegro
	15. Víctor Pérez	Francisco de P. Méndez
	16. Nicolás Tortolero	Luis García de Quevedo
	17. Enrique Omaña	Apolonio Pinzón
	18. Ramón Corral	Mariano Ruiz
México	1. Jesús Fuentes y Muñiz	Ricardo M. Campos
	2. Manuel Sánchez Facio	Roberto Santaella
	3. Eduardo L. Gallo	Luis Argandar
	4. Joaquín R. Verástegui	Rufino Gaxiola
	5. Pedro Azcué	Francisco Mejía
	6. Jesús Ayala	Felipe Quiñones
	7. Mariano Zúñiga	Jacobo Carrera y García
	8. Miguel Güinchard	Francisco Azpe
	9. Eduardo Franco	José S. Encisco
	10. Francisco Gochicoa	Jacinto Aguado y Barón
	11. Florencio Flores	José Gordillo
	12. Gumesindo Enríquez	Manuel Valenzuela
	13. Ramón Riveroll	Joaquín Zendejas
	14. Eduardo Viñas	Joaquín Trejo
	15. Manuel Ticó	*Benito Juárez Maza*
	16. Pascual Cejudo	Juan de Dios Arias
Michoacán	1. Miguel Mesa	Luis Valdés
	2. Manuel Orellana y N.	Wenceslao Rubio
	3. Pedro Eiquihua	Felipe López Romano
	4. J. Vicente Villada	Germán Contreras
	5. Juan B. Acosta	Trinidad G. de la Vega
	6. Juan B. de la Torre	Ignacio Juárez Sosa
	7. José del Villar	Felipe Rivera
	8. *Aristeo Mercado*	Maximiano Rocha
	9. Antonio Traslosheros	Ramón Sánchez
	10. Agustín Rivera y Río	Francisco A. Lerdo
	11. Néstor López	Demetrio Méndez
	12. Manuel Urquiza	Victoriano Pérez
	13. Serapión Fernández	Vincente Moreno
	14. Andrés Zenteno	José Dolores del Río
	15. *Manuel A. Mercado*	Francisco Villanueva
Morelos	1. Luis Flores	Juan Ocampo
	2. Jesús H. Preciado	Juan N. Govantes

	3. *Delfín Sánchez*	*Apolinar Castillo Ramírez*
	4. *Francisco Bulnes*	*Antonio Tovar*
Nuevo León	1. *Emetrio de la Garza*	Ricardo M. Cuéllar
	2. Antonio A. Elizondo	Julio Olvera
	3. Juan de Dios Treviño	Jesús Antonio Echavarría
	4. Joaquín Peña	Emilio Cárdenas
Oaxaca	1. Luis Pérez	*Manuel Dublán*
	2. Manuel E. Goytia	Manuel Castilla Portugal
	3. *Martín González*	*José Yves Limantour*
	4. José María Castellano	José Toro
	5. Félix Romero	Manuel Díaz Ordaz
	6. *Albino Zertuche*	Luis García Luna
	7. Carlos Alvarez	Ignacio Alvarez
	8. Ignacio Vázquez	Enrique Neve
	9. *Agustín Pradillo*	Esteban Cházari
	10. Francisco Pérez	Nicolás López Garrido
	11. Amado Banuet	Leopoldo Rincón
	12. Pascual Fenochio	Juan Fenochio
	13. *Emilio Pimentel*	*Salvador Díaz Mirón*
	14. Manuel José Toro	*Miguel Castellanos Sánchez*
	15. Manuel Ramírez Varela	Rafael Chousal
	16. *Rosendo Pineda*	Cenobio López
Puebla	1. *Agustín Pradillo*	Miguel Blanco
	2. Francisco Ibarra Ramos	José M. Cantú
	3. Vidal Escamilla	Atenógenes Carrasco
	4. Vincente Moreno	Lauro Luno
	5. Francisco González	Aurelio Madrid
	6. Manuel Santibáñez	Víctor Méndez
	7. Ignacio Torres Adalid	José Torres Adalid
	8. Apolonio Angulo	Cástulo Vera
	9. Pedro J. García	José Gordillo e Irazábal
	10. Telésforo Barroso	Juan Fenochio
	11. Antonio G. Esperón	Miguel Guerrero
	12. Manuel Romero Ancona	Miguel Serrano
	13. Joaquín de la Barreda	Manuel Galindo
	14. Enrique Mont	Wenceslao Mont
	15. Manuel Bueno	Jesús García
	16. Ramón Riveroll y Cinta	Antonio Gamboa
	17. Emilio L. Carsi	Francisco García
	18. Miguel R. Méndez	Miguel Salas
	19. Diego de la Peña	Manuel E. Ayala
	20. Manuel Márquez Galindo	Gonzalo Esteva
Querétaro	1. Luis M. Rubio	Manuel Garrido
	2. Rafael Chousal	José M. Echeverría
	3. José María Romero	José Encisa
San Luis Potosí	1. Francisco Bermúdez	Jesús Villalobos
	2. Angel Carpio	Eduardo Panha
	3. Manuel Muro	Bruno E. García

State	Deputy	Alternate
	4. Silvestre López Portillo	Rafael Manrique
	5. Ramón Fernández	Agustín R. Ortiz
	6. Francisco Bustamante	Darío Reyes
	7. Ignacio López Portillo	Rafael Díez Gutiérrez
	8. Alberto López Hermosa	José Verástegui
	9. *Bernardo Reyes*	Antonio Rivas Mercado
	10. *Justino Fernández*	Adolfo Flores
	11. Manuel Orellana	Alberto Palacios
	12. Lorenzo Ceballa	Jesús Martel
Sinaloa	1. *Justo Sierra*	*Eustaquio Buelna*
	2. Marcos Carrillo	Manuel Thomas Terán
	3. Julio Espinosa	Florencio Vega
	4. Francisco Barroso	Juan B. Rojo
Sonora	1. Saturnino Ayón	Javier Fernández
	2. *Angel Ortiz Monasterio*	Javier Torres Rivas
	3. Leonardo Fortuno	Ricardo Egea
Tabasco	1. *Manuel Sánchez Mármol*	Manuel Zapata Vera
	2. José Patricio Nicoli	Mariano Pedrero
Taumaulipas	1. Juan Guerrero	Francisco Fuentes Farías
	2. Domingo López de Lara	Francisco L. de Saldaña
	3. Casimiro Castro	Demetrio Salazar
Tlaxcala	1. Mariano Muñoz de Cota	Mariano Grajales Murphy
	2. Teodoro Rivera	Juan Zayas
	3. Joaquín Salazar y Murphy	Agustín Picazo Cuevas
Veracruz	1. Julián F. Herrera	Enrique Llorente
	2. Fernando Andrade Párraga	Enrique Llorente
	3. Mauro S. Herrera	Efrén M. Reina
	4. Ramón Rodríguez Rivera	Francisco B. Barrientos
	5. Romualdo Pasquel	Gustavo Esteva
	6. José González Pérez	J. Camarillo
	7. Emeterio Ruiz	Juan Argüelles
	8. *Ignacio Pombo*	Amado Talavera
	9. *Teodoro Dehesa*	Pedro Landero
	10. Donaciano Lara	*Salvador Díaz Mirón*
	11. Agustín Cerdán	Antonio Rodríguez Guerra
Yucatán	1. Waldemaro G. Cantón	Ricardo Ituarte
	2. Vicente Herrera	Antonio Peralta
	3. Francisco Ogarrio	Manuel Gutiérrez
	4. Juan A. Esquivel	Eduardo Bermúdez
	5. *Francisco Cantón*	Fernando Peraza
	6. Antonio Cisneros	Estanislao Velasco
	7. Arturo Shields	Cirilo Gutiérrez
	8. Tomás Salazar	Francisco Prida y Arteaga
Zacatecas	1. Francisco Acosta	Francisco Calderón
	2. José Barrera	Pedro Belaunzarán

3.	Ramón Bolaños	Juan Bolaños
4.	Miguel Canales	Jesús Canales
5.	*Manuel González Cosío*	Fernando San Salvador
6.	*Rosendo Márquez*	Ricardo Moreno
7.	*Simón Sarlat*	Faustino Michel
8.	Manuel G. Solana	Manuel S. Caballero
9.	Lauro Cavazos	Hilarión Frías y Soto
10.	Carlos Argais	Mariano Ledesma

1886–88 (13th Legislature)

State	Deputy	Alternate
Aguascalientes	1. *Alejandro Vázquez Mercado*	Ignacio M. Marín
	2. Miguel Güinchard	Rafael Sagredo
	3. Agapito Silva	Alberto M. Dávalos
	4. Diego Ortigoza	Mateo Guererro
Baja California	1. Antonio Gómez	Rodolfo F. Nieto
Campeche	1. Manuel T. Peniche	Nicolás Urcelay
	2. *Román S. Lascuraín*	Luis Miranda e Iturbe
Chiapas	1. Martín Morales	Eduardo Esparza
	2. Jesús Oliver	Magín Llaven
	3. Román Pino	Bernardo M. Vaca
	4. *Manuel Ortega Reyes*	José A. Velasco
	5. *Manuel Carrascosa*	José J. Rivas
Chihuahua	1. Leopoldo Rincón	Antonio A. Mena
	2. Fernando Zetina	*Porfirio Parra*
	3. *Jesús E. Valenzuela*	Lauro Carrillo
	4. Manuel Rincón	Tito Arriola
Coahuila	1. Pedro Acuña	Luis Navarro
	2. Enrique Baz	Juan S. Galán
Colima	1. Manuel Cortés	*Enrique O. de Lamadrid*
	2. Francisco C. Palencia	*Miguel García Topete*
Distrito Federal	1. *Pedro Rincón Gallardo*	Miguel Sánchez Tagle
	2. Guillermo Prieto	*Emilio Rabasa*
	3. Francisco Rincón	Darío Vasconcelos
	4. C. Luis Labastida	Jesús Labastida
	5. *José Yves Limantour*	Enrique Landa
	6. *Roberto Núñez*	Ignacio Bejarano
	7. Antonio Carbajal	Ramón Guererro
	8. Tomás Reyes Retana	José Cuéllar
	9. *Trinidad García*	Ignacio Maldonado
	10. Alberto Terreros	Andrés Gutt
Durango	1. Alberto Sante Fe	Manuel Tebar
	2. Rafael Salcido	Manuel Valenzuela

State	Deputy	Alternate
	3. Francisco Escobar y V.	Juan Almazán
	4. Faustino Michel	Ignacio Michel
Guanajuato	1. Joaquín Chico	Julio Arancivia
	2. *Francisco de P. Casteneda*	Enrique Mont
	3. Ramón Alcázar	Enrique Omana
	4. *José María Lozano*	Saturnino Ayón
	5. *Angel Ortiz Monasterio*	
	6. Rafael Pérez Gallardo	Lauro Cavazos
	7. Mariano Robles	Javier Torres Rivas
	8. *Carlos Olaguíbel y Arista*	Vicente Mora
	9. Francisco G. Cosmes	José Barrera
	10. *Mariano Escobedo*	Agustín Morales
	11. Antonio Cisneros Cámara	Arturo Cisneros Cámara
	12. Luis Olivo	Antonio León Traslosheros
	13. *Emeterio de la Garza*	Juan de Argomedo
	14. Francisco Malo	Francisco García López
	15. Enrique Mackintosh	Juan B. Acosta
	16. Francisco García Morales	Ramón Riveroll y Cinta
	17. Diego A. Berea	Florencio Riestra
	18. Manuel García Ramírez	Sixto Moncada
Guerrero	1. Julio T. Alvarez	José M. Arce
	2. Manuel Guillén	Amado Berdeja
	3. *Marcelo León*	Ignacio Maldonado Morón
	4. Juan Gutiérrez	Carlos Ferrer y Crespo
	5. Mariano Ortiz	José R. Tamayo
	6. Juan Hidalgo	Eduardo Román
	7. Manuel I. Zamora	José E. Celada
	8. José Epigmenio Pineda	Cirilo R. Heredia
Hidalgo	1. Carmen de Ita	Manuel Garrido
	2. *José M. Gamboa*	José Márquez Muñoz
	3. *Gabriel Mancera*	Francisco Portilla
	4. Manuel Mirus	José M. Delgado
	5. *Juan B. Castelló*	Joaquín Ramírez
	6. *Julio Zárate*	Luis Rivas Góngora
	7. *Simón Cravioto*	Emilio Islas
	8. *Juan A. Mateos*	Rafael David
	9. *Pedro L. Rodríguez*	Gabriel Islas
	10. Juan José Baz	Manuel Gómez Parada
	11. Manuel Unda	Francisco Alfaro
Jalisco	1. Francisco Sepúlveda	Francisco Sáenz Moras
	2. Mariano Coronado	Pedro J. Olasagarre
	3. Estanislao Cañedo	Carlos Villegas
	4. Martín González	Antoni Gil Ochoa
	5. *Alfonso Lancaster Jones*	Daniel Palacios
	6. Darío Balandrano	Ventura Gómez Alatorre
	7. Apolonio Casillas	Ignacio Vallejo
	8. Antonio Riva y Echeverría	Ignacio L. Montenegro
	9. Eduardo Bermúdez	Francisco José Zavala
	10. *Apolinar Castillo Ramírez*	Cipriano M. Covarrubias

	11. *Francisco Romero*	Florencio Riestra
	12. *Pedro Landázuri*	Lorenzo García
	13. *Pedro A. Galván*	Juan Dablau
	14. Luis Medrano	Ignacio Viscarra
	15. Arnulfo García	Carlos Gómez Luna
	16. *Ireneo Paz*	Luis G. Quevedo
	17. *Ramón Rodríguez Rivera*	Apolonio Pinzón
	18. *Luis Pombo*	*Mariano Ruiz*
México	1. Jesús Fuentes y Muñiz	Ricardo Campos
	2. Juan Bribiesca	Maury González
	3. Cristóbal Chapital	Luis Argandar
	4. Manuel Ticó	*Benito Juárez Maza*
	5. Eduardo M. Franco	José E. Enciso
	6. *Agustín Arroyo de Anda*	Rufino Gaxiola
	7. Pedro de Azcué	Juan Uribe
	8. Florencio Flores	Pedro Sandoval
	9. Maríano Zúñiga	Augusto Rojas
	10. Diego de la Peña	Juan Dublán
	11. Pascual Cejudo	Juan D. Arias
	12. Ignacio G. Heras	Jesús Quirós
	13. Jesús Ayala	José T. Ferrer
	14. *Francisco de P. Gochicoa*	Carlos Mayorga
	15. *Gustavo Baz*	Ignacio Fernández Ortigosa
	16. José Rafael Alvarez	Joaquín Zendejas
Michoacán	1. Francisco de S. Menocal	Ignacio Ojeda Berdusco
	2. Juan de la Torre	Felipe Rivera
	3. Mariano Muñoz de Cote	Alfonso E. López
	4. Onofre Ramos	Vicente Maciel
	5. José María Romero	Eduardo Carrión
	6. *Manuel A. Mercado*	Rafael Herrera
	7. *Ricardo Hornedo*	Manuel M. Galindo
	8. *Rafael Reyes Spíndola*	Octavio Reyes Spíndola
	9. Carlos Argais	Alejandro Abarca
	10. José M. Arce	Darío Vasconcelos
	11. *Francisco Vélez*	Angel Carrión
	12. Néstor López	Francisco García
	13. Serapión Fernández	Agapito Silva
	14. *Aristeo Mercado*	Arturo Paz
	15. José A. Puebla	Macedonio Gómez
Morelos	1. *Francisco Bulnes*	Leopoldo Zamora
	2. *Gilberto Crespo*	Manuel Zapata Vera
	3. Manuel U. Preciado	Pedro Bustamante
	4. Antonio Tovar	Manuel Flores
Nuevo León	1. Pedro J. Morales	Eduardo García
	2. Manuel Serrano	Platón García Delgado
	3. Manuel Z. Doria	Francisco Martínez Salazar
	4. Carlos F. Ayala	Pedro Garza
Oaxaca	1. *Gregorio Chávez*	Juan N. Castellanos
	2. Manuel E. Goytia	Francisco García Alonso

State	Deputy	Alternate
	3. *Martín González*	Esteban Cházari
	4. *José María Castellanos*	José Toro
	5. *Antonio Ramos*	Federico Sandoval
	6. *Albino Zertuche*	Luis García Luna
	7. José Ignacio Alvarez	Juan Dublán
	8. Ignacio Vázquez	Carlos Alvarez
	9. *Agustín Pradillo*	Pedro García de León
	10. Francisco Pérez	Nicolás López Garrido
	11. Amado Banuet	Manuel Soto
	12. Pascual Fenochio	Juan Fenochio
	13. *Emilio Pimentel*	Alonzo Mariscal
	14. Francisco Iriarte	Rodolfo Sandoval
	15. Manuel Ramírez Varela	Eduardo García
	16. *Rosendo Pineda*	Gerardo Toledo
Puebla	1. José de J. López	Manuel Carsi
	2. *Agustín Pradillo*	Diódoro Batalla
	3. *Francisco Mejía*	Emilio Carsi
	4. Francisco Ibarra Ramos	Enrique Marañón
	5. Manuel Dargui	Rafael Serrano Aguirrezábal
	6. Manuel Santibáñez	Modesto R. Martínez
	7. *Miguel Serrano*	Enrique Sort
	8. *Mucio G. Martínez*	Jesús García
	9. Juan H. Revueltas	Atenógenes N. Carrasco
	10. Vidal Escamilla	Juan Fenochio
	11. Manuel Romero Ancona	Uriel Alatriste
	12. Telésforo Barrosa	José Gordillo Irazábal
	13. Joaquín de la Barreda	Manuel Galindo
	14. Wenceslao Rubio	Daniel Palacio
	15. Manuel Bueno	Mauro G. Rebollo
	16. Eulalio Núñez	Antonio Gamboa
	17. Antonio G. Esperón	Ramón Miranda
	18. Miguel R. Méndez	Cástulo Zenteño
	19. Luis Garfías	Abraham Sosa
	20. Manuel Márquez Galindo	Miguel A. Salazar
Querétaro	1. Fernando M. Rubio	José Izito
	2. Rafael Chauzal	Rafael García Martínez
	3. *Eulalio Vela*	Angel M. Padilla
	4. Angel M. Domínguez	José Vivanco
San Luis Potosí	1. Francisco Bermúdez	Jesús Villalobos
	2. Angel Carpio	Ramón de la Garza
	3. *Justino Fernández*	Filomeno Mata
	4. Manuel Orellana y N.	Alberto Palacios
	5. Ramón Fernández	Agustín R. Ortiz
	6. Francisco Bustamante	Darío Reyes
	7. Ignacio López Portillo	Rafael Díez Gutiérrez
	8. Alberto López Hermosa	José Verástegui
	9. *Bernardo Reyes*	Antonio Rivas Mercado
	10. *Justino Fernández*	Adolfo Flores
	11. Manuel Orellana	Alberto Palacios
	12. Lorenzo Ceballa	Jesús Martel

Sinaloa	1. *Justo Sierra*	*Eustaquio Buelna*
	2. Marcos Carrillo	Manuel Thomas Terán
	3. Julio Espinosa	Florencio Vega
	4. Francisco Barroso	Juan B. Rojo

Sonora	1. Saturnino Ayón	Javier Fernández
	2. *Angel Ortiz Monasterio*	Javier Torres Rivas
	3. Leonardo Fortuno	Ricardo Egea

| Tabasco | 1. *Manuel Sánchez Mármol* | Manuel Zapata Vera |
| | 2. José Patricio Nicoli | Mariano Pedrero |

Taumaulipas	1. Juan Guerrero	Francisco Fuentes Farías
	2. Domingo López de Lara	Francisco L. de Saldaña
	3. Casimiro Castro	Demetrio Salazar

Tepic	1.	
	2. *Antonio Pliego y Pérez*	Manuel Gutiérrez Nájera
	3. Enrique Mejía	Manuel Dublán y Maza

Tlaxcala	1. Mariano Muñoz de Cota	Mariano Grajales Murphy
	2. Teodoro Rivera	Juan Zayas
	3. Joaquín Salazar y Murphy	Agustín Picazo Cuevas

Veracruz	1. José M. Cuesta y Lagos	Joaquín G. Solana
	2. Julián F. Herrera	Efrén M. Reyna
	3. Enrique Llorente Rechu	Manuel García Méndez
	4. José M. Gómez	José Antonio Villegas
	5. Manuel S. Herrera	Angel Lucido Cambas
	6. Rafael Rodríguez Talavera	Manuel Levi
	7. José González Pérez	Gaudencio González Llave
	8. *Ignacio Pombo*	Lorenzo Fernández
	9. José Manuel Jáuregui	Manuel S. Vela
	10. Donaciano Lara	Domingo Bureau
	11.	

Yucatán	1. Waldemaro G. Cantón	Ricardo Ituarte
	2. Pedro Inclán	Antonio Peralta
	3. Ignacio Gómez del Campo	Manuel Gutiérrez
	4. Salvador Dondé	Eduardo Bermúdez
	5. Teodosio Canto	José Dolores Aranda Arceo
	6. Nicolás Tuñón Cañedo	Estanislao Velasco
	7. Cirilo F. Gutiérrez	Manuel M. Arredondo
	8. Demetrio Salazar	Ramón Prida

Zacatecas	1. Rafael Jiménez	Ramón Romero
	2. Agustín Cerdán	Pedro Belauzarán
	3. Francisco Acosta	Nazario Lomas
	4. Francisco Vázquez	Longinos M. Chávez
	5. *Manuel González Cosío*	Agustín Lozano
	6. Ramón Bolaños	Juan Bolanos
	7. Alonso Mariscal	Zeñón Ibarra
	8. Luis Torres	*Manuel Sierra Méndez*
	9. *Sóstenes Rocha*	Celedonio Mexía
	10. Ricardo Moreno	Jesús Valenzuela

1888–90 (14th Legislature)

State	Deputy	Alternate
Aguascalientes	1. Ricardo Egea	Diego Pérez Ortigosa
	2. Miguel Güinchard	Rafael Sagredo
	3. Agapito Silva	Mateo Guerrero
	4. Jesús Díaz de León	
Baja California	1. Antonio Gómez	Rodolfo F. Nieto
Campeche	1. Manuel T. Peniche	Nicolás Urcelay
	2. *Román S. Lascuráin*	Javier Santamaría
Chiapas	1. Martín Morales	Emilio G. Cantón
	2. Federico Méndez Rivas	Abel Rivera
	3. Román Pino	Emilio G. Baz
	4. Jesús Oliver	Magín Llaven
	5. Pedro Ancuña	Antonio Prado
Chihuahua	1. Leopoldo Rincón	*Porfirio Parra*
	2. Fernando Zetina	Ramón Guerrero
	3. *Jesús E. Valenzuela*	Pedro Bustamante
	4. Manuel Rincón	Roberto Santa María
Coahuila	1. *Ignacio Escudero*	Miguel Gómez
	2. Juan S. Galán	Frumencio Fuentes
Colima	1. Francisco C. Palencia	Severo Campo
	2. Jesús M. Cerda	Joaquín Pita
Distrito Federal	1. *Pedro Rincón Gallardo*	Ignacio Belarano
	2. *Guillermo Prieto*	*Emilio Rabasa*
	3. Francisco Rincón	Alonso Rodríguez Miramón
	4. C. Luis Labastida	Jesús Labastida
	5. *José Yves Limantour*	*Emilio Pardo*
	6. *Roberto Núñez*	Joaquín Salazar y Murphy
	7. *José María Gamboa*	Guillermo Pérez
	8. Tomás Reyes Retana	Hilarión Frías y Soto
	9. *Trinidad García*	Ignacio Maldonado
	10. *Agustín Arroyo de Anda*	Gabriel María Islas
Durango	1. Alberto Sante Fe	Emilio Islas
	2. Rafael Salcido	Emilio G. Saravia
	3. Juan Gutiérrez	Miguel Amador
	4. Faustino Michel	Ignacio Michel
Guanajuato	1. Rafael Pérez Gallardo	Lauro Cavazos
	2. Maríano Robles	Javier Torres Rivas
	3. *Mariano Escobedo*	Julio Arancivia
	4. *Carlos de Olaguíbel y A.*	Vicente Moreno
	5. Ramón Alcázar	Enrique Omana
	6. Enrique Mackintosh	Francisco Urueta
	7. Francisco G. Cosmes	José Barrera

	8. *Francisco de P. Castañeda*	Francisco García Morales
	9. Luis Olivo	José Cantú
	10. Joaquín Chico	Diego de A. Berea
	11. Manuel García Ramírez	Sixto Moncada
	12. Alberto Malo	Antonio Cisneros Cámara
	13. Emilio Baz	Eduardo J. Velázquez
	14. Enrique Mont	Francisco Ruiz
	15. Francisco García López	Tomás Chávez
	16. *Angel Ortiz Monasterio*	Manuel Reyes
	17. Domingo López de Lara	Antonio León Traslosheros
	18. José Patricio Nicoli	Ignacio L. Montenegro
Guerrero	1. Julio J. Alvarez	Jose M. Arce
	2. Manuel Guillén	Emilio Islas
	3. *Marcelo León*	Ignacio Maldonado Morón
	4. Mariano Ortiz de M.	Francisco Cortés
	5. Eutimio Cervantes	Manuel Roa
	6. Francisco Escobar y V.	Pedro Ramírez
	7. Alberto Lombardo	Ignacio D. Salas
	8. José T. Gómez	Alejandro Argandar
Hidalgo	1. Manuel Gómez Parada	Jesús Rodríguez
	2. Ramón F. Riveroll	Luis Rivas Góngora
	3. *Gabriel Mancera*	Miguel M. Ansúrez
	4. Manuel Inda	Francisco Portilla
	5. Enrique Sort	Silviano Riquelme
	6. Manuel Mirus	Francisco Alfaro
	7. *Simón Cravioto*	Hilarión Frías y Soto
	8. *Julio Zárate*	Vicente Luengas
	9. *Pedro L. Rodríguez*	Gabriel Islas
	10. Carmen de Ita	Emilio Islas
	11. *Juan A. Mateos*	Manuel Garrido
Jalisco	1. Francisco Sepúlveda	Francisco Martínez Gallardo
	2. Mariano Coronado	José M. Gómez
	3. Salvador Cañedo	*José López Portillo*
	4. *Martín González*	Nicolás España
	5. Francisco Rincón Gallardo	Daniel Palacios
	6. *Eduardo Rincón Gallardo*	Carlos Villegas
	7. *Gustavo Baz*	Luis Chousal
	8. Antonio Riva y Echeverría	Ignacio L. Montenegro
	9. *Rosalino Martínez*	Francisco Sáinz Meraz
	10. *Luis C. Curiel*	Prisciliano Benítez
	11. *Francisco Romero*	Florencio Riestra
	12. *Pedro Landázuri*	Pedro García
	13. *Pedro A. Galván*	Juan Dublán
	14. Luis Medrano	Luis Vizcarra
	15. Arnulfo García	Carlos Gómez Luna
	16. *Ireneo Paz*	Eduardo Medina
	17. *Ramón Rodríguez Rivera*	Miguel Gómez
	18. *Luis Pombo*	*Mariano Ruiz*
México	1. Jesús Fuentes y Muñiz	Eugenio Zubieta
	2. Juan Bribiesca	Diego María Ortigoza

State	Deputy	Alternate
	3. Ignacio García Heras	Pedro Sandoval
	4. Manuel Ticó	*Benito Juárez Maza*
	5. Eduardo M. Franco	Manuel Garibay
	6. Diego de la Peña	Alfonso L. Velasco
	7. Alberto Terreros	Rufino Gaxiola
	8. Florencio Flores	Manuel F. Soto
	9. Pedro Azcué	Pedro Escudero y Pérez G.
	10. *Ramón Gómez Villavicencio*	Fernando Cantón y Fresas
	11. Eduardo Bermúdez	Joaquín Cendejas
	12. Mariano Zúñiga	Augusto Rojas
	13. Jesús Ayala	Francisco Cortés
	14. *Francisco de P. Goicochea*	Antonio Prado
	15. *Manuel Gutiérrez Nájera*	Luis Argandar
	16. José Rafael Alvarez	Manuel Flores
Michoacán	1. Francisco de S. Menocal	Antonio Pérez Gil
	2. Juan de la Torre	Felipe Rivera
	3. *Francisco A. Vélez*	*Félix M. Alcérreca*
	4. *Angel M. Padilla*	Octavio Reyes Spíndola
	5. José María Arce	Darío Vasconcelos
	6. *Rafael Reyes Spíndola*	Arturo Paz
	7. Emilio Ruiz	Antonio Prado
	8. José M. Romero	Alberto Bianchi
	9. Onofre Ramos	Luis Chousal
	10. *Manuel A. Mercado*	Rafael Herrera
	11. Ricardo Hornedo	Manuel M. Galindo
	12. Serapión Fernández	Agapito Silva
	13. José Antonio Puebla	Melchor Ocampo Manso
	14. *Aristeo Mercado*	Luis Escandón
	15. Rafael Rodríguez Talavera	Ricardo B. Suárez
Morelos	1. *Francisco Bulnes*	Leopoldo Zamora
	2. *Gilberto Crespo*	Manuel Zapata Vera
	3. Manuel U. Preciado	Pedro Bustamante
	4. *Antonio Tovar*	José Cazarín
Nuevo León	1. Pedro J. Morales	Antonio García Garza
	2. Manuel Serrano	Platón García Delgado
	3. Manuel Z. Doria	Francisco Martínez Salazar
	4. Carlos J. Ayala	Francisco E. Reyes
Oaxaca	1. *Gregorio Chávez*	Juan N. Castellanos
	2. Francisco Uriarte	Rodolfo Sandoval
	3. *Martín González*	Esteban Cházari
	4. José María Castellanos	José Toro
	5. Amado Banuet	Manuel Soto
	6. *Albino Zertuche*	Luis García Luna
	7. *Emilio Pimentel*	Juan Fenochio
	8. Ignacio Vázquez	Carlos Alvarez
	9. *Agustín Pradillo*	Manuel Gómez
	10. Francisco Pérez	Nicolás López Garrido
	11. Manuel Ramírez Varela	Miguel F. González

	12. Pascual Fenochio	Juan Meixueiro
	13. José Ignacio Alvarez	Joaquín María Ruiz
	14. *Juan de Dios Peza*	Juan Muñoz Cano
	15. Manuel E. Goytia	Crisóforo Canseco
	16. *Rosendo Pineda*	Pío Ortega
Puebla	1. José de J. López	Manuel Carsi
	2. *Agustín Pradillo*	Juan B. Acosta
	3. Francisco Pocheros	Joaquín Pita
	4. Manuel Santibáñez	Modesto R. Martínez
	5. Moisés Rojas	Manuel Emiliano Ayala
	6. Vital Escamilla	Juan Fenochio
	7. *Miguel Serrano*	Juan de Dios Almazán
	8. *Mucio G. Martínez*	Jesús García
	9. Miguel de la Peña	Uriel Alatriste
	10. Telésforo Barroso	Manuel Valenzuela
	11. *Sóstenes Rocha*	Eduardo Velasco
	12. Joaquín de la Barreda	Miguel Galindo y Galindo
	13. Manuel Bueno	Mauro G. Rebollo
	14. Manuel Darqui	Daniel Palacios
	15. Eulalio Núñez	Antonio Gamboa
	16. Antonio G. Esperón	Agustín Romero
	17. *Francisco Mejía*	José María Cuevas
	18. Antonio Méndez	Vicente Llamas
	19. Luis Garfías	Abraham Sosa
	20. Manuel Márquez Galindo	Manuel Cerón
Querétaro	1. Rafael Chousal	Rafael García Martínez
	2. Leónardo F. Fortuño	Lorenzo Gorostiaga
	3. Carlos Argaiz	Agustín R. Olloqui
	4. Fernando María Rubio	Ignacio Martínez Uribe
San Luis Potosí	1. *Justino Fernández*	Alejandro Garrido
	2. Manuel Orellana Nogueras	Alberto Palaciosa
	3. Angel Carpio	Lorenzo García
	4. José María Prieto Garza	Gabriel Durán
	5. *Eduardo Dublán*	Jesús Villalobos
	6. Miguel Lebrija	*Pablo Verástegui*
	7. *Blas Escontría*	Agustín R. Ortíz
	8. Jesús Martel	Jesús R. España
	9. Francisco Bustamante	Vicente Morales
	10. Vacant	
	11. Manuel Muró	Marcos Vives
	12. Lorenzo Ceballos	Rómulo E. Vidales
Sinaloa	1. *Justo Sierra*	Ignacio Bejarano
	2. Marcos Carrillo	Manuel Thomas Terán
	3. Jesús F. Uriarte	Celso Gaxiola
	4. Francisco D. Barroso	Manuel Sierra Méndez
Sonora	1. Angel M. Domínguez	Lucas Arvisu
	2. *Rafael Izábal*	Gabriel Monteverde
	3. Darío Balandrano	Eugenio L. Fuentes

State	Deputy	Alternate
Tabasco	1. *Joaquín D. Casasús*	Manuel Zapata Vera
	2. *Abraham Bandala*	Luis Flores
Tamaulipas	1. Manuel de León	Teófilo Ramírez
	2. Ismael Rodríguez	Guillermo Obregón
	3. *Juan B. Castelló*	Gregorio Cortina Basadre
Tepic (Nayarit)	1. Guadalupe López	Francisco Rivas Gómez
	2. *Antonio Pliego y Pérez*	*Manuel Sierra Méndez*
	3. Enrique Mexía	*Benito Juárez Maza*
Tlaxcala	1. Teodoro Rivera	Anastacio Pérez
	2. Manuel Andrade	Ignacio Cerón
	3. Pablo Ochoa	Amado García
Veracruz	1. José Manuel Jáuregui	Manuel García Méndez
	2. Enrique Llorente Rocha	Manuel García Méndez
	3. *Ismael Salas*	Angel Lúcido Cambas
	4. Agustín Cerdán	José Antonio Villegas
	5. Donaciano Lara	Domingo Bureau
	6. Mauro S. Herrera	Modesto L. Herrera
	7. *Ignacio Pombo*	Lorenzo Fernández
	8. José González Pérez	Gaudencio González Llave
	9. Manuel S. Vila	José María Melgar
	10. Manuel Levi	Juan Cházaro Soler
	11. José María Cuesta	Lorenzo K. Ferrer
Yucatán	1. Waldemaro G. Cantón	Pedro Ordóñez
	2. Pedro Laclau	Felipe Rosas
	3. Ignacio Gómez del Campo	José González de González
	4. Salvador Dondé	Gabriel María Islas
	5. Teodosio Canto	José Dolores Aranda Arceo
	6. Nicolás Tuñón Cañedo	Estanislao Velasco
	7. Cirilo F. Gutiérrez	José R. Mena
	8. Demetrio Salazar	Ramón Prida
Zacatecas	1. Alonso Mariscal	Fernando Vega
	2. Vacant	
	3. Francisco Acosta	Nazario Lomas
	4. Francisco Vázquez	Manuel M. Salcedo
	5. Agustín Lozano	Juan Bolaños
	6. Bernabé Loyola	Manuel Plowes Valero
	7. Eugenio Barreiro	Manuel Valenzuela
	8. Rafael Jiménez	Fausto Moguel
	9. *Alfredo Chavero*	Pedro Belanzarán
	10. Wenceslao Rubio	*Manuel Sierra Méndez*

1890–92 (15th Legislature)

State	Deputy	Alternate
Aguascalientes	1. Ricardo Egea	Jesús Fructuoso López
	2. Miguel Güinchard	Rafael Sagredo

	3. Agapito Silva	Ignacio Marín
	4. Diego Pérez Ortigoza	Nicolás López Garrido
Baja California	1. Antonio Gómez	Rodolfo F. Nieto
Campeche	1. Manuel T. Peniche	Eduardo Castillo Llavalle
	2. *Román S. Lascuráin*	Javier Santa María
Chiapas	1. *Miguel Utrilla*	Martín Morales
	2. Federico Méndez Rivas	José Mora
	3. Román Pino	Ermilo G. Cantón
	4. Jesús Oliver	Magín Llaven
	5. Pedro Acuña	Joaquín Paino
Chihuahua	1. Ignacio de la Torre y M.	Leopoldo Rincón
	2. Fernando Zetina	Ramón Guerrero
	3. *Jesús E. Valenzuela*	Pedro Bustamante
	4. Manuel Flores	Roberto Santa María
Coahuila	1. Alejandro Elguezábal	Miguel Gómez y Cárdenas
	2. Daniel García	Frumencio Fuentes
Colima	1. *Ignacio M. Escudero*	Ernesto Ritter
	2. Francisco C. Palencia	Severo Campero
Distrito Federal	1. *Pedro Rincón Gallardo*	Ignacio Bejarano
	2. *Guillermo Prieto*	Gabriel Islas
	3. Francisco Rincón	*Emilio Rabasa*
	4. C. Luis Labastida	Jesús Labastida
	5. *José Yves Limantour*	*Emilio Pardo*
	6. *Roberto Núñez*	Joaquín Salazar y Murphy
	7. *José María Gamboa*	Guillermo Pérez
	8. Tomás Reyes Retana	Hilarión Frías y Soto
	9. *Trinidad García*	Ignacio Maldonado
	10. *Agustín Arroyo de Anda*	Manuel Olivera y Toro
Durango	1. Alberto Sante Fe	Emilio Islas
	2. Rafael Salcido	Emilio G. Saravia
	3. Juan Gutiérrez	Miguel Amador
	4. Faustino Michel	Ignacio Michel
Guanajuato	1. *Mariano Escobedo*	Julián Arancivia
	2. Ramón Alcázar	Enrique Omana
	3. Enrique Mackintosh	Trinidad Ortega
	4. Rafael Pérez Gallardo	Lauro Cabazos
	5. Fernando González	Antonio Rivas Mercado
	6. Francisco G. Cosmes	José Barrera
	7. Luis Olivo	José Cantú
	8. *Carlos de Olaguíbel y A.*	Vicente Moreno
	9. Manuel García Ramírez	Sixto Moncada
	10. Joaquín Chico	Diego de A. Berea
	11. Alberto Malo	Eduardo J. Velázquez
	12. Emilio Baz	Carlos García
	13. Enrique Mont	Francisco Ruiz

State	Deputy	Alternate
	14. Francisco García López	Lorenzo García
	15. *Angel Ortiz Monasterio*	Carlos Díaz Infante
	16. Domingo López de Lara	Antonio León Traslosheros
	17. José Patricio Nicoli	Ignacio L. Montenegro
	18. Ignacio Ibargüengoitia	Antonio Cisneros Cámara
Guerrero	1. Vicente Sánchez	José M. Arce
	2. Manuel Guillén	Emilio Islas
	3. *Marcelo León*	Ignacio Maldonado Morón
	4. Mariano Ortiz de M.	Francisco Cortés
	5. Eutimio Cervantes	Jesús Barrera
	6. *Buenaventura Anaya*	Emilio E. García
	7. Alberto Lombardo	Pedro Ramírez
	8. José J. Gómez	Rafael Nájera
Hidalgo	1. Francisco Espinosa	Manuel Gómez Parada
	2. Ramón María Riveroll	Ramón F. Riveroll y C.
	3. *Gabriel Mancera*	Manuel Fernández Soto
	4. *Emilio Pardo, Jr.*	Manuel Garrido
	5. Enrique Sort	Rafael Casco
	6. Manuel Mirus	Alberto Sánchez
	7. *Simón Cravioto*	Hilarión Frías y Soto
	8. Ismael Islas	Vicente Luengas
	9. *Pedro L. Rodríguez*	Rafael García Martínez
	10. Carmen de Ita	Emilio Islas
	11. *Juan A. Mateos*	Jesús Rodríguez
Jalisco	1. Francisco Sepúlveda	Francisco Martínez Gallardo
	2. Mariano Coronado	José M. Gómez
	3. *Luis Pérez Verdía*	Joaquín Silva
	4. Antonio Riva y Echeverría	Luis Vizcarra
	5. Francisco Rincón Gallardo	Daniel Palacios
	6. Joaquín Escoto	Carlos Villegas
	7. Luis Chausal	Juan R. Zavala
	8. Martín González	Nicolás España
	9. *Rosalino Martínez*	Manuel Carsi
	10. *Luis C. Curiel*	Prisciliano Benítez
	11. *Francisco Romero*	Florencio Riestra
	12. *Pedro Landázuri*	Luis Velasco Ruz
	13. Juan Dublán	*José López Portillo y R.*
	14. Manuel M. Seoane	Ignacio L. Montenegro
	15. Arnulfo García	Ponciano Guzmán
	16. *Ireneo Paz*	Antonio Arias
	17. Miguel Zagaceta	José G. González
	18. *Luis Pombo*	Manuel M. Tortolero
México	1. Jesús Fuentes y Muñiz	Joaquín Salazar y Murphy
	2. Juan Bribiesca	Francisco Bezarez
	3. Ignacio García Heras	Eugenio Zubieta
	4. Ignacio de la Torre y M.	Guillermo Pérez Valenzuela
	5. Manuel Ticó	Manuel Garibay
	6. Diego de la Peña	Alfonso L. Velasco
	7. Alberto Terreros	Ricardo Domínguez

	8. Florencio Flores	Jacobo Mercado
	9. Pedro Azcué	Narciso Zermeño
	10. *Ramón Gómez Villavicencio*	Agustín Lascano
	11. Julián Montiel	Joaquín Zendejas
	12. Enrique Mexía	Augusto Rojas
	13. Jesús Ayala	Pedro Sandoval y Gual
	14. *Francisco de P. Goicochea*	Guillermo Valleto
	15. *Manuel Gutiérrez Nájera*	Luis Aragandar
	16. Macedonio Gómez	José Rafael Alvarez
Michoacán	1. Francisco S. Menocal	Nicolás Menocal
	2. Juan de la Torre	Felipe Rivera
	3. *Francisco A. Vélez*	*Francisco Vélez, Jr.*
	4. *Angel M. Padilla*	Octavio Reyes Spíndola
	5. Enrique Landa	Darío Vasconcelos
	6. *Rafael Reyes Spíndola*	Arturo Paz
	7. Emilio Ruiz	
	8. José María Romero	Diego Díaz Barriga
	9. *Aristeo A. Mercado*	Melchor Ocampo Manzo
	10. *Manuel A. Mercado*	Rafael Herrera
	11. *Ricardo Hornedo*	Manuel M. Galindo
	12. Onofre Ramos	Ignacio Moreno
	13. Gonzalo A. Esteva	Francisco C. García
	14. Serapión Fernández	Víctoriano Pérez
	15. Rafael Rodríguez Talavera	Andrés Iturbide
Morelos	1. *Francisco Bulnes*	Manuel Ríos y Peña
	2. *Gilberto Crespo*	José Cazarín
	3. Manuel V. Preciado	Felipe Salazar
	4. *Antonio Tovar*	Ramón Quiroz
Nuevo León	1. *Francisco M. Ramírez*	Jesús M. Cerdán
	2. Manuel Serrano	Espiridión Benavides
	3. Manuel T. Doria	Encarnación Coronado
	4. Carlos F. Ayala	Manuel Morales Treviño
Oaxaca	1. Francisco Uriarte	Esteban Cházari
	2. Juan N. Castellanos	Crisóforo Canseco
	3. *Martín González*	Juan Prieto
	4. José María Castellanos	José Toro
	5. Amado Banuet	Jesús Acebedo
	6. Luis García Luna	Enrique Pérez Rubio
	7. *Emilio Pimentel*	Manuel Martínez Gracida
	8. Ignacio Vázquez	
	9. *Agustín Pradillo*	Rafael Casco
	10. Pascual Fenochio	Andrés Portillo
	11. Manuel Ramírez Varela	Fausto Moguel
	12. *Benito Juárez Maza*	Manuel H. San Juan
	13. José Ignacio Alvarez	Gildardo Gómez
	14. Manuel Ricardo Rincón	Francisco Hernández
	15. Manuel E. Goytia	Francisco Rincón y Pérez
	16. *Rosendo Pineda*	Juan Ogarrio
Puebla	1. José de J. López	Francisco Sáenz Meraz
	2. *Agustín Pradillo*	Juan B. Acosta

State	Deputy	Alternate
	3. Francisco Poseros	Ignacio L. Cortez
	4. Manuel Santibáñez	Fidel Régules
	5. Moisés Rojas	Modesto R. Martínez
	6. Vidal Escamilla	Mauro G. Rebollo
	7. *Miguel Serrano*	Eduardo Arrioja
	8. *Mucio P. Martínez*	Jesús García
	9. *Miguel de la Peña*	Uriel Alatriste
	10. Telésforo Barroso	Manuel Valenzuela
	11. *Sóstenes Rocha*	Eduardo Velásquez
	12. Joaquín de la Barreda	José L. Alvarez
	13. Manuel Bueno	Juan D. Almazán
	14. Manuel Darqui	Juan Hernández
	15. Eulalio Núñez	Antonio Gamboa
	16. Antonio G. Esperón	José de Jesús Rabago
	17. *Francisco Mejía*	Agustín Romero
	18. Víctor Méndez	Vicente Llamas
	19. Luis Garfías	Abraham Sosa
	20. Manuel Márquez Galindo	Apolonio Casillas
Querétaro	1. Rafael Chousal	Lorenzo Gorostiaga
	2. Leónardo F. Fortuño	Rafael García Martínez
	3. Carlos Argaiz	Agustín R. Olloqui
	4. Fernando María Rubio	Ignacio Martínez Uribe
San Luis Potosí	1. *Justino Fernández*	Alejandro Garrido
	2. Manuel Orellana Nogueras	Alberto Palacios
	3. Angel Carpio	José Guadalupe Rostro
	4. José María Prieto Garza	Gabriel Durán
	5. *Eduardo Dublán*	Jesús R. Espana
	6. Miguel Lebrija	*Pablo Verástegui*
	7. *Blas Escontría*	Camilo Arriaga
	8. Jesús Martel	Lorenzo García
	9. Francisco Bustamante	Vicente Morales
	10. Manuel Muró	Angel Flores
	11. Manuel González	Manuel Medina
	12. Lorenzo Ceballos	Rómulo E. Vidales
Sinaloa	1. *Justo Sierra*	Ignacio Bejarano
	2. Marcos Carrillo	Manuel Thomas Terán
	3. Jesús F. Uriarte	Celso Gaxiola
	4. Francisco de P. Barroso	*Eduardo Pankhurst*
Sonora	1. Angel M. Domínguez	Enrique Quijada
	2. *Rafael Izábal*	Víctor Aguilar
	3. Darío Balandrano	Manuel Alatorre
Tabasco	1. *Joaquín D. Casasús*	Manuel Zapata Vera
	2. *Abraham Bandala*	Luis Flores
Tamaulipas	1. Manuel de León	Teófilo Ramírez
	2. Ismael Rodríguez	Guillermo Obregón
	3. *Juan B. Castelló*	Gregorio Cortina Basadre

Tepic (Nayarit)	1. Guadalupe López	Francisco Rivas Gómez
	2. *Antonio Pliego y Pérez*	*Manuel Sierra Méndez*
	3. Simón Parra	*Francisco de la Barra*
Tlaxcala	1. *José González Porras*	Ignacio Gómez del Campo
	2. Manuel Andrade	Amado García
	3. Teodoro Rivera	Eugenio Zubieta
Veracruz	1. José Manuel Jáuregui	Manuel García Méndez
	2. Enrique Llorente Rocha	Gustavo A. Esteva
	3. *Julio Zárate*	Angel Lúcido y Cambas
	4. Agustín Cerdán	José Antonio Villegas
	5. Donaciano Lara	Domingo Bureau
	6. Mauro F. Herrera	Modesto L. Herrera
	7. José M. Cuesto y Lagos	Lorenzo R. Ferrer
	8. Manuel Levi	Juan N. César
	9. Manuel S. Vila	José María Melgar
	10. Juan Cházaro Soler	Lorenzo Fernández
	11. José Antonio Gamboa	Gandencio González Llave
Yucatán	1. Waldemaro G. Cantón	Pedro Ordóñez
	2. Pedro Laclau	Vidal Castillo
	3. Benjamín Bolaños	Perfecto Villamil
	4. Salvador Dondé	Gabriel María Islas
	5. Juan de Dios Peza	Perfecto Avila
	6. Vacant	
	7. Cirilo F. Gutiérrez	José R. Mena
	8. Demetrio Salazar	Ramón Prida
Zacatecas	1. Alonso Mariscal	José Lámbarri
	2. *Adalberto A. Esteva*	Manuel C. Aguilar
	3. Jesús M. Rábago	Manuel C. Aguilar
	4. Francisco Vázquez	Francisco Ortega
	5. Agustín Lozano	Juan Bolaños
	6. *Joaquín Obregón González*	Ramón Corona
	7. Eugenio Barreiro	Manuel Valenzuela
	8. Rafael Jiménez	Pedro A. Herrera
	9. *Alfredo Chavero*	Ramón Romero
	10. Wenceslao Rubio	Francisco Ledesma

1892–94 (16th Legislature)

State	Deputy	Alternate
Aguascalientes	1. Ricardo Egea	Jesús Díaz de León
	2. Miguel Güinchard	Rafael Sagredo
	3. Juan Avendaño	Jesús Rábago
	4. Diego Pérez Ortigosa	Julio D. Vera
Baja California	1. Antonio Gómez	Miguel Melgarejo
Campeche	1. Manuel T. Peniche	Eduardo Castillo Lavalle
	2. *Román S. Lascuráin*	Javier Santa María

State	Deputy	Alternate
Chiapas	1. *Miguel Utrilla*	José Mora
	2. Federico Méndez Rivas	*Víctor Manuel Castillo*
	3. Román Pino	Abelardo Domínguez
	4. Jesús Oliver	Magín Llaven
	5. Juan Acuña	Pedro Acuña
Chihuahua	1. Ignacio de la Torre y M.	Canuto Elías
	2. Fernando Zetina	Lorenzo Arellano
	3. *Jesús E. Valenzuela*	Buenaventura Becerra
	4. José Manuel Flores	*Enrique C. Creel*
Coahuila	1. Alejandro Elguezábal	Miguel Gómez y Cárdenas
	2. Daniel García	Frumencio Fuentes
Colima	1. *Ignacio M. Escudero*	Ernesto Ritter
	2. Francisco C. Palencia	Severo Campero
Distrito Federal	1. *Guillermo Prieto*	Esteban Cházari
	2. Luis G. Labastida	Jesús Labastida
	3. *José Yves Limantour*	Julio Limantour
	4. *Roberto Núñez*	Carlos Casasús
	5. *José María Gamboa*	Angel Pola
	6. Tomas Reyes Retana	Emilio G. Saravia
	7. *Trinidad García*	Ricardo Domínguez
	8. *Agustín Arroyo de Anda*	Alonso Rodríguez Miramón
	9. *Pablo Macedo*	Pedro Ceballos
	10. *Emilio Pardo, Jr.*	Federico V. Riva Palacios
Durango	1. Alberto Sante Fe	Felipe P. Gavilán
	2. Rafael Salcido	José I. Icaza
	3. Miguel Amador	
	4. Faustino Michel	Ignacio Michel
Guanajuato	1. *Mariano Escobedo*	Alberto Ruiz Alvarez
	2. Ramón Alcázar	Enrique Omana
	3. Enrique Mackintosh	Trinidad Ortega
	4. Rafael Pérez Gallardo	Lauro Cavazos
	5. Antonio Rivas Mercado	Vicente Moreno
	6. Francisco G. Cosmes	José Barrera
	7. *Carlos de Olaguíbel y A.*	Julio Arancivia
	8. Luis Olivo	José Cantú
	9. Manuel García Ramírez	Sixto Moncada
	10. Joaquín Chico	Diego de A. Berea
	11. Alberto Malo	Eduardo J. Velázquez
	12. Emilio Baz	Carlos García
	13. Enrique Mont	Manuel M. Seoane
	14. Francisco García López	Antonio León Traslosheros
	15. *Angel Ortiz Monasterio*	Carlos Díaz Infante
	16. Domingo López de Lara	Javier Torres Rivas
	17. José Patricio Nicoli	Ignacio L. Montenegro
	18. Ignacio Ibargüengoitia	Antonio Cisneros Cámara
Guerrero	1. Vicente Sánchez	José M. Arce
	2. Manuel Guillén	Jesús Morán

	3. *Marcelo León*	Benjamín J. Garibay
	4. Ignacio O. Montesinos	Pascual Luna Lara
	5. Antonio Cervantes	Andrés Díaz Millán
	6. *Buenaventura Anaya y Aranda*	Emilio E. García
	7. Alberto Lombardo	Francisco Martínez López
	8. Pedro Miranda	Valentín Gómez Farías
Hidalgo	1. Francisco Espinosa	Manuel Gómez Parada
	2. Ramón María Riveroll	Guillermo Vélez
	3. *Gabriel Mancera*	Francisco Portilla
	4. *Manuel Sánchez Mármol*	Manuel Garrido
	5. Enrique Sort	Rafael García Martínez
	6. Manuel Mirus	Guillermo Pascoe
	7. *Simón Cravioto*	Jesús Rodríguez
	8. Ismael Salas	Felipe de J. Isunza
	9. *Pedro L. Rodríguez*	Agapito J. Martínez
	10. Carmen de Ita	Jesús M. Rábago
	11. *Luis Pérez Verdía*	Carlos K. Ruiz
Jalisco	1. Francisco Sepúlveda	Gabriel Aguirre
	2. Mariano Coronado	Luis G. Palomar
	3. *Juan A. Mateos*	Nicolás de la Peña
	4. Antonio Riva y Echeverría	Tomás V. Gómez
	5. Francisco Rincón Gallardo	Agustín Domínguez
	6. Joaquín María Escoto	Narciso Corvera
	7. Manuel Algara	José María Gutiérrez
	8. *Martín González*	Apolonio Pinzón
	9. *Rosalino Martínez*	Manuel Carsi
	10. *Luis C. Curiel*	Manuel Bustamante
	11. *Francisco Romero*	Aurelio González H.
	12. *Pedro Landázuri*	Paulino Preciado
	13. Celso G. Ceballos	Eliseo Madrid
	14. *Rafael de Zayas Enríquez*	Juan R. Zavala
	15. Arnulfo García	José Antonio Barba
	16. *Ireneo Paz*	Jorge Delorme
	17. Miguel Sagaseta	Felipe Robledo
	18. Manuel Briseño Ortega	Manuel Galván
México	1. Ignacio García Heras	Teodoro Zúñiga
	2. Juan Bribiesca	Alfredo Garrido
	3. Manuel de León	Juan Berriozábal
	4. Jose María Castro	Ignacio Gómez del Campo
	5. Genaro Raigosa	Joaquín García Luna
	6. Julián Montiel	Jacobo Mercado
	7. Enrique Mexía	Alberto Sánchez
	8. *Ramón Gómez Villavicencio*	Arturo Paz
	9. Pedro Azcué	Joaquín Romo
	10. Enrique Flores	José C. Téllez
	11. Manuel Ticó	Joaquín Salazar y Murphy
	12. Pedro Miranda	Diego de la Peña
	13. Alberto Terreros	Ricardo Domínguez
	14. Macedonio Gómez	Francisco Cardona
	15. *Manuel Gutiérrez Nájera*	Juan Rodríguez
	16. *Francisco de P. Gochicoa*	Benito Sánchez

State	Deputy	Alternate
Michoacán	1. Francisco S. Menocal	Miguel Silva
	2. Juan de la Torre	Felipe Rivera
	3. *Francisco A. Vélez*	Francisco Vélez, Jr.
	4. *Fernando González*	Germán Contreras
	5. Enrique Landa	Salvador D. González
	6. *Rafael Reyes Spíndola*	Jacobo Mercado
	7. Emilio Ruiz	Rafael Montaño Ramiro
	8. Jose María Romero	Diego Diaz Barriga
	9. *Angel Padilla*	*Gabriel Aguirre*
	10. *Manuel A. Mercado*	*Luis G. Caballero*
	11. Ricardo Hornedo	Federico Bravo
	12. Onofre Ramos	Antonio Treviño
	13. Angel M. Polo	Francisco C. García
	14. Serapión Fernández	Antonio Vizcaíno
	15. *Francisco Bulnes*	Constantino Mota
Morelos	1. *Gilberto Crespo*	José Cazarín
	2. *Antonio Tovar*	José Luciano Varela
	3. Manuel V. Preciado	Felipe Salazar
	4. Rafael Rodríguez Talavera	Manuel Ríos y Peña
Nuevo León	1. *Francisco M. Ramírez*	Jesús M. Cerda
	2. Manuel Serrano	Epitacio Resendis
	3. Manuel Z. Doria	Encarnación Coronado
	4. Carlos F. Ayala	Lorenzo Sepúlveda
Oaxaca	1. Francisco Uriarte	Ramón Prida
	2. Juan N. Castellaños	Joaquín Payno
	3. Crisóforo Canseco	Jesús Acevedo
	4. Jose María Castellanos	Patricio León
	5. Juan Dublán	Agustín Robles Arenas
	6. Luis García Luna	Manuel Bustamante
	7. *Emilio Pimentel*	Francisco Magro
	8. Ignacio Vázquez	Francisco Rincón
	9. Rafael Casco	Cruz Martínez
	10. Pascual Fenochio	Manuel Martínez Gracida
	11. Manuel Ramírez Varela	Albino López Garzón
	12. *Benito Juárez Maza*	Mariano Benavides
	13. Jose Ignacio Alvarez	Gildardo Gómez
	14. Manuel E. Rincón	Juan Prieto
	15. *Luis Pombo*	Leopoldo Rincón
	16. *Rosendo Pineda*	Enrique Montero
Puebla	1. Jose de J. López	Francisco Sáenz Meraz
	2. *Agustín Pradillo*	Ignacio Barda
	3. Francisco Poceros	Gerardo Márquez
	4. Manuel Santibáñez	Emilio Alvarez
	5. Manuel Escudero y Pérez	Modesto R. Martínez
	6. Vital Escamilla	Manuel López Cabanzo
	7. *Miguel Serrano*	Domingo Echegaray
	8. Dámaso Sánchez	José María Márquez
	9. Francisco Dehesa	Enrique Romero
	10. Telésforo Barroso	Herculano Torres

	11. *Sóstenes Rocha*	Eduardo Velásquez
	12. Manuel Espinosa de los M.	Manuel Márquez Galindo
	13. Manuel Bueno	Juan de Dios Almazán
	14. Manuel Darqui	Guillermo Pérez
	15. Eulalio Núñez	Valeriano Vergara
	16. Gerardo Silva	Uriel Alatriste
	17. *Francisco Mejía*	Fortunato Nava
	18. Víctor Méndez	Tomás Ramos
	19. Luis Garfías	José Luis Bello
	20. Joaquín de la Barreda	Agustín Fernández
Querétaro	1. Rafael Chousal	Rafael García Martínez
	2. Leonardo F. Fortuño	Juan Orozco
	3. *Félix M. Alcérreca*	Agustín Ruiz Olloqui
	4. Fernando María Rubio	José Izita
San Luis Potosí	1. *Justino Fernández*	Vicente Morales
	2. Manuel Orellana Nogueras	Alberto L. Palacios
	3. Angel Carpio	José Guadalupe Rostro
	4. Jose María Prieto Garza	Gabriel Durán
	5. *Eduardo Dublán*	Jesús R. España
	6. Miguel Lebrija	*Pablo Verástegui*
	7. *Blas Escontría*	Camilo Arriaga
	8. Jesús Martel	Lorenzo García
	9. Francisco Bustamante	Alejandro Garrido
	10. Manuel Muró	Angel Flores
	11. Francisco Macín	Buenaventura Ortiz
	12. Lorenzo Ceballos	Rómulo E. Vidales
Sinaloa	1. *Justo Sierra*	Luis M. de Castro
	2. Rafael Izábal	Juan Zaldívar
	3. Jesús F. Uriarte	Manuel Altorre
	4. Francisco de P. Barroso	José Rentería
Sonora	1. Angel M. Domínguez	Alberto Morales
	2. Manuel Thomas Terán	Enrique Monteverde
	3. Darío Balandrano	Francisco Salcido
Tabasco	1. *Joaquín D. Casasús*	Carlos Casasús
	2. *Abraham Bandala*	Luis Flores
Tamaulipas	1. Manuel González	Manuel Medina
	2. Ismael Rodríguez	Manuel de la Cruz
	3. *Juan B. Castelló*	Francisco Gutiérrez
Tepic (Nayarit)	1. Guadalupe López	Francisco Rivas Gómez
	2. *Antonio Pliego y Pérez*	Loreto Gutiérrez
	3. Simón Parra	*Francisco de la Barra*
Tlaxcala	1. *José González Porras*	Pomposo Picazo
	2. Manuel Andrade	Plutarco Montiel
	3. Teodoro Rivera	Amado García
Veracruz	1. Felipe Arellano	Manuel G. Méndez
	2. Enrique Llorente Rocha	José Antonio Márquez

State	Deputy	Alternate
	3. *Julio Zárate*	Gaudencio de la Llave
	4. Agustín Cerdán	Francisco S. Ortiz
	5. Donaciano Lara	Luis Valle
	6. Mauro S. Herrera	Leopoldo M.Núñez
	7. Rafael Herrera	Guillermo Obregón
	8. Manuel Levi	Ignacio Vado
	9. Manuel S. Vila	José E. Domínguez
	10. Juan Cházaro Soler	José F. Gómez
	11. José Antonio Gamboa	Amado Talavera
Yucatán	1. Waldemaro G. Cantón	José Vidal Castillo
	2. Pedro Laclau	Pedro Ordóñez
	3. Benjamín Bolaños	Demetrio Traconis García
	4. Salvador Dondé	Albino Manzanilla
	5. *Juan de Dios Peza*	Ignacio Gamboa
	6. Ignacio Bejarano	José María Osorno
	7. Cirilo F. Gutiérrez	Juan Gamboa
	8. Demetrio Salazar	Serapio Baqueiro
Zacatecas	1. Alonso Mariscal	Carlos F. Chávarri
	2. *Adalberto A. Esteva*	Manuel Valerio Ortega
	3. Jorge Carmona	Marcos S. Casteldi
	4. Francisco Vázquez	Genaro García
	5. Agustín Lozano	Ramiro J. Elorduy
	6. *Joaquín Obregón González*	Crispin Aguilar y Bobadilla
	7. Eugenio Barreiro	Manuel Vallejo
	8. Eduardo Carrillo	Rafael Carvajal
	9. *Alfredo Chavero*	José Lámbarri
	10. Wenceslao Rubio	Manuel Valenzuela

1894–96 (17th Legislature)

State	Deputy	Alternate
Aguascalientes	1. *Mariano Escobedo*	Alberto Pérez Alvarez
	2. Miguel Güinchard	Rafael Sagredo
	3. José Vega	Jesús Rábago
	4. Diego Pérez Ortigosa	Jesús Díaz de León
Baja California	1. Rodolfo F. Nieto	Alberto Correa
Campeche	1. Manuel T. Peniche	Eduardo Castillo Lavalle
	2. *Román S. Lascuraín*	Javier Santa María
Chiapas	1. *Víctor Manuel Castillo*	José Lino García
	2. Federico Méndez Rivas	José Mora
	3. Román Pino	Adolfo Díaz Rugama
	4. Jesús Oliver	Magín Llaven
	5. Francisco Cosmes	Ignacio Romero Vargas
Chihuahua	1. Bernardo Urueta	*Porfirio Parra*
	2. Francisco Albístegui	Francisco Portillo
	3. *Jesús E. Valenzuela*	Lorenzo J. Arellano
	4. Martín González	Francisco Martínez López

Coahuila	1. Epifanio Reyes	Hilarión Frías y Soto
	2. Rafael Ramos Arizpe	Melchor G. Cárdenas
Colima	1. *Ignacio M. Escudero*	Ernesto Ritter
	2. Francisco C. Palencia	Enrique de Lamadrid
Distrito Federal	1. *Guillermo Prieto*	Manuel G. Prieto
	2. Luis G. Labastida	Jesús Labastida
	3. *José Yves Limantour*	Julio Limantour
	4. *Roberto Núñez*	*Carlos Casasús*
	5. *José María Gamboa*	Angel Pola
	6. Tomás Reyes Retana	Alberto Arellano y Millán
	7. *Trinidad García*	Salvador Echegaray
	8. *Agustín Arroyo de Anda*	Alonso Rodríguez Miramón
	9. *Pablo Macedo*	Rafael Arrillaga
	10. *Emilio Pardo, Jr.*	*Federico Gamboa*
Durángo	1. Alberto Santa Fe	Fernando Téllez Girón
	2. Rafael Salcido	José I. Icaza
	3. Leopoldo Rincón	Juan N. Flores y Quijar
	4. Faustino Michel	
Guanajuato	1. *Eduardo Liceaga*	*Gildardo Gómez*
	2. Joaquín Chico	Francisco Mejía
	3. Pedro Ocampo	Alberto Lombardo
	4. Manuel Anaya	Moisés R. González
	5. Ramón Alcázar	Rafael Casco
	6. *Francisco de P. Gochicoa*	José Tornel
	7. *Rosendo Pineda*	Archibaldo Guedea
	8. *Pablo Escandón y Barrón*	José Mijares Anorga
	9. Cecilio F. Estrada	Antonio Rivas Mercado
	10. Ignacio Ibargüengoitia	Francisco de P. del Río
	11. Uriel Alatriste	Luis Aguilar
	12. Juan de Argomedo	José Bribiesca Saavedra
	13. Manuel Carrillo	Joaquín M. Ruiz
	14. José Manuel de Santo	Fernando Vega
	15. Sebastián Camacho	Ignacio Icaza
	16. Alberto Leal	Alberto Leal
	17. José Fernández	Daniel García
	18. *Ismael Salas*	José María Santo
Guerrero	1. Vicente Sánchez	Perfecto Montalvo
	2. Manuel Guillén	Julián Deloya
	3. *Marcelo León*	José María Caneda
	4. Félix P. Alvarez	Rafael Icaza
	5. Eutimio Cervantes	Leopoldo Viramonte
	6. *Carlos de Olaguíbel*	Ignacio Burgoa
	7. Emilio E. García	Damián Flores
	8. Alejandro Elguésabal	Miguel Castro
Hidalgo	1. Francisco Espinosa	Manuel Gómez Parada
	2. Ramón María Riveroll	Guillermo Vélez
	3. *Gabriel Mancera*	Rafael García Martínez
	4. Prisciliano Benítez	Severo Carrasco Pérez
	5. Domingo López de Lara	Heriberto Barrón

State	Deputy	Alternate
	6. Manuel Mirus	José Delgado
	7. *Simón Cravioto*	Jesús Rodríguez
	8. Emilio G. Baz	Alfredo Saavedra
	9. *Pedro L. Rodríguez*	José Landero y Cos
	10. Carmen de Ita	Simón Andoaga
	11. José Patricio Nicoli	*Rafael Cravioto*
Jalisco	1. Francisco Sepúlveda	Heriberto Barrón
	2. Mariano Coronado	José A. Casillas
	3. *Juan A. Mateos*	Salvador Vega Limón
	4. Antonio Riva y Echeverría	Tomás V. Gómez
	5. *Manuel Sierra Méndez*	Nicolás España
	6. Joaquín María Escoto	*Carlos Díaz Dufoo*
	7. Manuel Algara	Carlos Villegas
	8. Luis G. Galván	José María Macías
	9. *Rosalino Martínez*	José María Arce
	10. Tomás Morán	Manuel Bustamante
	11. *Francisco Romero*	Florencio Riestra
	12. *Pedro Landázuri*	Juan Gutiérrez
	13. Celso G. Ceballos	Adolfo Cámara
	14. *Rafael de Zayas Enríquez*	Francisco Macías
	15. Ignacio Mañón y Valle	Eduardo Portu
	16. *Ireneo Paz*	Ignacio L. Montenegro
	17. Miguel Sagaseta	Carlos Gómez
	18. Luis Pérez Verdía	Jacinto Montaña
México	1. Ignacio García Heras	Joaquín García Luna
	2. Juan Bribiesca	Nicolás Bribiesca
	3. Manuel de León	Diego de la Peña
	4. *Manuel Domínguez*	Francisco de Landa
	5. Américo Lara	Juan Berriozábal
	6. Julián Montiel	Samuel Morales Pereira
	7. Enrique Mexía	Alberto Sánchez
	8. *Ramón Márquez Galindo*	Joaquín Salazar y Murphy
	9. Pedro Azcué	Luis Zepeda
	10. Guillermo Pérez V.	Francisco Cardona
	11. *Emilio Pardo*	Rafael Pardo
	12. *Manuel Sánchez Mármol*	José Zayas
	13. Alberto Terreros	Arturo Paz
	14. Miguel Villalobos	Luis Espinosa
	15. *Manuel Gutiérrez Nájera*	Juan Pérez Gálvez
	16. *Angel Ortiz Monasterio*	*Francisco J. Gaxiola*
Michoacán	1. *Luis G. Caballero*	*Carlos Díaz Dufoo*
	2. Juan de la Torre	Felipe Rivera
	3. *Francisco A. Vélez*	Francisco Vélez, Jr.
	4. *Fernando González*	Enrique Mackintosh
	5. Enrique Landa	Gregorio Aldasoro
	6. *Rafael Reyes Spíndola*	Rafael Hinojosa
	7. Emilio Ruiz	Agapito Silva
	8. José María Romero	Rafael Díaz Barriga
	9. *Manuel A. Mercado*	Jacobo Mercado
	10. *Angel Padilla*	Arturo Mercado

	11. Ricardo Hornedo	Federico Bravo
	12. Onofre Ramos	Agustín Pliego y Pérez
	13. Angel M. Polo	Francisco C. García
	14. Serapión Fernández	Antonio Vizcaíno
	15. *Francisco Bulnes*	Manuel Flores
Morelos	1. *Gilberto Crespo*	José Casarín
	2. *Antonio Tovar*	Joaquín Bezne Irigoyen
	3. Manuel V. Preciado	José Aristeo Ochoa
	4. Ignacio de la Torre	Juan Belaunzarán
Nuevo León	1. *Francisco M. Ramírez*	Jesús M. Cerda
	2. Manuel Serrano	Marcelo Salinas
	3. Manuel Z. Doria	Rafael Flores Fernández
	4. Carlos F. Ayala	Lorenzo Sepúlveda
Oaxaca	1. Francisco Uriarte	Ramón Prida
	2. Juan N. Castellanos	Guillermo Meijueiro
	3. Juan Prieto	Jesús Acevedo
	4. José María Castellanos	Próspero Alvarez
	5. Juan Dublán	Agustín Robles Arenas
	6. Luis García Luna	Rafael Bolaños Cacho
	7. José Agustín Domínguez	Leopoldo Rincón
	8. Ignacio Vázquez	*Francisco Alfaro*
	9. *Emilio Pimentel*	José Zorrilla Tejeda
	10. Pascual Fenochio	Aureliano Hernández
	11. Andrés Cruz Martínez	Albino López Garzón
	12. *Benito Juárez Maza*	*Félix Díaz*
	13. José Ignacio Alvarez	*Gildardo Gómez*
	14. Manuel E. Rincón	Joaquín Ogarrio
	15. *Luis Pombo*	Manuel Martínez Gracida
	16. Manuel Santibáñez	Andrés Portillo
Puebla	1. José de J. López	Francisco Sáenz Meraz
	2. *Agustín Pradillo*	Manuel Flores
	3. *Roberto Gayol*	Emilio Zertuche
	4. Melesio T. Alcántara	Emilio Alvarez
	5. Manuel Escudero y Pérez	Modesto R. Martínez
	6. Vital Escamilla	Manuel López Cabanzo
	7. *Miguel Serrano*	Domingo Echegaray
	8. *Gregorio Mendizábal*	Pascual Luna Lara
	9. Francisco Dehesa	Enrique Romero
	10. Telésforo Barroso	Herculano Torres
	11. *Eduardo Velázquez*	Manuel María Arrioja
	12. Ramón Bolaños	Luis Gómez Daza
	13. Manuel Contreras	Adolfo Díaz Rugama
	14. *Pablo Martínez del Río*	Miguel Muñoz
	15. Eulalio Núñez	Valeriano Vergara
	16. Gerardo Silva	Joaquín María Ruiz
	17. Javier Algara	Pedro Santres
	18. Víctor Méndez	Tomás Ramos
	19. Luis Garfías	Emilio Salgado
	20. Joaquín de la Barreda	Agustín Fernández

State	Deputy	Alternate
Querétaro	1. Rafael Chousal	Tomás Noriega
	2. Leónardo F. Fortuño	Juan Orozco
	3. *Félix M. Alcérreca*	Agustín Ruiz Olloqui
	4. Fernando María Rubio	José Izita
San Luis Potosí	1. *Justino Fernández*	Vicente Morales
	2. Manuel Orellana Nogueras	Alberto L. Palacios
	3. Angel Carpio	Lorenzo García
	4. José María Prieto Garza	Rafael Manríquez
	5. *Eduardo Dublán*	Adolfo Flores
	6. Miguel Lebrija	*Pablo Verástegui*
	7. *Blas Escontría*	Camilo Arriaga
	8. Jesús Martel	Paulino F. Almanza
	9. Francisco Bustamante	Alejandro Garrido
	10. Manuel Muró	Alberto López Hermosa
	11. Francisco Macín	Buenaventura Ortiz
	12. Lorenzo Ceballos	Rómulo E. Vidales
Sinaloa	1. Vicente Riva Palacio	Luis Martínez de Castro
	2. Rafael Izábal	Juan Zaldívar
	3. Jesús F. Uriarte	Manuel Alatorre
	4. Francisco de P. Barroso	Manuel Betancourt
Sonora	1. Angel M. Domínguez	Franciso de P. Morales
	2. Manuel Thomas Terán	Enrique Monteverde
	3. Darío Balandrano	Francisco Salcido
Tabasco	1. *Joaquín D. Casasús*	Carlos Casasús
	2. Ismael Rodríguez	Luis Flores
Tamaulipas	1. Manuel González	Ramón Gómez y Villavicencio
	2. *José González Porras*	Francisco Fuentes Farías
	3. *Juan B. Castelló*	Francisco Gutiérrez
Tepic (Nayarit)	1. Guadalupe López	Francisco Rivas Gómez
	2. *Antonio Pliego y Pérez*	Loreto Gutiérrez
	3. *Francisco de la Barra*	Antonio Zaragoza
Tlaxcala	1. *Abraham Bandala*	*Rafael Rodríguez Talavera*
	2. Manuel Andrade	Plutarco Montiel
	3. Teodoro Rivera	Amado García
Veracruz	1. Enrique Llorente Rocha	José E. Domínguez
	2. *Felipe Arellano*	Ignacio Vado
	3. *Julio Zárate*	Eduardo Melgar
	4. Agustín Cerdán	Ignacio M. del Castillo
	5. Donaciano Lara	Guillermo Obregón
	6. Mauro S. Herrera	Guillermo Valleto
	7. Rafael Herrera	Juan de Dios Rodríguez
	8. Manuel Levi	José Agustín Castro
	9. Antonio Falcón	Ramón Prado
	10. José Antonio Gamboa	Ignacio M. Luchichi
	11. Juan Cházaro Soler	José F. Gómez

Yucatán	1. Waldemaro G. Cantón	José Vidal Castillo
	2. Pedro Laclau	Pedro Ordóñez
	3. Benjamín Bolaños	Demetrio Traconis García
	4. Salvador Dondé	Albino Manzanilla
	5. *Juan de Dios Peza*	Ermilo G. Cantón
	6. Ignacio Bejarano	Genaro V. Cervera
	7. Cirilo F. Gutiérrez	Juan Gamboa
	8. Demetrio Salazar	Serapio Baqueiro
Zacatecas	1. Alonso Mariscal	Carlos F. Chavarrí
	2. *Adalberto A. Esteva*	Alberto R. Elorduy
	3. Jorge Carmona	Manuel Arrioja
	4. Gregorio Aldazoro	Miguel Canales
	5. Agustín Lozano	Julián Hornedo
	6. *Genaro García*	José de la Cueva
	7. Eugenio Barreiro	Samuel Morales Pereyra
	8. Marcos Simón Casteldi	Rafael Carbajal
	9. *Alfredo Chavero*	Perfecto Montalvo
	10. Wenceslao Rubio	Mariano Ledesma

1896–98 (18th Legislature)

State	Deputy	Alternate
Aguascalientes	1. *Mariano Escobedo*	Mariano Escobedo, Jr.
	2. Miguel Güinchard	Rafael Sagredo
	3. José Vega	Jesús Rábago
	4. Adolfo Fenochio	Jesús Díaz de León
Baja California	1. Antonio Salinas y Carbó	Alfonso Garay
Campeche	1. Manuel T. Peniche	Jesús Contreras
	2. Diego Pérez Ortigosa	Magín Llaven
Chiapas	1. Román Pino	Manuel de Trejo
	2. *Víctor Manuel Castillo*	Rafael Villa
	3. Federico Méndez Rivas	Abelardo Domínguez
	4. José Villasaña	Daniel Zepeda
	5. Juan Berriozábal	Manuel Garfías Salinas
Chihuahua	1. Bernardo Urueta	Francisco de P. Portillo
	2. *Francisco Albístegui*	*Porfirio Parra*
	3. *Jesús E. Valenzuela*	Lorenzo J. Arellano
	4. Ignacio M. Luchichi	Jesús Arellano
Coahuila	1. Epifanio Reyes	Hilarión Frías y Soto
	2. Rafael Ramos Arizpe	Melchor G. Cárdenas
Colima	1. Francisco C. Palencia	*Enrique O. de la Madrid*
	2. *Ignacio M. Escudero*	Ernesto Ritter
Distrito Federal	1. *Guillermo Prieto*	Adolfo Díaz Rugama
	2. Luis G. Labastida	*Francisco Alfaro*
	3. Julio Limantour	Ernesto Chavero

State	Deputy	Alternate
	4. Alonso Rodríguez Miramón	Agustín Lazo
	5. *José María Gamboa*	Luis Salazar
	6. Tomás Reyes Retana	Francisco Portilla
	7. *Trinidad García*	José Portilla
	8. *Agustín Arroyo de Anda*	Antonio Grande Guerrero
	9. *Pablo Macedo*	Alberto Icaza
	10. *Emilio Pardo, Jr.*	Eduardo Noguera
Durángo	1. Alberto Sante Fe	Alberto Casa Madrid
	2. Roberto Orrantía	José Ignacio Icaza
	3. Leopoldo Rincón	Fernando Téllez Girón
	4. Faustino Michel	Ignacio Michel
Guanajuato	1. *Eduardo Liceaga*	*Gildardo Gómez*
	2. Manuel Carrillo Antillón	Joaquín M. Ruiz
	3. Pedro Ocampo	Alberto Lombardo
	4. Francisco Montaño Ramiro	Moisés R. González
	5. Ignacio Ibargüengoitia	José Sauto y Sauto
	6. *Francisco de P. Gochicoa*	Alberto Malo
	7. Rafael Lavista	Archibaldo Guedea
	8. *Pablo Escandón y Barrón*	José Mijares Anorga
	9. Cecilio F. Estrada	Antonio Rivas Mercado
	10. Nicolás del Moral	Rafael Casco
	11. Jesús Casco	*Francisco Mejía*
	12. Juan de Argomedo	Luis A. Aguilar
	13. José Bribiesca Saavedra	Manuel Llamosa
	14. José Manuel de Santo	Fernando Vega
	15. *Sebastián Camacho*	José Ignacio Icaza
	16. Ramón Alcázar	*Felipe Arellano*
	17. Carlos Chico	Daniel García
	18. *Ismael Salas*	José María Santo
Guerrero	1. Manuel Guillén	Isidro Rojas
	2. *Marcelo León*	Carlos Mercenario
	3. Félix P. Alvarez	José María Villalvaso
	4. Eutimio Cervantes	Manuel Cervantes
	5. *Carlos de Olaguíbel*	Alberto Ruiz Alvarez
	6. Alejandro Elguesábal	Aurelio de Canales
	7. Julio Alvarez	Alberto Sánchez
	8. *Francisco Romero*	Francisco Martínez López
Hidalgo	1. Francisco Espinosa	*Carlos Díaz Dufoo*
	2. Ramón María Riveroll	Arnulfo García
	3. *Gabriel Mancera*	Jesús Rodríguez
	4. *Rafael Cravioto*	Manuel García Ramírez
	5. Domingo López de Lara	Juan Gutiérrez
	6. Manuel Mirus	Antonio Grande Guerrero
	7. *Simón Cravioto*	Rafael Oropeza
	8. Federico V. Riva Palacio	Rodolfo Izunza
	9. *Pedro L. Rodríguez*	Vicente Pérez
	10. Carmen de Ita	Manuel Garrido
	11. Aurelio Melgarejo	Moisés Rojas

Jalisco		
	1. Francisco Sepúlveda	Severo Carrasco Pérez
	2. Prisciliano M. Benítez	Diódoro Contreras
	3. *Juan A. Mateos*	Ramón R. Prado
	4. Antonio Riva y Echeverría	Diego Baz
	5. *Manuel Sierra Méndez*	Rafael Linares
	6. Joaquín María Escoto	Eduardo Portu
	7. Manuel Algara	Carlos Gómez Luna
	8. Luis G. Galván	Alonso Fernández
	9. Bartolomé Carbajal	Rafael Dorantes
	10. Tomás Moran	José Ana Casillas
	11. Juan Manuel Betancourt	Manuel Galván
	12. *Pedro Landázuri*	Francisco M. Silva
	13. Celso G. Ceballos	Bernardo Echauri
	14. Manuel Serrato	Emeterio de la Garza
	15. *Rafael de Zayas Enríquez*	Florencio Riestra
	16. *Ireneo Paz*	Manuel M. Tortolero
	17. Miguel Sagaseta	Ignacio L. Montenegro
	18. Luis Pérez Verdía	Agustín Pascal

México		
	1. Ignacio García Heras	Manuel Ruiz Sandoval
	2. Juan Bribiesca	Ignacio Burgoa
	3. Manuel Plata	Ramón Prida
	4. *Manuel Domínguez*	Enrique Pérez Rubio
	5. Américo Lara	Roberto García
	6. Julián Montiel	*Francisco J. Gaxiola*
	7. Enrique Mexía	Francisco Martínez López
	8. *Ramón Márquez Galindo*	Arturo Paz
	9. Pedro Azcué	Alfredo Garrido
	10. Guillermo Pérez V.	Juan Pérez Gálvez
	11. *Emilio Pardo*	Rafael Pardo
	12. *Manuel Sánchez Mármol*	Felipe G. Cantón
	13. Alberto Terreros	Jesús Rodríguez
	14. *Juan Villegas*	Antonio González
	15. Alberto González de León	Aurelio J. Venegas
	16. Juan de Dios Chousal	Manuel Auza

Michoacán		
	1. *Luis G. Cabellero*	Miguel Mesa
	2. Juan de la Torre	Felipe Rivera
	3. *Francisco A. Vélez*	Francisco Vélez, Jr.
	4. *Fernando González*	Enrique Mackintosh
	5. *Rafael Reyes Spíndola*	Celerino Luviano
	6. Enrique Landa	Juan B. Maciel
	7. Emilio Ruiz	Primitivo Ortiz
	8. Fausto Moguel	Onofre Ramos
	9. José María Romero	Carlos Eiquihua
	10. *Angel Padilla*	Francisco Martínez López
	11. *Francisco Bulnes*	Félix Lemus Olaneta
	12. *Manuel A. Mercado*	Jacobo Mercado
	13. Luis Pliego y Pérez	Alfonso Garay
	14. Serapión Fernández	Víctoriano Pérez
	15. Miguel M. Acosta	Agapito Silva

Morelos		
	1. *Gilberto Crespo*	José Casarín
	2. *Antonio Tovar*	Manuel Sales Zepeda

State	Deputy	Alternate
	3. Manuel V. Preciado	Enrique de Olavarría
	4. Ignacio de la Torre	Pedro M. López
Nuevo León	1. *Francisco M. Ramírez*	Jesús M. Cerda
	2. Manuel Serrano	Marcelo Salinas
	3. Manuel Z. Doria	Francisco Salazar
	4. Carlos F. Ayala	Lorenzo Sepúlveda
Oaxaca	1. Juan N. Castellanos	Federico Zorrilla
	2. Francisco Uriarte	Manuel Escobar
	3. Juan Prieto	Aureliano Hernández
	4. José María Castellanos	Lauro Cejudo
	5. Juan Dublán	Ricardo A. Romero
	6. Luis García Luna	*Miguel Bolaños Cacho*
	7. Aurelio Valdivieso	José Agustín Domínguez
	8. Manuel Santibáñez	Luis Moncada
	9. *Emilio Pimentel*	Francisco Magro
	10. Pascual Fenochio	Francisco Gutiérrez Cortina
	11. Andrés Cruz Martínez	Gildardo Gómez
	12. *Benito Juárez Maza*	Guillermo Meixueiro
	13. José Antonio Alvarez	José Ignacio Alvarez
	14. Manuel E. Rincón	Joaquín Ogarrio
	15. *Luis Pombo*	Andrés Ruiz
	16. *Rosendo Pineda*	Constantino Chapital
Puebla	1. Carlos Martínez Peregrina	Rafael Izunza
	2. *Miguel Serrano*	Emilio López Vaal
	3. Melesio T. Alcántara	Uriel Alatriste
	4. *Roberto Gayol*	Diego Martínez
	5. *Agustín Pradillo*	Manuel Flores
	6. Vital Escamilla	Tomás E. Ramos
	7. José Wenceslao González	Natal Pesado
	8. *Gregorio Mendizábal*	Adolfo Díaz Rugama
	9. Enrique Pazos	Modesto R. Martínez
	10. Telésforo Barroso	José Antonio de la Peña
	11. *Eduardo Velázquez*	Emilio Alvarez
	12. Mariano Ruiz	Enrique Romero Obregón
	13. Antonio Ramos	Joaquín Payno
	14. *Pablo Martínez del Río*	Manuel Amador
	15. Eulalio Núñez	Pascual Luna Lara
	16. *Lauro Carrillo*	Emilio Zertuche
	17. Javier Algara	Fernando Lavalle
	18. *Roberto Núñez*	Francisco Cosmes
	19. Luis Garfías	Luis G. Daza
	20. Joaquín de la Barreda	Angel Cabrera
Querétaro	1. Rafael Chousal	Domingo Barrios Gómez
	2. Leónardo F. Fortuño	Juan Orozco
	3. *Félix M. Alcérreca*	Agustín Ruiz Olloqui
	4. Fernando María Rubio	Ignacio Goytia
San Luis Potosí	1. *Justino Fernández*	Vicente Morales
	2. Manuel Orellana Nogueras	Alberto L. Palacios
	3. Angel Carpio	Lorenzo García

	4. José María Prieto Garza	Rafael Manrique de Lara
	5. *Eduardo Dublán*	Adolfo Flores
	6. Miguel Lebrija	*Pablo Verástegui*
	7. *Blas Escontría*	Camilo Arriaga
	8. Jesús Martel	Paulino F. Almanza
	9. Francisco de la Maza	Alejandro Garrido
	10. Alberto López Mermosa	Manuel Muró
	11. José E. de Landa	Adolfo Díaz Rugama
	12. Francisco Vázquez	Juan J. Farías
Sinaloa	1. *Angel Lúcido Cambas*	Juan Gutiérrez
	2. *Rafael Izábal*	Juan Zaldívar
	3. Francisco D. Barroso	Francisco Martínez López
	4. *Guillermo Pous*	Arturo Paz
Sonora	1. Angel M. Domínguez	Francisco de P. Morales
	2. Manuel Thomas Terán	Enrique Monterde
	3. Darío Balandrano	Carlos Garza Cortina
Tabasco	1. *Joaquín D. Casasús*	Manuel Mestre
	2. Ismael Rodríguez	Andrés C. Sosa
Tamaulipas	1. Manuel González	Ramón Gómez y Villavicencio
	2. Emilio Alvarez	Francisco Fuentes
	3. *Juan B. Castelló*	Guillermo Obregón
Tepic (Nayarit)	1. Guadalupe López	Francisco Rivas Gómez
	2. *Antonio Pliego y Pérez*	Tomás Mancera
	3. Ignacio Gómez del Campo	Antonio Zaragoza
Tlaxcala	1. Agustín Mora	Modesto Martínez
	2. Manuel Andrade	Pedro Ordóñez
	3. Teodoro Rivera	Rafael Serrano Aguirrezábal
Veracruz	1. *Leandro M. Alcolea*	*Félix Díaz*
	2. Modesto L. Herrera	Ignacio Vado
	3. Enrique Llorente Rocha	Manuel Gómez Velasco
	4. Francisco Dehesa	Enrique Herrera Moreno
	5. Donaciano Lara	Guillermo Obregón
	6. Mauro S. Herrera	Guillermo Valleto
	7. Rafael Herrera	Agustín Avendaño
	8. Manuel Levi	Francisco J. Muñoz
	9. Antonio Gamboa	Eduardo Melgar
	10. Juan Cházaro Soler	José F. Gómez
	11. Rafael Rodríguez Talavera	Ignacio M. del Castillo
Yucatán	1. *Cástulo Zenteno*	José Palomeque
	2. Pedro Laclau	José R. Avila V.
	3. Benjamín Bolaños	Demetrio Traconis García
	4. Salvador Dondé	Albino Manzanilla
	5. *Juan de Dios Peza*	Ermilo G. Cantón
	6. Ignacio Bejarano	Genaro V. Cervera
	7. Cirilo F. Gutiérrez	Ignacio Gamboa
	8. Demetrio Salazar	José Encarnación Maldonado

State	Deputy	Alternate
Zacatecas	1. Alonso Mariscal	Manuel Valenzuela
	2. *Adalberto A. Esteva*	Jesús María Castañeda
	3. Jorge Carmona	Carlos J. Chavarrí
	4. Gregorio Aldasoro	Rafael T. Ruiz
	5. Agustín Lozano	José María Lámbarri
	6. *Genaro García*	Arturo de la Cueva
	7. Adolfo Hegewich	Adolfo de la Isla
	8. Marcos Simón Casteldi	Ramón del Hoyo
	9. *Alfredo Chavero*	Rafael Carvajal
	10. Wenceslao Rubio	Francisco J. Ortega

1898–1900 (19th Legislature)

State	Deputy	Alternate
Aguascalientes	1. *Mariano Escobedo*	Mariano Escobedo, Jr.
	2. Miguel Güinchard	Jesús Díaz de León
	3. José Vega	José Ferrel
	4. Adolfo Fenochio	Jesús M. Rabago
Baja California	1. Antonio Salinas y Carbó	Luis Grajales
Campeche	1. Manuel T. Peniche	José Guadalupe Hinojosa
	2. Ignacio Canseco	Luis Alvarez
Chiapas	1. Román Pino	Manuel Garfías Salinas
	2. *Víctor Manuel Castillo*	Antonio Maza
	3. Federico Méndez Rivas	Miguel Huidobro de Azua
	4. José Villasaña	Abelardo Domínguez
	5. Juan Berriozábal	Jesús O. Argüello
Chihuahua	1. Bernardo Urueta	Francisco de P. Portillo
	2. *Francisco Albístegui*	*Porfirio Parra*
	3. Ignacio M. Luchichi	Jesús Arellano
	4. *Jesús E. Valenzuela*	Eduardo Castillo del Valle
Coahuila	1. Hilarión Frías y Soto	*Venustiano Carranza*
	2. Rafael Ramos Arizpe	Melchor G. Cárdenas
Colima	1. *Enrique O. de la Madrid*	Ignacio Michel
	2. *Ignacio M. Escudero*	Ernesto Ritter
Distrito Federal	1. *Pablo Macedo*	Ignacio Sánchez
	2. *Emilio Pardo, Jr.*	Emilio Baz
	3. *Francisco Sosa*	Juan de Pérez Gálvez
	4. Luis G. Labastida	Agustín M. Lazo
	5. Julio Limantour	Ernesto Chavero
	6. Alonso Rodríguez Miramón	Manuel Barreiro
	7. *José María Gamboa*	Ignacio Capetillo
	8. Tomás Reyes Retana	Alberto Icaza
	9. Manuel E. Rincón	Eduardo Noguera
	10. Enrique Olavarría y F.	Agustín Alfredo Núñez

Durango	1. Rafael Salcido	Fernando Zárraga
	2. Leopoldo Rincón	Juan N. Flores Quijar
	3. Roberto Orrantía	*Agustín Arroyo de Anda*
	4. Manuel Nacoechea	Gilberto Montiel Estrada

Guanajuato	1. *Eduardo Liceaga*	*Juan de Dios Peza*
	2. Indalecio Ojeda	Felipe Arellano
	3. Cecilio F. Estrada	Rafael Lavista
	4. Jesús Morales	Luis A. Aguilar
	5. Lorenzo Elizaga	Antonio Rivas Mercado
	6. Julio López Masse	Francisco Montaño Ramiro
	7. *Pablo Escandón y Barrón*	José Sauto y Sauto
	8. Alejandro Elguezábal	Archibaldo Guedea
	9. Jesús Loera	Nicolás del Moral
	10. *Francisco Mejía*	Ismael Zúñiga
	11. José María de Sauto	*Gildardo Gómez*
	12. Juan de Argumedo	José Briesca Saavedra
	13. *Francisco de P. Gochicoa*	Juan Hernández y Marín
	14. José Manuel de Sauto	Fernando Vega
	15. *Ismael Salas*	Moisés R. González
	16. Carlos Chico	Daniel García
	17. Manuel Carrillo Antillón	Rafael Casco
	18. Ignacio Ibargüengoitia	Manuel de Sales Zepeda

Guerrero	1. *Manuel Guillén*	José G. González
	2. Carlos Flores	Carlos Mercenario
	3. Mariano Ruiz	Fidencio Hernández
	4. Manuel Larrañaga Portugal	Ricardo Hornedo
	5. *Carlos de Olaguíbel*	Aldofo Díaz Rugama
	6. Ramón Corona	Ramón Prado
	7. Francisco Romero	Demetrio Sodi
	8. Aurelio Cadena y Marín	Luis G. Valdés

Hidalgo	1. Francisco Espinosa	*Carlos Díaz Dufoo*
	2. *Porfirio Parra*	Aurelio D. Canale
	3. José Domínguez Peón	Galo de Ita
	4. Domingo López de Lara	Francisco Moctezuma
	5. Manuel Mirus	Jesús Rodríguez
	6. *José Castellot*	Carlos López
	7. Luis Martínez de Castro	Jesús Díaz de León
	8. Manuel García Ramírez	Luis Hernández
	9. José María Garza Ramos	Bernabé Bravo
	10. Carmen de Ita	Tomás Mancera
	11. Aurelio Melgarejo	Rafael Manrique de Lara

Jalisco	1. Joaquín M. Escoto	Jesús Fructuoso López
	2. Prisciliano M. Benítez	Diódoro Contreras
	3. *Juan A. Mateos*	Francisco Urquiega
	4. Antonio Riva y Echeverría	Margarita García
	5. *Manuel Sierra Méndez*	Rafael Linares
	6. Bartolomé Carbajal	Amado M. Rivas
	7. Tomás Morán	José Ana Casillas
	8. Manuel Algara	Carlos Gómez Luna
	9. *Pedro Landázuri*	Carlos K. Ruiz

State	Deputy	Alternate
	10. Manuel Cervantes	Manuel M. Tortolero
	11. Luis G. Galván	Leopoldo Valencia
	12. Juan D. Rodríguez	Manuel Galván
	13. Luis Pérez Verdía	Francisco P. de Echeverría
	14. Nicolás Menocal	
	15. *Ireneo Paz*	Carlos Villegas
	16. *Rafael de Zayas Enríquez*	Manuel Prieto
	17. Genaro Pérez	Florencio Riestra
	18. Celso G. Ceballos	Eduardo Portu
México	1. Ignacio García Heras	Manuel Ruiz Sandoval
	2. Enrique Pérez Rubio	Jesús Rodríguez
	3. Manuel Para	Francisco Moctezuma
	4. Manuel Domínguez	Arturo Paz
	5. Carlos Casasús	Juan de Pérez Gálvez
	6. Julián Monticl	Rafael Pérez Gallardo
	7. Francisco Martínez López	Trinidad Pliego
	8. *Ramón Márquez Galindo*	Joaquín Oropeza
	9. Pedro Azcué	Joaquín Villada Cardoso
	10. Antonio de la Peña	Luis Riba y Cervantes
	11. Rafael Pardo	Manuel Illanes
	12. *Manuel Sánchez Mármol*	Alfredo Garrido
	13. Alberto Terreros	Salvador Vega Limón
	14. Antonio González	Miguel Avalos
	15. Alberto González de León	José Estrada
	16. Juan de Dios Chousal	Manuel Auza
Michoacán	1. *Luis G. Caballero*	Ulises Valdés
	2. *Rafael Reyes Spíndola*	Constancio Idiáques
	3. *Francisco A. Vélez*	Francisco Vélez, Jr.
	4. *Fernando González*	Enrique Mackintosh
	5. *Francisco Bulnes*	Celerino Luvianos
	6. Enrique Landa	Manuel Villaseñor
	7. Emilio Ruiz	Ridel Régules
	8. Fausto Moguel	Agapito Solórzano
	9. José María Romero	Aurelio Pérez
	10. *Angel Padilla*	Eduardo Viñas
	11. Juan de la Torre	Manuel Mercado
	12. Luis Pliego y Pérez	Alfonso Garay
	13. Jacobo Mercado	Everardo Hégensack
	14. Serapión Fernández	Manuel Barrios
	15. Miguel M. Acosta	Florentino Díaz
Morelos	1. *Gilberto Crespo*	José Casarín
	2. Antonio Tovar	Manuel Ramírez
	3. Manuel V. Preciado	Aristeo Calderón
	4. Ignacio de la Torre	Ramón Oliveros
Nuevo León	1. *Francisco M. Ramírez*	Jesús M. Cerda
	2. Manuel Serrano	Arnulfo Berlanga
	3. Manuel Z. Doria	Andrés Noriega
	4. Eleuterio del Valle	Lorenzo Sepúlveda

Oaxaca		
	1. Juan N. Castellanos	Darío Vasconcelos
	2. Manuel Escobar	Federico Zorrilla
	3. *Miguel Bolaños Cacho*	Gonzalo Espinosa
	4. José María Castellanos	Esteban Maqueo
	5. Juan Dublán	Juan Prieto
	6. Luis García Luna	Simón Parra
	7. Aurelio Valdívieso	Mariano Salgado
	8. Manuel Santibáñez	Francisco J. Carrero
	9. *Emilio Pimentel*	Lauro Cejudo
	10. Pascual Fenochio	Mariano Benavides
	11. Andrés Cruz Martínez	Guillermo Meixueiro
	12. *Benito Juárez Maza*	Manuel G. Escandón
	13. José Antonio Alvarez	José Ignacio Alvarez
	14. *Trinidad García*	Joaquín Ogarrio
	15. *Luis Pombo*	Enrique González Gaviño
	16. *Rosendo Pineda*	*Antonio Ramos Pedrueza*

Puebla		
	1. Carlos Martínez Peregrina	Alfredo Sandoval
	2. *Miguel Serrano*	Pedro Rangel
	3. Francisco Iturbide	Manuel Amador
	4. *Roberto Gayol*	Uriel Alatriste
	5. *Agustín Pradillo*	Manuel Flores
	6. Manuel Villaseñor	José Guadalupe Hinojosa
	7. Ignacio Muñoz	Eduardo Arrioja
	8. *Gregorio Mendizábal*	Manuel Lacroix
	9. Enrique Pazos	José Antonio de la Peña
	10. Telésforo Barroso	*Lauro Carrillo*
	11. Carlos Saavedra	Joaquín de la Barreda
	12. Enrique Romero Obregón	Rafael Marín González
	13. Joaquín Payno	Joaquín Pita
	14. *Pablo Martínez del Río*	Diego Martínez
	15. Eulalio Núñez	Delfino Arrioja
	16. José Issac Narváez	Rafael Hernández
	17. Javier Algara	Tomás E. Ramos
	18. *Roberto Núñez*	Francisco Cosmes
	19. Luis Garfías	Ramón Varela
	20. José Portilla	Ignacio M. Marín

Querétaro		
	1. Rafael Chousal	Domingo Barrios Gómez
	2. Leónardo F. Fortuño	Luis Sámano
	3. *Félix M. Alcérreca*	Agustín Ruiz Olloqui
	4. Fernando María Rubio	Eduardo Noguera

San Luis Potosí		
	1. *Justino Fernández*	Lorenzo García
	2. Manuel Orellana Nogueras	Alberto L. Palacios
	3. Jesús Martel	Alejandro Garrido
	4. José Vega	Alonso Fernández
	5. *Eduardo Dublán*	Marcos Vives
	6. Miguel Lebrija	*Pablo Verástegui*
	7. *Blas Escontría*	Camilo Arriaga
	8. Angel Carpio	Rafael Manrique
	9. Francisco de la Maza	Paulino Almanza
	10. Alberto López Mermosa	Adolfo Flores
	11. José E. de Landa	José Díez Gutiérrez
	12. Francisco Vázquez	Francisco Martínez

State	Deputy	Alternate
Sinaloa	1. *Angel Lucido Cambas*	Manuel Garrido N.
	2. Juan Garduño	Manuel Serrato
	3. Francisco D. Barroso	Juan Zaldívar
	4. *Guillermo Pous*	Arturo Paz
Sonora	1. Angel M. Domínguez	Franciso de P. Morales
	2. Manuel Thomas Terán	Ernesto Peláez
	3. Darío Balandrano	Carlos Garza Cortina
Tabasco	1. *Joaquín D. Casasús*	Manuel Mestre
	2. Ismael Rodríguez	Manuel de León
Tamaulipas	1. Manuel González	Antonio Domínguez
	2. Emilio Alvarez	José Antonio Gamboa
	3. *Juan B. Castelló*	Guillermo Obregón
Tepic (Nayarıt)	1. Francisco Rivas Gómez	Melesio Parra
	2. *Antonio Pliego y Pérez*	Felipe Rocha
	3. Ignacio Gómez del Campo	Antonio Zaragoza
Tlaxcala	1. Agustín Mora	Modesto Martínez
	2. Manuel Andrade	Manuel Rivera
	3. Teodoro Rivera	José N. Macías
Veracruz	1. *Leandro M. Alcolea*	Félix Díaz
	2. Modesto L. Herrera	Trinidad Herrera
	3. Enrique Llorente Rocha	Juan de Dios Rodríguez
	4. Francisco Dehesa	Eduardo Megal
	5. Donaciano Lara	Guillermo Obregón
	6. Mauro S. Herrera	Guillermo Valleto
	7. Rafael Herrera	Guillermo Obregón
	8. Manuel León	Gabriel Zárate
	9. Francisco J. Muñoz	Manuel Muñoz Landero
	10. *Salvador Díaz Mirón*	Isidro Rojas
	11. Rafael Rodríguez Talavera	Ignacio M. del Castillo
Yucatán	1. *Cástulo Zenteno*	José Clotilde Baqueiro
	2. Pedro Laclau	Manuel Domínguez Elizalde
	3. Benjamín Bolaños	Ramón Riveroll
	4. Salvador Dondé	Gonzalo Peón
	5. *Francisco Cantón Rosado*	Audomaro Reyes Sánchez
	6. *Emeterio de la Garza*	Felipe Cantón
	7. Cirilo F. Gutiérrez	Federico Peraza Rosado
	8. Demetrio Salazar	Angel M. Polo
Zacatecas	1. Alonso Mariscal	Manuel Valenzuela
	2. *Adalberto A. Esteva*	Ernesto Enríquez
	3. Eutimio Cervantes	Joaquín Irigoyen
	4. Gregorio Aldasoro	Juan Gutiérrez
	5. Agustín Lozano	Joaquín Sandoval
	6. *Genaro García*	José María Lámbarri
	7. Adolfo Hegewich	Ezequiel A. Chávez
	8. Marcos Simón Casteldi	Eduardo F. Arteaga

| | 9. *Alfredo Chavero* | Roberto García |
| | 10. Javier Osorno | Francisco J. Ortega |

1900–1902 (20th Legislature)

State	Deputy	Alternate
Aguascalientes	1. *Mariano Escobedo*	Mariano Escobedo, Jr.
	2. Miguel Güinchard	Jesús Díaz de León
	3. Francisco Ramírez	José Ferrel
	4. *Angel Ortiz Monasterio*	Francisco Rincón Gallardo
Baja California	1. Antonio Salinas y Carbó	Manuel Rivera
Campeche	1. Francisco G. Cosío	José Méndez Estrada
	2. Ignacio Canseco	Adalberto Quijano
Chiapas	1. Román Pino	Ezequiel Chávez
	2. *Víctor Manuel Castillo*	Domingo Chanona
	3. Federico Méndez Rivas	José Antonio Rivera
	4. José Villasaña	Enrique Torres Torija
	5. Tomás Macmanus	Carlos E. Margáin
Chihuahua	1. Bernardo Urueta	Francisco de P. Portillo
	2. Rafael Aguilar	Miguel Márquez
	3. Ignacio M. Luchichi	Jesús Arellano
	4. *Jesús E. Valenzuela*	Luis G. Palomar
Coahuila	1. Hilarión Frías y Soto	Alfredo E. Rodríguez
	2. Rafael Ramos Arizpe	Manuel Lazo Aldape
Colima	1. Ignacio Michel	Francisco Santa Cruz, Jr.
	2. *Ignacio M. Escudero*	José Camarena
Distrito Federal	1. *Pablo Macedo*	Ignacio Sánchez
	2. *Emilio Pardo, Jr.*	Emilio Baz
	3. Francisco Sosa	Juan Pérez Gálvez
	4. Luis G. Labastida	Agustín M. Lazo
	5. Julio Limantour	Rafael Cabañas
	6. Alonso Rodríguez Miramón	Tomás Noriega
	7. *José María Gamboa*	Ricardo del Río
	8. Carlos Flores	Alberto Icaza
	9. Manuel E. Rincón	Eduardo Noriega
	10. Enrique Olavarría y F.	Fidel Régules
Durango	1. *Enrique Creel*	Jesús M. Rábago
	2. Leopoldo Rincón	Juan N. Flores y Quijar
	3. Enrique Montero	*Agustín Arroyo de Anda*
	4. Manuel Nacoechea	Gilberto Montiel Estrada
Guanajuato	1. *Eduardo Liceaga*	*Juan de Dios Peza*
	2. Indalecio Ojeda	Felipe Arellano
	3. Cecilio F. Estrada	*Antonio Ramos Pedrueza*
	4. Jesús Morales	Luis A. Aguilar
	5. Lorenzo Elizaga	Antonio Rivas Mercado

State	Deputy	Alternate
	6. Julio López Masse	Francisco Montaño Ramiro
	7. *Pablo Escandón y Barrón*	José Sauto y Sauto
	8. Alejandro Elguezábal	Archibaldo Guedea
	9. Jesús Loera	Ignacio O. Ocádiz
	10. *Francisco Mejía*	Ricardo Suárez Gamboa
	11. José María de Sauto	*Gildardo Gómez*
	12. Juan de Argumedo	José Bribiesca Saavedra
	13. *Francisco de P. Gochicoa*	Luis Samano
	14. José Manuel de Sauto	Fernando Vega
	15. *Ismael Salas*	Moisés R. González
	16. Carlos Chico	Daniel García
	17. Manuel Carrillo Antillón	Rafael Casco
	18. Ignacio Ibargüengoitia	Manuel de Sales Zepeda
Guerrero	1. Manuel Guillén	José G. González
	2. Ramón Cosío González	Gabriel González Mier
	3. Adolfo Fenochio	Ricardo Hornedo
	4. *Carlos de Olaguíbel*	Ramón Reinoso
	5. Ramón Corona	Ignacio Capetillo
	6. Francisco Romero	Demetrio Sodi
	7. Alonso Guide	Aurelio Cadena
	8. Fidencio Hernández	Mauricio Scheleske
Hidalgo	1. *Carlos Díaz Dufoo*	Nicolás Menocal
	2. *Porfirio Parra*	Aurelio D. Canale
	3. José Domínguez Peón	Galo de Ita
	4. Domingo López de Lara	Francisco Moctezuma
	5. Manuel Mirus	Jesús Rodríguez
	6. *José Castellot*	Luis Hernández
	7. Luis Martínez de Castro	Jesús Díaz de León
	8. Mariano Ruiz	Heriberto Barrón
	9. José María Garza Ramos	Bernabé Bravo
	10. Carmen de Ita	Tomás Mancera
	11. *Gabriel Mancera*	Porfirio Díaz, Jr.
Jalisco	1. Joaquín M. Escoto	Antonio Maza
	2. Prisciliano M. Benítez	Diódoro Contreras
	3. *Juan A. Mateos*	Jesús M. Rábago
	4. Antonio Riva y Echeverría	Manuel J. Othón
	5. *Manuel Sierra Méndez*	Eleuterio del Valle
	6. Bartolomé Carbajal	Ernesto Enríquez
	7. Tomás Morán	Juan Gutiérrez
	8. Manuel Algara	Luis Palomar
	9. *Pedro Landázuri*	Celso G. Ceballos
	10. Manuel Cervantes	Ignacio Moreno
	11. José María Ortiz	Luis G. Galván
	12. Juan D. Rodríguez	Manuel Galván
	13. Luis Pérez Verdía	Eduardo Portu
	14. Vicente Luengas	Nicolás Menocal
	15. *Ireneo Paz*	Carlos Villegas
	16. *Rafael de Zayas Enríquez*	Manuel Prieto
	17. Genaro Pérez	Francisco de P. Echeverría
	18. Manuel M. Plata	*Querido Moheno*

México	1. Ignacio García Heras	Celso García
	2. Enrique Pérez Rubio	Javier Santa María
	3. Ernesto Chavero	Roberto García
	4. Manuel Domínguez	Arturo Paz
	5. Carlos Casasús	Juan de Pérez Galvéz
	6. Julián Montiel	Rafael Pérez Gallardo
	7. Francisco Martínez López	Luis G. Valdés
	8. *Ramón Márquez Galindo*	Carlos Chaix
	9. Pedro Azcué	Vicente Villada Cardoso
	10. Antonio de la Peña	Miguel Avalos
	11. Rafael Pardo	Manuel G. Rueda
	12. *Manuel Sánchez Mármol*	*Francisco Javier Gaxiola*
	13. Aurelio Melgarejo	Salvador Vega Limón
	14. Antonio González	*Roberto Esteva Ruiz*
	15. Alberto González de León	Jesús Urueta
	16. Juan de Dios Chousal	Manuel Auza
Michoacán	1. José María Romero	Manuel Mercado, Jr.
	2. *Angel Padilla*	Eduardo Viñas
	3. Juan de la Torre	José Canedo
	4. Luis Pliego y Pérez	Alfonso Garay
	5. Jacobo Mercado	Salvador González
	6. Serapión Fernández	Lorenzo Larrauri
	7. Julián Villarreal	*Miguel Silva González*
	8. *Luis G. Caballero*	Antonio Ramírez G.
	9. *Rafael Reyes Spíndola*	Constancio P. Idiáquez
	10. *Francisco A. Vélez*	Francisco Vélez, Jr.
	11. Fernando González	Enrique Mackintosh
	12. *Francisco Bulnes*	José Isidro Yáñez
	13. Enrique Landa	Manuel Villaseñor
	14. Emilio Ruiz y Silva	Fidel Régules
	15. Fausto Moguel	Pedro Argüelles
Morelos	1. *Gilberto Crespo*	José Casarín
	2. *Antonio Tovar*	José Aristeo Ochoa
	3. Manuel V. Preciado	Amador Espinosa
	4. Ignacio de la Torre	Francisco M. Rodríguez
Nuevo León	1. Manuel Cantú Treviño	Jesús María Cerda
	2. Manuel Serrano	Arnulfo Berlanga
	3. Lorenzo Sepúlveda	Andrés Noriega
	4. *José López Portillo*	Adolfo Zambrano
Oaxaca	1. Juan N. Castellanos	Manuel G. Prieto
	2. Manuel Escobar	Federico Zorrilla
	3. *Miguel Bolaños Cacho*	Gonzalo Espinosa
	4. José María Castellanos	Roberto García
	5. Juan Dublán	Manuel Martínez Mont
	6. Luis García Luna	Simón Parra
	7. Aurelio Valdivieso	Manuel G. Escandón
	8. Francisco J. Carrera	Enrique González Gaviño
	9. *Emilio Pimentel*	Simón Parra
	10. Pascual Fenochio	Antonio Maza
	11. Andrés Cruz Martínez	Guillermo Meixueiro
	12. *Benito Juárez Maza*	José Inés Dávila

State	Deputy	Alternate
	13. José Antonio Alvarez	José Ignacio Alvarez
	14. *Trinidad García*	Joaquín Ogarrio
	15. *Luis Pombo*	Enrique González Gaviño
	16. *Rosendo Pineda*	*Antonio Ramos Pedrueza*
Puebla	1. Carlos Martínez Peregrina	Alfredo Sandoval
	2. *Miguel Serrano*	José María Macías
	3. Francisco Iturbide	Rómulo Farrera
	4. *Roberto Gayol*	Uriel Alatriste
	5. *Agustín Pradillo*	Manuel Flores
	6. Joaquín Villada	Manuel G. Rueda
	7. Ignacio Muñoz	Emilio López Vaal
	8. Gregorio Mendizábal	Manuel Lacroix
	9. Enrique Pazos	Enrique Orozco
	10. Telésforo Barroso	Joaquín Calero
	11. Carlos Saavedra	Joaquín de la Barreda
	12. Ismael Zúñiga	Enrique Romero Obregón
	13. Joaquín Payno	José Antonio de la Peña
	14. *Pablo Martínez del Río*	Willehado Flores Ruiz
	15. Eulalio Núñez	José Rafael Hernández
	16. Constancio P. Idiáquez	Enrique Marín
	17. Javier Algara	Fernando C. Lavalle
	18. *Roberto Núñez*	Francisco Cosmes
	19. Luis Garfías	Ramón Varela
	20. *Lauro Carrillo*	José Portilla
Querétaro	1. Rafael Chousal	Alfonso Garay
	2. Leónardo F. Fortuno	Luis Samano
	3. *Félix M. Alcérreca*	Domingo Barrios Gómez
	4. Fernando María Rubio	Eduardo Noguera
San Luis Potosí	1. *Justino Fernández*	Joaquín Arguinzóniz
	2. Manuel Orellana Nogueras	Alberto L. Palacios
	3. Jesús Martel	Alejandro Garrido
	4. Alonso Fernández	Rafael Manrique
	5. *Eduardo Dublán*	Juan C. Bonilla
	6. Miguel Lebrija	Luis Espinosa Y Cuevas
	7. Mariano Fortuno	Antonio de P. Rodríguez
	8. José Méndez Estrada	Antonio Vázquez
	9. Francisco de la Maza	Francisco G. de Cosío
	10. Alberto López Hermosa	Ignacio Paulo
	11. José E. de Landa	José Barrenechea
	12. Fernando Camacho	Manuel S. Soriano
Sinaloa	1. Jesús Fructuoso López	Manuel Garrido N.
	2. Juan Garduño	Manuel Serrato
	3. *Rafael de Zayas Enríquez*	Juan Zaldívar
	4. *Guillermo Pous*	Arturo Paz
Sonora	1. Angel M. Domínguez	Arturo Iturriaga
	2. Esteban Mercenario	Ernesto Peláez
	3. Darío Balandrano	Carlos Garza Cortina
Tabasco	1. Joaquín D. Casasús	Manuel Mestre
	2. Ismael Rodríguez	Manuel de León

Tamaulipas	1. Manuel González	Antonio Domínguez
	2. Emilio Alvarez	Ricardo Suárez Gamboa
	3. *Juan B. Castelló*	Guillermo Obregón

Tepic (Nayarit)	1. Francisco Rivas Gómez	Melesio Parra
	2. *Antonio Pliego y Pérez*	Felipe Rocha
	3. Ignacio Gómez del Campo	Antonio Zaragoza

Tlaxcala	1. Agustín Mora	Modesto Martínez
	2. Manuel Andrade	Baldomero Andrade
	3. Teodoro Rivera	Melesio Parra

Veracruz	1. *Leandro M. Alcolea*	Rafael Alcolea
	2. Modesto L. Herrera	Angel Jiménez Prieto
	3. *Agustín Aragón*	Carlos Tejeda Guzmán
	4. Francisco Dehesa	Eduardo Melgar
	5. Donaciano Lara	Enrique Doleire
	6. *Félix Díaz*	Ramón García Núñez
	7. Guillermo Obregón	Enrique Herrera
	8. Manuel Levi	Trinidad Herrera
	9. Francisco J. Muñoz	Manuel Muñoz Landero
	10. *Salvador Díaz Mirón*	Isidro Rojas
	11. Rafael Rodríguez Talavera	Ignacio M. del Castillo

Yucatán	1. Rafael Dávila	Luciano Vargas
	2. Pedro Laclau	Luis F. Urcelay
	3. Benjamín Bolaños	Ramón Riveroll
	4. Salvador Dondé	Delio Moreno Cantón
	5. *Francisco Cantón Rosado*	Audomaro Reyes Sánchez
	6. *Emeterio de la Garza*	Manuel Domínguez Elizalde
	7. Cirilo F. Gutiérrez	Rafael Dorantes
	8. Demetrio Salazar	Alfonso Cámara y Cámara

Zacatecas	1. Isidro Rojas	Manuel S. Caballero
	2. *Adalberto A. Esteva*	Rafael Carbajal
	3. Eutimio Cervantes	Enrique Caloca
	4. Gregorio Aldasoro	Juan Gutiérrez
	5. Agustín Lozano	Joaquín Sandoval
	6. *Genaro García*	Ernesto Enríquez
	7. Adolfo Hegewich	Daniel Aguilar
	8. Marcos Simón Casteldi	Eduardo F. Arteaga
	9. *Alfredo Chavero*	Roberto García
	10. Alonso Mariscal y Piña	Javier Osorno

1902–04 (21st Legislature)

State	Deputy	Alternate
Aguascalientes	1. *Mariano Escobedo*	José Herrán
	2. Miguel Güinchard	Ignacio N. Marín
Baja California	1. Antonio Salinas y Carbó	Gastón J. Vives
Campeche	1. Francisco G. Cosío	Luis García Mezquita
	2. Ignacio Canseco	Eulogio Pereira Escobar

State	Deputy	Alternate
Chiapas	1. Román Pino	Ezequiel Chávez
	2. *Víctor Manuel Castillo*	Javier Santa María
	3. José María Villasaña	Onofre Ramos
	4. Francisco Rincón Gallardo	Enrique Torres Torija
	5. *Ignacio M. Escudero*	José Camargo
Chihuahua	1. Bernardo Urueta	Francisco de P. Portillo
	2. Eduardo Novoa	Jesús Rábago
	3. *Miguel Bolaños Cacho*	Jesús Arellano
	4. *Jesús Urueta*	Juan Zaldívar
	5. *Enrique C. Creel*	Rafael Aguilar
	6. *Porfirio Parra*	*José Trinidad Alamillo*
Coahuila	1. Hilarión Frías y Soto	Ignacio Alcocer
	2. Rafael Ramos Arizpc	Eduardo Lobatón
	3. Alfredo E. Rodríguez	José García Rodríguez
	4. *Manuel Garza Aldape*	Manuel de la Fuente
	5. *Francisco M. Ramírez*	José Ferrel
Colima	1. Ignacio Michel	José Manuel Othón
Distrito Federal	1. *Roberto Núñez*	Francisco G. Cosmes
	2. *Pablo Macedo*	Jesús Galindo y Villa
	3. *Manuel Flores*	Alberto Icaza
	4. *Emilio Pardo*	Rafael Angel de la Peña
	5. Luis G. Labastida	Isidro Díaz Lombardo
	6. Julio M. Limantour	Luis Riba y Cervantes
	7. *Francisco Sosa*	Agustín Lazo
	8. *Francisco Bulnes*	Luis Velasco Rus
	9. Juan de Pérez Gálvez	Luis Elguero
Durango	1. *Pablo Martínez del Río*	Juan N. Flores y Quijar
	2. Nicolás Menocal	Gustavo A. Esteva
	3. Enrique Montero	Gilberto Montiel Estrada
	4. Manuel Necoechea	Tomás Macmanus
	5. Angel Gutiérrez	Rafael Martínez Freg
	6. Jesús Menjarás	Alberto Flores
Guanajuato	1. *Eduardo Licéaga*	*Juan de Dios Peza*
	2. Indalecio Ojeda	*Felipe Arellano*
	3. Cecilio F. Estrada	*Antonio Ramos Pedrueza*
	4. Jesús Morales	Luis A. Aguilar
	5. Lorenzo Elizaga	Antonio Rivas Mercado
	6. Julio López Masse	Francisco Montaño Ramiro
	7. *Pablo Escandón y Barrón*	José Sauto y Sauto
	8. Alejandro Elguezábal	Archibaldo Guedea
	9. Jesús Loera	Ignacio O. Ocádiz
	10. Rafael Dávila	Javier Torres Rivas
	11. José María de Sauto	*Gildardo Gómez*
	12. Juan de Argumedo	José Bribiesca Saavedra
	13. *Francisco de P. Gochicoa*	*Angel Ortiz Monasterio*
	14. José Manuel de Sauto	Fernando Vega
	15. Salvador Echegaray	Luis Samano
	16. Carlos Chico	Daniel García

| | 17. Manuel Carrillo Antillón | Rafael Casco |
| | 18. Ignacio Ibargüengoitia | Juan Chapital |

Guerrero	1. Manuel Guillén	Eduardo Noguera
	2. Adolfo Fenochio	Isidro Rojas
	3. *Carlos de Olaguíbel*	Ignacio Burgoa
	4. Pedro Laclau	Hesiquio Marañón
	5. Francisco Romero	Francisco J. Meléndez
	6. Aurelio Cadena y Marín	Francisco Ortega M.
	7. Fidencio Hernández	Luis García
	8. Ramón Reynoso	Efrén Villalvaso

Hidalgo	1. *Carlos Díaz Dufoo*	Francisco Moctezuma
	2. Ignacio Sánchez	Carlos Tejeda Guzmán
	3. José Domínguez Peón	José Peón del Valle
	4. Pedro Argüelles	Armando Santa Cruz
	5. Manuel Mirus	Angel Jiménez Prieto
	6. *Emeterio de la Garza*	Antonio Grande Guerrero
	7. Mariano Ruiz	Heriberto Barrón
	8. José María Garza Ramos	Manuel Torres Sagaseta
	9. Carmen de Ita	Luis Hernández
	10. *Gabriel Mancera*	Galo de Ita

Jalisco	1. Joaquín M. Escoto	José G. González
	2. Diódoro Contreras	Francisco de P. Portilla
	3. *Juan A. Mateos*	Jesús Arellano
	4. José Rincón Gallardo	Francisco Magro
	5. *Ramón Corona*	Macario Nieto y Tello
	6. Bartolomé Carbajal	Amado M. Rivas
	7. Tomás Morán	Ignacio Moreno
	8. Manuel Algara	José de J. Anaya
	9. *Pedro Landázuri*	José R. Avila
	10. Manuel Cervantes	Francisco Macías Gutiérrez
	11. Jesús Rodríguez	Florencio Riestra
	12. *Luis Pérez Verdía*	Ignacio L. Montenegro
	13. Juan de Dios Rodríguez	Carlos Carral
	14. Enrique Pazos	Francisco Martínez Negrete
	15. *Ireneo Paz*	Ricardo Curiel
	16. *Rafael de Zayas Enríquez*	Eduardo Portu
	17. Genaro Pérez	Francisco de P. Echeverría
	18. *Manuel M. Plata*	*Querido Moheno*
	19. Manuel Martínez del Río	José Méndez Estrada

México	1. Ignacio García Heras	Arturo Paz
	2. Enrique Pérez Rubio	Ignacio Capetillo
	3. Ernesto Chavero	Juan Gutiérrez
	4. *Félix M. Alcérreca*	*Trinidad Alamillo*
	5. Carlos Casasus	*Samuel García Cuéllar*
	6. Manuel Villaseñor	Eduardo Noguera
	7. Francisco Martínez López	Ignacio L. de la Barra
	8. *Ramón Márquez Galindo*	Aurelio Canale
	9. Benjamín Bolaños	José Ignacio Icaza
	10. Antonio de la Peña	Miguel Avalos
	11. Rafael Pardo	Juan de Pérez Gálvez
	12. *Manuel Sánchez Mármol*	Roberto García

State	Deputy	Alternate
	13. Aurelio Melgarejo	*Roberto Esteva Ruiz*
	14. Antonio González	Javier Torres Rivas
	15. Alberto González de León	Salvador Esquino
	16. Juan de Dios Chousal	Manuel Auza
Michoacán	1. Pedro Martínez López	Nicolás Menocal
	2. Eduardo Viñas	Salvador Vega Limón
	3. Juan de la Torre	Fidel Régules
	4. Jacobo Mercado	Manuel Mercado
	5. Alfonso Garay	Lauro Arancivia
	6. Serapión Fernández	Tomás E. Pellicer
	7. Julián Villarreal	Alberto Correa
	8. *Luis G. Caballero*	Roque Macouzet
	9. *Rafael Reyes Spíndola*	Luis G. Arriaga
	10. *Francisco A. Vélez*	Francisco Vélez, Jr.
	11. *Fernando González*	*Federico Gamboa*
	12. *Enrique de Olavarría*	Ismael Pizarro Suárez
	13. Enrique Landa	Carlos Parra
	14. Emilio Ruiz y Silva	Salvador Cortés Rubio
	15. *Agustín Aragón*	Héctor Díaz
	16. *Gustavo A. Baz*	Ulises Valadés
Morelos	1. *Antonio Tovar*	Luis G. Urbina
	2. Manuel V. Preciado	Manuel Escudero y V.
	3. Ignacio de la Torre	Felipe Ruiz de Velasco
Nuevo León	1. *José López Portillo*	Adolfo Zambrano
	2. Manuel Serrano	Arnulfo Berlanga
	3. Lorenzo Sepúlveda	Andrés Noriega
	4. Jesús M. Cerda	Arnulfo Botello
	5. Francisco Martínez Baca	Francisco Salazar
	6. Diego de A. Berea	Mario Peña
Oaxaca	1. Juan N. Castellanos	Manuel M. Mimiaga
	2. Manuel Escobar	Francisco Belmar
	3. *Ignacio M. Luchichi*	Constantino Chapital
	4. José María Castellanos	Francisco Armendáriz
	5. Juan Dublán	Rafael Bolaños Cacho
	6. Luis García Luna	Simón Parra
	7. Aurelio Valdivieso	Andrés Portillo
	8. Francisco J. Carrera	Enrique González Gaviño
	9. *Emilio Pimentel*	Marcial Salinas
	10. Pascual Fenochio	Enrique Fenochio
	11. Andrés Cruz Martínez	
	12. *Benito Juárez Maza*	Juan Prieto
	13. José Antonio Alvarez	José Ignacio Alvarez
	14. Victoriano Fuentes	Ramón Bolaños
	15. *Luis Pombo*	Federico Pombo
	16. *Rosendo Pineda*	José Inés Dávila
Puebla	1. Carlos Martínez Peregrina	Pomposo Bonilla
	2. *Miguel Serrano*	Arturo Hurriaga
	3. *Roberto Gayol*	Tomás E. Ramos

	4. Alonso Rodríguez Miramón	Manuel E. Mercado
	5. Joaquín Villada	José Guadalupe Tonque
	6. Pedro de Azcué	José Antonio de la Peña
	7. Mariano Fortuño	Francisco L. Fortuño
	8. Vicente Luengas	Manuel Haro Mateos
	9. Telésforo Barroso	Enrique Marín
	10. Carlos Saavedra	Joaquín Pita
	11. Ismael Zúñiga	Adalberto Niño de Rivera
	12. Homero Bandala	Gildardo Gómez
	13. Demetrio Salazar	Fernando C. Lavalle
	14. Eulalio Núñez	Carlos Bello
	15. Constancio Peña Idiáquez	Sergio Bonilla
	16. Javier Algara	Rafael Martínez Carrillo
	17. Ricardo del Río	Angel W. Cabrera
Querétaro	1. Rafael Chousal	Ignacio Solares
	2. Agustín Mora	Luis F. Garfías
	3. *Félix M. Alcérreca*	Domingo Barrios Gómez
	4. Fernando María Rubio	Eduardo Noguera
San Luis Potosí	1. Manuel Orellana Nogueras	Alberto L. Palacios
	2. Jesús Martel	Joaquín Arguinzóniz
	3. Alonso Fernández	Antonio Vázquez
	4. Alberto López Hermosa	Adolfo Flores
	5. Miguel Lebrija	Luis Espinosa y Cuevas
	6. Lázaro B. Caballero	Ernesto Peláez
	7. Francisco de la Maza	Rafael Manrique
	8. Fernando Camacho	Pedro Barrenechea
	9. Alfredo Chavero	Enrique Romero Obregón
	10. José de Landa	Alejandro Garrido
Sinaloa	1. José Portilla	Norberto Domínguez
	2. Juan Garduño	Domingo Uriarte
	3. Luis Martínez de Castro	Miguel Retes
	4. *Guillermo Pous*	Enrique G. Martínez
	5. Juan García Brito	Enrique Romero
Sonora	1. Angel M. Domínguez	Ernesto Peláez
	2. Antonio Maza	Gustavo Torres
	3. Darío Balandrano	Carlos Garza Cortina
	4. *Víctoriano Salado Alvarez*	Manuel Uruchurtu
Tabasco	1. *Joaquín D. Casasús*	Manuel Mestre
	2. José Castellot	Manuel de León
	3. Rosalino Martínez	Gabriel González Mier
Tamaulipas	1. Domingo López de Lara	Luis Labat
	2. Ricardo Suárez Gamboa	Manuel M. Hinojosa
	3. *Juan B. Castelló*	Antonio Domínguez V.
	4. José María de la Vega	Antonio Rivera G.
Tepic (Nayarit)	1. Francisco Rivas Gómez	Juan González Quintanilla
	2. *Antonio Pliego y Pérez*	Felipe Rocha
	3. Ramón Cosío González	Luis Elguero

State	Deputy	Alternate
Tlaxcala	1. Modesto R. Martínez	Ignacio Carranza
	2. Miguel V. Avalos	Plutarco Montiel
	3. Teodoro Rivera	Rosalío Cahuantzi
Veracruz	1. *Leandro M. Alcolea*	Rafael Alcolea
	2. Modesto L. Herrera	Marcario Melo y Téllez
	3. Mauricio Scheleske	Manuel Galván
	4. Francisco Dehesa	Eduardo Melgar
	5. Donaciano Lara	Francisco J. Huarte
	6. *Félix Díaz*	Luis G. Senties
	7. Guillermo Obregón	Enrique Herrera
	8. Manuel Levi	Trinidad Herrera
	9. Francisco J. Muñoz	Manuel Muñoz Landero
	10. *Salvador Díaz Mirón*	Hesiquio Marañón
	11. Rafael Rodríguez Talavera	Ignacio M. del Castillo
	12. *Gregorio Mendizábal*	Trinidad González de la Vega
	13. Ignacio Muñoz	Leopoldo Villarreal
	14. *Trinidad García*	Roberto García
	15. Leopoldo Rincón	Leopoldo Núñez
	16. *Adalberto A. Esteva*	José Teófilo Ochoa
Yucatán	1. *Manuel Calero y Sierra*	Demetrio Molina
	2. Fernando Duret	Luis Vidal y Flor
	3. *Manuel Sierra Méndez*	Francisco Robleda
	4. Salvador Dondé	Enrique Fernández Granados
	5. *Francisco Cantón Rosado*	Néstor Rubio Alpuche
Zacatecas	1. Benjamín de Gyves	José María Echeverría
	2. Eutimio Cervantes	Gilberto García
	3. Gregorio Aldasoro	Cayetano de la Parra
	4. Agustín Lozano	Francisco Huarte
	5. *Genaro García*	Fernando Rosso
	6. Adolfo Hegewich	Jesús Morales
	7. Marcos Simón Casteldi	Manuel Soto
	8. Alonso Mariscal y Piña	Francisco Aguirre

1904–06 (22nd Legislature)

State	Deputy	Alternate
Aguascalientes	1. Francisco G. de Cosío	Jesús Díaz de León
	2. Ignacio Canseco	Valentín Gómez Farías
Baja California	1. Antonio Salinas y Carbo	Enrique Fernández Castelló
Campeche	1. Melesio Parra	Constantino Chapital
	2. José Aréchiga	Sebastián García
Chiapas	1. Eduardo Novoa	Jesús M. Rábago
	2. *Víctor Manuel Castillo*	Juan Andrade
	3. José Echeverría	Antonio Rubio Rocha
	4. Francisco Rincón Gallardo	Enrique Torres Torija
	5. *Ignacio M. Escudero*	José Camargo
	6. Fausto Moguel	Mauricio Iralda

Chihuahua	1. Bernardo Urueta	Francisco de P. Portillo
	2. *Ezequiel A. Chávez*	Antonio Mena
	3. Leopoldo Ortega	Vicente Vallada
	4. *Antonio Ramos Pedrueza*	Jesús Urueta
	5. *Enrique C. Creel*	*Juan Sánchez Azcona*
	6. *Porfirio Parra*	Gabriel Aguirre
Coahuila	1. Hilarión Frías y Soto	Andrés Sánchez Juárez
	2. Rafael Ramos Arizpe	Isaac Siller
	3. Alfredo E. Rodríguez	Ignacio Alcocer
	4. *Manuel Garza Aldape*	Encarnación Dávila
	5. Gregorio Ruiz	José Ferrel
Colima	1. Ignacio Michel	Balbino Dávalos
Distrito Federal	1. *Roberto Núñez*	Francisco G. Cosme
	2. *Pablo Macedo*	Jesús Galindo y Villa
	3. *Manuel Flores*	Alberto Icaza
	4. *Pablo Martínez del Río*	Eduardo R. García
	5. Luis G. Labastida	Luis G. Labastida, Jr.
	6. Julio M. Limantour	Luis Riba y Cervantes
	7. *Francisco Sosa*	Tomás E. Ramos
	8. *Francisco Bulnes*	Luis Velasco Rus
	9. Manuel Zamacona e Inclán	Heriberto Barrón
Durango	1. Rafael Pardo	Gilberto Montiel Estrada
	2. Nicolás Menocal	Crispín Aguilar
	3. Luis A. Aguilar	Alberto Flores
	4. Daniel García	Cirilio Gutiérrez
	5. Angel Gutiérrez	Agustín Lazo
	6. Jesús Monjaraz	Carlos Zarco
Guanajuato	1. *Eduardo Liceaga*	*Juan de Dios Peza*
	2. Indalecio Ojeda	*Felipe Arellano*
	3. Cecilio F. Estrada	José M. Garza Ramos
	4. Enrique Montero	Francisco Montaño Ramiro
	5. Lorenzo Elizaga	Antonio Rivas Mercado
	6. Jesús Morales	Manuel Torres Sagareta
	7. *Pablo Escandón y Barrón*	José Sauto y Sauto
	8. Manuel Guillén	Damián Flores
	9. Ramón Huerta	Archibaldo Guedea
	10. Rafael Dávila	Agustín Torres Rivas
	11. José María de Sauto	*Gildardo Gómez*
	12. Juan de Argumedo	José Bribiesca Saavedra
	13. *Francisco de P. Gochicoa*	Gustavo A. Esteva
	14. José Manuel de Sauto	Fernando Vega
	15. Jesús Loera	José Antonio Gamboa
	16. Carlos Chico	Salvador Echegaray
	17. Manuel Carrillo Antillón	Rafael Casco
	18. Juan Chapital	Daniel Reyes Retana
Guerrero	1. *Francisco Alfaro*	Enrique Baz
	2. Adolfo Fenochio	Rafael García Martínez
	3. *Carlos Díaz Dufoo*	Antonio Reyna
	4. Pedro Laclau	Carlos Garza Cortina

State	Deputy	Alternate
	5. *Jesús Urueta*	Juan Zaldívar
	6. *Juan A. Hernández*	Aurelio Cadena y Marín
	7. Juan Pérez Gálvez	Carlos Guevara Alarcón
	8. Ramón Reynoso	Matías Chávez
Hidalgo	1. *Carlos Olaguíbel y Arista*	Antonio Grande Guerrero
	2. Ignacio Sánchez	Salvador Quevedo y Z.
	3. José Domínguez Peón	José Peón del Valle
	4. Francisco Romero	Manuel Torres Sagaseta
	5. Manuel Mirus	Armando y Santa Cruz
	6. *Emeterio de la Garza*	Luis G. Otero
	7. Federico Hernández	Luis Hernández
	8. *Gabriel Mancera*	José Macías
	9. Carmen de Ita	Galo de Ita
	10. Juan A. Mateos	Manuel S. Rodríguez
Jalisco	1. Enrique Pazos	Lucio I. Gutiérrez
	2. *Luis Pérez Verdía*	Fortunato Arce
	3. Pedro Argüelles	Antonio Grande Guerrero
	4. José Rincón Gallardo	Pelegrín Prida
	5. *Ramón Corona*	Enrique González Gaviño
	6. Bartolomé Carbajal	Juan Belaunzarán
	7. Tomás Morán	José María Najar
	8. Manuel Algara	Carlos Prieto
	9. *Pedro Landázuri*	Francisco Magro
	10. Ramón C. Castañeda	José R. Aspe
	11. Joaquín Payno	Rafael O. Cortes
	12. Diódoro Contreras	Francisco Munguía Torres
	13. Juan de Dios Rodríguez	Carlos Carral
	14. Raúl Dehesa	José G. González
	15. *Ireneo Paz*	Luis I. Ruiz
	16. *Julio Guerrero*	Ricardo Curiel
	17. Genaro Pérez	Pedro Suárez
	18. *Manuel M. Plata*	*Querido Moheno*
	19. Manuel Martínez del Río	José Méndez Estrada
México	1. *José M. de la Vega*	Ignacio García Heras
	2. Enrique Pérez Rubio	Ignacio Capetillo
	3. Ernesto Chavero	Juan Gutiérrez
	4. Manuel Cervantes	Luis Manuel Rojas
	5. Carlos Casasús	José Portillo
	6. Manuel Villaseñor	Eduardo Noguera
	7. Emilio Ruiz y Silva	Joaquín García Luna
	8. *Ramón Márquez Galindo*	Aurelio Canale
	9. Benjamín Bolaños	Isidro Díaz Lombardo
	10. Antonio de la Peña	Francisco M. de Olabuíbel
	11. Eduardo Henkel	Luis V. Galván
	12. Enrique Landa	Gonzalo E. García
	13. Aurelio Melgarejo	*Roberto Esteva Ruiz*
	14. Pedro Martínez López	*Samuel García Cuéllar*
	15. Julián Villareal	Antonio Barbabosa
	16. Juan de Dios Chousal	Manuel Auza

Michoacán	1. Antonio González	Enrique González Gaviño
	2. *Ricardo García Granados*	Salvador Vega Limón
	3. Juan de la Torre	Fidel Régules
	4. Jacobo Mercado	Hipólito Reyes
	5. Alfonso Garay	Manuel Mercado, Jr.
	6. Serapión Fernández	Ernesto Enríquez
	7. Alberto González de León	Francisco G. García
	8. *Luis G. Caballero*	Javier Santa María
	9. *Rafael Reyes Spíndola*	*Francisco M. de Olaguíbel*
	10. *Francisco A. Vélez*	Francisco Vélez, Jr.
	11. Joaquín Sandoval	Carlos Parra
	12. *Enrique de Olavarría*	Francisco Carranza
	13. *Manuel Sánchez Mármol*	
	14. Francisco Martínez López	Samuel Contreras
	15. *Agustín Aragón*	José de las Muñecas
	16. Francisco de Landa y E.	Mauricio García
Morelos	1. *Antonio Tovar*	Luis G. Urbina
	2. Manuel V. Preciado	José María Carbajal
	3. Ignacio de la Torre	Luis Flores
Nuevo León	1. *José López Portillo*	Adolfo Zambrano
	2. Manuel Serrano	Arnulfo Berlanga
	3. Lorenzo Sepúlveda	Francisco Flores Saldaño
	4. Jesús M. Cerda	Arnulfo Botello
	5. Francisco Martínez Baca	Francisco Salazar
	6. Diego de A. Berea	José A. Muguerza
Oaxaca	1. Juan N. Castellanos	Ignacio Burgoa
	2. Manuel Escobar	Manuel M. Mimiaga
	3. *Ignacio M. Luchichi*	Andrés Portilla
	4. José María Castellanos	José Zorrilla
	5. Juan Dublán	Rodolfo Franco
	6. Antonio Rivas Mercado	Rafael Aguilar
	7. *Angel Ortiz Monasterio*	Gonzalo Espinosa
	8. Francisco J. Carrera	Enrique González Gaviño
	9. *Emilio Pimentel*	Simón Parra
	10. Pascual Fenochio	Demetrio Bolaños Cacho
	11. Andrés Cruz Martínez	Constantino Chapital
	12. *Benito Juárez Maza*	Joaquín Rivero y Heras
	13. José Antonio Alvarez	Joaquín Ogarrio
	14. Víctoriano Fuentes	Julio E. de Morales
	15. *Luis Pombo*	Federico Pombo
	16. *Rosendo Pineda*	Guillermo A. Esteva
Puebla	1. Carlos Martínez Peregrina	Ernesto Espinosa Bravo
	2. *Miguel Serrano*	Samuel Contreras
	3. *Roberto Gayol*	Tomás E. Ramos
	4. Alonso Rodríguez Miramón	Enrique González Gaviño
	5. *Manuel Carrascosa*	Eduardo Biaben
	6. Pedro de Azcué	Fortunato Hernández
	7. Maríano Fortuno	Francisco L. Fortuno
	8. Fernando Camacho	Manuel Haro Mateos
	9. *Rafael Hernández Madero*	Joaquín Pita

State	Deputy	Alternate
	10. *Alfredo Chavero*	Carlos Meijueiro
	11. Miguel Lebrija	Adalberto Niño de Rivera
	12. Homero Bandala	Clemente Escalona
	13. Demetrio Salazar	Fernando C. Lavalle
	14. Eulalio Núñez	Carlos Bello
	15. Constancio Peña Idiáquez	Sergio Bonilla
	16. Juan Garduño	Juan Gutiérrez
	17. *Guillermo Pous*	Angel W. Cabrera
Querétaro	1. Rafael Chousal	Alberto Chousal
	2. Agustín Mora	Ignacio Solares
	3. *Félix M. Alcérreca*	Domingo Barrios Gómez
	4. Fernando María Rubio	Eduardo Noguera
Quintana Roo	1. *Mariano Ruiz*	Vicente Villada
San Luis Potosí	1. Alberto L. Palacios	Joaquín Arguinzóniz
	2. Jesús Martel	Arturo Paz
	3. Alonso Fernández	David Reyes Retana
	4. Alberto López Hermosa	Adolfo Flores
	5. Ismael Zúñiga	Andrés Cuéllar y García
	6. José Carral	Antonio Echávarri
	7. *Agustín Pradillo*	Joaquín Villada
	8. Vicente Luengas	Octavio B. Cabrera
	9. Carlos M. Saavedra	Alejandro Garrido
	10. José de Landa	Luis Espinosa
Sinaloa	1. *José Portilla*	Luis García de Letona
	2. Javier Algara	Agustín Torres Rivas
	3. Luis Martínez de Castro	Domingo Uriarte
	4. Ricardo del Río	Arturo Paz
	5. Juan García Brito	José Lozano Vivanco
Sonora	1. Ricardo Suárez Gamboa	José L. Cosío
	2. Pomposo Bonilla	Carlos Aguirre Pellegría
	3. *Victoriano Salado Alvarez*	Juan de Arzamendi
	4. José Mena	Eduardo Portu
Tabasco	1. *Joaquín D. Casasús*	Manuel Mestre
	2. José Castellot	Horacio Jiménez
	3. Rosalino Martínez	Gabriel González Mier
Tamaulipas	1. Ramón Rabasa	Alejandro Ainslie
	2. Angel M. Domínguez	Luis Grajales
	3. *Juan B. Castelló*	Antonio Domínguez V.
	4. Antonio Maza	Fermín Legorreta
Tepic (Nayarit)	1. Ramón Bolaños Cacho	Luis Labat
	2. Gregorio Aldasoro	Pedro del Villar
	3. Benjamín de Gyves	José Vargas
Tlaxcala	1. Modesto R. Martínez	José N. Macías
	2. Francisco A. Dehesa	Ignacio Carranza
	3. Teodoro Rivera	Rafael Martínez Freg

Veracruz	1. *Leandro M. Alcolea*	Rafael Alcolea
	2. Modesto L. Herrera	Luis G. Sentíes
	3. Mauricio Scheleske	Manuel Fernández
	4. Miguel V. Avalos	Manuel Galván
	5. Francisco J. Huarte	Erén M. Reyna
	6. *Félix Díaz*	*Diódoro Batalla*
	7. Guillermo Obregón	Enrique Herrera
	8. Manuel Leví	Trinidad Herrera
	9. Francisco J. Muñoz	Manuel Muñoz Landero
	10. *Salvador Díaz Mirón*	Hesiquio Marañón
	11. Rafael Rodríguez Talavera	Ignacio M. del Castillo
	12. *Gregorio Mendizábal*	Trinidad González de la Vega
	13. Ignacio Muñoz	Leopoldo Villarreal
	14. *Trinidad García*	Luis Rebollar
	15. Leopoldo Rincón	Leopoldo Núñez
	16. *Adalberto A. Esteva*	Aristeo Ochoa
Yucatán	1. *Manuel Calero y Sierra*	Néstor Rubio Alpuche
	2. Fernando Duret	Francisco Robledo
	3. *Manuel Sierra Méndez*	Luis Vidal y Flor
	4. Salvador Dondé	Yanuario Manzanilla
	5. *Francisco Cantón Rosado*	Elidoro Rosado
Zacatecas	1. Ramón Cosío González	Daniel R. Aguilar
	2. Eutimio Cervantes	Trinidad Alamillo
	3. *Antonio Pliego Pérez*	
	4. Agustín Lozano	Ignacio L. de la Barra
	5. *Genaro García*	Francisco Urquiaga
	6. Adolfo Hegewich	Prisciliano Figueroa
	7. Julio López Masse	Andrés Ortega
	8. Alonso Mariscal y Piña	Guilebaldo Llanas

1906–08 (23rd Legislature)

State	Deputy	Alternate
Aguascalientes	1. Francisco G. de Cosío	Luis Lara Pardo
	2. Ignacio Canseco	Carlos S. Aguilar
Baja California	1. Antonio Salinas y Carbó	Gastón J. Vives
Campeche	1. Melesio Parra	Alberto Carbó
	2. José Aréchiga	*Miguel Lanz Duret*
Chiapas	1. Eduardo Novoa	Jesús M. Rábago
	2. *Víctor Manuel Castillo*	Gonzalo Ortega
	3. José Echeverría	Ignacio Michel
	4. Enrique Torres Torija	Miguel Utrilla
	5. Cirilio Gutiérrez	Samuel Contreras
	6. Eduardo Viñas	Fausto Moguel
Chihuahua	1. Bernardo Urueta	Enrique González Martínez
	2. *Ezequiel A. Chávez*	Simón Parra
	3. José María Gamboa	José Urueta
	4. *Antonio Ramos Pedrueza*	Justo Prieto

State	Deputy	Alternate
	5. *Juan Sánchez Azcona*	Angel Pola
	6. *Porfirio Parra*	Eugenio Esquerro
Coahuila	1. Rafael R. Arizpe	Encarnación Dávila
	2. Alfredo E. Rodríguez	Ignacio Alcocer
	3. *Manuel Garza Aldape*	Ricardo Curiel
	4. *Francisco M. Ramírez*	José Ferrel
	5. Alberto Guajardo	Carlos Pereyra
Colima	1. Ignacio Michel	Ernesto Mora
Distrito Federal	1. *Roberto Núñez*	Francisco G. Cosmes
	2. *Pablo Macedo*	Luis E. Ruiz
	3. *Manuel Flores*	Alberto Correa
	4. *Pablo Martínez del Río*	Eduardo R. García
	5. Luis G. Labastida	Luis G. Labastida, Jr.
	6. Julio M. Limantour	Ignacio Burgoa
	7. Andrés Sánchez Juárez	José Sánchez Juárez
	8. José Romero	*Samuel García Cuéllar*
	9. *José Algara*	Heriberto Barrón
Durango	1. Rafael Pardo	Jesús Galindo y Villa
	2. Nicolás Menocal	Manuel Mateos
	3. Luis A. Aguilar	Jesús Salcido y Avilez
	4. Daniel García	Carlos Zarco
	5. Angel Gutiérrez	Carlos Carral
	6. Manuel Zamacona	José M. Luján
Guanajuato	1. *Eduardo Licéaga*	*Juan de Dios Peza*
	2. Indalecio Ojeda	*Felipe Arellano*
	3. Juan Chico	José M. Garza Ramos
	4. Enrique Montero	Francisco Montaño Ramiro
	5. Lorenzo Elizaga	Antonio Rivas Mercado
	6. Jesús Morales	José Sauto y Sauto
	7. *Pablo Escandón y Barrón*	Melchor Ayala
	8. Damián Flores	Francisco Fernández Castelló
	9. Francisco Fernández I.	Agustín Torres Rivas
	10. Luis Vidal y Flor	Archibaldo Guedea
	11. José María de Sauto	Ricardo Otero
	12. Juan de Argumedo	José Bribiesca Saavedra
	13. *Francisco de P. Gochicoa*	Juan Zaldívar
	14. José Manuel de Sauto	Fernando Vega
	15. Jesús Loera	Eduardo Iturbide
	16. Carlos Chico	Salvador Echegaray
	17. Manuel Carrillo Antillón	Rafael Casco
	18. Juan Chapital	Daniel Reyes Retana
Guerrero	1. *Francisco Alfaro*	Enrique Baz
	2. Adolfo Fenochio	Rafael García Martínez
	3. *Carlos Díaz Dufoo*	Carlos Guevara Alarcón
	4. Pedro Laclau	Alberto Rivera
	5. *Jesús Urueta*	José J. González
	6. *Juan A. Hernández*	Aurelio Cadena y Marín

| | 7. Juan Pérez Gálvez | Gildardo Gómez |
| | 8. Ramón Reynoso | Faustino Estrada |

Hidalgo	1. *Carlos Olaguíbel y Arista*	Luis Hernández
	2. Ignacio Sánchez	Salvador Quevedo y Z.
	3. José Domínguez Peón	José Peón del Valle
	4. Francisco Romero	Manuel Torres Sagaseta
	5. Manuel Mirus	Armando y Santa Cruz
	6. *Emeterio de la Garza*	Ignacio Fernández Ortigosa
	7. Fidencio Hernández	*Francisco M. de Olaguíbel*
	8. *Gabriel Mancera*	Ignacio Durán
	9. Carmen de Ita	Antonio Grande Guerrero
	10. Juan A. Mateos	Gabriel Silva y Valencia

Jalisco	1. Enrique Pazos	Genaro Cervera
	2. *Luis Pérez Verdía*	Eduardo Bermúdez
	3. Pedro Argüelles	Rafael O. Cortes
	4. José Rincón Gallardo	Pelegrín Prida
	5. *Ramón Corona*	Juan Gutiérrez
	6. Jesús Monjaras	Ricardo Crombé
	7.	Lucio I. Gutiérrez
	8. Manuel Algara	Carlos Prieto
	9. Francisco Magro	Francisco Munguía Torres
	10. Ramón C. Castañeda	José R. Aspe
	11. Joaquín Payno	Luis Lara Pardo
	12. *Joaquín Redo*	Antonio Juambeltz
	13. Juan de Díos Rodríguez	Ignacio L. Montenegro
	14. Juan Osorio	Luis González de la Vega
	15. *Ireneo Paz*	
	16. *Julio Guerrero*	Ricardo Curiel
	17. Genaro Pérez	Felipe Valencia
	18. *Manuel M. Plata*	*Querido Moheno*
	19. Manuel Martínez del Río	Manuel R. Uruchurtu

México	1. *José M. de la Vega*	Ignacio García Heras
	2. Enrique Pérez Rubio	Agustín Alfredo Núñez
	3. Ernesto Chavero	Francisco M. de Olaguíbel
	4. Manuel Cervantes	Gonzalo E. Garces
	5. Carlos Casasús	Manuel Castañares
	6. Manuel Villaseñor	J. de Jesús Pliego
	7. Emilio Ruiz y Silva	Martín Suárez Gómez
	8. *Ramón Márquez Galindo*	Gabriel Aguillón
	9. Benjamín Bolaños	Franco Urquiaga
	10. Antonio de la Peña	Manuel Rojas
	11. Eduardo Henkel	Felipe Berriozábal
	12. Enrique Landa	*Francisco Gaxiola*
	13. Aurelio Melgarejo	Franco M. de Arredondo
	14. *Rafael de Zayas Enríquez*	Manuel Medina Garduño
	15. *Julián Villarreal*	Ernesto Enríquez
	16. Juan de Dios Chousal	Eduardo García

Michoacán	1. Enrique González Gaviño	Miguel Silva
	2. *Ricardo García Granados*	*Guillermo Pous*
	3. Juan de la Torre	Ulises Valdés

State	Deputy	Alternate
	4. Jacobo Mercado	Ignacio Durán
	5. Alfonso Garay	Ismael Pizarro Suárez
	6. Serapión Fernández	Rafael García Martínez
	7. Alberto González de León	José Vargas
	8. *Luis G. Caballero*	Felipe Iturbide
	9. *Rafael Reyes Spíndola*	Guillermo Fitzmaurice
	10. *Francisco A. Vélez*	Francisco Vélez, Jr.
	11. Joaquín Sandoval	Manuel Mercado, Jr.
	12. *Enrique de Olavarría*	Héctor Díaz Mercado
	13. Agustín Lozano	Salvador Vega Limón
	14. *José N. Macías*	Ladislao Belina
	15. *Agustín Aragón*	Aurelio Pérez
	16. Francisco de Landa y E.	Leandro Ibarra
Morelos	1. *Antonio Tovar*	Ramón Olivera
	2. *Justo Sierra*	José María Carbajal
	3. Ignacio de la Torre	Felipe Ruiz de Velasco
Nuevo León	1. *José López Portillo*	Adolfo Zambrano
	2. Tomás Macmanus	Arnulfo Berlanga
	3. Lorenzo Sepúlveda	Francisco Flores Saldaña
	4. Jesús M. Cerda	José Berruecos Tornel
	5. Juan Robles Linares	Agustín Torres Rivas
	6. José María García Ramos	José A. Muguerza
Oaxaca	1. Juan N. Castellanos	Ignacio Burgoa
	2. Manuel Escobar	Rodolfo Franco
	3. *Ignacio M. Luchichi*	Andrés Portilla
	4. José María Castellanos	Joaquín Camacho
	5. Juan Dublán	Ramón Pardo
	6. Rafael Aguilar	Gonzalo Espinosa
	7. *Angel Ortiz Monasterio*	Honorato Bolaños
	8. Francisco J. Carrera	Jacobo L. Grandison
	9. Marcial Salinas	Luis Mario Saavedra
	10. Enrique Fenochio	Salvador Bolaños Cacho
	11. Andrés Cruz Martínez	Manuel M. Mimiaga
	12. *Benito Juárez Maza*	Lorenzo García
	13. José Igancio Alvarez	Joaquín Ogarrio
	14. Víctoriano Fuentes	Julio E. de Morales
	15. *Luis Curiel*	José Zorrilla
	16. *Rosendo Pineda*	Guillermo A. Esteva
Puebla	1. Carlos Martínez Peregrina	Lorenzo Goroztiaga
	2. *Miguel Serrano*	Francisco Martínez Baca
	3. Carlos Garza Cortina	Luis G. Valdez
	4. Alonso Rodríguez Miramón	Ernesto Espinosa Bravo
	5. *Manuel Carrascosa*	Carlos Prieto
	6. Pedro de Azcué	Rafael Cortés
	7. Mariano Fortuno	Francisco L. Fortuño
	8. Fernando Camacho	Maurilio Iralda
	9. *Rafael Hernández Madero*	Manuel Haro Mateos
	10. *Alfredo Chavero*	Luis Riba y Cervantes
	11. Miguel Lebrija	Carlos Pereyra
	12. Homero Bandala	Joaquín Pita

	13. Demetrio Salazar	Sergio Bonilla
	14. *Ramón Manterola*	Luis Grajales
	15. Constancio Peña Idiáquez	Samuel García
	16. Juan Zayas Guarneros	Juan Gutiérrez
	17. *Guillermo Pous*	Angel W. Cabrera
Querétaro	1. Rafael Chousal	Alberto Chousal
	2. Prisciliano Maldonado	Domingo Barrios Gómez
	3. *Félix M. Alcérreca*	Miguel R. Soberón
	4. Fernando María Rubio	Ignacio Solares
Quintana Roo	1. Mariano Ruiz	Vicente Villada
San Luis Potosí	1. Alberto L. Palacios	Joaquín Arguinzóniz
	2. Arturo Paz	Octavio B. Cabrera
	3. *Alonso Fernández*	Francisco Olaguíbel
	4. Alberto López Hermosa	José López Moctezuma
	5. Ismael Zúñiga	Jacinto Cortina
	6. José Carral	Manuel Pereda
	7. *Agustín Pradillo*	Joaquín Villada
	8. Vicente Luengas	Roberto Irizar
	9. Carlos M. Saavedra	Adolfo Flores
	10. José de Landa	Rafael I. González
Sinaloa	1. *Juan García Brito*	Lorenzo Pérez Castro
	2. José Portilla	José C. Castelló
	3. Luis Martínez de Castro	Antonio Grande Guerrero
	4. Javier Algara	Alberto C. Carbó
	5. Ricardo del Río	Domingo Uriate
Sonora	1. Ricardo Suárez Gamboa	José L. Cosío
	2. Sergio Bonilla	Tomás E. Ramos
	3. *Rosalino Martínez*	Gabriel González Mier
	4. José Mena	Eduardo Castelazo
Tabasco	1. Cesáreo Garza	Ismael Pizarro Suárez
	2. José Castellot	Agustín Shulze Rincón
	3. *Victoriano Salado Alvarez*	Domingo León
Tamaulipas	1. Ramón Prida	Matías Guerra
	2. Pedro Rendón	Manuel Fernández Verna
	3. *Juan B. Castelló*	Antonio Domínguez V.
	4. Antonio Maz	Fermín Legorreta
Tepic (Nayarit)	1. Ramón Bolaños Cacho	Leopoldo Romano
	2. Gregorio Aldasoro	Guadalupe Trueba
	3. Francisco Rivas Gómez	Juan de Mata Román
Tlaxcala	1. Modesto R. Martínez	Pascual Santaella
	2. Francisco A. Dehesa	Ricardo M. Sousa
	3. Rafael Martínez Freg	Ignacio Carranza
Veracruz	1. *Leandro M. Alcolea*	Rafael Alcolea
	2. Modesto L. Herrera	Gonzalo Herrera
	3. Enrique D'Oleire	Trinidad González

State	Deputy	Alternate
	4. Raúl Dehesa	Rómulo Ferrara
	5. Francisco J. Huarte	Efrén M. Reyna
	6. *Félix Díaz*	*Diódoro Batalla*
	7. Guillermo Obregón	Francisco de P. Senties
	8. Manuel Levi	Trinidad Herrera
	9. Luis G. Sentíes	Leopoldo M. Núñez
	10. *Salvador Díaz Mirón*	Hesiquio Marañón
	11. Rafael Rodríguez Talavera	Ignacio M. del Castillo
	12. *Gregorio Mendizábal*	Joaquín Maas
	13. Ignacio Muñoz	Leopoldo Villarreal
	14. Carlos Romero	Luis Rebollar
	15. Leopoldo Rincón	Manuel Galván
	16. *Adalberto A. Esteva*	Aristeo Ochoa
Yucatán	1. *Manuel Calero y Sierra*	Néstor Rubio Alpuche
	2. Fernando Duret	Lorenzo Pérez Castro
	3. *Manuel Sierra Méndez*	Manuel Marrón Aguirre
	4. Salvador Dondé	Yanuario Manzanilla
	5. Julio S. Novoa	Leopoldo Alcalde
Zacatecas	1. Alvaro Rodríguez	José Higinio Escobedo
	2. Eutimio Cervantes	*José Trinidad Alamillo*
	3. *Antonio Pliego Pérez*	Guillermo de la Parra
	4. Ignacio L. de la Barra	Flavio Macías
	5. *Genaro García*	José L. García
	6. Adolfo Hegewich	Isidro Rojas
	7. Julio López Masse	Luis Angel Malda
	8. Alonso Mariscal y Piña	Rafael Noriega

1908–10 (24th Legislature)

State	Deputy	Alternate
Aguascalientes	1. Francisco G. de Cosío	Jesús Díaz de León
	2. Ignacio Canseco	
Baja California	1. Antonio Salinas y Carbo	Gastón J. Vives
Campeche	1. Melesio Parra	Manuel Sota Riva
	2. José Aréchiga	*Miguel Lanz Duret*
Chiapas	1. Eduardo Novoa	Jesús M. Rábago
	2. *Víctor Manuel Castillo*	Fernando Castañón
	3. José Echeverría	Victoriano Palafox
	4. Enrique Torres Torija	César Castellanos
	5. Emilio Alvarez	Leopoldo Rabasa
	6. Eduardo Viñas	Gregorio Culebro
Chihuahua	1. Bernardo Urueta	Justo Prieto
	2. *Ezequiel A. Chávez*	Simón Parra
	3. Fructuoso García	José María Gamboa
	4. *Federico Gamboa*	Heriberto Barrón
	5. *Antonio Ramos Pedrueza*	Luis Terrazas
	6. *Porfirio Parra*	Gabriel Aguirre

Coahuila	1. Rafael R. Arizpe	Francisco Villar
	2. Alfredo E. Rodríguez	Mariano Viesca y Arispe
	3. *Manuel Garza Aldape*	Ignacio Alcoer
	4. Gregorio Ruiz	*José Trinidad Alamillo*
	5. Alberto Guajardo	Carlos Pereyra

| Colima | 1. Ignacio Michel | Francisco Robles |

Distrito Federal	1. *Roberto Núñez*	Roberto Núñez, Jr.
	2. *Pablo Macedo*	Luis E. Ruiz
	3. *Manuel Flores*	Francisco Espinosa
	4. Guillermo Fitz Maurice	Perfecto Nieto
	5. Julio M. Limantour	Eduardo García
	6. *Francisco Olaguíbel*	*Samuel García Cuéllar*
	7. Andrés Sánchez Juárez	José Sánchez Juárez
	8. Ricardo R. Guzmán	Tomás Ramos
	9. José Romero	Tobías Núñez

Durángo	1. Rafael Pardo	Jesús Salcido y Avilez
	2. Nicolás Menocal	Carlos Zarco
	3. Luis A. Aguilar	José María Luján
	4. Daniel García	Luis de la Parra
	5. Angel Gutiérrez	Generoso Garza
	6. Manuel Zamacona	Lázaro Pavía

Guanajuato	1. *Eduardo Liceaga*	*Juan de Dios Peza*
	2. Indalecio Ojeda	Manuel Zapata Vera
	3. Bonifacio Olivares	José María Garza Ramos
	4. Enrique Montero	Francisco Montaño Ramiro
	5. Lorenzo Elizaga	Antonio Rivas Mercado
	6. Jesús Morales	José Sauto y Sauto
	7. *Pablo Escandón y Barrón*	Carlos Corona
	8. Francisco Fernández C.	Melchor Ayala
	9. Francisco Fernández I.	Albino Acereto
	10. Luis Vidal y Flor	Archibaldo Guedea
	11. José Chico	Ricardo Otero
	12. Juan de Argumedo	José Bribiesca Saavedra
	13. *Francisco de P. Gochicoa*	Manuel Romero Ibáñez
	14. Fernando Vega	Luis Vieyra
	15. Jesús Loera	Alberto Facha
	16. Tirso Inurreta	Luis Grajales
	17. Rafael Casco	David Reyes Retana
	18. Juan Chapital	Eduardo Iturbide

Guerrero	1. *Francisco Alfaro*	Eugenio Zubieta
	2. Adolfo Fenochio	José Landero Granados
	3. *Carlos Díaz Dufoo*	José Y. Yáñez
	4. Pedro Laclau	Manuel Sagaceta Vega
	5. José Castelló, Jr.	Arturo Alvaradejo
	6. *Juan A. Hernández*	Aurelio Cadena y Marín
	7. Juan Pérez Gálvez	Faustino Estrada
	8. Ramón Reynoso	Francisco Ortega

Hidalgo	1. Andrés Ruiz y Silva	Regino González
	2. *Mariano Ruiz*	Vicente Villada
	3. José Domínguez Peón	José Peón del Valle

State	Deputy	Alternate
	4. Francisco Romero	José L. Cossio
	5. Manuel Mirus	Armando y Santa Cruz
	6. *Emeterio de la Garza*	Manuel Torres Sagaceta
	7. Fidencio Hernández	Antonio Grande Guerrero
	8. *Gabriel Mancera*	José Zayas Guarneros
	9. Carmen de Ita	Luis Hernández
	10. Juan A. Mateos	Santiago Enríquez de Rivera
Jalisco	1. *Rafael Zubarán Capmany*	Sabino Orozco
	2. *Luis Pérez Verdía*	Antonio Ayala Ríos
	3. Pedro Argüelles	Joaquín Silva
	4. José Rincón Gallardo	Gustavo A. Esteva
	5. *Ramón Corona*	Manuel Castañares
	6. Jesús Monjaras	Ignacio Burgoa
	7. Manuel Algara	Jesús Galindo y Villa
	8. Francisco Magro	Luis García de Letona
	9. Alberto Correa	Manuel M. Tortolero
	10. Eduardo Delhumeau	Lucio Y. Gutiérrez
	11. *Joaquín Redo*	Antonio Juambeltz
	12. Juan de Dios Rodríguez	Celso G. Ceballos
	13. Juan Orozco	Ignacio L. Montenegro
	14. *Ireneo Paz*	Eduardo Prieto Basabe
	15. Luis Velasco Rus	Juan R. Orci
	16. Genaro Pérez	Octaviano de la Mora
	17. José María Vega	*Querido Moheno*
	18. Manuel Martínez del Río	Francisco Escudero
	19. José R. Aspe	Enrique Pérez Arce
México	1. Ignacio García Heras	Eduardo García
	2. Enrique Pérez Rubio	Amador Cárdenas
	3. Ernesto Chavero	Gonzalo E. Garcés
	4. Manuel Cervantes	Manuel Macías
	5. Carlos Casasús	Lorenzo Pérez Castro
	6. Manuel Villaseñor	Francisco Urquiaga
	7. Emilio Ruiz y Silva	Luis Lara Pardo
	8. *Ramón Márquez Galindo*	Manuel Torres Sagaceta
	9. Benjamín Bolaños	Tomás E. Ramos
	10. Antonio de la Peña	Gabriel T. Aguillón
	11. Eduardo Henkel	J. de Jesús Pliego
	12. Enrique Landa	Luis Manuel Rojas
	13. Aurelio Melgarejo	Manuel Castillo
	14. Manuel Fernández Berna	Angel Pola
	15. Lenar Chávez	Rafael Lara León
	16. *Julián Villarreal*	Ernesto Enríquez
Michoacán	1. Enrique González Gaviño	Aurelio Pérez
	2. *Ricardo García Granados*	Samuel Conteras
	3. Juan de la Torre	Jenaro Cervera
	4. Jacobo Mercado	Manuel Mercado, Jr.
	5. Alfonso Garay	Enrique Garay
	6. Alberto Gonalez de León	Gabriel García
	7. *Luis G. Caballero*	Francisco Icaza
	8. *Luis G. Caballero*	Ismael Pizarro Suárez
	9. *Francisco A. Vélez*	Francisco Vélez, Jr.

	10. Joaquín Sandoval	Leandro Ibarra
	11. *Enrique de Olavarría*	Manuel Mateos
	12. Salvador Vega Limón	Rafael Mancera
	13. Manrique Moheno	Ladislao Belina
	14. *José N. Macías*	Héctor Díaz Mercado
	15. *Agustín Aragón*	Perfecto Méndez Padilla
	16. Francisco de Landa y E.	Ulises Valdés
Morelos	1. *Antonio Tovar*	Manuel Ignacio Oropeza
	2. Ignacio de la Torre	José María Carbajal
	3. *Justo Sierra*	Felipe Ruiz de Velasco
Nuevo León	1. *José López Portillo*	Adolfo Zambrano
	2. Tomás Macmanus	Arnulfo Berlanga
	3. Lorenzo Sepúlveda	Francisco Flores Saldaña
	4. Jesús M. Cerda	Crispiano Madrigal
	5. Juan Robles Linares	Rafael García Martínez
	6. José María García Ramos	Carlos Basave
Oaxaca	1. Juan N. Castellanos	Luis Mario de Saavedra
	2. Manuel Escobar	Honorato Bolaños
	3. *Ignacio M. Luchichi*	José Zorrilla
	4. José María Castellanos	Rodolfo Franco
	5. Eutimio Cervantes	Luis Flores Guerra
	6. Manuel H. San Juan	Julio E. de Morales
	7. Rafael Aguilar	Guillermo A. Esteva
	8. Manuel Fernández Ortigosa	Nicolás Varela
	9. Francisco Carrera	Rafael Hernández
	10. Enrique Fenochio	Gonzalo Espinosa
	11. Andrés Cruz Martínez	Manuel Jiménez Ramírez
	12. *Benito Juárez Maza*	Demetrio Bolaños Cacho
	13. José Igancio Alvarez	Joaquín Ogarrio
	14. Víctoriano Fuentes	*Francisco Modesto Ramírez*
	15. *Luis Curiel*	Rodolfo Pardo
	16. *Rosendo Pineda*	Ignacio Burgoa
Puebla	1. Carlos Martínez Peregrina	Lorenzo Goroztiaga
	2. *Miguel Serrano*	Manuel Larrañaga Portugal
	3. Carlos Garza Cortina	Mariano Bonilla
	4. Carlos Aguilar	Manuel Romero Palafox
	5. José R. Avila	Marcos Antonio Carranco
	6. *Manuel Carrascosa*	Manuel Amador
	7. Pedro de Azcué	Agustín Alfredo Núñez
	8. Fortunato Hernández	Jesús M. de la Fuente
	9. Maríano Fortuño	Guillermo Obregón
	10. Fernando Camacho	Daniel González
	11. *Rafael Hernández Madero*	Joaquín Pita
	12. Alberto L. Palacios	José Antonio de la Peña
	13. Demetrio Salazar	José A. Loaeza
	14. *Ramón Manterola*	Julián Morineau
	15. Constancio Peña Idiáquez	Ernesto Espinosa Bravo
	16. Juan Zayas Guarneros	Rafael Marín
	17. *Guillermo Pous*	Angel W. Cabrera
Querétaro	1. Rafael Chousal	Alberto Chousal
	2. Prisciliano Maldonado	Antonio Alvarez Rul

State	Deputy	Alternate
	3. *Félix M. Alcérreca*	Ignacio Solares
	4. Fernando María Rubio	Domingo Barrios Gómez
Quintana Roo	1. *Mariano Ruiz*	Vicente Villada
San Luis Potosí	1. Alberto López Hermosa	Octaviano Cabrera
	2. Arturo Paz	*Encarnación Ipiña*
	3. Joaquín Paullada	Miguel A. Quijano
	4. José de Jesús Anaya	José López Moctezuma
	5. Ismael Zúñiga	Roberto Irizar
	6. José Carral	Mariano Palau
	7. *Agustín Pradillo*	Joaquín Villada
	8. Viccnte Luengas	Antonio F. López
	9. José de Landa	Adolfo Flores
	10. Carlos M. Saavedra	Rafael L. González
Sinaloa	1. Manuel R. Uruchurtu	Julián Morineau
	2. *José Portilla*	José C. Castelló
	3. Luis Martínez de Castro	Francisco de P. Millán
	4. Javier Algara	Gabriel Silva
	5. Ricardo del Río	Antonio Larriba
Sonora	1. Ricardo Suárez Gamboa	Rafael Cortés
	2. Sergio Bonilla	Tomás E. Ramos
	3. Gabriel González Mier	Manuel Marrón Aguirre
	4. José Mena	Eduardo Castelazo
Tabasco	1. Césareo Garza	Domingo León
	2. José Castellot	Nicandro L. Melo
	3. *Victoriano Salado Alvarez*	Manuel H. Nava
Tamaulipas	1. Ramón Prida	Luis G. Marrón Velasco
	2. Pedro Rendón	Guillermo Obregón, Jr.
	3. Ignacio Durán	Alberto Pro
	4. Antonio Maza	Alfredo Fernández Castelló
Tepic (Nayarit)	1. José Casarín	Salvador Chousal
	2. Gregorio Aldasoro	Guadalupe Trueba
	3. Francisco Rivas Gómez	Leopoldo Romano
Tlaxcala	1. Modesto R. Martínez	Manuel Macías
	2. Francisco A. Dehesa	Pascual Santaella
	3. Rafael Martínez Freg	Manuel Torres Sagaceta
Veracruz	1. *Leandro M. Alcolea*	Samuel García
	2. Modesto L. Herrera	Gonzalo Herrera
	3. Enrique D'Oleire	José Luis Requeña
	4. Raúl Dehesa	Trinidad González Vega
	5. Julio Monteverde	Rafael Alcolea
	6. Francisco J. Ituarte	Leopoldo M. Núñez
	7. *Félix Díaz*	*Diódoro Batalla*
	8. Guillermo Obregón	Ramón F. Cadena
	9. Manuel Levi	Trinidad Herrera

	10. *Salvador Díaz Mirón*	Hesiquio Marañón
	11. Rafael Rodríguez Talavera	Ignacio M. del Castillo
	12. *Gregorio Mendizábal*	Manuel Castañares
	13. Ignacio Muñoz	Leopoldo Villarreal
	14. *Manuel Calero*	Ramón M. Dehesa
	15. Leopoldo Rincón	Aristeo Ochoa
	16. *Adalberto A. Esteva*	Agustín Torres Rivas
Yucatán	1. Carlos Ramiro	Elías Amábilis
	2. Fernando Duret	Jenaro Cervera
	3. *Manuel Sierra Méndez*	Leopoldo Alcalde
	4. Salvador Dondé	Juan López Peniche
	5. Julio S. Novoa	Januario Manzanilla
Zacatecas	1. Alvaro Rodríguez	Daniel R. Aguilar
	2. *Antonio Pliego Pérez*	Antonio Bulnes Cabares
	3. Ignacio L. de la Barra	Cornelio Echegaray
	4. Juan Fenochio	Aurelio Gavatón
	5. *Genaro García*	Luis Martínez de Castro
	6. Adolfo Hegewich	Francisco Medina Barrón
	7. Julio López Masse	Guillermo Parra
	8. Alonso Mariscal y Piña	Guilebaldo Llamas

1910–12 (25th Legislature)

State	Deputy	Alternate
Aguascalientes	1. Antonio Tovar	Jesús Díaz de León
	2. Ignacio Canseco	Bandelio Contreras
Baja California	1. Francisco Bulnes	José Arce
Campeche	1. Melesio Parra	Manuel Aznar Preciat
	2. José Aréchiga	Aurelio Patiño
Chiapas	1. Eduardo Novoa	Jesús M. Rábago
	2. Fausto Moguel	Alejandro García
	3. Artemio del Valle	Leopoldo Rabasa
	4. Enrique Torres Torija	César Castellanos
	5. Juvencio Robles	Fernando de Gyves
	6. Manuel Larrañaga Portugal	Manuel Sagaseta Vega
Chihuahua	1. Bernardo Urueta	Francisco Asúnsolo
	2. *Ezequiel A. Chávez*	Simón Parra
	3. Fructuoso García	Pablo Prida
	4. *Federico Gamboa*	Juan Rondero
	5. *Antonio Ramos Pedrueza*	Espiridión Provencio
	6. Celso Acosta	Reinaldo Ramos
Coahuila	1. Rafael R. Arizpe	Luis del Toro
	2. Eliezer Espinosa	Mariano Viesca y Arispe
	3. José Echeverría	Dionisio García Fuentes
	4. Gregorio Ruiz	*José Trinidad Alamillo*
	5. *Carlos Pereyra*	Antonio Rodríguez

State	Deputy	Alternate
Colima	1. Ignacio Michel	Francisco Santa Cruz
Distrito Federal	1. *Roberto Núñez*	Roberto Núñez, Jr.
	2. *Pablo Macedo*	Luis E. Ruiz
	3. *Manuel Flores*	Francisco Espinosa
	4. Guillermo Fitz Maurice	Manuel Lascuráin
	5. *Miguel Lanz Duret*	Eduardo García
	6. *Francisco Olaguíbel*	Tomás Ramos
	7. Andrés Sánchez Juárez	José Sánchez Juárez
	8. Antonio Peñafiel	Joaquín de Haro
	9. José Romero	Agustín M. Lazo
Durango	1. Rafael Pardo	Adrián Castillo
	2. Nicolás Menocal	Carlos Zarco
	3. Luis A. Aguilar	Jesús Salcido Avilás
	4. Daniel García	Samuel García
	5. Angel Gutiérrez	Javier Icaza
	6. Eleuterio Martínez	Lázaro Pavía
Guanajuato	1. *Eduardo Licéaga*	Francisco Morales
	2. Indalecio Ojeda	Carlos Alvarez
	3. Bonifacio Olivares	Honorato Bolaños
	4. Enrique Montero	Francisco Montaño Ramiro
	5. Lorenzo Elizaga	Guillermo Novoa
	6. Santiago Sierra	José Sauto y Sauto
	7. *Pablo Escandón y Barrón*	Carlos Corona
	8. Melchor Ayala	Francisco Fernández C.
	9. Francisco Fernández I.	Enrique Langenscher
	10. Luis Vidal y Flor	Archibaldo Guedea
	11. Nicéforo Guerrero	Ricardo Otero
	12. Juan de Argumedo	José Bribiesca Saavedra
	13. Luis Espinosa y Cuevas	Eduardo Iturbide, Jr.
	14. Bernabé de la Parra	Luis Vieyra
	15. Jesús Loera	Luis Morales Cortázar
	16. Tirso Inurreta	Carlos Hoth
	17. Rafael Casco	David Reyes Retana
	18. Juan Chapital	Albino Acereto
Guerrero	1. Manuel Sagaseta Vega	Francisco Munguía
	2. Adolfo Fenochio	Teófilo del Castillo
	3. *Carlos Díaz Dufoo*	Alberto Jiménez
	4. Pedro Laclau	José Landero Granados
	5. Jesús Urias	Manuel Olea
	6. *Juan A. Hernández*	Aurelio Cadena y Marín
	7. Juan Pérez Gálvez	Arturo Alvaradejo
	8. Abraham Bandala	Ramón Reynoso
Hidalgo	1. Andrés Ruiz y Silva	Regino González
	2. *Mariano Ruiz*	Vicente Villada
	3. José Peon del Valle	Francisco Rosete
	4. Francisco Romero	Agustín M. Lazo
	5. Manuel Mirus	Armando I. Santa Cruz
	6. Joaquín González Ortega	José María Valero

	7. Javier Torres Rivas	Fidencio Hernández
	8. Jesús Lujan	*José María Luján*
	9. Carmen de Ita	Carlos Sánchez Mejorada
	10. Juan A. Mateos	Herón Rodríguez
Jalisco	1. *Luis Pérez Verdía*	Joaquín P. Riveroll
	2. Salvador Chousel	Joaquín Silva
	3. José Luciano Varela	Salvador de la Rosa
	4. *José María Gamboa*	Eduardo Prieto Basave
	5. Carlos Aguirre	Gustavo A. Esteva
	6. Jesús Monjarás	Antonio Ayala y Ríos
	7. Manuel Algara	Enrique Pérez Arce
	8. Francisco Magro	Marco Antonio Barranco
	9. J. Isaac Aceves	Lucio I. Gutiérrez
	10. *Eduardo Delhumeau*	Felipe Valencia
	11. *Joaquín Redo*	Ignacio L. Montenegro
	12. Juan de Dios Rodríguez	Jesús Z. Moreno
	13. Juan Orozco	José María Lozano
	14. Miguel Zárate	Manuel M. Tortolero
	15. Luis Velasco Rus	Enrique Rodríguez Miramón
	16. Genaro Pérez	Julián Morineau
	17. José María Vega	*Querido Moheno*
	18. Alberto Crespo	Francisco V. Escalante
	19. José R. Aspe	Gabriel Silva Valencia
México	1. Francisco Millán	Benito Sánchez Valdés
	2. *José María Lozano*	Antonio Cárdenas
	3. Ernesto Chavero	Julio Cecilio Santana
	4. Arturo Alvaradejo	Antonio Alvarez Rul
	5. Manuel Villaseñor	Francisco Urquiaga
	6. Emilio Ruiz y Silva	Luis Manuel Rojas
	7. *Ramón Márquez Galindo*	Rubén Valenti
	8. Benjamín Bolaños	Eduardo García
	9. Antonio de la Peña	Juan R. Ororci
	10. Eduardo Henkel	Tomás E. Ramos
	11. Enrique Landa	Luis Angel Malda
	12. Aurelio Melgarejo	Manuel del Castillo
	13. Manuel Fernández Berna	José de la Vega
	14. Llenar Chávez	Martín Suárez Gómez
	15. *Julián Villarreal*	Gabriel F. Aguillón
	16. Carlos Casasús	Adolfo E. Grajales
Michoacán	1. *Nemesio García Naranjo*	Ernesto Enríquez
	2. *Ricardo García Granados*	José Delgado
	3. Juan de la Torre	Eduardo González
	4. Jacobo Mercado	Ulises Valdés
	5. Alfonso Garay	Enrique Garay
	6. *Luis G. Caballero*	Manuel Mercado
	7. *Rafael Reyes Spíndola*	José Reyes Spíndola
	8. *Francisco A. Vélez*	Francisco Vélez, Jr.
	9. Rafael Alcolea	Juan de la Orta
	10. José N. Macías	Héctor Díaz Mercado
	11. Salvador Vega Limón	Ismael Pizarro Suárez
	12. Gabriel González Mier	Ladislao Belina
	13. Francisco de Landa	José María Silva

State	Deputy	Alternate
	14. Alberto González de León	Ramón Murguía
	15. Joaquín Sandoval	Luis G. Zumaya
	16. Ricardo Molina	Alberto Guillén
Morelos	1. Francisco González de C.	Ignacio Ortega
	2. Ignacio de la Torre	Alberto Sánchez
	3. *Justo Sierra*	Fernando Reyes Durán
Nuevo León	1. Carlos Herrera	Eduardo I. Martínez
	2. Amador Cárdenas	Eulalio Sanmiguel
	3. J. F. de P. Maldonado	Pablo V. González
	4. Jesús M. Cerda	Agustín Garza Galindo
	5. Juan Robles Linares	Rafael García Martínez
	6. José María García Ramos	Celso Canales
Oaxaca	1. Juan N. Castellanos	*Francisco Modesto Ramírez*
	2. Manuel Escobar	José Zorrilla
	3. *Ignacio M. Luchichi*	Manuel Palacios Silva
	4. José María Castellanos	Joaquín Ogarrio
	5. *Samuel García Cuéllar*	Eutimio Cervantes
	6. Manuel H. San Juan	Adolfo G. Silva
	7. Rafael Aguilar	Isuaro Figueroa
	8. Manuel Fernández Ortigosa	Carlos Benavides
	9. Francisco Carrera	Ignacio Burgoa
	10. Enrique Fenochio	Manuel María Mimiaga
	11. Andrés Cruz Martínez	Juan Acevedo y Camacho
	12. *Benito Juárez Maza*	Wenceslao García
	13. José Ignacio Alvarez	Luis M. Saavedra
	14. Víctoriano Fuentes	Nicanor Cruz
	15. *Luis Curiel*	Pablo Prida
	16. *Rosendo Pineda*	Angel Pola
Puebla	1. Carlos Martínez Peregrina	Federico López
	2. *Miguel Serrano*	Samuel Contreras
	3. Carlos Garza Cortina	Rafael Serrano
	4. Carlos Aguilar	Enrique Santibáñez
	5. José R. Avila	Joaquín Pita
	6. *Manuel Carrascosa*	Francisco Flores
	7. Pedro de Azcué	Aquiles Centella
	8. Eduardo Mestre Ghigliazza	Ernesto Solís
	9. Fortunato Hernández	Rafael Marín
	10. Fernando Camacho	Ernesto Espinosa
	11. *Rafael Hernández Madero*	Alejandro D. Ainslie
	12. Alberto L. Palacios	Modesto Tamariz
	13. Demetrio Salazar	Ernesto Mora
	14. *Ramón Manterola*	Leonardo Viramontes
	15. Constancio Peña Idiáquez	Delfino Arrioja
	16. Juan Zayas Guarneros	Francisco Lozano
	17. *Guillermo Pous*	Angel W. Cabrera
Querétaro	1. Rafael Chousal	Alberto Chousal
	2. Prisciliano Maldonado	Agustín Alfredo Núñez
	3. *Félix M. Alcérreca*	Ignacio Solares
	4. Fernando María Rubio	Samuel Contreras

Quintana Roo   1. Antonio Salinas Carbó

San Luis Potosí
1. Alberto López Hermosa — Samuel García
2. Arturo Paz — *Encarnación Ipiña*
3. Joaquín Paullada — José López Moctezuma
4. José de Jesús Anaya — Gabriel Aguillón
5. Ismael Zúñiga — Miguel A. Quijano
6. José Carral — *Miguel Lanz Duret*
7. Joaquín Maas — Tomás Berlanga
8. Vicente Luengas — Miguel V. Avalos
9. Julián Morineau — Adolfo Flores
10. Luis Riba y Cervantes — Rafael I. González

Sinaloa
1. Manuel R. Uruchurtu — Julián Morineau
2. José Portilla — Santiago J. Sierra
3. Luis Martínez de Castro — Mario Bulnes
4. Javier Algara — Antonio Larriba
5. Ricardo del Río — Francisco Alcalde

Sonora
1. Ricardo Suárez Gamboa — Lucio I. Gutiérrez
2. Sergio Bonilla — Avelino Espinosa
3. José Mena — Eduardo Castelazo
4. José Castellót, Jr. — Aurelio D. Canale

Tabasco
1. Carlos A. Saavedra — Joaquín Oropeza
2. Manrique Moheno — Domingo León
3. Ignacio Bravo Betancourt — Manuel Pasalaga

Tamaulipas
1. Ramón Prida — Manuel Mateos Cejudo
2. Pedro Rendón — Luis G. Marrón Velasco
3. Ignacio Durán — Alberto Pró
4. Antonio Maza — Cayetano Garza Cortina

Tepic (Nayarit)
1. José Casarín — Ignacio Galván
2. Gregorio Aldasoro — Guadalupe Trueba
3. Francisco Rivas Gómez — Luis Martínez de Castro

Tlaxcala
1. Horacio Lolanne — Rafael Anzúres
2. Francisco A. Dehesa — Gildardo Márquez
3. José Juan Tablada — Manuel Cuéllar

Veracruz
1. *Diódoro Batalla* — Eduardo M. Cauz
2. Manuel Mercado — Carlos E. Ramírez
3. Enrique D'Oleire — José Luis Requena
4. Raúl Dehesa — Trinidad González Vega
5. Julio Monteverde — Rafael Alcolea
6. Francisco J. Ituarte — Leopoldo M. Núñez
7. *Félix Díaz* — Telésforo Ocampo
8. Guillermo Obregón — Ramón F. Cadena
9. Manuel Leví — Trinidad Herrera
10. *Salvador Díaz Mirón* — Hesiquio Marañón
11. Rafael Rodríguez Talavera — Gonzalo Herrera
12. *Gregorio Mendizábal* — Juan B. Delgado
13. Ignacio Muñoz — Leopoldo Villarreal
14. *Manuel Calero* — Felipe Salazar

State	Deputy	Alternate
	15. Leopoldo Rincón	Aristeo Ochoa
	16. *Adalberto A. Esteva*	Samuel García
Yucatán	1. Carlos Ramiro	Agustín Torres Rivas
	2. Fernando Duret	Pedro Solís Cámara
	3. *Manuel Sierra Méndez*	Alonso Aznar Mendoza
	4. Salvador Dondé	Juan R. Orci
	5. Julio S. Novoa	Manuel Romero Palafox
Zacatecas	1. Alvaro Rodríguez	*Nemesio García Naranjo*
	2. *Antonio Pliego Pérez*	Vicente F. Zárate
	3. Ignacio L. de la Barra	Telésforo Ocampo
	4. José González Ortega	Fernando Sansalvador
	5. *Genaro García*	Enrique C. Andrade
	6. Adolfo Hegewich	Adolfo Medina
	7. Juan R. Orci	Higinio A. Escobedo
	8. Alonso Mariscal y Piña	Luis Martínez de Castro, Jr.

1912–14 (26th Legislature)

State	Deputy	Alternate
Aguascalientes	1. Eduardo J. Correa	Demetrio Rizo
	2. Román Morales	Carlos A. Sala López
Baja California	1. Antonio G. Canalizo	Miguel L. Cornejo
Campeche	1. Salvador Martínez Alomía	José Ferrer MacGregor
	2. *Juan Zubarán*	Francisco Perera Escobar
Chiapas	1. Jesús Martínez Rojas	Diego Coello Lara
	2. Rómulo Farrera	Virgilio Figueroa
	3. Manuel Rovelo Argüello	Eleuterio Aguilar
	4. César Castellanos	Leopoldo de la Vega
	5. Adolfo E. Grajales	Enoch Paniagua
	6. *Querido Moheno*	Lisandro López
	7. Virgilio Figueroa	Teófilo Castillo Corzo
Chihuahua	1. None elected	
	2. None elected	
	3. None elected	
	4. None elected	
	5. None elected	
	6. None elected	
Coahuila	1. *Roque González Garza*	Serapio Aguirre
	2. *Gustavo A. Madero*	Salvador Benavides
	3. Rafael L. Hernández	Hilario Carrillo
	4. *Eliseo Arredondo*	Jorge E. Von Versen
	5. *Adrián Aguirre Benavides*	Hilario Delgado
Colima	1. *Arturo Gómez*	Manuel R. Alvarez

Distrito Federal		
	1. *Carlos Trejo y Lerdo*	Emanuel Amor
	2. Marcos López Jiménez	Néstor Monroy
	3. *Jesús Urueta*	Rafael Moya
	4. *Eduardo F. Hay*	*Marcelino Dávalos*
	5. *Jorge Vera Estañol*	Antonio Maza
	6. Mauricio Gómez	*Rafael Pérez Taylor*
	7. Silvestre Anaya	Eduardo R. Velázquez
	8. Alfredo Ortega	Daniel Leal
	9. Adolfo Orive	Manuel Origel
	10. Carlos B. Zetina	Ricardo Ramírez
	11. *Luis Cabrera*	Pablo Salinas y Delgado
	12. *Juan Sánchez Azcona*	Carlos Argüelles

Durango		
	1. *Ignacio Borrego*	Manuel Loaeza
	2. Pedro B. Alvarez	Zeferino Murga
	3. Vacant	
	4. Adalberto Ríos	Manuel del Real Alfaro
	5. *Luis Zubiría y Campa*	Alberto Flores
	6. Vacant	
	7. Vacant	

Guanajuato		
	1. Alejandro M. Ugarte	Federico Villaseñor
	2. Enrique Bordes Mangel	Fernando Chico
	3. Gonzalo Ruiz	Isaac Aguilar
	4. Manuel F. Villaseñor	Alberto Sánchez Vallejo
	5. Carlos Vargas Galeana	Enrique del Moral
	6. José Villaseñor	Benedicto Navarro
	7. Miguel Díaz Infante	Wenceslao Torres Camarena
	8. Manuel Malo y Juvera	David Rincón Gallardo
	9. *José María de la Vega*	*Manuel G. Aranda*
	10. Flavio González	Enrique Mendoza y Albarrán
	11. *José Natividad Macías*	Salvador Puente
	12. Ramón Mújica Leyva	Francisco Díaz Barriga
	13. Miguel Castelazo Fuentes	Francisco de P. Mendoza
	14. Joaquín Ramos Roa	José Ma. Hernández
	15. Francisco de G. Arce	Pedro de G. Arce
	16. Angel Rivero Caloca	Felipe Ortiz
	17. Florencio Cabrera	Juan Pizarro Suárez
	18. Pablo Lozada	Celso Ledesma

Guerrero		
	1. Alfonso G. Alarcón	Eduardo Mendoza
	2. Rafael del Castillo C.	Simón Ventura
	3. Vacant	
	4. José María Acevedo	José de Jesús Nieto
	5. Eduardo Neri	Bonifacio Rodríguez
	6. Faustino Estrada	Luis G. Flores
	7. Vacant	
	8. Vacant	

Hidalgo		
	1. Ricardo Pascoe	J. Guadalupe Nava
	2. José M. Montaño	Javier Piña y Aguayo
	3. Manuel Gea González	Antonio Gea González
	4. Francisco de la Peña	Florencio Hernández
	5. Manuel Ramírez Castillo	Alfredo Vite

State	Deputy	Alternate
	6. *Alfonso Cravioto*	Salvador Guerrero
	7. Luis Jasso	Rafael Delgado
	8. *Francisco Romero*	José María Lezama
	9. Alfonso Varela	Manuel Ortiz
	10. Jesús del Rosal	Antonio Guerrero
Jalisco	1. *Francisco Escudero*	Salvador Garibay
	2. Manuel F. de la Hoz	Luis B. de la Mora
	3. Ismael Palomino	J. Guadalupe Sánchez
	4. Rafael de la Mora	Juan N. Nieto
	5. Jacobo Romo	Antonio Rivera de la Torre
	6. Gonzalo del Castillo N.	Zenón de la Torre
	7. *José María Lozano*	Tomás Rosales
	8. Juan L. Lomelí	Juan Pérez Sahagún
	9. Victoriano Aceves	Miguel Palomar y Vizcarra
	10. *Rodolfo Reyes*	Salvador Jiménez Loza
	11. Luis Manuel Rojas	Francisco González Arias
	12. Enrique Alvarez del C.	Carlos G. Villaseñor
	13. Gabriel Vargas	Jacinto Robles Martínez
	14. Jesús Camarena	Miguel R. Martínez
	15. *Jorge Delorme y Campos*	Epitacio Silva
	16. Ignacio Galván	Jorge Silva
	17. Pascual Alva	Lorenzo Llano y Valdés
	18. Jacinto Cortina	Mauro Velasco
	19. José González Rubio	Eustaquio Mendoza
	20. Carlos Corona	Juan N. Córdoba
México	1. Salvador Moreno Arriaga	Rodolfo Argüelles
	2. *Francisco M. de Olaguíbel*	Joaquín M. Madrid
	3. Demetrio López	Aurelio J. Venegas
	4. *Guillermo Ordorica*	Rafael N. Millán
	5. Tranquilino Navarro	Alberto Ronces
	6. Juan Galindo y Pimentel	Francisco Pérez Carbajal
	7. Luis G. Chaparoo	Luis G. Becerril
	8. José J. Reynoso	Jesús Ramírez
	9. *Isidro Fabela*	Emilio López
	10. Vicente Pérez	Ernesto Enríquez
	11. Antonio Aguilar	Manuel Aguirre
	12. Emilio Cárdenas	Gregorio Ledesma
	13. Javier Torres Rivas	Luis G. Zaldívar
	14. Manuel Urquidi	Gustavo Garmendia
	15. Pedro Galicia Rodríguez	Jesús Ramos
	16. Mariano Vicencio	José Antonio Carrasco
Michoacán	1. José Ortiz Rodríguez	Melesio Alvarez
	2. *Pascual Ortiz Rubio*	Antonio Carranza
	3. José Oceguera	Andrés Iturbide
	4. Felipe Rivera	Luis G. Sobreyra
	5. Adolfo M. Isassi	Alberto Castañeda
	6. Enedino Colín	Carlos Echenique
	7. Celerino Luviano	*Manuel Padilla*
	8. José Trinidad Carrión	José Gaytán
	9. Agapito Solórzano S.	Luis G. Arriaga
	10. Leopoldo Hurtado Espinosa	Jesús Silva

	11. José Silva Herrera	Julio Valladares
	12. Jesús Munquía Santoyo	Manuel Olivera
	13. Vacant	
	14. *Francisco Elguero*	José Méndez Padilla
	15. Perfecto Méndez Padilla	
	16. Rafael Reyes	Próspero Herrera
	17. Joaquín Torres	Francisco Lozano
Morelos	1. Patricio Leyva	Luis G. Malváez
	2. Valentín del Llano	Antonio D. Melgarejo
	3. Francisco Canale	
Nuevo León	1. Alfonso Madero	Manuel Amaya
	2. Jesús M. Aguilar	Florentino Caso
	3. José M. de la Garza	Francisco Benítez Leal
	4. *Nemesio García Naranjo*	Pablo Salazar
	5. Miguel Alardín	N. Rincón Ríos
	6. Jesús H. Treviño	Juan C. Hernández
Oaxaca	1. José Mayoral	Alfonso Suárez
	2. Carlos Cerqueda	Carlos Barroso
	3. Francisco Munguía	Nicolás Varela
	4. José M. García Ramos	Moisés Ramírez
	5. Eleazar del Valle	Demetrio Calvo
	6. *Francisco M. Ramírez*	Demetrio Calvo
	7. Eusebio P. León	Lorenzo Mayoral
	8. *Miguel Bolaños Cacho*	Eliseo Gómez Añorve
	9. Prisciliano Maldonado	Victoriano González
	10. Luis G. Vázquez	Edmundo Pastelín
	11. Abraham Castellanos	Ramón Castillo Isassi
	12. Fidencio Hernández	Guillermo Meixueiro
	13. Guillermo Meixueiro	Fidencio Hernández
	14. Miguel de la Llave	Luis Meixueiro
	15. *Crisóforo Rivera Cabrera*	Porfirio Pereyra
	16. Adolfo C. Gurrión	Severo Castillejos
Puebla	1. Ignacio Pérez Salazar	José G. Pacheco
	2. Rodolfo Bello	Tomás Fourlong
	3. *Rosendo Márquez*	Juan O'Farrill
	4. Enrique M. Ibáñez	Juan P. Hernández
	5. José Mariano Pontón	Baraquiel M. Alatriste
	6. Enrique Rodiles Maniau	Ignacio Avalos
	7. Luis G. Guzmán	Leopoldo García Veyrán
	8. Emilio Ibáñez	Alberto O'Farrill
	9. Luis G. Unda	Ismael Palafox
	10. Benamín Balderas Márquez	Francisco Arenas Pérez
	11. *Luis T. Navarro*	Carlos Aldeco
	12. Octaviano Couttolene	José Couttolene
	13. Alfredo Alvarez	Vicente Lombardo, Jr.
	14. *Pascual Luna y Parra*	Marcario González
	15. Manuel F. Méndez	Nemorio Rivera
	16. Gabriel M. Oropesa	Adolfo Lechuga
	17. *Alfonso Cabrera*	José Dolores Pérez
	18. Alfredo Vergara	Carlos C. Vargas

State	District/Deputy	Alternate
Querétaro	1. Juan N. Frías	Luis F. Pérez
	2. Manuel Pérez Romero	Amador E. Ugalde
	3. Constantino Llaca	Eduardo G. Escanlán
	4. Rómulo de la Torre	Alonzo M. Veraza
Quintana Roo	1. Aurelio Canale	Juan Jiménez
San Luis Potosí	1. *Juan Sarabia*	Agustín Mayo Barrenechea
	2. Pedro Antonio Santos	Mauricio Dávalos
	3. Enrique O'Farrill	Valentín Flores
	4. *Rafael Nieto*	Francisco Gómez
	5. Rutilio Berlanga	Miguel L. Quijano
	6. Moisés García	Eduardo Arizmendi
	7. Julián Ramírez Martínez	Daniel A. Martínez
	8. José Rodríguez Cabo	Carlos Gobea
	9. Samuel M. Santos	Enrique M. Espinosa
	10. *Rafael Curiel*	Santos Pérez
Sinaloa	1. Francisco Verdugo Fálquez	José de Jesús Moncayo
	2. *J. Felipe Valle*	Francisco C. Aragón
	3. Carlos M. Esquerro	*Ignacio Noris*
	4. Vacant	
	5. Pedro R. Zavala	Benjamín Trasviñas
Sonora	1. *Roberto V. Pesqueira*	Joaquín Corella
	2. *Carlos E. Randall*	Agustín A. Roa
	3. Aureliano Mendívil	José J. Obregón
	4. Francisco R. Velázquez	Agustín Rodríguez
Tabasco	1. *Félix F. Palavicini*	Marcos E. Becerra
	2. Gerónimo López Llergo	Manuel Gregorio Zapata
	3. Tirso Inurreta	Pedro P. Romero
Tamaulipas	1. Antonio Domínguez V.	Francisco Treviño
	2. Leandro Peña	Antonio J. Hernández
	3. Telésforo Villasana	Tarquino Jiménez
	4. Armando Z. Ostos	Luis Ramírez de Alba
Tepic (Nayarit)	1. Nicolás Muñoz Ruiz	Carlos Pesqueira
	2. Miguel Ortíz Sánchez	Gabino Navarro
	3. *Luis Castillo Ledón*	Lucas Marín
Tlaxcala	1. Isaac Barrera	Narciso Paredes
	2. Gerzayn Ugarte	Emiliano Ramírez Luna
	3. *Eduardo Tamariz*	Manuel Sánchez Gavito
Veracruz	1. Francisco T. Mascareñas	Moisés N. Ramos
	2. Francisco M. Ostos	Gonzalo Herrera
	3. J. Trinidad Herrera	Leonardo Zenil Martínez
	4. Ignacio Peláez	Gabriel Jiménez
	5. *José de J. Núñez y D.*	Teodomiro Gutiérrez
	6. José R. Azpe	Francisco Suinaga
	7. Gregorio Ruiz	Gustavo Bello
	8. Miguel Hernández J.	Francisco de P. Rendón

	9. *Salvador Díaz Mirón*	*Adalberto A. Esteva*
	10. Ignacio Muñoz	Rafael Carbajal Cházaro
	11. Tomás Braniff	Antonio Médiz Bolio
	12. Manauel Carvajal	Fernando Castellanos
	13. *Heriberto Jara*	Pánfilo Méndez
	14. Gustavo A. Esteva	Samuel García
	15. Francisco Arias	Jorge Ruiz
	16. José Castellot, Jr.	Tirso W. Cházaro
	17. Luis Vidal y Flor	F. Tejeda y Llorca
	18. Gabriel F. Figueroa	Luis R. Colina
	19. *José Manuel Puig*	Francisco Robleda
Yucatán	1. Serapio Rendón	Lorenzo Ancona Pérez
	2. *Antonio Ancona Albertos*	Alvaro Medina Ayora
	3. Alonso Aznar Mendoza	Manuel Evia Cervera
	4. Víctor Moya Zorrilla	Roberto Casellas Díaz
	5. Albino Acereto	Siegfred Figueroa
	6. *José I. Novelo*	Eudaldo Ferráez
Zacatecas	1. Luis Mora Castillo	Luis M. Flores
	2. Francisco Zezati	Jesús B. González
	3. Luis Rodarte	Enrique L. Flores
	4. *Aquiles Elorduy*	Jesús Sánchez
	5. Enrique García	Luis Villaseñor
	6. Vacant	Samuel Dávila
	7. J. Trinidad Luna	Enrique Luna y Román
	8. Elías Amador	Lorenzo Gallardo

1913–14 (26th Legislature)

State	Deputy	Alternate
Aguascalientes	1. Eduardo J. Correa	Demetrio Rizo
	2. Jesús A. Martínez	David Revilla
Baja California	1. Daniel Hidalgo	Alberto P. Preciado
Campeche	1. Juan H. Brito	Salvador Dondé
	2. Julián Quintero	Eduardo Hurtado
Chiapas	1. Federico W. Esponda	Lauro Castro
	2. Ezequiel Burguete	Manuel Romero Palafox
	3. Manuel Rovelo Argüello	Eduardo Castro
	4. Rubén Valentí	Manrique Moheno
	5. Manuel M. Escobar	Bernardo Martínez Baca
	6. Andrés Contreras	Gustavo Serrano
	7. Angel Pola	Arturo G. Serrano
Chihuahua	1. None elected	
	2. None elected	
	3. None elected	
	4. None elected	
	5. None elected	
	6. None elected	

State	District/Deputy	Alternate
Coahuila	1. Emilio Campa	Pascual Hernández
	2. Vacant	
	3. Vacant	
	4. Rafael Arispe Ramos	Pompeyo Mier
	5. Juan Lanz	Francisco Dávila
Colima	1. Manuel R. Alvarez	Arturo Millán
Distrito Federal	1. Nicolás Bejarano	Octavio Barona
	2. Gabriel Huerta	Joaquín Zerecero
	3. Eugenio Paredes	Antonio Paredes
	4. Vicente Calero	Daniel Maass
	5. Víctor Manuel Corral	Javier Algara
	6. Carlos Aguila	Luis de Legarreta
	7. Manuel M. Guasque	Manuel Huerta
	8. Manuel Vidaurrázaga	Manuel Guasque, Jr.
	9. *Carlos Trejo y Lerdo de T.*	Andrés Bermejillo
	10. Jesús M. Rábago	Juan M. Bribiesca
	11. José M. Soriano	Fernando Noriega
	12. Fernando Camacho	Ricardo Tapia Fernández
Durango	1. None elected	
	2. None elected	
	3. None elected	
	4. None elected	
	5. None elected	
	6. None elected	
	7. None elected	
Guanajuato	1. Ponciano Aguilar	José Balmaceda
	2. Gilberto Rincón Gallardo	Antonio Flores
	3. Juan Fernández de Castro	Urbano González
	4. José Sauto	Prudencio Hernández
	5. Agustín Lanuza	Rafael Pérez Vásquez
	6. Enrique Leal	Salomé Garza Aldape
	7. Juan Olivares	Jesús D. Ibarra
	8. *Alfonso Teja Zabre*	Joaquín Ederro
	9. José Elguero	Enrique Campa Cos
	10. Benjamín Bravo	Manuel R. Briones
	11. Alfonso de la Lama	Reynaldo Lazcano
	12. Daniel R. Aguilar	Ricardo Guzmán
	13. José Castellot, Jr.	Antonio R. Villagómez
	14. Bonifacio Olivares	Eusebio Ortega
	15. Enrique Baz	Emilio González Caballero
	16. Liborio Fuentes	Cipriano Espinosa
	17. Eulalio Díaz González	Enrique Chico González
	18. Tomás Casas	Elpidio Manrique
Guerrero	1. Alberto Quiroz	Tito Hernández
	2. Antonio Morea	Manuel Toledo
	3. Angel M. Reyes	Luis Berdejo
	4. Gonzalo Zúñiga	Manuel Olea
	5. Carlos Guevara Alarcón	Francisco Olea
	6. Miguel Montúfar	Manuel Aburto

	7. Tomás Moreno	Enrique A. López
	8. Otilio Ortiz	Manuel Vega
Hidalgo	1. Agustín Bretón	Aurelio Blanquet, Jr.
	2. Javier de Moure	Manuel Lazeano
	3. Vacant	
	4. Manuel Corral	Eduardo Martínez
	5. Fernando Gil	Ruperto Serna
	6. Carlos Sánchez Mejorada	José de Landero
	7. Luis Noriega	Simón Orozco
	8. Daniel Vergara Lope	Cristóbal García
	9. Leopoldo Kiel	Angel Hermosillo
	10. Vicente Garrido Alfaro	Emilio Barranco Pardo
Jalisco	1. Jesús Camarena	Alberto Quintero
	2. Manuel F. de la Hoz	Ludalecio Dávila
	3. José Gutiérrez Hermosillo	Mauro Villaseñor
	4. Rafael de la Mora	Manuel S. Ordaz
	5. Ricardo Gómez Robelo	Bernardo Reyna
	6. José Juan Tablada	Octaviano de la Mora
	7. José Rincón Gallardo	Abraham Contreras
	8. Benjamín Camarena	Agustín Basave
	9. José Palomar y Vizcarra	Leoncio R. Blanco
	10. Manuel Cuesta Gallardo	Julio S. Arce
	11. *Miguel Ahumada*	Jesús Guzmán
	12. Salvador Garibay	Lorenzo I. Calderón
	13. Miguel Suárez del Real	Pascual Amelio
	14. José Luis Velasco	Jesús Quinard
	15. Jesús Hernández y García	Severiano Pérez Jiménez
	16. Carlos Corona	Ignacio Luquín
	17. Francisco de P. Bravo	Cástulo Gallardo
	18. Pascual Alva	Ignacio L. Montenegro
	19. Aurelio Camarena	Juan S. Castro
	20. Joaquín Palencia	Fortino España
México	1. Ignacio de la Torre	Ignacio Burgoa
	2. José Posada Ortiz	Rafael Bernal
	3. Eduardo Viñas	Demetrio López
	4. Ignacio Montes de Oca	Eduardo Henkel
	5. Juan Venegas	Francisco Pérez Carbajal
	6. Alfonso Castillo	Gustavo Graf
	7. José I. Rebollar	Antonio Barbabosa
	8. *Francisco M. de Olaguíbel*	Aurelio J. Venegas
	9. Ramón Díaz	Juan Galindo Pimentel
	10. Cruz González	Benito Sánchez Valdez
	11. Joaquín Piña	Joaquín Madrid
	12. *José Refugio Velasco*	Wulfrano Vásquez
	13. Ignacio M. Corona	Jesús Pliego
	14. Vicente Pliego Carmona	*Antonio Pliego Pérez*
	15. Alfonso Noriega	Luis Riba y Cervantes
	16. José López Moctezuma	Ignacio L. Pliego
Michoacán	1. Francisco Pascual García	Eduardo Santoyo
	2. Felipe Iturbide	Manuel M. Bonilla

State	District/Deputy	Alternate
	3. Angel López Negrete	Francisco Asúnsolo
	4. Frumencio Fuentes	Luis Sobrevía
	5. Luis G. Navarro	Jesús Solórzano Pliego
	6. Rafael López	Manuel R. Calderón
	7. Vacant	
	8. Julio C. Bandala	Luis Macouzet
	9. Luis Fernández	Joaquín Bolaños Cacho
	10. José Ma. Garza Aldape	Luis G. Alvarez
	11. Moisés Guerrero	Carlos Noriega
	12. Antonio Guerra Juárez	Silviano Hurtado
	13. Eduardo Villagrán	Rafael Campuzano
	14. *Francisco Elguero*	
	15. Perfecto Méndez Padilla	Arcadio Dávalos
	16. Alfonso Baz	Hermenegildo Heredia
	17. Carlos Ezeta	Ciro Castillo
Morelos	1. Antonio Escandón	Manuel Cañas
	2. Joaquín García Pimentel	Manuel Martínez del Campo
	3. Vicente Vertíz	Miguel Díaz
Nuevo León	1. *Ignacio Morelos Zaragoza*	Juan J. Buchard
	2. Jorge Warden	Octavio Barocio
	3. Enrique Ballesteros	Andrés Noriega
	4. *Emeterio de la Garza, Jr.*	Pablo Salazar
	5. Ignacio Morelos Zaragoza	José Morelos Zaragoza
	6. Fernando Ancira	Jacinto Barrera
Oaxaca	1. Tereso I. Luna	José María Núñez
	2. Miguel Bolaños, Jr.	Miguel Jiménez Ramírez
	3. Javier Icaza Landa	Luis Bustamante
	4. Miguel Montes de Oca	Cristóbal A. Pareyón
	5. Joaquín Bustamante	Carlos Barroso
	6. Genaro Pérez	Constantino Chapital
	7. Julio Cavero	Fortino Figueroa
	8. Laureano López Negrete	Manuel H. San Juan
	9. Eugenio G. Maldonado	Demetrio Calvo
	10. Benjamín Bolaños	Luis Maqueo Castellanos
	11. Enrique Villegas	Esteban Maqueo C.
	12. Luis Ballesteros	Francisco Ramírez del R.
	13. Salvador Bolaños Cacho	Julio Fenelón
	14. Leopoldo Naranjo	Arnulfo Miranda
	15. Rafael Rábago	Ramón Castillo
	16. José F. Díaz González	Enrique Vasconcelos
Puebla	1. Javier Rojas	Serafín de la Torre
	2. Ignacio Pérez Salazar	Angel Sela
	3. *Pascual Luna y Parra*	Manuel M. Márquez
	4. Manuel A. Mercado	Juan M. Quintana
	5. Fausto E. Miranda	J. Antonio Huesca
	6. Ignacio Michel y Parra	Pedro Loyola
	7. Miguel Guadalajara	Amado Cantú
	8. Jesús Quiroz	José González Pacheco
	9. José María Camacho	Manuel Mirus
	10. Juan Escalante	Juan Hernández

	11. José García Rodríguez	José Sarmiento
	12. Renato A. Lizardi	Octaviano Couttolenc
	13. Gustavo Maass	Ricardo Rubio
	14. Luis G. Pradillo	Sotero Ojeda
	15. Ruberto Zaleta	Lucio Pinillos
	16. Francisco Venegas	Rafael Serrano
	17. Pío Camarena	Atenedoro Monroy
	18. *Eduardo Tamariz*	Francisco Traslosheros
Querétaro	1. Felipe Ruiz de Cabañas	Salvador Domínguez
	2. Luis Pérez Bolde	Juan Manuel Noriega
	3. Agustín Rubio	Francisco R. Lozada
	4. Juan Muñoz Fuentes	Adolfo de la Isla
Quintana Roo	1. Julián G. Villaseñor	Luis Amado
San Luis Potosí	1. Alberto L. Palacios	Pedro Díez Gutiérrez
	2. Alberto López Hermosa	Manuel Rivera
	3. Miguel Múzquiz Blanco	Fernando Rodríguez
	4. Antonio Médiz Bolio	Carlos Grande
	5. Juventino Romero	Vicente Warnes
	6. Simón Mitre	Antonio Alcocer
	7. Ignacio B. Guevara	Vicente Montes de Oca
	8. Rafael Arias Pereyra	Alvaro Alvarez
	9. Octavio Mancera	Manuel Galán
	10. Julián Carrillo	Diego Gutiérrez
Sinaloa	1. Carlos A. Ferrer	Juan R. Saís
	2. *Joaquín Redo*	Francisco Alcalde, Jr.
	3. Juan Vasavilbaso	Ramón Ponce de León
	4. Antonio Ortega y Medina	Francisco Guarneros
	5. Francisco Montero	Rafael Miranda
Sonora	1. Miguel Ordorica	Francisco Canale
	2. None elected	
	3. None elected	
	4. None elected	
Tabasco	1. Eduardo Rubio	Eduardo Graham
	2. Arturo Tapia	Mariano Olivera
	3. Remigio Uruchurtu	Telésforo Salazar
Tamaulipas	1. Vacant	
	2. Manuel Olea	Aurelio Collado
	3. José A. del Castillo	Francisco Dosal
	4. Ricardo López y Parra	Luis Berrueco Serna
Tepic (Nayarit)	1. Leopoldo Romano	Carlos Pesquera
	2. Enrique Hurtado	Pablo Rodríguez Castro
	3. Ignacio Martínez Ochoa	Gabino Navarro
Tlaxcala	1. Rafael Loaiza	Geronimo Aguilar
	2. Miguel Viveros	Rafael Anzures
	3. Enrique Sánchez González	Santiago Garibay

State	Deputy	Alternate
Veracruz	1. Eduardo M. Mateos	Juan N. Alejandre
	2. Rafael Roqueñé	Manuel Jiménez
	3. Vicente Sánchez Gutiérrez	Bernardo González
	4. Joaquín R. Grajales	Enrique Herrera
	5. Virgilio Villanueva	Guillermo Pous
	6. Francisco Cánovas	Manuel Vásquez
	7. Jorge Huerta	Francisco Ochoa
	8. Rubén Bouchez	Ramón T. Riverol
	9. *Salvador Díaz Mirón*	Maríano Domínguez
	10. Severino Herrera Moreno	Manuel I. Lestrade
	11. Emilio del Toro	Rafael O. Cortés
	12. Antonio del Palacio	Roberto Argüelles Bringas
	13. Luis S. Malpica	Francisco Grajales
	14. Francisco Arenas	Pedro Senties
	15. *Francisco de P. Aspe*	Vicente Gutiérrez Zamora
	16. Luis del Toro	Adalberto A. Esteva
	17. Mario Maass	Juan H. Caboda
	18. Miguel Domínguez Palacios	Sebastián Hernández
	19. Mario Díaz Mirón	Gabriel Carballo
Yucatán	1. Miguel Mendoza Ayora	José Trinidad Molina
	2. Manuel Meneses Duque	Fernando Solís Cano
	3. Gerardo Manzanilla	Francisco Robledo
	4. Arcadio Escobedo Guzmán	Clemente Gutiérrez
	5. Ricardo Ortiz	Roberto Castilla Rivas
	6. Miguel Peón	Guillermo Ziáurriz
Zacatecas	1. José C. Delgado	José Pérez Espino
	2. Heriberto Ramos Cuevas	Aurelio Castañeda
	3. Aurelio Ruelas	José Bonilla
	4. Vacant	
	5. *Genaro García*	José Vásquez
	6. Vacant	
	7. José Espinosa Rondero	Guillermo López de Lara
	8. Vacant	

1916–17 (Constitutional Convention)

State	Deputy	Alternate
Aguascalientes	1. Aurelio L. González	Archibaldo E. Pedroza
	2. *Daniel Cervantes*	Gonzalo Ortega
Baja California	1. Ignacio Roel	Matías Gómez
Campeche	1. Juan Zubarán	Fernando Galeano
	2. Herminio Pérez Abreu	Enrique Arias Solís
Chiapas	1. Enrique Suárez	Francisco Rincón
	2. Enrique D. Cruz	Lisandro López
	3. No election	
	4. No election	

	5. Cristóbal Ll. Castillo	Amadeo Ruiz
	6. *J. Almilcar Vidal*	
	7. Daniel A. Zepeda	Daniel Robles

Chihuahua	1. No election	
	2. Manuel M. Prieto	
	3. No election	
	4. No election	
	5. No election	
	6. No election	

Coahuila	1. *Manuel Aguirre Berlanga*	José Rodríguez González
	2. *Ernesto Meade Fierro*	Toribio de los Santos
	3. *José María Rodríguez*	Eduardo Guerra
	4. Jorge von Verson	Silviano Pruneda
	5. *Manuel Cepeda Medrano*	José N. Santos

Colima	1. *Francisco Ramírez V.*	J. Concepción Rivera

Distrito Federal	1. *Ignacio L. Pesqueira*	Claudio M. Tirado
	2. Lauro López Guerra	Javier Rayón
	3. Gerzayn Ugarte	Ernesto Garza Pérez
	4. Amador Lozano	Serapio Aguirre
	5. *Félix F. Palavicini*	Francisco Cravioto
	6. Rafael Martínez	Carlos Duplán
	7. Rafael L. de los Ríos	Román Rosas y Reyes
	8. Arnulfo Silva	Amancio Gracia García
	9. Antonio Norzagaray	Francisco Espinosa
	10. Fernando Vizcayno	Clemente Allande
	11. Ciro B. Ceballos	Isidro Lara
	12. Alfonso Herrera	Gabriel Calzada

Durango	1. *Silvestre Dorador*	Carlos Rivera
	2. *Rafael Espeleta*	Francisco A. Pérez
	3. Antonio Gutiérrez	Mauro R. Moreno
	4. *Fernando Castaños*	Salvador Castaños
	5. Fernando Gómez Palacios	Celestino Simental
	6. *Alberto Terrones B.*	Antonio P. Hernández
	7. Jesús de la Torre	Jesús Silva

Guanajuato	1. Ramón Frausto	Apolonio Sánchez
	2. Vicente M. Valtierra	Pedro R. Arizmendi
	3. *José Natividad Macías*	Enrique Pérez
	4. José López Lira	J. Jesús Patiño
	5. David Peñaflor	Luis M. Alcocer
	6. José Villaseñor Lomelí	Juan Garcidueñas
	7. Antonio Madrazo	Santiago Manrique
	8. *Hilario Medina*	Federico González
	9. *Manuel G. Aranda*	Alberto Villafuerte
	10. *Enrique Colunga*	Félix Villafuerte
	11. Ignacio López	José Serrato
	12. *Alfredo Robles Domínguez*	Francisco Díaz Barriga
	13. *Fernando Lizardi*	David Ayala
	14. Nicolás Cano	Pilar Espinosa

State	Deputy	Alternate
	15. Gilberto M. Navarro	Sabás González Rangel
	16. Luis Fernández Martínez	Miguel Hernández Murillo
	17. Vacant	Francisco Rendón
	18. Carlos Ramírez Llaca	Guillermo J. Carrillo
Guerrero	1. Fidel Jiménez	Jesús A. Castañeda
	2. *Fidel Guillén Zamora*	
	3. No election	
	4. No election	
	5. No election	
	6. *Francisco Figueroa*	José Castrejón Fuentes
	7. No election	
	8. No election	
Hidalgo	1. Antonio Guerrero	Benjamín García
	2. Leopoldo Ruiz	Erasmo Trejo
	3. Alberto M. González	Antonio Peñafiel
	4. No election	
	5. *Rafael Vega Sánchez*	Eustorgio Sánchez
	6. No election	
	7. *Alfonso Cravioto*	Lauro Albuquerque
	8. *Matías Rodríguez*	Crisóforo Aguirre
	9. Ismael Pintado Sánchez	Alfonso Sosa
	10. Refugio M. Mercado	Leoncio Campos
	11. Alfonso Mayorga	J. González
Jalisco	1. *Luis Manuel Rojas*	Carlos Cuervo
	2. *Marcelino Dávalos*	Tomás Morán
	3. Federico E. Ibarra	Luis G. Gómez
	4. Manuel Dávalos Ornelas	Francisco Villegas
	5. Francisco Martínez del C.	Manuel Martínez del C.
	6. Bruno Moreno	Gilberto Dalli
	7. Gaspar Bolaños V.	Manuel Bouquet
	8. Manuel Castañeda	Alberto Macías
	9. Juan de Dios Robledo	Rafael Degollado
	10. Jorge Villaseñor	José Jorge Farías
	11. *Amado Aguirre*	Salvador Brihuega
	12. José Solórzano	Gabriel González Franco
	13. *Ignacio Ramos Praslow*	Rafael Obregón
	14. Francisco Labastida I.	
	15. José Manzano	Miguel R. Martínez
	16. *Joaquín Aguirre Berlanga*	Pablo R. Suárez
	17. *Esteban B. Calderón*	Conrado Oseguera
	18. *Paulino Machorro y Narváez*	Bernardino Germán
	19. Sebastián Allende	Carlos Villaseñor
	20. Rafael Ochoa	Gregorio Preciado
México	1. Aldegundo Villaseñor	
	2. Fernando Moreno	Salvador Z. Sandoval
	3. Enrique O'Farrill	Abraham Estévez
	4. Guillermo Ordorica	Prócoro Dorantes
	5. No election	

	6. No election	
	7. No election	
	8. *José J. Reynoso*	Apolinar C. Juárez
	9. Jesús Fuentes Dávila	Gabriel Calzada
	10. Macario Pérez	Artemio Basurto
	11. Antonio Aguilar	José D. Aguilar
	12. Juan Manuel Guiffard	Emilio Cárdenas
	13. José E. Franco	Manuel A. Hernández
	14. Enrique A. Enríquez	Carlos L. Angeles
	15. Donato Bravo Izquierdo	Modesto Romero Valencia
	16. *Rubén Martí*	David Espinosa
Michoacán	1. Francisco Ortiz Rubio	José P. Ruiz
	2. *Alberto Peralta*	Rubén Romero
	3. *Cayetano Andrade*	Carlos García de León
	4. Salvador Herrejón	Uriel Avilez
	5. Gabriel R. Cervera	Enrique Parra
	6. Onésimo López Couto	Francisco Martínez González
	7. *Salvador Alcaraz*	Sidronio Sánchez Pineda
	8. *Pascual Ortiz Rubio*	*Manuel Martínez Sepúlveda*
	9. *Martín Castrejón*	Roberto Sepúlveda
	10. *Martín Castrejón*	Alberto Alvarado
	11. José Alvarez	Vicente Medina
	12. José Silva Herrera	Ignacio Gómez
	13. Rafael Márquez	Joaquín Silva
	14. Amadeo Betancourt	Abraham Mejía
	15. *Francisco J. Múgica*	Antonio Navarrete
	16. *Jesús Romero Flores*	Luis G. Guzmán
	17. Florencio G. González	José de la Peña
Morelos	1. Antonio Garza Zambrano	Armando Emparán
	2. José L. Gómez	
	3. Alvaro L. Alcázar	Enrique C. Ruiz
Nuevo León	1. Manuel Amaya	Luis Guimbarda
	2. *Nicéforo Zambrano*	Lorenzo Sepúlveda
	3. Luis Ilizaliturri	Wenceslao Gómez Garza
	4. Ramón Gómez	Adolfo Cantú Jáuregui
	5. Reynaldo Garza	J. Jesús Garza
	6. *Agustín Garza González*	Plutarco González
Oaxaca	1. *Salvador González Torres*	Francisco León C.
	2. Israel del Castillo	Juan Sánchez
	3. Leopoldo Payán	Manuel Santaella
	4. Luis Espinosa	José Vázquez V.
	5. No election	
	6. No election	
	7. No election	
	8. No election	
	9. Manuel Herrera	Pablo Allende
	10. No election	
	11. *Manuel García Vigil*	Pastor Santa Ana
	12. *Porfirio Sosa*	José Honorato Márquez
	13. No election	

State	Deputy	Alternate
	14. Celestino Pérez	Antonio Salazar
	15. *Crisóforo Rivera Cabrera*	Miguel Ríos
	16. Genaro López Miró	José F. Gómez
Puebla	1. *Daniel Guzmán*	Salvador R. Guzmán
	2. Rafael P. Cañete	Enrique Contreras
	3. Miguel Rosales	Federico Ramos
	4. Gabriel Rojano	Rafael Rosete
	5. *David Pastrana Jaimes*	Jesús Domínguez
	6. *Froylán C. Manjárrez*	Manuel A. Acuña
	7. Antonio de la Barrera	Luis G. Bravo
	8. José Rivera	Aurelio M. Maja
	9. Epigmenio A. Martínez	Anacleto Merino
	10. *Pastor Rouaix*	Ireneo Villarreal
	11. *Luis T. Navarro*	Rómulo Munguía
	12. Porfirio del Castillo	Celerino Cano
	13. *Federico Dinorín*	Joaquín Díaz Ortega
	14. *Gabino Bandera y Mata*	
	15. Leopoldo Vázquez Mellado	Ricardo Márquez Galindo
	16. Gilberto de la Fuente	Manuel A. Nieva
	17. *Alfonso Cabrera*	Agustín Cano
	18. José Verástegui	Cándido Nieto
Querétaro	1. Juan N. Frías	Enrique B. Domínguez
	2. *Ernesto Perusquía*	Julio Herrera
	3. José María Truchuelo	J. Jesús Rivera
	4. No election	
San Luis Potosí	1. Samuel de los Santos	Filiberto Ayala
	2. Arturo Méndez	
	3. *Rafael Cepeda*	Rafael Martínez Mendo
	4. *Rafael Nieto*	Cosme Dávila
	5. Dionisio Zavala	Enrique Córdova Cantú
	6. Gregorio A. Tello	
	7. Julián Ramírez Martínez	
	8. No election	
	9. No election	
	10. *Rafael Curiel*	Hilario Menéndez
Sinaloa	1. Pedro R. Zavala	Juan Francisco Vidales
	2. *Andrés Magallón*	José C. Valdés
	3. Carlos M. Esquerro	
	4. *Cándido Avilez*	Primo B. Beltrán
	5. *Emiliano C. García*	Antonio R. Castro
Sonora	1. *Luis G. Monzón*	Cesáreo G. Soriano
	2. *Flavio A. Borques*	Manuel Padrés
	3. *Ramón Ross*	Angel Porchas
	4. Eduardo C. García	*Juan de Dios Borjórquez*
Tabasco	1. *Rafael Martínez de Escobar*	Fulgencio Casanova
	2. Antenor Sala	Santiago Ocampo
	3. Carmen Sánchez Magallanes	Luis Gonzali

Tamaulipas	1. *Pedro A. Chapa*	Alejandro C. Guerra
	2. Zeferino Fajardo	Daniel S. Córdova
	3. Emiliano P. Nafarrete	José María Herrera
	4. Fortunato de Leija	Félix Acuña

Tepic (Nayarit)	1. *Cristóbal Limón*	
	2. *Cristóbal Limón*	Marcelino Cedaño
	3. *Juan Espinosa Bávara*	Guillermo Bonilla

Tlaxcala	1. Antonio Hidalgo	Felipe Xicoténcatl
	2. Modesto González Galindo	Juan Torrentera
	3. Ascencio Tepal	Fausto Centeno

Veracruz	1. No election	
	2. *Saúl Rodiles*	Alberto Herrera
	3. *Adalberto Tejada*	Enrique Meza
	4. Benito G. Ramírez	Heriberto Román
	5. Rodolfo Curti	Jenaro Ramírez
	6. Eliseo L. Céspedes	Rafael Díaz Sánchez
	7. Adolfo G. García	Joaquín Bello
	8. *Josafat B. Márquez*	Augusto Aillaud
	9. Alfredo Solares	Gabriel Malpica
	10. Alberto Román	Martín Cortina
	11. *Silvestre Aguilar*	Miguel Limón Uriarte
	12. Angel Juarico	Domingo A. Jiménez
	13. *Heriberto Jara*	Salvador González García
	14. Victorio E. Góngora	Epigmenio H. Ocampo
	15. *Cándido Aguilar*	Carlos L. Gracidas
	16. Marcelo Torres	Moisés Rincón
	17. Galdino H. Casados	Donanciano Zamudio
	18. Juan de Dios Palma	León Medel
	19. Fernando A. Pereyra	Antonio Ortiz Ríos

Yucatán	1. *Antonio Ancona Albertos*	Ramón Espada
	2. Enrique Recio	Rafael Gamboa
	3. Héctor Víctoria	Felipe Valencia
	4. Manuel González	Felipe Carrillo
	5. Miguel Alonso Romero	Juan N. Ortiz

Zacatecas	1. Adolfo Villaseñor	Rafael Simoní Castelvi
	2. Julián Adame	Rodolfo Muñoz
	3. Jairo R. Dyer	Narciso González
	4. No election	
	5. Rosendo A. López	Samuel Castañón
	6. No election	Andrés L. Arteaga
	7. Antonio Cervantes	
	8. *Juan Aguirre Escobar*	Jesús Hernández

1917–18 (27th Legislature)

State	Deputy	Alternate
Aguascalientes	1. J. Concepción Saucedo	Silvestre Trujano
	2. Enrique Muñoz	Abraham Cruz

State	Deputy	Alternate
Baja California	1. José T. Cantú	Juan Velásquez
	2. Modesto C. Rólland	Eduardo S. Carrillo
Campeche	1. *Juan Zubarán Capmany*	Francisco Perera Escobar
	2. Julio Zapata B.	Francisco M. Paoli
Chiapas	1. *Emilio Araujo*	Raúl Pola Muñoz
	2. Enrique Suárez	Miguel Castillo
	3. Isaac Rojas Dugelay	Herminio Cancino
	4. Vacant	
	5. Ricardo Carrascosa	
	6. Pedro A. Cristiani	César Córdoba
	7. Raúl Gutiérrez Orantes	Rafael Ortega, Jr.
Chihuahua	1. Manuel H. Segovia	
	2. Vacant	
	3. Vacant	
	4. Manuel M. Prieto	Gregorio Martínez R.
	5. Vacant	
	6. Vacant	
	7. Andrés Ortiz	Enrique Soto Peimbert
Coahuila	1. *Manuel Cepeda Medrano*	Pedro Gil Farías
	2. Gustavo Gámez	Andrés L. Viesca
	3. *Aarón Sáenz*	Enrique Viesca Lobatón
	4. Aureliano Esquivel	Arturo Carranza
	5. *Jacinto B. Treviño*	José N. Santos
Colima	1. *Salvador Saucedo*	Juan Torres Virgen
Distrito Federal	1. *Eduardo Hay*	Juan Tirso Reynoso
	2. *Rafael Martínez de Escobar*	Joaquín Martínez
	3. *Filomeno Mata*	Rodrigo Cárdenas
	4. *Jesús Urueta*	Benjamín Marín
	5. *Ernesto Aguirre Colorado*	Ignacio Rodríguez M.
	6. Rafael Martínez	Federico de la Colina
	7. Luis I. Mata	Guadalupe García García
	8. Jesús Acuña	Enrique C. Osornio
	9. Mauricio Gómez	Rafael Alducín
	10. *Manuel García Vigil*	Adolfo Abreu Sala
	11. *Adolfo Cienfuegos y Camus*	Luis A. Peredo
	12. *Miguel A. Peralta*	Ramiro Manzanos
Durango	1. Manuel Vargas	Carlos S. Benítez
	2. Francisco Arreola R.	Luis Bernal
	3. Antonio Gutiérrez	Mauro R. Moreno
	4. *Alfonso Breceda*	Alberto Echeverría
	5. Daniel Sánchez	Alberto Ruiz
	6. Jesús J. Villarreal	José Acevedo
	7. Jesús de la Torre	Jesús Silva
Guanajuato	1. Francisco Medina	Alberto C. Franco
	2. Manuel G. Aranda	Catarino Partida
	3. Ricardo López F.	Telésforo Pérez

	4. Jesús López Lira	Jesús Patiño
	5. Reynaldo Narro	Juan Carrión
	6. José Villaseñor	Francisco Soto
	7. *Antonio Madrazo*	José D. Torres
	8. *Hilario Medina*	Felipe Espinosa
	9. Luis Fernández Martínez	Santiago Reyes
	10. Francisco de P. Mendoza	Luis Gil
	11. Ignacio López	Francisco Sánchez
	12. *Alfredo Robles Domínguez*	Francisco Díaz Barriga
	13. *José Siurob*	José Aguilar
	14. Federico Montes	Leovino Zavala
	15. Ezequiel Ríos Landeros	Crescenciano Aguilera
	16. Miguel Hernández Garibay	*Enrique Colunga*
	17. Roberto Sepúlveda	Pedro Ulloa
	18. Carlos Ramírez Llaca	Lucas Contreras
Guerrero	1. Manuel Bello	Julián Otero
	2. Pedro Uruñuela	Luis Méndez
	3. Vacant	
	4. Aurelio Velázquez	Hipólito Herrera
	5. Simón Ventura	Fortunato Silva
	6. Eduardo Neri	Miguel Rodríguez
	7. Vacant	
	8. Vacant	
Hidalgo	1. *Efrén Rebolledo*	Jesús Bravo Terán
	2. Nicasio Jurado	Arturo Jiménez
	3. Alberto M. González	Antonio Peñafiel
	4. Samuel H. Mariel	Angel M. Toledo
	5. *Rafael Vega Sánchez*	Eustorgio Sánchez
	6. Jesús Silva	Rodrigo M. Lara
	7. *Alfonso Cravioto*	Lauro Albuquerque
	8. Crisóforo Aguirre	
	9. Manuel Lailson Banuet	Rodolfo M. Lara
	10. Daniel Téllez Escudero	Domingo Ortega
	11. Eduardo Cisneros	Gonzalo López
Jalisco	1. Salvador Escudero	José Mora Ibarra
	2. Justo González	Alberto V. de la Peña
	3. Cristóbal Limón	Enrique Gómez Salcedo
	4. *Juan M. Alvarez del C.*	Ezequiel Ortega
	5. *Francisco Martín del Campo*	Manuel Martín del C.
	6. Manuel Dávalos Ornelas	Mariano Camberos
	7. Juan Tirso Reynoso	Jesús Argüelles
	8. J. Pascual Alejandre	Francisco Cornejo
	9. Juan de Dios Robledo	Manuel Martínez Valadez
	10. José Figueroa	Antonio Cortés
	11. José González Ibarra	Manuel Pérez Brambila
	12. José Solórzano	Aurelio M. Fernández
	13. Arturo J. Higareda	José Mares
	14. Efrén Aguirre	Miguel San Juan
	15. José García de Alba	J. Jesús Chávez
	16. *Joaquín Aguirre Berlanga*	Enrique Gómez Salcedo
	17. Rosendo A. Soto	Bruno María
	18. Basilio Badillo	Juan Ortega

State	Deputy	Alternate
	19. José Manzano	Federico Mendoza Vizcaíno
	20. Ramón Blancarte	Francisco López
México	1. Isidro Izquierdo	Enrique del Castillo
	2. Tomás Valle	Antonio Sanabria
	3. Arturo Ruiz Estrada	José Alva Reza
	4. Guillermo Ordorica	Prócoro Dorantes
	5. Austreberto P. Castañeda	Julio Pomposo
	6. Vacant	
	7. Francisco González	Ernesto Garza Pérez
	8. Carlos Campero	José del Toro
	9. Ismael Díaz González	Anastasio Meza
	10. José Federico Rocha	Facundo Rodea
	11. Valentín Flores Garza	José D. Aguilar
	12. Emilio Cárdenas	Eduardo E.Palacios
	13. Alvaro Pruneda	Pedro Ortiz
	14. José Morales Hesse	Tirso Inurreta, Jr.
	15. Donato Bravo Izquierdo	Modesto Romero Valencia
	16. Juan A. Ruiz	Alfonso Ortega
Michoacán	1. Porfirio García de León	José P. Ruiz
	2. *Cayetano Andrade*	Jesús Díaz Barriaga
	3. Martín Barragán	Enrique Ochoa
	4. Uriel Avilés	Francisco Patiño Borja
	5. Enrique Parra	Federico Téllez
	6. Onésimo López Couto	Francisco Martínez González
	7. *Salvador Alcaraz*	Waldo López Celis
	8. Salvador González Torres	Bruno Valdés
	9. José Gaytán	José Vásquez
	10. Candor Guajardo	Eduardo G. Alcázar
	11. Rafael Cano	José Lira
	12. José Silva Herrera	J. Jesús Hurtado
	13. Vacant	
	14. Amadeo Betancourt	Lázaro Cárdenas
	15. Antonio Navarrete	Francisco Múgica Pérez
	16. *Francisco J. Múgica*	Francisco Mercado
	17. Emiliano Gómez S.	Manuel Hurtado Juárez
Morelos	1. No election	
	2. No election	
	3. No election	
Nuevo León	1. Jonás García	Autero G. Roel
	2. Marciano González	Santos Ríos
	3. Ramón Gámez	José S. Moreno
	4. Vidal Garza Pérez	Fortunato Zuazua
	5. Rosalío Alcocer	Miguel Rosas
	6. Cecilio Garza González	*Aarón Sáenz*
Oaxaca	1. Flavio Pérez Gasga	Ernesto Rosas
	2. Isaac Olivé	José Leyva
	3. Juan M. Otero	Félix Méndez
	4. Alfonso S. Pardo	Hermenegildo Esperanza
	5. *Manuel Rueda Magro*	Juan G. Vasconcelos

	6. Aurelio M. Peña	Pedro Camacho
	7. Vacant	
	8. Severiano Avendaño	Francisco Castellanos
	9. Isaac Cancino Gómez	Vicente Vásquez P.
	10. Carlos R. Montiel	Eduardo Guerrero
	11. José M. Ortega	Melquiades Marroquín
	12. Pedro Ramírez, Jr.	Liborio Ramírez
	13.	
	14. Germán Gay Baños	Alejandro M.Vásquez
	15. Francisco Arlanzón	Roberto Rivero
	16. *Crisóforo Rivera Cabrera*	Santiago Hernández
	17. Genaro López Miro	José F. Gómez
Puebla	1. *Porfirio del Castillo*	Casimiro González
	2. *Luis Sánchez Pontón*	Ezequiel López
	3. *José M. Sánchez*	Celerino Rojas
	4. Luis M. Hernández	José H. Castro
	5. Rafael R. Rojas	Miguel Carranco
	6. *Froylán C. Manjárrez*	Ignacio Avalos
	7. Antonio de la Barrera	Agustín Verdín
	8. José Rivera	José Alberto Tapia
	9. Pablo García	Enrique Castillo
	10. Joaquín Paredes Colín	Faustino García
	11. Modesto González Galindo	Victoriano C. Juárez
	12. Manuel M. Guerrero	Juan Carrasco
	13. *Gabino Bandera y Mata*	Abraham Perdomo Leal
	14. *Luis Cabrera*	Pedro Molina
	15. A. Pineda	Demetrio Santa Fe
	16. Gonzalo Lechuga V.	Rubén F. Muñoz
	17. Lauro González	Federico Cabrera
	18. Ernesto Hernández	Mariano Lechuga
Querétaro	1. Jerónimo Hernández	Juan Rivas Tagle
	2. Bernardo Rodríguez Saro	Alberto Ugalde Uribe
	3. Gabriel J. Córdova	Benigno Trejo
	4. Rómulo de la Torre	Casimiro Pedraza
Quintana Roo	1. Joaquín Lanz Galera	Octavio A. González
San Luis Potosí	1. *Aurelio Manrique*	Teodoro Rigal
	2. *José C. Cruz*	Lauro A. Berumen
	3. José S. Pedroza	Lauro S. Segura
	4. Cosme Dávila	Lamberto Rocha
	5. Dionisio Zavala	Isidoro Z. Alvardo
	6. Juan Francisco Barragán	Carlos Navarro
	7. Enrique Anaya	Julián Ramírez Martínez
	8. José Moctezuma	Luis Morales
	9. Hilario Hermosillo	Antonio García
	10. *Rafael Curiel*	Eustorgio González
Sinaloa	1. Emilio Z. López	Eliseo Leyzaola
	2. *Andrés Magallón*	Armando Franco Rojo
	3. Mariano Rivas	Vicente Guerrero
	4. Filberto C. Villarreal	José L. Sánchez
	5. Angel Gaxiola, Jr.	Francisco Barnóin

State	Deputy	Alternate
Sonora	1. *Roberto V. Pesqueira*	Jesús M. González
	2. *Carlos Plank*	Luis L. León
	3. Alejo R. Bay	Angel Porchas
	4. Gustavo Padrés	Eduardo C. García
Tabasco	1. *Rafael Martínez Escobar*	Fulgencio Casanova
	2. Nicolás Cámara	Francisco Castellanos
	3. Federico Martínez de E.	
Tamaulipas	1. *Pedro A. Chapa*	Régulo Flores
	2. Daniel S. Córdoba	Baldomero Sánchez
	3. Raúl Garate	Telésforo Villasana
	4. *Emilio Portes Gil*	Salvador R. Delgado
Tepic (Nayarit)	1. J. de Jesús Ibarra	Pedro Elías
	2. José R. Padilla	Rosendo González Rubio
	3. Rafael Aveleyra	José Ahumada
Tlaxcala	1. Santiago Meneses	Anastasio Meneses
	2. Anastasio Hernández	Miguel Domínguez
	3. Marcelo Portillo	Fausto Zenteno
Veracruz	1. Silvestre Aguilar	José Casas Rodríguez
	2. Eugenio Méndez	Nicolás Caballero
	3. Alberto C. Herrera	
	4. *Adalberto Tejeda*	Enrique Meza
	5. Benito Ramírez G.	Filiberto Román
	6. Jenaro Ramírez	Efrén Méndez
	7. Eliseo L. Céspedes	Daniel Muñoz Estefan
	8. Adolfo G. García	Joaquín Bello
	9. *Josafat B. Márquez*	Augusto Aillaud
	10. Gabriel Malpica	Octavio Bueno
	11. Alberto Román	Ezequiel F. Ameca
	12. Manuel Carrillo Iturriaga	Antonio Marín Garrido
	13. *Heriberto Jara*	Salvador González García
	14. Rubén Basáñez	Joaquín Correa
	15. José Pereyra Carbonell	Agustín G. Arrazola
	16. José Pesqueira	Manuel Altamirano
	17. Benito Fentanes	Benito González
	18. Salvador Torres Berdón	Teodoro C. Gilbert
	19. Juan Medina	Sotero Vargas
Yucatán	1. *Antonio Ancona Albertos*	Manuel Berzunza
	2. *J. D. Ramírez Garrido*	Eladio Domínguez
	3. Rafael Manzanilla Tejero	J. Dolores Conde
	4. J. Cleofas Echeverría	Antonio Gual García
	5. Enrique Sánchez	Tenorio Edmundo Bolio
	6. *Miguel Alonso Romero*	Delfín Sánchez
Zacatecas	1. Eliseo García	Miguel Chávez
	2. Rafael Márquez	Samuel M. Moreno
	3. Jairo R. Dyer	Federico Carranza

4. Rafael F. Arellano   Gilberto Vásquez
5. Cuauhtémoc Esparza   Rafael Castro
6. Juan R. Lizalde   Epigmenio Sandoval
7. J. Trinidad Luna E.   Antonio Cervantes
8. *Juan Aguirre Escobar*   Manuel Olvera

1918–20 (28th Legislature)

State	Deputy	Alternate
Aguascalientes	1. Juan Díaz Infante	J. Trinidad Pedroza
	2. Enrique Fernández Ledesma	Juan Parga
Baja California	1. José T. Cantú	Juan Velásquez
	2. Vacant	
Campeche	1. Arturo Baledón Gil	Alfonso Quintana
	2. Conrado Ocampo	Benjamín Negroe G.
Chiapas	1. *Emilio Araujo*	Alfonso J. Cruz
	2. Enrique Suárez	Jenaro Ruiz de Chávez
	3. Herminio Cancino	Artidoro Pinto
	4. Francisco Araujo	Ricardo Carrascosa
	5. Raúl Gutiérrez Orantes	Mariano García
	6. César A. Lara	Joaquín Gallegos
	7. Luis Espinosa	Efraín Toledo
Chihuahua	1. Andrés Ortiz	Vito Aguirre
	2. Alejandro Velásquez	Jesús Gómez Salas
	3. Octavio M. Trigo	Pilar M. Juárez
	4. Jesús N. González	Daniel Mijares Perea
	5. Enrique Soto Peimbert	Liborio Chávez Franco
	6. Manuel Chávez M.	Manuel H. Segovia
	7.	
Coahuila	1. *Ernesto Meade Fierro*	José de la Luz Valdés
	2. Gustavo Gámez	Salvador Valero González
	3. *Alfredo Breceda*	Manuel H. Flores
	4. *Jesús Rodríguez de la F.*	Alberto Villarreal
	5. *Francisco L. Treviño*	Apolonio R. Martínez
Colima	1. *Salvador Saucedo*	Fernando Cruz
Distrito Federal	1. Francisco Cravioto G.	Alfredo Zayas
	2. Jerónimo Hernández	Cutberto Ramírez
	3. Rafael L. de los Ríos	Tomás H. Gasca
	4. Paulino Fontes	Rafael Zerecero
	5. Alfredo Rodríguez	Ramón Blancarte
	6. Miguel Gómez Noriega	Alberto Sánchez
	7. Guillermo E. Cordero	José Morales Gómez
	8. Mariano D. Urdanivia	Alberto L. de Guevara
	9. Ezequiel Ríos Landeros	Ignacio de la Hidalgo
	10. Rafael Cárdenas	Manuel García G.

State	Deputy	Alternate
	11. Jenaro Palacios Moreno	Luis Mondragón
	12. Federico Silva	Enrique Cervantes Olivera
Durango	1. José Ignacio Mena	Antonio Rosales
	2. Manuel Fierro	Antonio Camacho
	3. Antonio Gutiérrez	Javier Lozada Cabrera
	4. *Alfonso Breceda*	Alberto Echeverría
	5. Marino Castillo Nájera	Antonio Fernández
	6. Miguel Espinosa	Liborio Espinosa y E.
	7. Jesús de la Torre	Jesús Silva
Guanajuato	1. Francisco Medina	Margarito Sánchez
	2. Carlos García	Pedro P. Arizmendi
	3. Juan E. Macías	Justo A. Pedroza
	4. Francisco Madrid	Federico Garma
	5. José Luis Patiño	Agustín Gutiérrez
	6. José Villaseñor	Salvador Villaseñor
	7. Mariano Leal	J. Guadalupe Núñez
	8. Manuel Gutiérrez de V.	J. Rafael López
	9. Francisco Orozco Muñoz	Liborio Crespo
	10. José A. Roaro	José Nieto Aguilar
	11. Jesús Pérez Vela	José Aguilar
	12. Ramón Martínez del Río	Agustín Lira
	13. Ramón García Ruiz	Salvador Albarrán
	14. Federico Montes	Leóbino Zavala
	15. Benjamín Méndez	Sabás González Rangel
	16. Luis Fernández Martínez	Miguel M. Hernández
	17. Ernesto Alcocer	Pantaleón Delgado
	18. Camino Hernández Loyola	Arturo Ducoing
Guerrero	1. Vacant	
	2. Vacant	
	3. Vacant	
	4. Vacant	
	5. Vacant	
	6. *Gabino Bandera y Mata*	Juan N. Vicario
	7. *David Pastrana Jaimes*	José Rodríguez Leal
	8. José Castilleja	José Próspero Cervantes
Hidalgo	1. *Efrén Rebolledo*	Rafael López Serrano
	2. Leopoldo E. Camarena	Enrique Vásquez
	3. Pablo Aguilar	Carlos Hoyo
	4. Samuel H. Mariel	Carlos M. Andrade
	5. Narciso Paz	José Rojo Herrera
	6. Aniceto Ortega	Rafael Rojas
	7. Federico de la Colina	Miguel A. Hidalgo
	8. *Matías Rodríguez M.*	Enrique González
	9. Ignacio Ruiz Martínez	Félix Franco
	10. Francisco César Morales	Carlos Gómez
	11. Antonio Guerrero	Alfonso Mayorga
Jalisco	1. *Paulino Machorro y N.*	Luis G. Gámiz
	2. Salvador Escudero	José Mora Ibarra

3. J. Guadalupe Ruvalcaba — Luis Castillo
4. *Juan M. Alvarez del C.* — Rafael Sánchez Lira
5. *Francisco Martín del Campo* — José Delgadillo
6. *J. Guadalupe de Anda* — Manuel Montero
7. Manuel Lomelí — Darío Cruz
8. Vacant — José Pascual Alejandre
9. Antonio Valadez Ramírez
10. José Pascual Alejandre — Luis Flores Guillén
11. Vacant — Manuel Pérez Brambila
12. José Solórzano — José S. Corona
13. Julián Villaseñor Mejía — Luis Corona
14. *José María Cuéllar* — Bandelio Bernal
15. José García de Alba — J. Jesús Chávez
16. *Joaquín Aguirre Berlanga* — Salvador Pérez Arce
17. Rosendo A. Soto — Bruno María
18. Basilio Badillo — Juan Ortega
19. Carlos Galindo — Ignacio Enríquez
20. Ramón Blancarte — Francisco López

México

1. Carlos L. Angeles — Alberto S. Mejía
2. Atanasio Gutiérrez — Darío López
3. Ponciano López — Leopoldo Esteves
4. Guillermo Ordorica — Prócoro Dorantes
5. Diego Vilchis — Crescencio Camacho
6. Francisco Pérez Carbajal — Inocente Campuzano
7. Francisco Aguirre León — Jesús Ballesteros
8. José Federico Rocha — Luis G. Plascencia
9. Ismael Díaz González — Manuel M. Vega
10. Isauro Castillo Garrido — José del Río
11. Antonio Aguilar — José D. Aguilar
12. Emilio Cárdenas — Saúl Rubio
13. Felipe de la Barrera — Othón Salcedo
14. José Morales Hesse — Manuel Hernández Bravo
15. Donato Bravo Izquierdo — Jesús Sotres y Olaco
16. Antonio Quesada

Michoacán

1. Luis Breña — Pedro A. Luna
2. *Uriel Avilés* — José Alfonso Sáenz
3. Martín Barragán — Isidoro Núñez
4. *Leopoldo Zincúnegui T.* — Rafael Sánchez Vigil
5. Enrique Parra — José Sánchez Anaya
6. Estanislao Peña — Mauro Patiño
7. Humberto Villela — Rafael Santibáñez
8. Vacant
9. José Gaitán — Nicandro Villaseñor
10. Juan de Dios Avellaneda — Nicandro Villaseñor
11. J. Isaac Arriaga — Ignacio Villegas
12. José Silva Herrera — Carlos León
13. Alejandro R. Aceves — Andrés Amezola
14. Abraham Mejía — Gustavo Maciel
15. Prisciliano Carriedo — Isaac C. Alfaro
16. Rafael Reyes — Francisco Mercado
17. José M. Soto — Alfonso Valdés

State	Deputy	Alternate
Morelos	1. No election	
	2. No election	
	3. No election	
Nayarit	1. José María Ruiz	Ramón Bayardo
	2. Lucas Bravo	Aurelio Partida
	3. *Juan Espinosa Bávara*	*Luis Castillo Ledón*
Nuevo León	1. Gregorio Morales Sánchez	Antonio Moreno
	2. *Santiago Roel*	Luis F. Elizondo
	3. Carlos E. Támez	José B. y Berlanga
	4. José P. Saldaña	Santiago Salinas
	5. Miguel Rosas	José M. González
	6. Marciano González	Leandro Garza Leal
Oaxaca	1. *Manuel García Vigil*	Pablo Allende
	2. Miguel E. Schulz y A.	Guadalupe F. Martínez
	3. Genaro V. Vásquez	Ramón Palacios Toro
	4. Antonio Villalobos	Pedro Camacho
	5. Porfirio Pastor	Alfredo Altamirano
	6. Francisco Valladares	Isaac Velasco
	7. Vacant	
	8. Adalberto Lazcano	José Tapia
	9. José Guadalupe García	Benjamín L. de Guevara
	10. Carlos Bravo	Marcos Juárez
	11. Isaac Olivé	Emigdio Alfaro
	12. Justo Alencaster Roldán	Pedro A. Vega
	13. Vacant	
	14. Vacant	
	15. Francisco Arlanzón	Cutberto A. Díaz
	16. Porfirio Ruiz	Plutarco Gallegos
	17. Cosme D. Gómez	Francisco Robles
Puebla	1. Unknown	Juan Vigueras
	2. Unknown	Unknown
	3. *José M. Sánchez*	Antonio Ortega
	4. Luis Felipe Contreras	Manuel Montes
	5. Rafael R. Rojas	Miguel Carranco
	6. *Eduardo Arrioja Isunza*	Aurelio Madrid Avila
	7. Samuel R. Malpica	Juan Aguilar
	8. Eulogio Hernández	Rafael J. Ruiz
	9. Pablo García	Antonio Marín Palacios
	10. Benjamín Balderas	Francisco Gálvez
	11. Roberto Camacho	Pedro Z. Maceda
	12. Roberto Castro	Alberto Guerrero
	13. Antonio Medina	Eduardo Guerrero
	14. Constantino Molina	José Córdova
	15. Fortunato Méndez	Leopoldo Vásquez Mellado
	16. Pablo Silva	Juan C. Salas
	17. Federico Cabrera	Federico Pérez Fernández
	18. Sabino Rodríguez	Antonio Lazcano

Querétaro	1. José Verástegui	Felipe B. Díaz
	2. Julio Herrera	Lamberto Retana
	3. *José Siurob*	Aurelio Díaz Guevara
	4. Rómulo de la Torre	Alejo Altamirano

| Quintana Roo | 1. Joaquín Lanz Galera | Enrique M. Barragán |

San Luis Potosí	1. Arturo Méndez	Antonio Morales
	2. Horacio Ezeta	Bernardo L. Bandala
	3. Unknown	Lauro S. Segura
	4. Alfonso Fuentes Barragán	Pablo Sánchez Infante
	5. Dionisio Zavala	Alfonso Cárdenas
	6. Carlos Navarro	Pedro Francisco Sauceda
	7. Franco Verástegui	Juan D. Cervantes
	8. Ignacio Moctezuma	Rafael Castillo Vega
	9. Nicasio Sánchez Salazar	Samuel L. Vásquez
	10. Antonio M. García	Gabriel Torres Garza

Sinaloa	1. *Roberto Casas Alatriste*	Eliseo Quintero
	2. Feliciano Gil	Antonio R. Pérez
	3. Félix A. Mendoza	Jesús Vizcarra
	4. Emiliano Z. López	Alfredo Horne
	5. Emiliano C. García	Antonio R. Castro

Sonora	1. Gildardo Gómez	Ladislao Bailón
	2. Gustavo Padrés	Manuel M. Méndez
	3. *Francisco R. Serrano*	Arturo J. Valenzuela
	4. José Pesqueira	Jesús T. Ruiz

Tabasco	1. Manuel Andrade	Francisco Montellanos
	2. José Ferrel	Raúl Mendoza Cuesta
	3. Francisco Castellanos D.	Luis Aguilera C.

Tamaulipas	1. Herminio S. Rodríguez	Francisco Flores Santos
	2. Candelario Garza	Antonio Castro
	3. Francisco Martínez S.	Unknown
	4. Eliseo L. Céspedes	Unknown

Tlaxcala	1. José de la Luz Ortiz	Abel Carro
	2. José Sánchez R.	José María Suárez
	3. Modesto González G.	Adalberto Cortés

Veracruz	1. *Manlio Fabio Altamirano*	Erasmo O. Romero
	2. Francisco Tejeda Llorea	Joel Flores
	3. *Enrique Meza*	Hermelindo Beltrán
	4. Damián Alarcón	Porfirio Hernández V.
	5. Victorio Lorandi	Teodomiro T. Gutiérrez
	6. Miguel F. Fernández	Carlos González C.
	7. Francisco Reyes	Manuel Betancourt
	8. Adolfo G. García	Miguel Mora
	9. Amado J. Trejo	Pedro Rendón
	10. José M. Mancisidor	Unknown
	11. Unknown	Jenaro Angeles

State	Deputy	Alternate
	12. Unknown	Francisco Ortega
	13. Unknown	Martín Torres
	14. Miguel Limón	Enrique Segura
	15. Rubén Basáñez	Carlos L. Gracidas
	16. Rodolfo Cancela	Samuel M. Tello
	17. Alfonso Castro	Rafael Hoyos
	18. Luis G. Carrión	Julián Moreno
	19. Juan Manuel Giffard	Natividad Chable
Yucatán	1. Agustín Franco	Gordiano Ortiz
	2. Manuel Romero Cepeda	Francisco Rodríguez
	3. José Castillo Torre	Manuel Castilla Solís
	4. Alvaro Rivera Castillo	Rodolfo Gamboa
	5. José María Hurtalde	Bernabé Escalante
	6. Edmundo Bolio	Antonio L. Quintal
Zacatecas	1. Alfonso Toro	Jenaro Borrego
	2. Ignacio E. Martínez	Pedro Adame
	3. Oscar II. León	Francisco Amézaga
	4. J. Rudecindo Bertamen	Alfredo Reveles
	5. Cuauhtémoc Esparza	Ignacio Velasco
	6. Angel H. Huerta	Juan Martínez V.
	7. José Macías Rubalcaba	Francisco Bañuelos
	8. Matías Ramos	Lucio Frías

1920–22 (29th Legislature)

State	Deputy	Alternate
Aguascalientes	1. Pedro de Alba	Carlos Lomelí Alba
	2. Rodrigo Palacio	Jesús de Lara
Baja California	1. Ricardo Romero	Gustavo Appel
	2. Enrique von Borstel	Juan H. Mendoza
Campeche	1. *Juan Zubarán Capmany*	Lorenzo Mier y Terán
	2.	Felipe Bracho
Chiapas	1. Luis Espinosa	Amadeo Ruiz
	2. Vacant	
	3. Jaime A. Solís	Mileiades Carrascosa
	4. Vacant	
	5. *José Castañón*	Raimundo Enríquez
	6. César A. Lara	Antonio Martínez
	7. Agustín Castillo	Edrulfo Escandón
Chihuahua	1. Socorro García	Ramón Vargas Flores
	2. *Norberto Domínguez*	Francisco Chávez Holguín
	3. Liborio Chávez Franco	Eduardo Quesada
	4. Luis L. León	Francisco Tovar y Pérez
	5. Manuel Rico G.	Enrique Seinfert
	6. Alejandro Velásquez	Francisco Acosta y Plata
	7. Rafael Balderrama	Fausto Aguirre

Coahuila	1. *Miguel Alessio Robles*	Daniel Cerda
	2. Aureliano J. Mijares	Leopoldo Pimentel
	3. Francisco Guerrero V.	Vicente Rivera
	4. Fidel Ramírez M.	Martin V. González
	5. Andrés Gutiérrez Castro	Hermilo Calderón S.

| Colima | 1. *Salvador Saucedo* | José Campero |

Distrito Federal	1. Herminio Pérez Abreu	Gustavo S. Martínez
	2. *Rafael Martínez de Escobar*	Abraham González
	3. *José Inés Novelo*	Emigdio Hidalgo Catalán
	4. *Vito Alessio Robles*	Francisco Chevannier
	5. Jesús M. Garza	Rubén Vizcarra
	6. Rafael Ramos Pedrueza	Fernando León
	7. *Ernesto Aguirre Colorado*	Pedro Luna
	8. Rafael Lara G.	Ramón Velasco
	9. *Roberto Casas Alatriste*	León G. Rojas
	10. Octavio Paz	Carlos Aragón
	11. Jorge Prieto Laurens	José Dolores Pérez
	12. Carlos Argüelles	Melesio Jiménez

Durango	1. *Ignacio Borrego*	Luis Zubiría y Campa
	2. Lorenzo Gámiz	Juan J. Palacios
	3. Salvador Franco Urías	Alberto Sánchez
	4. Rodrigo Gómez	Alberto Terrones Benítez
	5. Emilio Gandarilla	Vicente Galindo
	6. Liborio Espinosa y Elenes	Miguel Espinosa y Elenes
	7. Aquilino Emilio Rama	José R. Dávila

Guanajuato	1. Ramón Velarde	Fidencio García
	2. Nicolás Cano	Heriberto Morales
	3. Carlos Chico	Ignacio de Ibarrondo
	4. Unknown	Unknown
	5. Unknown	Unknown
	6. Francisco Soto	Maríano Loza
	7. *Agustín Arroyo Ch.*	José Rodiles C.
	8. Manuel Gutiérrez de V.	J. Rafael López
	9. Enrique Fernández Martínez	Ramón León
	10. Antonio D. Maldonado	Vicente Mendoza Oliveros
	11. Gilberto Sánchez	Manuel Aguilar
	12. Lucas Lira	Sebastián Rocha
	13. Vicente Alvarez	Luis Montaño
	14. José Méndez	José María Nieto
	15. José Ascensión Aguilera	Manuel Vertiz
	16. Enrique Hernández Alvarez	Simeón Ortuño
	17. Roberto Sepúlveda	José M. Sota
	18. Lucas Contreras	Arturo Ducoing

Guerrero	1. Custodio Valverde	Demetrio Ramos
	2. *Fidel Guillén*	Francisco Vásquez
	3. Juan B. Salazar	Rafael Torres
	4. *Miguel F. Ortega*	Agustín Vieyra
	5. *Adolfo Cienfuegos y Camus*	Crescencio A. Miranda
	6. Trinidad Mastache	José M. Caneda

State	Deputy	Alternate
	7. Urbano Lavín	Gildaro R. Gama
	8. *José Inocente Lugo*	Isidoro Cervantes
Hidalgo	1. Luis Paredes	Crisóforo Aguirre
	2. Leopoldo E. Camarena	Enrique Vásquez
	3. Abel Hernández Coronado	Leopoldo Esquivel
	4. Jesús E. Azuara	Polquinto Cobos
	5. Francisco de la Peña	Jesús J. Guerrero
	6. Estanislao Olguín	Jorge A. Olguín
	7. Francisco Castrejón	Elías Elías
	8. Santiago Rodríguez López	J. Trinidad Oviedo
	9. Francisco López Soto	Angel Morales
	10. Alfonso Gómez	Alfonso de Ita
	11. Erasmo Trejo	Ricardo Garibay
Jalisco	1. *José G. Zuno Hernández*	Gustavo R. Cristo
	2. Federico N. Solórzano	Francisco Gutiérrez Mejía
	3. Pablo H. Sánchez	Tomás L. Rubalcaba
	4. *Juan M. Alvarez del C.*	Luis Alvarez del Castillo
	5. Salvador Serrano H.	Manuel Gutiérrez Aguilar
	6. Gumaro Villalobos	Francisco Z. Moreno
	7. Manuel Lomelí	Andrés Mora
	8. Manuel Navarro	José de Jesús Aguilar
	9. Antonio Valadez Ramírez	Enrique Arévalo
	10. Juan Bravo y Juárez	Javier Enciso
	11. Carlos Cuervo	Constantino Alcalá
	12. Reinaldo Esparza Martínez	Herminio Ortiz
	13. José Maqueo Castellanos	Florencio Topete
	14. *José María Cuéllar*	Miguel San Juan
	15. Augusto Aillaud	Gabriel Blanco
	16. Ignacio Luquín	José Sánchez
	17. José C. Miramontes	Miguel S. del Real
	18. Unknown	Job Chávez
	19. *Basilio Badillo*	Carlos B. Munguía
	20. Natalio Espinosa	Lauro Bracamontes
México	1. Enrique del Castillo	Vicente C. Abasta
	2. José Luis Solórzano	Manuel Lara
	3. David Montes de Oca	Rafael Castañeda
	4. Bernardo de la Vega	Roberto Otáñez
	5. José Remedios Colón	Waldo Cienfuegos
	6. Arturo Alarcón	Julio Pomposo Gorostieta
	7. Atanasio Gutiérrez	Carlos Pichardo
	8. Abraham Franco	Fernando Moreno
	9. Angel Alanís Fuentes	Artemio Garduño
	10. Leopoldo Guadarrama	Benjamín Arcos
	11. Isauro Castillo Garrido	Heriberto E. Enríquez
	12. Vacant	
	13. Tranquilino Salgado	Eduardo Fernández
	14. Felipe de la Barrera	Gabino Hernández
	15. Antonio Manero	Manuel M. Rodríguez
	16. Prócoro Dorantes	Rafael Monterrubio
	17. Leopoldo Vicencio	Mariano Vicencio

Michoacán		
	1. *Uriel Avilés*	José P. Ruiz
	2. *Manuel Padilla*	Antonio Díaz
	3. Bibiano Ibarra	José Molina
	4. *Leopoldo Zincúnegui T.*	Francisco Patiño Borja
	5. José Sánchez Anaya	Rafael Reyes Pérez
	6. J. Antonio Couto	Carlos Riva Palacio
	7. Martín Barragán	Isaac Montenegro
	8. Constantino Rivera	Silvestre Ch. Marroquín
	9. Eduardo Larís Rubio	José Victoria
	10. Ignacio C. Villegas	Rafael Cano
	11. Silvano Hurtado	Emigdio Santa Cruz
	12. Rafael M. González	Braulio Alcázar
	13. José Bravo Betancourt	Ramón Sánchez Arriola
	14. Uriel Navarro	Alberto Méndez
	15. Prisciliano Carriedo	Florentino Melgoza
	16. Luis Guzmán	Francisco Mercado
	17. José M. Soto	José Navarrete

Morelos		
	1. Leopoldo Reynoso Díaz	Albino Ortiz
	2. *Mariano Montero Villar*	Rafael Barajas
	3. Francisco de la Torre	Rodolfo Magaña

Nayarit		
	1. Francisco Trejo	Pedro E. Elías
	2. Lucas Bravo	Aurelio Partida
	3. Ricardo A. Alvarez	José María Ledón

Nuevo León		
	1. *Miguel D. Martínez Rendón*	José María Díaz
	2. Francisco González y G.	Julio Leal
	3. Francisco Garza	Manuel Barreda
	4. Juan Quiroga	Alberto Chapa
	5. *Pedro A. Chapa*	Roberto Morelos Zaragoza
	6. M. Agustín González	I. Avala Villarreal

Oaxaca		
	1. *Manuel García Vigil*	Eduardo Vasconcelos
	2. José Leyva	Apolonio Aguilar
	3. Manuel G. Toro	Gabriel Pérez
	4. *Francisco Modesto R.*	Próspero Bolaños
	5. Manuel Franco Cerqueda	Celestino Pérez
	6. Miguel G. Calderón	Gustavo E. Velasco
	7. Joaquín Acevedo	Arturo Osorio
	8. Adalberto Lazcano	Otilio Silva y Castillo
	9. Israel del Castillo	Pedro Altamirano
	10. Eduardo Guerrero	Juan Antonio Orozco
	11. Francisco Castillo	Heraclio Ramírez
	12. Joaquín Ogarrio Meixueiro	
	13. Ignacio C. Reyes	Maximiliano Cenobio
	14. Onésimo González	Secundino Sánchez
	15. Alfonso Pérez Gasga	Abraham Velásquez
	16. *Crisóforo Rivera Cabrera*	Francisco Lobo Villalobos
	17. Cosme D. Gómez	Ciro Martínez

Puebla		
	1. *José M. Sánchez*	Luis Sánchez de Cima
	2. Clemente Munguía	Gonzalo Maceda
	3. Antonio Ortega	Fidel Vélez

State	Deputy	Alternate
	4. Manuel Montes	Alfonso María Figueroa
	5. Carlos Sánchez Pontón	Cosme del Raso
	6. *Eduardo Arrioja Isunza*	Guillermo Escobedo
	7. Vacant	
	8. Unknown	José Alberto Tapia
	9. *Porfirio del Castillo*	Antonio María Palacios
	10. Francisco J. Barbosa	Gabriel Tejada
	11. Godofredo Guzmán Peláez	Heliodoro Marín
	12. Alberto Guerrero	Jesús Hermoso
	13. José Gálvez	Leopoldo Gómez León
	14. Claudio N. Tirado	Miguel Angel Cuevas
	15. Manuel F. Méndez	Antonio Hernández
	16. J. Melquíades Vergara	Luis Cabrera
	17. Vacant	
	18. Leobardo L. Lechuga	Jesús L. Téllez
Querétaro	1. *José Siurob*	Ramón Bueno
	2. Francisco Ramírez Luque	Enrique Herrera
	3. Constantino Llaca	Ciro Montes Vargas
	4. Filemón Basaldúa	Reinaldo Montes
Quintana Roo	1. Enrique M. Barragán	*J. Amílcar Vidal*
San Luis Potosí	1. *Aurelio Manrique*	Graciano Sánchez
	2. *Antonio Díaz Soto y Gama*	J. Ciriaco Cruz
	3. Arnulfo Portales	Ricardo Almanza Gordoa
	4. Luis Castro y López	Cosme Dávila
	5. Juan Angel Morales	Octaviano Rangel
	6. Flavio B. Ayala	Valentín Narváez
	7. Víctor del Pino	Buenaventura Robles
	8. Angel Silva	Gabriel Martínez
	9. Agustín E. Vidales	Antonio García
	10. Ildefonso Peña	Pedro Altamirano
Sinaloa	1. Francisco Ramos Esquer	Enrique Zazueta Bátiz
	2. José Gómez Luna	Abraham Salcido
	3. Macedonio B. Gutiérrez	José Siordia
	4. J. Joaquín Silva	Eleuterio Aguilar, Jr.
	5. Fernando B. Martínez	Filiberto R. Quintero
Sonora	1. *Froylán C. Manjárrez*	Manuel O. Villegas
	2. *Juan de Dios Borjórquez*	Angel Castillo Nájera
	3. Alejo Bay	Luis A. Aldaco
	4. Gustavo P. Serrano	Guillermo Macalpín
Tabasco	1. Federico Martínez de E.	Victorino Ramón P.
	2. *José Domingo Ramírez G.*	Candelario Damián
	3. Fernando Aguirre Colorado	Daniel J. Castillo
Tamaulipas	1. Herminio S. Rodríguez	Donaciano Echavarría
	2. Candelario Garza	Domingo García
	3. Eliseo L. Céspedes	José F. Montesinos
	4. *Emilio Portes Gil*	Ignacio Angeles

Tlaxcala	1. Mauro Angulo	Abel Carro
	2. Moisés Huerta	Felipe Xóchihua
	3.	

Veracruz	1. José H. Romero	Roberto J. Peralta
	2. Joel Flores	José María Argüelles
	3. Miguel Ramírez	Luis Melo
	4. Benito Ramírez G.	Enrique Barón Obregón
	5. Teodomiro T. Gutiérrez	Raimundo Pérez Reyes
	6. Francisco Reyes	Arturo Almazán
	7. Adolfo G. García	José de Jesús Roa
	8. *Manlio Fabio Altamirano*	Luis G. Morales
	9. Adolfo Contreras	Flavio Galván
	10. Miguel B. Fernández	Casimiro Cruz Muñoz
	11. *Arturo Campillo Seyde*	Juan B. Sariol
	12. *Enrique Meza*	Samuel Herrera
	13. Guillermo Rodríguez	Severino Méndez
	14. Jesús Z. Moreno	Luis Rodríguez
	15. Manuel Zapata	Clemente Gabay
	16. Manuel Tello Romero	Antonio Martínez
	17. Francisco Tejeda Llorea	Juan Joachín
	18. Manuel E. Miravete	Andrés Pérez Cadena
	19. Aurelio P. Márquez	Bernardo H. Simoncen

Yucatán	1. *Felipe Carrillo Puerto*	Gustavo Arce
	2. Edmundo B. Cantón	Juan Zárate
	3. Benjamín Carrillo Puerto	Delfín Sánchez
	4. Edmundo Bolio	Federico Carrillo
	5. Manuel Berzunza	Gustavo C. Correa
	6. Miguel Alonzo Romero	Anastasio Manzanilla

Zacatecas	1.	
	2. Jesús B. González	Salvador Alatorre
	3. Leopoldo Estrada	Justo M. Sánchez
	4. J. Rudecindo Berumen	José F. Brilanti
	5. Manuel García Rojas	Ignacio Velasco
	6. Tereso Reyes	Juan Manuel Dávila
	7. *Roque Estrada*	José Macías Rubalcaba
	8. Daniel Castañeda Nigra	Juan M. Hernández

1922–24 (30th Legislature)

State	Deputy	Alternate
Aguascalientes	1. Rafael Quevedo	Melitón Perea
	2. Rodrigo Palacio	Isaac Díaz de León
Baja California	1. Ricardo Covarrubias	Francisco L. García
	2. Enrique von Borstel	Alberto Alvarado H.
Campeche	1. Eduardo Mena Córdova	Manuel Osorno
	2. José Certucha	Arturo Shiels D.
Chiapas	1. Luis Espinosa	Victórico Grajales
	2. César Martínez Rojas	Miguel Castillo H.

State	Deputy	Alternate
	3. Jaime A. Solís	Milcíades Carrascosa
	4. Agustín Castillo	Aarón Castellanos
	5. Luis Ramírez Corzo	Manuel Gris
	6. J. Enríquez Domínguez	Francisco Flores R.
	7. Julio Esponda	Enrique F. Toledo
Chihuahua	1. Angel G. Castellanos	Manuel F. Monzón
	2. Rafael V. Balderrama	Francisco Chávez Holguín
	3. José Sáenz Juárez	Casimiro E. Almeida
	4. *Luis L. León*	Manuel M. Prieto
	5. Pedro Ignacio Chacón	Nicolás Pérez
	6. Manuel Chávez M.	José A. Luján
	7. Luis A. Aldaco	Emilio Aguirre
Coahuila	1. Lorenzo Dávila	Conrado C. García
	2. *Adrián Aguirre Benavides*	Manuel H. Rodríguez
	3. Otilio González	José García Ureña
	4. Enrique Breceda	Reginaldo Cepeda
	5. Carlos Garza Castro	Federico de Luna
	6. Jacobo Cárdenas	José Garza Cabello
	7. Elpidio Barrera	Marcelino de Hoyos T.
Colima	1. *Francisco Solórzano Béjar*	Enrique Rivera Quevedo
	2. Salvador Vizcarra	Manuel Gudiño
Distrito Federal	1. Ezequiel Salcedo	Salvador López Olivares
	2. Mariano Samayoa	Jerónimo Hernández
	3. Carlos Argüelles	Manuel Cárdenas
	4. *Rafael Pérez Taylor*	Armando Salcedo
	5. Luis G. Malváez	Gilberto Rubalcaba
	6. Martín Luis Guzmán	Severino Bazán
	7. Antonio Valadez Ramírez	Antonio Yáñez Salazar
	8. *Roque González Garza*	Eduardo F. Islas
	9. Gustavo Arce	Armando Vargas
	10. Mauricio Gómez	Francisco Flores
	11. José F. Gutiérrez	Carlos Ortiz
	12. *Luis N. Morones*	Fernando Rodarte
	13. Rubén Vizcarra	Isaías Juárez
	14. Romeo Ortega	Florentino Miranda
	15. *Froylán C. Manjárrez*	Policarpio Mercado
Durango	1. Marino Castillo Nájera	Miguel Galván Rivas
	2. Lorenzo Gámiz	José M. Miranda
	3. Salvador Franco Urías	Juan Pablo Estrada
	4. Rodrigo Gómez	Alberto Terrones Benítez
	5. Emilio Gandarilla	Carlos Andrade
	6. Liborio Espinosa y Elenes	Miguel Espinosa y Elenes
	7. Aquilino Emilio Rama	José R. Dávila
Guanajuato	1. José A. Guerra	Luis Rangel
	2. Jesús López Lira	Juan Mora
	3. Quirino S. Trillo	Ignacio de Herrondo

	4. Ramón Velarde	Salvador Carrera
	5. Manuel Ortiz	Manuel Ayala
	6. Ezequiel Ríos Landeros	Juan G. Abascal
	7. Ignacio García Téllez	David Gutiérrez de Velasco
	8. José J. Razo	Francisco Sánchez H.
	9. *Federico Medrano*	Miguel León
	10. *Agustín Arroyo Ch.*	Roberto Sepúlveda
	11. Manuel Hernández Galván	Joaquín Quintana
	12. Lucas Lira	Maximiliano Villalobos
	13. *Alberto Peralta*	Isauro Rivera
	14. José M. Gutiérrez	José Gil Lámbarri
	15. José Ascensión Aguilera	Everardo Soto
	16. Enrique Hernández Alvarez	Mónico Aguiñaga
	17. Francisco Olivares	José M. Benítez
	18. Gustavo M. Bravo	José María Hernández L.

Guerrero	1. Ismael Carmona	Juan R. Escudero
	2. Ignacio Pérez Vargas	José D. López
	3. Rafael Torres	Melitón Caamaño
	4. Refugio Cervantes	Ignacio Andraca
	5. Arturo Martínez Adame	Arturo Nava
	6. Moisés G. Herrera	Carlos Flores
	7. José Castilleja	Florencio M. Salgado
	8. *Ezequiel Padilla*	Desiderio Borja

Hidalgo	1. Enrique Trejo Martínez	Angel Vadillo
	2. Adalberto Lazcano Carrasco	Manuel María Lazcano
	3. Celso Ruiz	Pedro P. Pérez
	4. Daniel Cerecedo Estrada	Faustino R. Mendoza
	5. Fernando Herrera	Gerardo Hernández
	6. J. Trinidad Cano	Francisco M. Austria
	7. Norberto Aranzábal	Rodolfo Asiáin
	8. *Matías Rodríguez*	Octaviano Flores
	9. Felipe Díez Martínez	Manuel Lailson Banuet
	10. Juvencio Nochebuena	Tomás Rueda
	11. Vacant	

Jalisco	1. Alfredo Romo	Francisco Vidrio Pérez
	2. Benigno Palencia	Eugenio López Guerra
	3. Aldolfo Hernández Marín	Primitivo González
	4. *Juan M Alvarez del C.*	Dionisio L. Gómez
	5. *Francisco Escudero*	Atalo S. Montoya
	6. Francisco Z. Moreno	Abraham González
	7. Juan de Dios Robledo	Ismael Lozano
	8. Manuel Navarro	Pedro Ibarra González
	9. José de Jesús Cuéllar	José Torres H.
	10. *José G. Zuno Hernández*	J. Guadalupe Estrada
	11. Carlos Cuervo	Enrique del Río
	12. Reinaldo Esparza Martínez	Francisco Grajeda
	13. *Daniel Benítez*	Elías F. Hurtado
	14. *José María Cuéllar*	Miguel San Juan
	15. Fernando Valencia	Agustín García de Alba
	16. Alberto Pérez Rojas	Fernando Martín del Campo

State	Deputy	Alternate
	17. Prisciliano Valdés	Ignacio Sánchez Valdés
	18. Paulino Manzano	Felipe Pérez
	19. Aurelio Sepúlveda	Joaquín Gutiérrez
	20. Francisco González G.	Reinaldo Esparza
México	1. Jesús M. Díaz	José I. González
	2. Roberto Nieto	David Jiménez
	3. Demetrio Hinostrosa	Juan Torres Osorio
	4. David Montes de Oca	Antonio Izquierdo
	5. José Alva Reza	H. Pedro D'Oleire
	6. Roberto Otáñez	José Estrada Hernández
	7. Clemente Trueba	Leopoldo Pérez
	8. Pedro Laguna	Francisco B. Valero
	9. *Isidro Fabela*	Lauro Medrano
	10. *Filberto Gómez*	Agustín López
	11. Eduardo Zarza	Luis G. Ramírez
	12. José Guadalupe López	Enrique Jacob
	13. Arturo J. Valenzuela	Alberto Rodríguez
	14. *Gilberto Fabila*	Wenceslao Labra
	15. Luis Manuel Díaz	Manuel M. Rodríguez
	16. Prócoro Dorantes	Adolfo Rivera
	17. Mariano Vicencio	Ignacio M. Monroy
Michoacán	1. Enrique Parra	Luis Díaz
	2. José Pérez Gil y Ortiz	Luis Pérez Gil
	3. José Barriga Zavala	José Rincón Tovar
	4. Vidal Solís	Jesús Torres Caballero
	5. Federico Villegas	Maclovio Yáñez
	6. Agustín Gómez Campos	Maurilio López Núñez
	7. *Salvador Alcaraz Romero*	Celerino Luviano
	8. Joaquín Silva	Víctor Sotelo
	9. Jesús Magaña Soto	Joaquín Muñoz
	10. Ignacio C. Villegas	Gabriel Avila
	11. Emigdio Santacruz	Carlos Mendoza
	12. *Alfredo Alvarez*	Jesús F. Maciel
	13. Antonio Valladares	Atanasio Pineda
	14. Ramón Sánchez Arriola	Mariano Ramírez
	15. Rubén C. Navarro	David Marín Quiroz
	16. Salvador Murguía	Luis Méndez
	17. Torcuato Lemus	Lázaro V. Ramírez
	18. Enrique Ramírez	José Gómez
	19. Miguel A. Quintero	Inocencio Pérez
Morelos	1. *Mariano Montero Villar*	Albino Ortiz
	2. Leopoldo Reynoso Díaz	Ismael Velasco
	3. Vicente Aranda	Salvador S. Saavedra
Nayarit	1. Marcos Esmerio	Ignacio Morales
	2. Ismael Romero	Everardo Peña Navarro
	3. Apolonio R. Guzmán	Mateo Magallón
Nuevo León	1. Miguel D. Martínez Rendón	Daniel Colchado
	2. Francisco González y G.	Jesús M. Gutiérrez

	3. Francisco Garza	Lázaro B. Casas
	4. Juan Quiroga	Amado Villarreal
	5. Carlos Roel	Juan I. Martínez
	6. Eduardo Súllivan	Epifanio Martínez Ayala

Oaxaca
1. Eduardo Vasconcelos — Marcelino Muciño
2. Miguel de la Llave — Joaquín Corres
3. Genaro V. Vásquez — Otilio J. Madrigal
4. José Reyes San Germán — Alfonso Francisco Ramírez
5. Joaquín Ogarrio Meixueiro — Cenobio Antonio Márquez
6. Onésimo González — Pedro Hernández
7. Ricardo Delgado — Ramón Castañeda
8. José Pérez Acevedo — Gilberto Torres
9. Israel del Castillo — Eduardo Vasconcelos
10. Manuel Díaz Chávez — Bartolo Castillo
11. Leovigildo Bolaños — Abraham López
12. *Francisco Modesto Ramírez* — José García Ramos
13. Fermín E. Díaz — Samuel González
14. Miguel G. Calderón — Rodolfo Zorrilla
15. Roberto Rivero — Abelardo Márquez Galán
16. Camilo Flores Olvera — Rufino García
17. José F. Gómez — Arturo Larrañaga

Puebla
1. Luis Sánchez de Cima — Severo Reza
2. Gonzalo Bautista — Jesús Castillo
3. *Porfirio del Castillo* — César Garibay
4. *Roberto Casas Alatriste* — Rafael Pérez de León
5. Francisco I. Montoya — Sebastián Rojas
6. *Eduardo Arrioja Isunza* — Guillermo Escobedo
7. *Gilberto Bósques* — Eugenio Fuentes
8. Ricardo Reyes Márquez — Ezequiel Rosas
9. Francisco Hernández — Enrique Castillo
10. Fernando F. Franco — Francisco Barbosa
11. Guillermo Castillo Tapia — Prisciliano Ruiz
12. Alberto Guerrero — Pedro Díaz Murueta
13. José Gálvez — Pablo Landero León
14. Wenceslao Macín — Rufino A. Landero
15. Arnulfo Pérez H. — Enrique Carmona y R.
16. Sealtiel Oliver y C. — César Lechuga
17. Gonzalo E. González — Miguel Márquez Rivera
18. Porfirio Hernández — Francisco R. Pérez

Querétaro
1. Francisco Ramírez Luque — J. Cruz Hernández
2. Enrique B. Domínguez — Francisco Martínez
3. Juan Pastoriza — Eduardo Moreno
4. *José Siurob* — Policarpo Olvera

Quintana Roo
1. Enrique M. Barragán — Fernando González M.

San Luis Potosí
1. *Aurelio Manrique* — Ramón F. Hernández
2. *Antonio Díaz Soto y Gama* — Graciano Sánchez
3. Manuel Dávalos Aragón — David Zárate
4. Justino Compeán — Manuel R. Gómez
5. Jorge Prieto Laurens — Jesús Canal

State	Deputy	Alternate
	6. José P. Camacho	Miguel Solís
	7. Alfonso Gama	Rómulo Amarillas
	8. Gabriel Martínez	Aurelio L. Rodríguez
	9. Agustín E. Vidales	José María Rivera
	10. Adolfo Altamirano	Daniel Torres Garza
Sinaloa	1. *Juan de Dios Bátiz*	Ernesto Verdugo
	2. *Cándido Avilés*	Manuel Valdés
	3. Salomé Vizcarra	Carlos Bouttier
	4. Angel Montoya A.	Alejandro G. Castro
	5. Francisco de P. Alvarez	Antonio R. Castro
Sonora	1. José E. Peraza	Emeterio R. Aguayo
	2. Julián S. González	Apolonio L. Castro
	3. Manuel M. Méndez	Guillermo C. Miranda
	4. Alberto Gutiérrez	Enrique Terrazas
	5. Antonio G. Rivera	Federico J. Valenzuela
Tabasco	1. Justo A. Santa Anna	Manuel O. Nieto
	2. Alfonso Casanova C.	Homero Margalli G.
	3. Isaac Olivé	Alejandro Ruiz
Tamaulipas	1. Policarpo Rodríguez	Alejandro G. Guerra
	2. Candelario Garza	*Emilio Portes Gil*
	3. *Emilio Portes Gil*	Pedro Romero
	4. Eliseo L. Céspedes	Eduardo Benavides
	5. Rafael Garibay	Miguel Sánchez Saldaña
Tlaxcala	1. Pedro Suárez	Vicente Chavarría
	2. Moisés Huerta	Miguel Domínguez
	3. Aurelio M. Peña	Adalberto Cortés
Veracruz	1. Adolfo Azueta	Juan L. Alexandre
	2. *Enrique Meza*	Rosendo Bridat
	3. Isauro Barranco	Nabor Chagoya
	4. Enrique Barón Obregón	Luis R. Reyna
	5. Luis G. Márquez	Ricardo Hernández
	6. *Manlio Fabio Altamirano*	Alejandro Vernett
	7. Efrén D. Marín	Manuel Zapata
	8. Guillermo Rodríguez	Francisco Méndez
	9. Antonio Sánchez Rebolledo	José A. Murrieta
	10. Enrique L. Soto	Cipriano Villanueva Garza
	11. José Ismael Aguado	Ruperto S. García
	12. Carlos Puig y Casauranc	Enrique C. Huerta
	13. Guillermo Fernández	Juan Galicia
	14. *Arturo Campillo Seyde*	Arcadio Hernández
	15. Rubén Basáñez	Jorge Meléndez
	16. José Villanueva Garza	Martín C. Jiménez
	17. Juan Joachín	Miguel Vives Ruiz
	18. Manuel Miravete	Julio Cadena
	19. *José Manuel Puig y Casauranc*	Manuel A. Limón

Yucatán	1. *José Castillo Torre*	Aurelio Velásquez
	2. Arturo Cisneros Canto	Eladio Domínguez
	3. José de la Luz Mena	José E. Ancona
	4. Luis Torregrosa	Rafael Gamboa
	5. José María Iturralde	Fernando Gamboa B.
	6. Miguel Cantón	Rafael Cebada T.
Zacatecas	1. Enrique García	Leopoldo I. Hernández
	2. Jesús B. González	León J. Oteo
	3. Francisco Olivier	Federico M. Gutiérrez
	4. Ignacio Sánchez Campa	J. Angel Acevedo
	5. J. Jesús Velásquez	Manuel García Rojas
	6. Tereso Reyes	Antonio D. Carrillo
	7. Leopoldo Estrada	Leocadio Frías Quiarte
	8. Isidro Cardona	Manuel Olvera

1924–26 (31st Legislature)

State	Deputy	Alternate
Aguascalientes	1. Rafael Quevedo	Isaac Díaz de León
	2. *Manuel Carpio*	José M. Ortega
Baja California	1. Ricardo Covarrubias	Ignacio F. Loaiza
	2. Enrique von Borstel M.	Manuel Gómez Jiménez
Campeche	1. Silvestre Pavón Silva	Emilio Martínez Preciat
	2. Eduardo R. Mena Córdova	F. Enrique Angly Lara
Coahuila	1. Jacobo Cárdenas	José Martínez y Martínez
	2. *Vicente Santos Guajardo*	Mariano Chavero
	3. Cándor Guajardo	Ambrosio Rodríguez
	4. Elpidio Rodríguez	Roberto J. Robledo
	5. Antonio Garza Castro	José María Ibarra
	6. Marcos A. Hernández	Aureliano L. Cadena
Colima	1. *Francisco Solórzano Béjar*	Enrique Rivera Quevedo
	2. José Llerenas	Juan de la Cruz García
Chiapas	1. Julio Esponda	Francisco Aranjo
	2. Jesús Z. Nucamendi	Fiacro E. López
	3. César Martínez Rojas	Miguel Castillo, Jr.
	4. Benjamín Mijangos	Evaristo Bonifaz
	5. Manuel Rabasa	Martín Paredes
	6. Milcíades Carrascosa	Ventura Castro
	7. *Luis Ramírez Corzo*	Luis Monroy Aguirre
Chihuahua	1. José U. Escobar	Samuel Carlisle
	2. Francisco García Carranza	Isauro Medina
	3. *Mariano Irigoyen*	Abelardo S. Amaya
	4. Antonio Corona	Benito Martínez Miller
	5. *Francisco R. Almada*	Elisco Prieto
	6. José Calles	Mariano Guillén
	7. Antonio Fuentes	Rodrigo Aguilera

State	Deputy	Alternate
Distrito Federal	1. *Leopoldo Zincúnegui Tercero*	Manuel Balderas
	2. Guillermo Zárraga	Alfonso Márquez P.
	3. *Luis L. León*	Gorgonio Estrada
	4. Gustavo Durón González	Raúl Prieto
	5. *Rafael Martínez de Escobar*	Arnulfo Silva
	6. Gonzalo González	Ramón Reyes
	7. Miguel Yépez Solórzano	Antonio Aldrete
	8. *Romeo Ortega*	Ricardo González Montero
	9. Justo A. Santa Anna	Carlos Aragón
	10. José F. Gutiérrez	Elías F. Hurtado
	11. Ernesto Prieto	Felipe Avila
	12. *Luis N. Morones*	Ricardo Treviño
	13. *Eduardo Delhumeau, Jr*	José Remedios López
	14. Rafael Ponce de León	Antonio Espinosa y Rodríguez
	15. Amílcar Zentella	Ricardo López F.
Durango	1. Alejandro Antuna	José D. Quiroga
	2. Salvador Reyes Avilés	Laureano Martinez
	3. Juan Pablo Estrada	Leopoldo Martínez
	4. Rodrigo Gómez	Felipe Gómez
	5. Ramón Martínez	José G. Fabela
	6. *Alberto Terrones Benítez*	Guillermo S. Seguín
	7. Benjamin Borrego Martínez	Fernando J. Silveyra
Guanajuato	1. José A. Guerra	Manuel Rangel
	2. *Enrique Fernández Martínez*	Manuel G. Aranda
	3. Constantino Llaca	Francisco Bedia
	4. Juan B. Bravo	Manuel Sánchez
	5. Felipe Muñoz	J. Jesús Rea
	6. Juan G. Abascal	Jesús Silva Ruiz
	7. Isauro Lolía	Juan Araryo
	8. Ignacio García Téllez	Pascual J. Padilla
	9. *Federico Medrano V.*	Pulcherio Pérez Pardo
	10. Angel Aragón	Manuel Tamayo
	11. *Agustín Arroyo Ch.*	Fermín Montenegro
	12. *Cayetano Andrade*	Francisco Díaz Barriga
	13. *José Aguilar y Maya*	Leopoldo Alcántar
	14. José M. Gutiérrez	Esteban Bueno
	15. *Benjamín Méndez, Jr.*	Adolfo Obregón
	16. Enrique Hernández Alvarez	Leandro Jaso
	17. Francisco Olivares Gutiérrez	J. Pilar Rivera
	18. Lucas Contreras	Arturo Ducoing
Guerrero	1. Desiderio Borja	Héctor Varelea
	2. Camerino T. Ocampo	Adrián Gómez
	3. Magarito Gómez	Manuel B. Toledo
	4. *Ezequiel Padilla*	*Galo Soberón y Parra*
	5. *Alberto Vásquez del Mercado*	Alejandro Sánchez
	6. J. Refugio Cervantes	Ramón Ibarra
	7. Juan B. Salazar	Leonides Moctezuma

	8. Daniel L. Barrera	Alfonso O. Guevara
	9. Justino M. Castro	Santiago Solano
	10. Manuel López	Francisco Maldonado

Hidalgo

1. Camerino Campos — Emiliano Esparza
2. José L. Galván — Alfredo Madrid
3. Leonardo M. Hernández — Heliodoro López
4. Oscar B. Santander — Cesáreo I. García
5. Artemio Basurto — Francisco de la Peña, Jr.
6. *Juvencio Nochebuena* — Erasmo Angeles
7. Alberto Cravioto — Alberto Angeles
8. Román Monroy — Nicomedes Falcón
9. Francisco López Soto — Floro M. Parra
10. Santiago Hernández — Leobardo I. Mercado
11. Anastasio Arciniega — Efraín Ledesma

Jalisco

1. Alfredo Romo — Francisco Vidrio Pérez
2. José V. Gómez Cano — Carlos Ortiz M.
3. Gustavo R. Cristo — Luis J. Abitia
4. *José María Cuéllar* — Leopoldo Cuéllar
5. Juan B. Izábal — Miguel Rábago Soto
6. David Orozco — Manuel Ortega
7. Ricardo Covarrubias — Francisco Aceves Orozco
8. Francisco Z. Moreno — Daniel Macías
9. Antonio Valadez Ramírez — José de Jesús Cuéllar
10. Ramón Córdova — Longinos Casillas
11. Margarito Ramírez — J. Guadalupe de Anda
12. David S. López — Enrique Vásquez L.
13. Fernando Martín del Campo — Salvador Zuno Hernández
14. J. Jesús Otero — Luis García
15. Francisco D. Flores — Ruperto García
16. Romualdo Parra — Francisco Camacho
17. Benigno Palencia — Severiano Lozano
18. Felipe Pérez — Isidoro Morales Palafox
19. Julián Villaseñor Mejía — Casimiro Castillo
20. Justo González — Elpidio Robles
21. Alberto González — Martíniano Sendis
22. Juan Madrigal — Fernando Chávez
23. Carlos Cuervo — Emilio Hernández

México

1. Jesús M. Díaz — Fernando Garcés
2. Roberto Nieto — Manuel R. Calderón
3. *David Montes de Oca* — Margarito Gómez
4. Roberto Otáñez — Adrián López Gómez
5. Demetrio Hinostrosa — Zenón Suárez
6. Telésforo Flores Peña — Efrén Sámano
7. *Gilberto Fabila* — Juan Manuel Patiño
8. Ramón Anaya — Jorge A. Vargas
9. Clemente Trueba — Francisco J. Téllez
10. Filiberto Gómez — Lorenzo Robles
11. Arturo J. Valenzuela — Alfredo M. Ezeta
12. Enrique Jacob — Plácido García
13. Benito Zorraquin — Ernesto Ríos

State	Deputy	Alternate
	14. Mariano García M.	*Wenceslao Labra, Jr.*
	15. Luis Manuel Díaz	Manuel Rodríguez Ayala
	16. Prócoro Dorantes	José de la Sierra
	17. Rómulo A. Villavicencio	Ramón Madrigal
Michoacán	1. José Pérez Gil y Orta	Pascual Cortés
	2. Víctorino Flores	Demetrio Maciel
	3. Luis Díaz	Juan Alvarado Díaz
	4. Vidal Solís	Alfredo León
	5. *Silvestre Guerrero*	Salvador Guerrero
	6. *Carlos Riva Palacio*	Manuel Avilés
	7. José María Sánchez Pineda	Clicerio V. Carvajal
	8. Joaquín Silva	Rafael Montalván
	9. Pedro M. Martínez	Francisco Rivera Díaz
	10. Efraín Pineda	Diódoro Torres
	11. *Melchor Ortega*	Juan Ayala
	12. Alfredo Alvarez Treviño	Antonio Espinosa Gutiérrez
	13. J. Jesús Pineda	Ignacio Martínez
	14. Rafael Picazo	J. Jesús Gudino
	15. Octavio Magaña	Pedro Pérez
	16. Rafael Alvarez y Alvarez	Alfonso Leñero Ruiz
	17. *Jesús Romero Flores*	Melesio Moreno R.
	18. Ernesto Aceves	Rafael Padilla Ramírez
	19. José Valdovinos Garza	José Rodríguez
Morelos	1. Eugenio Mier y Terán	Luis G. Campo
	2. Vicente Anzures	Ernesto Pinzón
	3. Silvano Sotelo	Santos Quevedo
Nayarit	1. Agustín Arriola Valadez	Bernardo M. León
	2. Ismael Romero Gallardo	Antonio Villarreal
	3. José de la Peña	Pedro López S.
Nuevo León	1. Timoteo R. Martínez	Manuel Villarreal
	2. Porfirio Pérez Salinas	Protasio Flores
	3. Cruz C. Contreras	Jesús María Fernández
	4. Jesús Santos Mendiola	Cosme Villarreal
	5. Juan I. Martínez	Aurelio Garza González
	6. José Martínez Campos	Crescencio de la Garza G.
Oaxaca	1. Rafael Hernández Pimentel	Emilio Alvarez
	2. Election nullified, October 9, 1924	
	3. *Genaro V. Vásquez*	Otilio Jiménez Madrigal
	4. Rufino Zavaleta	Juvencio Larrañaga
	5. *Manuel Rueda Margo*	Manuel Franco Cerqueda
	6. José García Ramos	Cecilio Cruz Palacios
	7. Librado G. López	Rosendo Pérez
	8. Rafael E. Melgar	Fermín E. Díaz
	9. Alberto Vargas	José Guadalupe García
	10. Pedro A. Vásquez	Manuel B. Albuerne
	11. Adolfo Arias	Héctor Fierro

	12. José Pérez Acevedo	Antonio Gómez Tamariz
	13. *Alfonso F. Ramírez*	Rafael Cruz Pombo
	14. *José Castillo Larrañaga*	Efrén Narváez
	15. Francisco Arlanzón	Juan Reyes Saavedra
	16. *Francisco López Cortés*	Samuel Villalobos
	17. Amado Fuentes B.	Efrén N. Mata

Puebla

1. Luis Sánchez de Cima — Donaciano Jiménez
2. *Pastor Rouaix* — Juan Pérez
3. *José María Sánchez* — Rosendo Medrano
4. Jesús Ponce — Rafael H. Rodríguez
5. Juan Domínguez Martínez — Federico Tosqui
6. Reynaldo Nuncio — Samuel R. Malpica
7. Jesús Zafra — José López Guillemín
8. *Ricardo Reyes Márquez* — J. Trinidad Hernández
9. Luciano M. Sánchez — Ignacio González
10. Marino Pérez — Matías Montiel
11. Alfredo Ortega Martínez — Andrés Gasca Mendoza
12. Manuel M. Guerrero — Andrés Sosa
13. *Vicente Lombardo Toledano* — Jorge Avila Parra
14. *Wenceslao Macip* — Pedro Molina
15. *Gonzalo Bautista* — Leopoldo Vásquez Mellado
16. Salustio Cabrera — Eduardo Moreno
17. Gonzalo E. González — Guillermo Quirós
18. Aarón L. Valderrábano — Luis Santos Martínez

Querétaro

1. José Veraza y Rubio — Antonio Martínez
2. J. Trinidad Obregón — Aurelio Briones
3. *José Siurob* — Miguel G. Herrera
4. Ildefonso de la Peña — Ignacio Urbiloa Reyna

Quintana Roo

1. Fernando González Madrid — Alfonso Orozco

San Luis Potosí

1. Antonio Trujillo Espinosa — Cecilio Leos
2. Enrique Henshaw — Julián Adams
3. Arnulfo Portales — Benito Flores
4. *Antonio Díaz Soto y Gama* — José Narváez
5. Pedro Merla — Arturo Torres
6. José P. Camacho — Rafael Sánchez
7. Manuel Orta — José María Méndez
8. Jezaúr Pérez — Francisco Ariceaga
9. Antonio M. García — Melitón Uribe y Mendoza
10. *Gonzalo N. Santos* — Juan Alvares

Sinaloa

1. Cosme Alvarez — Ignacio L. Zavala
2. Manuel Riveros — Filiberto Mora y Ochoa
3. *Juan de Dios Bátiz* — Fernando Cuén
4. *Fausto A. Marín* — José Bernal y M.
5. Antonio López Sorcini — Francisco Peregrina
6. Salomé Vizcarra, Jr. — Martiniano H. Osuna

Sonora

1. *Emiliano Corella M.* — Pedro R. Dávila
2. Agustín Rodríguez — Francisco Celaya
3. Alberto Sáinz — Abelardo B. Sobarzo

State	Deputy	Alternate
	4. *Ramón Ramos*	Benjamin Peñúñuri
	5. Jesús M. Aguirre	Roberto A. Morales
Tabasco	1. Pablo Azcona	Manuel Jiménez
	2. Carlos Puig y Casauranc	Ovidio Jasso
	3. Juan Aguilar Ficachi	Alejandro Ruiz
Tamaulipas	1. Gregorio Garza Salinas	Leonides Guerra
	2. Agustín Aguirre Garza	Angel Cárdenas
	3. *Emilio Portes Gil*	Lorenzo de la Garza
	4. Juan A. Veites	Manuel J. Garza
	5. Santiago Chávez	Emilio Herrera
Tlaxcala	1. Florencio Zainos y Lumbreras	Felipe Xicohténcatl
	2. Filiberto E. Arenas	Arnulfo Tapia
	3. Eduardo Fernández de Lara	Juan Vásquez Ramírez
Veracruz	1. Election nullified, October 9, 1925	
	2. Hilario Menéndez	Enrique Núñez
	3. Isaac Velásquez	Cecilio Gómez
	4. Damián Alarcón	Rogelio A. Garmendia
	5. Luis G. Márquez	Alfonso Luna Méndez
	6. *Manlio Fabio Altamirano*	Antonio Fierro
	7. Guillermo Rodríguez	Gabriel Moctezuma, Jr.
	8. Gabriel Aguillón Guzmán	Vicente A. Cortés
	9. Enrique L. Soto	Angel D. Hernández
	10. Victorio Lorandi	Gonzalo Fernández
	11. Juan B. Sariol	Genaro Andrade
	12. Eulalio Martínez	Pedro López
	13. Martín Torres	Carlos Andrade
	14. *Arturo Campillo Seyde*	Teodoro Villegas
	15. Anselmo Mancisidor	Francisco Galán
	16. *Alejandro Cerísola*	Alvaro Cano Carrera
	17. *Pedro C. Rodríguez*	Tomás Pérez Morteo
	18. Primitivo R. Valencia	Manuel Azamar
	19. Andrés Gómez	Daniel Cinta
Yucatán	1. José E. Ancona	José Pérez Rosado
	2. Rodulfo Izquierdo	Samuel Espadas
	3. *José Castillo Torre*	Abelardo Gual García
	4. *Neguib Simón*	José N. Salazar A.
	5. Luis Torregrosa	Ernesto Rivero Díaz
	6. Ariosto Castellanos C.	Regino Escalante Rosado
Zacatecas	1. Election nullified, October 9, 1924	
	2. Leocadio Guerrero	José Dávila Díaz
	3. Pedro Belaunzarán	Guillermo C. Aguilera
	4. Luis R. Reyes	Rigoberto V. y Valdés
	5. *J. Jesús Delgado*	José D. Hernández

	6. *Lauro G. Caloca*	Ramiro Talancón
	7. J. Trinidad Luna Enríquez	Fidel B. Serrano
	8. Celestino Castro	J. Cruz N. Veloz

1926–28 (32nd Legislature)

State	Deputy	Alternate
Aguascalientes	1. Rafael Quevedo	Antonio Espinosa
	2. Isaac Díaz de León	Julio Ramírez
Baja California	1. José María Tapia	Rafael Souza
	2. Gilberto Isaís	Cuauhtémoc Hidalgo
Campeche	1. Raymundo Poveda C.	José del G. Hernández P.
	2. Eduardo R. Mena Córdova	Emilio Martínez Preciat
Coahuila	1. Juan L. Morales	Francisco A. Moreno
	2. Eduardo C. Loustaunau	Eduardo L. Perales
	3. Manuel Mijares V.	Domingo Valdés Llano
	4. Elpidio Barrera	Lázaro Solís
	5. Antonio Garza Castro	Gustavo Salinas
	6. Domingo Acosta	Lázaro Guedea
	7. Francisco de Valle	Adolfo Mondragón
Colima	1. José Llerenas	Napoleón Ramos Salido
	2. Francisco J. Silva	Salvador González
Chiapas	1. Max Cenobio Robles	Rafael Pascasio Gamboa
	2. Carlos Flores Tovilla	Adolfo Suárez
	3. Amet Ramos Cristiani	J. Amilcar Vidal
	4. Evaristo Bonifaz	Lindoro Castellanos
	5. Jamie A. Solís	Emilio Esponda
	6. *José Castañón*	Raymundo E. Enríquez
	7. Ulises Vidal	Policarpo Rueda
Chihuahua	1. Juan Salas Porras	Samuel Carlisle
	2. Pedro M. Fierro	Casimiro F. Almeida
	3. Nicolás Pérez	Manuel Romero
	4. Francisco G. Rodríguez	Roberto G. Galindo
	5. *Ramón Ramos*	José María Caraveo
	6. Rafael V. Balderrama	Inocente Rubio L.
	7. Bernardo R. Hasbach	Antonio Fuentes
Distrito Federal	1. Eulalio Martínez	Severino A. Olín
	2. Joaquín de la Peña	Enrique M. Bonilla
	3. Manuel Balderas	Antonio Espinosa y Rodríguez
	4. *Arturo Campillo Seyde*	Saturino Almada
	5. Samuel O. Yúdico	Antonio Ramos
	6. Gonzalo González	Elías F. Hurtado
	7. *Genaro V. Vásquez*	Indalecio Cruz Velasco
	8. *Gonzalo N. Santos*	Pedro Quevedo
	9. Juan Lozano	Rafael Villanueva
	10. José F. Gutiérrez	Honorato Hernández

State	Deputy	Alternate
	11. Ernesto Prieto	Inocencio Medina
	12. Ricardo Treviño	José de la Luz Valdéz
	13. Carlos Aragón	J. Trinidad Vivas
	14. Arturo de Saracho	Rafael Cruz
	15. José Moreno Salido	Ismael M. Lozano
Durango	1. *Silvestre Dorador*	José A. Albístegui
	2. Pedro Alvarez	Rosalio Quiñones
	3. Daniel R. Gutiérrez	J. Jesús Castro
	4. Election nullified on October 18, 1926	
	5. Carlos Andrade	José Ramón Valdés
	6. Jesús Salas Barrasa	Erasmo Barrasa
	7. Fernando Arenas	Santiago Hernández
	8. Liborio Espinosa y Elenes	J. Donaciano Rubio
Guanajuato	1. Nicolás Cano	José E. Troncoso
	2. Enrique Bordes Mangel	Luis G. Belaunzarán
	3. Gustavo Caballero	Luis A. Manrique
	4. Juan B. Bravo	Javier Sánchez
	5. *Ernesto Hidalgo*	Pío Mendoza
	6. Salvador Villaseñor	Manuel Cross
	7. Francisco Alvarez, Jr.	Rómulo Rodríguez
	8. Francisco Ramírez Escamilla	Salomón Torres Neri
	9. José González	Alberto Guerrero
	10. Estanislao Cortés Teixeira	Roberto de la Cerda
	11. Basiliso Ortega	Joaquín Quintana
	12. *José Aguilar y Maya*	Sebastián Rocha
	13. Melchor García	J. Dolores Villarreal
	14. Joaquín Torreblanca	Luis G. Corona
	15. Manuel Espinos	Tomás González
	16. *Vicente Cortés Herrera*	Mónico Rangel
	17. Pedro Suárez	Alberto Loyola
	18. Felipe Doria	Antonio Mata
Guerrero	1. Desiderio Borja	Luis Bedolla, Sr.
	2. José Castilleja	Adrián Gómez
	3. Amadeo Melendez	Emigdio Hidalgo Catalán
	4. *Alfonso L. Nava*	José Rueda Bravo
	5. Francisco S. Carreto	Francisco Rodríguez
	6. Alberto Méndez	Nicolás C. Fonseca
	7. Miguel Andrew Almazán	Rafael Torres Avilés
	8. Guillermo R. Miller	Jesús L. López
	9. Refugio Cervantes	Ramón Peralta
	10. Manuel López	Francisco Maldonado, Jr.
Hidalgo	1. Juan Manuel Delgado	Rodolfo Vera
	2. *Javier Rojo Gómez*	Justo Rivero
	3. José H. Romero	Aurelio B. Chapa
	4. Enrique Medécigo Rosas	José Rivera Careta
	5. Fernando Herrera	Manuel Herrera
	6. Honorato Austria	Heriberto Castillo

	7. Atanasio Hernández V.	David Licona
	8. Lauro Albuquerque	Juan Cruz
	9. Francisco López Soto	José Bernal Castillo
	10. Luis Sánchez Mejorada	Crescencio Ibarra Olivares
	11. Ismael Pintado Sánchez	Manuel Gómez
Jalisco	1. Alfredo Romo	Francisco Vidrio Pérez
	2. Justo González	Pablo Martínez Ortiz
	3. Alberto Meza Ledesma	Fermín Labastida
	4. Ignacio Vizcarra	Gregorio González Yáñez
	5. Juan B. Izábal	Manuel Rábago Soto
	6. David Orozco	Manuel Ortega
	7. Ricardo Covarrubias	Salvador Toral M.
	8. Francisco Z. Moreno	Carlos M. Muñoz
	9. José Radillo	José María López González
	10. *José Guadalupe de Anda*	Ismael M. Lozano
	11. Margarito Ramírez	Jesús M. Herrera
	12. J. Ascensión de la Cruz	Juan Ochoa
	13. Narciso Mejía	Fernando Guijarro Cázares
	14. Joaquín Vidrio	Luis García
	15. *Esteban García de Alba*	Félix Ramos
	16. Benigno Palencia	Ramón Delgado
	17. José Zataray	Francisco Camacho
	18. Ignacio H. Santana	Federico Santana
	19. Manuel H. Ruiz	Salvador Higareda
	20. Severiano Lozano	Víctor Preciado
	21. Alberto González	Julio Sánchez
	22. Juan Madrigal	Fernando Chávez
	23. Fernando González Madrid	Timoteo R. Martínez
México	1. Enrique A. Enríquez	Mario Sánchez Curiel
	2. Margarito Gómez	Manuel Alvarez
	3. Augusto Aillaud	Hiram Garduño
	4. Adrián López Gómez	Heriberto D'Oleire
	5. Zenón Suárez	Luis Izquierdo
	6. Víctor Díaz de León	Bernardo Pérez Guzmán
	7. *Gilberto Fabila*	Ernesto Ramos
	8. Eucario López	Antonio M. Luna
	9. Ramón Anaya	Francisco J. Téllez
	10. Filiberto Gómez	Lorenzo Robles
	11. David Montes de Oca	José Jiménez
	12. Manuel Aguayo	Alberto Romo Flores
	13. Armando P. Arroyo	Delfino Nájera
	14. Wenceslao Labra	Manuel Basauri
	15. Fernando E. Escamilla	Abelardo Montaño
	16. Manuel Riva Palacio	Pedro Trueba
	17. José Luis Solórzano	Félix García
Michoacán	1. José Aguilar	Demetrio Maciel
	2. Victorino Flores	Alberto Pichardo
	3. Luis Díaz	Manuel Díaz
	4. *Leopoldo Zincúnegui Tercero*	Luis Estrada
	5. *Silvestre Guerrero*	José Rivera

State	Deputy	Alternate
	6. *Arturo Bernal*	Manuel Avilés
	7. José María Sánchez Pineda	Luis E. Juárez
	8. José Carrasco Sandoval	Jesús Torres Zamudio
	9. Alberto Oviedo Mota	José Gómez Hurtado
	10. Efraín Pineda	José Pimentel
	11. *Melchor Ortega*	Leobardo Paz
	12. Silviano Hurtado	Jesús Hurtado Z.
	13. Austreberto Muratalla Torres	Ildefonso Duarte C.
	14. Rafael Picazo	José Cisneros
	15. Octavio Magaña	Rafael Coria
	16. Rafael Alvarez y Alvarez	Agustín Alcocer M.
	17. Agustín Méndez Macías	Genaro Melgosa
	18. Ernesto Aceves	Rafael Padilla Ramírez
	19. *Juan Abarca Pérez*	Victorino Flores
Morelos	1. Silvano Sotel	Neguib Simón
	2. *Gildardo Magaña*	Manuel Magaña
	3. Eugenio Mier y Terán	M. Solís Domínguez
Nayarit	1. Antioco Rodríguez	José Ramón Narváez
	2. Ismael Romero Gallardo	Luis Romero Gallardo
	3. Pedro López S.	Luis Frías
Nuevo León	1. Francisco Garza	Cristóbal Díaz
	2. Jesús Santos Mendiola	Amador Saldaña
	3. Felizardo C. Villarreal	Hilario Contreras Molina
	4. Francisco A. Cárdenas	José Garay Chapa
	5. Francisco Garza Nieto	Jesús Garza Martínez
	6. Juan A. Saldaña	Santiago Salinas
Oaxaca	1. Romeo Ortega	Aristeo V. Guzmán
	2. Emilio Alvarez	Ezequiel Canseco Barroso
	3. Carlos T. Robinson	Juan Alcázar
	4. Rufino Zavaleta	Manuel Díaz Chávez
	5. Pablo Baranda	Manuel Ardillas
	6. José García Ramos	Ambrosio González
	7. Leopoldo Melgar	Gonzalo Díaz
	8. *Rafael E. Melgar*	Indalecio Cruz Velasco
	9. Ricardo Luna	Segundo Arenasa
	10. Lorenzo Mayoral	Pedro Manuel Avendaño
	11. Marcelo C. Mejía	Jorge Meixueiro
	12. Manuel Téllez Sill	Constantino Belmar
	13. Leopoldo Gómez Añorve	Arnulfo Villegas Garzón
	14. José Gómez	Manuel Santaella Odriozola
	15. Francisco Arlanzón	Rafael González
	16. Alfonso F. Ramírez	Alberto Reyes Gil
	17. Heliodoro Charis	Genaro López Miro
Puebla	1. Eduardo Moneda	Emilio H. Flores
	2. *Pastor Rouaix*	Fernando Pacheco
	3. Luciano M. Sánchez	Faustino L. Allende
	4. Joaquín Lórenz	Juan Aparicio
	5. Benjamín Aguillón Guzmán	Vicente Beneites

6. Pedro B. Limón — *Antonio Díaz Soto y Gama*
7. Antonio Islas Bravo — Rafael Cebada
8. *Ricardo Reyes Márquez* — Trinidad Hernández
9. Francisco Hernández — Alfonso Castillo Gil
10. Arturo Flores López — Rafael Herrera Alvarado
11. Salustio Hernández — Luis G. Ibáñez
12. Humberto Barros — Hilario Galicia
13. Vicente Lombardo Toledano — Jorge Avila Parra
14. Constantino Molina — Gaspar Allende
15. *Gonzalo Bautista* — Javier N. Luna
16. Salustio Cabrera — Moisés Vergara
17. Enrique Hernández — Juan N. Esquitín
18. Ricardo Márquez Galindo — Lorenzo Oropeza
19. Abraham Lucas — Fidel Herrera

Querétaro

1. José Veraza y Rubio — Antonio Romo Ruiz
2. Aurelio Briones — Inocencio Ramírez
3. Agustín Casas — Carlos Osuna
4. Ildefonso de la Peña — Porfirio Rubio

Quintana Roo

1. Candelario Garza — Ignacio Fuentes

San Luis Potosí

1. Antonio Trujillo Espinosa — Rafael H. Chávez
2. José Santos Alonso — Basilio Ortega
3. Ernesto Martínez Macías — Manuel Montante
4. Florencio Galván — Cesáreo Vásquez
5. Epifanio Castillo — Darío Rangel
6. Valentín Aguilar — J. Guadalupe Alonso
7. Manuel Orta — Dagoberto de la Torre
8. Fernando Moctezuma — Esteban Segura
9. Arnulfo Portales — Mariano Martínez
10. *Gonzalo N. Santos* — Leopoldino J. Ortiz
11. Juan Enrique Azuara — Miguel Ortiz
12. Antonio M. García — Jesús Angeles

Sinaloa

1. Francisco A. Rivera — Marcelino Z. Herrera
2. Manuel Riveros — Alejandro López Beltrán
3. Fernando Cuen — Macario Gaxiola
4. Cuauhtémoc Ríos — Teódulo Gutiérrez
5. Rodolfo G. Robles — Manuel Rodríguez Gutiérrez
6. Mariano Rivas — Pedro Cáceres

Sonora

1. Carlos B. Maldonado — Emeterio R. Aguayo
2. Jesús G. Lizárraga — Alvaro V. Carrillo
3. Arturo C. Ortega — Francisco Barreras
4. Ricardo Topete — Aurelio Peñúñuri, Jr.
5. Adalberto Encinas — Guillermo E. Romo

Tabasco

1. Bartolo Flores — Manuel Figarola
2. Alcides Caparrosa — Juan Lugo
3. Alejandor Ruiz S. — Antonio del Valle Pardo

Tamaulipas

1. Enrique Medina — Aurelio Cavazos
2. Rafael Zamudio — Leoncio Torres

State	Deputy	Alternate
	3. Pedro Romero	Carlos Darío Ojeda
	4. Juan Rincón	Arturo G. Pizano
	5. Benito Juárez Ochoa	Genaro G. Ruiz
Tlaxcala	1. Francisco Aguirre León	David González
	2. Moisés Rosalio García	Rosendo Ramírez
	3. Inés Aguilar	Alejandro Solís
Veracruz	1. Luis G. Márquez	Macario G. Alvarez
	2. Carlos Puig y Casauranc	Gaspar Méndez
	3. José C. López	Froylán G. Fuentes
	4. Gabriel Aguillón Guzmán	José Ramírez, Jr.
	5. Andrés E. Gómez	Milcíades Garizurieta
	6. *Alejandro Cerisola*	Gonzalo N. Cruz
	7. *Manlio Fabio Altamirano*	Carlos Ulibarri K.
	8. Ramón C. Mora	Heriberto Juárez
	9. Eduardo F. Garrido	Miguel M. Sánchez
	10. Enrique L. Soto	Flavio D. Galván
	11. Francisco J. González	Baraquiel Hernández
	12. José J. Araiza	Prisciliano Ruiz
	13. Ascanio Fernández Pinto	Antonio B. Rojas
	14. Alberto Méndez R.	Arnulfo Sierra
	15. Teodoro E. Villegas	Alfonso Mendívil
	16. Guillermo Rodríguez	Raúl Ruiz
	17. *Pedro Palazuelos L.*	Pedro Madrid
	18. Eduardo Cortina	Angel Venegas
	19. Pedro C. Rodríguez	Francisco E. Espinosa
	20. Manuel Castellanos Quinto	Gerardo Ramírez
	21. Carlos Real	Miguel R. Aguilar
Yucatán	1. Víctor Rendón	Waldemaro Ceballos Castilla
	2. Samuel Espadas C.	Aurelio Velásquez
	3. José E. Ancona	Mariano Correa Espinosa
	4. Ariosto Castellanos C.	Gualberto Carrillo
	5. Manuel Castilla Solís	Félix Rosado Iturralde
	6. Luis Torregrosa	Julio Castillo Pasos
Zacatecas	1. Enrique Enciso	Manuel Arellano
	2. Lamberto Elías	Celestino Castro
	3. Guillermo C. Aguilera	Gregorio R. Rivera
	4. Antonio Cisneros	Joel Morales
	5. J. Jesús Delgado	Lázaro Correa
	6. Gabriel Macías	J. Trinidad Camino
	7. J. Trinidad Luna Enríquez	Ladislao E. Rodríguez
	8. Juan Zenón Aguilar	Luis Juárez

1928–30 (33rd Legislature)

State	Deputy	Alternate
Aguascalientes	1. Juan C. Alvarado	Jesús P. Cornejo
	2. Rafael Quevedo	Enrique Montero M.

| Baja California | 1. Flavio J. Bórquez | Luis G. Valdés |
| | 2. Nemesio Vargas | Francisco García Bareño |

| Campeche | 1. José del C. Hernández Pino | Manuel J. Mex |
| | 2. Angel Castillo Lanz | Luis Fernando Sotelo |

Coahuila	1. Rómulo Moreira	Juan Martínez Negrete
	2. Eduardo C. Loustaunau	Blas Quintero
	3. Manuel Mijares V.	Salvador de la Torre
	4. Alfredo I. Moreno	Rodolfo Ceballos Cancino
	5. Antonio Garza Castro	Agustín Rodríguez
	6. Raymundo Cervera	Rafael Urista
	7. Adolfo Mondragón	Ignacio Risa Jiménez

| Colima | 1. Pablo Hernández | Tomás Arias |
| | 2. Francisco J. Silva | *Francisco Solórzano Béjar* |

Chiapas	1. Juan M. Esponda	Enrique Ochoa
	2. Raymundo E. Enríquez	Moisés A. Calderón
	3. Evaristo Bonifaz	Rodolfo A. Navarro
	4. Horacio Lacroix	Enoch Escobar
	5. Carlos M. Jiménez	César Ruiz
	6. Pedro Cerísola	Emilio Esponda
	7. Ernesto Constantino Herrera	Antonio León
	8. Rafael Cal y Mayor	Enrique R. Sapién

Chihuahua	1. Rafael Romero	Víctor Rivera Vásquez
	2. Miguel E. Yáñez	Salvador Santana
	3. José Valenzuela	José A. Espejo
	4. Antonio Corona	Marcelo Madrid
	5. Francisco Aldaco	Alfonso Olivas
	6. Práxedes Giner D.	Julián Luján Caballero
	7. Francisco Orpinel	Francisco Monzón

Distrito Federal	1. Aníbal M. Cervantes	Rafael Mallén, Jr.
	2. Ernesto Verdugo	Ignacio H. Santana
	3. Manuel Balderas	Carlos A. de la Vega
	4. Rafael Cruz	Miguel Orrico Caparroso
	5. Arturo de Saracho	José María Gutiérrez
	6. Enrique Medina	Pedro Quevedo
	7. Alfonso Romandía Ferreira	Carlos Noriega Hope
	8. Adalberto Encinas	Alfonso Aguilar G.
	9. Rafael Sánchez Lira	Adolfo Sánchez L.
	10. Ernesto Prieto	Manuel Robles
	11. Ricardo Topete	Francisco V. Rivas
	12. Carlos Almazán	Abigail Quiroz
	13. Tomás A. Robinson	Jesús Vidales M.
	14. *Aurelio Manrique, Jr.*	José M. Ferrer
	15. *Gustavo A. Uruchurtu*	Ismael M. Lozano

Durango	1. Francisco Pérez	Fidel Raudry
	2. Pedro Alvarez	Arturo Farías
	3. Daniel R. Gutiérrez	Jesús Castro
	4. Alfonso Cruz	Margarito Machado Q.

State	Deputy	Alternate
	5. José Ramón Valdez	J. Donaciano Sosa
	6. Jesús Salas Barraza	Erasmo Barraza
	7. Fernando Arenas	Alejandro Balderrama
	8. Liborio Espinosa y Elenes	J. Bautista Elenes
Guanajuato	1. Octavio Mendoza González	José Serrano
	2. Enrique Fernández Martínez	Enrique Hernández A.
	3. Ramón V. Santoyo	Arturo Bailleres
	4. Edmundo Domenzáin	Manuel Sánchez R.
	5. *Enrique Romero Courtade*	Napoleón Negrete
	6. Ramón Velarde	José Pimentel
	7. Francisco Alvarez, Jr.	Pascual Urtaza G.
	8. José Rodríguez C.	Jesús Hernández Alcalá
	9. *Federico Medrano V.*	Alfonso González
	10. J. Jesús Yáñez Maya	Prócoro Esquivel
	11. Basilio Ortega	Luis G. Cabrera
	12. Adolfo Vallejo Gómez	Francisco Díaz Barriga
	13. David Ayala	Adolfo O. Corral
	14. Esteban Bueno	Domingo Luna
	15. Joaquín Torreblanca	Ramón V. Santoyo
	16. Federico Hernández A.	Enrique Fernández Martínez
	17. Francisco Briones	Raúl Cordero
	18. *Ernesto Hidalgo*	Mariano Vértiz
	19. Salvador López Moreno	Jesús Patiño
	20. Carlos Valdés	Ramón Pérez Villalobos
	21. *José Aguilar y Maya*	Salvador Albarrán
Guerrero	1. Desiderio Borja	Luis Bedolla
	2. Adrián Gómez	Rufino Salgado R.
	3. Amadeo Meléndez	Eugenio Vildosola
	4. *Alfonso L. Nava*	David Próspero Cardona
	5. Francisco S. Carreto	Juvencio Sánchez
	6. Alberto Méndez	Manuel García
	7. Maurilio Vázquez Melo	Julián Romero
	8. José Castilleja	Amado G. Sandoval
	9. Roberto García Infante	Enrique Lobato
	10. Plácido A. Maldonado	Luis Rodríguez
Hidalgo	1. Ernesto P. Sánchez	Eduardo J. Paredes
	2. Leopoldo E. Camarena	Eliseo G. Nava
	3. Jesús H. Romero	Benito Calva
	4. Jesús Medecigo Rosas	Emilio Vargas
	5. Fernando Herrera	Faustino D. Mendoza
	6. Honorato Austria	Leonides Torres
	7. *Bartolomé Vargas Lugo*	Atilano Rincón
	8. Juan Cruz O.	Gregorio Hernández
	9. José P. Arroyo	José Bernal Castillo
	10. Daniel Olivares	Moisés Calderón
	11. Otilio Villegas	Salvador Melo
Jalisco	1. Alfredo Romo	José Pérez Corona
	2. Manuel Hernández y Hernández	Carlos Gutiérrez Santacruz

3. Juan C. García — José Morales M.
4. *José María Cuéllar* — Luis Alvarez del Castillo
5. José Germán — Xavier Enciso
6. David Orozco — J. Guadalupe Rivera
7. José V. Gómez Cano — Manuel González Verdía
8. *J. Guadalupe de Anda* — Francisco Z. Moreno
9. Maríano Torres H. — Inocencio Cuéllar
10. José Zataray — José A. Castañeda
11. Arcadio E. Padilla — Regino Ibarra González
12. Ramón Madrigal — Eliseo Novoa
13. Enrique Díaz de León — Fernando Guijarro Cázares
14. Julio Díaz — Luis García
15. Esteban García de Alba — Félix Ramos
16. Jesús Otero — Ignacio Santana
17. J. Rodrigo Camacho — Severiano Lozano
18. Benigno Palencia — Federico Santana
19. Manuel H. Ruiz J. — Guadalupe Santana
20. Francisco Labastida I. — Ignacio Reynoso
21. Alberto González — Ponciano Guzmán
22. Juan B. Izábal — Daniel Velasco
23. Fernando González Madrid — Florentino Cuervo

México

1. Zenón Suárez — Luis Ramírez de Arellano
2. Manuel Alvarez — Mario Sánchez Curiel
3. Felipe Estrada — Jesús López Zetina
4. Augusto Aillaud — Bernardo de la Vega
5. Abelardo Montaño — Luis Manuel Díaz
6. Adrián López Gómez — Manuel Sánchez Cabrera
7. Eucario López — Juan Manuel Patiño
8. David Montes de Oca — Martín Arias, Jr.
9. Rafael M. Legorreta — Juan Chacón
10. Fortino Hernández — Daniel Herrera
11. Enrique M. Bonilla — Esteban S. Huitrón
12. Armando P. Arroyo — Lorenzo Barnerí
13. Delfino Nájera — Adrián Legaspi
14. Wenceslao Labra — Ignacio Gómez A.
15. Salvador Navarro — Abelardo Montaño
16. Manuel Riva Palacio — Pedro Trueba
17. José Luis Solórzano — Lorenzo Robles

Michoacán

1. Alberto Aceves — Salvador Ramos
2. Ernesto Aceves — Francisco Arroyo de Ando
3. Luis Díaz — José Rodríguez Corona
4. *Leopoldo Zincúnegui Tercero* — José Vallejo Samano
5. Lorenzo Robles — Antonio M. Luna
6. Manuel Avilés — Onofre Vásquez
7. José María Sánchez Pineda — Jenaro Arredondo
8. Luis Méndez — Santiago Hernández
9. José Gaitán — Federico Montaño
10. Efraín Pineda — Alejandro Rizo
11. *Melchor Ortega* — Leobardo Paz
12. Silviano Hurtado — Jesús Hurtado Z.
13. J. Gabino Carranza — Antonio Ruiz F.

State	Deputy	Alternate
	14. Rafael Picazo	Alfredo Anaya
	15. Octavio Magaña	Luis G. Torres
	16. Florentino Melgoza	Manuel Magaña
	17. Melesio Moreno R.	José Chavolla
	18. Rodolfo Ramírez	José Villegas
	19. *Juan Abarca Pérez*	Florentino Zaragoza
Morelos	1. Silvano Sotelo	Juan Salazar
	2. Manuel Magaña	Porfirio Palacios
	3. Enrique Espinosa	Bernardo Rodríguez
Nayarit	1. Guillermo Ponce de León	Manuel Bustamante
	2. Antioco Rodríguez	Ramón Parra R.
	3. Enrique Espinosa	Bernardo Rodríguez
Nuevo León	1. Antonio García González	Antonio de P. Gutiérrez
	2. Alberto Galván	Alfonso N. Barjáu
	3. Enrique O. Garza	Pedro Villarreal
	4. Santiago Salinas	Conrado C. Espinosa
	5. Carlos Osuna	Julio L. Leal
	6. Edmundo Martínez	Maximiliano Berrones
Oaxaca	1. Ramón Pardo	Carlos H. Rueda
	2. Manuel Téllez Sill	Constantino Esteva
	3. Lorenzo Mayoral Pardo	Gustavo Alvarez
	4. Rufino Zavaleta	Rubén Rosas Espejo
	5. Jorge Meixueiro	Justo López
	6. José García Ramos	Ricardo Luna
	7. Alberto Sáinz	Otilio Jiménez Madrigal
	8. *Rafael E. Melgar*	Manuel Santaella Odriozola
	9. Mauro Vásquez	Gustavo Quiroga
	10. Demetrio Bolaños Cacho	Manuel Díaz Chávez
	11. Amado Fuentes B.	Maríano Rodas
	12. *Alfonso Francisco Ramírez*	David F. Ramírez
	13. Antolín Jiménez	Belisario Robles
	14. Leopoldo Melgar	Roberto Rivero
	15. Francisco Arlanzón	Vulfrano Esteves
	16. Francisco López Cortés	Fernando I. Guzmán
	17. Prisciliano M. López	Fidel Pineda
Puebla	1. Conrado C. Rochíu	Miguel G. Muñoz
	2. Gonzalo González	Alfonso R. Salas
	3. Rafael Cárdenas	Ricardo Gutiérrez
	4. Antonio Montes	Miguel Cordero
	5. José Luis Moreno	Buenaventura Cordero
	6. Manuel Aradillas	Luis A. Sarmiento
	7. Gonzalo Bautista	Manuel Valdés Bravo
	8. Miguel Andrew Almazán	Juan Ibarra
	9. Ricardo Reyes Márquez	Enrique Morales
	10. Ignacio de la Mora	Luis Hernández Cházaro
	11. José Bravo Izquierdo	Enrique Montes de Oca
	12. Miguel Barbosa M.	Everardo Gómez
	13. Joaquín Lórenz	Felipe Doria

	14. Juan R. Delgado	Porfirio B. Vargas
	15. Benjamín Aguillón Guzmán	Angel Rendón
	16. Constantino Molina	Abraham Contreras
	17. Abraham Lucas	Elpidio Barrios
	18. Salustio Cabrera	Laureano de la Llave
	19. Luis Flores	Arnulfo Zamora
	20. Ricardo Márquez Galindo	Job Sánchez
	21. Crisóforo Ibáñez	Moisés Santos M.
Querétaro	1. Rodolfo Torreblanca	Ambrosio Guerrero
	2. Fernando E. Escamilla	Pablo S. Montes de Oca
	3. Daniel Mendoza	Alfredo Nieto Camacho
	4. Ambrosio Guerrero	Otilio Trejo
Quintana Roo	1. Librado Abitia	Alfonso Orozco
San Luis Potosí	1. José Santos Alonso	Leopoldino J. Ortiz
	2. *Antonio Díaz Soto y Gama*	Valentín Aquilar
	3. Tomás Tapia	Ernesto Martínez Macías
	4. Epifanio Castillo	Rómulo Guerrero
	5. Antonio García Pedraza	Teodoro Salazar
	6. Florencio Galván	Antonio García
	7. Manuel Orta	Dagoberto de la Torre
	8. Fernando Moctezuma	Esteban Segura
	9. Alfonso E. Plancarte	Jorge Velásquez
	10. *Gonzalo N. Santos*	Braulio M. Romero
	11. Juan Enrique Azuara	Andrés Zárate
	12. Marciano C. Salazar	Elfego Reyes
Sinaloa	1. Francisco A. Rivera	Ignacio Terrazas, Jr.
	2. Alejandro López Beltrán	Rómulo Zárate Escalante
	3. Filiberto Mora y Ochoa	Antonio Amézquita
	4. Cristóbal Bon Bustamante	Jesús María Tarriba
	5. J. Francisco Ferreira	Jenaro Escobosa
	6. Mariano Alvarez, Jr.	Alberto Tirado
	7. Mariano Rivas	Pedro Cáceres
Sonora	1. Melitón R. Hernández	Maximiliano Zúñiga
	2. Alfredo Iruretagoyena	José Carmelo
	3. Felizardo Almada	Ignacio Salazar Q.
	4. Enrique Terrazas	Antonio C. Encinas
	5. Manuel P. Torres	Octavio Flores García
Tabasco	1. Francisco Trujillo Gurría	Trinidad Malpica H.
	2. Manuel Garrido Lacroix	Leobardo Magaña
	3. J. Guadalupe Aguilera M.	Alejandro Ruiz S.
	4. Augusto Hernández Olivé	Víctor Fernández Manero
Tamaulipas	1. Práxedis Balboa, Jr.	Loreto Garza, Jr.
	2. *Marte R. Gómez*	Jesús Treviño
	3. Gustavo González	Gregorio H. Pedraza
	4. Manuel Tárrega	Antonio Balandrano
	5. Rutilio Camacho	Manuel Alvarez

State	Deputy	Alternate
Tlaxcala	1. Carlos Fernández de Lara	Vicente L. Benéitez
	2. Moisés Rosalio García	Rosendo Ramírez
	3. Mauro Angulo	Ignacio Avalos
Veracruz	1. Luis G. Márquez	Crescenciano de la Garza
	2. Carlos Puig Casauranc	Jacinto Hernández Barragán
	3. Enrique Meza	Eugenio C. Avila
	4. Juan P. Sariol	Miguel Barranco
	5. Andrés E. Gómez	Antonio Cabrera
	6. *Alejandro Cerísola*	Víctor Gudini
	7. Luis de la Sierra	*Josafat Márquez*
	8. Ramón C. Mora	Roberto Guzmán Carrillo
	9. Enrique L. Soto	Rafael Aguilar, Jr.
	10. Guillermo Rodríguez	Joaquín Alarcón
	11. Modesto Solís Domínguez	Antonio García Quevedo
	12. Gabriel Aguillón Guzmán	Vicente Loyo
	13. José Moreno Salido	Hilarión Madrazo
	14. Hernán Laborde	Adalberto Lara Pardo
	15. Teodoro E. Villegas	José Aguila
	16. Roberto A. Morales	Epigmenio Guzmán
	17. *Pedro Palazuelos Léycegui*	Faustino A. Mateos
	18. Eduardo Cortina	Francisco Rodríguez Celís
	19. Pedro C. Rodríguez	Rogelio Hernández R.
	20. Francisco J. González	Rafael Silva Alvarez
	21. Carlos Real	Bernardo G. Mortera
Yucatán	1. *Antonio Médiz Bolio*	César Alayola Barrera
	2. Pablo García Ortiz	Max Peniche Vallado
	3. Rodulfo Izquierdo	Antonio Aguilar
	4. Ariosto Castellanos Cárdenas	Silvio Hernández Lope
	5. Bernardino Enríquez	Humberto Monforte
	6. Pedro Solís Cámara	Armando Escalante
Zacatecas	1. Enrique Enciso	Vicente Romero
	2. Ursulo A. García	Simón D. Robledo
	3. Guillermo C. Aguilera	Enrique Delgado
	4. León García	Epigmenio Talamantes
	5. Gabriel Macías	Luis Dávila
	6. Juan Ramón Lizalde	Reynaldo Herrera
	7. J. Jesús Luna E.	Ladislao E. Rodríguez
	8. Juan Zenón Aguilar	Francisco Serrano

1930–32 (34th Legislature)

State	Deputy	Alternate
Aguascalientes	1. *Juan G. Alvarado*	José Loera
	2. Pedro Quevedo	Alberto del Valle
Baja California	1. José María Dávila	Manuel Monter
	2. Ignacio L. Cornejo	Braulio Maldonado

Campeche
1. Angel Castillo Lanz — Luis F. Sotelo R.
2. Fausto Bojórquez Castillo — Armando Abreu y Abreu

Chiapas
1. Alvaro Cancino — Carlos Maldonado
2. Juan M. Esponda — Abelardo Domínguez
3. Enoch Escobar — Emilio Contreras
4. Antonio León — Constantino Aceituno

Chihuahua
1. Cipriano Arriola — Carlos Aguilar U.
2. Enrique Hernández Gómez — Jesús Lugo
3. Simón Puentes — José E. Tapia
4. Enrique Soto Peimbert — Santiago V. Almada

Coahuila
1. Ricardo Ainslie R. — Arnulfo M. Zaldívar
2. Manuel Mijares V. — Santos Castañeda
3. Alfredo I. Moreno — Jesús González Lobo
4. Raymundo Cervera — Severo Jiménez

Colima
1. Pedro Cervantes — Wenceslao R. Olea
2. Blas Dueñas — Pedro Gudiño

Distrito Federal
1. Samuel Villarreal, Jr. — Salvador Neri
2. Angel Ladrón de Guevara — Tomás H. Gasca
3. Ismael M. Lozano — Julián B. Lafón
4. José Morales Hesse — Isaac Cancino Gómez
5. *Ismael Salas* — José de Luna Sánchez
6. José Pérez Gil y Ortiz — Francisco Macías Sauza
7. Cosme Mier y Riva Palacio — Fernando Linares G.
8. Tiburcio G. Altamirano — Raúl P. Velasco
9. José Torres H. — Luis Medina

Durango
1. José Ramón Valdez — Clemente S. Ceniceros
2. Liborio Espinosa y Elenes — Miguel Espinosa y Elenes
3. Lorenzo Gámiz — Juan Fernández Albarrán

Guanajuato
1. Enrique Fernández Martínez — Enrique Hernández Alvarez
2. *Federico Medrano V.* — Eduardo Díaz Infante
3. Salvador López Moreno — J. Jesús Patiño
4. Basiliso Ortega — Luis G. Cabrera
5. *Enrique Romero Courtade* — Juan Rico
6. Adolfo Vallejo Gómez — José Escutia Rosiles
7. David Ayala — Salvador Albarrán
8. *Ernesto Hidalgo* — Francisco Rocha
9. Ramón V. Santoyo — Benjamín Méndez Aguilar

Guerrero
1. Rufino Salgado R. — Adrián Gómez
2. Luis Cruz Manjárrez — Isidro Mejia
3. José Rueda Bravo — Ambrosio Calvo B.
4. Antonio Moyado B. — Gonzalo Ramírez Rayón
5. Ocampo N. Bolaños — Nabor A. Ojeda
6. Leopoldo Reynoso Díaz — Manuel M. López

Hidalgo
1. José Rivera — J. Refugio Guerrero S.
2. Daniel Olivares — Juan Marañón

State	Deputy	Alternate
	3. Carlos Velázquez Méndez	Margarito Gómez
	4. Ernesto Viveros	Wilfrido Osorio
	5. Juan Cruz Oropeza	Juan López
	6. Otilio Villegas	Homero Beltrán Hernández
Jalisco	1. Manuel Hernández y Hernández	Ruperto García
	2. David Orozco	Francisco Z. Moreno
	3. *J. Jesús González Gallo*	Tiburcio Muñoz
	4. José V. Gómez Cano	Inocencio S. Cuéllar
	5. Manuel H. Ruiz	Alfonso Durán
	6. Esteban García de Alba	J. Félix Ramos
	7. Heliodoro de la Mora	José T. Ceballos
	8. Fernando Basulto Limón	Aureliano Santana
	9. J. Leopoldo Cuéllar	Isidro Niz
	10. José Manuel Chávez	Alberto Z. González
	11. José Zataray	Francisco Javier Huizar
	12. Sebastián Allende	Everardo Topete
México	1. Manuel Riva Palacio	Oliverio Esquinca Aguilar
	2. Wenceslao Labra	José Jiménez
	3. Armando P. Arroyo	Esteban S. Huitrón
	4. Ignacio Gómez A.	Fortino Hernández
	5. Delfino Nájera	David Montes de Oca
	6. Adrián López Gómez	Luis Ramírez de Arellano
	7. Rafael M. Legorreta	Bernardo Gómez
	8. Felipe Estrada	Mario Sánchez Curiel
	9. Zenón Suárez	Adrián Legaspi
Michoacán	1. Enrique Morelos N.	Francisco Corona N.
	2. Manuel Medina Chávez	Alberto Coria
	3. Ernesto Soto Reyes	José Paul
	4. Alfonso Leñero Ruiz	Ernesto Pardo
	5. Rafael Picazo	Luis Morales
	6. Silviano Hurtado	Luis G. Zumaya
	7. Efraín Pineda	J. Jesús Cornejo V.
	8. Manuel Avilés	Andrés Landa y Piña
	9. *Donaciano Carreón*	Juan Manuel Carrillo
Morelos	1. J. Guadalupe Pineda	Francisco Alarcón
	2. Leopoldo Heredia	Juventino Pineda E.
Nayarit	1. Francisco Trejo	Luis G. Hernández
	2. Gregorio Díaz C.	Evaristo Lerma Ríos
Nuevo León	1. *Plutarco Elías Calles, Jr.*	Jesús E. Treviño
	2. Amel Barocio García	Liborio Bortoni
	3. Martín Quiroga	Jesús Garza Ríos
Oaxaca	1. Mauro M. Vásquez	Gonzalo Altamirano C.
	2. Enrique Liekens	Mariano Rodas
	3. Jorge Meixueiro	Roberto Salinas

	4. Wilfrido C. Cruz	Ricardo Vásquez Crespo
	5. Amado Fuentes B.	Roberto Ortiz Gris
	6. Francisco Arlanzón	Próculo Vielma
	7. Julio Bustillos	Antonio Castillo B.
	8. *Alfonso Francisco Ramírez*	Leoncio Villegas
	9. Anastasio García Toledo	Artemio López Cortés
	10. *Rafael E. Melgar*	Agustín Ortiz
Puebla	1. Joaquín Lórenz	Gabriel Sánchez Guerrero
	2. Bernardo Chávez	Telésforo Salas
	3. Antonio Montes	Manuel Rivera
	4. Fernando R. González	Salvador Fidel Ibarra
	5. Fermín E. Díaz	Guillermo Ibarra
	6. Gonzalo Bautista	Paulino B. Castillo
	7. Juan R. Delgado	Calixto Casillas
	8. Manuel Aradillas	Enrique Montes de Oca
	9. Ramón Galindo	Job S. Sánchez
	10. Francisco J. Domínguez	Francisco R. Pérez
Querétaro	1. Federico Gutiérrez Pastor	Benito Frías
	2. Saturnino Osornio	Juan Reyes del Campillo
Quintana Roo	1. Ricardo Suárez Escalante	Manuel Junco C.
San Luis Potosí	1. José Santos Alonso	Ranulfo Zárate Ortega
	2. Marciano C. Salazar	Andrés Zárate S.
	3. *Gonzalo N. Santos*	Juan Enrique Azuara
	4. Fernando Moctezuma	Manuel Orta
	5. Epifanio Castillo	Florencio Galván
	6. Tomás Tapia	Pilar García
	7. Antonio García Pedraza	Epifanio Berrones
Sinaloa	1. José R. de Saracho	Ramón García Cárdenas
	2. *Juan de Dios Bátiz*	Jesús Abitia
	3. Filberto Mora y Ochoa	Cristóbal Bon Bustamante
Sonora	1. Walterio Pesqueria	Enrique Mexía
	2. Emiliano Corella M.	Miguel Bernal
	3. Miguel A. Salazar	Marcelino Aranda
Tabasco	1. Homero Margalli G.	Arnulfo Pérez H.
	2. César A. Rojas	Víctor Fernández Manero
Tamaulipas	1. Manuel Tarrega	Martín Aréchiga, Jr.
	2. Graciano Sánchez	Leopoldo D. Muñiz
	3. Práxedis Balboa, Jr.	Salvador Razo
Tlaxcala	1. Moisés Rosalío García	Felipe Xicotencatl
	2. Carlos Fernández de Lara	Vicente L. Benéitez
Veracruz	1. Luis G. Márquez	Salvador Coss
	2. Agapito Barranco	Onofre Morales
	3. *Alejandro Cerísola*	Eustergio Aldana

State	Deputy	Alternate
	4. Guillermo Rodríguez	Longinos Herrera
	5. Manuel Jasso	Isauro Acosta
	6. Enrique L. Soto	Manuel Almanza
	7. Modesto Solís Domínguez	Carlos Zapata Vela
	8. Francisco A. Mayer	Tomás Sosa
	9. Carlos Darío Ojeda	Aurelio Uscanga
	10. Pedro C. Rodríguez	Guillermo García Zamudio
	11. Francisco J. González	Manuel E. Miravete
	12. Odilón Patraca Limón	Abelardo B. Rodríguez
Yucatán	1. *Neguib Simón*	Mario Negrón P.
	2. Manuel J. Sabido	Carlos Duarte Moreno
	3. Rafael Cebada T.	Augusto Molina Ramos
	4. Miguel Rosado	Ernesto Cervera
Zacatecas	1. Lamberto Elías	Luis de la Fuente
	2. J. Manuel Reyes	Guillermo Lópcz W.
	3. Francisco Bañuelos	Constantino Cervantes
	4. J. Jesús Delgado	José Falcón

1932–34 (35th Legislature)

State	Deputy	Alternate
Aguascalientes	1. Juan G. Alvarado	Gonzalo R. Rubalcava
	2. Pedro Quevedo	Jesús Guerra L.
Baja California del Norte (Territory)	1. Armando R. Pareyón	José María Rodríguez
Baja California del Sur (Territory)	1. Braulio Maldonado	Jesús Castro
Campeche	1. Angel Castillo Lanz	Luis F. Sotelo Regil
	2. Fernando Enrique Angli Lara	Manuel Osorno Castellanos
Coahuila	1. Ricardo Ainslie R.	Juan Martínez L.
	2. Manuel Mijares V.	Miguel de los Cobos
	3. Francisco Saracho	Moisés Carranza
	4. Severo Jiménez Cadena	Juan García H.
Colima	1. Manuel G. Orozco	Zenaido Jiménez
	2. Daniel Cárdenas Mora	Prisciliano Valencia
Chiapas	1. Alvaro Cancino	Enrique Ochoa
	2. Juan M. Esponda	Enoch Escobar
	3. Efraín Poumián	Antonio Vera G.
	4. Martín G. Cruz	Efraín Aranda O.
	5. Antonio León	Glustein Cruz

Chihuahua

1. Cipriano Arriola — Dionisio Torres
2. Casimiro E. Almedia — Gustavo Chávez
3. Octavio M. Trigo — Juan Aquilar G.
4. *Francisco R. Almada* — Efraín Chaparro
5. Angel Posada — Abraham Oros y Oros

Distrito Federal

1. *Luis L. León* — Rodolfo Zamudio
2. José Morales Hesse — Isaac Cancino Gómez
3. Ismael M. Lozano — Angel Olvera C.
4. *Ismael Salas* — Carlos Torres
5. Vicente L. Benéitez — Jacinto Castillo
6. Lamberto Ortega — Luis Alcaraz Macías
7. Samuel Villarreal, Jr. — José Gallardo
8. José María Dávila — Carlos A. Calderón
9. Cosme Mier y Riva Palacio — Maclovio Torrijos
10. José Torres H. — Facundo Calderas
11. Guillermo Zárraga — Arturo Galán
12. Tomás A. Robinson — Agustín Jiménez Chávez

Durango

1. José Alejandro Albístegui — Guillermo Arellano
2. Dionisio Ortiz Acosta — Roberto López Franco
3. Fernando Arenas — José Tavizón
4. Alejandro Antuna López — Enrique Fabela Peimbert

Guanajuato

1. Alfonso Fernández — Alfredo Chagoyán
2. *Melchor Ortega* — José Rodríguez C.
3. Epigmenio Alvarez — Alfonso González
4. Federico Montes — Catarino B. Aranda
5. J. Jesús Yáñez Maya — J. Melquíades Ruiz
6. Ernesto Martínez Macías — José Alfredo Ortega
7. Rafael Patiño — Tomás Guzmán
8. David Ayala — Saturnino Esquivel
9. Luis Martínez Vértiz — Miguel Herrera
10. Enedino Ortega — Emilio González Domenzáin

Guerrero

1. *Ezequiel Padilla* — Abraham González
2. Dimpno Mendiola Flores — Miguel Saavedra, Jr.
3. Luis Bedolla — Alberto C. Reyes
4. Angel Barrios — Jesús Morales
5. Cirilo R. Heredia — Alfonso E. Delgado
6. Angel Tapia Alarcón — Feliciano Radilla

Hidalgo

1. Carlos Velázquez Méndez — Raymundo Enríquez
2. Ambrosio Ordaz H. — Daniel Olivares
3. José Rivera — Francisco Mendoza
4. Arcadio Cornejo — Eustolio Becerra
5. José Lugo Guerrero — Leonardo Ramírez
6. Otilio Villegas — Pascual Morales
7. Homero Beltrán Hernández — Fortino González

Jalisco

1. J. Leopoldo Cuéllar — Luis V. García
2. Arturo Bouquet — Salvador Pedroza Guerra
3. J. Jesús Gutiérrez Casillas — León Acero
4. Macedonio S. Barrera — Cecilio Camarena

State	Deputy	Alternate
	5. Juan Aviña López	Jerónimo Sahagún
	6. Clemente Sepúlveda	Matías Romo
	7. Manuel F. Ochoa	J. Félix Valencia
	8. Florencio Topete	Salvador Rodríguez
	9. Ponciano Guzmán	Manuel Palomera Calleja
	10. José Manuel Chávez	Alfonso G. Ceballos
	11. José Zataray	Agustín Rivera
	12. Everardo Topete	Jesús R. Gutiérrez
	13. Miguel Moreno	Manuel González Vargas
México	1. Manuel Riva Palacio	Agustín Rocha
	2. Armando P. Arroyo	Oliverio Esquinca Aguilar
	3. *Gilberto Fabila*	Margarito Hernández
	4. José Mozo	David González
	5. Antonio Romero	Luis Sánchez
	6. Ignacio Gómez A.	Porfirio Ramírez
	7. Wenceslao Labra	José Jiménez
	8. Felipe Estrada	Abelardo Montaño
	9. Bernardo Gómez	Jesús López Zetina
	10. Adrián Legaspi	Juan Manuel Patiño
Michoacán	1. Gabino Vázquez	Ernesto Ruiz Solís
	2. Carlos González Herrejón	Emilio Toledo Sosa
	3. Alberto Bremauntz	Federico Castillo
	4. Enrique Ramírez	Ramón Angel
	5. Luis García Amezcua	J. Socorro Quiroz
	6. Agustín Leñero	Francisco Hernández
	7. Alberto Coria	Gabriel Zamora
	8. J. Jesús Ordorica	Fortino González
	9. Francisco A. Martínez	Víctor Sotelo
	10. Ricardo Carrillo Durán	Sacrovir Patiño
	11. Primitivo Juárez	Vidal Jiménez
Morelos	1. Agapito M. Albarrán	Jacinto Leyva
	2. J. Refugio Bustamante	Jesús Gutiérrez
Nayarit	1. Guillermo Flores Muñoz	Tomás Rojas Cardiel
	2. Marcos Jiménez	José González Maxemín
Nuevo León	1. Jesús C. Treviño	Luis Bueno
	2. Antonio G. Garza	Alfredo Montemayor
	3. Dionisio García Leal	Federico Z. González
	4. Generoso Chapa Garza	Baudelio Duarte
Oaxaca	1. Amado Fuentes B.	Mariano Rodas
	2. Enrique Liekens	Víctor Olivera
	3. Julio Bustillos	Enrique D. Chávez
	4. Constantino Esteva	Enrique Reyes
	5. Andrés Ruiz	José León de la Rosa
	6. *Manuel Rueda Magro*	Edmundo Jiménez
	7. *Rafael E. Melgar*	Antolín Jiménez
	8. Jesús Castillo Merino	Rodolfo E. Herrera

	9. Roberto Rivero	Isidro Montesinos López
	10. Flavio Pérez Gasga	Rodolfo Navarro
	11. Wilfrido C. Cruz	Antonio Carreño

Puebla
1. Antonio Arellano — Jerónimo Cabral
2. Bernardo L. Bandala — Antonio Moro
3. *Froylán C. Manjárrez* — Rafael Cortés
4. Rafael Lara Grajales — Sabas Rebolledo
5. *Eduardo Arrioja Isunza* — Ernesto Santillana
6. Carlos Soto Guevara — Fidel Cortés F.
7. Manuel Aradillas — Manuel Leal R.
8. Manuel M. Moreno — Manuel G. Molina
9. Gonzalo Bautista — Silvestre Pérez
10. Víctor Ortiz — Eduardo Guerra
11. Paz Faz Risa — Silverio Trejo

Querétaro
1. Fidencio Osornio — Juan Reyes del Campillo
2. Severiano Montes — Noradino Rubio

San Luis Potosí
1. José Santos Alonso — José María Acevedo, Jr.
2. Epifanio Castillo — Bruno Flores
3. Antonio García Pedraza — Epifanio Berrones
4. Tomás Tapia — Pilar García
5. Fernando Moctezuma — José L. Hernández
6. *Gonzalo N. Santos* — Juan Enrique Azuara
7. Andrés Zárate Sánchez — Graciano Sánchez

Sinaloa
1. José R. de Saracho — Cecilio Rivera
2. Antonio Amézquita — Eligio Abitia
3. Cristóbal Bon Bustamante — Luis G. Bringas
4. Enrique Pérez Arce — Víctor Hernández

Sonora
1. Alejandro Lacy, Jr. — Flavio F. Bórquez
2. Andrés H. Peralta — Brígido Navarrete E.
3. Francisco L. Terminel — Antonio A. Siqueiros

Tabasco
1. Daniel T. Castillo — Manuel J. Andrade
2. Manuel Lastra Ortiz — José María Silva Trujillo

Tamaulipas
1. Fernando Gómez — Miguel de los Santos Garza
2. Rafael Treviño Solís — Leonardo C. Moctezuma
3. Jesús Aguirre Siller — Antonio Peralta

Tlaxcala
1. Samuel Mendoza — Lino Mixcoatl
2. Moisés Rosalío García — Manuel M. Hernández

Veracruz
1. Guillermo Rodríguez — Mario González Cruz
2. Agapito Barranco — Miguel Ramírez
3. Manuel Maples Arce — Francisco Rabatté
4. Luis G. Márquez — Carlos Bauza
5. Carolino Anaya — Gonzalo N. Cruz
6. Manuel Jasso — Manuel Landa
7. Francisco J. González — Juan S. León
8. Viterbo Silva — Ignacio García

State	Deputy	Alternate
	9. Juan C. Peña	Neftalí Trujillo
	10. Eduardo Cortina	Carlos Lucio
	11. Carlos Darío Ojeda	Juan Belmonte G.
	12. Pedro C. Rodríguez	Serapio Aguilar
	13. Antonio Hipólito H.	Agustín G. Alvarado
	14. Eugenio Méndez Aguirre	Miguel Alemán
Yucatán	1. Fernando López Cárdenas	Cecilio Dorantes Chi
	2. Antonio Méndez	Rogerio Milán Heredia
	3. Alvaro López Patrón	Eleuterio Novelo
	4. Mario Negrón Pérez	Víctor Mena P.
Zacatecas	1. Enrique Arana Aguirre	Ambrosio Acosta
	2. Ursulo Pinedo	José Salomé Zapata
	3. *Leobardo Reynoso*	Aristeo Saldívar
	4. Paulino Pérez	Antonio G. Guzmán

APPENDIX D

Directors of Federal Departments and Agencies, 1884–1934

Attorney General of the Federal District and Federal Territories

Attorney General

Paulino Machorro Narváez	14 Sept. 1915–27 Jan. 1918
Carlos I. Meléndez	28 Jan. 1918–17 Sept. 1919
José Martínez Sotomayor	18 Sept. 1919–17 July 1920
Manuel I. Fierro	18 July 1920–2 Nov. 1923
Angel Alanís Fuentes	8 Nov. 1923–23 Jan. 1925
Everardo Gallardo	24 Jan. 1925–25 Jan. 1926
Juan Correa Nieto	26 Jan. 1926–30 Nov. 1928
José Aguilar y Maya	1 Dec. 1928–4 Feb. 1930
Nicéforo Guerrero	5 Feb. 1930–1 July 1931
José Hernández Delgado	13 July 1931–4 Sept. 1932
José Trinidad Sánchez Benítez	5 Sept. 1932–30 Nov. 1934
Raúl Castellano, Jr.	1 Dec. 1934–30 Nov. 1937

Department of the Federal District (Central Department, 1929–30; governor of the Federal District, 1884–1928)

Director General

José Ceballos	3 Dec. 1884–18 Apr. 1893
Manuel Domínguez	19 Apr. 1893–16 July 1893
Pedro Rincón Gallardo	17 July 1893–2 Aug. 1896
Nicolás Islas y Bustamante	3 Aug. 1896–7 Aug. 1896
Rafael Rebollar	8 Aug. 1896–7 Oct. 1900
Guillermo de Landa y Escandón	8 Oct. 1900–7 Dec. 1900
Ramón Corral	8 Dec. 1900–2 Jan. 1903
Guillermo de Landa y Escandón	3 Jan. 1903–2 May 1911
Samuel García Cuéllar	3 May 1911–19 May 1911
Alberto García Granados	20 May 1911–1912
Ignacio Rivero	3 Aug 1912–20 Aug. 1912
Federico González Garza	21 Aug. 1912–2 Feb. 1913
Samuel García Cuéllar	25 Feb. 1913–24 Feb. 1914

Ramón Corona Mac Entee	25 Feb. 1914–17 Aug. 1914
Alfredo Robles Domínguez	18 Aug. 1914–9 Sept. 1914
Heriberto Jara	10 Sept. 1914–21 Nov. 1914
Juan Gutiérrez R.	22 Nov. 1914–25 Nov. 1914
Vicente Navarro	26 Nov. 1914–3 Dec. 1914
Manuel Chao	4 Dec. 1914–31 Dec. 1914
Vito Alessio Robles	1 Jan. 1915–26 Jan. 1915
Gildardo Magaña	12 Mar. 1915–9 June 1915
César López de Lara	11 June 1915–20 July 1915
Gildardo Magaña	22 July 1915–2 Aug. 1915
César López de Lara	3 Aug. 1915–6 Apr. 1917
Gonzalo G. de la Mota	7 April 1917–3 May 1917
César López de Lara	4 May 1917–21 Jan. 1918
Alfredo Breceda	22 Jan. 1918–20 Aug. 1918
Arnulfo González Medina	21 Aug. 1918–20 Jan. 1919
Alfredo Breceda	21 Jan. 1919–26 Feb. 1919
Benito Flores	27 Feb. 1919–27 May 1919
Manuel Rueda Magro	28 May 1919–6 May 1920
Miguel Gómez Noriega	7 May 1920– 6 July 1920
Celestino Gasca	8 July 1920–24 Oct. 1923
Ramón Ross	25 Oct. 1923–14 Dec. 1923
Abel S. Rodríguez	15 Dec. 1923–10 Feb. 1924
Ramón Ross	11 Feb. 1924–20 June 1926
Francisco R. Serrano	21 June 1926–19 June 1927
Primo Villa Michel	20 June 1927–30 Nov. 1928
José Manuel Puig Casauranc	1 Jan. 1929–31 May 1930
Crisóforo Ibáñez	1 June 1930–7 Oct. 1930
Lamberto Hernández	8 Oct. 1930–15 Oct. 1931
Enrique Romero Courtade	16 Oct. 1931–20 Oct. 1931
Lorenzo Hernández	21 Oct. 1931–19 Jan. 1932
Vicente Estrada Cajigal	20 Jan. 1932–25 Aug. 1932
Manuel Padilla	26 Aug. 1932–2 Sept. 1932
Juan G. Cabral	5 Sept. 1932–15 Dec. 1932
Aarón Sáenz	16 Dec. 1932–15 June 1935

Secretary General

Nicolás Islas y Bustamante	1888–96
Angel Zimbrón	1896–1906
Ricardo R. Guzmán	1906–10
Ignacio Burgoa	1910–11
José Antonio Rivera G.	1911–14
Moisés García	1914–15
Joaquin Jurado	1915

Note: Archival records from 1915–35 are unavailable since the earthquake in 1985.

Department of Health (1917)

Director General

José María Rodríguez	3 May 1917–10 Sept. 1919
Gabriel M. Malda	1 June 1920–30 Nov. 1924
Aquilino Villanueva	30 Nov. 1928–6 Feb. 1930
Rafael Silva	7 Feb. 1930–19 Jan. 1932
Gastón Melo	20 Jan. 1932–25 Oct. 1933

Manuel F. Madrazo   26 Oct. 1933–30 Nov. 1934
Abraham Ayala González   1 Dec. 1934–15 June 1935

Secretariat of Agriculture (1914, 1920–35)

Secretary
Manuel Garza Aldape   17 Feb. 1914–9 July 1914
Carlos Rincón Gallardo   10 July 1914–14 July 1914
Antonio I. Villarreal   1 June 1920–26 Nov. 1921
Unknown   27 Nov. 1921–21 Apr. 1922
Ramón P. de Negri   22 Apr. 1922–30 Nov. 1924
Luis L. León   1 Dec. 1924–30 Nov. 1928
Marte R. Gómez   1 Dec. 1928–5 Feb. 1930
Manuel Pérez Treviño   5 Feb. 1930–1 Sept. 1931
Saturnino Cedillo   1 Sept. 1931–15 Oct. 1931
Francisco S. Elías   21 Oct. 1931–30 Nov. 1934
Tomás Garrido Canabal   1 Dec. 1934–10 June 1935

Secretariat of Communications and Public Works (1891)

Secretary
Manuel González Cosío   13 Mar. 1891–21 Oct. 1895
Francisco Z. Mena   14 Nov. 1895–22 Dec. 1907
Leandro Fernández   23 Dec. 1907–24 Mar. 1911
Norberto Domínguez   25 Mar. 1911–25 May 1911
Manuel Bonilla   26 May 1911–26 Nov. 1912
Jaime Gurza   27 Nov. 1912–18 Feb. 1913
David de la Fuente   19 Feb. 1913–13 Sept. 1913
José María Lozano   15 Sept. 1913–14 Oct. 1913
José María Lozano   19 Feb. 1914–18 May 1914
Arturo Alvaradejo   10 July 1914–13 July 1914
Isaac Bustamante   14 July 1914–13 Aug. 1914
Pascual Ortiz Rubio   1 June 1920–16 Feb. 1921
Faustino Real   17 Feb. 1921–14 July 1921
Amado Aguirre   15 July 1921–30 Nov. 1924
Adalberto Tejeda   1 Dec. 1924–25 Aug. 1925
Eduardo Ortiz   26 Aug. 1925–20 June 1926
Ramón Ross   21 June 1926–30 Nov. 1928
Javier Sánchez Mejorada   1 Dec. 1928–5 Feb. 1930
Juan Andrew Almazán   5 Feb. 1930–14 Oct. 1931
Carlos Blake   15 Oct. 1931–20 Oct. 1931
Gustavo P. Serrano   21 Oct. 1931–19 Jan. 1932
Miguel N. Acosta   20 Jan. 1932–21 Nov. 1934
Mariano Moctezuma   22 Nov. 1934–30 Nov. 1934
Rodolfo Elías Calles   1 Dec. 1934–15 June 1935

Subsecretary
Santiago Méndez   13 Mar. 1891–21 Oct. 1895
Santiago Méndez   21 Oct. 1895–22 Dec. 1907
Gilberto M. Montiel   23 Dec. 1907–1 April 1911
Francisco Nicolau   2 Apr. 1911–25 May 1911
Francisco Nicolau   26 May 1911–22 June 1911
Manuel Urquidi   23 June 1911–6 Nov. 1911

Manuel Urquidi	6 Nov. 1911–
José F. Covarrubias	–27 Nov. 1912
José F. Covarrubias	27 Nov. 1912–18 Feb. 1913
Rafael M. Vázquez	19 Feb. 1913–14 Aug. 1913
Adolfo de la Lama	15 Aug. 1913–13 Sept. 1913
Arturo Alvaradejo	15 Sept. 1913–9 July 1914
Isaac Bustamante	10 July 1914–14 July 1914
Ignacio Bonillas	21 Aug. 1914–1 May 1917*
Manuel Rodríguez Gutiérrez	Feb. 1918–30 May 1920
Manuel Rodríguez Gutiérrez	31 May 1920–8 June 1920
José Morales Hesse	9 June 1920–30 Nov. 1920
José Morales Hesse	1 Dec. 1920–31 Dec 1920
Faustino F. Roel	1 Jan. 1921–16 Feb. 1921
José I. Lugo	17 Feb. 1921–14 July 1921
Faustino F. Roel	15 July 1921–
Eduardo Ortiz	1923–30 Nov. 1924
Eduardo Ortiz	1 Dec. 1924–20 June 1926
Carlos G. Blake	5 Feb. 1930–14 Oct. 1931
Mariano Moctezuma	5 Sept. 1932–21 Nov. 1934
Francisco L. Terminal	1 Feb. 1935–15 June 1935

*Bonillas acted as secretary of communications, although President Carranza never named anyone officially to the position.

Secretariat of Foreign Relations

Secretary

José Fernández	1 Dec. 1884–18 Dec. 1884
Joaquín Baranda	19 Dec. 1884–18 Jan.1885
Ignacio Mariscal	19 Jan. 1885–13 May 1890
Manuel Azpíroz	14 May 1890–15 Sept. 1890
Ignacio Mariscal	16 Sept. 1890–5 Jan. 1898
Manuel Azpíroz	6 Jan. 1898–11 Jan. 1898
Ignacio Mariscal	12 Jan. 1898–16 Apr. 1910
Enrique C. Creel	4 May 1910–24 Mar. 1911
Francisco León de la Barra	25 Mar. 1911–25 May 1911
Victoriano Salado Alvarez	26 May 1911–26 June 1911
Bartolomé Carvajal y Rosas	27 June 1911–5 Nov. 1911
Manuel Calero	6 Nov. 1911–9 Apr. 1912
Pedro Lascuráin	15 Jan. 1913–18 Feb. 1913
Francisco León de la Barra	19 Feb. 1913–8 July 1913
Carlos Pereyra	9 July 1913–27 July 1913
Manuel Garza Aldape	28 July 1913–10 Aug. 1913
Federico Gamboa	11 Aug. 1913–24 Sept. 1913
Antonio Peña y Reyes	25 Sept. 1913–30 Sept. 1913
Querido Moheno	1 Oct. 1913–17 Feb. 1914
José López Portillo	18 Feb. 1914–9 July 1914
Francisco S. Carvajal	10 July 1914–13 July 1914
Rafael Díaz Iturbide	16 July 1914–13 Aug. 1914
Isidro Fabela	21 Aug. 1914–26 Nov. 1914
Jesús Urueta	12 Dec. 1914–18 June 1914
Jesús Acuña	24 June 1914–21 Apr. 1916
Cándido Aguilar	26 Apr. 1916–30 Nov. 1916

Ernesto Garza Pérez	1 May 1917–3 Feb. 1918
Cándido Aguilar	*4 Feb. 1918–8 Nov. 1918*
Ernesto Garza Pérez	*9 Nov. 1918–18 Mar. 1919*
Salvador Diego Fernández	19 Mar. 1919–18 May 1919
Ernesto Garza Pérez	19 May 1919–31 May 1919
Salvador Diego Fernández	1 June 1919–12 Oct. 1919
Hilario Medina	13 Oct. 1919–31 Mar. 1920
Alberto C. Franco	1 Apr. 1920–21 May 1920
Juan Sánchez Azcona	1 June 1920–14 June 1920
Miguel Covarrubias	15 June 1920–3 Aug. 1920
Cutberto Hidalgo	4 Aug. 1920–13 Jan. 1921
Aarón Sáenz	14 Jan 1921–26 Jan. 1921
Alberto J. Pani	27 Jan. 1921–26 Sept. 1923
Aarón Sáenz	27 Sept. 1923–30 Apr. 1927
Genaro Estrada	1 May 1927–19 Jan. 1932
Manuel C. Téllez	20 Jan. 1932–31 Dec. 1932
José Manuel Puig Casauranc	1 Jan. 1933–11 Oct. 1933
Enrique Jiménez Domínguez	12 Oct. 1933–7 Nov. 1933
José Manuel Puig Casauranc	8 Nov. 1933–30 Nov. 1933
Emilio Portes Gil	1 Dec. 1934–15 June 1935

Subsecretary

José Fernández	11 Feb. 1884–30 Dec. 1884
Andrés C. Vázquez	1 Feb. 1885–15 Oct. 1885
Eduardo Garay	16 Oct. 1885–15 Sept. 1886
José T. de Cuéllar	16 Sept. 1886–30 Dec. 1886
Manuel Díaz Mimiaga	1 Jan. 1887–15 Sept. 1887
José T. de Cuéllar	15 Sept. 1887–30 Apr. 1890
Manuel Azpíroz	3 May 1890–2 Feb. 1899
José María Gamboa	4 Feb. 1899–19 Aug. 1901
José Algara	4 Oct. 1901–10 Mar. 1908
Federico Gamboa	14 Mar. 1908–7 Dec. 1910
Victoriano Salado Alvarez	12 Dec. 1910–26 June 1911
Bartolomé Carvajal y Rosas	26 June 1911–9 Jan. 1912
Julio García	9 Jan. 1912–22 Feb. 1913
Carlos Pereyra	22 Feb. 1913–15 July 1913
Antonio Peña y Reyes	15 Sept. 1913–1 Oct. 1913
Querido Moheno	1 Oct. 1913–7 Oct. 1913
Francisco M. de Olaguíbel	7 Oct. 1913–13 Feb. 1914
Genaro Fernández McGregor	Feb. 1914–23 Feb. 1914
Roberto A. Esteva Ruiz	23 Feb. 1914–10 July 1914
Rafael Díaz Iturbe	11 July 1914–12 Aug. 1914
José Ortiz Rodríguez	18 Dec. 1914–14 Jan. 1915
Jesús Urueta	15 Jan. 1915–23 June 1916
Juan Neftali Amador	21 Apr. 1916–10 Aug. 1916
Alfonso M. Siller	2 Dec. 1916–15 Feb. 1917
Ernesto Garza Pérez	15 Feb. 1917–28 May 1919
Hilario Medina	13 Oct. 1919–31 Mar. 1920
Cutberto Hidalgo	14 June 1920–30 Nov. 1920
Aarón Sáenz	1 Dec. 1920–2 Mar. 1924
Genaro Estrada	3 Mar. 1924–4 Feb. 1930
José Vázquez Schiaffino	6 Feb. 1930–21 Jan. 1932
Fernando Torreblanca Contreras	21 Jan. 1932–3 June 1935

Secretariat of Government

Secretary
Manuel Romero Rubio	1 Dec. 1884–3 Oct. 1895
Manuel González Cosío	21 Oct. 1895–11 Jan. 1903
Ramón Corral	16 Jan. 1903–25 Mar. 1911
Emilio Vázquez Gómez	26 May 1911–2 Aug. 1911
Alberto García Granados	2 Aug. 1911–27 Oct. 1911
Rafael Hernández Madero	28 Oct. 1911–5 Nov. 1911
Abraham González	6 Nov. 1911–17 Feb. 1912
Jesús Flores Magón	26 Feb. 1912–25 Nov. 1912
Rafael Hernández Madero	27 Nov. 1912–18 Feb. 1913
Victoriano Huerta	19 Feb. 1913–19 Feb. 1913
Alberto García Granados	19 Feb. 1913–24 Apr. 1913
Vacant	24 Apr. 1913–12 June 1913
Aureliano Urrutia	13 June 1913–14 Sept. 1913
Manuel Garza Aldape	6 Oct. 1913–9 Feb. 1914
Adolfo de la Lama	10 Feb. 1914–13 July 1914
José María Luján	14 July 1914–13 Aug. 1914
Eliseo Arredondo	21 Aug. 1914–25 Nov. 1914
Rafael Zubarán Capmany	26 Nov. 1914–23 June 1915
Jesús Acuña	24 June 1915–2 Mar. 1916
Manuel Aguirre Berlanga	1 May 1916–21 May 1920
Gilberto Valenzuela	1 June 1920–3 Aug. 1920
José Inocencio Lugo	4 Aug. 1920–30 Nov. 1920
Plutarco Elías Calles	1 Dec. 1920–29 Sept 1923
Enrique Colunga	5 Oct. 1923–30 Nov. 1924
Romeo Ortega	1 Dec. 1924–7 Jan. 1925
Gilberto Valenzuela	8 Jan. 1925–25 Aug. 1925
Adalberto Tejeda	26 Aug. 1925–18 Aug. 1928
Felipe Canales	30 Nov. 1928–28 Apr. 1929
Carlos Riva Palacio	29 Apr. 1929–4 Feb. 1930
Emilio Portes Gil	5 Feb. 1930–27 Aug. 1931
Lázaro Cárdenas	28 Aug. 1931–15 Oct. 1931
Manuel C. Téllez	21 Oct. 1931–19 Jan. 1932
Juan José Ríos Ríos	20 Jan. 1932–2 Sept. 1932
Eduardo Vasconcelos	5 Sept. 1932–8 May 1934
Narciso Bassols	9 May 1934–30 Sept. 1934
Juan de Dios Bojórquez	1 Oct. 1934–15 June 1935

Subsecretary
Manuel Antonio Mercado	*1882–1900*
Miguel S. Macedo	1906–11
Matías Chávez	1911
Federico González Garza	1911–12
Ignacio Alcocer	1913–14
Eliseo Arredondo	20 Aug. 1914–
Manuel Aguirre Berlanga	1 Apr. 1916–4 Dec. 1917
Gilberto Valenzuela	1920
José Inocencio Lugo	1 Dec. 1920–30 Dec. 1922
Gilberto Valenzuela	31 Dec. 1922–13 Nov. 1923
Daniel Benítez	14 Nov. 1923–30 Nov. 1924
Primo Villa Michel	1925

Felipe Canales	1 Dec 1928–28 Apr. 1929
Octavio Mendoza González	30 Apr. 1929–1931
Silvestre Guerrero	22 Oct. 1931–1932
Eduardo Vasconcelos	21 Jan. 1932–4 Sept. 1932
Juan C. Cabral	16 Dec. 1932–30 Nov.1934
Francisco Ramírez Villarreal	1 Jan. 1935–18 June 1935

Secretariat of Industry and Commerce (Secretariat of National Economy, 1933–47; Secretariat of Industry and Commerce, 1917–32; Secretariat of Development, Colonization, Industry, and Commerce, 1861–1917)

Secretary

Carlos Pacheco	1 Dec. 1884–21 Mar. 1891
Manuel Fernández Leal	8 Jan. 1892–11 Jan. 1903
Manuel González Cosío	12 Jan. 1903–21 Mar. 1905
Blas Escontría	24 Mar. 1905–20 May 1907
Olegario Molina	20 May 1907–25 Mar. 1911
Manuel Marroquín Rivera	25 Mar. 1911–25 May 1911
Manuel Calero	26 May 1911–11 July 1911
Rafael Hernández Madero	12 July 1911–26 Nov. 1912
Manuel Bonilla	27 Nov. 1912–18 Feb 1913
Alberto Robles Gil	19 Feb. 1913–7 July 1913
Adolfo de la Lama	8 July 1913–10 Aug. 1913
Manuel Garza Aldape	11 Aug. 1913–8 Feb. 1914
Eduardo Tamariz y Sánchez	9 Feb. 1914–10 July 1914
Pastor Rouaix	14 July 1914–13 Aug. 1914
Pastor Rouaix	26 Aug. 1914–30 Apr. 1917
Alberto J. Pani	1 May 1917–30 Nov. 1918
León Salinas	22 Jan. 1919–31 May 1919
Plutarco Elías Calles	21 Oct. 1919–1 Feb. 1920
León Salinas	22 Feb. 1920–21 May 1920
Jacinto B. Treviño	1 June 1920–20 Nov. 1920
Rafael Zubarán Capmany	1 Dec. 1920–26 Dec. 1921
Miguel Alessio Robles	27 Feb. 1922–23 Oct. 1923
Manuel Pérez Treviño	30 Oct. 1923–30 Nov. 1924
Luis N. Morones	1 Dec. 1924–31 July 1928
José Manuel Puig Casauranc	1 Aug. 1928–31 Dec. 1928
Ramón P. de Negri	1 Jan. 1929–4 Feb. 1930
Luis L. León	5 Feb. 1930–7 Oct. 1930
Aarón Sáenz	8 Oct. 1930–19 Jan. 1932
Abelardo L. Rodríguez	20 Jan. 1932–2 Aug. 1932
Primo Villa Michel	8 Aug. 1932–30 Nov. 1934
Francisco J. Múgica	1 Dec. 1934–15 June 1935

Subsecretary (Oficial Mayor 1884–1900)

Manuel Fernández Leal	2 Dec. 1884–30 Nov. 1892
Gilberto Crespo y Martínez	2 Dec. 1892–30 Nov. 1900
Gilberto Montiel	1 Dec. 1900–11 Jan. 1903
Andrés Aldasoro	1 Dec. 1903–21 Mar. 1905
Guillermo Beltrán	21 Mar. 1905–5 Mar. 1907
Andrés Aldasoro	21 Apr. 1907–26 May 1909
Manuel Calero	26 May 1909–11 Aug. 1909
Andrés Aldasoro	11 Aug. 1909–11 Apr. 1911

Francisco Díaz Lombardo   1 June 1911–18 Feb. 1913
Antonio Escandón   14 July 1914–12 Aug. 1914

Note: Archival records for 1915–35 are unavailable.

Secretariat of Justice (Department of Justice, 1917–20; Secretariat of Justice, Public Instruction, and Fine Arts, 1891–1917; Secretariat of Justice and Public Instruction, 1861–91)

Secretary

Joaquín Baranda	1 Dec. 1884–10 Apr. 1901
Justino Fernández	19 Apr. 1901–15 May 1905
Justino Fernández	16 May 1905–24 Mar. 1911
Demetrio Sodi	25 Mar. 1911–25 May 1911
Rafael Hernández Madero	26 May 1911–11 July 1911
Manuel Calero	12 July 1911–5 Nov. 1911
Manuel Vázquez Tagle	6 Nov. 1911–18 Feb. 1913
Rodolfo Reyes	19 Feb. 1913–11 Sept. 1913
Adolfo de la Lama	15 Sept. 1913–14 July 1914
Eduardo Preciat Castillo	19 July 1914–13 Aug. 1914
Manuel Escudero y Verdugo	8 Sept. 1914–17 Aug. 1915
Roque Estrada	18 Aug. 1915–9 Sept. 1916
Pascual Morales y Molina	10 Sept. 1916–30 Apr. 1917
Miguel Román	3 May 1917–21 May 1920

Secretariat of Public Education (Department of Public Instruction and Fine Arts, 1917–21; Secretariat of Public Instruction and Fine Arts, 1905–1916)

Secretary

Justo Sierra	1 Dec. 1905–23 Mar. 1911
Jorge Vera Estañol	24 Mar. 1911–25 May 1911
Francisco Vázquez Gómez	26 May 1911–27 Oct. 1911
Miguel Díaz Lombardo	6 Nov. 1911–25 Feb. 1913
José María Pino Suárez	26 Feb. 1912–18 Feb. 1913
Jorge Vera Estañol	19 Feb. 1913–13 June 1913
Manuel Garza Aldape	14 June 1913–11 Aug. 1913
José María Lozano	11 Aug. 1913–15 Sept. 1913
Eduardo Tamariz y Sánchez	17 Sept. 1913–20 Sept. 1913
Nemesio García Naranjo	21 Sept. 1913–14 July 1914
Rubén Valenti	14 July 1914–13 Aug. 1914
Félix F. Palavicini	25 Aug. 1914–25 Sept. 1916
Alfonso Cravioto	26 Sept. 1916–18 Nov. 1916
Juan León	18 Nov. 1916–28 Feb. 1917
José Natividad Macías	3 May 1917–21 May 1920
José Vasconcelos	1 Dec. 1920–2 July 1924
Bernardo J. Gastélum	2 July 1924–30 Nov. 1924
José Manuel Puig Casauranc	1 Dec. 1924–22 Aug. 1928
Moisés Sáenz	23 Aug. 1928–29 Nov. 1928
Ezequiel Padilla	30 Nov. 1928–4 Feb. 1930
Aarón Sáenz	5 Feb. 1930–8 Oct. 1930
Carlos Trejo y Lerdo de Tejada	9 Oct. 1930–8 Dec. 1930
José Manuel Puig Casauranc	9 Dec. 1930–21 Sept. 1931

Alejandro Cerísola	22 Sept. 1931–15 Oct. 1931
Narciso Bassols	21 Oct. 1931–8 May 1934
Eduardo Vasconcelos	9 May 1934–30 Nov. 1934

Subsecretary

Justo Sierra	1901–05
Ezquiel A. Chávez	1905–1910
Alberto J. Pani	1911
Enrique González Martínez	1913
Nemesio García Naranjo	1913
Rubén Valenti	1914
Alfonso Cravioto	1914–15
Félix F. Palavicini	1915–16
Alfonso Cravioto	1916–17
Bernardo J. Gastélum	1921–24
Moisés Sáenz	1925–28
Carlos Trejo y Lerdo de Tejada	1930
Alejandro Cerísola	1931

Secretariat of the Treasury and Public Credit

Secretary

Manuel Dublán	1 Dec. 1884–31 May 1891
Benito Gómez Farías	12 June 1891–30 Oct. 1891
Matías Romero	1 Jan. 1892–7 May 1893
José Yves Limantour	8 May 1893–25 May 1911
Ernesto Madero	26 May 1911–18 Feb. 1913
Toribio Esquivel Obregón	19 Feb. 1913–26 July 1913
Enrique Gorostieta	14 Aug. 1913–5 Oct. 1913
Adolfo de la Lama	6 Oct. 1913–9 July 1914
Gilberto Trujillo	10 July 1914–13 Aug. 1914
Felícitos Villarreal	14 Aug. 1914–18 Sept. 1914
Carlos M. Esquerro	19 Sept. 1914–29 Sept. 1914
José J. Reynoso	30 Sept. 1914–21 Nov. 1914
Rafael Nieto	22 Nov. 1914–13 Dec. 1914
Luis Cabrera	14 Dec. 1914–1 May 1917
Rafael Nieto	2 May 1917–5 Apr. 1919
Luis Cabrera	6 Apr. 1919–19 May 1920
Aureliano Mendívil	20 May 1920–2 June 1920
Salvador Alvarado	3 June 1920–30 Nov. 1920
Adolfo de la Huerta	1 Dec. 1920–25 Sept. 1923
Alberto J. Pani	26 Sept. 1923–28 Jan. 1927
Luis Montes de Oca	16 Feb. 1927–20 Jan. 1932
Rafael Mancera Ortiz	21 Jan. 1932–14 Feb. 1932
Alberto J. Pani	15 Feb. 1932–28 Sept. 1933
Plutarco Elías Calles	29 Sept. 1933–31 Dec. 1933
Marte R. Gómez	1 Jan. 1934–30 Nov. 1934

Subsecretary (1900)

Roberto Núñez	21 Dec. 1900–6 Oct. 1904
Luis G. Labastida	6 Oct. 1904–26 Jan. 1905
Roberto Núñez	26 Jan. 1905–24 May 1911
Jaime Gurza	24 May 1911–13

Gilberto Trujillo	12 July 1914–12 Aug. 1914
José J. Reynoso	30 Aug. 1914–21 Nov. 1914
Rafael Nieto	Dec. 1914–4 May 1919
Francisco G. Sada Muguerza	1920
Manuel Gómez Morín	1920–21
Salvador Urbina Frías	1922
Manuel Padrés	1 Dec. 1922–25 Sept. 1923
Alberto Mascareñas Navarro	1 Dec 1924–1925
José Vázquez Schiaffino	1925
Octavio Dubois Méndez	8 June 1925–15 Feb. 1927
Rafael Mancera Ortiz	12 Feb. 1930–16 Feb. 1932
Octavio Dubois Méndez	16 Feb. 1932–28 Sept. 1933
Marte R. Gómez Segura	29 Sept. 1933–1 Jan. 1934
Alfonso González Gallardo	1 Mar. 1934–30 Nov. 1934
Efraín Buenrostro	1 Dec. 1934–31 Dec. 1937

Note: The oficial mayor was the second–ranked position until 1900.

Oficial Mayor

José Antonio Gamboa	1 Dec. 1884–26 May 1892
José Yves Limantour	27 May 1892–9 May 1893
Roberto Núñez	17 May 1893–23 Apr. 1900
Francisco de P. Cardona	13 Oct. 1900–2 Mar. 1903
Manuel Necoechea	2 Mar. 1903–1 May 1903
Francisco de P. Cardona	1 May 1903–31 Dec. 1903
Manuel Necoechea	1 Jan. 1904–1 Mar. 1905
Luis G. Labastida	1 Mar. 1905–29 May 1906
R. G. Revuelta	12 Dec. 1906–10 July 1911
Carlos M. Esquerro	18 Oct. 1913–30 Sept. 1914
Rafael Nieto	21 Nov. 1914–27 Dec. 1914
Enrique Rodríguez Maniau	15 Jan. 1915–9 Mar. 1915
Manuel Padilla	10 Mar. 1915–10 June 1915
Rafael N. Millán y Alva	1916
Antonio Madrazo	20 Oct. 1916–14 Nov. 1918
Alberto de la Canal	26 May 1919–
Octavio Dubois Méndez	1 Jan. 1924–8 June 1925
Rafael Mancera Ortiz	18 Feb. 1927–11 Feb. 1930
Luis Sánchez Pontón	12 Feb. 1930–1931
Alfonso Herrera Salcedo	16 Feb. 1932–1933
Alfonso González Gallardo	7 Oct. 1933–1 Mar. 1934
José Raymundo Cárdenas del Río	1 Aug. 1935–28 Nov. 1940

Secretariat of War and Navy

Secretary

Pedro Hinojosa	1 Dec. 1884–19 Mar. 1896
Felipe Berriozábal	20 Mar. 1896–9 Jan. 1900
Bernardo Reyes	25 Jan. 1900–24 Dec. 1902
Francisco Z. Mena	16 Jan. 1903–15 Mar. 1905
Manuel González Cosío	21 mar. 1905–25 May 1911
Eugenio Rascón	26 May 1911–15 July 1911
José González Salas	18 July 1911–5 Mar. 1912
Angel García Peña	5 Mar. 1912–18 Feb. 1913

Manuel Mondragón	19 Feb. 1913–12 June 1913
Aureliano Blanquet	13 June 1913–9 July 1914
José Refugio Velasco	10 July1914–13 Aug. 1914
Eduardo Hay	21 Aug. 1914– 7 Sept. 1914
Jacinto B. Treviño	8 Sept. 1914–26 Sept. 1914
Ignacio L. Pesqueira	27 Sept. 1914–12 Mar. 1916
Alvaro Obregón	13 Mar. 1916–1 May 1917
Jesús Agustín Castro	3 May 1917–6 Apr. 1918
Juan José Rios	7 Apr. 1918–18 Feb. 1920
Francisco L. Urquizo	22 Feb. 1920–21 May 1920
Plutarco Elías Calles	1 June 1920–20 Nov. 1920
Benjamín Hill	1 Dec. 1920–14 Dec. 1920
Enrique Estrada	15 Dec. 1920–1 Dec. 1921
Francisco R. Serrano	2 Dec. 1921–30 Nov. 1924
Joaquín Amaro	1 Dec. 1924–1 Mar. 1929
Plutarco Elías Calles	2 Mar. 1929–18 May 1929
Joaquín Amaro	20 May 1929–14 Oct. 1931
Plutarco Elías Calles	15 Oct. 1931–30 July 1932
Abelardo L. Rodríguez	2 Aug. 1932–2 Sept. 1932
Pablo Quiroga	5 Sept. 1932–31 Dec. 1932
Lázaro Cárdenas	1 Jan. 1933–15 June 1933
Pablo Quiroga	28 June 1933–30 Nov. 1934

Subsecretary

Alejandro Pezo	28 Apr. 1896–24 Dec. 1902
Juan Villegas	24 Dec. 1902–4 Mar. 1903
Luis del Carmen Curiel	4 Mar. 1903–29 Nov. 1907
José María Mier	29 Nov. 1907–1 Nov. 1909
Ignacio Salamanca	1 Nov. 1909–25 May 1911
Juan M. Durán	26 May 1911–18 July 1911
José González Salas	19 July 1911–30 Oct. 1911
Manuel M. Plata	31 Oct. 1911–21 Feb. 1913
Manuel M. Velázquez	22 Feb. 1913–14 June 1913
Felipe Mier	15 June 1913–1 Nov. 1913
Felipe Angeles	1 Nov. 1913–8 Mar. 1914
Gustavo Salas Ochoa	9 Mar. 1914–26 Sept. 1914
Ignacio L. Pesqueira	27 Sept. 1914–13 Mar. 1916
No official information	13 Mar. 1916–2 May 1917
Jesús Agustín Castro	3 May 1917–7 Apr. 1918
Juan José Ríos y Ríos	8 Apr. 1918–17 Sept 1919
Francisco L. Urquizo Benavides	18 Sept. 1919–31 May 1920
Francisco R. Serrano	1 June 1920–26 Nov. 1920
Enrique Estrada	1 Dec. 1920–31 Jan. 1931
Francisco R. Serrano	1 Feb. 1921–3 Mar. 1922
Roberto Cruz Díaz	4 Mar. 1922–4 Nov. 1923
Francisco R. Manzo	5 Nov. 1923–1 Oct. 1924
Joaquín Amaro	1 Dec 1924–26 July 1925
Miguel Piña, Jr.	1 Oct. 1925–10 July 1928
Abundio Gómez	11 Dec 1928–1 June 1929
Matías Ramos Santos	1 June 1929–11 Aug. 1930
Pablo Quiroga	11 Aug. 1930–1 Apr. 1931
Abelardo L. Rodríguez	16 Oct. 1931–20 Jan. 1932
Pablo Quiroga	21 Jan. 1932–30 June 1933
Manuel Avila Camacho	1 July 1933–31 Oct. 1937

Convention Governments (Nov. 6, 1914–Oct. 10, 1915)

Presidents
Eulalio Gutiérrez	6 Nov. 1914–15 Jan. 1915
Roque González Garza	16 Jan. 1915–9 June 1915
Francisco Lagos Cházaro	10 June 1915–10 Oct. 1915

Secretariat of Agriculture

Secretary
Manuel Palafox	1 Jan. 1915–27 Mar. 1915
Vacant	28 Mar. 1915–10 June 1915
Manuel Palafox	14 June 1915–10 Oct. 1915

Secretariat of Communications

Secretary (all were subsecretaries; no secretaries were named)
José Rodríguez Cabo	4 Dec. 1914–15 Jan. 1915
José Vázquez Schiaffino	16 Jan. 1915–10 June 1915
Federico Cervantes	14 June 1915–10 Oct. 1915

Secretariat of Development

Secretary
Valentín Gama	4 Dec. 1914–16 Jan. 1915
Carlos Patoni	17 Jan. 1915–9 Mar. 1915
Antonio Castilla	10 Mar. 1915–10 June 1915
Alberto B. Piña	14 June 1915–10 Oct. 1915

Secretariat of Foreign Relations

Secretary
Vacant	6 Nov. 1914–31 Dec. 1914
José Ortiz Rodríguez	1 Jan. 1915–16 Jan. 1915
Vacant	16 Jan. 1915–9 Mar. 1915
Ismael Palafox	10 Mar. 1915–10 June 1915
Ignacio Borrego	14 June 1915–10 Oct. 1915

Secretariat of Government

Secretary
Vacant	6 Nov. 1914–31 Dec. 1914
Lucio Blanco	1 Jan. 1915–15 Jan. 1915
Alfredo Güinchenne	16 Jan. 1915–10 June 1915
José Quevedo	14 June 1915–10 Oct. 1915

Secretariat of Justice

Secretary

Miguel Alessio Robles	6 Nov. 1914–31 Dec. 1914
Rodrigo Gómez	1 Jan. 1915–27 Mar. 1915
Vacant	28 Mar. 1915–10 June 1915
Miguel Mendoza López S.	14 June 1915–10 Oct. 1915

Secretariat of Public Instruction

Secretary

José Vasconcelos	6 Nov. 1914–15 Jan. 1915
Ramon López Velarde	16 Jan. 1915–20 Jan. 1915
Joaquín Ramos Roa	21 Jan. 1915–10 June 1915
Otilio Montaño	15 June 1915–28 July 1915
Vacant	29 July 1915–10 Oct. 1915

Secretariat of the Treasury

Secretary

Manuel N. Robles	20 Nov. 1914–3 Dec. 1914
Felícitos Villarreal	4 Dec. 1914–15 Jan. 1915
Enrique Rodiles Maniau	16 Jan. 1915–9 Mar. 1915
Manuel Padilla	10 Mar. 1915–10 June 1915
Luis Zubiría y Campa	14 June 1915–10 Oct. 1915

Secretariat of War and Navy

Secretary

José Isabel Robles	6 Nov. 1914–15 Jan. 1915
Alfredo Serratos	16 Jan. 1915–27 Mar. 1915
Vacant	28 Mar. 1915–23 May 1915
Francisco V. Pacheco	24 May 1915–10 Oct. 1915

APPENDIX E

Ambassadors to Cuba, France,
the Soviet Union, United Kingdom,
and the United States, 1900–1934

CUBA

Minister

Gilberto Crespo y Martínez	1 July 1902–16 Feb. 1906
José F. Godoy	17 Feb. 1906–14
Heriberto Jara	1917–20
Antonio Fernández Ferrer	1922–23
Arturo de Saracho	1924–25
Romeo Ortega	1925–27
Carlos Trejo y Lerdo de Tejada	1 Apr. 1927–30
Adolfo Cienfuegos y Camus	16 Mar. 1930–33
Octavio Reyes Spíndola	1933–34 (in charge)
Alfonso Cravioto	1934–36

FRANCE

Minister

Sebastián de Mier	1901–12
Miguel Díaz Lombardo	4 Mar. 1912–13
Francisco León de la Barra	1913–14
Alberto J. Pani	1918–20
Rodolfo Nervo	1922
Alfonso Reyes	1924
Alberto J. Pani	1927–31
Emilio Portes Gil	1931
Alfonso Castelló	1931–33
Francisco Castillo Nájera	1933–35
Marte R. Gómez	1 Jan. 1935–30 Apr. 1936

SOVIET UNION

Minister

Pedro Rincón Gallardo	26 June 1900–07
Carlos Américo Lera	20 June 1907–2 Jan. 1912
Bartolomé Carbajal y Rosas	3 Jan. 1912–13
Miguel Covarrubias	1913
Basilio Badillo	1 Nov. 1922–28
Jesús Silva Herzog	1928–1930
None	1930–35

UNITED KINGDOM

Minister

Sebastián de Mier	14 Mar. 1900–01
Alfonso Lancaster Jones	1901–03
Pedro Rincón Gallardo	1903–05
Miguel Covarrubias	1907–11
Miguel de Beístegui	20 June 1911–23 Apr. 1912
Miguel Covarrubias	24 Apr. 1912–13
Bartolomé Carbajal y Rosas	1913
Salvador Diego Fernández	1919–20
Juan F. Urquidi	1922 (in charge)
Alfonso de Rosenweig Díaz	1925 (in charge)
Gilberto Valenzuela	23 Sept. 1925–28
Leopoldo Ortiz	1929–31
Alberto Mascareñas	1931–33
Javier Sánchez Mejorada	1933–31 Dec. 1934
Leonides Andreu Almazán	1 Jan. 1935–31 Dec. 1935

UNITED STATES

Ambassador

Manuel Azpíroz	30 Mar. 1899–1905
Joaquín D. Casasús	1905–06
Enrique C. Creel	18 Dec. 1906–09
Francisco León de la Barra	27 Feb. 1909–24 Mar. 1911
Gilberto Crespo y Martínez	13 July 1911–18 Apr. 1912
Manuel Calero	19 Apr. 1912–6 Jan. 1913
Angel Algara y Romero de Terreros	1913 (in charge)
Eliseo Arredondo	1915
Ignacio Bonillas	1917–20
Manuel C. Téllez	1920–24 (in charge)
Manuel C. Téllez	1924–31
José Manuel Puig Casauranc	1931–32
Fernando González Roa	1932–34
Francisco Castillo Nájera	1 Jan. 1935–

APPENDIX F

Governors, 1884–1934

AGUASCALIENTES

Hornedo, Francisco G.	1 Dec. 1883–30 Nov. 1887
Vázquez del Mercado, Alejandro	1 Dec. 1887–30 Nov. 1895
Arellano, Rafael	1 Dec. 1895–99
Sagredo, Carlos	1899–1903
Vázquez del Mercado, Alejandro	1903–25 May 1911
Ruiz de Chávez, Felipe	26 May 1911–27 May 1912
Fuentes Dávila, Alberto	7 June 1912–13
García Hidalgo, Carlos (Gen.)	1 Mar. 1913–14
Ruelas, Miguel (Gen.)	1914
Lomelí, Aniceto	1914
García Hidalgo, Carlos (Gen.)	1914
Fuentes Dávila, Alberto	24 Sept. 1914–15 Oct. 1914
Elizondo, Víctor (Gen.)	4 Nov. 1914–28 Jan. 1915
Díaz, Benito (Gen.)	28 Jan. 1915–10 July 1915
Estrada, Roque (Gen.)	22 July 1915–4 Aug. 1915
Triana, Martín (Gen.)	5 Aug. 1915–13 July 1916
Osuna, Gregorio (Gen.)	14 July 1916–16 Jan. 1917
Norzagaray, Antonio (Gen.)	17 Jan. 1917–11 June 1917
González, Aurelio L.	11 June 1917–Apr. 1920
Medina, Victorino	Apr. 1920–30 Nov. 1920.
Arellano Valle, Rafael	1 Dec. 1920–23
Elizalde, José María	1923–23 Oct. 1923
Lomelí, Manuel	1924–25
Azpeitía, Benjamín	24 Oct. 1925–26
Reyes Barrientos, Francisco	1926
Díaz de León, Isaac	1926–27
De la Mora, Benjamín	1928
Carpio, Manuel	1929–4 Nov. 1929
Quevedo, Rafael	1930–31
Zamarripa, Guadalupe	1932
Osornio, Enrique	1 Dec. 1932–30 Nov. 1936

BAJA CALIFORNIA

Torres, Luis E. (Gen.)	1888–94
Sanginés, Agustín (Col.)	25 June 1894–25 Feb. 1902
Arróniz, Abraham (Col.)	25 Sept. 1902–8 Feb. 1903
Vega, Celso (Col.)	9 Feb. 1903–28 June 1911
Ptanick, Carlos	1912–13
Espinosa y Ayala, José Dolores	1913
Gómez, Miguel V.	1913
Vázquez, Francisco N. (Col.)	1913–14
Zárate, David	1914
Avilés, Baltasar	1914
Zárate, David	1914
Cantú Jiménez, Esteban (Col.)	1915–20
Balarezo, Manuel	1920–21
Ibarra, Epigmenio, Jr.	1921–22
Lugo, José Inocente	1922–23
Rodríguez, Abelardo (Gen.)	1923–29
Tapia Freyding, José María (Col.)	1929–30
Bernal, Arturo (Gen.)	1930
Trejo y Lerdo de Tejada, Carlos	1930–31
Olachea Avilés, Agustín (Gen.)	1931–35

BAJA CALIFORNIA DEL SUR

Arróniz, Abraham (Col.)	1900–02
Sanginés, Agustín (Col.)	1902–11
Díez, Santiago	1911–13
Cota, Federico	1913
Osuna, Gregorio (Lt. Col.)	1913–14
Amezcua, Manuel (Maj.)	1914
Cornejo, Miguel L.	1914
Carrillo, Eduardo S.	1914
Ortega, Félix	1915
Angulo, Urbano (Maj.)	1915–16
Moreno, Enrique	1916–17
Lacroix Rovirosa, Francisco	1917
Mezta, Manuel (Gen.)	1917–20
Arriola, Agustín	1920–24
Piña, Miguel (Gen.)	1924
Abitia, Librado	1924–25
Esquerro, Carlos H.	1925–27
Galindo, Daniel	1927
Aguirre, Amado (Gen.)	1927–29
Olachea Avilés, Agustín (Gen.)	1929–31
García de Alba, Ruperto (Gen.)	1931–32
Domínguez Cota, Juan (Gen.)	1932–38

CAMPECHE

Montalvo, Juan	15 Nov. 1883–15 Sept. 1887
Ferrer, José Trinidad	16 Sept. 1887–24 Apr. 1888
Durán, Onecífero	25 Apr. 1888–15 Sept. 1888
Kerlegand, Joaquín Z.	16 Sept. 1888–15 Sept. 1891
Preve, Leocadio	16 Sept. 1891–15 Sept. 1895
Montalvo, Juan	16 Sept. 1895–18 Nov. 1898
Gutiérrez MacGregor, Carlos	19 Nov. 1898–1 Apr. 1902

Castellot, José	2 Apr. 1902–9 Aug. 1902
García Mezquita, Luis	10 Aug. 1902–14 June 1903
Castellot, José	15 June 1903–25 June 1903
García Mezquita, Luis	26 June 1903–14 June 1905
Ruz, José	15 June 1905–20 June 1905
Aznar y Cano, Tomás	21 June 1905–8 Aug. 1910
García Gual, José	9 Aug. 1910–24 May 1911
Suzarte Campos, Gustavo	25 May 1911–15 June 1911
Sabás Flores, Román	16 June 1911–26 June 1911
Espinosa, Urbano	27 June 1911–15 Sept. 1911
Castilla Brito, Manuel	16 Sept. 1911–13 June 1913
Rivera, Manuel (Gen.)	4 July 1913–9 Sept. 1914
Mucel, Joaquín (Gen.)	10 Sept. 1914–16 Sept. 1919
Arias Solís, Enrique	17 Sept. 1919–5 May 1920
Arceo Z., Eduardo	17 May 1920–17 Feb. 1921
Gómez Briceño, Enrique	18 Feb. 1921–11 Aug. 1921
Ferrer Vega, Guillermo	12 Aug. 1921–Nov. 1921
Flores, Ramón Félix	Nov. 1921 15 Sept. 1923
Castillo Lanz, Angel	16 Sept. 1923–15 Sept. 1927
Pavón Silva, Silvestre	16 Sept. 1927–28 Dec. 1928
Bojórquez C., Ramiro	29 Dec. 1928–15 Sept. 1931
Romero Esquivel, Benjamín	16 Sept. 1931–16 Sept. 1935

CHIAPAS

Ramírez, José María	1 Dec. 1883–30 Nov. 1887
Carrascosa, Manuel	1 Dec. 1887–30 Nov. 1891
Rabasa, Emilio	1 Dec. 1891–26 Feb. 1894
Moguel, Fausto	27 Feb. 1894–30 Nov. 1895
León, Francisco C. (Col.)	1 Dec. 1895–11 Oct. 1899
Pimentel, Rafael	12 Oct. 1899–25 Dec. 1905
Rabasa, Ramón	26 Dec. 1905–27 May 1911
Rovelo Argüello, Manuel	17 Aug. 1911–29 Nov. 1911
Gordillo León, Reynaldo	15 Dec. 1911–12
Guillén, Flavio	29 Jan. 1912–19 Mar. 1913
Gordillo León, Reynaldo	20 Mar. 1913–18 July 1913
Palafox, Bernardo A. (Gen.)	19 July 1913–13 Aug. 1914
Castro, Jesús Agustín (Gen.)	13 Sept. 1914–28 May 1915
Corral, Blas (Gen.)	29 May 1915–24 Sept. 1916
Villanueva, Pablo (Col.)	25 Sept. 1916–1 Dec. 1919
Morales y Molina, Pascual (Gen.)	2 Dec. 1919–8 Mar. 1920
González, Alejo G. (Gen.)	9 Mar. 1920–31 Nov. 1920
Fernández Ruiz, Tiburcio (Gen.)	1 Dec. 1920–20 Nov. 1924
Córdoba, César	1 Jan. 1925–19 May 1925
Vidal, Carlos A. (Gen.)	20 May 1925–4 Apr. 1927
Martínez Rojas, Federico	31 Oct. 1927–Mar. 1928
Coutiño, Amador	Mar. 1928–30 Nov. 1928
Enríquez, Raymundo E.	1 Dec. 1928–30 Nov. 1932
Grajales, Victorio (Gen.)	1 Dec. 1932–22 Sept. 1936

CHIHUAHUA

González Esquivel, Celso	9 Apr. 1884–3 Oct. 1884
Pacheco, Carlos (Gen.)	4 Oct. 1884–8 Dec. 1884
Fuero, Carlos (Gen.)	9 Dec. 1884–27 July 1885
Maceyra, Félix F.	28 July 1885–10 June 1887
Pacheco, Carlos (Gen.)	11 June 1887–87

Carrillo, Lauro (Col.)	1887–92
Pimentel, Rafael	5 June 1892–3 Oct. 1892
Ahumada, Miguel (Col.)	4 Oct. 1892–1903
Terrazas, Luis (Gen.)	1903–04
Creel, Enrique	18 Aug. 1904–10 Apr. 1910
Sánchez, José María	11 Apr. 1910–5 Dec. 1910
Terrazas, Alberto	6 Dec. 1910–30 Jan. 1911
Ahumada, Miguel (Col.)	31 Jan. 1911–9 June 1911
González, Abraham	10 June 1911–23 Feb. 1913
Rábago, Antonio (Gen.)	23 Feb. 1913–30 May 1913
Mercado, Salvador R. (Gen.)	30 May 1913–Nov. 1913
Villa, Francisco (Gen.)	8 Dec. 1913–7 Jan. 1914
Chao, Manuel (Gen.)	8 Jan. 1914–12 May 1914
Avila, Fidel (Gen.)	20 May 1914–22 Dec. 1915
Enríquez, Ignacio C. (Col.)	23 Dec. 1915–11 May 1916
Treviño, Francisco L. (Gen.)	12 May 1916–4 Dec. 1916
González, Arnulfo (Gen.)	5 Dec. 1916–3 July 1918
Enríquez, Ignacio C. (Gen.)	3 July 1918–14 Nov. 1918
Ortiz, Andrés	15 Nov. 1918–29 Feb. 1920
Angulo, Melquíades	29 Feb. 1920–13 Mar. 1920
Salinas, Emilio (Gen.)	13 Mar. 1920–26 Apr. 1920
Gómez Luna, Alfonso (Gen.)	29 Apr. 1920–8 May 1920
Gameros, Tomás	20 May 1920–14 June 1920
Rodríguez, Abel S.	14 June 1920–3 Oct. 1920
Enríquez, Ignacio C. (Gen.)	4 Oct. 1920–5 Apr. 1924
Talavera, Reinaldo	5 Apr. 1924–3 Oct. 1924
Almeida, Jesús Antonio (Col.)	4 Oct. 1924–15 Apr. 1927
Mascareñas, Manuel	15 Apr. 1927–8 May 1927
Orozco E., Fernando	8 May 1927–3 Oct. 1928
Caraveo, Marcelo (Gen.)	4 Oct. 1928–8 Apr. 1929
León, Luis L.	13 Apr. 1929–3 July 1929
Almada, Francisco R.	6 Dec. 1929–15 July 1930
Escobar, Rómulo	15 July 1930–14 Aug 1930
Ortiz, Andrés	1930–31
Fierro, Roberto (Gen.)	2 Nov. 1931–4 July 1932
Salido, Eduardo	4 July 1932–3 Oct. 1932
Quevedo, Rodrigo M. (Gen.)	4 Oct. 1932–3 Oct. 1936

COAHUILA

Cervantes, Julio María (Gen.)	10 Dec. 1884–90
Garza Galán, José María (Gen.)	1890–93
Múzquiz, José María	1893–94
Arizpe y Ramos, Francisco	18 Feb. 1894–14 Aug. 1894
Cárdenas, Miguel	15 Aug. 1894–16 Aug. 1909
De la Peña, Prágedis	17 Aug. 1909–31 Nov. 1909
Del Valle, Jesús	1 Dec. 1909–28 May 1911
Carranza, Venustiano	29 May 1911–7 Mar. 1913
Blánquez, Manuel M.	8 Mar. 1913–19 Oct. 1913
Alcocer, Ignacio	20 Oct. 1913–30 Oct. 1913
Maas Aguila, Joaquín (Gen.)	1 Nov. 1913–17 Nov. 1913
Velasco, José Refugio (Gen.)	18 Nov. 1913–20 Nov. 1913
De la Peña, Prágedis	21 Nov. 1913–1 Feb. 1914
Maas Aguila, Joaquín (Gen.)	2 Feb. 1913–20 May 1914
Robles, José Isabel (Gen.)	21 May 1914–23 May 1914
Acuña, Jesús	24 May 1914–5 Jan. 1915

Angeles, Felipe (Gen.)	6 Jan. 1915–11 Jan. 1915
Ramírez, Santiago (Gen.)	12 Jan. 1915–16 May 1915
Gutiérrez, Luis (Gen.)	17 May 1915–14 June 1915
Madero González, Raúl (Gen.)	15 June 1915–19 June 1915
Pereyra, Orestes (Gen.)	20 June 1915–3 Sept. 1915
De la Huerta, Adolfo	4 Sept. 1915–5 Sept. 1915
Espinosa Mireles, Gustavo	6 Sept. 1915–6 Apr. 1917
Neira González, Bruno	7 Apr. 1917–11 Nov. 1917
Breceda Mercado, Alfredo	12 Nov. 1917–14 Dec. 1917
Espinosa Mireles, Gustavo	15 Dec. 1917–5 May 1920
Cadena Rojas, Porfirio (Gen.)	6 May 1920–26 May 1920
Gutiérrez, Luis	27 May 1920–30 Nov. 1921
González Medina, Arnulfo (Gen.)	1 Dec. 1921–30 Oct. 1923
Garza García, Juan	31 Oct. 1923–25 June 1924
Farías, Miguel	25 June 1924–25 Nov. 1924
Rodríguez, Elpidio	26 Nov. 1924–4 Oct. 1925
Ainslie R., Ricardo	5 Oct. 1925–30 Nov. 1925
Pérez Treviño, Manuel (Gen.)	1 Dec. 1925–30 Nov. 1929
Ortiz Garza, Nazario	1 Dec. 1929–30 Nov. 1933
Valdés Sánchez, Jesús	1 Dec. 1933–30 Nov. 1937

COLIMA

García, Esteban	1 Nov. 1883–31 Oct. 1887
Gómez, Gildardo	1 Nov. 1887–27 Nov. 1893
Santa Cruz, Francisco (Col.)	1893–8 May 1902
De la Madrid, Enrique O.	9 May 1902–18 May 1911
García Topete, Miguel	19 May 1911–31 Oct. 1911
Alamillo, José Trinidad	1 Nov. 1911–8 Apr. 1913
Jaramillo, Julián (Gen.)	12 Apr. 1913–12 Oct. 1913
Hernández, Juan A. (Gen.)	13 Oct. 1913–13 Jan. 1914
Delgadillo, Antonio (Gen.)	14 Jan. 1914–19 July 1914
Calderón, Esteban Baca (Gen.)	24 Nov. 1914–5 Jan. 1915
Ríos, Juan José (Gen.)	6 Jan. 1915–29 June 1917
Valle, J. Felipe	30 June 1917–31 Oct. 1919
Alvarez García, Miguel	1 Nov. 1919–31 Oct. 1923
Hurtado Suárez, Gerardo	1 Nov. 1923–20 Apr. 1925
Solórzano Béjar, Francisco	4 May 1925–31 Oct. 1927
Cervantes, Laureano	1 Nov. 1927–6 Aug. 1931
Torres Ortiz, Pedro	10 Aug. 1931–19 Nov. 1931
Saucedo, Salvador	20 Nov. 1931–22 Aug. 1935

DURANGO

Flores, Juan Manuel (Gen.)	1884–30 Jan. 1897
Fernández, Leandro	1897
Santa Marina, Juan	1897–1904
Fernández, Esteban	1904–11
Saravia y Murúa, Emiliano G.	1 Aug. 1911–2 Nov. 1911
Alonso y Patiño, Luis	2 Nov. 1911–Feb. 1912
Saravia y Murúa, Emiliano G.	Feb. 1912–14 Sept. 1912
Patoni, Carlos	15 Sept. 1912–13 Jan. 1913
Perea, Jesús	Feb. 1913–3 July 1913
Rouaix, Pastor	4 July 1913–Sept. 1914
Ceniceros, Severino	28 Sept. 1914–13 Oct. 1914
Saravia y Murúa, Emiliano G.	15 Dec. 1914–15

García, Maximo (Gen.)	Aug. 1915–Oct. 1915
Arrieta, Mariano (Gen.)	Oct. 1915–Jan. 1916
Castaños, Fernando	28 Jan. 1916–28 Feb. 1916
González, Arnulfo (Gen.)	26 June 1916–1 July 1916
Maycotte, Fortunato (Gen.)	1916–15 Oct. 1916
Gavira, Gabriel (Gen.)	Oct. 1916–Apr. 1917
Osuna, Carlos (Gen.)	Apr. 1917–Aug. 1917
Arrieta, Domingo (Gen.)	1 Aug. 1917–20
Nájera, Enrique R.	12 May 1920–15 Sept. 1920
Castro, Jesús Agustín (Gen.)	16 Sept. 1920–15 Sept. 1924
Nájera, Enrique R.	16 Sept. 1924–July 1928
Amaya, Juan Gualberto (Gen.)	16 Sept. 1928–3 Mar. 1929
Terrones Benítez, Alberto	15 Mar. 1929–17 Sept. 1931
Rouaix, Pastor	18 Sept. 1931–Sept. 1932
Real, Carlos (Gen.)	Sept. 1932–31 Dec. 1935

GUANAJUATO

Rocha y Portú, Pablo (Gen.)	14 Mar. 1884–30 May 1885
González Flores, Manuel (Gen.)	31 May 1885–8 May 1893
Obregón González, Joaquín	11 May 1893–3 May 1911
Aranda, Enrique O.	4 May 1911–3 June 1911
Castelazo, Juan B.	4 June 1911–30 Nov. 1911
Lizardi, Víctor José	1 Dec. 1911–3 July 1913
Cuéllar, Rómulo (Gen.)	4 July 1913–28 July 1914
De la Garza, Pablo A. (Gen.)	5 Aug. 1914–17 Nov. 1914
Camarena, Pablo (Col.)	18 Nov. 1914–17 Jan. 1915
Serratos, Abel B. (Col.)	18 Jan. 1915–10 May 1915
Siurob, José (Gen.)	11 May 1915–21 Dec. 1916
Dávila, Fernando	22 Dec. 1916–14 Apr. 1917
Ponce de León, Pedro	14 Apr. 1917–14 June 1917
Alcocer, Agustín	15 June 1917–19 Sept. 1919
Alcocer, Fernando	1 Sept. 1919–25 Sept. 1919
Montes, Federico (Gen.)	25 Sept. 1919–26 Feb. 1920
Villaseñor, Toribio	27 Feb. 1920–26 Apr. 1920
De Ezcurdia, Agustín	27 Apr. 1920–10 May 1920
Colunga, Enrique	12 May 1920–15 Sept. 1920
Madrazo, Antonio	16 Sept. 1920–25 Sept. 1923
Colunga, Enrique	26 Sept. 1923–3 Oct. 1923
García Téllez, Ignacio	4 Oct. 1923–2 Nov. 1923
Soto, Jesús S.	3 Nov. 1923–22 Apr. 1924
Sierra, Arturo	22 Apr. 1924–30 Nov. 1924
Colunga, Enrique	1 Dec. 1924–18 Sept. 1927
Mendoza González, Octavio	18 Sept. 1927–25 Sept. 1927
Arroyo Ch., Agustín	26 Sept. 1927–25 Sept. 1931
Hernández Alvarez, Enrique	26 Sept. 1931–1 June 1932
Reynoso, José J.	4 June 1932–25 Sept. 1932
Ortega, Melchor	26 Sept. 1932–25 Sept. 1935
Yáñez Maya, J. Jesús	26 Sept. 1935–16 Dec. 1935

GUERRERO

Alvarez, Diego (Gen.)	1882–85
Arce, Francisco O. (Gen.)	1885–Nov. 1893
Mercenario, Antonio (Col.)	1893–1901
Mora, Agustín	1901–04

Guevara Alarcón, Carlos	1904
Guillén, Manuel	1904–07
Saavedra, Silvano	1907
Flores, Damián	1907–11
Figueroa, Francisco	1911
Lugo, José Inocente	1911–13
Zozaya, Manuel (Gen.)	1913–14
Salgado, Jesús H. (Gen.)	1914
Blanco, Julián (Gen.)	1914–15
Díaz, Simón (Lt. Col.)	1915–16
Mariscal, Silvestre G. (Gen.)	1916–Dec. 1917
Adams, Julio	Dec. 1917–18
Figueroa, Francisco	1918–21
Neri, Rodolfo	1921–29 Nov. 1923
Lavín, Urbano	30 Nov. 1923–24 Mar. 1924
Neri, Rodolfo	25 Mar. 1924–31 Mar. 1925
López, Héctor F. (Gen.)	1 Apr. 1925–1 Feb. 1928
Martínez, Enrique (Col.)	2 Feb. 1928–28
Castrejón, Adrián (Gen.)	1928–25 Mar. 1933
Guevara, Gabriel M. (Gen.)	1 Apr. 1933–Nov. 1935

HIDALGO

Cravioto, Simón (Col.)	1 Apr. 1881–31 Mar. 1885
Cravioto, Francisco (Gen.)	1 Apr. 1885–30 Oct. 1897
Rodríguez, Pedro Ladislao	30 Nov. 1897–1911
González, Joaquín	1911
Silva, Jesús	1911
Rosales, Ramón (Gen.)	1911–12
Lara, Miguel	16 Oct. 1912–16 Mar. 1913
Rosales, Ramón (Gen.)	1 Apr. 1913–4 July 1913
Sanginés, Agustín (Gen.)	5 July 1913–4 Aug. 1914
Flores, Nicolás (Gen.)	Sept. 1914–21
Azuara, Amado (Gen.)	1921–2 Nov. 1923
Azuara, Antonio (Gen.)	3 Nov. 1923–31 Mar. 1925
Rodríguez, Matías (Col.)	1 Apr. 1925–31 Mar. 1929
Vargas Lugo, Bartolomé	1 Apr. 1929–31 Mar. 1933
Viveros, Ernesto	1 Apr. 1933–31 Mar. 1937

JALISCO

Tolentino, Francisco (Gen.)	1 Mar. 1883–28 Feb. 1886
Corona, Ramón (Gen.)	1 Mar. 1886–11 Nov. 1889
Bárcena, Mariano	13 Nov. 1889–21 Oct. 1890
Curiel, Luis (Gen.)	22 Oct. 1889–30 Apr. 1891
Galván, Pedro A. (Gen.)	1 Mar. 1891–12 Dec. 1891
Santa Cruz, Francisco (Col.)	13 Dec. 1891–1 Mar. 1893
Curiel, Luis (Gen.)	2 Mar. 1893–10 Jan. 1903
Ahumada, Miguel (Col.)	1 Mar. 1903–25 Jan. 1911
Zavala, Juan R.	26 Jan. 1911–28 Feb. 1911
Cuesta Gallardo, Manuel	1 Mar. 1911–24 Mar. 1911
Robles Gil, Alberto	1 June 1911–12
López Portillo y Rojas, José	1912–14
Mier, José María (Gen.)	Feb. 1914–July 1914
Diéguez, Manuel M. (Gen.)	12 July 1914–18 Oct. 1917
Degollado, Emiliano	19 Oct. 1917–23 Feb. 1918

Bouquet, Manuel	24 Feb. 1918–30 Apr. 1919
Castellanos y Tapia, Luis	1 Mar. 1919–20
Ramos Praslow, Ignacio (Col.)	1920
Labastida Izquierdo, Francisco (Col.)	1920–28 Feb. 1921
Badillo, Basilio	1 Mar. 1921–17 Mar. 1922
Valadez Ramírez, Antonio	18 Mar. 1922–28 Feb. 1923
Zuno Hernández, José Guadalupe	1 Mar. 1923–23 Mar. 1926
Barba González, Silvano	1926–27
Ramírez, Margarito (Gen.)	23 Apr. 1927–7 Aug. 1929
Cuéllar, José María	1929–30
García de Alba, Ruperto (Gen.)	1930–31
Robledo, Juan de Dios	1931–32
Allende, Sebastián	1 Apr. 1932–28 Feb. 1935

MÉXICO

Zubieta, José	9 Mar. 1881–4 Mar. 1885
Lalanne, Jesús	5 Mar. 1885–9 Mar. 1886
Zubieta, José	10 Mar. 1886–18 Mar. 1889
Villada, José Vicente (Gen.)	19 Mar. 1889–6 May 1895
Villada, Eduardo	7 May 1895–4 Mar. 1897
Villada, José Vicente (Gen.)	5 Mar. 1897–17 May 1904
González, Fernando (Gen.)	18 May 1904–30 Apr. 1909
Castillo, Carlos	1 May 1909–24 May 1911
Hidalgo, Rafael M.	25 May 1911–8 Oct. 1911
Medina Garduño, Manuel	9 Oct. 1911–11 Mar. 1913
León de la Barra, Francisco	12 Mar. 1913–11 July 1913
Beltrán, Joaquín (Gen.)	12 July 1913–6 Aug. 1914
Murguía, Francisco (Gen.)	27 Aug. 1914–30 Nov. 1914
Baz, Gustavo	15 Dec. 1914–18 Oct. 1915
Morales Molina, Pascual (Gen.)	19 Oct. 1915–21 Aug. 1916
Cepeda, Rafael	22 Aug. 1916–14 Jan. 1917
Tejada, Carlos	15 Jan. 1917–19 June 1917
Millán, Agustín (Gen.)	20 June 1917–5 Sept. 1918
García Luna, Joaquín	6 Sept. 1918–3 Mar. 1919
Millán, Agustín (Gen.)	4 Mar. 1919–20
López, Darío	1920
Gómez, Abundio (Gen.)	5 Aug. 1920–7 Feb. 1921
Campos Mena, Manuel	8 Feb. 1921–15 Sept. 1921
Gómez, Abundio (Gen.)	16 Sept. 1921–15 Sept. 1925
Riva Palacio, Carlos	16 Sept. 1925–15 Sept. 1929
Gómez, Filiberto (Col.)	16 Sept. 1929–15 Sept. 1933
Solórzano, José Luis	16 Sept. 1933–27 June 1936

MICHOACÁN

Dorantes, Prudenciano	11 Sept. 1883–Sept. 1885
Jiménez, Mariano (Gen.)	Sept. 1885–2 June 1891
Mercado, Aristeo	3 June 1891–13 May 1911
Silva, Miguel	1911
Ortiz, Primitivo	1911–15 Sept. 1912
Silva, Miguel	16 Sept. 1912–19 May 1913
Garza González, Jesús	30 July 1913–June 1914
Sánchez, Gertrudis G. (Col.)	2 Aug. 1914–2 Mar. 1915
Robles, José I. (Gen.)	3 Mar. 1915–5 Apr. 1915
Elizondo, Alfredo (Gen.)	26 Apr. 1915–18 Feb. 1917

Rentería Luviano, José (Gen.)	19 Feb. 1917–6 Aug. 1917
Ortiz Rubio, Pascual (Gen.)	6 Aug. 1917–5 July 1920
Múgica, Francisco J. (Gen.)	22 Sept. 1920–9 Mar. 1922
Sánchez Pineda, Sidronio	9 Mar. 1922–24 Jan. 1924
Pulido, Ponciano	25 Jan. 1924–23 Feb. 1924
Guerrero, Silvestre	24 Feb. 1924–15 Sept. 1924
Ramírez, Enrique (Gen.)	16 Sept. 1924–30 Mar. 1928
Méndez, Luis	31 Mar. 1928–15 Sept. 1928
Cárdenas, Lázaro (Gen.)	16 Sept. 1928–3 Dec. 1934
Serrato, Benigno (Gen.)	16 Sept. 1934–3 Dec. 1934
Sánchez Tapia, Rafael (Gen.)	1934–35

MORELOS

Flores y Caso, Luis	1 Oct. 1884–13 Mar. 1885
Tovar, Antonio	14 Mar. 1885–24 May 1885
Preciado, Jesús H. (Gen.)	25 May 1885–4 Feb. 1895
Alarcón, Manuel (Gen.)	5 Feb. 1895–15 Dec. 1908
Flores y Caso, Luis	16 Dec. 1908–08
Escandón y Barrón, Pablo (Col.)	1908–7 May 1911
Leyva, Francisco	8 May 1911–June 1911
Carreón, Juan	June 1911–3 Oct. 1911
Figueroa, Ambrosio	4 Oct. 1911–21 July 1912
Villamar, Aniceto	5 Aug. 1912–31 Nov. 1912
Leyva, Patricio	1 Dec. 1912–7 Apr. 1913
Robles, Juvencio (Gen.)	17 Apr. 1913–3 Sept. 1913
Jiménez Castro, Adolfo (Gen.)	2 Oct. 1913–16 Mar. 1914
Bretón, Agustín (Gen.)	17 Mar. 1914–15 May 1915
Mejía, Gregorio G.	16 May 1914–19 June 1914
Ojeda, Pedro (Gen.)	20 June 1914–13 Aug. 1914
De la O, Genovevo (Gen.)	30 Sept. 1914–May 1915
Vázquez, Lorenzo (Gen.)	14 Aug. 1915–2 May 1916
Carreón, Dionisio (Gen.)	16 Aug. 1916–19
Not in functions	1917–Jan. 1919
Aguilar, José G. (Col.)	Jan. 1919–19
Rodríguez, Juan María	7 Jan. 1920–23 Apr. 1920
Flores, Luis	24 Apr. 1920– July 1920
Parres, José G.	10 July 1920–13 Dec. 1923
Ortega, Alfredo	23 Dec. 1923–22 Sept. 1924
Velasco, Ismael	4 Oct. 1924–7 Sept. 1925
Rojas Hidalgo, Joaquín	10 Oct. 1925–24 Feb. 1926
Alcázar, Alvaro L.	25 Feb. 1926–12 June 1926
Del Llan, Valentín	13 June 1926–31 Aug. 1926
Figueroa, Alfonso María	1 Sept. 1926–19 Mar. 1927
Puente, Ambrosio	20 Mar. 1927–12 Mar. 1930
Estrada Cajigal, Vicente	17 May 1930–16 May 1934
Bustamante, Jorge Refugio	17 May 1934–6 May 1938

NAYARIT (TEPIC)

Romano, Leopoldo	25 Jan. 1880–21 May 1897
Rocha y Portú, Pablo	22 May 1897–30 Dec. 1904
Ruiz, Mariano (Gen.)	31 Dec. 1904–24 May 1911
Espinosa, Martín	24 May 1911–19 May 1913
Migoni, Agustín F.	2 June 1913–17 Oct. 1913
Gil, Miguel	18 Oct. 1913–21 Dec. 1913
Servín, Domingo	1 Jan. 1914–16 May 1914

Dozal, Juan	3 June 1914–June 1915
Torres S., Juan	–24 Apr. 1917
Ferreira, Jesús M.	25 Apr. 1917–31 Dec. 1917
Santos Godínez, José (Gen.)	31 Dec. 1917–19 Mar. 1919
Santiago, Francisco D. (Gen.)	19 Mar. 1919–27 Feb. 1920
Ibarra, Fernando S.	28 Feb. 1920–20 Apr. 1920
Arreola, Salvador	21 Apr. 1920–11 June 1920
Santos Godínez, José (Gen.)	12 June 1920–27 Sept. 1921
Corona, Federico R.	27 Sept. 1921–31 Dec. 1921
Villanueva, Pascual	1 Jan. 1922–31 Jan. 1925
De la Peña, José	1 Jan. 1926–5 Feb. 1927
Velarde, Ricardo	6 Feb. 1927–27
Ramírez Romano, Francisco	1927–28
Baca Calderón, Esteban (Gen.)	1928
Anguiano, Francisco	1929
Cristo, Gustavo R.	1929–31 Dec. 1930
Castillo Ledón, Luis	1 Jan. 1930–7 Aug. 1931
Espinosa Sánchez, Juventino	7 Aug. 1931–33
Azcárraga, Gustavo B.	28 Sept. 1933–31 Dec. 1933
Parra, Francisco	1 Jan. 1934–31 Dec. 1937

NUEVO LEÓN

García, Canuto	1883–85
Garza García, Genaro	1885
Reyes, Bernardo (Gen.)	1885–87
Garza Ayala, Lázaro	1887–89
Reyes, Bernardo (Gen.)	1889–1900
Benítez Leal, Pedro	1900–02
Reyes, Bernardo (Gen.)	1902–09
Mier, José María (Gen.)	1909–10
Chapa, Leobardo	1910–11
Villarreal, Viviano L.	1911–13
Treviño, Gerónimo	24 Feb. 1913–27 Mar. 1913
Botello, Salomé	1913–14
Villarreal, Antonio I.	1914–15
Madero, Raúl	13 Feb. 1915–18 May 1915
De la Garza, Pablo A.	1915–17
Ricaut, Alfredo (Gen.)	24 Mar. 1917–29 June 1917
Zambrano, Nicéforo	1917–19
Santos, José E. (Gen.)	1919–20
González, Porfirio G. (Gen.)	13 May 1920–4 Feb. 1921
García, Juan Manuel	1921–22
Támez, Ramiro	1922–23
Pérez, Alfredo	1923
Treviño Martínez, Anastacio A.	1923
González, Porfirio G. (Gen.)	25 Dec. 1923–16 Oct. 1925
Siller, Jerónimo	1925–27
Sáenz, Aarón (Gen.)	1927–31
Cárdenas, Francisco A.	1931–33
Quiroga, Pablo	1933–27 Sept. 1935

OAXACA

Jiménez, Mariano (Gen.)	4 Jan. 1883–30 Nov. 1884
Mier y Terán, Luis (Gen.)	1 Dec. 1884–17 Feb. 1886
Canseco, Agustín	18 Feb. 1886–17 May 1886

Mier y Terán, Luis (Gen.)	18 May 1886–25 Feb. 1887
Canseco, Agustín	26 Feb. 1887–30 Nov. 1888
Zertuche, Albino (Gen.)	1 Dec. 1888–4 May 1890
Chávez, Gregorio (Gen.)	16 May 1890–30 Nov. 1894
González, Martín (Gen.)	1 Dec. 1894–6 June 1902
Bolaños Cacho, Miguel	7 June 1902–30 Nov. 1902
Pimentel, Emilio	1 Dec. 1902–4 May 1911
Díaz Quintas, Heliodoro	8 June 1911–23 Sept. 1911
Juárez Maza, Benito	24 Sept. 1911–21 Apr. 1912
Bolaños Cacho, Miguel	20 Aug. 1912–14 July 1914
Canseco, Francisco	15 July 1914–30 Nov. 1914
Dávila, José Inés	7 Dec. 1914–19 Aug. 1915
Castro, Jesús Agustín (Gen.)	20 Aug. 1915–31 Mar. 1917
Jiménez Méndez, Juan (Gen.)	1 Apr. 1917–9 July 1919
Eustaquio Vázquez, Francisco	10 July 1919–29 Jan. 1920
Rodríguez, Alfredo	30 Jan. 1920–4 May 1920
Acevedo, Jesús	5 May 1920–28 Oct. 1920
Bravo, Carlos	29 Oct. 1920–15 Dec. 1920
García Vigil, Manuel (Gen.)	16 Dec. 1920–3 Mar. 1924
Ibarra, Isaac M. (Gen.)	4 Mar. 1924–30 Nov. 1924
Jiménez, Onofre	1 Dec. 1924–7 Dec. 1925
Vázquez, Genaro	8 Dec. 1925–30 Nov. 1928
López Cortés, Francisco	1 Dec. 1928–30 Nov. 1932
García Toledo, Anastasio	1 Dec. 1932–30 Nov. 1936

PUEBLA

Enciso, Ignacio	1884–85
Márquez, Rosendo (Gen.)	11 Feb. 1885–20 Sept. 1892
Martínez, Mucio P. (Gen.)	121 Sept. 1892–Mar. 1911
Sandoval, Miguel	1911
Mora, Agustín	1911
Isunza, Rafael	1911–20 Sept. 1911
Canete, Rafael P.	21 Sept. 1911–24 Dec. 1911
Meléndez, Nicolás	25 Dec. 1911–13
Carrasco, Juan B.	1 Feb. 1913–1 June 1913
Maas Flores, Juan (Gen.)	June 1913–15 Jan. 1914
Hernández, Juan (Gen.)	22 Jan. 1914–14 July 1914
Muñoz Ovando, Francisco	1914
Coss, Francisco (Gen.)	1914
Espinosa, Rafael	1915
Coss, Francisco (Gen.)	1915
Cervantes, Luis G.	1915–16
Castro, Cesáreo (Gen.)	1 Apr. 1916–17
Cabrera, Alfonso	1917–20
Rojas, Rafael (Gen.)	8 May 1920–16 June 1920
Sánchez Pontón, Luis	1920–21
Sánchez Rojas, José María (Gen.)	20 June 1921–18 Feb. 1922
Manjárrez, Froylán C.	2 Mar. 1922–23
Lombardo Toledano, Vicente	1923
Guerrero, Alberto	1923–24
Sánchez Rojas, José María (Gen.)	1924
Moreno, Enrique	1924–25
Osorio, Arturo	1925
Macip, Wenceslao	1925

Tirado, Claudio N.	1925–26
Montes, Manuel P. (Gen.)	1926–27
Bravo Izquierdo, Donato (Gen.)	1927–29
Andreu Almazán, Leonides	1929–33
Crisóstomo Bonilla, Juan	1933
Mijares Palencia, José (Gen.)	1933–37

QUERÉTARO

Olvera, Rafael	1 Oct. 1883–31 Sept. 1887
González de Cosío, Francisco	1 Oct. 1887–26 Mar. 1911
Isla, Adolfo	27 Mar. 1911–16 May 1911
Veraza, Alfonso	17 May 1911–26 June 1911
Septién, José Antonio	27 June 1911–31 Sept. 1911
Loyola, Carlos M.	1 Oct. 1911–29 Sept. 1913
Chicarro, Joaquín F.	30 Sept. 1913–13 July 1914
Septién, José Antonio	14 July 1914–30 July 1914
Montes Alanís, Federico (Gen.)	1 Aug. 1914–28 Nov. 1914
Elizondo, Teodoro	29 Nov. 1914–17 Jan. 1915
Bravo, Gustavo M.	17 Jan. 1915–30 Mar. 1915
Siurob, José (Gen.)	31 Mar. 1915–5 May 1916
Montes Alanís, Federico (Gen.)	6 May 1916–29 Mar. 1917
Salinas, Emilio (Gen.)	30 Mar. 1917–30 June 1917
Perusquía, Ernesto	1 July 1917–31 Sept. 1919
Argaín, Salvador	1 Oct. 1919–5 May 1920
de la Torre, Rómulo	19 May 1920–31 Sept. 1920
Truchuelo, José M.	1 Oct. 1920–30 Sept. 1923
Ramírez Luque, Francisco	1 Oct. 1923–15 Dec. 1923
de la Peña, Joaquín	16 Dec. 1923–25 Aug. 1924
Malo Juvera, Julián	26 Aug. 1924–18 July 1925
Llaca, Constantino	19 July 1925–31 Sept. 1927
Araujo, Abraham	1 Oct. 1927–25 June 1929
Vázquez Mellado, Angel	26 June 1929–5 July 1929
Anaya, Ramón	6 July 1929–30 Sept. 1931
Osornio, Saturnino	1 Oct. 1931–30 Sept. 1935

QUINTANA ROO

Molina Solís, Olegario	1 Feb. 1902–11
Sánchez Rivera, Manuel (Gen.)	16 Sept. 1912–11 Nov. 1912
Eguía Lis, Rafael	1913–15
Alvarado, Salvador (Gen.)	1915
May Pech, José Francisco (Gen.)	1915–16
Plank, Carlos (Gen.)	1916
Vidal, Carlos A. (Col.)	1916–17
Solís, Octaviano	1917–18
Estrada, Mateo (Gen.)	1918–20
Isamarripa, Isaías (Gen.)	1920–21
Coral Heredía, Pascual (Gen.)	26 Jan. 1921–Apr. 1921
Abitia, Librado (Col.)	1921–23
Rojas, Atanacio (Gen.)	1923
Abitia, Librado (Col.)	16 May 1924–Aug. 1924
Barocio, Enrique (Col.)	5 Sept. 1924–Jan. 1925
Aguirre, Amado (Gen.)	Jan. 1925–May 1925
Garza, Candelario	1926
Ancona Albertos, Antonio	1926–27

Siurob, José (Gen.)	1927–30
Campillo Seyde, Arturo (Gen.)	1930–31
Bañuelos, Félix (Gen.)	1931–22 Mar. 1934*
Melgar, Rafael (Gen.)	1935–40

*No federal territory of Quintana Roo existed from March 23, 1934 to January 10, 1935; it was annexed to Campeche and Yucatán.

SAN LUIS POTOSÍ

Díez Gutiérrez, Pedro	1881–84
Díez Gutiérrez, Carlos (Gen.)	1885–98
Escontría, Blas	1898–05
Espinosa y Cuevas, José	1 Dec. 1905–11
Ipiña, José Encarnación	1911
Cepeda, Rafael (Gen.)	1911–13
García Hernández, Agustín	1913
Romero, Francisco (Gen.)	12 June 1913–15 May 1914
Velasco, José Refugio (Gen.)	116 May 1914–16 June 1914
Muñoz, Ricardo	1914
Gutiérrez, Eulalio (Gen.)	1914
Alvarez, Herminio	5 Dec. 1914–15
Kasperowits, José	1915
Flores, Adolfo	1915
Saravia, Emiliano	1915
Gavira, Gabriel (Gen.)	1915
Dávila, Vicente (Gen.)	1915–16
Chapoy, Federico (Col.)	1916–17
Breceda, Alfredo (Gen.)	1917
Barragán, Juan (Gen.)	1917–18
Martínez, Severino	1918–19
Nieto, Rafael	1919–23
Guerrero, Paulino	1923
Prieto Laurens, Jorge	1923
Manrique, Aurelio	1923–25
Cano, Abel	1925–27
Cedillo, Saturnino (Gen.)	1927–31
Turrubiartes, Ildefonso (Gov.)	1931–35

SINALOA

Martínez de Castro, Mariano	1881–84
Canedo, Francisco	1884–88
Martínez de Castro, Mariano	1888–92
Canedo, Francisco	1892–June 1909
Redo, Diego	1909–22 June 1911
Gaxiola Rojo, Celso	23 June 1911–6 Aug. 1911
Banderas, Juan M. (Gen.)	7 Aug. 1911–20 Sept. 1911
Rentería, Jorge	21 Sept. 1911–7 Feb. 1912
Paliza, Ruperto L.	29 June 1912–26 Sept. 1912
Riveros, Felipe	27 Sept. 1912–20 Mar. 1913
Legorreta, José (Gen.)	21 Mar. 1913–3 July 1913
Riveros, Felipe	4 July 1913–24 Nov. 1914
Rodríguez Gutiérrez, Manuel	25 Nov. 1914–20 Mar. 1916
Ibáñez, Isuaro	21 Mar. 1916–30 Apr. 1916
Flores, Angel (Gen.)	1 May 1916–Apr. 1917
Pesqueira, Ignacio L. (Gen.)	Apr. 1917–June 1917

Iturbe, Ramón F. (Gen.)	27 Sept. 1917–26 Dec. 1919
Vega, Alejandro R.	19 May 1920–23 Sept. 1920
Flores, Angel (Gen.)	24 Sept. 1920–15 Mar. 1923
Rivas, Manuel	16 Mar. 1923–24 Mar. 1924
Flores, Angel (Gen.)	24 Mar. 1924–30 Oct. 1924
Díaz, Victoriano	31 Oct. 1924–24
Vega, Alejandro	1 Jan. 1925–17 Sept. 1926
Bátiz, Juan de Dios (Gen.)	18 Sept. 1926–13 Nov. 1927
Páez, Manuel	14 Nov. 1927–31 Dec. 1929
Gaxiola, Macario (Gen.)	1 Jan. 1930–21 Dec. 1932
Páez, Manuel	1 Jan 1933–16 Dec. 1935

SONORA

Torres, Luis E. (Gen.)	1 Sept. 1883–31 Aug. 1895
Corral, Ramón	1 Sept. 1895–31 Aug. 1899
Ortiz, Celedonio C.	1 Sept. 1899–26 Aug. 1900
Izábal, Rafael	27 Aug. 1900–24 Jan. 1903
Torres, Luis E. (Gen.)	25 Jan. 1903–30 June 1903
Izábal, Rafael	1 July 1903–31 Aug. 1907
Torres, Luis E. (Gen.)	1 Sept. 1907–27 May 1911
Gayou, Eugenio H.	1 June 1911–3 July 1911
Randall, Carlos E.	4 July 1911–31 Aug. 1911
Maytorena, José María (Gen.)	1 Sept. 1911–25 Feb. 1913
Pesquiera, Ignacio L. (Col.)	26 Feb. 1913–25 Mar. 1913
*García, Francisco H. (*Gen.).	1 Apr. 1913–16 Mar. 1914
Maytorena, José María (Gen.)	Mar. 1914–5 Oct. 1914
Randall, Carlos E.	6 Oct. 1914–4 Aug. 1915
*Calles, Plutarco E. (*Gen.)	5 Aug. 1915–16 Aug. 1917
Soriano, Cesáreo G.	17 Aug. 1917–18 July 1918
Calles, Plutarco E. (Gen.)	19 July 1918–31 Aug. 1919
de la Huerta, Adolfo	1 Sept. 1919–28 May 1920
Bórquez, Flavio A.	14 June 1920–19 Nov. 1920
Piña H., Miguel (Gen.)	2 Jan. 1921–1 May 1921
de la Huerta, Adolfo	2 May 1921–3 June 1922
Elías, Francisco S.	4 June 1922–3 Apr. 1923
de la Huerta, Adolfo	4 Apr. 1923–14 May 1923
Bórquez, Flavio A.	21 May 1923–31 Aug. 1923
Bay, Alejo	1 Sept. 1923–31 Aug. 1927
Topete, Fausto (Gen.)	1 Sept. 1927–3 Mar. 1929
Elías, Francisco S.	30 Apr. 1929–31 Aug. 1931
Calles, Rodolfo Elías	1 Sept. 1931–31 Aug. 1935

TABASCO

Mestre Gorgoll, Manuel	1 Oct. 1883–1 Feb. 1884
León, Lauro	1 Feb. 1884–24 July 1884
Mestre Gorgoll, Manuel	24 July 1884–31 Dec. 1884
Castillo, Eusebio	1 Jan. 1885–11 Mar. 1886
Valenzula, Policarpo	11 Mar. 1886–5 Apr. 1886
Castillo, Eusebio	5 Apr. 1886–21 Mar. 1887
Bandala, Abraham (Gen.)	23 Mar. 1887–30 Sept. 1888
Merino Jiménez, Calixto	10 Oct. 1888–1 Jan. 1889
Sarlat Nova, Simón	1 Jan. 1889–20 Mar. 1890
Merino Jiménez, Calixto	20 Mar. 1890–13 June 1890
Sarlat Nova, Simón	13 June 1890–1 Mar. 1891
Merino Jiménez, Calixto	1 Mar. 1891–11 Sept. 1891

Sarlat Nova, Simón	11 Sept. 1891–17 Aug. 1892
Kerlegand Flores, Joaquín Zeferino (Gen.)	17 Aug. 1892–1 Dec. 1892
Sarlat Nova, Simón	1 Dec. 1892–12 Mar. 1894
Bandala, Abraham (Gen.)	12 Mar. 1894–15 Aug. 1894
Sarlat Nova, Simón	15 Aug. 1894–31 Dec. 1894
Bandala, Abraham (Gen.)	1 Jan. 1895–31 Dec. 1910
Valenzuela, Policarpo	1 Jan. 1911–9 June 1911
Mestre Ghigliazza, Manuel	9 June 1911–28 Apr. 1913
Valdés, Agustín (Gen.)	28 Apr. 1913–30 Aug. 1913
Yarza, Alberto (Gen.)	30 Aug. 1913–1 Sept. 1914
Domínguez Suárez, Luis Felipe (Gen.)	1 Sept. 1914–30 Sept. 1914
Greene Ramírez, Carlos (Gen.)	1 Oct. 1914–2 Feb. 1915
Juárez, Aquileo (Col.)	2 Feb. 1915–27 Aug. 1915
Mújica, Francisco J. (Gen.)	10 Sept. 1915–13 Sept. 1916
Domínguez Suárez, Luis Felipe (Gen.)	14 Sept. 1916–8 Dec. 1917
Ruiz, Joaquín	9 Dec. 1917–4 June 1918
Hernández Hermosillo, Luis M. (Gen.)	5 June 1918–7 Oct. 1918
Jara, Heriberto (Gen.)	8 Oct. 1918–15 Jan. 1919
Vidal, Carlos A. (Gen.)	16 Jan. 1919–10 Mar. 1919
Greene Ramírez, Carlos (Gen.)	10 Mar. 1919–27 Oct. 1920
Aguilar Suárez, Primitivo	28 Oct. 1920–10 Jan. 1921
Garrido Canabal, Tomás	11 Jan. 1921–13 May 1921
Casanova Casao, Pedro	15 July 1921–31 Dec. 1921
Garrido Canabal, Tomás	1 Jan. 1922–3 Apr. 1926
Ruiz Sobredo, Santiago	4 Apr. 1926–28 Oct. 1926
Hernández Olivé, Augusto	29 Oct. 1926–31 Dec. 1926
Cruz, Ausencio Conrado (Capt.)	1 Jan. 1927–31 Dec. 1930
Garrido Canabal, Tomás	1 Jan. 1931–31 Dec. 1934

TAMAULIPAS

de León, Gregorio	Sept. 1884–87
Prieto, Alejandro	4 May 1888–3 May 1896
Mainero, Guadalupe	4 May 1896–9 Aug. 1901
Argüelles, Pedro (Col.)	1 Oct. 1901–3 May 1908
Castelló, Juan B.	4 May 1908–31 May 1911
Lara, Espiridión	1 June 1911–30 Nov. 1911
Guerra, Matías	30 Nov. 1911–4 Feb. 1912
Argüelles, Joaquín	5 Feb. 1912–4 May 1912
Guerra, Matías	5 May 1912–27 Apr. 1913
Argüelles, Joaquín	28 Apr. 1913–23 July 1913
Rábago, Antonio (Gen.)	24 July 1913–17 Nov. 1913
Caballero, Raúl (Gen.)	18 Nov. 1913–26 July 1916
Trejo Flores, Fidencio	26 July 1916–21 Feb. 1917
Osuna, Gregorio (Gen.)	22 Feb. 1917–16 July 1917
Ricaut, Alfredo (Gen.)	17 July 1917–20 May 1918
Osuna, Andrés	20 May 1918–9 Nov. 1919
González Villarreal, Francisco (Gen.)	10 Nov. 1919–3 May 1920
Morante, José	13 July 1920–15 Feb. 1921
López de Lara, César (Gen.)	16 Feb. 1921–7 Dec. 1923
López Padilla, Benecio (Gen.)	9 Dec. 1923–1 Feb. 1924
Garza, Candelario	13 Feb. 1924–29 Nov. 1924
Portes Gil, Emilio	5 Feb. 1925–30 Nov. 1928
Rincón, Juan	1 Dec. 1928–4 Feb. 1929
Castellanos, Francisco	5 Feb. 1929–4 Feb. 1933
Villarreal, Rafael	5 Feb. 1933–20 Nov. 1935

TLAXCALA

Rivera, Teodoro	1884–85
Cahuantzi, Próspero (Col.)	1885–1911
Kennedy, Diego L.	1911
Sánchez, Agustín	1911
Maldonado, Ramón M.	1911
Hidalgo Sandoval, Antonio	1911–13
Sánchez, Agustín	1913
Maldonado, Agustín	1913
Grajales, Mariano	1913
Yarza, Alberto (Gen.)	1913
Cuéllar Alarcón, Manuel	1913–14
García, Luis J.	1914
Rojas, Máximo (Gen.)	21 Aug. 1914–15 Jan. 1915
del Castillo, Porfirio (Col.)	1 Nov. 1915–15
Meneses Bonilla, Anastasio	1915–16
Machorro, Antonio M.	1916–17
Ríos Zertuche, Daniel	1917
Rojas, Máximo	1918–20
Mendoza, Ignacio	1920
Apango, Rafael	1921–25
Mendoza, Ignacio	1925–29
Vázquez Sánchez, Adrián	1929–33
Bonilla, Adolfo (Gen.)	1933–37

VERACRUZ

Cortés y Frías, José (Gen.)	15 Nov. 1883–30 Nov. 1884
Enríquez, Juan de la Luz	1 Dec. 1884–17 Mar. 1892
Alcolea, Leandro M.	1 Apr. 1892–31 Nov. 1892
Dehesa, Teodoro	1 Dec. 1892–19 June 1911
Aillaud, León	21 June 1911–Feb. 1912
Lagos Cházaro, Francisco	15 Feb. 1912–30 Nov. 1912
Pérez Rivera, Antonio	1 Dec. 1912–28 June 1913
Cauz, Eduardo C. (Gen.)	1913–14
Aguilar, Cándido (Gen.)	20 June 1914–15
Millán, Agustín (Gen.)	15 Oct. 1915–6 Jan. 1916
Jara, Heriberto (Gen.)	1916
Aguilar, Cándido (Gen.)	1916–20
Nava, Antonio	1920
Garzón Cossa, Gabriel	1920
Tejeda, Adalberto (Gen.)	1 Dec. 1920–30 Nov. 1924
Jara, Heriberto (Gen.)	1 Dec. 1924–27
Rodríguez, Abel S.	Oct. 1927–30 Nov. 1928
Tejeda, Adalberto (Gen.)	1 Dec. 1928–30 Nov. 1932
Vázquez Vela, Gonzalo	1 Dec. 1932–35

YUCATÁN

Rosado, Octavio (Gen.)	1 Feb. 1882–31 Jan. 1886
Palomino, Guillermo (Col.)	1 Feb. 1886–9 May 1889
Pío Manzano, Juan	10 May 1889–31 Jan. 1890
Traconís, Daniel (Gen.)	1 Feb. 1890–31 Jan. 1894
Peón, Carlos	1 Feb. 1894–17 Aug. 1897
Iturralde, José María	18 Aug. 1897–31 Jan. 1898
Cantón, Francisco (Gen.)	1 Feb. 1898–31 Jan. 1902
Molina Solís, Olegario	1 Feb. 1902–6 Mar. 1907

Muñoz Aristégui, Enrique	7 Mar. 1907–10 Mar. 1911
Curiel, Luis C.	11 Mar. 1911–5 June 1911
Pino Suárez, José María	6 June 1911–8 Aug. 1911
González, Jesús L.	9 Aug. 1911–6 Oct. 1911
Pino Suárez, José María	7 Oct. 1911–10 Nov. 1911
Cámara Valles, Nicolás	11 Nov. 1911–14 Mar. 1913
Escobedo, Arcadio	15 Mar. 1913–8 July 1913
Rascón, Eugenio (Gen.)	9 July 1913–9 Sept. 1913
Cortés, Prisciliano (Gen.)	10 Sept. 1913–6 Sept. 1914
Avila, Eleuterio (Col.)	7 Sept. 1914–19 Jan. 1915
V. de los Santos, Toribio	20 Jan. 1915–8 Feb. 1915
Ortiz Argumedo, Abel	9 Feb. 1915–18 Mar. 1915
Alvarado, Salvador (Gen.)	19 Mar. 1915–31 Jan. 1918
Castro Morales, Carlos	1 Feb. 1918–12 May 1920
Garrido Canabal, Tomás	13 May 1920–18 June 1920
Ancona Albertos, Antonio	26 July 1920–26 Nov. 1920
Ayuso O'Horibe, Hircano	27 Nov. 1920–1 May 1921
Berzunza, Manuel	2 May 1921–31 Jan. 1922
Carrillo Puerto, Felipe	1 Feb. 1922–11 Dec. 1923
Ricardez Broca, Juan	12 Dec. 1923–16 Apr. 1924
Iturralde Traconís, José María	12 May 1924–31 Jan. 1926
Torre Díaz, Alvaro	1 Feb. 1926–31 Jan. 1930
García Correa, Bartolomé	1 Feb. 1930–31 Jan. 1934
Alayola Barrera, César	1 Feb. 1934–4 Oct. 1935

ZACATECAS

Chávez, Marcelino M.	16 Sept. 1884–15 Sept. 1888
Aréchiga, Jesús (Gen.)	16 Sept. 1888–15 Sept. 1900
García Valdez, Genaro	16 Sept. 1900–3 Feb. 1904
Pankhurst, Eduardo G.	4 Feb. 1904–15 Sept. 1908
de P. Zárate, Francisco	16 Sept. 1908–24 May 1911
León García, José	15 June 1911–15 Sept. 1912
González, Rafael Guadalupe	16 Sept. 1912–21 Oct. 1912
Ceniceros y Villarreal, Rafael	22 Oct. 1912–22 Jan.1913
Rodríguez Real, Heraclio	23 Jan. 1913–27 Mar. 1913
Ceniceros y Villarreal, Rafael	1 Apr. 1913–24 May 1913
Delgado, José (Gen.)	17 June 1913–10 Nov. 1913
Canseco, Alberto (Gen.)	11 Nov. 1913–19 Feb. 1914
Medina Barrón, Luis	20 Feb. 1914–13 June 1914
de la Vega, Manuel Carlos	1 July 1914–8 Nov. 1914
Cervantes, José Trinidad	9 Nov. 1914–15 Jan. 1915
Natera, Pánfilo (Gen.)	16 Jan. 1915–15 Aug. 1915
Figueroa, Rómulo	16 Aug. 1915–26 Apr. 1916
Plank, Carlos	27 Apr. 1916–28 Oct. 1916
Estrada, Enrique (Gen.)	29 Oct. 1916–8 Apr. 1917
Estrada, Enrique (Gen.)	8 July 1917–6 May 1920
Vázquez, Francisco	7 May 1920–15 Sept. 1920
Moreno, Donato	16 Sept. 1920–26 Nov. 1923
Salcedo, Ezequiel	27 Dec. 1923–7 Apr. 1924
Delgado, José T.	8 Apr. 1924–9 Aug. 1924
Castañeda, Aureliano	16 Sept. 1924–19 Dec. 1925
Belauzarán, Pedro	20 Dec. 1925–2 Apr. 1926
Rodarte, Fernando	1 May 1926–15 Mar. 1928
Bañuelos, Francisco (Gen.)	16 Mar. 1928–1 Sept. 1928

Medina, Alfonso	16 Sept. 1928–28 May 1929
Delgado, J. Jesús	29 May 1929–31 Dec. 1929
Reyes, Luis R.	1 Jan. 1930–31 Jan. 1932
Ruiz, Leobardo (Gen.)	1 Feb. 1932–15 Sept. 1932
Ramos, Matías (Gen.)	16 Sept. 1932–15 Sept. 1936

APPENDIX G

National Executive Committees
of the National Revolutionary Party
(Partido Nacional Revolucionario, PNR),
1929–1935

1 DECEMBER 1928

Secretary general	Luis L. León
Treasury secretary	*Manuel Pérez Treviño*
Press secretary	*Manlio Fabio Altamirano*
Interior secretary	*Basilio Badillo*
Organization secretary	*Aarón Sáenz*
2nd organization secretary	*Manuel Pérez Treviño*
3rd organization secretary	David Orozco
4th organization secretary	*Bartolomé García Correa*

1929

President	*Manuel Pérez Treviño*
Secretary general	Luis L. León
Organization secretary	*Melchor Ortega*

11 FEBRUARY 1930

President	*Basilio Badillo*
Secretary general	*Matías Rodríguez*
Acts secretary	*Bartolomé García Correa*
Press secretary	*Melchor Ortega*
Finance secretary	David Orozco
Federal District secretary	*Gonzalo N. Santos*
Exterior secretary	Manuel Riva Palacio
Oficial mayor	Jorge Meixueiro

6 MAY 1930

President	*Emilio Portes Gil*
Secretary general	Genaro V. Vásquez

Acts secretary — *Pastor Rouaix*
Treasury secretary — Rafael Apango
Exterior secretary — Jesús Silva Herzog
Federal District secretary — José Pérez Gil y Ortiz

1930
President — *Lázaro Cárdenas*
Secretary general — Silvestre Guerrero
Treasury secretary — Elías Campos
Exterior and labor secretary — Valentín Aguilar
Sessions and agrarian secretary — Manuel Mijares V.
Press secretary — Manuel Jasso
Federal District secretary — José Pérez Gil y Ortiz

29 AUGUST 1931
President — *Manuel Pérez Treviño*
Secretary general — *Gonzalo N. Santos*
Acts and agrarian secretary — *Matías Rodríguez*
Exterior and labor secretary — *Manlio Fabio Altamirano*
Press secretary — *Rafael E. Melgar*
Federal District secretary — José Santos Alonso
Treasury secretary — *Juan de Dios Bátiz*
Oficial mayor — Lamberto Ortega

16 OCTOBER 1931
President — *Manuel Pérez Treviño*
Secretary general — Fernando Moctezuma
Treasury secretary — *Juan de Dios Bátiz*
Federal District secretary — Ernesto Soto Reyes
Press secretary — Juan R. Delgado
Acts and agrarian secretary — *Matías Rodríguez*
Exterior and labor secretary — Francisco A. Mayer
Oficial mayor — Lamberto Ortega

12 MAY 1933
President — *Melchor Ortega*
Secretary general — Fernando Moctezuma
Treasury secretary — Guillermo Flores Muñoz
Press secretary — Manuel Riva Palacio
Acts and agrarian secretary — *Matías Rodríguez*
Exterior and labor secretary — Julio Bustillos
Federal District secretary — José Morales Hesse
Oficial mayor — Lamberto Ortega

9 JUNE 1933
President — *Manuel Pérez Treviño*
Secretary general — *Bartolomé Vargas Lugo*
Treasury secretary — Guillermo Flores Muñoz
Press secretary — Alejandro Lacy, Jr.
Federal District secretary — José Morales Hesse
Acts and agrarian secretary — *Matías Rodríguez*
Exterior and labor secretary — Julián Garza Tijerina
Oficial mayor — Lamberto Ortega

25 AUGUST 1933

President	*Carlos Riva Palacio*
Secretary general	*Federico Medrano V.*
Treasury secretary	Guillermo Flores Muñoz
Federal District secretary	Julián Garza Tijerina
Press secretary	Alejandro Lacy, Jr.
Acts and agrarian secretary	*Matías Rodríguez*
Exterior and labor secretary	José Morales Hesse
Oficial mayor	Lamberto Ortega

29 DECEMBER 1933

President	*Carlos Riva Palacio*
Secretary general	Gabino Vázquez
Organization secretary	*Enrique Romero Courtade*
Press secretary	*Froylán C. Manjárrez*
Labor secretary	Gilberto Flores Muñoz
Agrarian secretary	*Gilberto Fabila*
Education secretary	*Federico Medrano*
Treasury secretary	Francisco Trejo

14 DECEMBER 1935

President	*Matías Ramos*
Secretary general	Antonio Villalobos
Organization secretary	Manuel F. Ochoa
Press secretary	*Ausencio C. Cruz*
Agrarian secretary	Angel Posada
Education secretary	Gustavo Segura
Labor secretary	Gilberto Flores Muñoz
Treasury secretary	Máximo Othón

APPENDIX H

Presidents of Mexico, 1884–1934

Porfirio Díaz	1 Dec. 1884–25 May 1911
Francisco León de la Barra	25 May 1911–6 Nov. 1911
Francisco I. Madero	6 Nov. 1911–18 Feb. 1913
Pedro Lascuráin	19 Feb. 1913
Victoriano Huerta	19 Feb. 1913–14 July 1914
Francisco S. Carvajal	14 July 1914–13 Aug. 1914
Venustiano Carranza	20 Aug. 1914–21 May 1920
Adolfo de la Huerta	1 June 1920–30 Nov. 1920
Alvaro Obregón	1 Dec. 1920–30 Nov. 1924
Plutarco Elías Calles	1 Dec. 1924–30 Nov. 1928
Emilio Portes Gil	1 Dec. 1928–4 Feb. 1930
Pascual Ortiz Rubio	5 Feb. 1930–3 Sept. 1932
Abelardo L. Rodríguez	4 Sept. 1932–30 Nov. 1934
Lázaro Cárdenas	1 Dec. 1934–30 Nov. 1940

APPENDIX II

Presidents of Mexico, 1884–1931

BIBLIOGRAPHIC ESSAY

BIOGRAPHICAL RESEARCH in Mexico, as in most Latin American countries, is a challenge to the scholar. Because of the scope of this work, it is impossible to eliminate all errors of fact. Contradictions abound in biographical information and, even more than in recent periods, erroneous information is repeatedly used in published sources. Although no biographies without multiple sources (although not necessarily cited), including at least one official source, appear in this book, this cannot guarantee complete accuracy, especially since government sources also are erroneous. Although I have been able to eliminate hundreds of errors in earlier biographical information, unfortunately, source limitations prevent my adding a number of personalities whose biographies merit inclusion. Resources are appreciably better in the latter part of the twentieth century than those available for the first half and for the end of the nineteenth century. Biographical research on politicians is hampered by the fact that governmental data are sparse and official records often inconsistent. The Mexican government itself did not take an interest in its own biographical record until the late 1950s, and the first government organization manual was not published until the 1940s (Dirección Técnica de Organización, *Directorio del gobierno federal*, 1947).

It would take many lifetimes to complete archival research on all the persons in this book, since they cover such a wide range of years and places. But several archival sources are essential. Most important, all information in the appendices, with the exception of governors, come from these sources. For example, information on Supreme Court justices are found in the individual court *Memorias* by year, and officeholders in the Chamber of Deputies and Senate are available in their institutional *Memorias*, in the "*juntas previas*" sections. Although the Senate and the Chamber of Deputies published a record of a chamber's activities, including a list of members and the districts they represented, the only copies I have found for these early years are in Mexican legislative archives. The Library of Congress has Senate records for part of the twentieth century. After I completed this research, the Senate published a multivolume work which includes, among other data, a complete list of senators from 1876 to 1988, the first published

list ever made available. Entitled *El senado mexicano, por la razón de las leyes,* vol. 2 (Mexico City: Senado, 1987), it is invaluable to researchers and is available from the Library of Congress.

Official records are critical for biographical information too. Many biographies contain incomplete or inaccurate information about political offices held, especially senatorial, deputy, and assistant secretaryships. However, government records can be confusing, because a person's name is misspelled, different spellings of a biographee's name are used in distinct years, or, as I soon learned, the same individual held more than one post simultaneously during the Porfiriato. Also, the Asociación de Diputados Constituyentes was a primary source of information for those represented at the 1917 convention. I am indebted to various national agencies' archival departments for providing me with records of *oficiales mayores,* subsecretaries, and secretaries.

The other type of national archival records of use to this type of collective biography can be found in the National University in Mexico City, which has kept the matriculation records of each student enrolling in the National Preparatory School and the professional schools which formed the National University. These records provide an excellent source of information on educated political figures, often giving information about date and place of birth, their relatives, a legal guardian, and parents' occupation. Also, they help to specify school years of our biographees.

The Secretariat of War has also published *Memorias,* which are quite informative. These include lists of promotions, and lists of officers, and their rank, according to specific battles, particularly during the French intervention. It is possible to connect many of the prominent political figures in the Porfiriato to their combat relationships in the 1860s and 1870s. For example, the *Escalafón general del ejército* (Mexico City, 1902) includes rank and name, and deaths in combat, of all officers from 1847 through 1901. José María Dávila, who had the cooperation of the Secretariat of National Defense, published *El ejército de la revolución* (Mexico City: Slyse, 1938), containing promotion data on that generation. It can be found at the Colegio de México. Also, the Secretariat of Foreign Relations has recorded some biographical information and the deaths of every person in charge of the ministry in its *Funcionarios de la Secretaría de Relaciones, desde el año de 1821 a 1940* (Mexico City, 1940).

Educational institutions have also provided helpful data. For example, Gabriel Cuevas's excellent *El glorioso Colegio Militar mexicano en un siglo 1824–1924* (Mexico City, 1937), provides a complete list, by military specialty, of all graduates from the Military College through 1924, a particularly useful source for the educational background of military politicians, especially Victoriano Huerta's generation. Similar sources for civil institutions are Julián Bonavit's *Fragmentos de la historia del Colegio Primitivo* (Morelia, 1910), and Agustín Lanuza's, *Historia del Colegio de Guanajuato* (Guanajuato, 1924), who provides a list of all graduates through 1922. The best biographical sources of alumni are Marte R. Gómez's *Biografías de*

agrónomos (Mexico: Escuela Nacional de Agricultura, 1976), which includes excellent biographies of agricultural engineering graduates through 1914, and the *Escuela Libre de Derecho aniversario de su fundacion, 1912–22* (Mexico City, 1922).

Hundreds of works were used which are not cited in the text or sources. Only those works, published and unpublished, which provided information on multiple individuals have been listed after each biography. Numerous biographies exist on prominent individuals, although very few, even on presidential figures, have been published in English. Two books serve as bibles to the Mexican collective biographer, regardless of the individual's century or occupation: Juan B. Iguíñez, *Bibliografía biográfica mexicana* (Mexico City: Universidad Nacional Autónoma de México, 1969), and Sara de Mundo Lo, *México*, volume two of the *Index to Spanish American Collective Biography* (Boston: G. K. Hall, 1982). Both are superb reference works which index prominent Mexicans by name, who in turn are cross-referenced to hundreds of sources. Mundo Lo also lists all of the major research libraries holding the cited works. These are a must for anyone pursuing biographical research on Mexico.

I am also extremely grateful to Peter H. Smith, whose analytical book (see below) benefited from my earlier biographical research. He has kindly donated all of his original files to this work. Although most of his early biographies from the 1900s consist of positional information, they provide a valuable cross-reference. Furthermore, his work on consititutional deputies (1916–17) includes thorough biographical data, and his archival lists of ambassadors proved invaluable.

I am equally indebted to Stuart Voss, a foremost regional historian, who cross-checked many of the biographies with his own archival research from local sources in northwestern Mexico, providing additional information and countering errors.

Finally, Charles A. Hale, whose recent work focuses on prominent nineteenth-century generations from the National Preparatory School, also compared biographical notes with my files.

Basically, four types of published sources on Mexican biography are available. There are books which cover prominent figures nationally, sometimes focused on occupation, sometimes not. Books which are biographical directories of locales, states, or regions provide a second category. There are regional histories which are so detailed that they contain bits and pieces of information on many relevant figures. And finally, some genealogical works, of a national or regional scope, exist.

The most complete category, although difficult to encounter, is state biographical directories, typically published by devoted local historians who have made it their life's work to write and revise these directories. Ideally, if a first-rate directory from each state were available, the task of a national biographer would be easy. The quality of these works varies considerably. Among the better examples of this type of book are the directories by Francisco R. Almada, whose *Diccionario de historia, geografía y biografía*

chihuahuenses (Chihuahua, 1968), and *Gobernadores del estado de Chihuahua* (Mexico City: Imprenta de la Cámara de Diputados, 1950) are outstanding sources on state governors and military figures. Almada also wrote earlier books on Colima and Sonora; the book on Colima has the same qualities.

Chihuahua has received the most attention, qualitatively, in the literature, as have northwestern states in general. One of the best regional works, very detailed on family backgound, is Joaquín Márquez Montiel's *Hombres célebres de Chihuahua* (Mexico: Editorial Jus, 1953). Another biographer, Pastor Rouaix, who himself is among our biographees, has written the *Diccionario geográfico, histórico y biográfico del estado de Durango* (Mexico: Instituto Pan Americano de Geografía e Historia, 1946), which is quite useful for the 1910s and 1920s. The other state which has received more than its share of attention is Veracruz, largely because of the work of Leonardo Pasquel, whose *Xalapeños distinguidos* (Jalapa: Editorial Citlaltepetl, 1975), and *La generación liberal Veracruzana* (Veracruz: Editorial Citlaltepetl, 1972), provide excellent biographical information on leading figures from Veracruz and its two major cities.

Another politician, one of the last surviving *constituyentes*, Jesús Romero Flores, who knew many personalities, writes about his home state in his *Diccionario michoacano de historia y geografía* (Morclia, 1960), and Jorge Fernando Iturribarría, a local intellectual and politician, has published many books about his *patria chica*, Oaxaca, including *La generación oaxaqueña del 57* (Mexico City, 1956). Abraham Pérez López's *Diccionario biográfico hidalguense* (San Salvador, Hidalgo, 1979), again written from a local historian's perspective, provides excellent biographies for Hidalgo. Enriqueta de Parrodi's *Sonora, hombres y paisajes* (Mexico City: Editorial Pafim, 1941), contains good biographical coverage of that state.

Some state directories, similar to those which are national in scope, focus only on political leaders, generally governors. In this category is Daniel Moreno's *Colima y sus gobernadores* (Mexico City: Ediciones Studium, 1953), a frank and critical survey of state leaders. Manuel Mestre Ghigliazza, who comes from a Tabasco political family, has focused more specifically on a chronology of state governors. While not strictly biographical, it relates some of the most detailed information on birthdates, deaths, and parents of many prominent state figures, especially in the early twentieth century. State biographical directories are very useful because they often include biographies of prominent figures from other regions whose careers took them from their native states, especially during the revolutionary period.

Many of these local directories are essential for gubernatorial figures. National directories and encyclopedias tend to omit prominent provincial figures. For example, Juan Alvarez Coral, *Galería de gobernadores de Quintana Roo* (Mexico City: Gobierno de Quintana Roo, 1975), provides very complete coverage for this state and former federal territory, although some of the biographies are rather sketchy. Many other provincial or local direc-

tories appear to have little to do with political figures, yet can prove extremely helpful. For example, Cayetano Andrade has written *Antología de escritores nicolaitas, 1540–1940* (Mexico City: Editorial Vanguardia Nicolaita, 1941), which includes useful biographies of writers who were graduates of the Colegio de San Nicolás, in Michoacán, many of whom were prominent political figures locally and nationally. In general, directories of writers and poets from individual states or regions are among the best published sources. For example, a typical literary source with these qualities is Hugo Aranda Pamplona, *Biobibliografía de los escritores del estado de México* (Mexico City: UNAM, 1978). Purely local directories are sometimes based on the most unusual criteria. For example, Ricardo Covarrubias, who has written other books used in this research, has a multivolume *Las calles de Monterrey*, containing excellent biographies, including family backgrounds, of figures who have had streets named after them. Similarly, Hugo Leight, *Las calles de Puebla* (Puebla, 1967), is a work of quality, but only a small number of streets have been blessed with names of political figures in Puebla.

National directories are uneven in quality and have been published sporadically, especially from the 1880s through the 1950s. Generally, among the most useful national biographical sources are those published by organizations or institutions which focus on their own membership or occupational constituencies. For example, Alberto María Carreño is responsible for *La Academia Mexicana Correspondiente de la Española, 1875–1945* (Mexico City: Secretaría de Educación Pública, 1946), which contains excellent, detailed biograpies of its members, many of whom were prominent political figures. Even more useful are the more than one hundred volumes of the Sociedad Mexicana de Geografía y Estadística's *Boletín de la Sociedad Mexicana de Geografía y Estadística*, which includes many biographies of its members in a biographical and obituary section. Another work, which focuses only on writers, many of whom were leading political figures, is Esperanza Velázquez Bringas and Rafael Heliodoro Valle's *Indice de escritores* (Mexico City: Herrero, 1928).

For the nineteenth century, among the better works are José F. Godoy, *Enciclopedia biográfica de contemporáneos* (Washington, D.C.: Globe Printing Office, 1898). It contains personalities from all nations, including Mexico. The most useful works of notable Mexicans include Ernesto de la Torre Villar, *Mexicanos ilustres* (Mexico City: Jus, 1979), whose biographies are qualitatively superior; Antonio García Cubas, *Diccionario geográfico, histórico y biográfico de los Estados Unidos Mexicanos* (Mexico City: Antigua Impresa de Murguía, 1888–91), available on microfilm at the Library of Congress; Francisco Sosa, the leading nineteenth-century Mexican biographer, whose *Biografías de mexicanos distinguidos* (Mexico City: Edición de la Secretaría de Fomento, 1884), provides details on family backgrounds of distinguished Mexicans after 1884; Ireneo Paz, grandfather of Octavio Paz and a leading nineteenth-century figure, offers *Album de la paz y el trabajo*

(Mexico City: Ireneo Paz, 1911), available on microfilm from Tulane University, and his *Los hombres prominentes de México* (Mexico City: La Patria, 1888), in English, available at The University of Texas-Austin and The University of California-Berkeley, is one of the best single sources because of family backgrounds and dates of positions held.

Nineteenth-century scholarship also produced a series of works dealing specifically with government officeholders. Among the best of these works are Lázaro Pavía's, *Apuntes biográficos de los miembros más distinguidos del poder judicial* (Mexico City: F. Barroso, 1893), available on microfilm at the Library of Congress, which provides biographies at all levels of fifty-nine judges; *Porfirio Díaz y su gabinete; estudios biográficos* (Mexico City: Tipografía de los Editores, 1889), by Alfonso Luis Velasco, has information not found elsewhere; Manuel García Purón has some excellent biographies of presidents, but very little on their parents, in his *México y sus gobernantes, biografías* (Mexico City: Porrúa, 1964). Interestingly, the only dissertation which has looked at national leadership during this period is that by Jacqueline Ann Rice, whose "The Porfirian Political Elite: Life Patterns of the Delegates to the 1892 Unión Liberal Convention" (University of California, Los Angeles, 1979) is a superb source of leading *científicos* and their family ties. Only one other analytical work includes biographical information, the two-volume study by François-Javier Guerra, *Le Mexique: De l'ancien régime a la revolution* (Paris: L'Harmattan, 1985), now available from the Fondo de Cultura Económica (1988). This excellent work includes a coded appendix of the biographies of the individuals analyzed, which primarily are political positions held. However, the coding system makes it extremely difficult to use for multiple biographies. Peter Smith's bibliography in *Labyrinths of Power, Political Recruitment in Twentieth-Century Mexico* (Princeton: Princeton University Press, 1979), provides a useful overview of other biographical sources used in this book.

The revolutionary period is very weak in the literature, and very few works stand out. Among the few exceptions is Alberto Morales Jiménez's *Hombres de la revolución mexicana* (Mexico City: Talleres Gráficos de la Nación, 1960), and the more unusual *Los compañeros de Zapata* (Morelos, 1980), whose author, Valentín López González, gathers biographical information on Zapatistas not found in any other sources, historical or biographical. Of course, the various editions of the *Diccionario Porrúa* are a good place to start, although the multivolume *Enciclopedia de México* often has better-quality biographies. Also, the earlier editions of Percy A. Martin's *Who's Who in Latin America* (Stanford: Stanford University Press, 1935, 1940) include some important figures from the 1920s and 1930s. My own *Mexican Political Biographies, 1935–81* (Tucson: University of Arizona Press, 1982) provides extensive information about descendants and cites hundreds of additional sources, including newspapers and magazines, with information about individual political families. Although women held no prominent posts during the 1884–1934 period, Rosalía O'Chumacero's excellent *Perfil y pensamiento de la mujer mexicana*, vol. 3 (Mexico City:

Editores Mexicanos Unidos, 1974) provides excellent biographical sources about women related to notable politicians.

A special cateogory, all by itself, is social directories. Typically, they do not provide complete biographies; rather, they contain specific information about prominent individuals, for example, firm represented. A classic source of this type is the *Blue Book of Mexico, 1901* (Mexico City, 1901).

Another unusual source, by the biographer of Tabasco, is Manuel Mestre Ghigliazza, *Efemeridades biográficos* (Mexico City: Antigua Librería Robredo, 1945), an excellent, indexed source by name and date of death of distinguished individuals who died between 1822 and 1945. In addition to their date of death, he often includes occupation and place and date of birth.

The most difficult material on which to obtain information is family background and parents' occupation. As I suggested in the introduction, this work attempts to provide a continuous picture of family ties among political leadership from the 1880s through the present, highlighting the importance of personal ties in Mexican politics. Consequently, I found genealogical works to be particularly useful. Unfortunately, these are spotty and far from complete. Among the best published books are Torsten Dahl's *Linajes en México* (Mexico City: Casa Editora de Genealogía Ibero Americana, 1967), which never went beyond the original first volume, a book national in scope. Other works focus on a region or on selected families. The best regional book is by José María Valdés Acosta, whose three-volume study of Yucatán families, *A través de las centurias* (Mérida, 1931), is an outstanding examination of important names and families from this state. Another regional study, but largely confined to names, dates of birth, and marriages, rather than backgound, is Rodolfo González de la Garza's *Mil familias de Tamaulipas, Nuevo León, Coahuila y Texas* (Mexico City, 1980), 2 vols. Three studies of families were particularly useful because they were tied into prominent political leaders: Matilde Ipiña de Corsi, *Cuatro grandes dinastías en los descendientes de los hermanos Fernández de Lima y Barragán* (San Luis Potosí, 1956), which covers the Díez Gutiérrez, Rodríguez Cabo, Barragán, Verástegui, and Ipiña families; José Miguel Quintana, *La familia Quintana y algunas de sus alianzas* (Mexico City, 1969), which reveals connections between the Sánchez Navarro and Quintana families; and Gonzalo Torres Martínez, *Los Torres de Jáen en México* (Mexico City: Editorial Jus, 1975), which has multiple political and economic elite families, cross-indexed throughout, making it one of the most useful reference sources.

Finally, dozens of local and national histories have been published. Few authors of national histories provide sufficiently detailed information of individual personalities to justify a page-by-page reading for biographical information. Many have been used in this work, but they are too numerous to cite here, or in the biographies themselves. Of special value are Ernest Gruening's *Mexico and Its Heritage* (New York: D. Appleton-Century, 1928), because Gruening had access to unpublished files from the Secretariat of Government, which reveal important information on state figures

in the 1920s; and John W. F. Dulles, *Yesterday in Mexico* (Austin: University of Texas Press, 1961), which takes a special interest in biographical anecdotes of personalities from 1915 to 1935.

The most useful histories for biographical information are local or regional in scope. The recent interest of North American and Mexican scholars has produced numerous books and articles which detail the interlocking relationship between political and economic elites. Again, these are well-known works, easily accessible to the researcher, and generally are not individually cited in the biographies. One unpublished study, because it focuses specifically on political elites, William S. Langston's "Coahuila in the Porfiriato, 1893–1911: A Study of Political Elites" (Ph.D. dissertation, Tulane University, 1980), deserves mention.